WHERE TO DRINK
BEER

WHERE TO DRINK
BEER

—

JEPPE JARNIT-BJERGSØ

Φ

THE EXPERTS' GUIDE
TO THE BEST BEER
PLACES IN THE WORLD

CONTENTS

KEY

Beer & food
The best of both worlds, these are places to enjoy outstanding beer paired with delicious food.

Beer garden
A hidden garden, a tiny terrace, or a table at the foot of a mountain, these are the very best outdoor spaces for drinking beer.

Local favorite
The neighborhood dive bar or beloved pub down the street, these are spots that locals return to time and again for beer.

Unexpected
The most unusual places to drink beer—from a train station, airplane, and ferry to a laundromat, naval base, and national park.

Wish I'd opened
The most admired and respected establishments, these are the ones beer experts so wish they had opened themselves.

Worth the travel
Near and far, these spots are so good that they warrant hopping on a train or plane to experience.

INTRODUCTION

When I started getting into beer in the late 1990s, most people perceived beer as a simple, uncomplicated social drink. In Denmark, where I grew up, the selection was uninspiring. It was basically a Carlsberg monopoly, catering to plain palates without any sort of refinement. I discovered my passion for beer while exploring the Belgian beers, which sparked my interest immediately. I would drive twelve hours to breweries like Rodenbach and Westvleteren and the famous lambic breweries in the Pajottenland and load up the car. I'd also drive to Antwerp to go to Kulminator, one of the most famous beer bars in the world, and explore their amazing vintage beer selection. I was obsessed.

Looking back to those times, it's amazing to think about how different the perception of beer is today, as well as how accessible craft beer has become overall. Around the world, the craft-beer scene has exploded, and an interesting selection of beer is no longer a twelve-hour drive away. If you know where to find it, good beer can be found in just about every locality, near and far. Across the globe, in big cities and small towns, craft breweries are popping up at a rapid rate. Likewise, it's no longer a rarity to find a wide range of serious craft beers in both bars and restaurants—if you know where to look.

What has always appealed to me about brewing is that beer is easily made by those who are passionate about it. Horticultural experience and hundreds of acres of land are not necessary, as with tending a vineyard for wines, and neither are the special equipment and knowledge necessary in distilling spirits. In other words, the barriers are low, and anyone can make a tremendous beer wherever or whoever they are. In that sense, it is a very democratic drink.

As I travel the world to brew beer, I am constantly on the lookout for that new local brewery making memorable beers or that hidden gem of a beer bar only the locals would know. That inside scoop is what this book is all about.

We've asked prestigious industry professionals from around the world to let us know where good local beer can be found, as well as what their favorite destination bars are. Through these answers, this book can be used as a travel guide to find outstanding beer no matter where in the world you find yourself. And when you travel as much as I do, that's pretty exciting. I hope you'll agree.

Jeppe Jarnit-Bjergsø

THE BEER EXPERTS

ALEX ACKER
Jing-A Taproom 1949 and Jing-A Brewpub Xingfucun, 1949 The Hidden City, Courtyard 4, Beijing and 57 Xingfucun Zhong Lu, Beijing
Cofounder and brewer at Jing-A Brewing Co., with a national distribution across twenty cities in China., Acker also has a brewpub and taproom.

AT&T Park 311	Unexpected
Cantillon Brewery 174	Wish I'd opened
Crux Fermentation Project 293	Beer garden
De Verloren Hoek 181	Beer & food
Jing-A Taproom 1949 87	Local favorite
Ma Che Siete Venuti A Fà 234	Worth the travel

TIM ADAMS
Oxbow Brewing Company, 274 Jones Woods Road, Newcastle
Founder of Oxbow Brewing Company, a small farmhouse brewery in rural Maine.

Andechs Monastery 198	Beer garden
Eventide Oyster Company 357	Beer & food
In de Verzekering tegen de Grote Dorst 169	Worth the travel
Novare Res Bier Café 357	Local favorite
Publican Tavern 350	Unexpected
Teppa Room 77	Wish I'd opened

GEORGE ALEXAKIS
The Hoppy Pub, Nikiforou Foka 6, Thessaloniki
Owner and founder of The Hoppy Pub, dedicated to finding and bringing the best beers to Greece.

Ayinger Bräustüberl 198	Beer garden
BierCaB 226	Beer & food
BierCaB 226	Wish I'd opened
KANAAL 254	Unexpected
Ma Che Siete Venuti A Fà 234	Worth the travel
The Hoppy Pub 255	Local favorite

ALEXIS ALEXIOU
Pivo Microbrewery, Asklipiou 36, Nicosia
Cofounder of Pivo Microbrewery with his two brothers, Alexiou studied in the Czech Republic for 11 years before returning to Cyprus.

Beer Factory 241	Beer & food
Cobbs Farm Shop & Kitchen 130	Unexpected
Green Cat Pivárium 242	Wish I'd opened
Pivo Microbrewery 256	Local favorite
Únětice Brewery 241	Beer garden
Únětice Brewery 241	Worth the travel

DANIELLE ALLEN
Two Birds Brewing, 136 Hall Street, Spotswood
Cofounder of Two Birds Brewing, Australia's first female-owned brewery.

Bar Josephine 62	Worth the travel
Plough Hotel 62	Beer & food
The Oaks Hotel 56	Beer garden
Two Birds Brewing 63	Local favorite
Ze Pickle 57	Wish I'd opened
Zesty Edibles at Gunabul Homestead 57	Unexpected

FAL ALLEN
Anderson Valley Brewing, 17700 Highway 253, Boonville
Brewmaster at Anderson Valley Brewing Company, Allen has also worked for Archipelago Brewing Company in Singapore, Red Hook Brewery in Seattle, and Pike Place as head brewer. He won the Brewers Association's Russell Schehrer Award for Innovation and Achievement in Craft Brewing, judges beer internationally, and has written extensively about beer.

Big Island Brewhaus 289	Beer & food
Bootshaus Restaurant im Hain 198	Beer garden
Golden West Saloon 282	Local favorite
Little River Inn 282	Unexpected
Szimpla Kert 243	Wish I'd opened

MONNA ALMENNINGEN
Flåmsbrygga Hotel, Flåmsbrygga, Flam
Almenningen works at Ægir BrewPub, a Norse Viking-style brewpub in Norway.

Ægir BrewPub 113	Beer & food
Ægir BrewPub 113	Beer garden
Ægir BrewPub 113	Local favorite
Ægir BrewPub 113	Unexpected
Ægir BrewPub 113	Wish I'd opened
Ægir BrewPub 113	Worth the travel

ROBERTO ALVES DA FONSECA
Menu Magazine, São Paulo
Journalist who writes about craft beer in Brazil, Alves da Fonseca began his career covering politics.

Bier Keller 446	Worth the travel
CATETO Pinheiros 447	Wish I'd opened
Cervejaria Walfänger 447	Beer garden
Empório Alto dos Pinheiros 447	Local favorite
La Fine Mousse 193	Beer & food
The Muddy Charles Pub 359	Unexpected

MIKE AMIDEI
Tørst, 615 Manhattan Avenue, New York City
Beverage director at Tørst, rated as the top global beer destination, Amidei has worked in almost every facet of the industry.

A la Bière comme à la Bière 194	Worth the travel
Andorra 188	Local favorite
Au Coin Mousse 187	Worth the travel
Berlucoquet 184	Beer & food
Biercafé Au Trappiste 186	Local favorite
Biérocratie 193	Local favorite
Bierspeciaal Café "De Paas" 156	Beer garden
Bizarro Café Coyoacan 428	Local favorite
Border Psycho Taproom 427	Local favorite
Bouneweger Stuff 185	Beer & food
Brasserie des Franches-Montagnes 187	Worth the travel

RICHARD AMMERMAN

Jing-A Brewing Co., 57 Xingfucun Zhong Lu, Beijing
Raised in Italy and the U.S., Ammerman runs marketing at
Jing-A Brewing.

OLOF ANDERSSON

O/O Brewing, Exportgatan 35, Gothenburg
Cofounder of O/O Brewing.

KATIE ANDREWS

Jimmy's No. 43, 43 East 7th Street, New York City
Andrews has worked for food and beer events for Karma
Foods (Jimmy Carbone) and Jimmy's No 43.

STEPHEN ANDREWS

Nøgne Ø, Gamle Rykene Kraftstation, Lunde 8, Grimstad
Barrel cellar manager at Nøgne Ø, Andrews has a Certificate
in Brewing from the Institute of Brewing and Distilling in
London.

PAUL ANSPACH

Anspach & Hobday, 118 Druid Street, London
Co-owner of Anspach & Hobday, Anspach's mission is to put
London back at the center of Europe for beer.

JILLIAN ANTONELLI

Hidden River Brewing Company, 1808 West Schuylkill Road,
Douglassville
Antonelli helps run a three-barrel, family-owned and -operated
brewpub in Pennsylvania.

BRUNO AQUINO
Lisbon
Creator of the beer website cervejasdomundo.com, the largest online beer community in Portugal, as well as founder of the first and only homebrewing contest in Portugal.

Café Restaurant Brouwerij de Beyerd 155.........Wish I'd opened
CASK Pub & Kitchen 150.....................................Worth the travel
Cerveteca Lisboa 220.................................Local favorite
Mid Hants Railway Watercress Line 133..................Unexpected
Nüetnigenough 177...................................Beer & food
The City Barge 146....................................Beer garden

LUIS ARCE
TicoBirra, various locations in San José
Co-owner of TicoBirra, the first brewing-supplies company in Costa Rica, Arce launched the first craft-beer festival there and founded the Costa Rican Craft Brewers Association.

Apotecario 433...Beer & food
De Garre 181................................Worth the travel
El Vaquero Brewpub 433...........................Local favorite
LB Bieren 434.............................Wish I'd opened
Pitcher & Piano Newcastle 136....................Beer garden
Pizzeria a la leña il Giardino 432.................Unexpected

ISAAC AROCHE
La Chingonería, Centeno 544, Mexico City
Owner of La Chingonería in Mexico.

Biergarten 428......................................Beer garden
El Deposito 429..................................Wish I'd opened
Hop The Beer Experience 2 429....................Worth the travel
Little Miss Brewing 304..........................Unexpected
Tasting Room 429.................................Local favorite
Terraza Cru Cru 429.............................Beer & food

DYLAN BADGER
Ausable Brewing Company, 765 Mace Chasm Road, Keeseville
Badger learned how to homebrew at age eighteen from his older brother, Dan. He attended the University of Vermont for Ecological Agriculture, focusing on hop production. After college, Badger farmed while his brothers planned their future brewery.

Liquids and Solids at the Handlebar 366.............Local favorite
Manhattan Pizza & Pub 372..................Wish I'd opened
The Farmhouse Tap & Grill 371...................Beer & food
The Ginger Man Austin 423...................Worth the travel
The Olde Mecklenburg Brewery 407.............Beer garden
The Skinny Pancake 373.........................Unexpected

LAURENȚIU BĂNESCU
Bere Zaganu, Bodeni 72, Maneciu-Ungureni
Cofounder of Zaganu, Bănescu is reviving craft beer in Romania.

Cellarmaker Brewing Company 311.................Worth the travel
Romanian Craft Beer Bar 249...................Local favorite

HANNAH BARNETT
10 Barrel Brewing Company, 62950 Northeast 18th Street, Bend
Pub events coordinator at 10 Barrel Brewing Company and founder of craft beer and culture at the blog Hop Fox.

Bar Gernika 289.................................Unexpected

Barbarian Brewing Downtown Tap Room 289........Local favorite
Bittercreek Alehouse 289........................Beer & food
Goodlife Brewing Company 293....................Beer garden
Spoken Moto 293.............................Wish I'd opened
White Labs Tasting Room 306.................Worth the travel

TONY BARRON
BrewDog, Balmacassie Industrial Estate, Ellon
UK operations manager for BrewDog in Scotland.

Bloomsbury Lanes 146............................Unexpected
Freshcraft 315...............................Beer & food
Freshcraft 315...............................Worth the travel
Meddlesome Moth 413.........................Wish I'd opened
Modern Times Beer 304........................Local favorite
Stone Brewing World Bistro &
  Gardens Liberty Station 305.................Beer garden

KELLAN BARTOSCH
Wiseacre Brewing Company, 2783 Broad Avenue, Memphis
Captain of Industry and Teller of Tales at Wiseacre Brewing Company, Kellan worked for Sierra Nevada Brewing Co. and is a Certified Cicerone and a beer magazine columnist.

12 South Taproom & Grill 412...............Wish I'd opened
Khyber Pass Pub 392..........................Unexpected
Sage 291.....................................Beer & food
Stanley's Farmhouse Pizza 423................Beer garden
Wiseacre Brewing Company 412.................Local favorite
Young Avenue Deli 412........................Worth the travel

TODD BEAL
Maritime Beer Report, 43 Blue Thistle Road, Halifax
Founder of the Maritime Beer Report blog, Beal writes about craft beer in the Canadian Maritimes and abroad.

BeerTime 254..................................Unexpected
Lagunitas Brewing Company 283...............Beer garden
Mikkeller Bar San Francisco 311.............Wish I'd opened
Novare Res Bier Café 357....................Worth the travel
Social Kitchen & Brewery 310................Beer & food
Stillwell 270...............................Local favorite

LORI BECK
Holy Grale, 1034 Bardstown Road, Louisville
Co-owner of Holy Grale in Kentucky, where craft beer is paired with local and seasonally driven food.

Lommerzheim 204.............................Beer & food
Moeder Lambic Fontainas 176.................Worth the travel
Prater Biergarten 211.......................Beer garden

RYAN BEDFORD
Five Boroughs Brewing Co., 215 47th Street, New York City
Bedford is the taproom and events manager at Five Boroughs.

Bohemian Hall and Beer Garden 379..........Beer garden
Madison Square Garden 378..................Unexpected
Proletariat 376............................Local favorite
Row 34 358.................................Beer & food
Toronado Pub 310..........................Worth the travel

MIRO BELLINI
Premium Beverages, Melbourne
Melbourne-based beer industry professional who runs beer events and education programs. A former beer sommelier and brewery tour guide, Bellini is cofounder of Melbourne's Good Beer Week and Brooklyn Brewery Ambassador for Australia and New Zealand.

Cookie 63...Beer & food
Loop Project Space & Bar 62.......................Unexpected
Moon Dog Craft Brewery 62.....................Local favorite
Section 8 63...Wish I'd opened
Terminus Hotel Fitzroy North 62...............Beer garden
The Royston Hotel 63...................................Worth the travel

SARAH BENNETT
Long Beach
Founding editor of *Beer Paper L.A.* and columnist for *Los Angeles Times.*

Beachwood BBQ 285...................................Local favorite
Highland Park Brewery 300........................Wish I'd opened
Tørst 386..Worth the travel
Uncle Henry's Deli 281.................................Unexpected

JOSHUA M. BERNSTEIN
New York City
Brooklyn-based journalist covering beer, spirits, food, and travel.

Bohemian Hall and Beer Garden 379.........Beer garden
Brooklyn Cider House 384.........................Beer & food
Covenhoven 384...Local favorite
Nahshel Grocery 385.....................................Unexpected
Novare Res Bier Café 357...........................Wish I'd opened

TIM BESECKER
Twin Elephant Brewing Company, 13 Watchung Avenue, Chatham
Cofounder of Twin Elephant Brewing Company in New Jersey, offering handcrafted ales and lagers brewed with locally sourced ingredients when available.

Barcade Jersey City 362.............................Wish I'd opened
Delirium Café 174...Worth the travel
Prohibition Pig 373..Beer & food
Radegast Hall & Biergarten 388.................Beer garden
The Stirling Hotel 364...................................Local favorite

TIM BLADES
New Wave Distribution, 4 Hope Street, Edinburgh
Account manager at New Wave Distribution.

Hawkshead Brewery & The Beer Hall 131...........Beer & food
House of the Trembling Madness 134.............Wish I'd opened
Salt Horse Beer Shop & Bar 140................Local favorite
The Local Taphouse 63..................................Beer garden
The Local Taphouse 63..................................Worth the travel
Westhill Service Station 139.......................Unexpected

KEVIN BLODGER
Union Craft Brewing, 1700 Union Avenue, Unit D, Baltimore
Cofounder of Union Craft Brewing, Blodger has worked for numerous breweries in Maryland, Washington, D.C., and Illinois.

Blue Pit BBQ & Whiskey Bar 404...............Beer garden
Map Room 350..Worth the travel
Max's Taphouse 404......................................Local favorite

GABRIEL BOCANEGRA
Zombier and BierCaB, Carrer de Muntaner 55, Barcelona
Owner of Zombier and BierCab in Spain.

BierCaB 226..Beer & food
BierCaB 226..Local favorite
Cafe Kulminator 168......................................Wish I'd opened
Ma Che Siete Venuti A Fà 234....................Worth the travel

STÉPHANE BOGAERT
Brasserie Saint Germain and Page 24, 26 Route d'Arras, Aix-Noulette
Cofounder of Brasserie Saint Germain in 2003 with his brother Vincent and friend Hervé Descamps, Bogaert discovered craft beer in Boston when studying abroad.

La Capsule 185...Local favorite
La Capsule 185...Worth the travel
Le Bloempot 185...Beer & food
Spuyten Duyvil 388..Beer garden

MATTEO BONFANTI
Birrificio Carrobiolo, Piazza Indipendenza 1, Monza
Brewer at Birrificio Carrobiolo in Italy.

Birra del Carrobiolo 232..............................Local favorite
Birreria Cassina 231.......................................Beer garden
Nüetnigenough 177..Beer & food
The Evening Star 132.....................................Worth the travel

NEIL BONTOFT
Preston
A beer fanatic from England, Bontoft has traveled the world to try great bars and taprooms.

Bundobust Manchester 133.........................Beer & food
Hoppy Ending 230...Unexpected
Tap & Bottles 134..Local favorite
Tap & Bottles 134..Wish I'd opened
The Pilcrow Pub 133.......................................Beer garden
Tørst 386..Worth the travel

JONATHAN BOYCE
Empties, Dublin
Founder, content creator, and interviewer for *Empties* craft-beer blog and a member of the Irish national homebrew club, Boyce is also a competitive homebrewer.

BRUS 126..Wish I'd opened
IMPRFCTO 227..Unexpected
Koelschip 126...Worth the travel
Mother Kelly's 146...Beer garden
The Brew Dock 142...Local favorite
Warpigs Brewpub 126....................................Beer & food

BRIAN BOYER
Mount Rushmore Brewing Company, 140 Mount Rushmore Road, Custer
Owner of Mount Rushmore Brewing Company in South Dakota with his wife, Janet.

AJ's Ore Car Saloon 343................................Wish I'd opened
Buglin' Bull Restaurant and Sports Bar 343...........Local favorite
Buglin' Bull Restaurant and Sports Bar 343........Worth the travel
Hofbräuhaus 214...Beer garden
Moonshine Gulch Saloon 343......................Unexpected
Scottsdale Beer Company 278....................Beer & food

BEN BRADLEY
Warfield Distillery & Brewery, 280 North Main Street, Ketchum
Cofounder of Warfield Distillery & Brewery.

Sheffield's Beer & Wine Garden 351	Beer garden
Sheffield's Beer & Wine Garden 351	Worth the travel
Totoco Eco-Lodge 432	Unexpected
Warfield Distillery & Brewery 290	Beer & food
Warfield Distillery & Brewery 290	Local favorite

BETH BRASH
Beervana, Wellington
Brash runs New Zealand's beer festival, Beervana, which brings together 14,000 people every year.

Bitter Phew 56	Worth the travel
Brew Union Brewing Company 68	Wish I'd opened
Golding's Free Dive 69	Local favorite
Ortega Fish Shack & Bar 70	Beer & food
The Mussel Inn 68	Beer garden
Westpac Stadium 70	Unexpected

ROB BRIGHT
BeerTengoku.com, Tokyo
Manager of the blog BeerTengoku.com, Bright also contributes reviews about Japanese beers and bars.

Beach Muffin 76	Wish I'd opened
Honolulu BeerWorks 288	Beer & food
Shinshu Osake Mura 81	Unexpected
The Faltering Fullback 147	Beer garden
The Smugglers Ale House 134	Worth the travel
Watering Hole 82	Local favorite

SIMON BRODERICK
Rye River Brewing Company, Dublin Road, Celbridge
Beer blogger and beer specialist at Rye River Brewing.

Airbräu 214	Unexpected
Bag Of Nails 130	Worth the travel
L. Mulligan Grocer 142	Beer & food
Sean's Bar 143	Beer garden
Simon Lambert & Sons 143	Local favorite
The Salt House 143	Wish I'd opened

CHRIS BROWN
Holy City Brewing, 4155 Dorchester Road, Charleston
Graduate of the American Brewers Guild, Brown is a founder and production manager at Holy City Brewing.

Brick Store Pub 400	Wish I'd opened
Brick Store Pub 400	Worth the travel
Craftsmen Kitchen & Tap House 410	Beer garden
EVO Pizzeria 411	Beer & food
Kudu Coffee and Craft Beer 411	Local favorite

ADAM BRUCKMAN
Fantasy Beer League, Atlanta
A former homebrewer, Bruckman's newest venture is Fantasy Beer League.

Brick Store Pub 400	Wish I'd opened
Chinesischer Turm 214	Beer garden
The Porter Beer Bar 400	Local favorite
The Porter Beer Bar 400	Worth the travel
Wrecking Bar Brewpub 400	Beer & food

RÉMI BRUSA
Les Bières de Midgard, 118 Rue Juiverie, Chambéry
Brusa he opened Les Bières de Midgard in Savoie in 2013.

Le K7 184	Unexpected
Les Bières de Midgard 184	Beer & food
Les Bières de Midgard 184	Local favorite
Uptown Freehouse 66	Beer garden
Uptown Freehouse 66	Worth the travel

BRYAN BRUSHMILLER
Burley Oak Brewing Company, 10016 Old Ocean City, Boulevard, Berlin
Owner of a brewery in rural Maryland that produces 4,000 barrels a year.

Atomic Liquors 291	Unexpected
Burley Oak Brewing Company 405	Local favorite
ChurchKey 418	Worth the travel
Falling Rock Tap House 314	Beer garden
Granville Moore's 419	Wish I'd opened
Ramen Suzukiya 358	Beer & food

SHAHEEN BUDHRANI
Bestbev, 158A Connaught Road West, Hong Kong
BJCP Certified Level Beer Judge and founder of the craft-beer distribution company Bestbev and Hong Kong's first beer-focused magazine, Coaster.

Black Isle Bar and Rooms 141	Wish I'd opened
Mikkeller Bar Singapore 100	Wish I'd opened
Second Draft 93	Beer & food
The Globe 92	Local favorite
The Water Poet 150	Beer garden

RICHARD BURHOUSE
Magic Rock Brewing, Willow Park Business Centre, Willow Lane, Huddersfield
Cofounder of Magic Rock Brewing with his brother, Jonny.

Bar Desy 218	Beer & food
Bierkeller Au Trappiste 186	Worth the travel
Craven Arms Pub & Cruck Barn 134	Beer garden
Magic Rock Tap 137	Local favorite
The Black Swan at Oldstead 134	Unexpected

NICK BUSH
Drifter Brewing Company, 156 Victoria Road, Cape Town
Founder and head brewer at Drifter Brewing Company in South Africa. Bush named Drifter after a boat his parents sailed on around the world for almost ten years.

BEERHOUSE 262	Worth the travel
Drifter Brewing Company 262	Local favorite

ALEX BUTLER
Sabaja Craft Brewery, Prishtina-Gjilan Highway, Hajvali
Butler began as a homebrewer in New York City and ended up in Kosovo, where he built a craft brewery with his friends.

Bohemian Hall and Beer Garden 379	Beer garden
Constellation Brands Marvin Sands Performing Arts Center 365	Unexpected
Ports Cafe 366	Beer & food
Soma Book Station 253	Local favorite
Tap & Mallet 367	Worth the travel
Young Lion Brewing Company Taproom 365	Wish I'd opened

MATTHEW BUTTIGIEG
Brew Haus, 38 Saint Barbara Bastion, Valletta
Buttigieg fell in love with beer in Belgium and in 2013 returned to Malta, where he imports premium craft beer from around the world.

67 Kapitali 222	Unexpected
Badass Burgers - Razzett L-Ahmar 222	Beer garden
Delirium Café 174	Wish I'd opened
Ryan's Pub 222	Beer & food
Ryan's Pub 222	Local favorite
Stone Brewing World Bistro & Gardens Berlin 208	Worth the travel

NEIL CALLAGHAN
Cigar City Brewing, 3924 West Spruce Street, Tampa
Advanced Cicerone and certified BJCP beer judge, Callaghan is El Lector (with a focus on beer education) for Cigar City Brewing in Florida.

Brick Store Pub 400	Worth the travel
Cigar City Brewing Company 399	Local favorite
Kalamazoo Beer Exchange 336	Wish I'd opened
Mekong Restaurant 414	Unexpected
The Publican 353	Beer & food
Vices & Versa 271	Beer garden

DOMINIC CALZETTA
Cellarmen's, 24310 John R Road, Hazel Park
Calzetta is an owner of Cellarmen's and has certifications from the Cicerone and Beer Judge programs.

Axle Brewing Company Livernois Tap 335	Beer garden
Cellarmen's 336	Local favorite
Kozy Lounge 336	Worth the travel
Mabel Gray 336	Beer & food
Marathon Grand Rapids 335	Unexpected
The Northman 352	Wish I'd opened

MARIO CANESTRELLI
Orbit Beers, Arch 228, Fielding Street, London
Brewer at Orbit Beers, which began when founder Robert Middleton traveled across his native Scotland in his VW campervan to visit every single brewery.

Griess Keller 204	Beer garden
Ma Che Siete Venuti A Fà 234	Worth the travel
Mahr's Bräu 199	Wish I'd opened
Nüetnigenough 177	Beer & food
Stormbird 146	Local favorite

BRUNO CARRILHO
Cerveja Musa, Rua do Açucar 83, Lisbon
Cofounder of Cerveja Musa, Carrilho and his team brewed their first batch of beer in 2016.

Cerveja Musa 220	Local favorite
Embaixada do Porto 221	Unexpected
Garage Beer Company 227	Worth the travel
Ground Burger 221	Beer & food
The Bear's Lair 279	Beer garden

ASHLEIGH CARTER
Bierstadt Lagerhaus, 2875 Blake Street, Denver
Cofounder and head brewer of Bierstadt Lagerhaus, an all-lager traditional brewery.

Barrels & Bottles Brewery 287	Local favorite
Hirschgarten 214	Beer garden

Matchbox 316	Unexpected
Schoenramer Brewery 201	Worth the travel

AUGIE CARTON
Carton Brewing Company, 6 East Washington Avenue, Atlantic Highlands
Cofounder of Carton Brewing Company, a small independent brewery in New Jersey.

Asbury Festhalle & Biergarten 361	Beer garden
Blind Tiger Ale House 377	Worth the travel
Boyle's Tavern 363	Local favorite
Newark Liberty International Airport 363	Unexpected

JASON CARTY
Arms 2 Artisans and Backward Flag Foundation Inc., 699 Challenger Way, Forked River
Executive director of Arms 2 Artisans and Backward Flag Foundation Inc.

Asbury Festhalle & Biergarten 361	Beer garden
Jay's Elbow Room 363	Local favorite
Jay's Elbow Room 363	Unexpected
Jessop's Tavern 396	Worth the travel
The Local Eatery and Pub 363	Wish I'd opened
Varga Bar 393	Beer & food

PHIL CASSELLA
Adirondack Brewery, 33 Canada Street, Lake George
Cassella is marketing director at Adirondack Brewery and High Peaks Distilling.

Eventide Oyster Company 357	Beer & food
Mohawk Taproom & Grill 368	Local favorite
Novare Res Bier Café 357	Worth the travel
Threes Brewing 385	Beer garden

COLLIN CASTORE
Seventh Son Brewing, 1101 North 4th Street, Columbus
Castore had the craft-beer bar Bodega, then started the beer and wine carryout Barrel and Bottle, which is still in operation. Since 2013 he is founder and partner of Seventh Son Brewing and is president of the Ohio Craft Brewing Association.

Finn's Manor 315	Beer garden
Great Notion Brewing and Barrel House 321	Beer & food
Hopleaf 352	Worth the travel
Seventh Son Brewing Company 342	Local favorite
The Porch 397	Unexpected

DIEGO CASTRO
Independent Beer Consultant, Buenos Aires
Cofounder of Somos Cerveceros Civil Association, BJCP judge since 2009, Cicerone program's certified beer server, teacher, and writer of beer.

Breoghan 449	Local favorite
Brouwerij De Halve Maan 180	Beer & food
Cafe Kulminator 168	Wish I'd opened
La Trappe Trappist 154	Beer garden
Stone Brewing World Bistro & Gardens Berlin 208	Worth the travel

LING WAN CHANG
Taiwan Head Brewers Brewing Company, No. 10, Chong An Street, New Taipei City
Chang is in marketing and PR for Head Brewers Brewing Co. in Taiwan.

Duckstein German Brewery & Restaurant 58	Beer & food
Mikkeller Bar Taipei 88	Local favorite
Russian River Brewery 284	Worth the travel
TIME Keeper 88	Beer garden

RAFI CHAUDRY
Torn Label Brewing Company, 1708 Campbell Street, Kansas City
CEO and cofounder of Torn Label Brewing Company.

Bir & Fud 233	Beer & food
Double Shift Brewing Company 339	Local favorite
Pizza Port Carlsbad 280	Worth the travel
Wedge Brewing Company 406	Beer garden

JING CHEN
BlackLab Brewhouse & Kitchen, Palau de Mar, Barcelona
Cofounder and director of BlackLab, with all house-brewed, award-winning beers.

BlackLab Brewhouse & Kitchen 226	Worth the travel
Fitgers Brewhouse 337	Local favorite

LIUBOMIR CHONOS
KANAAL, Bulevard Madrid 2, Sofia
Chonos is cofounder of KANAAL.

Amsterdam Roest 164	Beer garden
Kaapse Maria 156	Beer & food
KANAAL 254	Local favorite
Le Bar du Matin 175	Wish I'd opened
Moeder Lambic Original 176	Worth the travel

JOEY CHUNG
The Bottle Shop, 114 Man Nin Street, Hong Kong
Cales and events coordinator at The Bottle Shop.

Brewers Beer Bar 110	Worth the travel
Second Draft 93	Beer & food
The Beer Bay 92	Unexpected
The Bottle Shop 98	Beer garden
The Globe 92	Local favorite

LAURENT CICUREL
Mousquebières, 6 Avenue Jean Aicard, Paris
Co-owner of La Fine Mousse, Cicurel has a mission to bring craft beers to Paris.

Bar Gallia 195	Beer garden
La Capsule 185	Wish I'd opened
La Fine Mousse 193	Beer & food
La Fine Mousse 193	Local favorite
Moeder Lambic Original 176	Worth the travel

IONUT CIOBOTA
Red City Transylvania, Sura Mare, Sibiu
Ciobota is one of four friends who produce 1717 in collaboration with a small 200-year-old family-owned Bavarian nanobrewery.

Le Petit Naples 249	Beer & food
Szimpla 249	Local favorite

BRAD CLARK
Jackie O's Pub & Brewery, 25 Campbell Street, Athens
Oversees brewing for Jackie O's.

Harmar Tavern 343	Unexpected
Jackie O's 342	Local favorite
Map Room 350	Worth the travel
Oxbow Brewing Company 357	Beer & food
The Greenhouse Tavern 342	Beer & food
Three Penny Taproom 372	Wish I'd opened

MICHAEL CO STEPHEN
Nipa Brew, 9635 Kamagong Street, Makati City
Founder of Nipa Brew Craft Beers, a microbrewery in the Philippines.

Alamat Filipino Pub & Deli 98	Beer garden
Backyard Kitchen + Brew 99	Beer & food
Brewerkz Riverside Point 100	Worth the travel
Joe's Brew 98	Wish I'd opened
Los Indios Bravos Boracay 99	Unexpected
Nipa Brew 98	Local favorite

MARTIN COAD
Greenstar Brewing, 3800 North Clark Street, Chicago
Coad opened Greenstar Brewing at Uncommon Ground in 2014. He had worked for the homebrew store Brew and Grow in Chicago and was brewmaster for Hofbräuhaus Chicago.

Duseks Board & Beer 352	Beer & food
Hopleaf 352	Worth the travel
Piece Brewery and Pizzeria 353	Wish I'd opened
Resi's Bierstube 352	Beer garden
The Dock 353	Unexpected
Uncommon Ground 351	Local favorite

JOHNNIE COMPTON
Highway Manor Brewing, 2238 Gettysburg Road, Camp Hill
CEO and founder of Highway Manor Brewing, Compton has been brewing for 18 years.

Hunger-N-Thirst 370	Local favorite
Kensington Quarters 392	Beer & food
Lux Lounge 367	Beer garden
Mastracchio's Restaurant & Lounge 370	Unexpected
Monk's Café 392	Worth the travel

LARRY COOK
Dodge City Brewing Co., 701 3rd Avenue, Dodge City
Brewer at Dodge City Brewing Co., Cook is also an award-winning homebrewer and BJCP Certified Beer Judge.

Avery Brewing Company 286	Beer & food
Central Standard Brewing 402	Beer garden
Dodge City Brewing 401	Local favorite
Falling Rock Tap House 314	Wish I'd opened
Falling Rock Tap House 314	Worth the travel
Gella's Diner & Lb Brewing Company 401	Unexpected

ANDREW COOPER
Wild Beer Co., Lower Westcombe Farm, Evercreech
Cofounder of the Wild Beer Co., a brewery in the UK specializing in barrel-aged, wild, and mixed fermented beers.

Eleven Madison Park 376	Beer & food
Hauser & Wirth Somerset 136	Unexpected
Hive Beach Café 131	Beer garden
Row 34 358	Wish I'd opened

Stomping Ground Brewery & Beer Hall 62........Worth the travel
Wild Beer at Wapping Wharf 130............................Local favorite

CRAIG COOPER
Bach Brewing, Auckland
Founder of Bach Brewing, Cooper worked in Canada and
Australia before returning to New Zealand.
Craft Beer Market 268..Worth the travel
Galbraith's Alehouse 67......................................Beer & food
Little Creatures Brewing Fremantle 58.............Wish I'd opened
Lumsden Freehouse 67..Beer garden
The Beer Spot 67...Local favorite

TOBY COOPER
The Globe, Garley Building, 45–53 Graham Street, Hong
Kong
Owner of The Globe since 2003, Cooper is founding chairman
of the Craft Beer Association of Hong Kong.
Craft Wheat & Hops 263.......................................Unexpected
Crate Brewery & Pizzeria 147.............................Beer garden
Euston Tap 148...Wish I'd opened
The Harp 147..Worth the travel
Maverick's Beach Bar 93......................................Unexpected
Second Draft 93..Beer & food
Second Draft 93..Local favorite
The Taphouse 56...Worth the travel

RAZVAN COSTACHE
Bucharest
Writer at Universitatea de Bere in Romania, Costache is
passionate about beer.
Blind Tiger Ale House 377....................................Worth the travel
BrewDog Brussels 174...Wish I'd opened
Kaapse Maria 156...Beer & food
Mikkeller Bar Bucharest 249...............................Local favorite
Stone Arch 338...Unexpected
Surly Brewing Company 338................................Beer garden

COLBY COX
Roadhouse Brewing Company, 1225 Gregory Lane, Box 1686,
Jackson Hole
Cox, a garage brewer, and chef Gavin Fine brew big IPAs,
Belgians, and extreme beers in small batches in Wyoming.
They opened Roadhouse Brewing Company's production
brewery and tap room in 2017.
Cardrona Hotel 68...Beer garden
Hotel Cloudbase 440...Unexpected
Roadhouse Brewing Company
  Pub & Eatery 296..Local favorite
't Poatersgat 181..Worth the travel
The Bottle & Cork 396..Wish I'd opened
Über Tap Room & Cheese Bar 346......................Beer & food

ETHAN COX
Community Beer Works, 15 Lafayette Avenue, Buffalo
Founder and co-owner of Community Beer Works.
BeerBistro 275..Beer & food
KeyBank Center 365...Unexpected
Mr. Goodbar 365...Local favorite
Resi's Bierstube 352...Beer garden
The Well 389..Worth the travel
Toronado Pub 310...Wish I'd opened

MAXON COX
Wolves' Head Brewing Company, 219 South Walnut
Street, Muncie
Cox has worked at Wolves' Head Brewing Company in Indiana
since its opening in 2012 and is a graduate of the Midwest
Bartenders School.
The Heorot 334...Local favorite

BLAKE CRAWFORD
The Alementary Brewing Co., 58 Voorhis Lane, Hackensack
Brewer and chemical engineer Crawford teamed up with a
molecular biologist to create the Alementary Brewing Co.
in suburban New Jersey.
Ambulance Brew House 366................................Beer garden
Ambulance Brew House 366................................Worth the travel
Beer Culture 377...Wish I'd opened
Debonair Music Hall 364.......................................Unexpected
Jockey Hollow Bar & Kitchen 363......................Beer & food
The Cloverleaf Tavern 362...................................Local favorite

JACK CREGAN
Bison Beer, 7 East Street, Brighton
Director at Bison Beer in the UK.
Beer Bear 130..Unexpected
Mikkeller Bar Copenhagen 127..........................Wish I'd opened
Mother Kelly's 146..Worth the travel
The Brunswick 132...Beer garden
The Pond 132...Beer & food
The Pond 132...Local favorite

PETER CROWLEY
Haymarket Pub & Brewery and Haymarket Brewery &
Taproom, 737 West Randolph Street, Chicago, and 9301 Red
Arrow Highway, Bridgman
Owner of Haymarket Pub & Brewery and Haymarket Brewery
& Taproom, Crowley has more than twenty years' professional
brewing experience and has won fifteen GABF and WBC
awards.
Half Acre Beer Company 352...............................Local favorite
Hopleaf 352...Beer & food
Monk's Café 392..Worth the travel
Transient Artisan Ales 334....................................Unexpected

JOSEMARI CUERVO
Crows Craft Brewing & Distilling Co., 238 Anahaw Street,
Muntinlupa
Founder of Crows Craft Brewing & Distilling Co. In 2016,
Crows Craft started distilling spirits, and recently they
launched the 1st Philippine Craft Gin.
Bar Pintxos 98..Beer & food
Bar Pintxos 98..Local favorite
Hopsy 279..Unexpected
Russian River Brewery 284...................................Worth the travel

JAMES CUTHBERTSON
Dark Star Brewing, Star Road Industrial Estate,
Partridge Green
Managing director of Dark Star Brewing since 2017.
Craft Beer Co 147..Wish I'd opened
Lucky Beach 132...Unexpected
Red Lion & Sun 148..Beer garden
The Lockhart Tavern 137.......................................Beer & food
The Lockhart Tavern 137.......................................Local favorite
The Wenlock Arms 148...Worth the travel

CUYPERS
Het Nest Brouwerij , Beyntel 17, Oud-Turnhout
Brewery president and head of operations at Brouwerij Het Nest.

Bistrot Brussels Airport 174	Unexpected
In Den Spytighen Duvel 168	Local favorite
Monk's Café 392	Worth the travel
Teresa's Next Door 371	Beer & food

MELENTIJEVIĆ KOSARA DANGIĆ
Kabinet Brewery, Despota Stefana Lazarevića 11, Nemenikuće
Cofounder of the first Serbian craft brewery and the only greenfield brewery in the Balkans.

Endorfin Bar & Restaurant 252	Beer & food
Kabinet Brewery 253	Worth the travel
Kod Tome I Nade 253	Unexpected
Majstor Za Pivo 253	Local favorite
Omnipollos Hatt 118	Wish I'd opened
Samo Pivo 253	Beer garden

GUILLAUME DAVID
Brasserie de Sulauze, Chemin du Vieux Sulauze, Miramas
Cofounder and brewer at Brasserie de Sulauze in the South of France.

Brasserie de Sulauze 185	Beer garden
Fietje 185	Worth the travel
La cuisine de Zebuline et Zigoto 185	Beer & food

YVAN DE BAETS
Brasserie de la Senne, Chaussée de Gand 565, Brussels
Masterbrewer and cofounder of Brasserie de la Senne in Belgium, De Baets studied Brewing at Meurice Institute of Malting and Brewing Sciences, where he teaches. He is also a beer writer and an international beer judge.

Amtrak 418	Unexpected
La Buvette Saint-Sébastien 175	Beer garden
La Fleur en Papier Doré 175	Wish I'd opened
Le Coq 176	Local favorite
Les Brigittines 176	Beer & food
The Avenue Pub 403	Worth the travel

THEO DE BEER
Anvil Ale Brewery, Naledi Drive, Dullstroom
De Beer and his wife, Sarie, own Anvil Ale Brewery, which specializes in brewing European-style ales.

Afro Caribbean Brewery 262	Worth the travel
Anvil Ale House & Brewery 262	Beer garden
Anvil Ale House & Brewery 262	Local favorite
Anvil Ale House & Brewery 262	Wish I'd opened
Banana Jam Cafe 262	Beer & food
Sedgefield Craft Brewery 263	Unexpected

SHAWN DECKER
Sketchbook Brewing Co., 821 Chicago Avenue, Evanston
Founder and managing partner of Sketchbook Brewing Co., and faculty at School of the Art Institute of Chicago.

Bryggeri Helsinki 122	Beer & food
Covenhoven 384	Worth the travel
Fountainhead 352	Local favorite
Letná Beer Garden 241	Beer garden
Monhegan Brewing Company 357	Unexpected
Oxbow Brewing Company 357	Wish I'd opened

ÉLOI DEIT
Brasserie Dunham, 3809 Rue Principale, Dunham
Head brewer at Brasserie Dunham, Deit uses local ingredients in the spirit of a true farmhouse brewery.

Austin Beer Garden Brewing Company 422	Beer garden
Birreria Volo 274	Wish I'd opened
Birreria Volo 274	Worth the travel
Brasserie Dunham 270	Local favorite
Le Bateau de Nuit 271	Unexpected
The Publican 353	Beer & food

MATT DELUCA
Castle Island Brewing Co., 31 Astor Avenue, Norwood
Head brewer at Castle Island Brewing Co.

Prohibition Pig 373	Beer & food
Prohibition Pig 373	Worth the travel
Radegast Hall & Biergarten 388	Beer garden
Slab 358	Wish I'd opened
Three Needs Brewery & Taproom 372	Local favorite
Two Georges Waterfront Grille 396	Unexpected

CINDY DERAMA
Twin Elephant Brewing Company, 13 Watchung Avenue, Chatham Borough
Cofounder of Twin Elephant Brewing Company with her husband, Tim Besecker, and their friend Scott McLuskey in New Jersey.

Brouwerij lane 385	Wish I'd opened
Cigar City Brewing 399	Unexpected
Prohibition Pig 373	Beer & food
Radegast Hall & Biergarten 388	Beer garden
The Stirling Hotel 364	Local favorite
To Be In Brugge 181	Worth the travel

KATY DEWINTER
New Heights Brewing Company, 928 5th Avenue South, Nashville
Tasting-room manager at New Heights Brewing Company.

Borough Market 150	Unexpected
BrewDog Bristol 130	Worth the travel
Small Bar 305	Wish I'd opened
The Filling Station 412	Local favorite
The Pharmacy Burger Parlor & Beer Garden 413	Beer garden
Tiger!Tiger! 306	Beer & food

CHRISTOPHER DEWOLF
Hong Kong
Canadian journalist based in Hong Kong since 2007, DeWolf writes about beer, cities, architecture, and design.

Apex 320	Beer garden
In de Wildeman 163	Wish I'd opened
Second Draft 93	Beer & food
TAP: The Ale Project 93	Local favorite
The Beer Bay 92	Unexpected
Vices & Versa 271	Worth the travel

STEFANO DI GIOACCHINO
Wilk Craft Beer, Avenida 9, Calle 33, San Jose
Owner of Wilk Craft Beer, the first establishment in Costa Rica to specialize in craft beer.

Craic Irish Pub 433	Unexpected
Delirium Café 174	Worth the travel
Mikkeller Bar San Francisco 311	Wish I'd opened

PIETRO DI PILATO
BrewFist Brewery, Via Molinari 5, Codogno
Founder and head brewer at BrewFist Brewery in Italy.

ANA DIAS
5 e Meio, 48 Rua Quinta da Mata, Lisbon
Dias has collaborated with the microbrewery 5 e Meio since
2014.

JOE DICK
James Clay, Edinburgh
Account manager for Scotland at James Clay.

EVAN DOAN
Doan's Craft Brewing, 1830 Powell Street, Vancouver
Co-owner and cofounder of Doans Craft Brewing with his
brother Mike.

DOUG DOZARK
Cycle Brewing, 534 Central Avenue, Saint Petersburg
Owner of Cycle Brewing in Florida.

KEVIN DRAKE
Alibi Ale Works, 10069 Bridge Street, Truckee, and 204 East
Enterprise Street, Incline Village
Drake and Rich Romo founded Alibi Ale Works in 2014 in
Nevada, where they have a brewery. They also have a public
house and music venue in California.

SCOTT DRAKE
Wormtown Brewery, 72 Shrewsbury Street, Worcester
Cofounder of Wormtown Brewery, Drake has been brewing
since 2011.

MARK DRUTMAN
Craft Beer Cellar Waterbury, 3 Elm Street, Waterbury
Co-owner of Craft Beer Cellar Waterbury, Drutman, has nearly
fifteen years in the industry and is a Certified Cicerone.

JOHN DUFFY
The Beer Nut Blog, Dublin
A Dublin-based beer blogger since 2005.

OLIVIER DUPRAS
Brasserie Isle de Garde, 1039 Rue Beaubien Est, Montreal
Cofounder of Brasserie Isle de Garde, Dupras started as a
gypsy brewer. Since March 2017, they brew on-site.

MATTY ECK
Strangeways Brewing, 350 Lansdowne Road, Fredericksburg
Brewmaster at Strangeways Brewing in Virginia.

PETER EICHHORN
Mixology, Berlin
Contributing writer for *Mixology*.

PATRICK EJLERSKOV
WestEnd BrygCentral, Westend 5, Copenhagen
Owner and head brewer of the microbrewery WestEnd
BrygCentral in Denmark.

Café Dyrehaven 127................................Wish I'd opened
Café Rose Red 180................................Unexpected
Calverley's Brewery 131................................Beer garden
Fermentoren 127................................Local favorite
Øl & Brød 127................................Beer & food
Toronado Pub 310................................Worth the travel

ANDRÉ EK
Brekeriet Beer AB, Österleden 165, Landskrona
With his two brothers, Ek is cofounder of Brekeriet Beer AB, a
sour-beer brewery in Sweden.

BierCaB 226................................Worth the travel
Glam Café 252................................Unexpected
Mahr's Bräu 199................................Beer garden
Malmö Brewing Co & Taproom 113................Local favorite
Row 34 358................................Beer & food
The Porter Beer Bar 400................................Wish I'd opened

LAURI ELANGO
Vaat Brewery, Türi 6, Tallinn
A full-time beer enthusiast, Elango runs Vaat Brewery in
Estonia with three friends.

BierCaB 226................................Wish I'd opened
Koht 246................................Local favorite
Leib Resto ja Aed 247................................Beer & food
One Pint Pub 122................................Worth the travel
Pudel Baar 247................................Beer garden
Tallinn Airport 247................................Unexpected

ANNA ELLIS
Resurgence Brewing Company, 1250 Niagara Street, Buffalo
Social media and marketing manager at Resurgence Brewing
Company in New York.

Genesee Brew House 367................................Beer & food
McSorley's Old Ale House 376................Worth the travel
Rabbit Hole 327................................Wish I'd opened
Resurgence Brewing Company 365................Local favorite
Wolff's Biergarten Syracuse 368................................Beer garden

BARRY ELWONGER
Motorworks Brewing, 1014 9th Street West, Bradenton
Director of sales and marketing at Motorworks Brewing,
Elwonger is a Certified Cicerone and BJCP judge.

À la Mort Subite 174................................Worth the travel
Jester King Brewery 423................................Beer garden
Kickbacks Gastropub 397................................Wish I'd opened
The Explorium Brewpub 344................................Beer & food
The Independent Bar and Cafe 399................Local favorite
Tropicana Field 398................................Unexpected

ANDRES ERAZO
Cervecería Quiteña, Avenida Manuel Córdova Galarza
S4-187, Quito
Erazo has been brewing beer since 2011 at the family-owned
Cerceveria Quiteña in Ecuador.

Cafe Kulminator 168................................Worth the travel
Quiteña Craft Beer Company 441................Local favorite
Stone Brewing World Bistro &
   Gardens Liberty Station 305................................Beer & food

LASSE ERICSSON
Nynäshamns Ångbryggeri, Lövlundsvägen 4, Nynashamn
Ericsson is cofounder and brewer at Nynäshamns
Ångbryggeri.

Akkurat 119................................Local favorite
In de Wildeman 163................................Worth the travel
Kebenekaise Fjällstation 113................................Unexpected
Spezial-Keller 199................................Beer garden
Zum Franziskaner 118................................Beer & food

KEVIN ERSKINE
Coelacanth Brewing, 760 A West 22nd Street, Norfolk
Author, consultant, and distiller in the spirits and beer industry
in the U.S. and Scotland.

Coelacanth Brewing Company 414................Local favorite
Mekong Restaurant 414................................Worth the travel

RYAN EVANS
Bruz Beers, 1675 West 67th Avenue #100, Denver
Cofounder of Bruz Beers, Evans is responsible for the
brewery's operations.

Ale House 314................................Beer & food
Bruz Beers 314................................Local favorite
Delirium Café 174................................Wish I'd opened
Delirium Café 174................................Worth the travel
Recess Beer Garden 316................................Beer garden

PAUL FALLEN
Fallen Brewing, The Old Engine Shed, Station House, Kippen
Founder and managing director of Fallen Brewing, an award-
winning brewery on the site of the old Kippen railway station
in rural Stirlingshire.

Stone Brewing World Bistro &
   Gardens Escondido 281................................Worth the travel
Sugar Boat 139................................Beer & food
The Barton Arms 136................................Unexpected
The Bow Bar 139................................Wish I'd opened
The Holyrood 9A 139................................Local favorite
The Ship Inn Fife 140................................Beer garden

AIDY FENWICK
Brooklyn Brewery, 79 North 11th Street, New York City
Scottish brand ambassador at Brooklyn Brewery.

Bundobust Leeds 137................................Beer & food
Grunting Growler 140................................Local favorite
Hemelvaart Bier Cafe 141................................Unexpected
Little Leeds Beerhouse 138................................Wish I'd opened
Local Option 351................................Worth the travel
Trillium Brewing Company 359................................Beer garden

JEN FERGUSON
Hop Burns & Black, 38 East Dulwich Road, London
Co-owner of Hop Burns & Black, an award-winning beer, hot
sauce, and vinyl record shop.

Avalon Inn at Glastonbury Festival 136................Unexpected
Ortega Fish Shack & Bar 70................................Beer & food
Proletariat 376................................Wish I'd opened
Proletariat 376................................Worth the travel
Southampton Arms 148................................Beer garden
The Marble Arch Inn 133................................Local favorite

JUAN FERNÁNDEZ
Malte, Rúa Galera 47, A Coruña
Owner of Malte, a cervezoteca in the northwest of Spain that specializes in pairing food with beer.

BierCaB 226	Beer & food
El Lúpulo Feroz 218	Local favorite
Garage Beer Company 227	Wish I'd opened
Letraria Craft Beer Garden Porto 221	Beer garden
Nel Buco del Mulo 234	Unexpected

CHARLES FINKEL
The Pike Brewing Company, 1415 1st Avenue, Seattle
Founder and chairman of Merchant du Vin (the world's largest craft-beer importer), founder of The Pike Brewing Company in Seattle, and a renowned expert in pairing food with beer.

Ayinger Bräustüberl 198	Beer garden
Delta Sky Club 326	Unexpected
Pike Brewing Company 327	Local favorite
Pike Brewing Company 327	Worth the travel
Tankard & Tun 328	Beer & food
Ye Olde Cheshire Cheese 146	Wish I'd opened

JÖRG FINKELDEY
Brew Africa Consulting, Cape Town
Beer consultant at Brew Africa Consulting, Finkeldey is former owner of Camelthorn Brewing Company in Namibia.

Berg River Brewery 263	Local favorite
Brauerei-Gasthof Plank 201	Worth the travel
Mad Giant 262	Unexpected
Urban Brewing Company 263	Wish I'd opened
Waldwirtschaft Biergarten Großhesselohe 215	Beer garden

JOSEPH FINKENBINDER
Bionic Brew, Shahe Jie Pedestrian Street, Baishizhou
Founder of Bionic Brew, Finkenbinder kicked off Shenzhen's craft-beer scene in 2014 by opening its first underground tap room.

Bionic Brew 87	Local favorite
Tröegs Independent Brewing 370	Beer & food
Tröegs Independent Brewing 370	Worth the travel

CARLA FISHER
Backslope Brewing, 1107 9th Street West, Columbia Falls
General manager of Backslope Brewing, a company Fisher started with her husband in 2015.

Backslope Brewing 291	Beer & food
Backslope Brewing 291	Local favorite
Backslope Brewing 291	Wish I'd opened
Bonsai Brewing Project 291	Beer garden
HA Brewing Co. 291	Worth the travel

NEIL FISHER
WeldWerks Brewing Company, 508 8th Avenue, Greeley
Co-owner, cofounder, and head brewer of WeldWerks Brewing Co., named *USA Today*'s Best New Brewery in the U.S.

Monk's Café 392	Worth the travel
WeldWerks Brewing Company 287	Local favorite

WILL FISHER
Austin Street Brewery, 1 Industrial Way, Suite 8, Portland
Cofounder of Austin Street Brewery, Fisher is a self-taught homebrewer.

Novare Res Bier Café 357	Beer garden
Novare Res Bier Café 357	Wish I'd opened
Oxbow Blending & Bottling 357	Local favorite
Simmel Market Munich 215	Unexpected
Slab 358	Beer & food
Zeitgeist 310	Worth the travel

TONY FORDER
Ale Street News, Maywood
Forder is cofounder and editor of *Ale Street News*, covering craft beer in the U.S. for 25 years.

Birreria Le Baladin 232	Beer & food
Defiant Brewing Company 366	Local favorite
Falling Rock Tap House 314	Worth the travel
Ithaca Beer Company 366	Beer garden
Popeye 83	Wish I'd opened
Shell Station 367	Unexpected

AMELIA FRANKLIN
Laughing Monk Brewing, 1439 Egbert Avenue, San Francisco
Director of sales at Laughing Monk Brewing, a small-batch craft brewery that draws from Californian and Belgian heritage.

Burrito Union 337	Beer & food
Delirium Café 174	Worth the travel
Franklins Restaurant, Brewery, and General Store 405	Local favorite
Oriole Park at Camden Yards 405	Unexpected
Takoda 419	Beer garden
The Church Brew Works 370	Wish I'd opened

CHRIS FROSAKER
Hi-Wire Brewing, 2 Huntsman Place, Asheville
Co-owner of Hi-Wire Brewing in North Carolina, Frosaker manages two breweries.

Appalachian Vintner 406	Local favorite
Banger's Sausage House & Beer Garden 422	Beer garden
Euclid Hall 314	Beer & food
Fish Heads Bar and Grill 408	Unexpected
Toronado Pub 310	Wish I'd opened
Tørst 386	Worth the travel

JONO GALUSZKA
The Crafty Pint, Palmerston North
Award-winning beer writer based in New Zealand.

Brew Union Brewing Company 68	Beer garden
Christchurch International Airport 67	Unexpected
Galbraith's Alehouse 67	Wish I'd opened
Hashigo Zake 69	Local favorite
Logan Brown Restaurant 69	Beer & food

ALESSIO GATTI
Canediguerra, Via del Prato 11, Alessandria
Founder of Canediguerra brewery in Italy, Gatti started working as a professional brewer in 2006.

Beershop Maddalena 231	Unexpected
Bere Buona Birra 232	Wish I'd opened
Birreria Luna Turca 232	Beer garden
Birrificio Lambrate Adelchi 232	Worth the travel
Ranzani13 230	Beer & food
Scurreria Beer & Bagel 231	Local favorite

MATT GELSTHORPE

Bittercreek Alehouse, 246 North 8th Street, Boise
Gelsthorpe leads the beer buying for Bittercreek Alehouse
in Idaho, and previously curated the beer aisle at the Boise
Co-op.

Bittercreek Alehouse 289..Local favorite
Deschutes Brewery Public House 321.....................Beer & food
PreFunk Beer Bar Nampa 290..........................Wish I'd opened
Roper's Regal Beagle 332.....................................Unexpected
The Stumbling Monk 328........................Worth the travel
Urban Chestnut Brewing Company 341.................Beer garden

ULRIKE GENZ

Schneeule Brauerei, Edinburger Strasse 59, Berlin
Owner of fifth-generation family-owned Landbrauhaus
Hofstetten in Austria.

Beereau 209...Local favorite
Brauerei-Gasthaus zum Max 199.....................Worth the travel
Brauerei-Gasthof Müller 201...........................Beer & food
Køpi 210...Unexpected
St. Georgen Bräu Keller 199............................Beer garden

LAWRENCE GEORGE

Brick & Feather Brewery, 78 11th Street, Turners Falls
Cofounder of Brick & Feather in 2015 with his wife, George has
worked in breweries since 2007.

Armsby Abbey 361......................................Beer & food
Five Eyed Fox 361.......................................Local favorite
Toronado Pub 310.......................................Worth the travel

PARASKEVAS GIAGMOUROGLOU

Satyr Brews, various locations
A Greek gypsy brewer, Giagmouroglou showcases out-of-the
norm brews.

BRUS 126...Wish I'd opened
Euston Tap 148..................................Worth the travel
The Lazy Bulldog Pub 254..................Beer & food
The Local Pub 254.............................Local favorite

JERRY GNAGY

Against the Grain Brewery, 401 East Main Street, Louisville
Cofounder of Against the Grain Brewery, Louisville's first
brewer-owned brewery.

Edmund's Oast Restaurant 411.......................Beer & food
Holy Grale 402...Beer garden
Holy Grale 402...Local favorite
Local Option 351..Worth the travel
Sassy's 322..Wish I'd opened
State of Beer 409..Unexpected

MIKE GOGUEN

Fork and Bottle Restaurant, Allmendstrasse 20, Zurich
Goguen founded the restaurant Fork & Bottle in 2012 as an
extension of his catering company, Melt.

Banana Jam Cafe 262....................................Unexpected
BierCaB 226..Worth the travel
Russian River Brewery 284.............................Wish I'd opened
The International Beer Bar 188.........................Local favorite
The Monk's Kettle 310.....................................Beer & food
Warpigs Brewpub 126.....................................Beer garden

DANIEL GOH

Smith Street Taps, 335 Smith Street #02-062, Singapore
Founder of The Good Beer Company and co-owner of award-
winning craft-beer hawker stall Smith Street Taps. Goh is also
the editor of SpiritedSingapore.com.

Little Island Brewing Company 100.....................Local favorite
Mekong Restaurant 414....................................Beer & food
Mikkeller Bangkok 96......................................Wish I'd opened
Stone Brewing World Bistro &
    Gardens Berlin 208.......................................Beer garden
The Beer Farm 58..Worth the travel
The Hop Locker 149..Unexpected

ALBERTO GÓMEZ

In Peccatum Craft Beer, Polígono Industrial San Cibrao das
Viñas, Calle 13, Nave 16, Ourense
CEO and founder of In Peccatum Craft Beer.

BierCaB 226..Worth the travel
Bret 165...Beer garden
Brew Wild Pizza Bar 219..................................Wish I'd opened
Cervezoteca Malte 219.....................................Beer & food
Los Bandidos 246..Unexpected
Malte 219...Local favorite

HUGO GONÇALVES

Cerveja Depressão, Lisbon
Blogger at Cerveja Depressão.

Cerveteca Lisboa 220......................................Local favorite
Dieu du Ciel! 271...Worth the travel
Dois Corvos Cervejeira 221..............................Wish I'd opened
Tørst 386...Beer & food

TIM GORMLEY

Burial Beer Company, 40 Collier Avenue, Asheville
Cofounder and head brewer at Burial Beer Company.

Apex 320...Beer garden
Bambinos Pizzeria 326....................................Unexpected
Edmund's Oast Restaurant 411........................Worth the travel
Quinn's Pub 327..Beer & food
The Dray 326...Wish I'd opened
Wedge Brewing Company 406..........................Local favorite

JAMES GOULDING

Wild Beer Co., Lower Westcombe Farm, Evercreech
A brewer for almost ten years, Goulding works at The Wild
Beer Co., a farmhouse brewery.

Another 8 80..Worth the travel
Café Beermoth 133..Wish I'd opened
Headrow House 137...Beer garden
The Abyss 114...Unexpected
The Elgin 149...Beer & food
The Mermaid Clapton 149................................Local favorite

ROLAND GRABER

CraftGallery, Marktgasse 38, Bern
Graber and his wife, Karin, sell craft beer from more than
fifteen countries at their shop, CraftGallery.

Barbière 186..Beer garden
Bierkeller Au Trappiste 186...............................Local favorite
CraftGallery 187...Beer & food
Moment 187...Unexpected
The International Beer Bar 188..........................Wish I'd opened
Warpigs Brewpub 126......................................Worth the travel

DAVE GRANT

Fierce Beer, Kirkhill Industrial Estate, Aberdeen
Managing director at Fierce Beer and recipient of best beer award in Scotland.

Anchorage Brewing Company 278............................Beer garden
BrewDog Castlegate 138...Local favorite
City Beer Store 311...Worth the travel
MUSA 138...Local favorite
Stone Brewing World Bistro
& Gardens Escondido 281.................................Wish I'd opened
The Rake 149..Unexpected

RICK GREEN

Vancouver
Vancouver branch president of the Campaign for Real Ale, publisher of the *British Columbia Beer Blog*, executive director of the Craft Brewers Guild of British Columbia, and cofounder of the Vancouver Craft Beer Week festival.

Great Leap Brewing 86..Local favorite
Hofbräuhaus 214...Beer garden
Spinnakers Gastro Brewpub
& Guesthouses 269...Beer & food
Spinnakers Gastro Brewpub
& Guesthouses 269...Worth the travel
Tørst 386...Wish I'd opened
Yugong Yishan 87...Unexpected

GEOFF GRIGGS

Blenheim
Beer writer, commentator, and judge based in New Zealand.

Galbraith's Alehouse 67.....................................Wish I'd opened
Moa Brewery Bar 68...Local favorite
Tahi Cafe & Bar 67...Unexpected
The Anchor 136...Beer & food
The Bell Inn 130...Beer garden
The Falkland Arms 135.......................................Worth the travel

LAUREN GRIMM

Grimm Artisanal Ales, 990 Metropolitan Avenue, New York City
Cofounder of Grimm Artisanal Ales in Brooklyn.

Beer Table 377..Unexpected
Booze'n Blues 174..Worth the travel
Gold Star Beer Counter 387...................................Local favorite
Mekelburg's 384...Beer & food
The Well 389..Beer garden

CHARLES GUERRIER

Southeast Asia Brewers Conference, Singapore
Director of the Southeast Asian Brewers Conference, Guerrier has worked in the beer industry in Asia for more than 20 years.

'T Kelderke 177...Beer & food
Ant 'n Bee 80...Worth the travel
Bia Hoi Junction Hanoi 97......................................Unexpected
BiaCraft Artisan Ales 97......................................Wish I'd opened
Pasteur Street Brewing Company 97...................Local favorite
The Ship Inn Devon 131..Beer garden

MOLLY GUNN

The Porter Beer Bar, 1156 Euclid Avenue, Atlanta
Owner of The Porter Beer Bar.

Apex 320...Beer garden
Blind Tiger Ale House 377..................................Wish I'd opened

Cafe Kulminator 168..Worth the travel
One Flew South 400..Unexpected
The Porter Beer Bar 400..Local favorite
The Publican 353...Beer & food

VADIM GUROV

Zagovor Brewery, 1-Y Silikatnyy Pereulok, Moscow
Gurov is the cofounder of Zagovor Brewery.

Protokoll 208...Worth the travel
Ratio Beerworks 316..Beer garden
RULE Taproom 246..Local favorite
Sunset Grille & Tap Room 373...............................Beer & food
Taps Beer Bar 100...Unexpected

JAROSLAW GUZDA

Omerta Pub, Kupa 3, 31-057 Krakow
After a career in oil and fuel trading, Guzda followed his dream to open Omerta Pub, one of the oldest pubs in Poland.

Bir & Fud 233..Beer & food
Il Serpente 233...Unexpected
Omerta Pub 240...Local favorite
Open Baladin Roma 234....................................Worth the travel
Viva La Pinta 240..Beer garden

JAMIL HADDAD

Colonel Beer, Sea Side Road, Batroun
Founder of Colonel Beer—consisting of Colonel Microbrewery and Colonel Brewpub & Restaurant—Haddad was born and raised in Batroun, Lebanon.

Colonel Beer 104..Beer garden
Colonel Beer 104..Local favorite
Colonel Beer 104...Wish I'd opened
Stone Brewing World Bistro
& Gardens Berlin 208...Beer & food
Stone Brewing World Bistro
& Gardens Berlin 208.......................................Worth the travel
Taybeh Brewing Company 104..............................Unexpected

FELIX HAGAD

Bogsbrew Craft Beer, 69 Tapulanga Street, Bacolod City
A largely self-taught brewer, Hagad is head brewer at Bogsbrew Craft Beer in the Philippines.

Brewery Gastropub 99..Beer & food
Cafe Azucarera 99...Local favorite
Homegrown Bar 99...Beer garden
Inasal & Co 99...Unexpected
The Bottle Shop 98...Worth the travel

TOMAS HALBERSTAD

Dugges Bryggeri AB, Östra Björrödsvägen 12, Landvetter
Communications director at Dugges Brewery in Sweden.

Brewers Beer Bar 114..Local favorite
Brygg 111..Wish I'd opened
Glam Café 252..Unexpected
Muted Horn 210..Worth the travel
Spezial-Keller 199...Beer garden
Tørst 386...Beer & food

JEFF HALVORSON
Where the Wild Beers Are, Eagan
Halvorson is a beer traveler and cofounder of Where the Wild Beers Are festival in New York City and Minneapolis and Saint Paul.

't Brugs Beertje 181	Worth the travel
3 Fonteinen 169	Beer & food
Cock & Bull Farmhouse 399	Unexpected
Monk's Café 392	Wish I'd opened
New Glarus Brewing Company 346	Beer garden
Republic 338	Local favorite

DANNY HAMILTON
Craft Beer Pilgrimage Tours, 725 Yates Street, Victoria
Founder of Craft Beer Pilgrimage in British Columbia.

Cascade Brewing Barrel House 320	Beer garden
Delirium Café 174	Worth the travel
Schlenkerla 199	Beer & food
The Drake Eatery 269	Local favorite
The Salt House 143	Unexpected
Warpigs Brewpub 126	Wish I'd opened

TOM HANSON
Young Master Brewery, G/F Sungib Industrial Building 53 Wong Chuk Hang Road, Hong Kong
Lead brewer at Young Master Brewery.

Kafé België 158	Beer garden
Second Draft 93	Local favorite
St. John Bar and Restaurant 147	Beer & food
The Fat Cat 136	Worth the travel

MARK HATHERLY
Grand Brewing Luxembourg, 6 Rue Jean Monnet, Luxembourg
Founder of Grand Brewing Luxembourg and level one Cicerone Beer server. Hatherly also received second place for Beer of the Year at the Luxembourg Homebrew Championship in 2017.

Caulfield RSL 62	Beer garden
Liquid Bar 186	Local favorite
Rock Bottom Restaurant & Brewery 405	Unexpected
San Jose Original Joe's 283	Wish I'd opened
The Arygll 135	Beer & food
The Bird in Hand 135	Worth the travel

JEHAD HATU
Grunting Growler, 51 Old Dumbarton Road, Glasgow
Owner of Grunting Growler.

Alfie Byrne's by Galway Bay Brewery 142	Unexpected
Grunting Growler 140	Local favorite
Jabeerwocky Craft Beer Pub 240	Worth the travel
Six°North Glasgow 141	Beer & food

JERRY HAUCK
Monks House of Ale Repute and Gandy Dancer Brew Works, 420 East 8th Street, Sioux Falls
Owner of Monks, a purveyor and leader of craft beer in South Dakota.

Monks House of Ale Repute and Gandy Dancer Brew Works 343	Local favorite
Monks House of Ale Repute and Gandy Dancer Brew Works 343	Worth the travel
Surly Brewing Company 338	Beer & food

YUYA HAYASHI
Watering Hole, Sendagaya 5-26-5-103, Tokyo
Beer manager at Watering Hole since 2013.

Beer Pub Ishii 80	Local favorite
Blind Tiger Ale House 377	Worth the travel
Seibu Dome 77	Unexpected
T.Y. Harbor 82	Beer garden
The Ginger Man New York 378	Wish I'd opened

SUZANNE HAYS
Row 34, 383 Congress Street, Boston
Beer director at Row 34.

Armsby Abbey 361	Beer & food
Brewer's Fork 358	Local favorite
Kahn's Fine Wines and Spirits 333	Unexpected
Notch Brewery & Tap Room 360	Beer garden
The Publick House 359	Wish I'd opened
The Rathskeller 333	Worth the travel

MICHÈLE HENGST
Berliner Berg Brauerei, Kopfstrasse 59, Berlin
Manager of Berliner Berg, Hengst runs the marketing and sales for the brewery.

Bergschloss 210	Local favorite
eins44 210	Beer & food
Lager Lager 210	Unexpected
Omnipollos Hatt 118	Worth the travel
ÜberQuell Brauwerkstätten 203	Wish I'd opened
Urban Spree 208	Beer garden

KRIS HERTELEER
De Dolle Brouwers, Roeselarestraat 12B, Esen
A painter and former architect, Herteleer is owner and brewer of De Dolle Brouwers.

Cafe Kulminator 168	Worth the travel
Le Chef et Moi 181	Beer & food
Lokaalmarkt Roeselare 170	Unexpected
Oerbier De Dolle Brouwers 170	Local favorite

STEVE HINDY
Brooklyn Brewery, 79 North 11th Street, New York City
Founder and chairman of Brooklyn Brewery.

Blind Tiger Ale House 377	Wish I'd opened
Gramercy Tavern 377	Beer & food
Grunting Growler 140	Local favorite
Grunting Growler 140	Worth the travel
Namgay Artisanal Brewery 96	Unexpected
Rock Center Café 378	Beer garden

RICHARD HINKLE
Snowy Mountain Brewery & Pub, 601 Pic Pike Road, Saratoga
Brewmaster and brewery manager at Snowy Mountain Brewery at the Saratoga Hot Springs Resort in Wyoming.

Cambrinus 180	Worth the travel
Dry Dock Brewing Co - North Dock 186	Local favorite
Jester King Brewery 423	Beer & food
Joyride Brewing Company 286	Wish I'd opened
Minneapolis–Saint Paul International Airport 338	Unexpected
Snowy Mountain Brewery & Pub 296	Beer garden

MARK HODGES
Holiday Wine Cellar, 302 West Mission Avenue, Escondido
Hodges is a whiskey ambassador, a Mezcal enthusiast, and the head of Holiday Wine Cellar's craft-beer department, where he has worked since 2008.

Churchill's Pub & Grille 284	Beer & food
Nepenthe 280	Unexpected
O'Brien's Pub 304	Worth the travel
Pizza Port Solana Beach 285	Local favorite
Stone Brewing World Bistro & Gardens Escondido 281	Beer garden
Urge Gastropub & Common House 306	Wish I'd opened

NATHAN HOEFT
First Street Brewing Company, 119 North Saint Joseph Avenue, Hastings
Founder of First Street Brewing Company in Nebraska, Hoeft began as a homebrewer in 2005.

Fairfield Opera House Brewery & Grill 341	Unexpected
First Street Brewing Company 341	Local favorite
First Street Brewing Company 341	Wish I'd opened
Hofbräuhaus 214	Beer garden
Hofbräuhaus 214	Worth the travel
Sozo American Cuisine 341	Beer & food

RON HOGLUND
Front Range Brewing Company, 400 West South Boulder Road #1650, Lafayette
Owner and executive brewer of Front Range Brewing Company, Colorado's first independent craft brewery.

Falling Rock Tap House 314	Local favorite
Front Range Brewing Company 287	Beer & food
Hofbräuhaus 214	Beer garden
The Last Word Saloon 139	Worth the travel
Yard House Denver 317	Wish I'd opened

JOHN HOLL
Craft Beer & Brewing magazine, Jersey City
Senior editor of Craft Beer & Brewing magazine, previously at All About Beer and The New York Times. He is the author of The American Craft Beer Cookbook and cohost of Steal This Beer podcast.

Blind Tiger Ale House 377	Worth the travel
Lakefront Brewery 345	Beer garden
Pop's Kitchen and Taproom 370	Unexpected
The Ruck 369	Beer & food
WÜRSTBAR 362	Local favorite

NATASHA HONG
DRiNK Magazine, 4 Holland Close #07-11, Singapore
Singapore-based lifestyle journalist and editor at DRiNK Magazine.

Friends of Ham 137	Beer & food
Smith Street Taps 100	Local favorite
The Grove 137	Worth the travel
Warpigs Brewpub 126	Wish I'd opened

ANASTASIA HOWELL
Cask Republic New Haven, 179 Crown Street, New Haven
Assistant general manager at Cask Republic.

Cask Republic 356	Beer & food
Cask Republic 356	Beer garden
Cask Republic 356	Local favorite
Cask Republic 356	Unexpected
Cask Republic 356	Wish I'd opened
Cask Republic 356	Worth the travel

BILL HOWELL
Northwest Brewing News, Sterling
Freelance writer and homebrewer for more than twenty years.

Café Amsterdam 278	Local favorite
De Garre 181	Worth the travel
Falling Rock Tap House 314	Wish I'd opened
Golden Eagle Saloon 278	Unexpected
La Trappe Cafe 310	Beer & food
Stone Brewing World Bistro & Gardens Escondido 281	Beer garden

GEORGI HRISTOV
Ailyak Craft Beer and Feel Good Brew Co., Sofia
Founder of Ailyak Craft Beer, rated the best beer in Bulgaria on Ratebeer.com. In 2015, Ailyak participated in the World Expo in Milan at the Slow Food stand.

Bagri Restaurant 254	Beer & food
Camba Old Factory 200	Beer garden
FOB 230	Worth the travel
KANAAL 254	Local favorite

KYLE HURST
Big aLICe Brewing Company, 8-08 43rd Road, New York City
Hurst is the president and cofounder of Big aLICe Brewing Company.

Bohemian Hall and Beer Garden 379	Beer garden
First Draft Taproom & Kitchen 315	Wish I'd opened
John Brown Smokehouse 379	Unexpected
LIC Landing by COFFEED 380	Worth the travel
Milwaukee Burger Company 344	Beer & food
The Gutter Bar LIC 379	Local favorite

PYRY HURULA
Sori Brewing, Suur-Sõjamäe 14, Tallinn
Cofounder of Sori Brewing in Tallinn, Hurula travels around Finland and Estonia preaching craft beer.

Jopenkerk Haarlem 155	Wish I'd opened
Phantom Carriage Brewery 280	Worth the travel
Sori Taproom 123	Beer & food
Sori Taproom 123	Local favorite
Stone Brewing World Bistro & Gardens Escondido 281	Beer garden
Tallinn ferry 247	Unexpected

JACOBO IGUÍNIZ MINUTTI
Daz Craft Beer, San Pedro Cholula
Brewing since 2009, Iguíniz is founder of Daz Craft Beer, Salón Cervecero, and Cholula.

Cierva Dorada 430	Beer & food
Cierva Dorada 430	Local favorite
Cierva Dorada 430	Wish I'd opened
El Diablito Cholula 430	Unexpected
Hop The Beer Experience 2 429	Worth the travel
La Legendaria 432	Beer garden

NATE ILAOA
Flying Fox Brewing Company, P.O. Box 579, Pava'la'l
Ilaoa is the owner of Flying Fox Brewing Company in American Samoa.

TOSHI ISHII
Ishii Brewing Co., 458 South Marine Corps Drive #102, Tamuning
President and brewmaster at Ishii Brewing Co. in Guam, Ishii was flying brewer at Ishii Brewery Consulting in Japan, COO and brewmaster at YO-HO Brewing Co., and foreign exchange brewer at Stone Brewing Co. in California.

VENKATESH IYER
Leeds Brewery Co. Ltd., 3 Sydenham Road, Leeds
Head brewer at Leeds Brewery.

CHRIS JACKSON
Dark Side Brew Crew, New Mexico
"Stoutmeister" of the *Dark Side Brew Crew* blog, where he is editor and lead writer.

MARISA JACKSON
Back to School Brewing, Siu Wai Industrial Centre, 29–33 Wing Hong Street, Hong Kong
Cofounder of Back to School Brewing.

EDWARD JALAT-DEHEN
Brasserie de l'Être, 7 ter Rue Duvergier, Paris
Cobrewer at Brasserie de l'Être, founded in 2015.

GEOFFREY JANSEN VAN VUUREN
Amundsen Brewery
Bjørnerudveien 14, Oslo
General manager of Amundsen Brewery in Norway.

JEPPE JARNIT-BJERGSØ
Evil Twin Brewing, 1616 George Street, New York City
Globe-trotting personality behind Evil Twin Brewing, Jarnit-Bjergsø distributes to 30 countries and is opening a brewery in Ridgewood, Queens in New York City.

CHRISTIAN JAUSLIN
Biervesuche and Wortspiele, Winterthur
President of Wortspiele, a Swiss beer festival, Jauslin is also
a Doemens certified beer sommelier and the founder of
bierversuche.ch.

DUSTIN JEFFERS
Saltwater Brewery, 1701 West Atlantic Avenue, Delray Beach
Cofounder and head of operations at Saltwater Brewery in
Florida.

KYLE JEFFERSON
Pueblo Vida Brewing Co., 115 East Broadway Boulevard, Tucson
Founder and owner of Pueblo Vida Brewing Co., located in
Arizona.

QI JIANG
Wuhan No. 18 Brewery, 923 Jinghan Road, Wuhan
Master brewer at Whuan No. 18 Brewery and certified by
the Technische Universität München, Jiang is a national light
industry certified senior brewing technician. He is the only
Chinese brewer to win an International Beer Cup Champion
title and is also a BJCP-certified beer judge.

AARON JOHNSON
Cascadian Beer podcast
Johnson has a podcast on stories about craft beer in the
American Pacific Northwest.

CAMERON JOHNSON
Young Buck Brewing, 154 South Madison Street, Spokane
Founder of Young Buck Brewing in Washington, specializing in
barrel-aged sour beer styles.

MARIKA JOSEPHSON
Scratch Brewing Company, 264 Thompson Road, Ava
Co-owner and head brewer at Scratch Brewing Company.

DIMITRIJ JURISIC
Ghetto Brewing, Gozdna Pot 6, Koper
Founder and owner of Hoppiness Beershop, Jurisic is also the
founder, co-owner, and brewer at Ghetto Brewing in Slovenia.

JUHA-PEKKA JYLHÄ
Olutkellari blog, Muurame
Beer enthusiast, blogger, and author from Finland, Jylhä
has written about Finnish microbreweries, distilleries, and
wineries.

PEKKA KÄÄRIÄINEN
Bryggeri Helsinki and Lammin Sahti, Sofiankatu 2, Helsinki
Founder and owner of Bryggeri Helsinki and Lammin Sahti Oy, the oldest microbrewery in Finland.

Bryggeri Helsinki 122	Beer & food
Bryggeri Helsinki 122	Local favorite
Bryggeri Helsinki 122	Wish I'd opened

STEVE KAMP
Evil Horse Brewing Co., 1338 Main Street, Crete
Kemp started brewing at home in 1983 after a *Chicago Tribune* article about unique Christmas gifts, and he has been an American Homebrewers Association member since 1984. He was president of the Chicago Beer Society and is brewmaster at Evil Horse Brewing Co.

Brick Stone Brewery 332	Beer & food
Evil Horse Brewing Company 332	Local favorite
Guaranteed Rate Field 350	Unexpected
Maple Tree Inn 332	Wish I'd opened
Quenchers Saloon 350	Worth the travel
Sheffield's Beer & Wine Garden 351	Beer garden

AGGELOS KANIATSAKIS
Sknipa, 17 kilometres off Thessaloniki-Polygyros Road
In 2015, Kaniatsakis cofounded Sknipa, a microbrewery named after a Greek expression for getting drunk.

August Bar 255	Worth the travel
Beer Fabrica 255	Local favorite
Extravaganza 255	Beer garden
Primate Draft 255	Beer & food
The Bar L.A.B. 255	Wish I'd opened
The Hoppy Pub 255	Unexpected

YAZAN M. KARADSHEH
Carakale Brewing Co., 12a Fuhays, Um el fesh, Fuhays
Founder of Jordan's only microbrewery, Karadsheh is building a beer culture in Jordan.

Brouwerij Lane 385	Worth the travel
Carakale Brewing Company 104	Local favorite
Lowry Beer Garden 315	Beer garden
Tørst 386	Beer & food

STUART KEATING
Earthbound Beer, 2724 Cherokee Street, Saint Louis
Co-owner and brewer at Earthbound Brewing in Missouri, Keating uses experimental ingredients and historical styles.

Bridge Tap House and Wine Bar 340	Beer & food
Buoy Beer Company 292	Wish I'd opened
Saint Louis Hop Shop 340	Local favorite
Scratch Brewing Company 332	Worth the travel
The Civil Life Brewing Company 340	Beer garden
Will Rogers World Airport 410	Unexpected

CLAY KEEL
42 North Brewing Company, 25 Pine Street, East Aurora
Chief brewing officer at 42 North Brewing Company, Keel is a Siebel Institute-trained professional brewer, Certified Cicerone, and BJCP Beer Judge.

Fox Hollow Golf Course 344	Unexpected
Hopleaf 352	Beer & food
Jester King Brewery 423	Beer garden
Mr. Goodbar 365	Local favorite
The Stein & Vine 396	Worth the travel
Tørst 386	Wish I'd opened

NATHAN KEFFER
Bandido Brewing, Jose J. Olmedo E1-136, Quito
Cofounder of Bandido Brewing, an American-style microbrewery.

Cerveza Artesanal Santa Rosa 440	Local favorite
Great Divide Brewing Co 315	Worth the travel
Hopworks Urban Brewery 321	Beer & food
Odell 286	Beer garden
Tørst 386	Wish I'd opened
Venti's Cafe + Basement Bar 294	Unexpected

MATTHEW KELLY
Good George Brewing, 32A Somerset Street, Hamilton
Kelly runs sales at Good George Brewing in New Zealand and learned the ropes at Galbraith's Alehouse and 16 Tun.

Galbraith's Alehouse 67	Local favorite
Lagunitas Brewing Company 283	Beer garden
Lovebucket at the Food Workshop 66	Wish I'd opened
Mikkeller Bar San Francisco 311	Beer & food
Toronado Pub 310	Worth the travel
Zoo Brew 306	Unexpected

CANAAN KHOURY
Taybeh Brewing Company, Taybeh Road 1, Taybeh
Master brewer and chief engineer at Taybeh Brewing Company, Khoury is responsible for introducing IPAs and sour beers to the Palestinian beer market. In 2016, he received the JS Ford Award for the highest score in the international brewing and distilling exams.

Davis Beer Shoppe 281	Worth the travel
Radio Bar 104	Local favorite
Russian River Brewery 284	Beer & food
Taybeh Brewing Company 104	Unexpected

PAUL KIM
Off Color Brewing, 3925 West Dickens Avenue, Chicago
Brewer, sales representative, and bar manager at Off Color Brewing.

Covenhoven 384	Beer garden
Guaranteed Rate Field 350	Unexpected
Hopleaf 352	Wish I'd opened
The Mousetrap 351	Local favorite
The Publican 353	Beer & food
The Side Project Cellar 340	Worth the travel

DEVIN KIMBLE
Hong Kong Beer Company, Wah Shing Centre, 5 Fung Yip Street, Hong Kong
Co-owner and director of Hong Kong Beer Co., Hong Kong's oldest craft brewery.

Father's Office 284	Wish I'd opened
The Avenue Pub 403	Worth the travel
The Beer Bay 92	Unexpected
The Globe 92	Local favorite

SVILEN KIRILOVSKI
Sega Daily Newspaper, Sofia
Journalist and founder of the beer blog *Bforbeer*, Kirilovski is a homebrewer, member of the Bulgarian Homebrewers Association, and judge of homebrew competitions in Bulgaria.

Delirium Café 174	Worth the travel
Halbite 254	Beer garden
KANAAL 254	Local favorite

N'dey Bara Tangra 254.................................Unexpected
Rhombus Brewery 253................................Beer & food

ALASTAIR KIRK
Tarn Hows Brewery, Knipe Fold, Ambleside
A self-taught brewer, Kirk brews small batches of beers in the
English Lake District. He is director of Tarn Hows Brewery.
Beer Ambleside 131....................................Local favorite
Beer Ambleside 131....................................Unexpected
Le Poechenellekelder 176..........................Worth the travel
The Drunken Duck Inn and Restaurant 131..........Beer & food
The Drunken Duck Inn and Restaurant 131.........Beer garden
The Factory Tap 131...................................Wish I'd opened

NIKOS KOCHYLIS
Ale Box, Doiranis 36, Athens
A passionate homebrewer from Greece, Kochylis runs Ale
Box, one of the few homebrew shops in Greece to supply
microbreweries.
Arch Beer House 255..................................Beer garden
The Lazy Bulldog Pub 254..........................Beer & food
The Local Pub 254.....................................Local favorite

KEEGAN KONKOSKI KRAMER
**Liquids and Solids at the Handlebar, 6115 Sentinel Road, Lake
Placid**
Cofounder of Liquids and Solids at the Handlebar, a restaurant
and butcher shop in the Adirondack Mountains of New York.
Bangers & Lace Wicker Park 353.................Wish I'd opened
Hen of the Wood 372.................................Local favorite
Jester King Brewery 423............................Worth the travel
Lost Nation Brewing 372............................Beer garden

PETER KRAMMER
**Landbrauhaus Hofstetten, Adsdorf 5, Saint Martin in
Muhlkreis**
Fifth-generation brewer at Brauerei Hofstetten in Austria.
Camba Biererlebniswelt in Truchtlaching 201..........Beer garden
Chelsea Pub 242.......................................Local favorite
Köglerhof 242..Beer & food
The Brickmakers Pub & Kitchen 243...............Worth the travel

DANIEL KRAVITZ
Artisanal Brew Works, 41 Geyser Road, Saratoga Springs
General manager at Artisanal Brew Works.
Artisanal Brew Works 368..........................Beer garden
Barcade Williamsburg 387..........................Wish I'd opened
Coastline Beach Bar 426.............................Unexpected
Parker Pie Company 373.............................Beer & food
The Ruck 369..Local favorite
Tremont Taphouse 342...............................Worth the travel

ØYSTEIN KROGTOFT
Macondo Import, Trondheimsveien 2, Oslo
CEO of Macondo Import, a Norwegian beer and wine
importer.
Doktor Glas 114..Unexpected
Mikkeller Bar Copenhagen 127.....................Worth the travel
Nedre Foss Gård 112.................................Local favorite
Olympen 112..Beer & food
Omnipollos Hatt 118..................................Wish I'd opened
Zollpackhof Restaurant & Biergarten 210................Beer garden

STEFAN KRUEGER
Berlin Beer Week Orga, Berlin
Cofounder and organizer of annual Berlin Beer Week and
founder of Beergeeks distribution, an importing company.
Akkurat 119...Worth the travel
BrewDog Berlin 210...................................Local favorite
Stone Brewing World Bistro &
   Gardens Berlin 208.................................Beer & food
Stone Brewing World Bistro &
   Gardens Berlin 208.................................Beer garden
The Morrison 300.......................................Unexpected

VLADIMIR KUSHNYREV
Troubadour Brewery, 9 Deribasovskaya Street, Odessa
Founder of Troubadour Brewery in Ukraine, Kushnyrev is an
engineer by training and began brewing at home in 2013.
Arsenal Ribs 248.......................................Unexpected
Friends and Beer 248.................................Beer & food
Friends and Beer 248.................................Worth the travel
Pyvnoy Sad 249..Beer garden
Troubadur 249...Local favorite

KATHERINE KYLE
Blind Tiger Ale House, 281 Bleecker Street, New York City
General manager of Blind Tiger Ale House.
Apex 320...Wish I'd opened
Fifth Hammer Brewing Company 379...................Local favorite
Fluid State Beer Garden 285.........................Worth the travel
Gramercy Tavern 377.................................Beer & food
Newark Liberty International Airport 363...............Unexpected

KIMMO KYLLÖNEN
Hopping Brewsters Beer Company Oy, Sirkesalontie 3, Akaa
Archaeologist and historian, Kyllönen is a founding member of
Hopping Brewsters Beer Company Oy.
Gastropub Tuulensuu 115............................Beer & food
Keppana Kellari 115....................................Unexpected
Ravintola Mullikka 122...............................Local favorite

AITOR LABRADOR
Wort magazine, Carrer Ample 23, Barcelona
Labrador is a writer, an editor, and a beer geek based in
Barcelona.
BierCaB 226...Local favorite
El Birrot 218...Beer garden
Howling Hops Brewery and Tank Bar 147..........Wish I'd opened
La Barricona 218..Beer & food
La Llúdriga 218..Unexpected

JAMES LANDERS
Walking Man Brewing, 240 Southwest 1st Street, Stevenson
Head brewer at Walking Man Brewing.
Brouwer's Cafe 326...................................Beer & food
Brouwer's Cafe 326...................................Worth the travel
G & S Lounge 423.....................................Unexpected
Horse Brass Pub 321.................................Local favorite

JACOB LANDRY
Urban South Brewery, 1645 Tchoupitoulas Street, New Orleans
Founder of Urban South Brewery, Landry has developed a passion for craft beer while living in Europe.

Edmund's Oast Restaurant 411	Beer & food
Root Down 316	Unexpected
The Avenue Pub 403	Worth the travel
Urban South Brewery 404	Local favorite

JAMES LARSON
Enlightened Brewing Company, 2018 South 1st Street, Milwaukee
Co-owner and director of operations at Enlightened Brewing Company.

Cooperage Brewing Company 284	Worth the travel
Draft and Vessel 345	Wish I'd opened
Goodkind 345	Beer & food
Hubbard Park Lodge 345	Beer garden
Miller Park 345	Unexpected
Palm Tavern 345	Local favorite

JOHN LATTA
Nomad Brewing Co. and Experienceit Beverages, 5 Sydenham Road, Brookvale
General manager at Nomad Brewing Co., Latta also established Australia's premiere craft-beer distribution company, Experienceit Beverages.

Fette Sau 388	Beer & food
Manly Oval 56	Unexpected
Nomad Brewing Company 'The Transit Lounge' 56	Local favorite
Stone Brewing World Bistro & Gardens Berlin 208	Beer garden
Stone Brewing World Bistro & Gardens Escondido 281	Worth the travel
The Wheatsheaf Hotel 58	Wish I'd opened

THOMAS LAU
Thirsty Brothers Ltd., BoldWin Industrial Building, 16–18 Wah Sing Street, Hong Kong
Cofounder of Thirsty Brothers Ltd., a distribution agency focused on bringing better drinks to Hong Kong, Macau, and Taiwan.

Baird Beer Taproom Harajuku 81	Beer & food
Craft Beer Market Vancouver 269	Wish I'd opened
Goodbeer Faucets 82	Worth the travel
Melbourne Cricket Ground 63	Unexpected
The Roundhouse - Chicken + Beer 92	Local favorite

JUN LEE SANG
Made In PONG DANG, 222-1 Noksapyeong-daero, Seoul
General manager at Made in PONG DANG, Sang Jun was previously the general manager at Four Seasons and Pyrus, a craft-beer pub in Seoul.

Apex 320	Worth the travel
Cascade Brewing Barrel House 320	Beer garden
Mysterlee Brewing Company 86	Beer & food
The Booth Brewery Pangyo 86	Local favorite

MARIE-JOSÉE LEFEBVRE
Brasseurs du Monde, 3755 Rue Picard, Saint-Hyacinthe
Marketing and export coordinator at Brasseurs du Monde in Quebec, Lefebvre was the general manager of the Mondial de la Bière festival for 11 years.

Abbaye d'Orval 170	Unexpected
Birreria Le Baladin 232	Beer & food
Cantillon Brewery 174	Worth the travel
König Ludwig Schlossbrauerei 200	Beer garden
The Ginger Man 378	Local favorite

ANIKÓ LEHTINEN
Helsinki
Beer specialist, author, journalist, presenter, blogger, and trainer, based in Finland.

7Stern Bräu 243	Beer garden
Bier-Bier 122	Local favorite
Felső Kocsma 243	Unexpected
Mad Grill 219	Beer & food
Mikkeller Bar Copenhagen 127	Wish I'd opened
Tørst 386	Worth the travel

GERRIT LERCH
Galopper Des Jahres, Schulterblatt 73, Hamburg
Owner of Galopper des Jahres, a craft-beer bar in Germany.

Galopper des Jahres 202	Local favorite
Galopper des Jahres 202	Worth the travel
Prater Biergarten 211	Beer garden
Stone Brewing World Bistro & Gardens Berlin 208	Wish I'd opened
ÜberQuell Brauwerkstätten 203	Beer & food

PON LERTSAKDADET
Eleventh Fort Brewing Co., Samutprakan
Lertsakdadet is cofounder of Eleventh Fort Brewing Co.

HK Brewcraft 92	Unexpected
O'glee 96	Beer & food
O'glee 96	Local favorite
O'glee 96	Worth the travel

RICK LEVERT
Kinnegar Brewing, K2, Ballyraine Industrial Estate, Letterkenny
In 2011, LeVert founded Kinnegar, where he is director and head brewer.

Donegal Airport 141	Unexpected
Golgatha 211	Beer garden
Sunflower Public House 141	Worth the travel
The Bernard Shaw 142	Wish I'd opened
The Tap Room at Rathmullan House 142	Beer & food

KRIS LI
Jing-A Brewing Co., #57 Xingfu Middle Street, Lee World Building, Room 307, Beijing
Cofounder of Jing-A Brewing Co. with longtime friend Alex Acker.

Birreria Volo 274	Wish I'd opened
Hopfengarten 215	Beer garden
Jing-A Taproom 1949 87	Local favorite
Moeder Lambic Original 176	Worth the travel
Warpigs Brewpub 126	Beer & food

LEA LIMA

Cerveteca Lisboa, Praça das Flores 62, Lisbon
Lima is a designer from Portugal who was a bartender at
Cerveteca Lisboa.

Baladin Bologna 230	Beer & food
Cerveteca Lisboa 220	Local favorite
Cerveteca Lisboa 220	Wish I'd opened
Letraria Craft Beer Garden Porto 221	Beer garden
Monterey Bar 208	Worth the travel

DAVID LIN

Comrade Brewing, 7667 East Iliff Avenue #F, Denver
Founder and chairman of Comrade Brewing in Denver.

Bull & Bush Brewery 314	Beer & food
Falling Rock Tap House 314	Local favorite
Falling Rock Tap House 314	Worth the travel
Halls Wine & Spirits 413	Unexpected

YUHANG LIN

Cascadia International Distribution LLC, Taipei
Beer ambassador and cofounder of Cascadia International
Distribution.

Beachwood BBQ and Brewing Long Beach 282	Beer garden
Brouwer's Cafe 326	Worth the travel
Himmeriget 126	Wish I'd opened
Mikkeller Bar Taipei 88	Local favorite
The 'Pen at Safeco Field 327	Unexpected
Tørst 386	Beer & food

PATRICK LIVELY

Anthem Brewing Company, 908 Southwest 4th Street,
Oklahoma City
President and brewmaster of Anthem Brewing Co., Lively was
production manager at Coop Ale Works.

Euclid Hall 314	Beer & food
Halls Wine & Spirits 413	Unexpected
Novare Res Bier Café 357	Worth the travel
Solera Brewery 294	Beer garden
TapWerks Ale House & Cafe 410	Local favorite
The Patriarch Craft Beer House & Lawn 409	Wish I'd opened

CATERINA LODO

Martigny
Lodo is passionate about beer and has worked in marketing for
White Frontier Brewery.

CRAK TapRoom 235	Beer & food
CRAK TapRoom 235	Unexpected
Ma Che Siete Venuti A Fà 234	Worth the travel
WhiteFrontier Taproom 187	Local favorite

JAMES LONG

Barbarian Brewing, 5270 Chinden Boulevard, Boise
Head brewer at a boutique brewery in Idaho that focuses on
barrel-aged and mixed-fermentation beers.

Idaho City Grocery 290	Unexpected
PreFunk Beer Bar Nampa 290	Worth the travel
State & Lemp 290	Beer & food
The HandleBar Boise 290	Local favorite

ESPEN LOTHE

Kinn Bryggeri, Bjørndalvegen 30, Floro
Lothe founded Kinn Bryggeri in Norway in 2009.

Apollon 110	Local favorite
Charles & De 112	Beer & food
Katarina Ølkafe 119	Worth the travel
Olympen 115	Beer garden

BEN LOVE

Gigantic Brewing Company, 5224 Southeast 26th Avenue,
Portland
Brewmaster and co-owner of Gigantic Brewing Company,
Love previously brewed at Pelican and Hopworks.

Alibi Room 268	Worth the travel
Brouwerij 't IJ 162	Beer garden
JBS (Jazz, Blues, Soul) 82	Wish I'd opened
Providence Park 322	Unexpected
The Publican 353	Beer & food
Victory Bar 322	Local favorite

VALTER LOVERIER

LoverBeer, Strada Pellinciona 7, Marentino
Owner, founder, and brewer of LoverBeer.

Bici & Birra 233	Unexpected
BierCaB 226	Wish I'd opened
Dogana Torino 233	Local favorite
La Fine Mousse 193	Beer & food
Ma Che Siete Venuti A Fà 234	Worth the travel
Stone Brewing World Bistro & Gardens Liberty Station 305	Beer garden

ERIN LOWDER

Solemn Oath Brewery, 1661 Quincy Avenue, Naperville
General manager at Solemn Oath Brewery.

Bellwoods Brewery 275	Beer & food
Bellwoods Brewery 275	Beer garden
Map Room 350	Local favorite
Map Room 350	Worth the travel
MEATliquor 149	Unexpected
Zeitgeist 310	Wish I'd opened

LIAM LOWDON

Cerveza Artesanal Stier, Porfirio Diaz Machicado 270,
Cochabamba
Founder of Cervecería Artesanal Stier, Lowdon is German and
has been living in Bolivia for many years.

Clementina 442	Wish I'd opened
F House 442	Local favorite
Gustu 442	Beer & food
La Campana 442	Beer garden
Running Chaski Hostel 442	Worth the travel
The Spitting Llama Bookstore and Outfitter Cochabamba 442	Unexpected

ZACH MACK

Alphabet City Beer Co., 96 Avenue C, New York City
Owner of Alphabet City Beer Co. and Governors Island Beer
Co., Mack is also a beer, food, travel, wine, and spirits writer.

Dieu du Ciel! 271	Worth the travel
Euston Tap 148	Wish I'd opened
Proletariat 376	Local favorite
RC Otter's Eats 396	Unexpected
Zum Schneider NYC 376	Beer garden

PHILLIP MACNITT
Modern Times Beer, 3725 Greenwood Street, San Diego
A craft-beer evangelist and head of national sales
for Modern Times.

Bankers Hill Bar and Grill 304	Unexpected
Live Wire 304	Local favorite
McSorley's Old Ale House 376	Wish I'd opened
Toronado San Diego 306	Beer & food
Watering Hole 82	Worth the travel
Zeitgeist 310	Beer garden

BEN MAESO
Prison City Pub and Brewery, 28 State Street, Auburn
Head of brewing operations and head brewer at Prison City
Brewing in New York.

Moeder Lambic Fontainas 176	Worth the travel
Now & Later 368	Local favorite
Parker Pie Company 373	Unexpected
Row 34 358	Beer & food
Stone Brewing World Bistro & Gardens Escondido 281	Beer garden
Tap & Mallet 367	Wish I'd opened

CHRIS MAESTRO
BierWax, 556 Vanderbilt Avenue, New York City
Founder and principal owner of BierWax, a craft-beer and vinyl
record bar in Prospect Heights, Brooklyn.

C'est Cheese 367	Unexpected
JBS (Jazz, Blues, Soul) 82	Wish I'd opened
NaparBCN 227	Worth the travel
Tørst 386	Beer & food
Tørst 386	Local favorite

CHRIS MAIR
New Wave Distribution, 4 Hope Street, Edinburgh
Owner of New Wave Distribution, The Hanging Bat, Salt Horse
Beer Shop & Bar, and Koelschip Yard in Scotland.

Firestone Walker Brewing Company 280	Beer & food
Proletariat 376	Worth the travel
Salt Horse Beer Shop & Bar 140	Local favorite
Six Degrees North 138	Wish I'd opened
Stone Brewing World Bistro & Gardens Escondido 281	Beer garden
The Anderson 141	Unexpected

OLLI MAJANEN
Bryggeri Helsinki Brewery & Restaurant, Sofiankatu 2,
Helsinki
Co-owner and manager at the brewery and restaurant
Bryggeri Helsinki, Majanen began his beer journey in the early
1990s. He gained experience working in beer bars in Helsinki,
and in 1994 he was nominated Beer Entrepreneur of the Year.

28 Café 220	Unexpected
BierCaB 226	Wish I'd opened
Bryggeri Helsinki 122	Local favorite
Nørrebro Bryghus 127	Beer & food
Spezial-Keller 199	Beer garden
The White Horse 147	Worth the travel

MIKKO MÄKELÄ
HIISI Brewing Co., Puulaakintie 8, Jyväskylä
Mäkelä is one of the entrepreneurs behind HIISI, a Finnish
craft brewery known for its creative use of ingredients (rocks
from a sauna stove, quark, doughnuts) and Finnish mythology.
He is chairman of the board for the Finnish craft brewers
association, Pienpanimoliitto.

Bryggeri Helsinki 122	Beer & food
Craft Beer Helsinki 122	Beer garden
Mother Kelly's 146	Worth the travel
Omnipollos Hatt 118	Wish I'd opened
Tanssisali Lutakko 114	Unexpected
Vihreä Haltiatar 114	Local favorite

THERESA MALAFRONTE
Newport Storm Brewery, 293 JT Connell Highway, Newport
PR and events coordinator at Newport Storm Brewery in
Rhode Island, a microbrewery with more than 100 hand-
crafted distinctive brews.

Newport Storm Brewery 371	Local favorite

CHELSIE MARKEL
It's a Brew Life, Dillsburg
Co-creator and craft-beer writer at ItsABrewLife.com, based
in Pennsylvania.

Henlopen City Oyster House 396	Unexpected
Hunger-N-Thirst 370	Beer & food
Prohibition Pig 373	Worth the travel
Sabatini's Pizza 370	Wish I'd opened
Tired Hands Brew Café 369	Local favorite
Tröegs Independent Brewing 370	Beer garden

ITAY MAROM
Hashahen Brewery, Srigim-Li On
Gypsy brewer Marom's brand Mivshelet Hashakhen was
named best brewery in Israel in 2016.

BeerBazaar Basta 104	Local favorite
Birrificio Lambrate Adelchi 232	Worth the travel
Porter & Sons 104	Beer & food
Santorini Brewing Company 256	Unexpected

RUBEN MARTINEZ
Tê Tê Brewing Co., 43 An Phu, An Phu, D2, Ho Chi Minh City
Cofounder of Tê Tê Brewing Co. in Vietnam, Martinez started
his career in breweries as a designer.

Cervezas La Virgen 219	Beer & food
Cervezas La Virgen 219	Wish I'd opened
Rogue Ales Public House 310	Beer garden
Rogue Saigon Craft Beer 97	Local favorite
Zeitgeist 310	Worth the travel

NEIL MARZOLF
Rants and Raves Brewery, 308 North Jackson Street, Moscow
Marzolf opened Rants & Raves Brewery, home of Damn Good
Beer, in Idaho in 2016.

Rants and Raves Brewery 290	Beer garden
Rants and Raves Brewery 290	Local favorite

DAN MASON
Trailway Brewing Company, 280 Main Street, Fredericton
Co-owner of the Trailway Brewing Company, Mason learned
to brew with his father before starting a 1 BBL brewery in a
basement.

540 Kitchen and Bar 269...Beer & food
540 Kitchen and Bar 269...Local favorite
Bishop's Cellar 270...Unexpected
Stillwell 270...Wish I'd opened
Stillwell 270...Worth the travel
Stillwell Beergarden 270...Beer garden

PAUL MAYBEE
Maybee Brew Co., 559 Wilsey Road, Fredericton
Owner of Maybee Brew, a family-owned 10-barrell brewery in
New Brunswick.
Birreria Volo 274...Worth the travel
James Joyce Pub 270..Beer & food
James Joyce Pub 270..Local favorite
Stillwell 270...Wish I'd opened
Stillwell Beergarden 270..Beer garden

AARON MCCLAIN
Crafty Bastard Brewery, 6 Emory Place, Knoxville
Cofounder and brewer at Crafty Bastard, which he started
with Jen Parker in 2014.
Crafty Bastard Brewery 412.................................Local favorite
Echelon Bicycles 412...Unexpected
Suttree's High Gravity Tavern 412.........................Beer & food
The Porter Beer Bar 400....................................Worth the travel
Thirsty Monk 406...Wish I'd opened
Wedge Brewing Company 406...............................Beer garden

DJ MCCREADY
Sydney
McCready is from North Carolina. After homebrewing, he
became a head brewer, then developed the beer program at
Oskar Blues and taught at a brewing school. At 27, he headed
up a new craft brewery in Sydney and won Australia's most
coveted beer awards.
Augustiner Bräu 242..Worth the travel
Frankie's Pizza by the Slice 56................................Local favorite
Hot Water Brewing Company 69............................Unexpected
The Local Taphouse 63..Beer & food
The Oaks Hotel 56...Beer garden
Tørst 386...Wish I'd opened

SHANNON MCFARLANE
Tempest Brewing Co., Block 11, Tweedbank Industrial Estate,
Galashiels
Brand and marketing manager at Tempest Brewing.
BRUS 126...Beer & food
Brussels Airport 170...Unexpected
Cafe Kulminator 168..Beer garden
Salt Horse Beer Shop & Bar 140............................Local favorite
Shilling Brewing Company 140.........................Wish I'd opened
The Porter Beer Bar 400....................................Worth the travel

LYNN MCILWEE
Hops Canary, Vancouver
McIlwee lives in British Columbia, Canada, and has been
writing about beer since 2011 through her blog *Hops Canary*,
and for other publications.
Alibi Room 268...Local favorite
Café Rose Red 180..Wish I'd opened
Moeder Lambic Original 176............................Worth the travel
Nüetnigenough 177..Beer & food
The 'Pen at Safeco Field 327.................................Unexpected

STU MCKINLAY
Yeastie Boys, Wellington
A gypsy brewer, McKinlay is the founder of Yeastie Boys in
New Zealand.
Bundobust Manchester 133.....................................Beer & food
Taps Beer Bar 100...Unexpected
The Rake 149..Local favorite
The Wheatsheaf Hotel 58...................................Worth the travel

PABLO MEJIA
Cerveceria Jester, Santiago
Cofounder and brewer of Cerveceria Jester, a microbrewery
located in Santiago, Chile.
Pepperland Bar 448..Local favorite
Stone Brewing World Bistro &
  Gardens Liberty Station 305................................Beer garden
Tørst 386..Beer & food
Tørst 386...Worth the travel

EDGARS MELNIS
Labietis, Aristīda Briāna Street, 9a-2, Riga
Co-owner and head brewer of Labietis Brewery, Melnis helped
launch the homebrewing movement in Latvia ten years ago.
Delirium Café 174..Worth the travel
Fenix Food Factory 156...Beer & food
Labietis 248..Local favorite

KIM MERCADO
Brouwerij Lane, 78 Greenpoint Avenue, New York City
General manager of Brouwerij Lane in Greenpoint, Brooklyn.
Brushland Eating House 364....................................Unexpected
Ma Che Siete Venuti A Fà 234............................Worth the travel
Oxbow Brewing Company 357..........................Wish I'd opened
Parker Pie Company 373..Beer & food
Sunshine Laundry & Pinball Emporium 385...........Local favorite

JOHN MERKLIN
Beach Haus Brewery, 801 Main Street, Belmar
Cofounder of the Beach Haus Brewery in New Jersey.
Amendment 21 363...Wish I'd opened
Blend Bar & Bistro 362.....................................Worth the travel
Brickwall Tavern & Dining Room 362....................Beer & food
Brickwall Tavern & Dining Room 362....................Local favorite
Capital Craft 362...Unexpected
The Asbury Hotel 361...Beer garden

CHRIS MEYERS
Crane Brewing Company, 6515 Railroad Street, Raytown
Cofounder and co-owner of Crane Brewing Company.
Bier Station 339..Beer garden
Brewery Emperial 339..Beer & food
Crane Brewing 340...Local favorite
Crane Brewing 340...Worth the travel
Irish Pub House 340..Unexpected
Tapcade 339..Wish I'd opened

RORY MILLER
Ah! Brew Works Ltd., Sofia
Cofounder and co-owner of Ah! Brew Works Ltd., Miller is an American living in Bulgaria.

100 Beers 254	Local favorite
Butcher's Tears 165	Worth the travel
Engine House No. 9 296	Beer garden
McMenamins Market Street Pub 321	Beer & food
McMenamins Market Street Pub 321	Wish I'd opened
Tavern Rubin 253	Unexpected

MARISSA MILLS
Parallel 49 Brewing, 1950 Triumph Street, Vancouver
Mills is marketing manager at Parallel 49 Brewing.

Parallel 49 Brewing Company 269	Beer & food
Parallel 49 Brewing Company 269	Local favorite
Parallel 49 Brewing Company 269	Worth the travel

ANDREA MINA
Birrificio Abusivo, Via Venticinque Marzo 29/A, Domagnano
Mina co-founded Birrificio Abusivo with four friends in 2015.

Agriturismo I Muretti 230	Unexpected
Birrificio Abusivo 236	Local favorite
Caffè Divino 236	Beer & food
L'insolito Posto 236	Worth the travel
O'Osciad Pub 231	Wish I'd opened
Roxy Bar 236	Beer garden

PETE MITCHAM
Beer Blokes, Melbourne
A Melbourne-based beer writer, Mitcham has worked with major beer festivals and as a chef.

Les 3 Brasseurs 66	Unexpected
Les 3 Brasseurs 66	Worth the travel
Stomping Ground Brewery & Beer Hall 62	Local favorite
The Local Taphouse 63	Beer & food
The Palace Hotel 63	Beer garden

DANIEL MORAGA LEÓN
Wilk Craft Beer, Avenida 9, Calle 33, San Jose
León works at Wilk Craft Beer in Costa Rica and is an empirical brewer. He learned to brew with Stéfano Di Gioacchino.

Hoppy's Place 434	Beer garden
LB Bieren 434	Unexpected
Lupulus Beer Shop 433	Beer & food
Wilk Craft Beer 434	Local favorite
Wilk Craft Beer 434	Worth the travel

CODY MORRIS
Mollusk Brewing, 803 Dexter Avenue North, Seattle
Morris is the brewmaster at Mollusk Brewing.

Apex 320	Worth the travel
Bottleworks 326	Local favorite
Brouwer's Cafe 326	Wish I'd opened
Mashiko 326	Beer & food

PATRICK MORSE
Flagship Brewing Company, 40 Minthorne Street, New York City
Head brewer at Flagship Brewing Company, Morse has 12 years of professional brewing experience in Vermont, California, and Brooklyn.

Adobe Blues 389	Local favorite

Bohemian Hall and Beer Garden 379	Beer garden
Eagle Rock Brewery 300	Unexpected
Mekelburg's 384	Beer & food
Mekelburg's 384	Wish I'd opened
Mekelburg's 384	Worth the travel

TOD MOTT
Tributary Brewing Company, 10 Shapleigh Road, Kittery
A professional beer brewer since 1990, Mott is the owner of Tributary Brewing Company.

Blind Tiger Ale House 377	Worth the travel
Eataly NYC Flatiron 376	Beer garden
Ebenezer's Pub 356	Beer & food
Novare Res Bier Café 357	Local favorite
Novare Res Bier Café 357	Wish I'd opened
Santa Barbara Eco-Beach Resort 222	Unexpected

ANTONIS MOUSTAKAS
Ali Microbrewery of Thessaloniki, Block 19-building 9 Sindos, Thessaloniki
Founder and head brewer of Thessaloniki Microbrewery.

Bottle Shop: Canterbury 134	Unexpected
Bussey Beer Garden 150	Beer garden
De Vlaamsche Reus 154	Worth the travel
The Craft Beer Co. Islington 148	Wish I'd opened
The Foundry Brew Pub 134	Beer & food
The Hoppy Pub 255	Local favorite

JONATHAN MOXEY
Perennial Artisan Ales, 8125 Michigan Avenue, Saint Louis
Moxey is a brewer at Perennial Artisan Ales.

't Brugs Beertje 181	Worth the travel
Civil Life Brewing Company 340	Local favorite
Loreley Beer Garden 377	Beer garden
The Owl Farm 387	Wish I'd opened
The Publican 353	Beer & food

ERIK MOYNIHAN
Magpie Brewing Company, 1309 Donghoecheon, Jeju Island
CEO and founder of Magpie Brewing Company in South Korea, Moynihan splits his time between the retail operation in Seoul and the brewery on Jeju Island.

Barcade Williamsburg 387	Wish I'd opened
Bellwoods Brewery 275	Worth the travel
CGV Movie Theatre 86	Unexpected
Second Draft 93	Beer & food
Woori Super 86	Local favorite

MARCI MULLEN
Belfast Bay Brewing Company, 100 Searsport Avenue, Belfast
Director of operations at family-owned Belfast Bay Brewing Co. Mullen's father founded the brewery in 1996.

Front Street Pub 356	Beer & food
Front Street Pub 356	Local favorite
JetBlue Park 397	Unexpected
La Bodega 262	Worth the travel
McKays Public House 356	Beer garden

MIKE MURPHY
Holy Mountain Brewing, 1421 Elliott Avenue West, Seattle
Co-owner and operator of Holy Mountain Brewing.

Burial Beer Company 406	Beer garden
Monk's Café 392	Worth the travel

No Anchor 327...Beer & food
Slow Boat Tavern 328...............................Local favorite

MIKE MURPHY
Vierveien 1, Stavanger
Brewmaster at Lervig on the west coast of Norway, Murphy
previously worked at craft breweries in Rome and Denmark.
Ma Che Siete Venuti A Fà 234............................Worth the travel
Mahr's Bräu 199..Beer garden
Øst 109...Local favorite
Pizzarium 234...Unexpected
Sabi Omakase Restaurant 113........................Beer & food
Standard Tap 393..Wish I'd opened

NICOLÒ MUSSO
Open Baladin Torino, Piazzale Valdo Fusi, Turin
Nephew of Teo Musso from Baladin, Nicolò Musso was born
inside the world of craft beer and works at Open Baladin
Torino.
Birreria Le Baladin 232.....................................Beer garden
Lambiczoon 232..Worth the travel
Open Baladin Roma 234....................................Beer & food
Open Baladin Torino 233...................................Local favorite

TEO MUSSO
Birrificio Baladin, Piazza V Luglio 1944, 15, Piozzo
Master brewer and founder of Baladin, a brewpub and farm
brewery in a small village in Piedmont, Italy.
Baladin Caselle Aeroporto 231...........................Unexpected
Birreria Le Baladin 232......................................Beer garden
Birreria Le Baladin 232......................................Local favorite
Birreria Le Baladin 232......................................Wish I'd opened
Open Baladin Roma 234.....................................Worth the travel
Open Baladin Torino 233....................................Beer & food

DEAN MYERS
Brasserie Beck, 1101 K Street Northwest, Washington, D.C.
Myers was a sommelier who ditched wine for beer.
Evening Star Cafe 413.......................................Unexpected
Granville Moore's 419..Local favorite
Siren by RW 419..Beer & food
The Bier Garden 414..Beer garden
The NoMad Bar 378...Worth the travel

RICK NELSON
Oedipus Brewing, Gedempt Hamerkanaal 85, Amsterdam
Cofounder and head creative of Oedipus Brewing in
Amsterdam.
Belmont Station 320...Worth the travel
Campingplatz Wallberg 202................................Unexpected
Holy Grale 402...Wish I'd opened
In de Wildeman 163..Local favorite
Mahr's Bräu 199...Beer & food
Oedipus Brewing 164...Beer garden

AMY NEWELL-LARGE
Avery Brewing Company, 4910 Nautilus Court, Boulder
Hospitality manager at Avery Brewing Company in Colorado.
Avery Brewing Company 286..............................Beer & food
Crew Republic 201...Worth the travel
Elizabeth Station 295...Unexpected
Stone Brewing World Bistro &
   Gardens Escondido 281...................................Beer garden

Turf Tavern 135...Wish I'd opened
Wibby Brewing 287...Local favorite

DAVID NEWMAN
Pint and Jigger, 1936 South King Street, Honolulu
Owner and operator of Pint and Jigger, Newman is the former
U.S. Bartender's Guild president for Hawaii.
Banger's Sausage House & Beer Garden 422..........Beer garden
Falling Rock Tap House 314................................Worth the travel
Father's Office 284..Wish I'd opened
Murphy's Bar & Grill 288....................................Unexpected
Pint and Jigger 288..Beer & food
Village Bottle Shop & Tasting Room 288...............Local favorite

LUKE NICHOLAS
Epic Brewing Company, 230B Neilson Street, Auckland
The owner of Epic Brewing Company in New Zealand,
Nicholas has more than twenty years of brewing experience.
Galbraith's Alehouse 67......................................Beer & food
Jackie's Beer Nest 87...Wish I'd opened
The Beer Library 67..Unexpected
Toronado Pub 310...Worth the travel
Vultures' Lane 66..Local favorite
Zeitgeist 310..Beer garden

STEFAN NIETO
Ragnarok Brewery, César Borja Oe3–930, Quito
Founder of Ragnarök Brewery in Ecuador.
Barbudo Beer Garden 448...................................Beer garden
Barbudo Beer Garden 448...................................Worth the travel
Fuente Italia 448..Unexpected
La Candelaria 441..Beer & food
La Candelaria 441..Local favorite

BRIAN OAKLEY
Julian's, 318 Broadway, Providence
Oakley is a major part of the Providence, Rhode Island,
craft-beer scene. In 2015, with his partners Julian Forgue and
Randy Kass, he opened Pizza J. He is also the co-organizer of
Beervana Fest and Bacon & Beer.
Armsby Abbey 361...Beer & food
Cafe Kulminator 168...Beer garden
La Capsule 185...Worth the travel
The Dinghy 411...Unexpected
The Scurvy Dog 371..Local favorite

YUKO ODASHIMA
Marubeni Logistics Corporation, Tokyo
Odashima is a balcony hop farmer and a saison lover.
Beach Muffin 76...Unexpected
Cardiff Giant 384..Local favorite
Mekelburg's 384...Beer & food
Mission Dolores 387...Beer garden
Tired Hands Fermentaria 369.............................Worth the travel

FLAVIU ADRIAN ODORHEAN
Cluj Napoca
Odorhean started bartending in 2009, is a certified beer sommelier, and sells local craft beers at festivals and events in Romania.

Blend. Brews & Bites 249..Local favorite
Borough Market 150..Unexpected
Brouwerij 't IJ 162..Beer garden
In 't Spinnekopke 175..Beer & food
Mikkeller Bar Bucharest 249........................Wish I'd opened
Proeflokaal Arendsnest 164........................Worth the travel

SHAWNA O'FLAHERTY
TorontoBoozeHound, Toronto
Creative director for TorontoBoozeHound, O'Flaherty was trained at George Brown College in the Wine Specialist Certificate program.

Bar Hop BrewCo 275..Beer garden
Burdock Brewery 274........................Wish I'd opened
Rainhard Brewing Company 274........................Local favorite
Siem Reap Brewpub 96..Unexpected
Tørst 386..Beer & food
Vices & Versa 271..Worth the travel

NIKKI O'HANLON
Glasgow
Beer connoisseur and blogger O'Hanlon lives in Glasgow and is also a library assistant and a part-time artist.

BrewDog Glasgow 140..Local favorite
Hopworks Urban Brewery 321........................Beer & food
Inn Deep 140..Beer garden
Koelschip Yard 140........................Wish I'd opened
Tørst 386..Worth the travel

JAIME OJEDA
ConEspuma.com, Bellavista 0360, Santiago
Owner and brewmaster of Loom BrewPub, founder of ConEspuma.com, and a beer consultant.

Ateliê Wäls 446........................Wish I'd opened
Barnabeer 170..Unexpected
Barnabeer 170..Worth the travel
Emmett's Brewing Company West Dundee 333.......Beer & food
Loom 448..Local favorite

HIDENORI OKA
YO-HO Brewing Company, 1119-1 Otai, Saku, Nagano
Marketing director of YO-HO Brewing Company, one of Japan's leading craft breweries.

Omohara Beer Forest 82..Beer garden
Popeye 83..Worth the travel
Watering Hole 82..Beer & food
Yona Yona Beer Works 83..Local favorite
YYG Brewery & Beer Kitchen........................Wish I'd opened

BOB OLSON
Bolero Snort Brewery, 65 Railroad Avenue, Ridgefield Park
Founder of Bolero Snort in New Jersey, Olson started homebrewing in 2009.

Barcade Jersey City 362........................Wish I'd opened
Capital Craft 362..Beer & food
Moeder Lambic Fontainas 176........................Worth the travel
Pilsener Haus & Biergarten 362........................Beer garden
Prudential Center 363..Unexpected

The Dog & Cask 363..Local favorite

JURA OMELKA
Pivo Chomout, Dalimilova 18/92, Olomouc
Co-owner and brewer at Pivo Chomout in the Czech Republic.

Pivovar Chomout 240..Beer garden
Pivovar Chomout 240..Local favorite
Zlý Časy 241..Beer & food
Zlý Časy 241..Worth the travel

ROBERTO ORANO
White Pony Microbrewery and White Pony Pub, Corso Vittorio Emanuele II 185, Padua
CEO and master brewer of White Pony Microbrewery, Orano is based in Italy and brewing in Belgium He is also cofounder of White Pony Pub.

'Cause Beer Loves Food 163..Unexpected
Craft & Draft 165........................Wish I'd opened
La Tana 175..Beer & food
La Tana 175..Worth the travel
White Pony Pub 236..Local favorite

ANGELO ORONA
Craft King Consulting, Los Lunas
President and owner of Craft King Consulting in New Mexico, Orona is a national judge with the Beer Judge Certification Program and a Certified Cicerone.

Cervejaria Santa Therezinha 446........................Unexpected
Cochon Butcher 403..Beer & food
Delirium Café 174..Worth the travel
Garden District 419..Beer garden
Moeder Lambic Original 176........................Wish I'd opened
Sister Bar 292..Local favorite

JEFF ORR
Tool Shed Brewing Company, 801 30th Street Northeast, Calgary
An avid homebrewer, Orr and his friend opened Tool Shed Brewing Company in 2012.

Alibi Room 268..Worth the travel
Bluejacket 418........................Wish I'd opened
Chili's Grill & Bar Calgary Airport 268........................Unexpected
Craft Beer Market 268..Beer & food
Lagunitas Brewing Company 283........................Beer garden
National on 17th 268..Local favorite

FRANCISCO OYARCE
Bake and Beer, locations in Las Vegas and Viña del Mar
Founder of Bake and Beer, Oyarce is a BJCP beer judge and experiments with fermenting doughs.

Bar el Irlandés 449..Local favorite
Bardenor 449..Unexpected
Mikkeller Bar San Francisco 311........................Beer & food
Porterhouse Central 142..Worth the travel

MALIA PAASCH
The Birch, 1231 West Olney Road, Norfolk
Rigato started The Birch, specializing in craft beers and cheese.

Birreria Volo 274........................Wish I'd opened
Commonwealth Brewing Company 414........................Local favorite
Edmund's Oast Restaurant 411........................Beer & food
Max's Taphouse 404..Worth the travel

Spuyten Duyvil 388..............................Beer garden
The Barrel 410.....................................Unexpected

THOMAS PALMER
Mondo Brewing Company, 86 Stewart's Road, London
Cofounder of Mondo Brewing Company, Palmer started the
brewery in 2014 with Todd Matteson.
Amtrak Surfliner 300...............................Unexpected
BRUS 126...Worth the travel
Crown and Anchor 146.........................Local favorite
Euston Tap 148.................................Wish I'd opened
Stone Brewing World Bistro &
    Gardens Liberty Station 305..............Beer garden
Tired Hands Fermentaria 369....................Beer & food

STEFÁN PÁLSSON
Reykjavík
Author of *Beer: Around the World in 120 Pints*.
Björsetur Íslands 110.........................Wish I'd opened
Fiskmarkaðurinn 110.............................Beer & food
Loksins bar 110....................................Unexpected
Micro Bar 110....................................Local favorite
Skúli Craft Bar 110..............................Beer garden
The Royal Oak 139..............................Worth the travel

YVES PANNEELS
Het Geuzegenootschap, Frans Baetensstraat 45, Lennik
Member of HORAL (High Council for Traditional Lambic
Beers), Panneels organizes beer festivals in Belgium and Lovell,
Maine.
Cohiba Atmosphere Antwerp 168...............Unexpected
Ebenezer's Pub 356............................Worth the travel
Edison 170...Beer & food
In de Verzekering tegen de Grote Dorst 169.........Local favorite

MAYTE PARDO
Althaia Artesana, Plaça dels Furs 1, Altea
Pardo opened Althaia Artesana with her husband, a
microbrewery in Alicante, on the southern coast of Spain.
2D2Dspuma 227...................................Beer garden
Cervezas Althaia Artesana 219..................Local favorite
Cervezas Althaia Artesana 219...................Unexpected
La Boutique de la Cerveza 220................Worth the travel
Llúpol Celler de Cerveses 220................Wish I'd opened
Ruzanuvol Cerveceria Artesanal Ruzafa 220............Beer & food

JOSH PATTON
Wooden Robot Brewery, 1440 South Tryon Street, Suite 110,
Charlotte
CEO and cofounder of Wooden Robot Brewery, an urban
farmhouse brewery featuring local ingredients.
Brawley's Beverage 407.........................Local favorite
Delirium Café 174.............................Worth the travel
Wooden Robot Brewery 407......................Beer & food

ODIN PAUL
Brauhaus Goslar, Marktkirchhof 2, Goslar
Brewmaster at Brauhaus Goslar in Germany, Paul is a two-time
gold-medal-winning brewer.
Brauhaus Goslar 203............................Local favorite
Brauhaus Lemke am Alex 210.....................Beer & food
Heinrich - Das Wirtshaus 203....................Beer garden
Schadt's Brauerei Gasthaus 203...............Wish I'd opened

Stone Brewing World Bistro &
    Gardens Berlin 208.........................Worth the travel
Südsee-Badeparadies Kontiki-Bar 203................Unexpected

NICOLE PEARCE
Liquor Stores N.A., Ltd., Various
Alaska Region Beer Merchant for Liquor Stores N.A., Ltd.
Fitzgerald's Hotel and Restaurant 335................Unexpected
Glam Café 252.................................Worth the travel
Humpy's Great Alaskan Alehouse 278..........Local favorite
Stone Brewing World Bistro &
    Gardens Escondido 281......................Beer garden
Surly Brewing Company 338......................Beer & food
TeKu Tavern 328..............................Wish I'd opened

MATTHEW PENE
Eleven Madison Park, 11 Madison Avenue, New York City
Pene is maître d'hôtel at Eleven Madison Park, where he was
beer director.
As Is NYC 377.................................Wish I'd opened
Brooklyn Harvest Market Union Ave 388.........Unexpected
Carmine Street Beers 379......................Local favorite
Radegast Hall & Biergarten 388.................Beer garden
Radegast Hall & Biergarten 388................Worth the travel
The Cannibal Beer & Butcher 378................Beer & food

ALEXA PENTON
Slow Boat Brewing Company, 6 Nan Sanlitun Lu, Beijing
Marketing manager at Slow Boat Brewing Company, one of
Beijing's first craft breweries.
ChurchKey 418..................................Beer & food
ChurchKey 418.................................Worth the travel
Great Leap Brewing 86..........................Beer garden
Pasteur Street Brewing Company 97............Wish I'd opened
Popeye 83...Unexpected
Slow Boat Brewing Company 87..................Local favorite

FRANCISCO PEREIRA
Cerveja LETRA, 684 Avenida Professor Machado Vilela,
Vila Verde
Cofounder of Fermentum, a spin-off from Cerveja LETRA.
Cruzes Credo 220................................Unexpected
Letraria Craft Beer Garden Porto 221............Beer garden
Letraria Craft Beer Garden Porto 221..........Local favorite
Moeder Lambic Fontainas 176....................Beer & food
NaparBCN 227.................................Worth the travel

JAIME PEREZ
Cervecera Tierra y Libertad, Del Jardín Patiño, Limón
Head brewer and co-owner of Cercevera Tierra y Libertad
in Costa Rica, Perez was born in Mexico and learned to brew
in North Carolina.
Beer Study 407................................Worth the travel
Milltown 407....................................Beer garden
The Pipe and Pint 408...........................Unexpected
Thirsty Monk 406..............................Wish I'd opened
Wicked Weed Brewing Pub 407....................Beer & food
Wilk Craft Beer 434............................Local favorite

JACOBO PÉREZ LLISO

La Quince Brewery, Calle Echegaray 23, Madrid
Cofounder and head brewer of La Quince Brewery.

Brew Wild Pizza Bar 219...Local favorite
Estebenea 218...Unexpected
Kaapse Brouwers 156..Worth the travel
Pizza Port Solana Beach 285...Beer & food
Stone Brewing World Bistro
  & Gardens Escondido 281..Beer garden

ONDREJ PERNICA

Klínec-Katz, Prague
Gypsy brewer based in Czech Republic.

BeerGeek Bar 241...Local favorite
BeerGeek Bar 241..Wish I'd opened
BeerGeek Bar 241...Worth the travel
Kino Světozor 241...Unexpected
Letná Beer Garden 241...Beer garden

LUKE PESTL

Bellwoods Brewery, 124 Ossington Avenue, Toronto
The owner of Bellwoods Brewery in Toronto, Pestl and
cofounder Mike Clark have been brewing beer since 2012.

Ace Hotel & Swim Club 283..Unexpected
Birreria Volo 274..Local favorite
Dandylion 274...Beer & food
Moeder Lambic Original 176.....................................Worth the travel
Suarez Family Brewery 366......................................Wish I'd opened

JOSH PFRIEM

Pfriem Family Brewers, 707 Portway Avenue, Hood River
Pfriem started his brewing career at Utah Brewers
Cooperative, then worked for Chuckanut Brewery in
Washington and Full Sail Brewing Company in Oregon. In
2011, he became brewmaster and cofounder of Pfriem Family
Brewers.

3 Fonteinen 169...Beer & food
Augustiner-Keller 214..Beer garden
Belmont Station 320..Local favorite
Moeder Lambic Fontainas 176.................................Worth the travel
Portland Lobster Company 358.....................................Unexpected
Tørst 386..Wish I'd opened

CHUWY PHILLIPS

Yokohama
Based in Japan, Phillips writes beer reviews and is a
homebrewer.

Beach Muffin 76...Beer & food
DevilCraft Hamamatsucho 81...................................Wish I'd opened
Full Monty British Pub and Cider House 76...........Local favorite
Sylvans 77...Beer garden
The Wenlock Arms 148...Worth the travel

ERICH PHILLIPS

Cerevisia Craft Brewery, 9B Street 29, Phnom Penh
Phillips and his friends started Cerevisia Craft Brewery in 2013.

Botanico 96..Beer & food
Botanico 96...Beer garden
Botanico 96...Local favorite
Rhinegeist Brewery 342..Wish I'd opened
Rhinegeist Brewery 342...Worth the travel

DAVID PIÉ ALIANA

Rosses i Torrades, Consell de Cent, 192 Barcelona
Aliana is founder and owner of Rosses i Torrades, a cellar
bottle shop where you can drink beer while listening to music
on a vinyl record.

BierCaB 226...Beer & food
Bodega Fermín 226...Worth the travel
Forn Europa 227...Unexpected
La Bona Pinta 227..Local favorite
La Cervecita Nuestra De Cada Día 227......................Beer garden

CHRISTOPHER PILKINGTON

Põhjala Brewery, Serva 28, Tallinn
Pilkington is head brewer at Põhjala, where he joined shortly
after the company began. He previously worked at BrewDog.

Birrificio Lambrate Adelchi 232..............................Worth the travel
BRUS 126..Beer & food
Jing-A Taproom 1949 87..Wish I'd opened
Koht 246..Local favorite

ANDRÉ PINTADO

Passarola Brewing, Rua Adriano Correia de Oliveira 4A,
Lisbon
Cofounder of Passarola Brewing.

Akkurat 119...Worth the travel
Letraria Craft Beer Garden Porto 221........................Beer garden
Letraria Craft Beer Garden Porto 221......................Local favorite
Mikkeller Bar San Francisco 311..................................Beer & food

LOGAN PLANT

Beavertown Brewery Tap Room, Unit 17–18, Lockwood
Industrial Park, London
Owner and founder of Beavertown Brewery Tap Room.

Beavertown Brewery Tap Room 150........................Local favorite
Russian River Brewery 284..Beer & food
Santa Barbara Bowl 284...Unexpected
The Unicorn 136...Worth the travel

PAUL PLETT

St. Nicholas Brewing Company, 12 South Oak Street,
Du Quoin
Head brewer at St. Nicholas. After learning the ropes of
industrial brewing in North Bergen, Plett joined the team at
St. Nicholas in the fall of 2015.

St. Nicholas Brewing Company 332...........................Beer & food
St. Nicholas Brewing Company 332...........................Beer garden
St. Nicholas Brewing Company 332.........................Local favorite
St. Nicholas Brewing Company 332...........................Unexpected
St. Nicholas Brewing Company 332.......................Wish I'd opened
St. Nicholas Brewing Company 332......................Worth the travel

ANTON PLIGIN

Craft rePUBlic, Malyy Gnezdnikovskiy Pereulok 9/7, Moscow
Cofounder of Craft rePUBlic, one of the first craft-beer bars in
Moscow. It is recognized by *RateBeer* as the best Russian craft
beer for three consecutive years.

Ægir BrewPub 113...Unexpected
BierCaB 226...Worth the travel
Birch & Barley 418..Beer & food
Brouwcafé de Molen 155..Beer garden
Craft rePUBlic 246...Local favorite
The Alchemist 373..Wish I'd opened

JOE PLOOF
Hanging Hills Brewing Co., 150 Ledyard Street, Hartford
Cofounder of Hanging Hills Brewing in Connecticut.
ANXO Cidery and Pintxos Bar 418............................Beer & food
Hank's Saloon 384...Worth the travel
Mostodulce 235...Unexpected
The Courtyard Brewery 403....................................Beer garden
The Gate 386...Wish I'd opened
The Spigot 356..Local favorite

MAXIM POLIVANOV
Golodranets, Ulitsa Shaumyana, 67, Rostov-on-Don
Founder of craft-beer bar Golodranets, craft-beer boutique
Butylochka, Belgian lambic salon Bokalchik, and vegan craft-
beer café Koluchka, all in Russia.
Golodranets 246...Local favorite
In de Verzekering tegen de Grote Dorst 169......Worth the travel
In De Vrede 170..Beer & food
Scandinavian Airlines 110.......................................Unexpected
Warpigs Brewpub 126...Beer garden

JESSE PRALL
Rubber Soul Brewing Company, 1930 Northwood Drive,
Salisbury
Chief brewing officer at Rubber Soul Brewing. Prall was head
brewer at Appalachian Brewing Company in Pennsylvania and
worked with Sam Calagione at Dogfish Head Craft Brewery in
Delaware, where he stayed for ten years.
Falling Rock Tap House 314..................................Worth the travel
Frankford Hall 392...Beer garden
Paxtang Grill 370..Unexpected
The Pickled Pig Pub 396..Local favorite
Tröegs Independent Brewing 370.............................Beer & food

SUSAN PROM
Voyageur Brewing Company, 233 West Highway 61, Grand
Marais
Marketing manager for Voyageur Brewing Company.
Voyageur Brewing Company 337..............................Beer & food
Voyageur Brewing Company 337..............................Beer garden
Voyageur Brewing Company 337..............................Local favorite
Voyageur Brewing Company 337..........................Worth the travel

RON RAIKE
Playalinda Brewing Company, 5220 South Washington
Avenue, Titusville
Brewmaster at Playalinda Brewing Company, Raike has
more than thirty years of experience in brewing, brewery
management, and distribution.
Playalinda Brewing Company Brix Project 399.........Beer & food
Red Light Red Light 398..Local favorite
Red Light Red Light 398......................................Worth the travel

ERICK RAMIREZ
Corcovado Cerveceria Artesanal, San Pablo de Heredia, San
Rafael
CEO and founder of Corcovado Cerveceria Artesanal in Costa
Rica.
Casa Brew Garden 433..Beer garden
Maui Brewing Company 289..................................Worth the travel
Pecan Lodge 413..Beer & food
Stiefel Pub 434..Local favorite

REID RAMSAY
Beer Street Journal, Atlanta
Founder and chief content creator for the website Beer Street
Journal.
Brick Store Pub 400..Local favorite
Brick Store Pub 400..Worth the travel
Firestone Walker Brewing Company 280................Beer & food
Stone Brewing World Bistro &
  Gardens Liberty Station 305................................Beer garden
The Comet Pub & Lanes 401...................................Unexpected
The1up Colfax 316...Wish I'd opened

DEVON RANDALL
Arts District Brewing Co., 828 Traction Avenue, Los Angeles
Randall is head brewer of Arts District Brewing Co.
Barbara's at the Brewery 301................................Local favorite
Ladyface Ale Companie Alehouse &
  Brasserie 279...Beer & food
Stone Brewing World Bistro &
  Gardens Escondido 281......................................Beer garden
Three Weavers Brewing Company 300....................Unexpected
Toronado San Diego 306.....................................Worth the travel

BIER RANGER
Cubao Expo, 3 General Romulo Avenue, Quezon City
A blogger at BierRanger, Ranger has been tasting and writing
about beer in the Philippines for two decades.
13 Ubay St. Comfort Dining 99...............................Beer & food
13 Ubay St. Comfort Dining 99...............................Unexpected
Alamat Filipino Pub & Deli 98..............................Wish I'd opened
Sagada Cellar Door 98..Worth the travel
The Bottle Shop 98...Beer garden
The Bottle Shop 98..Local favorite

ANDRIS RASIŅŠ
Aldaris Brewery, Tvaika iela 44, Riga
A beer sommelier at Aldaris Brewery, Rasiņš was educated at
the Beer and Cider Academy in London.
Alus Celle 247...Local favorite
Jack's Abby Craft Lagers 360.................................Beer & food
Muted Horn 210..Worth the travel
Stone Brewing World Bistro &
  Gardens Berlin 208...Beer garden

KEVIN RAUB
Lisbon
A Portugal-based travel journalist and hops enthusiast, Raub
has written over 50 Lonely Planet travel guides and contributes
to international publications while in pursuit of perfect brews.
Brouwerij 't IJ 162...Beer garden
Burial Beer Company 406.....................................Local favorite
Father's Office 284...Beer & food
Funkatorium 406...Wish I'd opened
Mikkeller Bar Copenhagen 127...........................Worth the travel
Newark Liberty International Airport 363...............Unexpected

TAYLOR REES
Spangalang Brewery, 2736 Welton Street, Denver
Cofounder of Spangalang Brewery, Rees began his
professional brewing career at Great Divide Brewing
Company, where he became head brewer.
Falling Rock Tap House 314................................Local favorite
Falling Rock Tap House 314................................Worth the travel
Goed Zuur 315..Beer & food
Whole Foods Market Charlotte 407.........................Unexpected

LEE REEVE
Abrewcadabrew, Yokohama
Owner and operator of ABREWCADABREW, Japan's premier
homebrewing club, and co-founding partner of the WORLD
CIDER experience.
Cactus Burrito 76..Unexpected
Full Monty British Pub and Cider House 76...........Local favorite

JAMES RENWICK
Mornington Peninsula Brewery, 72 Watt Road, Mornington
Renwick joined Mornington Peninsula Brewery in 2010 as bar
staff while completing his marketing degree. Upon graduation
and after nine months of travel, he returned to the brewery as
marketing manager.
Altar Cervecería 440...Unexpected
Bright Brewery 58..Beer garden
New Belgium Brewing Company 286..............Wish I'd opened
Stomping Ground Brewery & Beer Hall 62...............Beer & food
The Bar at Carwyn Cellars 63..............................Local favorite
The Scratch Bar 57..Worth the travel

JULIE RHODES
Merchant du Vin, Seattle
Specializing in European beer imports, Rhodes has ten years
of experience in beer sales, marketing, and management.
Ayinger Bräustüberl 198......................................Beer garden
De Heeren van Liedekercke 169.........................Worth the travel
Goed Zuur 315...Local favorite
Kuma's Corner 350..Wish I'd opened
Sint-Jorishof 169..Beer & food
Whip In 423..Unexpected

SERGIO RIBENBOIM
Sergio's World Beers, 1605 Story Avenue, Louisville
The founder of Sergio's World Beers each year, Ribenboim
takes groups of beer lovers to Europe to visit breweries.
Delirium Café 174..Wish I'd opened
Sergio's World Beers 403.....................................Beer & food
Sergio's World Beers 403....................................Local favorite
Sergio's World Beers 403....................................Worth the travel

TRAVIS RICHARDS
Nothing's Left Brewing Co., 1502 East 6th Street, Tulsa
Brewer for large breweries in Oklahoma, Richards started
Nothing's Left Brewing Co.
33 Acres Brewing Company 269.............................Unexpected
Fassler Hall 410..Beer garden
McNellie's South City 410...................................Local favorite
Nothing's Left Brewing Co. 410...........................Worth the travel
Oak & Ore 409...Beer & food
Prairie Brewpub 410......................................Wish I'd opened

SAMUEL RICHARDSON
Other Half Brewing, 195 Centre Street, New York City
Cofounder and brewmaster at Other Half Brewing Co.
Bar Great Harry 384..Local favorite
Bohemian Hall and Beer Garden 379.......................Beer garden
Omnipollos Hatt 118..Beer & food
Watering Hole 82...Worth the travel

BIRGIT RIEBER
Wegro Institut für Bierkultur, Florianigasse 55/21, Vienna
COO of Wegro Institut für Bierkultur, Rieber is the daughter of
a southern German brewery family. She's also a beer journalist,
a consultant, and a judge at the European Beer Star.
Augustiner Bräu 242..Beer garden
Braugasthaus Altes Mädchen 202.........................Local favorite
Dolden Mädel Braugasthaus 209.........................Worth the travel
The Brickmakers Pub & Kitchen 243.......................Beer & food

ELEONORA RIGATO
Birra Cerqua, Via Broccaindosso 5, Bologna
Communication-specialist focused on food and beverage and
a craft-beer lover, Rigato is based in Italy.
Birra Cerqua 230...Local favorite
Birrificio Lambrate Adelchi 232...........................Wish I'd opened
Brooklyn Brewery 387.......................................Worth the travel
Ranzani13 230...Beer & food

DAVID ROBERTS
Bittercreek Alehouse, 246 North 8th Street, Boise
Beer buyer for Bittercreek Alehouse.
Bar Gernika 289..Local favorite
Bittercreek Alehouse 289...................................Worth the travel

DARREN (DOC) ROBINSON
Doctor's Orders Brewing, Sydney
Founder of Doctor's Orders Brewing, Darren (Doc) Robinson
brews unconvential beers. Since they don't have their own
brewery, they take over other breweries in Sydney.
Bitter Phew 56...Local favorite
Little Beer Quarter (LBQ) 69...............................Unexpected
Netherworld 57..Wish I'd opened
Stone Brewing World Bistro & Gardens
    Escondido 281..Beer & food
Watsons Bay Boutique Hotel 57...........................Beer garden
Wheatsheaf Hotel 58..Worth the travel

ESTÁCIO RODRIGUES
Instituto da Cerveja, Avenida dos Carinas 417, São Paulo
Sommelier at the Instituto de Cerveja in São Paulo, Rodrigues
was educated at the Italian Sommelier Association.
Ambar Craft Beers 447.......................................Local favorite
Empório Alto dos Pinheiros 447.............................Unexpected
Englischer Garten 214..Beer garden
ICB Factory Brewery 447.................................Wish I'd opened
Stone Brewing World Bistro &
    Gardens Berlin 208.......................................Worth the travel
The Burger Map 447...Beer & food

RAPHAEL RODRIGUES
All Beers, São Paulo
Journalist and a beer sommelier.
Empório Alto dos Pinheiros 447.............................Beer & food
Empório Alto dos Pinheiros 447............................Local favorite

Empório Alto dos Pinheiros 447..........................Wish I'd opened
In de Wildeman 163..Worth the travel

NICOLAS RODRIGUEZ ETCHELET
Breohan Cerveceria, Bolívar 862, Buenos Aires
Managing partner at Breoghan Brewery.
Breoghan 449..Local favorite
Bruder Beer Garden 449...Beer garden
The Gibraltar 449...Unexpected

STEPHEN ROGINSON
Batch Brewing Company, 1400 Porter Street, Detroit
Founder and owner of Batch Brewing Company, Detroit's first
nano brewery. It has won the Best of Craft Beer awards, and
was voted the best microbrewery or brewpub by *Metro Times*
and *Hour Detroit*.
8 Degrees Plato 335..Local favorite
Augustiner-Keller 214..Beer garden
HopCat 335..Wish I'd opened
Hopleaf 352...Worth the travel
Skúli Craft Bar 110...Unexpected
The Søvengård 336..Beer & food

WENDY ROIGARD
Valkyrie Brewing Company, 234 Dallas Street, Dallas
Director at BeerNZ, New Zealand's leading craft-beer
distributor, Roigard founded Valkyrie Brewing Company in 2011
and has won ten Brewers Guild of New Zealand awards over
the past four years.
Ilam Homestead 68..Beer garden
Systembolaget 113..Unexpected
The Laboratory 68...Local favorite
The Laboratory 68...Wish I'd opened
The Mussel Inn 68...Worth the travel
Twenty Seven Steps 68..Beer & food

CAMILO ROJAS SANCHEZ
Chelarte, Carrera 14, Bogotá
Founder of Chelarte Brewery, one of the first craft breweries in
Colombia, and a homebrewer since 2007.
Chelarte 440...Local favorite
ChurchKey 418...Wish I'd opened
ChurchKey 418...Worth the travel
Gustu 442...Unexpected
Schneider Bräuhaus 215...Beer garden
Sierra Nevada Taproom and Restaurant 281................Beer & food

JUSSI ROKKA
Olutneuvos Oy, Tykistonkatu 11, Helsinki
Helsinki-based freelance journalist specializing in beer and
beer education.
BeerTime 254..Unexpected
Café Abseits 199..Wish I'd opened
Ravintola Olo 123..Beer & food
Ravintola St. Urho's Pub 123.....................................Local favorite
Schlenkerla 199...Worth the travel
Spezial-Keller 199..Beer garden

EUGENIO ROMERO
Cerveceria Wendlandt, Boulevard Costero 248, Ensenada
Romero opened a brewpub in Ensenada and then a brewery,
Cerveceria Wendlandt, on the Pacific Ocean.

Stone Brewing World Bistro
& Gardens Liberty Station 305.............................Beer garden
Wendlandt El Sauzal 426..Worth the travel
Wendlandt Ensenada 426..Beer & food
Wendlandt Ensenada 426..Local favorite

OFER RONEN
Srigim Brewery Ltd., Commercial Centre, Srigim
Cofounder of Srigim Brewery Ltd. in Israel.
Dieu du Ciel! 271...Beer & food
KANAAL 254...Unexpected
Porter & Sons 104..Worth the travel
Srigim Beer Garden 104..Beer garden
Srigim Beer Garden 104..Local favorite
Tied House 282..Wish I'd opened

KELSEY ROTH
Exhibit A Brewing Company, 81 Morton Street, Framingham
General manager at Exhibit A Brewing Company and a
Certified Cicerone.
Big Star 353..Beer garden
Delirium Café 174...Worth the travel
Hopleaf 352..Wish I'd opened
Olde Magoun's Saloon 360..Local favorite
Row 34 358...Beer & food
The Quarters 360..Unexpected

LEIF ROTSAERT
Wildlife Brewing, 145 South Main Street, Victor
Head brewer at Wildlife Brewing in Idaho, an organization
that provides accessible premium craft beers throughout the
Yellowstone region.
Pagosa Brewing Company & Grill 287.....................Beer garden
Second Street Brewery 292...Beer & food
Second Street Brewery 292...Worth the travel
Wildlife Brewing 290..Local favorite

ARNAU ROVIRA
Cervesa Espiga, Carrer de Malet 12, nau n°3, Sant Llorenç
d'Hortons
Head brewer and founder of Cervesa Espiga, a craft brewery
in Catalonia.
Beer'linale 226...Beer & food
BierCaB 226..Wish I'd opened
BierCaB 226..Worth the travel
British Airways 148...Unexpected
CocoVail Beer Hall 226...Local favorite

JOHN ROWLEY
Rowley Farmhouse Ales, 1405 Maclovia Street, Santa Fe
Brewer at Rowley Farmhouse Ales, Rowley is an accomplished,
award-winning brewer.
Banger's Sausage House & Beer Garden 422..........Beer garden
Ebenezer's Pub 356...Beer & food
Majestic Marketplace 278...Unexpected
Moeder Lambic Fontainas 176....................................Worth the travel
Rowley Farmhouse Ales 292......................................Local favorite
Rowley Farmhouse Ales 292......................................Wish I'd opened

JARED RUDY

Norsemen Brewing Company, 830 North Kansas Avenue, Topeka

Cofounder of Norsemen Brewing Company in Kansas. The brewery supports the arts and community in Topeka, and in 2015, the owners founded Fat Back Associates Corp.

Boulevard Brewing Company 339......................Wish I'd opened
Boulevard Brewing Tours
  & Recreation Center 339...........................Worth the travel
Gella's Diner & Lb Brewing Company 401.................Beer & food
Kansas City Renaissance Festival 401.....................Unexpected
Norsemen Brewing Company 402.....................Local favorite

PATRICK RUE

The Bruery, 717 Dunn Way, Placentia

CEO and founder of The Bruery, Rue is also a Master Cicerone.

Armsby Abbey 361...Beer & food
ChurchKey 418..Worth the travel
Docent Brewing 283.....................................Local favorite
Jester King Brewery 423.................................Beer garden
Publican Tavern 350.......................................Unexpected
Toronado Pub 310.......................................Wish I'd opened

JOSH RUFFIN

Brasserie V, 1923 Monroe Street, Madison

Ruffin is a Certified Cicerone, a beer buyer at Madison's premier taproom, and a writer.

Belmont Station 320.....................................Wish I'd opened
Cask & Ale 344...Local favorite
Crow's Feet Commons 293.................................Beer garden
GB's Bottle Shop and Tasting Bar 398.....................Unexpected
Proletariat 376..Worth the travel
The Porter Beer Bar 400.................................Beer & food

TRIP RUVANE

Barley Creek Brewing Company, 1774 Sullivan Trail, Tannersville

Owner of Barley Creek Brewing Company in Pennsylvania.

Barley Creek Brewing Company 371......................Beer & food
Barley Creek Brewing Company 371......................Beer garden
Barley Creek Brewing Company 371......................Local favorite
Barley Creek Brewing Company 371......................Worth the travel
Cooper's Seafood House 371...............................Unexpected
Falling Rock Tap House 314.............................Wish I'd opened

KELLY RYAN

Fork & Brewer, 20A Bond Street, Wellington

Since 2001, Ryan has been brewing at Tui, Fyne Ales, Thornbridge, Good George, Brew Mountain, and now Fork Brewing. He has been an international beer judge since 2007.

Coopers Alehouse 57.....................................Unexpected
Fork & Brewer 69..Local favorite
Hallertau Brewery & Biergarten 67......................Beer garden
The Mussel Inn 68.....................................Worth the travel
The Sheffield Tap 136..................................Wish I'd opened
The Snowdrop Inn 132...................................Beer & food

KEVIN RYAN

Service Brewing Company, 574 Indian Street, Savannah

Cofounder and CEO of Service Brewing Company in Georgia.

Banger's Sausage House & Beer Garden 422..........Beer garden
Ben's Neighborhood Grill & Tap 401.....................Unexpected
Brick Store Pub 400...................................Worth the travel

Crystal Beer Parlor 401...................................Beer & food
The Warehouse Bar & Grille 401.........................Local favorite
Thirsty Monk 406......................................Wish I'd opened

KAROL SADŁOWSKI

Browar Profesja, Kwidzyńska 6e, Wrocław

Co-owner of Browar Profesja, a Polish craft brewery established in 2015 by passionate homebrewers.

Bistro Narożnik 240....................................Local favorite
Kurna Chata 240..Beer garden
Profesja Bar 240......................................Wish I'd opened
Taphouse 56..Worth the travel
Targowa - Craft Beer and Food 240.....................Beer & food

HÖSKULDUR SÆMUNDSSON

Ölgerðin Egill Skallagrímsson, Grjóthálsi 7–11, Reykjavik

Brand manager for Ölgerðin—Iceland's largest brewery—and teacher at the Beer School, Sæmundsson has also coauthored a book on beer with Stefán Pálsson.

Augustiner-Keller 214....................................Beer garden
Élesztő 243..Worth the travel
Nørrebro Bryghus 127....................................Beer & food
Skúli Craft Bar 110.....................................Local favorite
Warpigs Brewpub 126...................................Wish I'd opened

JOSTEIN SÆTHRE

Skumbag Oslo, Møllergata 32, Oslo

Brewer and owner of Skumbag, Sæthre is also a brewer at Grünerløkka Brewery.

Brygg 111..Wish I'd opened
Café Sara 111...Beer garden
Grünerløkka Brygghus 111...............................Local favorite
Håndverkerstuene 111...................................Beer & food
Humle & Malt 111.......................................Unexpected
Omnipollos Hatt 118...................................Worth the travel

CRISTINA SAEZ

Pirate Brew, 4 Claire-Waldoff-Strasse, Berlin

Founder of Pirate Brew.

BRLO Brwhouse 209....................................Beer garden
Hopfenreich 209...Local favorite
Rockaway Brewing Company 380.........................Unexpected
Rockaway Brewing Company 380.......................Worth the travel
Stone Brewing World Bistro
  & Gardens Berlin 208................................Beer & food

OLIVER SAN ANTONIO

Con-Con San Antonio, Makati City

A beer enthusiast and a lawyer in the Philippines, San Antonio writes about beer, food, and travel.

Cafe Kulminator 168..................................Worth the travel
Delirium Café 174.....................................Wish I'd opened
Hofbräuhaus 214...Beer garden
Russian River Brewery 284..............................Beer & food
The Bottle Shop 98.....................................Local favorite

PABLO SANTOS

Cervecería Moonshine, Calle 134a #50-30, Bogotá

Founder of Cervecería Moonshine, a microbrewery.

Cantillon Brewery 174................................Worth the travel
Cerveza Akumal 431.....................................Unexpected
Cevicheria Central 118 440.............................Beer & food
El Mono Bandido 440....................................Local favorite
La Birrería at Eataly 234..............................Wish I'd opened
Prater Biergarten 211..................................Beer garden

RICARDO SANTOS

2C - Arte Cervejeira, Tamega Park, Amarante
A professional brewer since 2013 and owner of 2C - Arte
Cervejeira, a microbrewery in Portugal.

Aduela 221	Beer garden
Catraio 221	Wish I'd opened
Catraio 221	Worth the travel
Letraria Craft Beer Garden Porto 221	Beer & food
Letraria Craft Beer Garden Porto 221	Local favorite

SAM SARMAD

Malting Pot, Rue Scarron 50, Brussels
Owner of the bottle shop Malting Pot since 2012 and beer
taster since 1998.

Dynamo - Bar de Soif 175	Local favorite
Elfo's Pub 235	Worth the travel
Nüetnigenough 177	Beer & food
Prosciutteria Del Corso 235	Unexpected

SARA SARTANG

Folk & Friends, Norr Mälarstrand 32, Stockholm
A beer devotee living in London, Sartang shifted her attention
to craft beer while working at Brewdog in Stockholm. Today
she works at Folk & Friends.

Kælderkold 226	Worth the travel
Lådan 118	Beer & food
Ölbryggan 118	Beer garden
Oliver Twist 119	Local favorite
Omnipollos Hatt 118	Wish I'd opened
Söderhallen Billiard 119	Unexpected

BRIAN SAUER

Pirate Republic Brewing, Woodes Rogers Walk, Nassau
Raised in Wisconsin, Sauer is the head brewer at Pirate
Republic Brewing Company in the Bahamas.

Bull & Bush Brewery 314	Beer & food
Burnhearts 345	Worth the travel
ChurchKey 418	Wish I'd opened
Pirate Republic Brewing 426	Beer garden
Pirate Republic Brewing 426	Local favorite

SEBASTIAN SAUER

Freigeist Bierkultur, Diepenlinchener Strasse 20, Stolberg
Sauer is a historical-beer fanatic and a gypsy brewer in
Germany.

Bierkeller Roppelt 200	Beer garden
Craftbeer Corner Coeln 203	Local favorite
Koryo Hotel 86	Unexpected
Pizza Port Carlsbad 280	Wish I'd opened
Schlenkerla 199	Worth the travel
The Publican 353	Beer & food

EM SAUTER

Pints and Panels, 1700 Stratford Avenue, Stratford
Founder and cartoonist of Pints and Panels, communications
manager at Two Roads, and advanced cicerone.

À La Mort Subite 174	Worth the travel
Beer Revolution 283	Wish I'd opened
East Side Restaurant 356	Beer garden
Hotel Posada Ecológica La Abuela 432	Unexpected
J Timothy's Taverne 356	Local favorite
The Sovereign 419	Beer & food

JESSE SCHEITLER

Lost Cabin Beer Co., 1401 West Omaha Street #3, Rapid City
Founder of Lost Cabin Beer Co.

Biergarten Haus 418	Beer garden
Falling Rock Tap House 314	Wish I'd opened
Goed Zuur 315	Beer & food
Great American Ball Park 342	Unexpected
Independent Ale House 343	Worth the travel
Lost Cabin Beer Co. 343	Local favorite

NATHANIEL SCHMIDT

Aguamala Cerveceria, Carretera Ensenada-Tijuana, El Sauzal
de Rodriguez
Schmidt is a marine biologist who began brewing beer in 2005
and founded Cerveceria Agua Mala in Baja California.

Coronado Brew Pub 281	Worth the travel
Deckman's 427	Unexpected
Mendocino Brewing Company Ale House 285	Beer garden
Microbrewery Aguamala 426	Local favorite
Microbrewery Aguamala 426	Wish I'd opened
Stone Brewing World Bistro & Gardens Escondido 281	Beer & food

FELIX SCHUESSLER

Gasthausbrauerei Alt-Giessen Brewpub, Westanlage 30–32,
Giessen
Brewer at Gasthausbrauerei Alt-Giessen brewpub, Schuessler
studied beer tourism in Germany.

Beercode Kitchen & Bar 233	Unexpected
Kraft Bräu 204	Beer & food
Naïv 203	Local favorite
Siebensternbräu 243	Beer garden
Taproom Jungbusch 198	Wish I'd opened
Zapotex 204	Worth the travel

TIM SCIASCIA

Cellarmaker Brewing Company, 1150 Howard Street, San
Francisco
Owner and head brewer of Cellarmaker Brewing Company,
Sciascia started his career by cleaning kegs at Marin Brewing
Company.

City Beer Store 311	Local favorite
Panama 66 305	Beer garden
Public House 311	Unexpected
The Hermosillo 300	Worth the travel
The Masonry 327	Beer & food
Toronado San Diego 306	Wish I'd opened

TIM SCOTT

BiaCraft Artisan Ales, 1 Lê Ngô Cát, Ho Chi Minh City
Cofounder and co-owner of BiaCraft Artisan Ales and Quán
Ụt Ụt in Ho Chi Minh City, Scott is from Australia and has been
living and working in Vietnam's food and beverage scene for
seventeen years.

Beer Komachi 77	Worth the travel
Pasteur Street Brewing Company 97	Local favorite
Quán Ụt Ụt 97	Beer & food
Taco Mac 400	Wish I'd opened

VASSILIS SEGOS
Dark Crops Brewery, 125 Artemidos, Athens
Owner of Dark Crops Brewery and a homebrewer since 2010, Segos won gold medals at the Greek Homebrewing Competition and a bronze at the AHA National Homebrew Competition.

Bibere 255	Unexpected
The Lazy Bulldog Pub 254	Beer & food
The Local Pub 254	Beer garden
The Local Pub 254	Local favorite
The Monk's Kettle 310	Wish I'd opened
The Monk's Kettle 310	Worth the travel

GEOFFREY SEIDEMAN
Honolulu BeerWorks, 328 Cooke Street, Honolulu
In 2014, Seideman and his wife, Charmayne, opened Honolulu Beer Works.

Bashamichi Taproom 76	Unexpected
Honolulu BeerWorks 288	Beer & food
Honolulu BeerWorks 288	Local favorite
Independence Beer Garden 392	Beer garden
Ortleib's 393	Worth the travel
Russian River Brewery 284	Wish I'd opened

RASMUS SEIDLER KREBS
Himmeriget, Åboulevard 27–1960, Frederiksberg
A seasoned bar owner, Seidler Krebs runs Himmeriget.

Kronborggade 3 127	Local favorite
Restaurant 108 126	Unexpected
Spuyten Duyvil 388	Wish I'd opened
Threes Brewing 385	Worth the travel
Tørst 386	Beer & food

BEN SELF
West Sixth Brewing, 501 West 6th Street, Lexington
Cofounder of West Sixth Brewing, a production craft brewery and taproom in a 140-year-old bread factory in Kentucky.

Englischer Garten 214	Worth the travel
Kentucky Native Café 402	Beer garden
Proof On Main 403	Beer & food
West Sixth Brewing 402	Local favorite

MARTIN SERRA
La Porteña Cerveceria Artesanal, Barrio de las Delicias, San Juan del Sur
Owner of La Porteña, a micro enterprise that produces small batches of beer, using traditional methods, in Nicaragua.

Botanicos Beer Garden 432	Beer garden
Botanicos Beer Garden 432	Wish I'd opened
Cerveceria La Cruz 449	Worth the travel
La Estación Central 432	Beer & food
San Juan del Sur Cervecería 432	Local favorite

LEO SEWALD
Seasons Craft Brewery, Rua Provenzano 333, Porto Alegre
Head brewer and cofounder of Seasons Craft Brewery in Brazil, known for its creative approach to brewing.

Augustiner-Keller 214	Beer garden
Bier Keller 446	Unexpected
Bier Markt Vom Fass 446	Local favorite
Novare Res Bier Café 357	Worth the travel
Pacific Beach Ale House 305	Wish I'd opened
Tipsy Cow 295	Beer & food

GRAYSON SHEPARD
Craft Consultants, 2-1-106 Shiroganecho, Shinjuku, Tokyo
Avid craft-beer drinker and owner of a craft-beer and spirits-focused consulting firm in Japan.

Aw Shucks Country Store 413	Unexpected
DevilCraft Kanda 80	Wish I'd opened
Himalaya Table 80	Beer & food
Hop-Scotch Craft Beer & Whiskey 80	Wish I'd opened
Sapporo Beer Garden 76	Beer garden
The Answer Brewpub 414	Worth the travel

BEN SHINKLE
3rd Turn Brewing, 10408 Watterson Trail, Louisville
Brewer at 3rd Turn Brewing, Shinkle has worked there since 2015.

3rd Turn Oldham Gardens 402	Beer garden
3rd Turn Oldham Gardens 402	Local favorite
Coconutz Sports Bar 433	Unexpected
Coconutz Sports Bar 433	Worth the travel
Monnik Beer Company 403	Beer & food
Thirsty Monk 406	Wish I'd opened

SCOTT SHOR
Edmund's Oast, 1081 Morrison Drive, Charleston
Operating partner of Edmund's Oast, the award-winning brewery, restaurant, taproom, and beverage store in South Carolina.

Edmund's Oast 411	Worth the travel
Euclid Hall 314	Beer & food
Kudu Coffee and Craft Beer 411	Local favorite
Tørst 386	Wish I'd opened

ISAAC SHOWAKI
Octopi Brewing, 1131 Uniek Drive, Waunakee
President of Octopi Brewing, Showaki has worked in beer consulting and managment and has an extensive knowledge of contract brewing.

La Fontelina Restaurant 230	Worth the travel
Merchant Madison 344	Local favorite
Octopi Brewing 346	Beer garden
Piece Brewery and Pizzeria 353	Beer & food
The Sovereign 419	Unexpected

RONALD SIEMSGLUESS
Brausturm Bierverlag, Eduardstrasse 46–48, Hamburg
Founder and managing director of craft-beer import and distribution company, Brausturm Bieverlag, and taproom and bottle shop, Beyond Beer.

Beyond Beer 202	Local favorite
Beyond Beer 202	Wish I'd opened
Muted Horn 210	Worth the travel
ÜberQuell Brauwerkstätten 203	Beer & food
Weisses Bräuhaus Kelheim 200	Beer garden

MARK SIGMAN
Relic Brewing Co., 95B Whiting Street, Plainville
Brewer and owner of Relic Brewing Co.

Cafe Cambrinus 180	Beer & food
Euclid Hall 314	Worth the travel
Independence Beer Garden 392	Beer garden
J Timothy's Taverne 356	Local favorite
Khyber Pass Pub 392	Unexpected
Novare Res Bier Café 357	Wish I'd opened

LINDA MERETE SKOGHOLT
Brus Bar and To Øl, Osterhausgate 11, Oslo and Slotsgade 2, Copenhagen
Partner and co-owner of Brus Bar Oslo and Brus Distribution (with Tore Gynther of Brus ApS), Skogholt is also a beer, wine, and sake sommelier.

Brus Bar 111	Local favorite
Café Kulminator 168	Worth the travel
Café Vlissinghe 180	Beer garden
Microkosmos Craft Beer 96	Unexpected
Moeder Lambic Fontainas 176	Wish I'd opened
Restaurant Barr 126	Beer & food

JENS SKRUBBE
Skrubbe.com, Stockholm
A freelance beer writer in Sweden, Skrubbe has worked at the Press Club in Stockholm and is an expert for the Belgian Club, Sweden's only subscription beer club.

Cafe Kulminator 168	Worth the travel
De Heeren van Liedekercke 169	Beer garden
Internationella Pressklubben 118	Local favorite
Les Brigittines 176	Beer & food
Moeder Lambic Fontainas 176	Wish I'd opened
't Velootje Bar Peculiar 169	Unexpected

MISCHA SMITH
Pasteur Street Brewing Company, 144 Pasteur Street, Ho Chi Minh City
Smith is the head of sales at Pasteur Street.

Bia Hoi Junction Ho Chi Minh 97	Unexpected
Liquid Laundry Kitchen & Brew 88	Wish I'd opened
Malt 97	Local favorite
Mill Street Brew Pub 275	Beer garden
The Globe 92	Beer & food
The Jersey Giant Pub & Restaurant 275	Worth the travel

KEVIN SMOLAR
Sun King Brewery, 135 North College Avenue, Indianapolis
Lab manager at Sun King Brewery in Indiana.

3 Floyds Brewpub 334	Beer & food
Beer Geeks 333	Worth the travel
Brewfest 333	Wish I'd opened
TGI Fridays 334	Unexpected
The Pint Room Bar 333	Local favorite
The Rathskeller 333	Beer garden

VANESSA SOBRAL
Caldereta Cervejas , Rua Wisard 397, São Paulo
Owner of Caldereta Cervejas.

Cervejaria Dogma 350	Local favorite
Ambar Craft Beers 447	Beer & food
Caldereta Cervejas Artesanais 448	Wish I'd opened
Empório Alto dos Pinheiros 447	Worth the travel
Mercado Municipal de Curitiba 446	Unexpected
Tito Biergarten 448	Beer garden

ALAN SPRINTS
Hair of the Dog Brewing Company, 61 Southeast Yamhill Street, Portland
Sprints started Hair of the Dog in 1993 and sells about 1,000 barrels of beer every year.

Apex 320	Beer garden
Café Kulminator 168	Worth the travel

Dexter Brewhouse 326	Beer & food
Horse Brass Pub 321	Local favorite
Shiga Kogen Brewery 77	Unexpected

NEMANJA STEFANOVIC
Tron Brewery, Olge Alkalaj 18/24, Belgrade
Founder of Tron Brewery, a pioneer of craft brewing in Serbia; cofounder of Hopsi Adria, which sells hops in the region; and board member of the Small Independent Brewers Association of Serbia.

Amsterdam Airport Schiphol 165	Unexpected
Bar Saša 2532	Beer & food
Pivo i Kobaja 253	Beer garden
Samo Pivo 253	Local favorite
Samo Pivo 253	Worth the travel

ALEC STEFANSKY
Uncommon Brewers, 303 Potrero Street, 40H, Santa Cruz
Founder and head brewer of Uncommon Brewers.

The Oasis Tasting Room & Kitchen 284	Beer & food
The Oasis Tasting Room & Kitchen 284	Local favorite

DAVID STEIN
Creature Comforts Brewing Co., 271 West Hancock Avenue, Athens
Cofounder and head brewer at Creature Comforts Brewing Co. in Georgia.

Banger's Sausage House & Beer Garden 422	Beer garden
Brick Store Pub 400	Local favorite
Edmund's Oast Restaurant 411	Beer & food
Rock & Brews Paia 289	Wish I'd opened
Stein's Market and Deli 404	Unexpected
The Avenue Pub 403	Worth the travel

MATTHEW STEINBERG
Exhibit A Brewing Company, 81 Morton Street, Framingham
Cofounder and head brewer of Exhibit A Brewing Company in Massachusetts.

Armsby Abbey 361	Beer & food
Luke's Beer and Wine Convenience Store 360	Unexpected
Seymour The Pub 360	Local favorite
The Dive Bar 361	Beer garden
The Publick House 359	Worth the travel
Trillium Brewing Company 359	Wish I'd opened

JOHN STEWART
Perrin Brewing Company, 5910 Comstock Park Drive, Comstock Park
The director of brewing operations at Perrin Brewing Company, Stewart previously worked at New Holland Brewing Co.

Brasserie V 344	Unexpected
Choice City Butcher & Deli 286	Worth the travel
Founders Brewing Company Grand Rapids 335	Beer garden
Pine Box 327	Wish I'd opened
Rezervoir Lounge 336	Local favorite
The Publican 353	Beer & food

PAUL STUART DEL ROSARIO

Fat Pauly's Handcrafted Ales & Lagers, Pala-O, Iligan City
Co-owner and manager at Fat Pauly's in the Philippines.

Fat Pauly's 99	Beer & food
Fat Pauly's 99	Beer garden
Fat Pauly's 99	Local favorite
Fat Pauly's 99	Worth the travel

JEFFREY STUFFINGS

Jester King Brewery, 13187 Fitzhugh Road, Austin
Cofounder of Jester King Brewery, a farmhouse brewery in
Texas Hill Country.

Austin Beer Garden Brewing Company 422	Beer garden
Backcountry Pizza & Taphouse 286	Worth the travel
Draught House Pub & Brewery 422	Local favorite
Holy Grale 402	Beer & food
Novare Res Bier Café 357	Wish I'd opened
Schera's Algerian-American Restaurant & Bar 334	Unexpected

ZAQ SUAREZ

Craftpeak, 15 West Walnut Street, Asheville
Suarez has run sales and distribution for Burial Beer Co.,
helped start the creative agency Craftpeak, and has written
about beer.

Edmund's Oast Restaurant 411	Beer & food
Moeder Lambic Fontainas 176	Worth the travel
PJ's Fast Food Mart 409	Unexpected
Royal American 411	Beer garden
The Whale 407	Local favorite
Tørst 386	Wish I'd opened

JULIO SUBERO

Importadora Cultura Cervecera, 341 Avenida Rómulo
Betancourt, Santo Domingo
Beer enthusiast and co-owner of Cultura Cervecera in the
Dominican Republic.

Cultura Cervecera 426	Local favorite
Cultura Cervecera 426	Wish I'd opened
Cultura Cervecera 426	Worth the travel
Sierra Nevada Taproom 408	Beer & food

PJ SULLIVAN

Wet City, 223 West Chase Street, Baltimore
Co-owner of Wet City, a craft-beer bar in Maryland.

Banger's Sausage House & Beer Garden 422	Beer garden
Mikkeller Tórshavn 110	Wish I'd opened
Tired Hands Fermentaria 369	Worth the travel
Venice Tavern 405	Unexpected
Wet City 405	Beer & food
Wet City 405	Local favorite

MAGNUS SVENSSON

BrewDog Bar Sweden, 56 Sankt Eriksgatan, Stockholm
Owner of BrewDog Bar Sweden.

Cycle Brewing 398	Worth the travel
Fermentoren 127	Wish I'd opened
Row 34 358	Beer & food
The Rover 114	Local favorite

LANA SVITANKOVA

Varvar Brewery, Starosilska 1e, Kiev
A Cicerone beer server and Provisional BJCP judge,
Svitankova is also a writer and the manager at Varvar brewery
in Kiev.

Alaus Biblioteka 248	Wish I'd opened
Augustiner Bräu 242	Beer garden
Bee Beer 219	Beer & food
BRLO Brwhouse 209	Worth the travel
Tripel B 233	Unexpected
Varvar Bar 248	Local favorite

JAMES TAI

Beeracolyte, New York City
A craft-beer consultant and educator, Tai worked with chef
Alain Ducasse and Ducasse Studios to develop the beer
program at the Empire City Casino expansion. He was on the
starting team for Whole Foods Beer Room, which now has
locations across the U.S. He is also a Certified Cicerone and
BJCP Certified Beer Judge.

Blind Tiger Ale House 377	Local favorite
DeCicco & Sons 366	Unexpected
Euston Tap 148	Worth the travel
Jupiter Taproom 280	Beer garden
The Monk's Kettle 310	Beer & food
Toronado Pub 310	Wish I'd opened

JAANIS TAMMELA

Tanker Brewery, Hoidla tee 9, Harjumaa
CEO and cofounder of Tanker Brewery, Tammela began as a
homebrewer in Tallinn.

Airbräu 214	Unexpected
BlackLab Brewhouse & Kitchen 226	Beer & food
BrewDog Tallinn 246	Wish I'd opened
Koht 246	Local favorite
Letraria Craft Beer Garden Porto 221	Beer garden
Tampa Bay Brewing Company 399	Worth the travel

BRETT TATE

Dust Bowl Brewing Co., 3000 Fulkerth Road, Turlock
Founder and owner of Dust Bowl Brewing Co.

Alvarado Street Brewery & Grill 282	Wish I'd opened
Dust Bowl Brewery Taproom 285	Local favorite
Euclid Hall 314	Beer & food
Incline Spirits & Cigars 291	Unexpected
McMenamins Edgefield 294	Beer garden
Stone Brewing World Bistro & Gardens Escondido 281	Worth the travel

TRACY TEACH

Cerveceria Teach, Calle Berlin 172, Lima
Founder of Cerveceria Teach in Peru.

Candlelight Inn 368	Beer & food
El Rincón de Bigote 442	Unexpected
Humboldt Cider Company Tap Room 281	Wish I'd opened
Molly's Irish Bar & Restaurant 442	Local favorite

DANIEL THOMBANSEN

Lippstädter Brauerei, Langestrasse 3, Lippstadt
Brewer at Lippstädter since 2000.

Braugasthaus Altes Mädchen 202	Beer & food
Braugasthaus Altes Mädchen 202	Worth the travel
Brauhaus Thombansen 204	Local favorite
Brauhaus Thombansen 204	Unexpected
Forsterbräu Meran 235	Beer garden

ERIN THOMPSON

Brugge Brasserie, 1011 East Westfield Boulevard, Indianapolis
A beer enthusiast and professional, Thompson works in
several roles at the Belgian-style brewery, Brugge Brasserie.

Holy Grale 402	Beer & food
Minneapolis–Saint Paul International Airport 338	Unexpected
The Koelschip 333	Local favorite
The Koelschip 333	Wish I'd opened
The Koelschip 333	Worth the travel
The Rathskeller 333	Beer garden

BRETT TIEMAN

23 Brewing Company, Number 100, Section 1, Xinhai Road
Tieman founded 23 Brewing Company with Matthew Frazar.

23 Public Craft Beer 88	Local favorite
Double Windsor 389	Worth the travel
Fette Sau 388	Beer & food
Grassroots & Fruit 88	Unexpected
Yard House Honolulu 288	Beer garden

EUGENE TOLSTOV

Victory Art Brew, Tolmacheva Street 49, Ivanteyevka
Cofounder and brewmaster at Victory Art Brew, one of the
first Russian craft breweries. Tolstov has been homebrewing
for ten years.

60 Degrees Bar & Brewery Helsinki Airport 123	Unexpected
Cafe Kulminator 168	Wish I'd opened
Craft rePUBlic 246	Local favorite
In de Verzekering tegen de Grote Dorst 169	Worth the travel
The Beer Plant 422	Beer & food
Trophy Ranch 413	Beer garden

KRAIG TORRES

Hop City Craft Beer & Wine, 1000 Marietta Street Northwest
#302, Atlanta
Founder and chief hophead of Hop City Craft Beer & Wine and
Barleygarden Kitchen & Craft Bar.

Barleygarden Kitchen & Craft Bar 399	Beer garden
Brick Store Pub 400	Worth the travel
ChurchKey 418	Wish I'd opened
Hopleaf 352	Beer & food
The Lobster Trap Restaurant 359	Unexpected
The Porter Beer Bar 400	Local favorite

JEREMIAH TRACY

Thirsty Monk Brewery & Pub, 92 Patton Avenue, Asheville
Tracy oversees postproduction and retail quality for Thirsty
Monk and trains its elite crew of beer nerds.

Hopleaf 352	Worth the travel
Jake's Billiards 408	Wish I'd opened
The Brew Pump 406	Local favorite
The Brewer's Kettle 408	Beer garden
Zillie's Island Pantry 408	Unexpected

CHRIS TREANOR

WhiteFrontier, Rue du Levant 99, Martigny
Treanor is master brewer at White Frontier and was previously
at Galway Bay Brewery.

BierCaB 226	Worth the travel
Bierkeller Au Trappiste 186	Unexpected
CRAK Taproom 235	Wish I'd opened
The Sovereign 419	Beer & food
Warpigs Brewpub 126	Beer garden
WhiteFrontier Taproom 187	Local favorite

ZAC TRIEMERT

Brickway Brewery and Distillery, 1116 Jackson Street, Omaha
A commercial brewer for sixteen years, Triemert received a
master's degree in brewing and distilling in Scotland. He is the
brewmaster at Brickway Brewery and Distillery.

Avery Brewing Company 286	Beer garden
Brickway Brewery & Distillery 341	Local favorite
Delirium Café 174	Worth the travel
Local Beer, Patio and Kitchen Downtown 341	Wish I'd opened
Stone Brewing World Bistro & Gardens Liberty Station 305	Beer & food
Target Field 338	Unexpected

MICHIKO TSUTSUI

Watering Hole, 5-26-5 Sendagaya, Tokyo
Owner of Watering Hole.

Bamboo Beer Pub 82	Local favorite
Blind Tiger Ale House 377	Wish I'd opened
Falling Rock Tap House 314	Worth the travel
The ABGB 422	Beer garden
The Skinny Pancake 373	Unexpected
Tørst 386	Beer & food

FELIPE VALENCIANO

Sin Corbata Cervecería Artesanal, San Francisco de Dos Ríos,
San Jose
Cofounder and head brewer at Sin Corbata Cervecería
Artesanal, Valenciano studied culinary arts in Costa Rica and
Cerveza Artesana, a beer academy in Barcelona.

BierCaB 226	Wish I'd opened
BierCaB 226	Worth the travel
Casa Félix 433	Local favorite
Hofbräuhaus 214	Beer garden
Mercado La California 434	Unexpected
NaparBCN 227	Beer & food

VALGEIR VALGEIRSSON
Borg Brugghús, Grjóthálsi 7-11, Reykjavík
Brewmaster at Borg Brugghús in Iceland, Valgeirsson has been brewing since 2004.

Amway Center 398	Unexpected
Bjórsetur Íslands 110	Beer garden
Bjórsetur Íslands 110	Local favorite
Moeder Lambic Original 176	Wish I'd opened
Tørst 386	Beer & food
't Velootje Bar Peculiar 169	Worth the travel

BENNY VAN AERSCHOT
Inglorious Brew Stars, Seraphin De Grootestraat 33, Antwerp
Cofounder of Inglorious Brew Stars, van Aerschot and his twin brother won Best Homebrew of Belgium and the Netherlands at the Brouwland Beer Competition.

BierCaB 226	Wish I'd opened
BierCaB 226	Worth the travel
Billie's Bier Kafétaria 168	Local favorite
Cafe Kulminator 168	Beer garden
Gollem 168	Beer & food
University Of Antwerp 168	Unexpected

DOROTHÉE VAN AGT
Bières Cultes, 40 rue Damrémont, Paris
Van Agt has worked in the beer industry for ten years and manages four beer shops in Paris.

Dieu du Ciel! 271	Worth the travel
Les Trois 8 195	Local favorite
Nüetnigenough 177	Beer & food
Stone Brewing World Bistro & Gardens Berlin 208	Beer garden

AART VAN BERGEN
Walhalla Craft Beer, Spijkerkade 10, Amsterdam
Founder of Walhalla Craft Beer, van Bergen started as a homebrewer.

'cause Beer loves Food 163	Beer & food
Ægir BrewPub 113	Wish I'd opened
HaarBarbaar 163	Unexpected
In de Wildeman 163	Worth the travel
Poesiat & Kater 165	Beer garden
Walhalla Craft Beer 164	Local favorite

NICK VAN BEUSEKOM
Uiltje Brewing Company, Bingerweg 25, Haarlem
Export manager at Uiltje Brewing Company in the Netherlands.

Uiltje Bar 155	Beer & food
Uiltje Bar 155	Local favorite
Uiltje Bar 155	Worth the travel
Uiltje Brewery & Taproom 155	Beer garden

PETER VAN DER AREND
Morebeer, Nieuwezijds Voorburgwal 250, Amsterdam
A beer enthusiast, van der Arend opened Proeflokaal Arendnest in 2000 and owns Beer Temple.

'cause Beer loves Food 163	Beer & food
BeerTemple 162	Local favorite
Toronado Pub 310	Worth the travel

KICK VAN HOUT
Brouwerij Oersoep, Waalbandijk 14D, Nijmegen
Cofounder of Brouwerij Oersoep, a new brewery in the Netherlands.

De Biertuin 164	Beer garden
De Nieuwe Winkel 154	Beer & food
In de Wildeman 163	Worth the travel
Proeflokaal Goesting 154	Worth the travel
STOOM beer & food 154	Local favorite

LINDA VAN LOON
Utrecht
Dutch beer enthusiast with a passion for brewing.

Bierreclame Museum 154	Beer garden
Café Derat 158	Local favorite
Cafe Kulminator 168	Worth the travel

FRANS VAN STADEN
Jack Black Brewing Co., 10 Brigid Road, Cape Town
Marketing coordinator at Jack Black's Brewing Co. in South Africa.

Banana Jam Cafe 262	Beer garden
Banana Jam Cafe 262	Worth the travel
Jack Black's Taproom 263	Beer & food
Jack Black's Taproom 263	Local favorite
Jack Black's Taproom 263	Wish I'd opened
Motherland Brewers 263	Unexpected

MATT VAN WYK
Alesong Brewing and Blending, 80848 Territorial Highway, Eugene
Cofounder and brewmaster at Alesong Brewing and Blending in Oregon.

Beergarden 293	Beer garden
De Garre 181	Wish I'd opened
Goed Zuur 315	Beer & food
Greenberry Store & Tavern 293	Unexpected
Saraveza 322	Worth the travel
The Bier Stein 294	Local favorite

DEL VANCE
Beerhive Pub, 128 South Main Street, Salt Lake City
Cofounder of Uinta Brewing Co. and The Bayou Bar, and founder of Beerhive Pub.

Beerhive Pub 294	Local favorite
McMenamins Edgefield 294	Beer & food
McSorley's Old Ale House 376	Wish I'd opened
McSorley's Old Ale House 376	Worth the travel
Stone Brewing World Bistro & Gardens Escondido 281	Beer garden
Water Tower Sports Pub 336	Unexpected

CHRIS VANDERGRIFT
LexBeerScene.com, Lexington
Manager at LexBeerScene.com, and organizer of the Lexington Fest of Ales and Lexington Craft Beer Week.

Edmund's Oast Restaurant 411	Unexpected
Hopleaf 352	Beer & food
Hopleaf 352	Worth the travel
Stone Brewing World Bistro & Gardens Escondido 281	Beer garden
West Sixth Brewing 402	Local favorite
West Sixth Brewing 402	Wish I'd opened

LEO E. VASILEIOU
Urban Brewing, Vault C, CHQ Building, Custom House Quay, Dublin
Raised in Greece, Vasileiou cofounded Urban Brewing, an Irish food and beer spot influenced by his travels.

Brewery Corner 143..Local favorite
Mikkeller Bar Copenhagen 127.................................Beer & food
Taphouse 56..Worth the travel
The Bull and Castle 142...Unexpected
Urban Brewing 142..Beer garden

MARIE-PIER VEILLEUX
Brasserie Harricana, 95 Rue Jean-Talon Ouest, Montreal
Cofounder and owner of Brasserie Harricana, a microbrewery in the Mile-Ex neighborhood.

Auberge Festive Sea Shack 271...............................Unexpected
Bellwoods Brewery 275.......................................Wish I'd opened
Brasserie Harricana 270...Beer & food
Isle de Garde Brasserie 270...................................Local favorite
Madame Boeuf and Flea 274.....................................Beer garden
Tørst 386...Worth the travel

GABRIELA VELASCO
Patán Ale House, 1281 Calle Morelos, Guadalajara
Owner of Patán Ale House, Velasco is dedicated to craft beer and promoting Mexican brands.

Blind Lady Ale House 304......................................Wish I'd opened
Club der Visionäre 208...Beer garden
El Grillo 428..Worth the travel
Patan Ale House 428..Local favorite
Pigs Pearls 428...Unexpected
Tiger!Tiger! 306...Beer & food

VASILIA VENIZELACOU
Northern Monk Brew Co., The Old Flax Store, Marshall Mills, Holbeck
Venizelacou runs sales operations at Northern Monk Brew Co. in England.

BRUS 126...Wish I'd opened
Bundobust Leeds 137..Beer & food
Café am Neuen See 211...Beer garden
Northern Monk Brew Company 138.........................Local favorite
Premier Store Farsley 138..Unexpected
Skúli Craft Bar 110..Worth the travel

MARCO VIDMAR
Sir William's Pub, Tavčarjeva Ulica 8a, Ljubljana
Vidmar lived in Switzerland, Slovenia, and Croatia before opening Sir William's Pub.

Augustiner Bräu 242...Beer garden
Élesztő 243...Worth the travel
Mastro Birraio 231..Beer & food
Sir William's Pub 252...Local favorite

MARTIN VOIGT
Vienna
Voigt is a homebrewer, a beer writer, a blogger, and a festival organizer.

Alibi Room 268...Beer & food
BRLO Brwhouse 209...Beer garden
Falling Rock Tap House 314....................................Worth the travel

Sports Authority Field at Mile High 316....................Unexpected
The Brickmakers Pub & Kitchen 243.......................Local favorite
Tribaun 242..Wish I'd opened

KARL VOLSTAD
Civil Society Brewing, 1200 Town Center Drive, Suite 101, Jupiter
Cofounder and owner of Civil Society Brewing, Jupiter's first microbrewery.

Boxelder Craft Beer Market 397..............................Local favorite
Row 34 358..Beer & food

LADISLAV VRTIŠ
Pivovar Raven, Mozartova 1, Pilsen
CEO and co-owner of Pivovar Raven in Czech Republic.

BeerGeek Bar 241...Local favorite
T-Anker Sunny Terrace 241.......................................Beer garden
Taphouse 56..Worth the travel

MILOS VUKSIC
Endorfin Bar & Restaurant, Braće Jugovića 3, Belgrade
Cofounder of Endorfin Bar & Restaurant in Serbia, a craft-beer shop and restaurant.

Bar Toto 386..Worth the travel
Endorfin Bar & Restaurant 252..................................Beer & food
Endorfin Bar & Restaurant 252...............................Local favorite
Majstor Za Pivo 253..Beer garden
Mikkeller Bar Berlin 208......................................Wish I'd opened

THOMAS WAGNER
Sol de Copan, Avenida El Mirador, Copán Ruinas
Founder of Sol de Copan brewery in Honduras, Wagner has been brewing for 27 years.

Schlössle Brauerei 201..Beer & food
Schlössle Brauerei 201..Beer garden
Schlössle Brauerei 201...Worth the travel
Sol de Copán 432...Local favorite
Sol de Copán 432...Unexpected

ALEX WALLASH
The Rare Barrel , 940 Parker Street, Berkeley
Part of the founding team at the Rare Barrel, Wallash is in charge of sales and marketing.

3 Fonteinen 169...Beer & food
Single Fin Bali 100..Worth the travel
Societe Brewing Company 305.................................Local favorite

JUSTIN WALSH
June Lake Brewing, 131 South Crawford Avenue, June Lake
The founder of June Lake Brewing with his wife, Sarah, in the Eastern Sierras.

Blind Lady Ale House 304...Beer & food
Clocktower Cellar 282..Local favorite
Minden Meat and Deli 291..Unexpected
Pizza Port Carlsbad 280..Worth the travel
The Brewing Lair 280...Beer garden

GRANT WANER
Tallgrass Brewing Co., 5960 Dry Hop Circle, Manhattan
Market manager of Tallgrass Brewing Co. in Kansas.

Bierkeller Au Trappiste 186....................................Local favorite
Little Thai 187..Unexpected
Tørst 386..Worth the travel

MERLIN WARD
Wartega, 33 35th Street, 6A, New York City
Head brewer and cofounder of Wartega, Ward is a Certified Cicerone and a BJCP judge.

Greenwood Park 386	Beer garden
Mekelburg's 384	Beer & food
Wartega Brewing 387	Local favorite

ZACH WARREN
The Answer Brewpub, 6008 West Broad Street, Richmond
Warren is a beer ambassador and a wine drinker.

ChurchKey 418	Worth the travel
High Street Brewery 294	Beer garden
Mekong Restaurant 414	Local favorite
Shift Drinks 322	Wish I'd opened
The Answer Brewpub 414	Beer & food
Third Street Dive 403	Unexpected

ADAM WATSON
Sloop Brewing Co., 1065 County Route 19, Elizaville
Cofounder and brewmaster at Sloop Brewing Co.

Bank Square Coffeehouse 364	Unexpected
Chinesischer Turm 214	Beer garden
Mekelburg's 384	Beer & food
Schatzi's Pub & Bier Garden 367	Local favorite
Seumas' Bar 141	Worth the travel

POLLY WATTS
Avenue Pub, 1732 Saint Charles Avenue, New Orleans
Owner of Avenue Pub.

ChurchKey 418	Beer & food
Moeder Lambic Fontainas 176	Worth the travel
The Avenue Pub 403	Local favorite

CHRISTIAN WEBER
Common Roots Brewing Company, 58 Saratoga Avenue, South Glens Falls
Cofounder of Common Roots Brewing Company, a father-son team, Weber specializes in high-quality beers combining old-world traditions with new-inspiration.

Henry Street Taproom 368	Local favorite
Moeder Lambic Fontainas 176	Worth the travel
Sugarbush Resort 373	Unexpected
The City Beer Hall 364	Beer & food
The Farmhouse Tap & Grill 371	Wish I'd opened
Wolff's Biergarten Albany 364	Beer garden

JARED WELCH
Southern Grist Brewing Company, 1201 Porter Road, Nashville
Cofounder of Southern Grist Brewing.

7venth Sun Brewing Company 397	Unexpected
Craft Brewed 412	Local favorite
Goed Zuur 315	Worth the travel
Longman & Eagle 351	Beer & food
Toronado Pub 310	Wish I'd opened
Trillium Brewing Company 359	Beer garden

ERIC WENTLING
Beerploma, Waconia
Wentling has been a homebrewer for more than 25 years and is a Minnesota beer blogger focusing on local craft beer and breweries.

Indeed Brewing Company and Taproom 337	Local favorite
Lupulin Brewing 337	Unexpected
Surly Brewing Company 338	Beer garden
The Happy Gnome 338	Beer & food
The Happy Gnome 338	Worth the travel

TRISTAN WHITE
Dragoon Brewing Co., 1859 West Grant Road #111, Tucson
Founder and manager at Dragoon Brewing Company, White coordinates the sales, distribution, and taproom staff.

Loews Ventana Canyon Resort 279	Beer & food
Reilly Craft Pizza & Drink 279	Beer garden
Saint Charles Tavern 279	Unexpected
Tap & Bottle Downtown 279	Local favorite
Toronado Pub 310	Worth the travel

STEPHEN WHITEHURST
Brighton Bier, Unit 10, Bell Tower Industrial Estate, Roedean Road, Brighton
Director of Brighton Bier, an award-winning craft brewery in the UK.

Beer Belly Tenma 77	Worth the travel
Brighton Bierhaus 132	Local favorite

BEN WHITNEY
Protokoll, Boxhagener Strasse 110, Berlin
Manager of Protokoll in Berlin, Whitney managed the Austin craft bar Craft Pride.

Banger's Sausage House & Beer Garden 422	Beer garden
Berta block Boulderhalle Berlin 211	Unexpected
Craft Pride 422	Worth the travel
Draught House Pub & Brewery 422	Wish I'd opened
Griffin Claw Brewing Company 334	Beer & food
Muted Horn 210	Local favorite

CHRISTOPHER WILLIAMS
Williams Bros. Brewing Co., Kelliebank, Alloa
Brewer at Williams Bros. Brewing Co., a family-run brewery in Scotland.

Fette Sau 388	Wish I'd opened
Inn Deep 140	Beer garden
Inn Deep 140	Local favorite
Mother Kelly's 146	Worth the travel
Of Love & Regret 405	Beer & food
Plum Market 335	Unexpected

DAVID WILLIAMS
moogBrew, 1 Copeland Cottages, Marsh Lane, Taplow
Owner and brewer at moogBrew, possibly the smallest brewery in the Thames Valley.

Curry Leaf Cafe 132	Beer & food
moogBREW 130	Beer garden
moogBREW 130	Local favorite
Rogue Ales Public House 310	Worth the travel

ZOE WILLIAMS
Port Jeff Brewing Company, 22 Mill Creek Road, Port Jefferson
Williams works at The Port Jeff Brewing Company on Long Island, New York.

C'est Cheese 367	Beer & food
Tap & Barrel 368	Local favorite
Tap & Barrel 368	Wish I'd opened
Tap & Barrel 368	Worth the travel

The Country Corner 366...Unexpected
Tommy's Place 367..Beer garden

CODY WILSON

Prairie Artisan Ales, 120 Southwest 8th Street, Krebs
Brand ambassador for Prairie Ales, Wilson was born and raised
in Oklahoma City. He got into craft beer when managing a
liquor store, The Well of OKC.

ChurchKey 418..Worth the travel
Holy Grale 402...Beer & food
Kings Beer and Wine 278..Unexpected
Mekelburg's 384..Wish I'd opened
Spuyten Duyvil 388..Beer garden
The Bunker Club 409.. Local favorite

MATT WINJUM

Rhombus Guys Brewing Company, 116 South 3rd Street,
Grand Forks
Winjum, with Arron Hendricks, is co-owner of Rhombus Guys.

Blue Moose Bar & Grill 337..................................Wish I'd opened
Rhombus Guys 342...Beer & food
Rhombus Guys 342...Local favorite
Rhombus Guys Brewing Company 342...................Beer garden
Rhombus Guys Brewing Company 342.............Worth the travel

TREVOR WIRTANEN

Oliphant Brewing, 350 Main Street, Suite 2, Somerset
Owner and brewer at Oliphant Brewing in Wisconsin.

Gasthaus Bavarian Hunter 338.................................Beer garden
LOLO American Kitchen
  and Craft Bar Stillwater 339..Beer & food
Oliphant Brewing 346...Local favorite
The Crash 180..Worth the travel
The Roost 143...Wish I'd opened
Tom's Burned Down Cafe 344.....................................Unexpected

JAEGA WISE

Wild Card Brewery, Unit 7 Ravenswood Industrial Estate,
London
Head brewer at Wild Card Brewery.

Hofbräuhaus 214...Wish I'd opened
Pitt Cue 146...Beer & food
Rock City 135...Unexpected
Stratford Haven 135...Worth the travel
The Chequers 150...Local favorite
Wild Card Brewery 150..Beer garden

DAVE WITHAM

Proclamation Ale Company, 298 Kilvert Street, Warwick
Founder of Proclamation Ale Company in Rhode Island.

Armsby Abbey 361..Beer & food
Novare Res Bier Café 357.......................................Worth the travel
Proclamation Ale Company 371.............................Local favorite
Tree House Brewing Company 360...................Wish I'd opened

CHRISTOPHER WONG

Hitachino HK Brewery, Heroes Beer Co., HK Brewcraft,
Second Draft, TAP-The Ale Project, 15 Cochrane Street,
Hong Kong
General manager at Hitachino HK Brewery, head brewer at
Heroes Beer Co., and co-owner of TAP-The Ale Project and
Second Draft.

Second Draft 93...Beer & food

Smith Street Taps 100...Beer garden
TAP: The Ale Project 93...Local favorite
The Globe 92..Unexpected
Toronado Pub 310..Worth the travel

SCOTT WOOD

The Courtyard Brewery, 1020 Erato Street, New Orleans
Owner and head brewer of The Courtyard Brewery.

Neighborhood 304...Wish I'd opened
Parleaux Beer Lab 404..Local favorite
Stein's Market and Deli 404.......................................Unexpected
Stone Brewing World Bistro
  & Gardens Escondido 281.....................................Beer garden
Toronado San Diego 306..Worth the travel
Whip In 423..Beer & food

CASEY WORKMAN

Chelawasi Public House and Beer Co., 104 Campo Redondo,
Arequipa
Owner and founder with his wife of the brewpub Chelawasi
Public House and Beer Co., which opened in 2014.

Apex 320...Beer garden
Chelawasi Public House 441.................................Local favorite
Great Notion Brewing and Barrel House 321............Beer & food
McMenamins Edgefield 294................................Wish I'd opened
Sierra Andina Brewing Company 441.......................Unexpected
The BeerMongers 320...Worth the travel

SHIRO YAMADA

Far Yeast Brewing Company, 4341-1 Kosuge Village,
Yamanashi
Managing director and founder of Far Yeast Brewing
Company.

Brasserie Beer Blvd. 81..Local favorite
Eat Me Restaurant 96...Beer & food
Far Yeast Tokyo Craft Beer & Bao 81...................Wish I'd opened
La Fine Mousse 193..Worth the travel
Scandinavian Airlines 113..Unexpected

IVAN YEO

The 1925 Brewing Co., 261 Joo Chiat Road, Singapore
Yeo is head chef and co-owner of The 1925, which he manages
with Eng Kuang and their uncle, Yeo King Joey.

Great Leap Brewing 86..Wish I'd opened
Great Leap Brewing 86...Worth the travel
Red Dot Brewhouse 100..Beer garden
The 1925 Brewing Company Restaurant 100..............Beer & food
The 1925 Brewing Company Restaurant 100.........Local favorite

ALESSANDRO ZECCHINATI

Bura Brew, Ulica Mate Vlasica 26/19, Poreč
Cofounder of Bura Brew, an independent brewery, Zecchinati
developed a passion for craft beer in Italy and Ireland.

Beer Garden PUB 252...Beer garden
Bura Brew 252..Wish I'd opened
Craft Room 252..Local favorite
Mastro Birraio 231..Beer & food
Mastro Birraio 231...Worth the travel

JASON ZEEFF
Michigan
Globe-trotting independent consultant who works with
Michigan breweries.
Craft Food & Beverage Co. 426...............................Unexpected
Founders Brewing Company Grand Rapids 335.....Local favorite
Independence Beer Garden 392................................Beer garden
Jolly Pumpkin Restaurant &
   Brewery Traverse City 337.....................................Beer & food
La Fine Mousse 193..Worth the travel
Local Option 351...Wish I'd opened

KRISJANIS ZELGIS
Malduguns, Parka iela 2A, Rauna
A Latvian poet who has worked in restaurants and breweries,
Zelgis is the brewer at Malduguns, where he launched a line of
literary-inspired beers called I Am Introvert.
Folkklubs ALA Pagrabs 247....................................Beer & food
Other Half Brewing 384.......................................Wish I'd opened
Shinshu Osake Mura 81......................................Worth the travel
Špunka 248...Unexpected
Taka 248..Local favorite
Tris Viri Laiva 248..Beer garden

ROB ZELLERMAYER
Ray's Growler Gallery, 8930 West North Avenue Wauwatosa,
Wisconsin
General manager at Ray's Growler Gallery.
Hopleaf 352..Worth the travel
Jolly Pumpkin 334..Beer & food
New Belgium Brewing Company 286......................Beer garden
Palm Tavern 345..Local favorite
Sunset Beer Company 300................................Wish I'd opened
The Globe Pub 351...Unexpected

KIRK ZEMBAL
Blindman Brewing, Bay F - 3413 53 Avenue, Lacombe
Cofounder of Blindman Brewing, Zembal is a beer geek.
Apex 320..Beer garden
Bailey's Taproom 320..Beer & food
Cheese Bar 320..Unexpected
The BeerMongers 320..Worth the travel
The Sugar Bowl Cafe 268......................................Local favorite
Tørst 386..Wish I'd opened

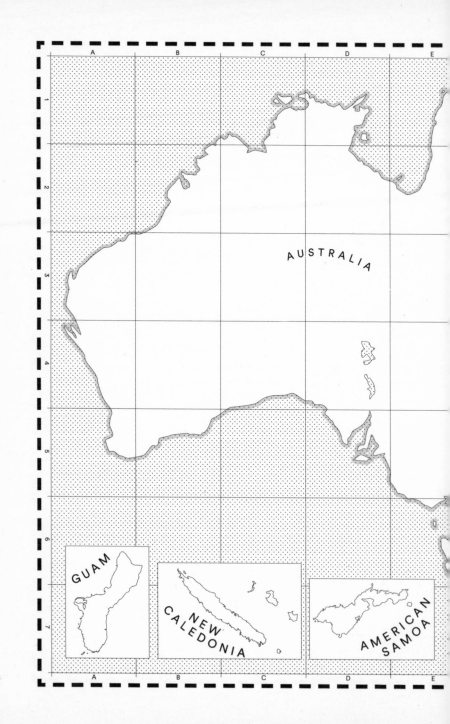

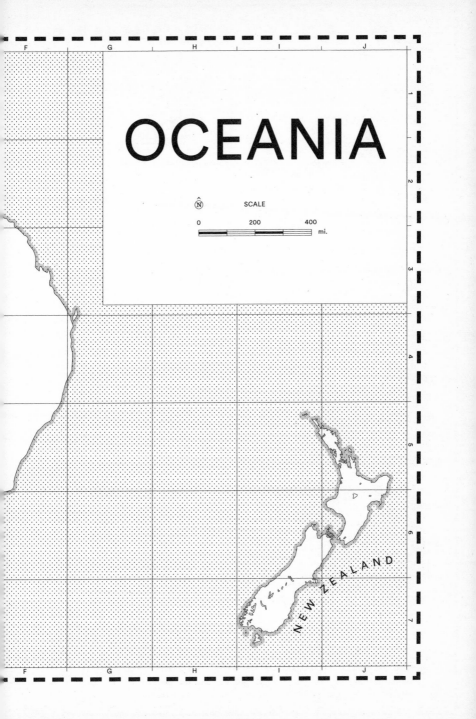

OCEANIA

SCALE

0   200   400   mi.

NEW ZEALAND

"THE BEST NATIONAL AND INTERNATIONAL BEER SELECTION IN ADELAIDE."

STU MCKINLAY P.58

"SCRATCH BAR IS QUIRKY AND JUST DOWNRIGHT AWESOME."

JAMES RENWICK P.57

"A FANTASTIC SELECTION OF GREAT DOMESTIC BEERS."

TOBY COOPER P.56

AUSTRALIA

"THE PERFECT BLEND OF ROTATING CRAFT BEERS, ARCADE AND PINBALL MACHINES, AND A FUN RELAXED VIBE."

DARREN (DOC) ROBINSON P.57

"AN ICONIC SYDNEY PUB WITH AN AMAZING COURTYARD FEATURING A GIANT OAK TREE IN THE MIDDLE."

DJ MCCREADY P.56

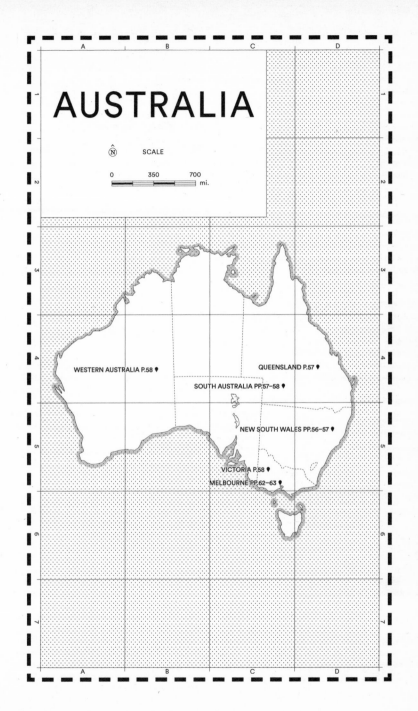

AUSTRALIA

N   SCALE

0   350   700
           mi.

WESTERN AUSTRALIA P.58

QUEENSLAND P.57

SOUTH AUSTRALIA PP.57–58

NEW SOUTH WALES PP.56–57

VICTORIA P.58

MELBOURNE PP.62–63

NOMAD BREWING COMPANY 'THE TRANSIT LOUNGE'

Recommended by
John Latta

5 Sydenham Road
Brookvale
Sydney
New South Wales 2100, Australia
+61 299074113
www.nomadbrewingco.com.au

Opening hours	Thur–Sun from 12 pm
Credit cards	Accepted
Type	Brewery and pub
Recommended for	Local favorite

"It features an astroturf car park beer garden, sun lounges and a bocce court, but there is also live music on weekends, an amazing dumpling bar, local pies on offer, pinball machines for a retro touch, and of course a massive lineup of beers."—John Latta

FRANKIE'S PIZZA BY THE SLICE

Recommended by
DJ McCready

50 Hunter Street
Central Business District
Sydney
New South Wales 2000, Australia
+61 299999999
www.frankiespizzabytheslice.com

Opening hours	Sat–Thur from 4 pm, Fri from 12 pm
Credit cards	Accepted
Type	Bar and entertainment venue
Recommended for	Local favorite

"The beer is pretty awesome. Frankie's keeps a beer nerd's variety of Aussie and international beers in stock while running a rock venue and dive bar."—DJ McCready

BITTER PHEW

Recommended by
Beth Brash,
Darren (Doc) Robinson

1/137 Oxford Street
Darlinghurst
Sydney
New South Wales 2010, Australia
www.bitterphew.com

Opening hours	Mon from 5 pm, Tue–Thur from 3 pm, Fri–Sun from 12 pm
Credit cards	Accepted
Type	Bar
Recommended for	Local favorite

THE TAPHOUSE

Recommended by
Toby Cooper

122 Flinders Street
Darlinghurst
Sydney
New South Wales 2010, Australia
+61 0293600088
www.taphousedarlo.com.au

Opening hours	Open 7 days from 12 pm
Credit cards	Accepted
Type	Bar
Recommended for	Worth the travel

"A fantastic selection of great domestic beers."
—Toby Cooper

MANLY OVAL

Recommended by
John Latta

Sydney Road & Belgrave Street
Manly
Sydney
New South Wales 2095, Australia
+61 299761699
www.manlyrugby.com.au

Opening hours	Variable
Credit cards	Not accepted
Type	Entertainment venue
Recommended for	Unexpected

"Finding good beer at sports venues in Australia is rare. Manly 1st Grade rugby is an exception to this rule, with a tent located on the far corner serving a nice lineup of local craft beers from Nomad and Yeastie Boys."—John Latta

THE OAKS HOTEL

Recommended by
Danielle Allen,
DJ McCready

118 Military Road
Neutral Bay
Sydney
New South Wales 2089, Australia
+61 299535515
www.oakshotel.com.au

Opening hours	Mon–Sat from 10 am, Sun from 12 pm
Credit cards	Accepted
Type	Beer garden and restaurant
Recommended for	Beer garden

"An iconic Sydney pub with an amazing courtyard featuring a giant oak tree in the middle. They also serve great food, and you can even grill your own steak on one of the outdoor barbecues."—DJ McCready

WATSONS BAY BOUTIQUE HOTEL

1 Military Road
Watsons Bay
Sydney
New South Wales 2030, Australia
+61 293375444
www.watsonsbayhotel.com.au

Recommended by
Toby Cooper

Opening hours...Always open
Credit cards...Accepted
Type...Beer garden and restaurant
Recommended for...Beer garden

BREWSKI BAR

22 Caxton Street
Brisbane
Queensland 4059, Australia
+61 733692198
www.brewskibar.com.au

Recommended by
Jeppe Jarnit-Bjergsø

Opening hours...Mon from 4 pm,
Tue–Sun from 12 pm
Credit cards...............................Accepted but not Amex
Type...Pub
Recommended for...Local favorite

Brewski is a great place for the beer nerd to explore. It carries a great range of beers from top-notch local breweries, and the heavy hitters from the wider Australian craft-beer scene. They round it off with a great selection of European and American beers as well. Hundreds of bottles means hundreds of options!

NETHERWORLD

186 Brunswick Street
Brisbane
Queensland 4006, Australia
+61 424156667
www.netherworldarcade.com

Recommended by
Darren (Doc) Robinson

Opening hours...Tue–Sun from 12 pm
Credit cards...Accepted
Type...Bar
Recommended for...Wish I'd opened

"The perfect blend of rotating craft beers, arcade and pinball machines, and a fun, relaxed vibe."
—Darren (Doc) Robinson

THE SCRATCH BAR

8/1 Park Road
Brisbane
Queensland 4064, Australia
+61 731079910
www.scratchbar.com

Recommended by
James Renwick

Opening hours.........Mon from 4 pm, Tue–Sun from 12 pm
Credit cards...Accepted
Type...Bar
Recommended for...Worth the travel

"Scratch Bar is quirky and just downright awesome."
—James Renwick

ZE PICKLE

37 Connor Street
Burleigh Heads
Queensland 4220, Australia
+61 756591091
www.zepickle.com

Recommended by
Danielle Allen

Opening hours...Mon–Fri from 5 pm,
Sat–Sun from 12 pm
Credit cards...Accepted
Type...Beer garden and restaurant
Recommended for...Wish I'd opened

ZESTY EDIBLES AT GUNABUL HOMESTEAD

9 Power Road
Gympie
Queensland 4570, Australia
+61 754823107
www.zestyedibles.com.au

Recommended by
Danielle Allen

Opening hours.............Mon–Fri from 9 am, Sat from 6 pm
Credit cards...Accepted
Type...Bar and restaurant
Recommended for...Unexpected

COOPERS ALEHOUSE

Adelaide Airport, Level 2
Shop 11–12
Adelaide
South Australia 5950, Australia
+61 882344059
www.adelaideairport.com.au

Recommended by
Kelly Ryan

Opening hours.....................................Open 7 days from 6 am
Credit cards...Accepted
Type...Restaurant
Recommended for...Unexpected

THE WHEATSHEAF HOTEL

39 George Street
Adelaide
South Australia 5031, Australia
+61 884434546
www.wheatsheafhotel.com.au

Recommended by
John Latta,
Stu McKinlay,
Darren (Doc) Robinson

Opening hours.............................Mon–Fri from 1 pm,
Sat–Sun from 12 pm
Credit cards...Accepted
Type................................Beer garden, microbrewery, and
entertainment venue
Recommended for...Wish I'd opened

"The focus is 100% beer and a great time, with food supplied by food trucks parked out front."—John Latta

"The Wheatsheaf has the best national and international beer selection in Adelaide, and its own small microbrewery out back, while also being one of the best small music venues in town."—Stu McKinlay

BRIGHT BREWERY

121 Great Alpine Road
Bright
Victoria 3741, Australia
+61 357551301
www.brightbrewery.com.au

Recommended by
James Renwick

Opening hours...................................Open 7 days from 11 am
Credit cards...Accepted
Type................................Beer garden and brewery
Recommended for.......................................Beer garden

LITTLE CREATURES BREWERY GEELONG

221 Swanston Street
Geelong
Victoria 3220, Australia
+61 352024009
www.littlecreatures.com.au

Recommended by
Marisa Jackson

Opening hours.......................................Mon–Fri from 10 am,
Sat–Sun from 8 am
Credit cards...Accepted
Type.............................Brewery and restaurant
Recommended for...Wish I'd opened

Melbourne, see pages 60–63

LITTLE CREATURES BREWING FREMANTLE

40 Mews Road
Fremantle
Western Australia 6160, Australia
+61 862151000
www.littlecreatures.com.au

Recommended by
Craig Cooper

Opening hours.......................................Mon–Fri from 10 am,
Sat–Sun from 9 am
Type.............................Brewery and restaurant
Recommended for...Wish I'd opened

DUCKSTEIN GERMAN BREWERY & RESTAURANT

9720 West Swan Road
Henley Brook
Western Australia 6055, Australia
+61 892960620
www.duckstein.com.au

Recommended by
Ling Wan Chang

Opening hours...................................Open 7 days from 11 am
Type.............................Brewery and restaurant
Recommended for...Beer & food

THE BEER FARM

177 Gale Road
Metricup
Western Australia 6280, Australia
+61 897557177
www.beerfarm.com.au

Recommended by
Daniel Goh

Opening hours...................................Open 7 days from 11 am
Credit cards...........................Accepted but not Amex
Type................................Beer garden and brewery
Recommended for...Worth the travel

"AN AMAZING SPACE."

ANDREW COOPER P.62

"THE FOUNDERS OF THE TAPHOUSE HAVE PLAYED A SIGNIFICANT ROLE IN ESTABLISHING THE CRAFT-BEER SCENE IN AUSTRALIA."

DJ MCCREADY P.63

MELBOURNE

"SLOW-COOKED LAMB SHOULDER, PIZZAS, BEER-BATTERED BREAM, AND EVEN BEER ICE CREAM!"

JAMES RENWICK P.62

"A WICKED DANCE FLOOR AND AN UNREAL BOTTLE MENU."

MIRO BELLINI P.62

MELBOURNE

1. THE BAR AT CARWYN CELLARS (P.63)
2. TERMINUS HOTEL FITZROY NORTH (P.62)
3. PLOUGH HOTEL (P.62)
4. BAR JOSEPHINE (P.62)
5. STOMPING GROUND BREWERY
   & BEER HALL (P.62)
6. MOON DOG CRAFT BREWERY (P.62)
7. COOKIE (P.63)
8. SECTION 8 (P.63)
9. LOOP PROJECT SPACE & BAR (P.62)
10. THE ROYSTON HOTEL (P.63)
11. MELBOURNE CRICKET GROUND (P.63)
12. THE PALACE HOTEL (P.63)
13. TWO BIRDS BREWING (P.63)
14. THE LOCAL TAPHOUSE (P.63)
15. CAULFIELD RSL (P.62)

MOON DOG CRAFT BREWERY

17 Duke Street
Abbotsford
Melbourne, Victoria 3067, Australia
+61 394282307

Recommended by
Miro Bellini

Opening hours	Wed–Fri from 4 pm, Sat–Sun from 12 pm
Credit cards	Accepted but not Amex
Type	Brewery
Recommended for	Local favorite

STOMPING GROUND BREWERY & BEER HALL

100 Gipps Street
Collingwood
Melbourne, Victoria 3066, Australia
+61 394151944
www.stompingground.beer

Recommended by
Andrew Cooper,
James Renwick

Opening hours	Open 7 days from 11:30 am
Credit cards	Accepted
Type	Brewery and bar
Recommended for	Worth the travel

"An amazing space at a brewery in Melbourne, genuinely fantastically designed. I keep going back. The design is quirky and original. It brings the outside in. It's a great space for passing the time."—Andrew Cooper

"This brewery has it all. The beer is phenomenal and diverse, ranging from Nitro NEIPAs to Blackberry Goses, and it is produced on-site direct to the taps. The food? Slow-cooked lamb shoulder, pizzas, beer-battered bream, and even beer ice cream!"—James Renwick

CAULFIELD RSL

4 Saint Georges Road
Elsternwick
Melbourne, Victoria 3185, Australia
+61 395283600
www.crsl.com.au

Recommended by
Mark Hatherly

Opening hours	Open 7 days from 10 am
Credit cards	Accepted
Type	Beer garden and restaurant
Recommended for	Beer garden

"Traditional Australian RSL atmosphere, with loads of sun in the afternoon."—Mark Hatherly

LOOP PROJECT SPACE & BAR

23 Meyers Place
Fitzroy
Melbourne, Victoria 3000, Australia
+61 396540500
www.looponline.com.au

Recommended by
Miro Bellini

Opening hours	Mon–Thur from 4:30 pm, Fri from 3 pm, Sat from 5 pm
Credit cards	Accepted
Type	Bar
Recommended for	Unexpected

"A wicked dance floor and an unreal bottle menu."
—Miro Bellini

TERMINUS HOTEL FITZROY NORTH

492 Queens Parade
Fitzroy North
Melbourne, Victoria 3068, Australia
+61 394813182
www.terminus.com.au

Recommended by
Miro Bellini

Opening hours	Mon–Thur from 4 pm, Fri–Sun from 12 pm
Credit cards	Accepted
Type	Beer garden and restaurant
Recommended for	Beer garden

BAR JOSEPHINE

295 Barkly Street
Footscray
Melbourne, Victoria 3011, Australia
+61 390770583

Recommended by
Danielle Allen

Opening hours	Open 7 days from 1 pm
Credit cards	Accepted
Type	Bar
Recommended for	Worth the travel

PLOUGH HOTEL

333 Barkly Street
Footscray
Melbourne, Victoria 3011, Australia
+61 396872878
www.ploughhotel.com.au

Recommended by
Danielle Allen

Opening hours	Open 7 days from 11:30 am
Credit cards	Accepted
Type	Bar and restaurant
Recommended for	Beer & food

COOKIE

Recommended by
Miro Bellini

252 Swanston Street
Melbourne City Centre
Melbourne, Victoria 3000, Australia
+61 396637660
www.cookie.net.au

Opening hours	Open 7 days from 12 pm
Credit cards	Accepted
Type	Restaurant
Recommended for	Beer & food

SECTION 8

Recommended by
Miro Bellini

27–29 Tattersalls Lane
Melbourne City Centre
Melbourne, Victoria 3000, Australia
+61 430291588
www.section8.com.au

Opening hours	Mon–Fri from 10 am, Sat–Sun from 12 pm
Credit cards	Not accepted
Type	Bar
Recommended for	Wish I'd opened

"It is an outdoor bar with cyclone fencing serviced out of two repurposed containers. The furniture is made of shipping pallets, and it's beautiful. "—Miro Bellini

MELBOURNE CRICKET GROUND

Brunton Avenue
Richmond

Recommended by
Thomas Lau

Melbourne, Victoria 3002, Australia
+61 396578888
www.mcg.org.au

Opening hours	Variable
Credit cards	Accepted
Type	Entertainment venue
Recommended for	Unexpected

THE ROYSTON HOTEL

Recommended by
Miro Bellini

12 River Street
Richmond
Melbourne, Victoria 3121, Australia
+61 394215000
www.roystonhotel.com.au

Opening hours	Wed–Sun from 12 pm, Mon–Tue from 4 pm
Credit cards	Accepted
Type	Pub
Recommended for	Worth the travel

THE LOCAL TAPHOUSE

Recommended by
Tim Blades,
DJ McCready,
Pete Mitcham

184 Carlisle Street
St Kilda
Melbourne, Victoria 3183, Australia
+61 395372633
www.thelocal.com.au

Opening hours	Open 7 days from 12 pm
Credit cards	Accepted
Type	Bar and restaurant
Recommended for	Beer & food

"The founders of the Taphouse have played a significant role in establishing the craft-beer scene in Australia."
—DJ McCready

THE PALACE HOTEL

Recommended by
Pete Mitcham

505–507 City Road
South Melbourne
Melbourne, Victoria 3205, Australia
+61 396823177
www.thepalacehotel.net.au

Opening hours	Open 7 days from 12 pm
Credit cards	Accepted
Type	Beer garden and pub
Recommended for	Beer garden

TWO BIRDS BREWING

Recommended by
Danielle Allen

136 Hall Street
Spotswood
Melbourne, Victoria 3015, Australia
+61 397620000
www.twobirdsbrewing.com.au

Opening hours	Thur–Fri from 4 pm, Sat–Sun from 12 pm
Credit cards	Accepted
Type	Brewery
Recommended for	Local favorite

THE BAR AT CARWYN CELLARS

877 High Street
Thornbury

Recommended by
James Renwick

Melbourne, Victoria 3071, Australia
+61 394841820
www.carwyncellars.com.au

Opening hours	Sun–Tue from 12 pm, Wed–Sat from 10 am
Credit cards	Accepted
Type	Bar
Recommended for	Local favorite

GUAM, AMERICAN SAMOA, NEW CALEDONIA & NEW ZEALAND

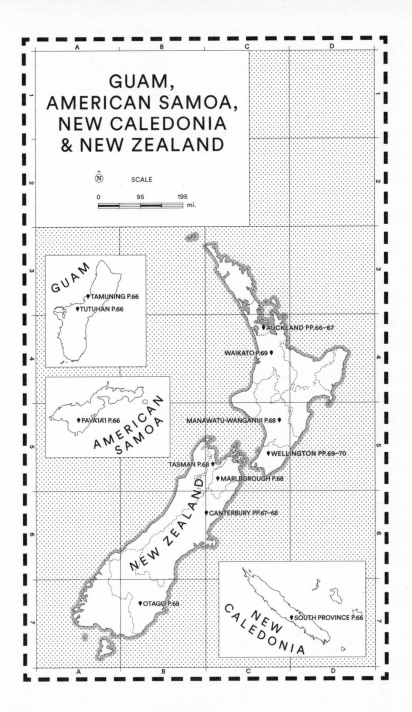

GUAM,
AMERICAN SAMOA,
NEW CALEDONIA
& NEW ZEALAND

N̂

SCALE

0   95   195
                    mi.

GUAM

♦ TAMUNING P.66
♦ TUTUHAN P.66

♦ PAVA'IA'I P.66

AMERICAN
SAMOA

♦ AUCKLAND PP.66–67

WAIKATO P.69 ♦

MANAWATU-WANGANUI P.68 ♦

♦ WELLINGTON PP.69–70

TASMAN P.68 ♦
♦ MARLBOROUGH P.68

♦ CANTERBURY PP.67–68

NEW ZEALAND

♦ OTAGO P.68

NEW
CALEDONIA

♦ SOUTH PROVINCE P.66

ISHII BREWING COMPANY

Suite 102 Northwest Plaza
458 South Marine Corps Drive
Tamuning 96931, Guam
+1 6714870868
www.ishiibrew.com

Recommended by
Toshi Ishii

Opening hours...................................Mon–Tue, Thur–Fri from
8:30 am, Sat from 1 pm
Credit cards..Not accepted
Type...Microbrewery
Recommended for..Wish I'd opened

SHAMROCKS

1180 Pale San Vitores Road
Tamuning 96913, Guam
+1 6719697726
www.shamrocksguam.com

Recommended by
Toshi Ishii

Opening hours.............................Open 7 days from 12 pm
Credit cards...Accepted
Type..Pub
Recommended for.......................................Local favorite

"This is the only bar in Guam that has all five styles of
Minagof (local craft beer)."—Toshi Ishii

NEX MINI MART

Building #50, Farenholt Avenue
Tutuhan 96910, Guam
+1 6714725559
www.mynavyexchange.com

Recommended by
Toshi Ishii

Opening hours.................................Open 7 days from 7 am
Credit cards...Accepted
Type...Retail
Recommended for...Unexpected

"This mini mart is in the Naval Exchange on the U.S. Naval
Base in Guam. They have local bottled beers, including
Minagof."—Toshi Ishii

FLYING FOX BREWING COMPANY

Highway 1
Pava'ia'i 96799, American Samoa
+1 6847311855
www.flyingfoxbeer.as

Recommended by
Nate Ilaoa

Opening hours......................................Mon–Sat from 11 am
Credit cards...Not accepted
Type..Pub
Recommended for...Local favorite

LES 3 BRASSEURS

33 Promenade Roger Laroque
Nouméa
South Province 98800, New Caledonia
+687 241516
www.cuenet.nc/3-brasseurs

Recommended by
Pete Mitcham

Opening hours..................................Open 7 days from 11 am
Credit cards..................................Accepted but not Amex
Type..Brewery and bar
Recommended for..Unexpected

"The only small-batch beer brewed in New Caledonia.
Great food and service, with sunset views."—Pete Mitcham

LOVEBUCKET AT THE FOOD WORKSHOP

309 Karangahape Road
Auckland Central
Auckland 1010, New Zealand
+64 98692469
www.lovebucket.co.nz

Recommended by
Matthew Kelly

Opening hours.......................................Tue–Sat from 4 pm
Credit cards...Accepted
Type...Restaurant
Recommended for.......................................Wish I'd opened

VULTURES' LANE

10 Vulcan Lane
Central Business District
Auckland 1010, New Zealand
+64 93007117
www.vultureslane.co.nz

Recommended by
Luke Nicholas

Opening hours..................................Open 7 days from 12 pm
Credit cards...Accepted
Type..Bar
Recommended for...Local favorite

"A good selection of rotating craft taps and friendly
staff."—Luke Nicholas

UPTOWN FREEHOUSE

224 Symonds Street
Eden Terrace
Auckland 1010, New Zealand
+64 93030637
www.uptownfreehouse.com

Recommended by
Rémi Brusa

Opening hours.............................Open 7 days from 11:30 am
Credit cards..................................Accepted but not Amex
Type...Beer garden
Recommended for..Beer garden

GALBRAITH'S ALEHOUSE

Recommended by
Craig Cooper,
Jono Galuszka,
Geoff Griggs,
Matthew Kelly,
Luke Nicholas

2 Mount Eden Road
Grafton
Auckland 1023, New Zealand
+64 93793557
www.alehouse.co.nz

Opening hours.................................Open 7 days from 12 pm
Credit cards..Accepted
Type...Pub
Recommended for...Beer & food

"A bastion of English-style cask-conditioned beer—and an excellent re-creation of an English pub—in the world's largest Polynesian city."—Geoff Griggs

"You can't help but love the place as soon as you walk in." —Jono Galuszka

LUMSDEN FREEHOUSE

Recommended by
Craig Cooper

444 Kyber Pass Road
Newmarket
Auckland 1023, New Zealand
+64 95501201
www.thelumsden.co.nz

Opening hours............................Open 7 days from 11:30 am
Credit cards..Accepted
Type...Beer garden and pub
Recommended for..Beer garden

HALLERTAU BREWERY & BIERGARTEN

1171 Coatesville-Riverhead Highway
Riverhead
Auckland 0892, New Zealand
+64 94125555
www.hallertau.co.nz

Recommended by
Kelly Ryan

Opening hours....................................Open 7 days from 11 am
Credit cards..Accepted
Type...Beer garden, brewery, and
entertainment venue
Recommended for..Beer garden

"It's fantastic for families, with a great beer garden and playground. It has awesome live music, an incredible menu, and of course, great beer brewed on-site. Hallertau does amazing beer and is one of the original barrel-aged and wild-beer producers in New Zealand. Funkonnay and Porter Noir are great choices if you like these styles. The setting is magical. They even have a winery and whiskey distillery on-site!"—Kelly Ryan

THE BEER SPOT

Recommended by
Craig Cooper

54 Northcote Road
Takapuna
Auckland 0627, New Zealand
+64 94802337
www.thebeerspot.co.nz

Opening hours.................................Open 7 days from 12 pm
Credit cards..Accepted
Type...Bar
Recommended for...Local favorite

TAHI CAFE & BAR

Recommended by
Geoff Griggs

1 Neville Street
Warkworth
Auckland 9020, New Zealand
+64 94223674
www.tahibar.com

Opening hours.......................................Tue–Sun from 11 am,
Mon from 3:30 pm
Credit cards..Accepted
Type...Bar
Recommended for...Unexpected

THE BEER LIBRARY

Recommended by
Luke Nicholas

363 Columbo Street
Christchurch
Canterbury 8023, New Zealand
+64 33792337
www.thebeerlibrary.co.nz

Opening hours.................................Open 7 days from 10 am
Credit cards..Not accepted
Type..Retail
Recommended for...Unexpected

"A deep selection of world-class craft beers." —Luke Nicholas

CHRISTCHURCH INTERNATIONAL AIRPORT

Recommended by
Jono Galuszka

30 Durey Road
Christchurch
Canterbury 8052, New Zealand
+64 33537777
www.christchurchairport.co.nz

Opening hours...Always open
Credit cards..Accepted
Type...Bar
Recommended for...Unexpected

ILAM HOMESTEAD

Recommended by
Wendy Roigard

87 Ilam Road
Christchurch
Canterbury 8041, New Zealand
+64 33642499
www.ilamhomestead.co.nz

Opening hours..Variable
Credit cards..Accepted
Type........................Bar, beer garden, and restaurant
Recommended for................................Beer garden

"The garden is stunning. They have many New Zealand
craft beers on tap and on hand pump."—Wendy Roigard

TWENTY SEVEN STEPS

Recommended by
Craig Cooper,
Wendy Roigard

16 New Regent Street
Christchurch
Canterbury 8011, New Zealand
+64 33662727
www.twentysevensteps.co.nz

Opening hours......................Open 7 days from 5 pm
Credit cards..Accepted
Type..Restaurant and bar
Recommended for................................Beer & food

THE LABORATORY

Recommended by
Wendy Roigard

17 West Belt
Lincoln
Canterbury 7608, New Zealand
+64 33253006
www.thelaboratory.co.nz

Opening hours........................Tue–Sun from 11 am
Credit cards..Accepted
Type...Bar
Recommended for................................Local favorite

BREW UNION BREWING COMPANY

41 Broadway Avenue
Palmerston North
Manawatu-Wanganui 4410
New Zealand
+64 62803146
www.brewunion.co.nz

Recommended by
Beth Brash,
Jono Galuszka

Opening hours......................Open 7 days from 11 am
Credit cards..Accepted
Type............................Brewery, pub, and beer garden
Recommended for............................Wish I'd opened

"Brew Union opened in 2016. An impressive Portland-style
brewpub, they offer excellent food, twenty-two taps, and
a mix of beers brewed on-site and from other independent
New Zealand breweries. The outdoor section is a
godsend."—Jono Galuszka

MOA BREWERY BAR

Recommended by
Geoff Griggs

258 Jacksons Road
Blenheim
Marlborough 7273, New Zealand
+64 93679492
www.moabeer.com

Opening hours......................Open 7 days from 11 am
Credit cards..Accepted
Type..Brewery and bar
Recommended for................................Local favorite

CARDRONA HOTEL

Recommended by
Colby Cox

2312 Cardrona Valley Road
Cardrona
Otago 9381, New Zealand
+64 34438153
www.cardronahotel.co.nz

Opening hours........................Open 7 days from 9 am
Credit cards..Accepted
Type........................Beer garden and restaurant
Recommended for................................Beer garden

THE MUSSEL INN

Recommended by
Beth Brash,
Wendy Roigard,
Kelly Ryan

1259 State Highway 60
Golden Bay
Tasman 7182, New Zealand
+64 35259241
www.musselinn.co.nz

Opening hours......................Open 7 days from 11 am
Credit cards..Accepted
Type...Pub
Recommended for............................Worth the travel

"A true destination pub at Golden Bay, one of New Zealand's
prize jewels for beautiful beaches and scenery. They brew
all their own beer, including the iconic Captain Cooker,
inspired by the first beer brewed in New Zealand by
Captain Cook. The pub itself is a single room. The outdoor
area that is somewhat magical, with big wooden tables and
swings scattered through the trees, has lots of shade during
the day. At night the trees light up and a fire pit provides
perfect beer-drinking surroundings."—Beth Brash

HOT WATER BREWING COMPANY

1043 Tairua Whitianga Road
Whenuakite
Waikato 3591, New Zealand
+64 78663830
www.hotwaterbrewingco.com

Recommended by
DJ McCready

Opening hours...................................Tue—Sun from 11 am
Type...Brewery
Recommended for...Unexpected

"While driving a camper van around New Zealand, we pulled up at a campground close enough to visit the famous Hot Water Beach, where you can dig your own mineral hot spring to laze in while looking out at the Pacific Ocean. That was awesome enough, but then we discovered the campground has a craft brewery attached, fittingly named Hot Water Brewing. Hot springs plus craft beer equals good times."—DJ McCready

FORK & BREWER

20A Bond Street
Wellington 6011, New Zealand
+64 44720033
www.forkandbrewer.co.nz

Recommended by
Kelly Ryan

Opening hours...................................Mon—Sat from 11:30 am
Credit cards...Accepted
Type...Brewery and pub
Recommended for...Local favorite

GOLDING'S FREE DIVE

14 Leeds Street
Wellington 6011, New Zealand
+64 43813616
www.goldingsfreedive.co.nz

Recommended by
Beth Brash

Opening hours...................................Open 7 days from 12 pm
Credit cards...Accepted
Type...Bar
Recommended for...Local favorite

"Tucked down Hannah's Laneway, with only a bright colored door and a flickering neon sign to give it away. Open the door, and it's like beer Narnia. This magical bar is filled with taxidermy, fairy lights, bucket lampshades, and *Star Wars* models. The friendly and knowledgeable staff can talk you through their perfectly curated seven-tap lineup, which changes daily so you know it's fresh."
—Beth Brash

HASHIGO ZAKE

25 Taranaki Street
Wellington 6011, New Zealand
+64 43847300
www.hashigozake.co.nz

Recommended by
Jono Galuszka

Opening hours...................................Open 7 days from 12 pm
Credit cards...Accepted
Type...Bar
Recommended for...Local favorite

"Hashigo Zake consistently has the best tap lineup and bottle list anywhere in Wellington and possibly the country. The service is always informative and helpful, while the space itself has enough corners to hide away. The food is always excellent—the meat pies are to die for—while the live music on Saturday nights is extremely good fun."—Jono Galuszka

LITTLE BEER QUARTER (LBQ)

6 Edward Street
Wellington 6011, New Zealand
+64 48033304
www.littlebeerquarter.co.nz

Recommended by
Darren (Doc) Robinson

Opening hours...................................Sun from 3 pm, Mon from 3:30 pm, Tue—Sat from 12pm
Type..Bar and restaurant
Recommended for...Unexpected

"Partially hidden up a laneway and around a corner is this enclave of craft beer with bistro food and a relaxed atmosphere. I'm never disappointed in the choice of beer or accompanying snacks."—Darren (Doc) Robinson

LOGAN BROWN RESTAURANT

192 Cuba Street
Wellington 6141, New Zealand
+64 48015114
www.loganbrown.co.nz

Recommended by
Jono Galuszka

Opening hours...................................Tue from 5:30 pm, Wed—Sat from 12:00 pm, Sun from 5:30 pm
Credit cards...Accepted
Type...Restaurant
Recommended for...Beer & food

"The team behind Logan Brown has been flying the flag for food and beer pairing in New Zealand long before it was fashionable."—Jono Galuszka

ORTEGA FISH SHACK & BAR

16 Majoribanks Street
Wellington 6011, New Zealand
+64 43829559
www.ortega.co.nz

Recommended by
Beth Brash,
Jen Ferguson

Opening hours	Open 7 days from 5:30 pm
Credit cards	Accepted
Type	Restaurant
Recommended for	Beer & food

"Wellington is a city for food and drink lovers, so you could pretty much throw an old beer can and be guaranteed to hit something amazing. But Ortega Fish Shack is among the best—a truly exceptional beer list, fantastic food, and some of the best service. Their beer list has more than fifty of New Zealand's finest beers, plus guest beers from around the world. What sets Ortega apart is the service—all of their staff are warm and natural hosts and exceptionally knowledgeable on all aspects of the beer and wine list and food. Try to sit at the bar and watch the masters at work."—Jen Ferguson

WESTPAC STADIUM

105 Waterloo Quay
Wellington 6140, New Zealand
+64 44733881
www.westpacstadium.co.nz

Recommended by
Beth Brash

Opening hours	Variable
Credit cards	Accepted
Type	Entertainment venue
Recommended for	Unexpected

"Wellington's local soccer team, the Phoenix, joined forces with Garage Project so you can drink great beer while watching a home game. The team even has its own special beer that's available only at the games for those Untappd badge chasers out there. In August the stadium hosts New Zealand's national beer event, Beervana, which has over sixty breweries pouring around 450 of New Zealand's best beer."—Beth Brash

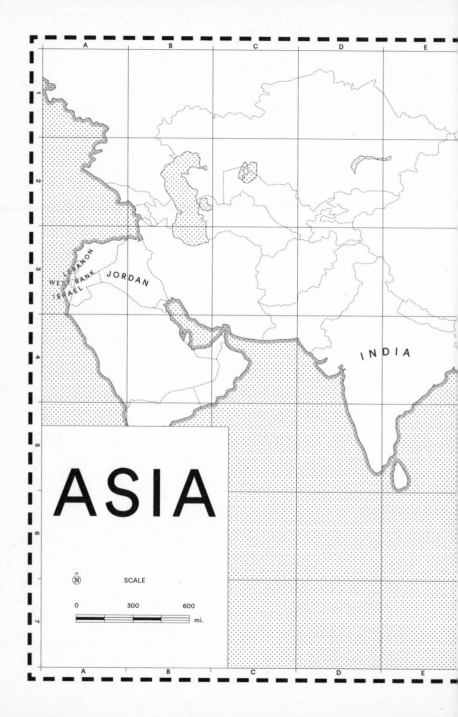

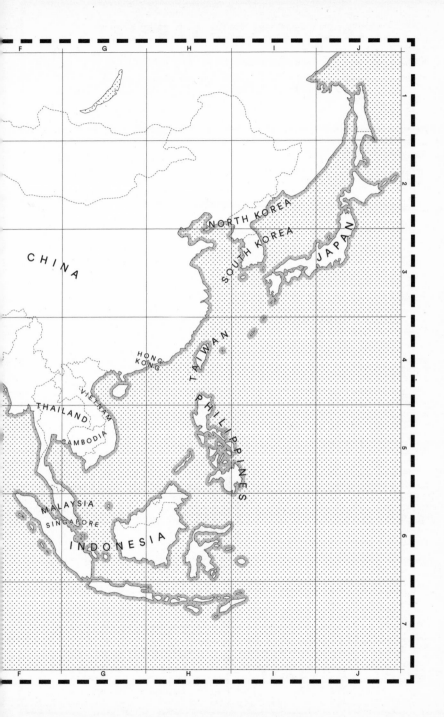

> **"THE WORLD'S LARGEST SELECTION OF THE WONDERFUL SHIGA KOGEN BEERS."**
> TIM ADAMS P.77

> "AMID A WARREN OF TINY STREETS AND NEON SITS THIS AMAZING LITTLE BREWERY-OWNED BAR WITH TEN TAPS AND GREAT FOOD."
> STEPHEN WHITEHURST P.77

JAPAN

> **"THE BEST BEERS, CIDERS, AND FOOD IN THE COUNTRY."**
> LEE REEVE P.76

> "UNBELIEVABLE BEERS MADE IN A 200-YEAR-OLD SAKE BREWERY."
> ALAN SPRINTS P.76

> "A TINY TAPROOM BY YOKOHAMA STATION THAT'S OOZING WITH CHARACTER."
> RICHARD AMMERMAN P.76

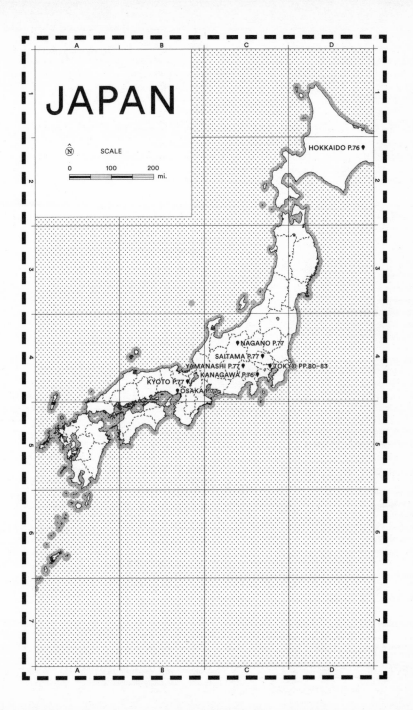

JAPAN

N

SCALE

0   100   200
mi.

HOKKAIDO P.76 ♥

♥ NAGANO P.77
SAITAMA P.77 ♥
YAMANASHI P.77 ♥   ♥ TOKYO PP.80–83
♥ KANAGAWA P.76 ♥
KYOTO P.77 ♥
♥ OSAKA P.77

SAPPORO BEER GARDEN

9-2-10, Kita 7-Jo Higashi
Higashi-ku
Sapporo
Hokkaido 065-0007, Japan
+81 120150550
www.sapporo-bier-garten.jp

Recommended by
Grayson Shepard

Opening hours	Open 7 days from 11:30 am
Credit cards	Accepted
Type	Beer garden
Recommended for	Beer garden

"Located in a 125-year-old former sugar factory and malt warehouse, the atmosphere is second to none."
—Grayson Shepard

CACTUS BURRITO

1045 Chitose
Takatsu-ku
Kawasaki-shi
Kanagawa 213-0022, Japan
+81 447770555
www.cactus-burrito.com

Recommended by
Lee Reeve

Opening hours	Sun–Fri from 5 pm, Sat from 12:30 pm
Credit cards	Not accepted
Type	Restaurant
Recommended for	Unexpected

"Authentic Mexican food with craft beer, run by two hard-working women."—Lee Reeve

BASHAMICHI TAPROOM

5-63-1 Sumiyoshi-cho
Naka Ward
Yokohama
Kanagawa 231-0013, Japan
+81 452644961
www.bairdbeer.com

Recommended by
Geoffrey Seideman

Opening hours	Mon, Wed–Fri from 5 pm, Sat–Sun from 12 pm
Credit cards	Accepted
Type	Bar
Recommended for	Unexpected

"Great beer and awesome barbecue."—Geoffrey Seideman

FULL MONTY BRITISH PUB AND CIDER HOUSE

Kitahara Building 102
Nishi Dori 41
Fukutomi-cho
Naka-ku
Yokohama
Kanagawa 231-0042, Japan
+81 453348787
www.fullmontyyokohama.com

Recommended by
Chuwy Phillips,
Lee Reeve

Opening hours	Tue–Sat from 5 pm, Sun from 4 pm
Credit cards	Not accepted
Type	Pub
Recommended for	Local favorite

"The best beers, ciders, and food in the country."
—Lee Reeve

THRASH ZONE

Tamura Building 1F
2-10-7 Tsuruya-cho
Kanagawa-ku
Yokohama
Kanagawa 221-0835, Japan
+81 455149947
www.beerdrinkinginternational.com

Recommended by
Richard Ammerman

Opening hours	Open 7 days from 12 pm
Credit cards	Not accepted
Type	Bar
Recommended for	Worth the travel

"A tiny taproom by Yokohama Station that's oozing with character. The owner bridges his experience in Japan's hardcore/thrash scene with his approach to brewing."
—Richard Ammerman

BEACH MUFFIN

8-3-22 Sakurayama
Zushi-shi
Kanagawa 249-0005, Japan
+81 468725204
www.beachmuffin.com

Recommended by
Rob Bright,
Yuko Odashima,
Chuwy Phillips

Opening hours	Thur–Sun from 11 am
Credit cards	Not accepted
Type	Bar
Recommended for	Beer & food

"Amazing vegan food with exceptional local craft beer, inside a beautifully designed building."—Rob Bright

BEER KOMACHI

Recommended by
Tim Scott

444 Hachiken-cho
Higashiyama-ku
Kyoto 605-0027, Japan
+81 757466152
www.beerkomachi.com

Opening hours	Mon, Wed–Fri from 5 pm, Sat–Sun from 3 pm
Credit cards	Accepted
Type	Pub
Recommended for	Worth the travel

SHIGA KOGEN BREWERY

1163 Hirao

Recommended by
Alan Sprints

Yamanouchi-machi
Shimotakai-gun
Nagano 381-0401, Japan
+81 269332155
www.tamamura-honten.co.jp

Opening hours	Mon, Wed–Fri from 1 pm, Sat–Sun from 11 am
Credit cards	Not accepted
Type	Brewery
Recommended for	Unexpected

"Unbelievable beers made in a 200-year-old sake brewery. They grow rice, fruit, and hops. They also have a cutting-edge barrel-aging program."—Alan Sprints

TEPPA ROOM

Recommended by
Tim Adams

Chalet Shiga
Yamanouchi-machi
Shimotakai-gun
Nagano 381-0401, Japan
+81 269342235
www.shigakogen.jp/chalet

Opening hours	Mon–Fri from 3 pm, Sat–Sun from 12 pm
Credit cards	Accepted but not Amex
Type	Bar
Recommended for	Wish I'd opened

"It's at the base of a sleepy ski resort in the Japanese Alps. It has the world's largest selection of the wonderful Shiga Kogen beers."—Tim Adams

BEER BELLY TENMA

Recommended by
Stephen Whitehurst

7-4 Ikeda-cho
Kita-ku
Osaka 530-0033, Japan
+81 663535005
www.beerbelly.jp/tenma

Opening hours	Fri–Wed from 3 pm
Credit cards	Not accepted
Type	Brewery and bar
Recommended for	Worth the travel

"This is owned by the wonderful Japanese brewery Minoh Beer. Amid a warren of tiny streets and neon sits this amazing little brewery-owned bar with ten taps and great food."—Stephen Whitehurst

SEIBU DOME

Recommended by
Yuya Hayashi

2135 Kamiyaamaguchi
Tokorozawa
Saitama 359-1153, Japan
+81 429251141
www.seibulions.jp

Opening hours	Variable
Credit cards	Accepted
Type	Bar
Recommended for	Unexpected

Tokyo, see pages 78–83

SYLVANS

Recommended by
Chuwy Phillips

6663-1 Funatsu Azakenmarubi
Fujikawaguchiko-machi
Minamitsuru-gun
Yamanashi 401-0301, Japan
+81 555832236
www.sylvans.jp

Opening hours	Fri–Wed from 11:30 am
Credit cards	Accepted
Type	Beer garden and restaurant
Recommended for	Beer garden

"Good German-style beer and a great garden and conservatory on the foothills of Mount Fuji."
—Chuwy Phillips

"IMPECCABLE BEER SERVICE AND OUTSTANDING STAFF."

CHARLES GUERRIER P.80

"TRADITIONAL JAPANESE SKEWERS WITH GREAT BEERS FROM BAIRD, INCLUDING SEASONAL AND LIMITED RELEASES."

THOMAS LAU P.81

TOKYO

"THE BEST NEIGHBORHOOD BAR IN JAPAN."

YUYA HAYASHI P.80

"THE PLACE EXUDES ENTHUSIASM FOR GOOD CRAFT BEER. THEY MANAGE TO GET GREAT BEER FROM AROUND JAPAN AND THE WORLD, BUT WHAT PULLS IT ALL TOGETHER IS THEIR GENUINE LOVE FOR CRAFT BEER AND GENEROSITY."

SAMUEL RICHARDSON P.82

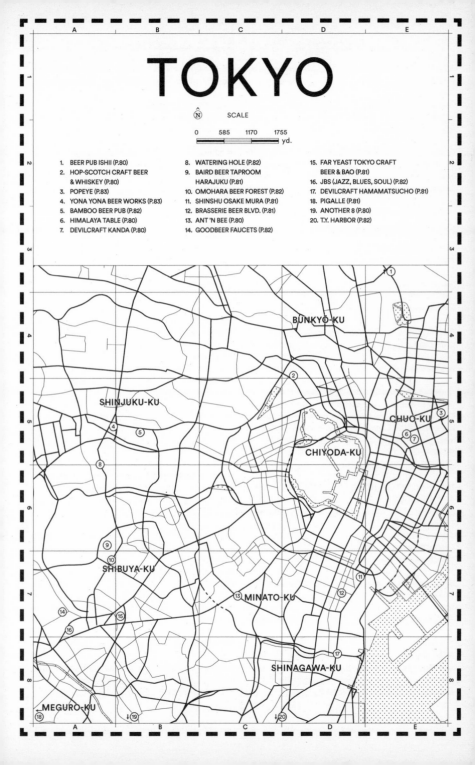

TOKYO

$\hat{N}$ SCALE

0   585   1170   1755
yd.

1. BEER PUB ISHII (P.80)
2. HOP-SCOTCH CRAFT BEER & WHISKEY (P.80)
3. POPEYE (P.83)
4. YONA YONA BEER WORKS (P.83)
5. BAMBOO BEER PUB (P.82)
6. HIMALAYA TABLE (P.80)
7. DEVILCRAFT KANDA (P.80)
8. WATERING HOLE (P.82)
9. BAIRD BEER TAPROOM HARAJUKU (P.81)
10. OMOHARA BEER FOREST (P.82)
11. SHINSHU OSAKE MURA (P.81)
12. BRASSERIE BEER BLVD. (P.81)
13. ANT 'N BEE (P.80)
14. GOODBEER FAUCETS (P.82)
15. FAR YEAST TOKYO CRAFT BEER & BAO (P.81)
16. JBS (JAZZ, BLUES, SOUL) (P.82)
17. DEVILCRAFT HAMAMATSUCHO (P.81)
18. PIGALLE (P.81)
19. ANOTHER 8 (P.80)
20. T.Y. HARBOR (P.82)

BUNKYO-KU

SHINJUKU-KU

CHUO-KU

CHIYODA-KU

SHIBUYA-KU

MINATO-KU

SHINAGAWA-KU

MEGURO-KU

BEER PUB ISHII

Recommended by
Yuya Hayashi

3-45-8 Sendagi
Bunkyō-ku
Tokyo 113-0022, Japan
+81 338287300
www.beerpub-ishii.com

Opening hours............Tue–Sat from 5 pm, Sun from 3 pm
Credit cards...Not accepted
Type..Bar
Recommended for.................................Local favorite

"The best neighborhood bar in Japan."—Yuya Hayashi

HIMALAYA TABLE

Recommended by
Grayson Shepard

3-5-5 Uchikanda
Chiyoda-ku
Tokyo 101-0047, Japan
+81 335254110
www.himalaya-table.info

Opening hours.............Mon–Fri from 5 pm, Sat from 3 pm
Credit cards..Accepted
Type..Restaurant
Recommended for.................................Beer & food

"A smallish bar and restaurant with ten taps, primarily
focused on domestic Japanese craft and Nepalese food.
The owner, Kubota-san, traveled extensively in Nepal and
also loves craft beer. He teamed up with a Nepalese chef to
focus on small plates and curries that go well with beer."
—Grayson Shepard

HOP-SCOTCH CRAFT BEER
& WHISKEY

Recommended by
Grayson Shepard

2-2-11 Fujimi
Chiyoda-ku
Tokyo 102-0071, Japan
+81 5031369699
www.hopscotchtokyo.com

Opening hours.............Mon–Fri from 5 pm, Sat from 3 pm
Credit cards..Accepted
Type..Pub
Recommended for.........................Wish I'd opened

"A tiny place that's practically standing room only but has
eight taps—mostly imports—a selection of whiskeys and
scotches, and a tiny kitchen. They have some of the best
nachos in Tokyo."—Grayson Shepard

DEVILCRAFT KANDA

Recommended by
Grayson Shepard

4-2-3 Nihonbashi-Muromachi
Chuo-ku
Tokyo 103-0022, Japan
+81 364358428
www.devilcraft.jp

Opening hours........Mon–Fri from 5 pm, Sat–Sun from 3 pm
Credit cards..Accepted
Type..Restaurant
Recommended for...........................Wish I'd opened

"The first of three outlets in Tokyo, DevilCraft Kanda has
fourteen craft beers on tap, along with Chicago-style
deep-dish pizza. Half the beers are from their own brewery,
while the rest are a mix of Japanese and international craft
beers. DevilCraft Kanda is fairly small and almost always
full, but the vibe is great. Reservations recommended."
—Grayson Shepard

ANOTHER 8

Recommended by
James Goulding

Yokogawa Building 1F
1-2-18 Shimomeguro
Meguro-ku
Tokyo 153-0064, Japan
+81 364179158
www.sakahachi.jp/another8

Opening hours....................................Open 7 days from 5 pm
Credit cards...Not accepted
Type..Bar
Recommended for...........................Worth the travel

"Absolutely stunning art direction—from the layout, bar,
tap handles, and glassware. I've never seen anything as
detailed or planned."—James Goulding

ANT 'N BEE

Recommended by
Charles Guerrier

5-1-5 Roppongi
Minato-ku
Tokyo 106-0032, Japan
+81 334781250

Opening hours....................................Open 7 days from 5 pm
Credit cards..Accepted
Type..Bar
Recommended for...........................Worth the travel

"A tiny basement bar off the chaos of Roppongi's main drag.
Impeccable beer service and outstanding staff."
—Charles Guerrier

BRASSERIE BEER BLVD.

Culture Center Building 2F
5-10-8 Shinbashi
Minato-ku
Tokyo 105-0004, Japan
+81 364359266
www.beerboulevard.com

Recommended by
Shiro Yamada

Opening hours........Mon–Fri from 11:45 am, Sat from 4 pm
Credit cards...Accepted
Type...Bar
Recommended for..Local favorite

"In addition to its good craft-beer selection, it offers Asahi
Super Dry in three serving styles. Very impressive."
—Shiro Yamada

DEVILCRAFT HAMAMATSUCHO

Risewell Bldg 1F
2-13-12 Hamamatsucho
Minato-ku
Tokyo 105-0013, Japan
+81 364358428
www.devilcraft.jp

Recommended by
Chuwy Phillips

Opening hours...Mon–Fri from 5 pm,
Sat–Sun from 12:30 pm
Credit cards...Accepted
Type..Restaurant
Recommended for..Wish I'd opened

SHINSHU OSAKE MURA

2-20-15 Shinbashi
Minato-ku
Tokyo 105-0004, Japan
+81 335725488
www.nagano-sake.com

Recommended by
Rob Bright,
Krisjanis Zelgis

Opening hours......................................Mon–Sat from 11 am
Credit cards...Not accepted
Type...Retail and bar
Recommended for..Unexpected

"A great little dive bar in the middle of Tokyo where you
can try famous beers and sakes from the Nagano region of
Japan."—Rob Bright

"The atmosphere there is always busy, but it feels
comfortable even though people are standing close to you.
Mostly local people after work. Price is also very friendly for
Tokyo. Would go back anytime."—Krisjanis Zelgis

PIGALLE

2-15-8 Taishido
Setagaya-ku
Tokyo 154-0004, Japan
+81 368052455
www.pigalle.tokyo

Recommended by
Jeppe Jarnit-Bjergsø

Opening hours.............Tue–Sat from 4 pm, Sun from 2 pm
Type...Bar
Recommended for...Worth the travel

Pigalle is a tiny, very unique beer bar in Tokyo that is owned
and operated by a very friendly husband and wife team. It's
truly one-of-a-kind.

BAIRD BEER TAPROOM HARAJUKU

1-20-13 Jingumae
Shibuya-ku
Tokyo 150-0001, Japan
+81 364380450
www.bairdbeer.com

Recommended by
Thomas Lau

Opening hours...Mon–Fri from 4 pm,
Sat–Sun from 12 pm
Credit cards...Accepted
Type...Bar
Recommended for...Beer & food

"Traditional Japanese skewers with great beers from Baird,
including seasonal and limited releases."—Thomas Lau

FAR YEAST TOKYO CRAFT BEER & BAO

2-6-8 Shibuya
Shibuya-ku
Tokyo 150-0002, Japan
+81 368740373
www.faryeast.com

Recommended by
Shiro Yamada

Opening hours.....................Open 7 days from 11:30 am
Credit cards...Accepted
Type...Bar
Recommended for..Wish I'd opened

GOODBEER FAUCETS

1-29-1 Shoto
Shibuya-ku
Tokyo 150-0046, Japan
+81 337705544
www.shibuya.goodbeerfaucets.jp

Recommended by
Thomas Lau

Opening hours..............................Mon–Fri from 4 pm,
Sat–Sun from 3 pm
Credit cards...Accepted
Type...Bar
Recommended for............................Worth the travel

"Knowledgeable staff, exciting beer selection, good
location, and great atmosphere."—Thomas Lau

JBS (JAZZ, BLUES, SOUL)

1-17-10 Dogenzaka
Shibuya-ku
Tokyo 150-0043, Japan
+81 334617788

Recommended by
Ben Love,
Chris Maestro

Opening hours........................Open 7 days from 2 pm
Credit cards...Not accepted
Type...Bar
Recommended for.............................Wish I'd opened

"JBS, owned and operated by Kobayashi-san, has attracted
visitors from around the world. It features over 11,000
records, which he curates along with his beer and whiskey
selections. An atmosphere like no other."—Chris Maestro

OMOHARA BEER FOREST

4-30-3 Jingumae
Shibuya-ku
Tokyo 150-0001, Japan
+81 354138747
www.sagaswhat.com/omoharabeer

Recommended by
Hidenori Oka

Opening hours..............................Mon–Fri from 4 pm,
Sat–Sun from 12 pm (summer)
Credit cards...Not accepted
Type..Beer garden
Recommended for.................................Beer garden

"Located in the very center of Harajuku-Omotesando. It's
open only in the summer. It serves quality beer from YO-HO
Brewing."—Hidenori Oka

WATERING HOLE

5-26-5 Sendagaya
Shibuya-ku
Tokyo 151-0051, Japan
+81 363806115
www.wateringhole.jp

Recommended by
Rob Bright,
Phillip MacNitt,
Hidenori Oka,
Samuel Richardson

Opening hours........................Open 7 days from 3 pm
Credit cards...Accepted
Type...Bar
Recommended for............................Worth the travel

"The place exudes enthusiasm for good craft beer. They
manage to get great beer from around Japan and the world,
but what pulls it all together is their genuine love for craft
beer and generosity."—Samuel Richardson

T.Y. HARBOR

2-1-3 Higashi-Shinagawa
Shinagawa-ku
Tokyo 140-0002, Japan
+81 354794555
www.tysons.jp/tyharbor

Recommended by
Yuya Hayashi

Opening hours..........................Mon–Fri from 11:30 am,
Sat–Sun from 11 am
Credit cards...Accepted
Type.......................................Beer garden and brewpub
Recommended for.................................Beer garden

"A brewpub beside a canal that offers a tremendous
view."—Yuya Hayashi

BAMBOO BEER PUB

1-31-3 Shinjuku
Shinjuku-ku
Tokyo 160-0022, Japan
+81 333525356
www.beerbamboo.jugem.jp

Recommended by
Michiko Tsutsui

Opening hours........................Open 7 days from 5 pm
Credit cards...Accepted
Type...Pub
Recommended for..............................Local favorite

"A small and cozy pub with a relaxed owner."
—Michiko Tsutsui

YONA YONA BEER WORKS

3-28-10 Shinjuku
Shinjuku-ku
Tokyo 160-0022, Japan
+81 353618147
www.yonayonabeerworks.com/shinjuku

Recommended by
Hidenori Oka

Opening hours............................Open 7 days from 11:30 am
Credit cards...Accepted
Type..Bar
Recommended for..Local favorite

"It's the official beer bar that serves a variety of craft beer from YO-HO Brewing, from American pale ales to barrel-aged beers."—Hidenori Oka

POPEYE

2-18-7 Ryogoku
Sumida-ku
Tokyo 130-0026, Japan
+81 336332120

Recommended by
Tony Forder,
Toshi Ishii,
Hidenori Oka,
Alexa Penton

Opening hours..............Mon–Fri from 5 pm, Sat from 3 pm
Credit cards...Accepted
Type..Bar
Recommended for...Worth the travel

"A huge variety of local and international beers, and it's close to the sumo stadium."—Alexa Penton

"THEY HAVE THE BEST SMOKED MEAT ANYWHERE IN CHINA, WITH BEERS TO MATCH." CHRISTOPHER PILKINGTON P.87

"THIS IS THE FIRST CRAFT-BEER BAR IN WUHAN, AND THE OWNER IS FAMOUS FOR BEING ONE OF THE FIRST PEOPLE IN CHINA TO PUSH THE CRAFT-BEER REVOLUTION." QI JIANG P.87

NORTH KOREA, SOUTH KOREA, CHINA, HONG KONG & TAIWAN

"GRITTY, URBAN, AND UNDERGROUND WITH HIGH-QUALITY BEER." JOSEPH FINKENBINDER P.87

"ENJOYING ONE OF THEIR WELL-CRAFTED BREWS WHILE RELAXING IN THE SHADE OF THEIR BEER GARDEN DURING THE WARMER MONTHS IS AN ABSOLUTE PLEASURE." RICK GREEN P.86

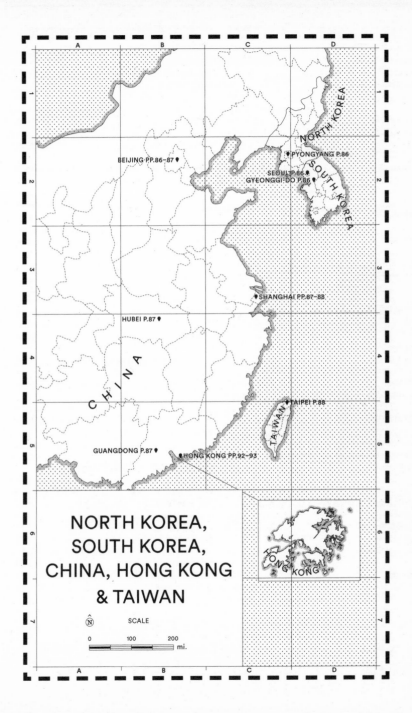

BEIJING PP.86–87 ♦

♦ PYONGYANG P.86

SEOUL P.86 ♦
GYEONGGI-DO P.86 ♦

NORTH KOREA

SOUTH KOREA

♦ SHANGHAI PP.87–88

HUBEI P.87 ♦

C H I N A

TAIWAN

♦ TAIPEI P.88

GUANGDONG P.87 ♦   ♦ HONG KONG PP.92–93

NORTH KOREA,
SOUTH KOREA,
CHINA, HONG KONG
& TAIWAN

N̂

SCALE

0   100   200
mi.

HONG KONG

KORYO HOTEL
Changgwang Street
Pyongyang 1001, North Korea
+850 23814937

Recommended by
Sebastian Sauer

Type...Bar and brewery
Recommended for.................................Unexpected

THE BOOTH BREWERY PANGYO
616 Pangyo-dong
Seongnam
Gyeonggi-do 13477, South Korea
+82 15444723
www.thebooth.co.kr/pangyo-brewery

Recommended by
Sang Jun Lee

Opening hours.................................Tue–Fri from 5 pm,
Sat–Sun from 2 pm
Type...Brewery
Recommended for.........................Local favorite

CGV MOVIE THEATRE
Seoul
South Korea
+82 15441122
www.cgv.co.kr

Recommended by
Erik Moynihan

Opening hours.................................Always open
Credit cards.......................................Accepted
Type.............................Entertainment venue
Recommended for............................Unexpected

"You can have a beer at the movies in Korea—even a few imported craft beers are available at many of the locations."
—Erik Moynihan

MYSTERLEE BREWING COMPANY
311 Dongmak-ro
Seoul 4156, South Korea
+82 232726337
www.mysterleebrewing.com

Recommended by
Sang Jun Lee

Opening hours.....................Open 7 days from 11:30 am
Credit cards.......................................Accepted
Type..Brewpub
Recommended for..........................Beer & food

WOORI SUPER
Kyoungnidan Alley
Seoul 04343, South Korea
+82 27987367

Recommended by
Erik Moynihan

Opening hours.................................Open 7 days from 9 am
Credit cards.......................................Accepted
Type...Retail
Recommended for.........................Local favorite

"The best selection of cans and bottles in the country and prices. It's next door to our bar."—Erik Moynihan

GREAT LEAP BREWING
#6 Doujiao Hutong
Di'Anmenwai Avenue
Beijing 100000, China
+86 1057171399
www.greatleapbrewing.com

Recommended by
Rick Green,
Marisa Jackson,
Alexa Penton,
Ivan Yeo

Opening hours.................................Open 7 days from 2 pm
Credit cards...........................Accepted but not Amex
Type...................................Brewery and bar
Recommended for.........................Worth the travel

"A very special place."—Marisa Jackson

"In a hidden alley in a converted Chinese-style courtyard house, surrounded by a high wall. Enjoying one of their well-crafted brews while relaxing in the shade of their beer garden during the warmer months is an absolute pleasure."—Rick Green

JING-A BREWPUB XINGFUCUN
57 Xingfucun Zhong Lu
Beijing 100001, China
+86 1065018883
www.jingabrewing.com

Recommended by
Richard Ammerman

Opening hours.....................Mon–Thur from 5 pm, Fri from
4 pm, Sat–Sun from 11 am
Credit cards.......................................Accepted
Type...............................Microbrewery and bar
Recommended for.........................Local favorite

JING-A TAPROOM 1949

1949 The Hidden City
Courtyard 4, Gongti Bei Lu
Beijing 100000, China
+86 1065018883
www.jingabrewing.com

Recommended by
Alex Acker,
Kris Li,
Christopher Pilkington

Opening hours	Mon–Wed from 5 pm, Thur–Fri from 5 pm, Sat–Sun from 11 am
Credit cards	Accepted
Type	Bar
Recommended for	Local favorite

"A stripped-down interior with a small speakeasy in the back. They have the best smoked meat anywhere in China, with beers to match."—Christopher Pilkington

PEIPING MACHINE TAPHOUSE

E101, 46 Fangjia Hutong
Beijing 100000, China
+86 1064011572

Recommended by
Richard Ammerman

Opening hours	Open 7 days from 5 pm
Credit cards	Accepted
Type	Bar
Recommended for	Wish I'd opened

"One of Beijing's only craft-beer bars located inside the inner city's ancient alleyways (hutongs). They have the biggest draught selection of any hutong bar, and the menu includes beers from small start-up breweries."—Richard Ammerman

SLOW BOAT BREWING COMPANY

6 South Sanlitun Street
Beijing 100027, China
+86 1065925388
www.slowboatbrewery.com

Recommended by
Alexa Penton

Opening hours	Open 7 days from 11 am
Credit cards	Accepted
Type	Brewery
Recommended for	Local favorite

YUGONG YISHAN

Zhang Zizhong Road 3-2
Beijing 100007, China
+86 1064042711
www.yugongyishan.com

Recommended by
Rick Green

Opening hours	Open 7 days
Credit cards	Not accepted
Type	Bar
Recommended for	Unexpected

"It's an alternative music venue featuring local and international acts in a Bohemian atmosphere. I came here thanks to an anniversary concert announcement in an English-language newspaper."—Rick Green

BIONIC BREW

Shahe Jie Pedestrian Street
Baishizhou, Nanshan District
Shenzhen
Guangdong 518000, China
+86 75586707005
www.bionicbrew.com

Recommended by
Joseph Finkenbinder

Opening hours	Open 7 days from 5 pm
Credit cards	Not accepted
Type	Microbrewery
Recommended for	Local favorite

"Gritty, urban, and underground with high-quality beer."
—Joseph Finkenbinder

Hong Kong, see pages 90–93

WUHAN NO.18 BREWING

923 Jinghan Road
Wuhan
Hubei 430000, China
+86 2782931718

Recommended by
Qi Jiang

Type	Brewery
Recommended for	Worth the travel

"This is the first craft-beer bar in Wuhan, and the owner is famous for being one of the first people in China to push the craft-beer revolution."—Qi Jiang

JACKIE'S BEER NEST

76 Zhaozhou Lu
Huangpu
Shanghai 200000, China
+86 13816502260

Recommended by
Luke Nicholas

Opening hours	Open 7 days from 11 am
Credit cards	Accepted
Type	Bar
Recommended for	Wish I'd opened

"So small and so good."—Luke Nicholas

LIQUID LAUNDRY KITCHEN & BREW

1028 Huaihai Middle Road
Xuhui District
Shanghai 200030, China
+86 2164459589
www.theliquidlaundry.com

Recommended by
Mischa Smith

Opening hours	Open 7 days from 11 am
Credit cards	Accepted
Type	Pub
Recommended for	Wish I'd opened

"The perfect blend of great craft beers and popular Asian nightlife. It balances the superfine line between a classic pub and an upscale nightclub."—Mischa Smith

GRASSROOTS & FRUIT

1 Shude Road
Magong City
Penghu 880, Taiwan
+886 982662194

Recommended by
Brett Tieman

Opening hours	Open 7 days from 3 pm
Credit cards	Not accepted
Type	Restaurant
Recommended for	Unexpected

"A highly regarded restaurant on a small outlying island. It features great local cuisine with freshly sourced ingredients and a nice selection of local Taiwan craft beer. A must-visit if you travel to Penghu."—Brett Tieman

23 PUBLIC CRAFT BEER

Number 100, Section 1
Xinhai Road
Da'an District
Taipei 106, Taiwan
+886 223632387

Recommended by
Brett Tieman

Opening hours	Open 7 days from 3:30 pm
Credit cards	Accepted
Type	Pub
Recommended for	Local favorite

"23 Public is 23 Brewing Company's inaugural tap room. The pub's twelve taps showcase 23 Brewing Company brews and its brewmasters' favorites from other local brands. Aside from offering one of the best beer selections in Taipei, 23 Public draws a wonderfully diverse clientele. The interior is minimally stylish but casual."—Brett Tieman

MIKKELLER BAR TAIPEI

Number 241, Nanjing West Road
Datong District
Taipei 103, Taiwan
+886 225586978
www.mikkeller.dk

Recommended by
Yuhang Lin,
Ling Wan Chang

Opening hours	Wed–Mon from 4 pm
Credit cards	Accepted
Type	Bar
Recommended for	Local favorite

"Mikkeller Taipei is just an eight-minute walk from Taipei's Beimen MRT Station (Songshan-Xindian Green Line). The bar has twenty-four taps, and besides Mikkeller beer on tap, you can also expect Mikkeller wine, spirits, and brews from other world-class breweries; they also serve cold-brew Taiwanese tea on tap. The interior design is inspired by Scandinavian style, but they keep the beauty of the historical building."—Ling Wan Chang

TIME KEEPER

Zhongxiao East Road
Nangang District
Taipei 371, Taiwan
+886 227839056

Recommended by
Ling Wan Chang

Opening hours	Open 7 days from 3 pm
Credit cards	Accepted
Type	Beer garden and pub
Recommended for	Beer garden

"Good food and craft beers brewed in Taiwan from a local brewer."—Ling Wan Chang

"THEY SERVE BEERS AT THE RIGHT TEMPERATURE, SO YOU DON'T NEED TO WARM UP YOUR STOUT WITH YOUR HANDS."

JOEY CHUNG P.93

"TOBY, THE OWNER, IS A LEGEND IN THE LOCAL BAR SCENE AND IS THE REAL GODFATHER OF CRAFT BEER IN THE FRAGRANT HARBOR."

DEVIN KIMBLE P.92

HONG KONG

"THEY OFFER A SEASONAL SELECTION FOR A BEER-PAIRED MENU, EACH TIME FOCUSING ON A DIFFERENT CITY IN JAPAN. IT'S RARE TO FIND SUCH GREAT JAPANESE FOOD AND CRAFT BEER TOGETHER, ESPECIALLY IN HONG KONG, DIRECTLY ABOVE THE AIRPORT EXPRESS TRAIN."

RICHARD AMMERMAN P.92

"INNOVATIVE AND TASTY FOOD PAIRED WITH A GREAT BEER SELECTION."

TOBY COOPER P.93

"THE LEADERS IN THE CRAFT-BEER SCENE OF HONG KONG."

MARISA JACKSON P.93

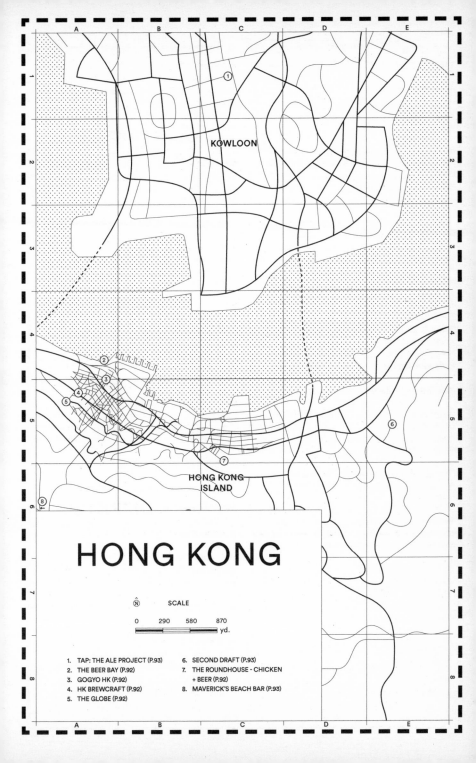

HONG KONG

N SCALE

0   290   580   870
yd.

1. TAP: THE ALE PROJECT (P.93)
2. THE BEER BAY (P.92)
3. GOGYO HK (P.92)
4. HK BREWCRAFT (P.92)
5. THE GLOBE (P.92)
6. SECOND DRAFT (P.93)
7. THE ROUNDHOUSE - CHICKEN
    + BEER (P.92)
8. MAVERICK'S BEACH BAR (P.93)

THE BEER BAY

Pier 3 and Pier 4
Central Ferry Piers
Hong Kong Island
Hong Kong 999077
+852 34817290

Recommended by
Joey Chung,
Christopher DeWolf,
Devin Kimble

Opening hours..........................Mon–Fri from 3 pm, Sat from
2:30 pm, Sun from 12:30 pm
Credit cards..Not accepted
Type...Beer garden
Recommended for...Unexpected

"This is a little bar stall next to the Central Ferry Piers.
Commuters grab a plastic cup of wine or a pint (!) of gin
and tonic before catching their ferries, but they also import
some very good craft beer from the UK. They have a number
of craft options on tap, including some local beer."
—Christopher DeWolf

THE GLOBE

Garley Building
43–53 Graham Street
Hong Kong Island
Hong Kong 999077
+852 25431941
www.theglobe.com.hk

Recommended by
Shaheen Budhrani,
Joey Chung, Marisa Jackson,
Devin Kimble, Mischa Smith,
Christopher Wong

Opening hours..................................Open 7 days from 10 am
Credit cards...Accepted
Type..Pub
Recommended for...Local favorite

"Toby, the owner, is a legend in the local bar scene and is the
real godfather of craft beer in the Fragrant Harbor."
—Devin Kimble

"Besides their high-quality British pub food, including
innovative savory pies, they are the leaders in the craft-beer
scene of Hong Kong."—Marisa Jackson

GOGYO HK

International Finance Centre Mall
Shop 3020, 3rd Floor, 8 Finance Street
Hong Kong Island
Hong Kong 999077
+852 23851366
www.gogyo.com.hk

Recommended by
Richard
Ammerman

Opening hours............................Open 7 days from 11:30 am
Credit cards...Accepted
Type...Restaurant
Recommended for..Beer & food

"Their kogashi (burned) miso ramen is legendary. They offer
a seasonal selection for a beer-paired menu, each time
focusing on a different city in Japan. It's rare to find such
great Japanese food and craft beer together, especially in
Hong Kong, directly above the airport express train."
—Richard Ammerman

HK BREWCRAFT

4/F, 15 Cochrane Street
Hong Kong Island
Hong Kong 999077
+852 59252739
www.hkbrewcraft.com

Recommended by
Pon Lertsakdadet

Opening hours............................Open 7 days from 11:30 am
Credit cards...Accepted
Type...Retail
Recommended for...Unexpected

"A great selection of craft-beer bottles from around the
world."—Pon Lertsakdadet

THE ROUNDHOUSE – CHICKEN
+ BEER

29 Amoy Street
Hong Kong Island
Hong Kong 999077
+852 28663330
www.roundhouse.com.hk

Recommended by
Thomas Lau

Opening hours..................................Open 7 days from 12 pm
Credit cards...Accepted
Type...Bar and restaurant
Recommended for...Local favorite

"The largest craft-beer selection on tap in Hong Kong."
—Thomas Lau

SECOND DRAFT

98 Tung Lo Wan Road
Hong Kong Island
Hong Kong 999077
+852 26560232

Recommended by
Shaheen Budhrani,
Joey Chung, Toby Cooper,
Christopher DeWolf,
Tom Hanson,
Edward Jalat-Dehen,
Erik Moynihan,
Christopher Wong

Opening hours	Mon–Fri from 12 pm, Sat–Sun from 11 am
Credit cards	Accepted
Type	Pub
Recommended for	Beer & food

"Second Draft is a taproom that's a great place to hang out with a group of craft-beer lovers. They have twenty-eight taps, from local to international craft beers. They serve beers at the right temperature, so you don't need to warm up your stout with your hands. Chef May Chow designed a great menu for pairing with craft beers. For example, their mapo tofu is made with a whole ball of burrata instead of the traditional tofu, and it comes with spicy minced pork and baby spinach. The result is amazing."—Joey Chung

"Innovative and tasty food paired with a great beer selection. Hong Kong's interpretation of pub food with clever well-conceived dishes."—Toby Cooper

"Second Draft has a really great beer selection. The bar itself is spacious and open and has this great vibe of retro Hong Kong being brought into modern times. The food is also great, curated by May Chow, who was voted Asia's best female chef. All around a great staff, too."—Tom Hanson

TAP: THE ALE PROJECT

15 Hak Po Street
Kowloon
Hong Kong 999077
+852 24682010

Recommended by
Christopher DeWolf,
Christopher Wong

Opening hours	Mon from 4 pm, Tue–Sun from 12 pm
Credit cards	Accepted
Type	Pub
Recommended for	Local favorite

"Great local beer selection and an amazing pub menu with local influences and a lovely staff. The beer-geek ritual is to head to 66 Hotpot, across the street, for the best mala chicken pot in town."—Christopher Wong

MAVERICK'S BEACH BAR

Pui O Beach
New Territories
Hong Kong 999077
+852 56628552
www.mavericks.hk

Recommended by
Toby Cooper

Opening hours	Fri from 5 pm, Sat–Sun from 11 am
Credit cards	Accepted
Type	Bar
Recommended for	Unexpected

"Laid-back, relaxed, really friendly owners, and fantastic location, right on the beach in Hong Kong."—Toby Cooper

"PERFECT PAIRING OF CRUSHABLE CRAFT BEERS AND AWESOME BARBECUE."
TIM SCOTT P.97

"LOUD, BOISTEROUS, ROWDY—EVERYTHING YOU COULD ASK FOR IN A BEER BAR!"
MISCHA SMITH P.97

"THE COMBINATION OF FOOD AND BEER IS SPLENDID."
SHIRO YAMADA P.96

SOUTH & SOUTHEAST ASIA

"A PIONEER. AND A LOT OF CHOICES IN A NATURAL COLD ENVIRONMENT, WITH FRESH AIR FROM THE MOUNTAINS."
BIER RANGER P.98

"THE FIRST BAR IN MUMBAI TO SUPPORT LOCAL INDEPENDENT CRAFT BEERS."
VENKATESH IYER P.96

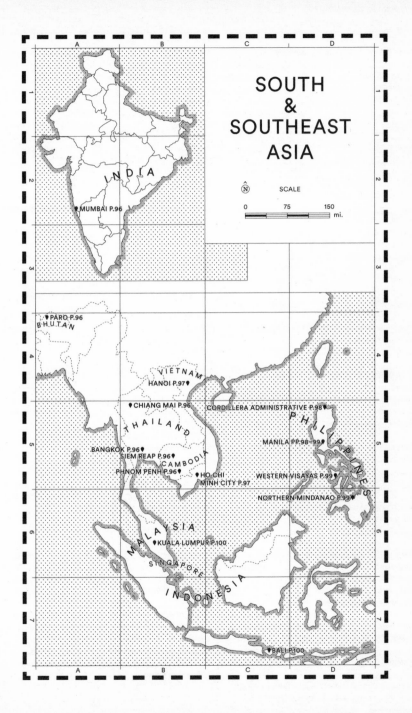

SOUTH & SOUTHEAST ASIA

$\widehat{N}$ SCALE

0   75   150
mi.

INDIA

♦ MUMBAI P.96

♦ PARO P.96
BHUTAN

VIETNAM
HANOI P.97

♦ CHIANG MAI P.96

THAILAND

CORDILLERA ADMINISTRATIVE P.98 ♦

PHILIPPINES

MANILA PP.98–99 ♦

BANGKOK P.96 ♦
SIEM REAP P.96 ♦
CAMBODIA
PHNOM PENH P.96 ♦
♦ HO-CHI
MINH CITY P.97

WESTERN VISAYAS P.99 ♦

NORTHERN MINDANAO P.99 ♦

MALAYSIA
♦ KUALA LUMPUR P.100

SINGAPORE

INDONESIA

♦ BALI P.100

NAMGAY ARTISANAL BREWERY

Dumsibu
Paro 11001, Bhutan
+975 17503688

Recommended by
Steve Hindy

Opening hours......................................Mon–Sat from 9 am
Credit cards...Not accepted
Type..Microbrewery
Recommended for..Unexpected

WOODSIDE INN

Woodhouse Road Colaba
Colaba
Mumbai 400001, India
+91 2222875752

Recommended by
Venkatesh Iyer

Opening hours......................................Mon–Fri from 11 am,
Sat–Sun from 10 am
Credit cards..Accepted but not Amex
Type..Pub
Recommended for..Worth the travel

"The first bar in Mumbai to support local independent craft beers."—Venkatesh Iyer

EAT ME RESTAURANT

Soi Pipat 2
Bangkok 10500, Thailand
+66 22380931
www.eatmerestaurant.com

Recommended by
Shiro Yamada

Opening hours......................................Open 7 days from 3 pm
Credit cards..Accepted
Type...Restaurant
Recommended for...Beer & food

"The combination of food and beer is splendid."
—Shiro Yamada

MIKKELLER BANGKOK

26 Ekkamai 10 Alley, Lane 2
Bangkok 10110, Thailand
+66 23819891
www.mikkellerbangkok.com

Recommended by
Daniel Goh

Opening hours......................................Open 7 days from 5 pm
Credit cards..Accepted but not Amex
Type...Bar and restaurant
Recommended for...Wish I'd opened

"There is great outdoor space at this far-flung outpost of Mikkeller. It's very cozy and has a lot of draft options, especially for Asia."—Daniel Goh

O'GLEE

Soi Ari 1
Bangkok 10400, Thailand
+66 641464983

Recommended by
Pon Lertsakdadet

Opening hours......................................Mon–Sat from 5:30 pm
Credit cards..Accepted but not Amex
Type..Pub
Recommended for...Beer & food

MICROKOSMOS CRAFT BEER

259 Moo 12
Chiang Mai 50170, Thailand
+66 859927005

Recommended by
Linda Merete Skogholt

Opening hours......................................Tue–Sat from 5 pm
Credit cards...Not accepted
Type...Beer garden
Recommended for..Unexpected

BOTANICO

9B Street 29
Phnom Penh 12200, Cambodia
+855 77943135

Recommended by
Erich Phillips

Opening hours..........Mon–Sat from 9 am, Sun from 10 am
Credit cards..Not accepted
Type........................Beer garden, bar, and restaurant
Recommended for...Beer garden

"For the most craft-brewed options in Cambodia."
—Erich Phillips

SIEM REAP BREWPUB

5 Street 05
Siem Reap Province 17259, Cambodia
+855 80888555
www.siemreapbrewpub.asia

Recommended by
Shawna O'Flaherty

Opening hours......................................Open 7 days from 11 am
Credit cards..Accepted
Type...Brewpub and restaurant
Recommended for..Unexpected

"Flights of six beers with the flight holder designed to hold ice, so it doesn't get hot while you drink in the tropical temperatures. The owner is extremely passionate about flavor and style. The food menu is creative, combining French and Cambodian dishes with lovely presentations."
—Shawna O'Flaherty

BIA HOI JUNCTION HANOI

Corner of Ta Hien
and Luong Ngoc Quyen
Hanoi 100000, Vietnam

Recommended by
Charles Guerrier

Opening hours..Variable
Credit cards...Not accepted
Type...Bar
Recommended for.....................................Unexpected

Bia Hoi Junction is a one-of-a-kind spot in the Old Quarter of Hanoi. Throngs of people go there to drink the locally made, sessionable, and affordable beer called Bia Hoi. It's definitely a hub of nightlife activities. It's also a great spot to enjoy some late-night street food.

BIACRAFT ARTISAN ALES

1 Lê Ngô Cát
Ho Chi Minh City 700000, Vietnam
+84 2839330903
www.biacraft.com

Recommended by
Charles Guerrier

Opening hours.....................Open 7 days from 11 am
Credit cards........................Accepted but not Amex
Type...Bar
Recommended for.............................Wish I'd opened

"They are huge supporters of the local craft industry. Fifty beer taps direct from the cold room in Ho Chi Minh City."
—Charles Guerrier

BIA HOI JUNCTION HO CHI MINH

Thai Van Lung
Ho Chi Minh City 700000, Vietnam

Recommended by
Mischa Smith

Opening hours..Variable
Credit cards...Not accepted
Type...Bar
Recommended for.....................................Unexpected

"These Bia Hoi places are very popular in Hanoi. We found one in Ho Chi Minh. Brewed fresh on-site every day, this 'gas beer,' or fresh beer, is more like beer-flavored water, served on ice to keep it cold. Loud, boisterous, rowdy—everything you could ask for in a beer bar."—Mischa Smith

MALT

46 Mac Thi Buoi
Ho Chi Minh City 700000, Vietnam
+84 918484763
www.maltsaigon.com

Recommended by
Mischa Smith

Opening hours........................Mon–Fri from 2 pm,
Sat–Sun from 12 pm
Credit cards...Accepted
Type...Pub
Recommended for..................................Local favorite

"A great selection of craft beers, fantastic cocktails, and great pub food. The outdoor courtyard is great, and there's a shuffleboard table."—Mischa Smith

PASTEUR STREET BREWING COMPANY

144 Pasteur Street
Ho Chi Minh City 700000, Vietnam
+84 2838239562
www.pasteurstreet.com

Recommended by
Charles Guerrier,
Alexa Penton
Tim Scott

Opening hours.....................Open 7 days from 11 am
Credit cards...Accepted
Type...Bar
Recommended for..................................Local favorite

QUÁN ỤT ỤT

60 Truong Sa, Quan Binh Thanh
Ho Chi Minh City 700000, Vietnam
+84 38400420
www.quanutut.com

Recommended by
Tim Scott

Opening hours.....................Open 7 days from 11 am
Credit cards........................Accepted but not Amex
Type......................................Bar and restaurant
Recommended for.............................Beer & food

"Perfect pairing of crushable craft beers and awesome barbecue."—Tim Scott

ROGUE SAIGON CRAFT BEER

13 Pasteur Street D1
Ho Chi Minh City 70000, Vietnam
+84 902365780

Recommended by
Ruben Martinez

Opening hours........................Open 7 days from 4 pm
Credit cards...Accepted
Type...Pub
Recommended for..................................Local favorite

SAGADA CELLAR DOOR
Lallal-ai, Patay
Sagada
Cordillera Administrative 2619, Philippines
+63 9175541345

Recommended by
Bier Ranger

Opening hours.....................Open 7 days from 2 pm
Credit cards...............................Not accepted
Type..Bar
Recommended for...................Worth the travel

ALAMAT FILIPINO PUB & DELI
5666 Don Pedro Street
Makati
Metropolitan Manila
National Capital Region 1209, Philippines
+63 9175302580

Recommended by
Stephen Michael Co,
Bier Ranger

Opening hours.....................Open 7 days from 6 pm
Credit cards...............................Not accepted
Type..Beer garden
Recommended for...................Beer garden

THE BOTTLE SHOP
Ground Floor
Tritan Ventures Building
Paseo de Magallanes
Makati
Metropolitan Manila
National Capital Region 1200, Philippines
+63 9178945076

Recommended by
Joey Chung,
Felix Hagad,
Bier Ranger,
Oliver San Antonio

Opening hours.....................Open 7 days from 2 pm
Credit cards...............................Accepted
Type..Bar, beer garden, and retail
Recommended for...................Beer garden

"A pioneer. And a lot of choices in a natural cold
environment, with fresh air from the mountains.
I've been to many places, but nothing compares to the
Bottle Shop."—Bier Ranger

JOE'S BREW
5834 Matilde Street
Makati
Metropolitan Manila
National Capital Region 1210, Philippines
+63 24000700

Recommended by
Stephen Michael Co

Opening hours.....................Tue–Sun from 5 pm
Credit cards...............................Accepted but not Amex
Type..Brewery and bar
Recommended for...................Wish I'd opened

"Brilliant decor and proper craft-beer glasses."
—Stephen Michael Co

NIPA BREW
9635 Kamagong Street
Makati
Metropolitan Manila
National Capital Region 1203, Philippines
+ 63 9273936968
www.nipabrew.com

Recommended by
Stephen Michael Co

Opening hours.....................Open 7 days from 5 pm
Credit cards...............................Accepted
Type..Brewery
Recommended for...................Local favorite

"This is the taproom of Nipa Brew, in a quiet neighborhood
just off the central business district of Makati."
—Stephen Michael Co

BAR PINTXOS
Don Gesu Building
Don Jesus Boulevard
Muntinlupa
Metropolitan Manila
National Capital Region 1780, Philippines
+63 28310065

Recommended by
Josemari Cuervo

Opening hours.....................Mon–Sat from 12 pm,
Sun from 11:30 am
Credit cards...............................Accepted
Type..Bar
Recommended for...................Local favorite

"It's my neighborhood bar, where I'm assured to walk
into friends of mine who regularly frequent the place.
Awesome food and fresh beer on tap."—Josemari Cuervo

BACKYARD KITCHEN + BREW

U.P. Town Center
Katipunan Avenue
Quezon City
Metropolitan Manila
National Capital Region 1104, Philippines
+63 9277261210

Recommended by
Stephen Michael Co

Opening hours.................................Open 7 days from 10 am
Credit cards...Accepted
Type..Restaurant
Recommended for...Beer & food

"The food and drink selection and pairings are spot on."
—Stephen Michael Co

13 UBAY ST. COMFORT DINING

13 Ubay Street
Quezon City
Metropolitan Manila
National Capital Region 1114, Philippines
+63 9178577159

Recommended by
Bier Ranger

Opening hours.................................Open 7 days from 11 am
Credit cards...Accepted
Type..Restaurant
Recommended for...Beer & food

FAT PAULY'S

Pala-O
Iligan City
Northern Mindanao 9200, Philippines
+63 9177063281

Recommended by
Paul Stuart del Rosario

Opening hours............Mon–Sat from 4 pm, Sun from 1 pm
Credit cards...Accepted
Type..Pub
Recommended for...Beer & food

BREWERY GASTROPUB

Paseo Verde Mall, Lacson Street
Bacolod
Western Visayas 6100, Philippines
+ 63 344740851

Recommended by
Felix Hagad

Opening hours.............................Open 7 days from 4:30 pm
Credit cards...Accepted
Type..Pub
Recommended for...Beer & food

CAFE AZUCARERA

89 C.L. Montelibano Avenue
Bacolod
Western Visayas 6100, Philippines
+63 344452867

Recommended by
Felix Hagad

Opening hours.................................Tue–Sun from 3 pm
Credit cards...Accepted
Type..Restaurant
Recommended for...Local favorite

HOMEGROWN BAR

Bacolod North Road
Bacolod
Western Visayas 6100, Philippines
+63 9173006136

Recommended by
Felix Hagad

Opening hours.................................Tue–Sun from 7 pm
Credit cards...Not accepted
Type...Beer garden
Recommended for...Beer garden

INASAL & CO

Liroville Street
Bacolod
Western Visayas 6100, Philippines
+63 344457770

Recommended by
Felix Hagad

Opening hours.................................Tue–Sun from 6 pm
Credit cards...Accepted
Type.................................Beer garden and restaurant
Recommended for..Unexpected

"Alfresco, and made from shipping containers. Very good
local cuisine."—Felix Hagad

LOS INDIOS BRAVOS BORACAY

Road 1A
Boracay
Western Visayas 5608, Philippines
+63 362882803
www.indiosbravosboracay.com

Recommended by
Stephen Michael Co

Opening hours.................................Open 7 days from 10 am
Credit cards...Accepted
Type...Restaurant and pub
Recommended for..Unexpected

"An amazing craft-beer selection near Boracay Beach."
—Stephen Michael Co

TAPS BEER BAR

A-0-3 One Residency, 1 Jalan Nagasari
Kuala Lumpur 50200, Malaysia
+60 321101560
www.tapsbeerbar.my

Recommended by
Vadim Gurov,
Stu McKinlay

Opening hours	Mon–Sat from 5 pm, Sun from 12 pm
Credit cards	Accepted
Type	Bar and restaurant
Recommended for	Unexpected

"Taps Beer Bar is an island paradise of craft beer in a largely
alcohol-free sea. It's a place where all traveling beer lovers
can feel at home."—Stu McKinlay

BREWERKZ RIVERSIDE POINT

Riverside Point
30 Merchant Road
Central Area
Singapore 058282, Singapore
+65 64387438
www.brewerkz.com

Recommended by
Stephen Michael Co

Opening hours	Open 7 days from 12 pm
Credit cards	Accepted
Type	Microbrewery and restaurant
Recommended for	Worth the travel

LITTLE ISLAND BREWING COMPANY

6 Changi Village Road #01-01/02
Changi
Singapore 509907, Singapore
+65 65439100
www.libc.co

Recommended by
Daniel Goh

Opening hours	Mon–Fri from 12 pm, Sat–Sun from 11 am
Credit cards	Accepted
Type	Microbrewery
Recommended for	Local favorite

SMITH STREET TAPS

335 Smith Street #02-062
Chinatown
Singapore 050335, Singapore
+65 94302750

Recommended by
Natasha Hong,
Christopher Wong

Opening hours	Tue–Sat from 6:30 pm
Credit cards	Not accepted
Type	Bar
Recommended for	Local favorite

THE 1925 BREWING COMPANY RESTAURANT

369 Jalan Besar
Kallang
Singapore 208997, Singapore
+65 62949215
www.the1925.com.sg

Recommended by
Ivan Yeo

Opening hours	Open 7 days from 10 am
Credit cards	Accepted but not Amex
Type	Brewery and pub
Recommended for	Local favorite

MIKKELLER BAR SINGAPORE

120 Prinsep Street
Rochor
Singapore 187937, Singapore
+65 63520950
www.mikkeller.dk

Recommended by
Shaheen Budhrani

Opening hours	Tue–Sun from 4 pm
Credit cards	Accepted
Type	Bar
Recommended for	Wish I'd opened

RED DOT BREWHOUSE

25A Dempsey Road #01-01
Tanglin
Singapore 247691, Singapore
+65 64750500
www.reddotbrewhouse.com.sg

Recommended by
Ivan Yeo

Opening hours	Mon–Sat from 12 pm, Sun from 10 am
Credit cards	Accepted
Type	Brewery and beer garden
Recommended for	Beer garden

SINGLE FIN BALI

Pantai Suluban, Jl. Labuan Sait
Uluwatu
Bali 80631, Indonesia
+62 361769941
www.singlefinbali.com

Recommended by
Alex Wallash

Opening hours	Open 7 days from 10 am
Credit cards	Accepted
Type	Bar
Recommended for	Worth the travel

"While the beer list is really only one to two beers long, the
Single Fin overlooks the Uluwatu surf break, where you can
watch world-class surfers ride epic waves."
—Alex Wallash

"A BEER GARDEN THAT OFFERS A VARIETY OF QUALITY CRAFT BEER. THERE ARE FREE TASTINGS FOR ALL BEERS."

OFER RONEN P.104

"A WIDE SELECTION OF ABOUT FIFTY BEERS WITH EXCELLENT FOOD."

ITAY MAROM P.104

MIDDLE EAST

"THE FRESHEST CRAFT BEER IN THE COUNTRY."

YAZAN M. KARADSHEH P.104

"ON TAP YOU'LL FIND REALLY INTERESTING BEERS THAT YOU CAN'T FIND IN THE MARKET. THEIR EXPERIMENTAL-BEER SELECTION COMBINES LOCAL INGREDIENTS, HERBS, AND SPICES."

CANAAN KHOURY P.104

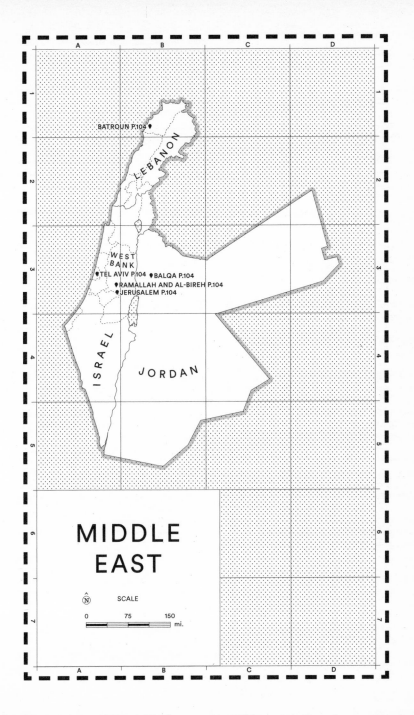

BATROUN P.104

LEBANON

WEST
BANK

TEL AVIV P.104   BALQA P.104

RAMALLAH AND AL-BIREH P.104

JERUSALEM P.104

ISRAEL

JORDAN

MIDDLE
EAST

N̂   SCALE

0   75   150   mi.

COLONEL BEER

Recommended by
Jamil Haddad

Sea Side Road
Batroun, Lebanon
+961 3743543
www.colonelbeer.com

Opening hours	Mon–Fri from 9 am
Credit cards	Accepted
Type	Beer garden and microbrewery
Recommended for	Beer garden

"Walking distance from the city's historic and touristic attractions and just feet from the sea."—Jamil Haddad

RADIO BAR

Recommended by
Canaan Khoury

Ramallah Main Street
Ramallah
Ramallah and al-Bireh 00972, West Bank
+970 22975333

Opening hours	Open 7 days from 4 pm
Credit cards	Accepted but not Amex
Type	Bar and restaurant
Recommended for	Local favorite

TAYBEH BREWING COMPANY

Recommended by
Jamil Haddad,
Canaan Khoury

Taybeh Road 1
Taybeh
Ramallah and al-Bireh, West Bank
+972 22898868
www.taybehbeer.com

Opening hours	Mon–Sat from 8 am
Credit cards	Accepted but not Amex
Type	Brewery
Recommended for	Unexpected

"On tap you'll find really interesting beers that you can't find in the market. Their experimental-beer selection combines local ingredients, herbs, and spices."—Canaan Khoury

SRIGIM BEER GARDEN

Recommended by
Ofer Ronen

Commercial Center
Srigim
Jerusalem District 99835, Israel
+972 732725313
www.srigim-beer.co.il

Opening hours	Thur from 8 pm, Fri–Sat from 10:30 am
Credit cards	Not accepted
Type	Beer garden
Recommended for	Beer garden

"The bar is a beer garden that offers a variety of quality craft beers. There are free tastings for all beers."—Ofer Ronen

BEERBAZAAR BASTA

Recommended by
Itay Marom

Rambam 1
Tel Aviv 9434247, Israel
+972 36125029
www.beerbazaar.co.il

Opening hours	Sun–Fri from 11 am, Sat from 7 pm
Credit cards	Accepted
Type	Bar
Recommended for	Local favorite

"This is the only place in Israel that focuses on local craft beers with the widest selection of Israeli craft beers (nearly 100)."—Itay Marom

PORTER & SONS

Recommended by
Itay Marom,
Ofer Ronen

Ha'Arbaa Street 14
Tel Aviv 6473914, Israel
+972 36244355
www.porterandsons.rest.co.il

Opening hours	Sun–Tue from 5 pm, Wed–Sat from 12 pm
Credit cards	Accepted
Type	Beer garden and restaurant
Recommended for	Beer & food

"A wide selection of about fifty beers with excellent food. This is a proper restaurant."—Itay Marom

CARAKALE BREWING COMPANY

12a Fuhays, Um el Fesh
Fuheis

Recommended by
Yazan M. Karadsheh

Balqa 11821, Jordan
+962 797285192
www.carakale.com

Opening hours	Thur from 6 pm, Fri–Sat from 2pm
Credit cards	Accepted
Type	Brewery
Recommended for	Local favorite

"The freshest craft beer in the country."
—Yazan M. Karadsheh

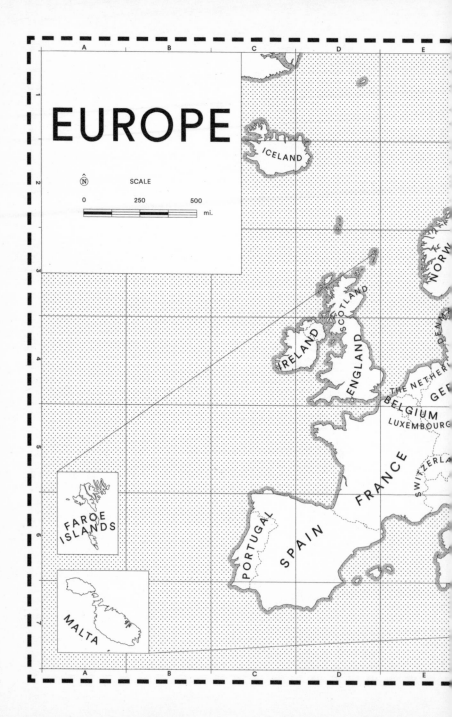

EUROPE

N

SCALE

0   250   500   mi.

ICELAND

NORW

DENMA

IRELAND

SCOTLAND

ENGLAND

THE NETHER

GER

BELGIUM

LUXEMBOURG

FRANCE

SWITZERLA

FAROE ISLANDS

PORTUGAL

SPAIN

MALTA

"ONE OF THE BEST CRAFT BREWERIES IN NORWAY AND ONE OF FLÅM'S BIGGEST ATTRACTIONS. THE BUILDING STYLE IS INSPIRED BY NORSE MYTHOLOGY, WITH THE EXTERIOR REMINISCENT OF A STAVE CHURCH."

MONNA ALMENNINGEN P.109

"IT IS JUST STUNNING."

KIMMO KYLLÖNEN P.111

ICELAND, FAROE ISLANDS, NORWAY, SWEDEN, FINLAND & DENMARK

"THIS HIP AND COZY BAR HAS ONE OF THE BEST TAP LISTS."

MIKE MURPHY P.109

"AN INCREDIBLE PLACE ON THE PATH OF A NORDIC FJORD."

ANTON PLIGIN P.109

ICELAND, FAROE ISLANDS, NORWAY, SWEDEN, FINLAND & DENMARK

SCALE

0   90   180 mi.

ICELAND
SKAGAFJÖRÐUR P.110
REYKJAVÍK P.110

STREYMOY P.110
FAROE ISLANDS

NORRBOTTEN P.113

FINLAND

CENTRAL FINLAND PP.114–115

PIRKANMAA P.115

SOGN OG FJORDANE P.113

NORWAY

SWEDEN

LIESJÄRVI P.115
TURKU P.115
HELSINKI PP.120–123

HORDALAND P.110

OSLO PP.111–112

ROGALAND P.113

SOLNA P.113
STOCKHOLM PP.116–119

VÄSTRA GOTALAND P.114

DENMARK

COPENHAGEN PP.124–127
SKÅNE P.113

LOKSINS BAR
Fálkavöllur 2
Keflavik International Airport
Keflavík
Reykjanesbær 235, Iceland
+354 7833332

Recommended by
Stefán Pálsson

Opening hours	Open 7 days from 4 am
Credit cards	Accepted
Type	Bar
Recommended for	Unexpected

"There is a long tradition in Iceland to start every trip abroad with a pint at the Keflavik International Airport, regardless of how early in the morning."—Stefán Pálsson

FISKMARKAÐURINN
Aðalstræti 12
Reykjavík 101, Iceland
+354 5788877
www.fiskmarkadurinn.is

Recommended by
Stefán Pálsson

Opening hours	Open 7 days from 11:30 am
Credit cards	Accepted
Type	Restaurant
Recommended for	Beer & food

MICRO BAR
Vesturgata 2
Reykjavík 101, Iceland
+354 8658389

Recommended by
Stefán Pálsson

Opening hours	Mon–Fri from 4 pm, Sat–Sun from 12 pm
Credit cards	Accepted
Type	Bar
Recommended for	Local favorite

SKÚLI CRAFT BAR
Aðalstræti 9
Reykjavík 101, Iceland
+354 5196455

Recommended by
Stefán Pálsson,
Stephen Roginson,
Höskuldur Sæmundsson,
Vasilia Venizelacou

Opening hours	Mon–Fri from 3 pm, Sat–Sun from 1 pm
Credit cards	Accepted
Type	Bar and beer garden
Recommended for	Beer garden

"Brilliantly situated in the center of Reykjavík, Skúli Craft Bar is lucky enough to be next to an open area with plenty of room for tables."—Stefán Pálsson

BJÓRSETUR ÍSLANDS
Hólar
Skagafjörður 551, Iceland

Recommended by
Stefán Pálsson,
Valgeir Valgeirsson

Opening hours	By appointment
Credit cards	Accepted
Type	Bar and microbrewery
Recommended for	Wish I'd opened

"Wow! This one is really far out of the way, in remote northern Iceland, at the agricultural Hólar University College. Ambitiously named 'The Icelandic Beer Center,' it has a shockingly big beer list at cheap prices (by Icelandic standards) and is a nonprofit, volunteer-run bar. Opening hours are flexible and based on when and if the staff bother to show up."—Stefán Pálsson

"They have the best prices in Iceland. Also, they have the smallest fully licensed brewery in Iceland, only fifty-liter batch sizes, which makes this bar the only place where their beer is available."—Valgeir Valgeirsson

MIKKELLER TÓRSHAVN
5 Bringsnagøta
Tórshavn
Streymoy 100, Faroe Islands
+298 411500
www.mikkeller.fo

Recommended by
PJ Sullivan

Opening hours	Sun–Thur from 5 pm, Fri–Sat from 4 pm
Credit cards	Accepted
Type	Bar
Recommended for	Wish I'd opened

APOLLON
Nygårdsgaten 2A
Bergen
Hordaland 5015, Norway
+47 55315943
www.apollon.no

Recommended by
Espen Lothe

Opening hours	Open 7 days from 10 am
Credit cards	Accepted
Type	Bar and retail
Recommended for	Local favorite

"A craft-beer bar and record store run by Einar Engelstad, a legendary culture writer."—Espen Lothe

BRUS BAR

Osterhaus Gate 11
Oslo 0183, Norway

Recommended by
Linda Merete Skogholt

Opening hours..................................Sun–Thur from 4 pm,
Fri–Sat from 2 pm
Credit cards..................................Accepted but not Amex
Type..Bar
Recommended for..................................Local favorite

"A tiny and cozy bar overflowing with crazy-good craft beers."—Linda Merete Skogholt

BRYGG

Storgata 7
Oslo 0155, Norway
www.brygg.no

Recommended by
Tomas Halberstad,
Jostein Sæthre

Opening hours..........................Mon–Fri from 7 am,
Sat from 11 am, Sun from 12 pm
Credit cards..Accepted
Type..Bar
Recommended for..................................Wish I'd opened

"They've gone all in, with a beer and cocktail bar, a ping-pong table, an open kitchen where food trucks can showcase their work, a thirty-kit Braumeister room where people can brew their own beer, taps for miles, and a bottle selection to match."—Tomas Halberstad

CAFÉ SARA

Hausmanns Gate 29
Oslo 0182, Norway
+47 22034000
www.cafesara.no

Recommended by
Stephen Andrews,
Jostein Sæthre

Opening hours...........Mon–Sat from 11 am, Sun from 1 pm
Credit cards..Accepted
Type...........................Beer garden and restaurant
Recommended for..Beer garden

"One of the most fascinating beer menus for draft beers in Oslo. The outdoor area is really nice, and a little secret if you don't know about it."—Jostein Sæthre

"Some of the best beer on tap and a few coolers with world-class bottles that people trade. Grab a nice bottle and a wineglass, and head to the hidden back garden."
—Stephen Andrews

GAASA

Storgata 36J
Oslo 0183, Norway
+47 45416469
www.gaasa.no

Recommended by
Geoffrey Jansen van Vuuren

Opening hours..................................Open 7 days from 4 pm
Credit cards..Accepted
Type..Beer garden
Recommended for..Beer garden

"With loads of outdoor seating in the courtyard and an ever-rotating tap list, this is the place to be."
—Geoffrey Jansen van Vuuren

GRÜNERLØKKA BRYGGHUS

Thorvald Meyers Gate 30B
Oslo 0555, Norway
+47 96622831
www.brygghus.no

Recommended by
Jostein Sæthre

Opening hours..................................Mon–Fri from 3 pm,
Sat–Sun from 12 pm
Credit cards..Accepted
Type..Brewery and pub
Recommended for..................................Local favorite

"An institution for beer enthusiasts."—Jostein Sæthre

HÅNDVERKERSTUENE

Rosenkrantz Gate 7
Oslo 0159, Norway
+47 22420750
www.hvks.no

Recommended by
Øystein Krogtoft,
Jostein Sæthre,
Geoffrey Jansen van Vuuren

Opening hours..Mon–Sat from 3 pm
Credit cards..Accepted
Type..Bar and restaurant
Recommended for..Beer & food

HUMLE & MALT

Oslo Airport, 2060 Gardermoen
Oslo 2061, Norway
+47 93045465
www.hmshost-umoe.com

Recommended by
Jostein Sæthre

Opening hours..................................Open 7 days from 10 am
Credit cards..Accepted
Type..Restaurant
Recommended for..Unexpected

NEDRE FOSS GÅRD

Nordregate 2
Oslo 0551, Norway
+47 92338293
www.nedrefossgaard.no

Recommended by
Øystein Krogtoft

Opening hours................................Mon–Sat from 11:30 am,
Sun from 12 pm
Credit cards..Accepted
Type..Bar and restaurant
Recommended for..Local favorite

OLYMPEN

Grønlandsleiret 15
Oslo 0190, Norway
+47 24101999
www.olympen.no

Recommended by
Espen Lothe

Opening hours..Mon–Fri from 11 am,
Sat–Sun from 12 pm
Credit cards..Accepted
Type..Restaurant
Recommended for..Beer & food

RØØR

Rosenkrantz Gate 4
Oslo 0159, Norway
www.roor.no

Recommended by
Geoffrey Jansen van Vuuren

Opening hours....................................Sun–Thur from 3 pm,
Fri–Sat from 1 pm
Credit cards..Accepted
Type..Bar
Recommended for..Local favorite

SCHOUSKJELLEREN MIKROBRYGGERI

2 Trondheimsveien
Oslo 0560, Norway
+47 21383930
www.schouskjelleren.no

Recommended by
Stephen Andrews

Opening hours..Sat–Thur from 4 pm,
Fri from 3 pm
Credit cards..Accepted
Type..Bar and brewery
Recommended for..Local favorite

"This basement haunt is like walking back in time. It's great
for cold nights in the city. It boasts a beautiful arched
brick ceiling and a roaring fireplace at the end of the room.
The bottle list is stellar, especially if you're looking for
lambics."—Stephen Andrews

CHARLES & DE

Langgaten 41
Sandnes
Rogaland 4306, Norway
+47 51683200
www.charlesogde.no

Recommended by
Espen Lothe

Opening hours..Mon–Sat from 9 am
Credit cards..Accepted but not Amex
Type..Restaurant
Recommended for..Beer & food

CARDINAL

Skagen 21
Stavanger
Rogaland 4006, Norway
+47 98204201
www.cardinal.no

Recommended by
Jeppe Jarnit-Bjergsø

Opening hours....................................Sun–Thur from 3 pm,
Fri–Sat from 12 pm
Credit cards..Accepted
Type..Pub
Recommended for..Local favorite

This has a pretty classic old-school pub interior but with
a huge list of well-curated craft beer.

ØST

Kvitsøygata 25
Stavanger
Rogaland 4014, Norway
+47 93431691
www.ostbar.no

Recommended by
Mike Murphy

Opening hours..Mon–Fri from 4 pm,
Sat–Sun from 1 pm
Credit cards..Accepted
Type..Bar
Recommended for..Local favorite

"It has a great rotating tap list. It has a chill interior—and
awesome deck and view—built in an old brewery from the
1850s. This hip and cozy bar has one of the best tap lists
around. Great selection."—Mike Murphy

SABI OMAKASE RESTAURANT

Pedersgata 38 Recommended by
Stavanger Mike Murphy
Rogaland 4013, Norway
+47 92543781
www.omakase.no

Opening hours..Thur–Sat from 8 pm
Credit cards...Accepted
Type...Restaurant
Recommended for...Beer & food

"Eivind, the sommelier, is excellent. He pairs beers but also mixes in sakes and wines to make the pairing perfect for the food. It takes the whole thing to the next level."
—Mike Murphy

ÆGIR BREWPUB

Flåmsbrygga Recommended by
Flåm Monna Almenningen,
Sogn og Fjordane 5742, Norway Aart van Bergen,
+47 57632050 Anton Pligin
www.aegirbrewery.com

Opening hours...................................Open 7 days from 12 pm
Credit cards...Accepted
Type...Brewpub
Recommended for.................................Worth the travel

"An incredible place on the path of a Nordic fjord. It has an amazing fireplace in the center of the pub and taps in the form of antlers."—Anton Pligin

"One of the best craft breweries in Norway and one of Flåm's biggest attractions. The building style is inspired by Norse mythology, with the exterior reminiscent of a stave church."
—Monna Almenningen

KEBENEKAISE FJÄLLSTATION

Nikkaluokta Recommended by
Norrbotten 981 99, Sweden Lasse Ericsson
+46 98055000
www.svenskaturistforeningen.se

Opening hours...Variable
Credit cards...Accepted
Type...Restaurant
Recommended for...Unexpected

"After walking nineteen kilometers from the parking area, the beer tastes extra good."—Lasse Ericsson

MALMÖ BREWING CO & TAPROOM

Bergsgatan 33 Recommended by
Malmö André Ek
Skåne 214 22, Sweden
+46 733921966
www.malmobrewing.com

Opening hours............Sun–Fri from 4 pm, Sat from 12 pm
Credit cards...Accepted
Type...Brewery
Recommended for...Local favorite

SYSTEMBOLAGET

Södra Förstadsgatan 50B Recommended by
Malmö Wendy Roigard
Skåne 211 43, Sweden
+46 40126771
www.systembolaget.se

Opening hours.....................................Mon–Sat from 10 am
Credit cards...Accepted
Type...Retail
Recommended for...Unexpected

"I found New Zealand craft beer there!"—Wendy Roigard

SCANDINAVIAN AIRLINES

Frösundaviks Allé 1 Recommended by
Solna Maxim Polivanov,
Solna Municipality 195 87, Sweden Shiro Yamada
+1 8002212350
www.flysas.com

Opening hours...Variable
Credit cards...Accepted
Type...Bar
Recommended for...Unexpected

Stockholm, see pages 116–119

THE ABYSS

35 Andra Langgatan
Gothenburg
Västra Götaland 413 27, Sweden
+46 31141512

Recommended by
James Goulding

Opening hours......................................Sun–Thur from 4 pm,
Fri–Sat from 3 pm
Credit cards...Accepted
Type...Pub
Recommended for.................................Unexpected

"An absolute dive-heavy metal bar. Nothing but bad lager on tap then a Swedish craft brewery selection in bottles. Very unexpected!"—James Goulding

BREWERS BEER BAR

Tredje Långgatan 8
Gothenburg
Västra Götaland 413 03, Sweden
+46 31147788
www.brewersbeerbar.se

Recommended by
Joey Chung,
Tomas Halberstad

Opening hours.....................Mon–Thur from 4 pm, Fri from
3 pm, Sat–Sun from 1 pm
Credit cards...Accepted
Type...Bar
Recommended for.................................Local favorite

"They are adventurous with their fourteen taps, sparing some for new and small brews. If you're hungry, their sourdough pizza is the best I've ever tried."—Joey Chung

DOKTOR GLAS

Linnégatan 56
Gothenburg
Västra Götaland 413 08, Sweden
+46 31241520
www.doktorglaslinnegatan.se

Recommended by
Øystein Krogtoft

Opening hours......................................Mon–Thur from 4 pm,
Fri from 3 pm, Sat–Sun from 1 pm
Credit cards...Accepted
Type...Bar and restaurant
Recommended for.................................Unexpected

ÖLREPUBLIKEN

Kronhusgatan 2B
Gothenburg
Västra Götaland 411 13, Sweden
+46 317113710
www.doktorglaslinnegatan.se

Recommended by
Olof Andersson

Opening hours..Mon–Fri from 11 am,
Sat from 1 pm, Sun from 2 pm
Credit cards...Accepted
Type...Bar
Recommended for.................................Local favorite

"This has been the watering hole for beer enthusiasts in Gothenburg for the last decade."—Olof Andersson

THE ROVER

Andra Langatan 12
Gothenburg
Västra Götaland 413 28, Sweden
+46 317750490
www.therover.se

Recommended by
Magnus Svensson

Opening hours......................................Mon–Thur from 4 pm,
Fri from 3 pm, Sat–Sun from 2 pm
Credit cards...Accepted
Type...Restaurant
Recommended for.................................Local favorite

TANSSISALI LUTAKKO

Lutakonaukio 3
Jyväskylä
Central Finland 40100, Finland
+358 14617866
www.jelmu.net

Recommended by
Mikko Mäkelä

Opening hours......................................Mon–Fri from 7 pm,
Sat–Sun from 8 pm
Credit cards.............................Accepted but not Amex
Type...Bar
Recommended for.................................Unexpected

VIHREÄ HALTIATAR

Kauppakatu 13
Jyväskylä
Central Finland 40100, Finland
+358 14618235

Recommended by
Juha-Pekka Jylhä,
Mikko Mäkelä

Opening hours......................................Tue–Sat from 6 pm
Credit cards...Accepted
Type...Bar
Recommended for.................................Local favorite

"Vihreä sure has a unique atmosphere. It's a small, cozy little pub on the quiet side of Jyväskylä. They have small and rare beer batches from their selection, which covers forty to fifty beers at a time. It's definitely worth a visit."
—Juha-Pekka Jylhä

Helsinki, see pages 120–123

KEPPANA KELLARI

Koivulantie 6   Recommended by
Liesjärvi 31350, Finland   Kimmo Kyllönen
+358 34355308
www.keppana.com

Opening hours......................Open 7 days from 12 pm
Credit cards...Accepted
Type...Bar and restaurant
Recommended for.......................................Unexpected

"It is just stunning."—Kimmo Kyllönen

GASTROPUB TUULENSUU

Hämeenpuisto 23   Recommended by
Tampere   Kimmo Kyllönen
Pirkanmaa 33210, Finland
+358 32141553
www.jelmu.net

Opening hours.............Sun–Fri from 3 pm, Sat from 12 pm
Credit cards...Accepted
Type..Pub
Recommended for....................................Beer & food

PANIMORAVINTOLA PLEVNA

Itäinenkatu 8   Recommended by
Tampere   Juha-Pekka Jylhä
Pirkanmaa 33210, Finland
+358 32601200
www.jelmu.net

Opening hours.......................................Mon–Sat from 11 am,
    Sun from 12 pm
Credit cards...Accepted
Type......................................Beer garden, bar, and brewery
Recommended for....................................Beer garden

PANIMORAVINTOLA KOULU

Eerikinkatu 18   Recommended by
Turku 20100, Finland   Juha-Pekka Jylhä
+358 22745757
www.panimoravintolakoulu.fi

Opening hours...................................Open 7 days from 11 am
Credit cards...Accepted
Type..........................Beer garden, brewery, and restaurant
Recommended for.......................................Beer garden

Copenhagen, see pages 124–127

"ONE OF THE BEST VINTAGE-BEER SELECTIONS IN THE WORLD FOCUSING ON LAMBIC AND GUEUZE."

GEOFFREY JANSEN VAN VUUREN P.119

"AWESOME, FUN DESIGN, GREAT BEER, AND PIZZA."

SAMUEL RICHARDSON P.118

STOCKHOLM

"THIS SNOOKER AND SHUFFLEBOARD SPOT FEELS LIKE YOUR AVERAGE POOL HALL HANGOUT UNTIL YOU GET TO THE BAR AND SEE THE SURPRISING CRAFT-BEER OPTIONS."

SARA SARTANG P.119

"AWESOME SELECTION OF BEERS."

STEFAN KRUEGER P.119

"THE BEST BELGIAN BEER BAR IN SCANDINAVIA."

JENS SKRUBBE P.118

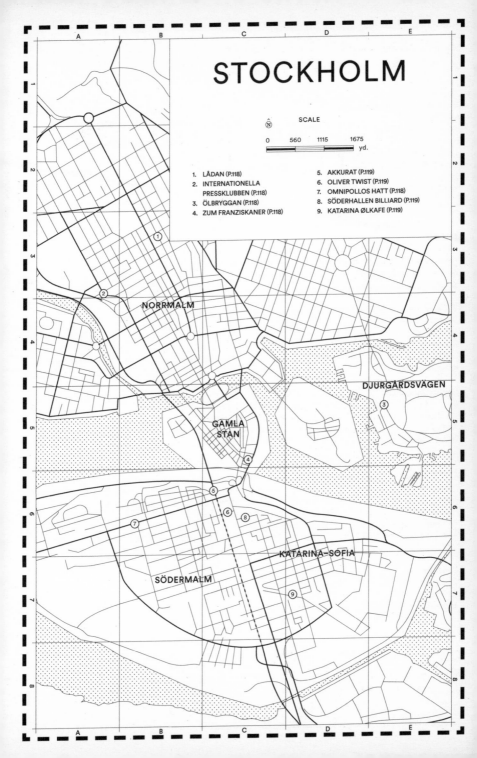

ÖLBRYGGAN

Djurgårdsvägen 40
Djurgårdsvägen
Stockholm 115 21, Sweden
+46 812131300
www.spiritmuseum.se

Recommended by
Sara Sartang

Opening hours	Tue–Sun from 1 pm
Credit cards	Accepted
Type	Beer garden
Recommended for	Beer garden

"A new installment in the Swedish craft-beer scene, tucked behind the Spiritmuseum, this quaint little outdoor beer garden brings craft beer to the waterfront. The staff are friendly and knowledgeable about beer and there's the backdrop of boats sailing by the old town—an excellent setting."—Sara Sartang

ZUM FRANZISKANER

Skeppsbron 44
Gamla Stan
Stockholm 111 30, Sweden
+46 84118330
www.zumen.se

Recommended by
Lasse Ericsson

Opening hours	Mon–Thur from 4 pm, Fri from 3 pm, Sat–Sun from 1 pm
Credit cards	Accepted
Type	Restaurant
Recommended for	Beer & food

OMNIPOLLOS HATT

Hökens Gata 1A
Katarina-Sofia
Stockholm 116 46, Sweden
+46 760838499
www.omnipolloshatt.com

Recommended by
Michele Hengst,
Øystein Krogtoft, Mikko
Mäkelä, Kosara Dangić
Melentijević,
Samuel Richardson,
Jostein Sæthre, Sara Sartang

Opening hours	Open 7 days from 12 pm
Credit cards	Accepted but not Amex
Type	Bar and restaurant
Recommended for	Wish I'd opened

"Awesome, fun design, great beer and pizza, and great people."—Samuel Richardson

"Omnipollos Hatt has brilliant beers, an extremely friendly staff, and incredible pizzas. There is never a dull moment in this quaint, trendy bar."—Sara Sartang

Their pizza is the real deal, but people are there for the beers. There is an amazing tap list of mostly Omnipollo beers, including their famous soft-serve beer (first in the world).

INTERNATIONELLA PRESSKLUBBEN

Vasagatan 50
Norrmalm
Stockholm 11120, Sweden
+46 08234870
www.pressklubben.se

Recommended by
Jens Skrubbe

Opening hours	Mon–Fri from 11 am, Sat from 4 pm
Credit cards	Accepted
Type	Bar
Recommended for	Local favorite

"The best Belgian beer bar in Scandinavia."—Jens Skrubbe

LÅDAN

Luntmakargatan 63
Norrmalm
Stockholm 113 58, Sweden
www.flippinburgers.se

Recommended by
Sara Sartang

Opening hours	Tue–Thur from 5 pm, Fri from 11 am, Sat from 12 pm
Credit cards	Accepted
Type	Restaurant
Recommended for	Beer & food

"It brings the classic combination of good burgers and good beers. They have different events, including Taco Tuesdays and craft brewery tap takeovers."—Sara Sartang

AKKURAT

Hornsgatan 18
Södermalm
Stockholm 118 20, Sweden
+46 86440015
www.akkurat.se

Recommended by
Joe Dick,
Lasse Ericsson,
Geoffrey Jansen van
Vuuren, Stefan Krueger,
André Pintado

Opening hours............................Mon–Thur, Sat from 3 pm,
Fri from 11 am, Sun from 6 pm
Credit cards..Accepted
Type...Bar
Recommended for..............................Worth the travel

"One of the best vintage-beer selections in the world
focusing on lambic and gueuze. A great rotating draft
list and an impressive whiskey selection makes this
my all-time favorite bar. The food is great too. I highly
recommend the Roquefort and bacon mussels. The
unmatched beer-cellar list is what keeps me coming back."
—Geoffrey Jansen van Vuuren

"Awesome selection of beers. Some have been in the cellar
for more than twenty years."—Stefan Krueger

The bottle list at Akkurat is very rightly legendary. On its
pages are many rare bottles, including several specially made
for Akkurat and available only here.

KATARINA ØLKAFE

Katarina Bangata 27
Södermalm
Stockholm 11639, Sweden
+46 86446443
www.katarinaolkafe.se

Recommended by
Espen Lothe

Opening hours..Mon–Fri from 5 pm,
Sat from 12 pm, Sun from 3 pm
Credit cards..Accepted
Type..Beer garden
Recommended for..Worth the travel

"Simple and lovely food, in just the right atmosphere."
— Espen Lothe

OLIVER TWIST

Repslagargatan 6
Södermalm
Stockholm 118 46, Sweden
+46 86400566
www.olivertwist.se

Recommended by
Sara Sartang

Opening hours....................................Mon–Fri from 11 am,
Sat–Sun from 12 pm
Credit cards..Accepted
Type...Pub
Recommended for..................................Local favorite

"Oliver Twist has the classic quaint London pub feel, but it is
backed with twenty-five taps of craft brews from all over
Sweden, Europe, and the United States and a daunting
bottle list of beers."—Sara Sartang

SÖDERHALLEN BILLIARD

Hornsgatan 61
Södermalm
Stockholm 118 49, Sweden
+46 87205680
www.biljarden.com

Recommended by
Sara Sartang

Opening hours.................................Open 7 days from 12 pm
Credit cards................................Accepted but not Amex
Type...Bar
Recommended for..................................Unexpected

"This snooker and shuffleboard spot feels like your
average pool-hall hangout until you get to the bar and see
the surprising craft-beer options."—Sara Sartang

"SUPERB HIGH-END CREATIVE NORDIC FOOD, WHICH PAIRS WELL WITH THE SHORT BUT WELL THOUGHT-OUT BEER LIST."

JUSSI ROKKA P.123

HELSINKI

"THIS IS THE PLACE IN HELSINKI WHERE A BEER GEEK WOULD GO FOR A GASTRONOMIC EXPERIENCE WITH BEER."

PYRY HURULA P.123

"A WIDE BEER SELECTION THAT CHANGES ALL THE TIME."

ANIKO LEHTINEN P.122

"THEY HAVE AN INSANE IMPORTED SELECTION OF BELGIAN GOODIES, AS WELL AS THE TOP LOCAL AND INTERNATIONAL BEERS."

LAURI ELANGO P.122

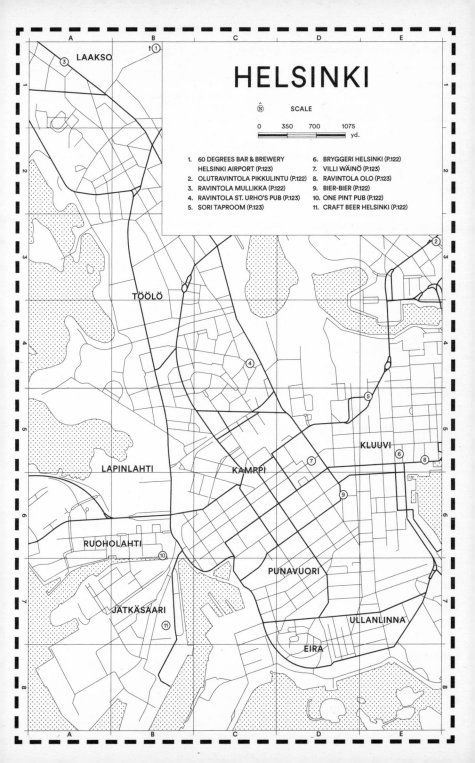

HELSINKI

(N̂)   SCALE

0   350   700   1075
yd.

1. 60 DEGREES BAR & BREWERY
   HELSINKI AIRPORT (P.123)
2. OLUTRAVINTOLA PIKKULINTU (P.122)
3. RAVINTOLA MULLIKKA (P.122)
4. RAVINTOLA ST. URHO'S PUB (P.123)
5. SORI TAPROOM (P.123)
6. BRYGGERI HELSINKI (P.122)
7. VILLI WÄINÖ (P.123)
8. RAVINTOLA OLO (P.123)
9. BIER-BIER (P.122)
10. ONE PINT PUB (P.122)
11. CRAFT BEER HELSINKI (P.122)

LAAKSO

TÖÖLÖ

LAPINLAHTI

KAMPPI

KLUUVI

RUOHOLAHTI

PUNAVUORI

JÄTKÄSAARI

ULLANLINNA

EIRA

BIER-BIER

Erottajankatu 13
Helsinki 00130, Finland
+358 106668451
www.bier-bier.fi

Recommended by
Aniko Lehtinen

Opening hours	Mon–Thur from 4 pm, Fri–Sat from 2 pm
Credit cards	Accepted
Type	Bar
Recommended for	Local favorite

"A wide beer selection that changes all the time. The staff are well educated and the atmosphere is amazing."
—Aniko Lehtinen

BRYGGERI HELSINKI

Sofiankatu 2
Helsinki 00170, Finland
+358 102352500
www.bryggeri.fi

Recommended by
Shawn Decker,
Pekka Kääriäinen,
Olli Majanen,
Mikko Mäkelä

Opening hours	Mon–Fri from 11 am, Sat from 12 pm
Credit cards	Accepted
Type	Restaurant
Recommended for	Beer & food

CRAFT BEER HELSINKI

Kap Hornin Katu 7
Helsinki 00220, Finland
www.craftbeerhelsinki.fi

Recommended by
Mikko Mäkelä

Opening hours	July 5–7 from 12 pm
Credit cards	Accepted
Type	Beer garden
Recommended for	Beer garden

OLUTRAVINTOLA PIKKULINTU

Klaavuntie 11
Helsinki 00910, Finland
+358 93215040
www.pikkulintu.fi

Recommended by
Jeppe Jarnit-Bjergsø

Opening hours	Mon–Fri from 3 pm, Sat–Sun from 12 pm
Credit cards	Accepted
Type	Pub
Recommended for	Worth the travel

Olutravintola Pikkulintu is simply a fantastic bar. Their rotating beer selection is top notch, and they highlight rare bottles from fan favorites, like Cantillon and 3 Fonteinen. There's a great food menu, a fantastic staff, and even an extensive whiskey selection if you aren't in the mood for beer.

ONE PINT PUB

Santakatu 2 B
Helsinki 00180, Finland
+358 923147208
www.onepintpub.com

Recommended by
Lauri Elango

Opening hours	Mon–Thur from 3 pm, Fri–Sun from 1 pm
Credit cards	Accepted
Type	Pub
Recommended for	Worth the travel

"A former Irish pub in Helsinki that today boasts a selection of craft beers. The pub is also an importer from a few great Estonian breweries. They have an insane imported selection of Belgian goodies, as well as the top local and international beers. They have a well-curated tap list and extremely knowledgeable staff. Cozy atmosphere and good prices too."—Lauri Elango

RAVINTOLA MULLIKKA

Mannerheimintie 130
Helsinki 00270, Finland
+358 95879889
www.mullikka.fi

Recommended by
Kimmo Kyllönen

Opening hours	Mon–Fri from 3 pm, Sat–Sun from 2 pm
Credit cards	Accepted
Type	Pub
Recommended for	Local favorite

"Cozy with friendly staff and a very nice selection of good Finnish craft beer from various breweries. Well worth a visit."—Kimmo Kyllönen

RAVINTOLA OLO

Pohjoisesplanadi 5
Helsinki 00170, Finland
+358 103206250
www.olo-ravintola.fi

Recommended by
Jussi Rokka

Opening hours.................................Tue–Sat from 6 pm
Credit cards..Accepted
Type..Restaurant
Recommended for..Beer & food

"Superb high-end creative Nordic food, which pairs well
with the short but well-thought out beer list."
—Jussi Rokka

RAVINTOLA ST. URHO'S PUB

Museokatu 10
Helsinki 00100, Finland
+358 958077222
www.urhospub.fi

Recommended by
Jussi Rokka

Opening hours.................................Open 7 days from 3 pm
Credit cards..Accepted
Type..Pub
Recommended for..Local favorite

60 DEGREES BAR & BREWERY
HELSINKI AIRPORT

Terminaali 1
Lentäjänkuja 3
Vantaa
Helsinki 01530, Finland
+358 505901095

Recommended by
Eugene Tolstov

Opening hours.................................Open 7 days from 5 am
Credit cards..Accepted
Type..Bar and brewery
Recommended for..Unexpected

"The beer selection is not like you would expect in a
European airport."—Eugene Tolstov

SORI TAPROOM

Vuorikatu 16
Helsinki 00100, Finland
+358 442438404
www.soritaproom.com

Recommended by
Pyry Hurula

Opening hours.................................Mon–Fri from 11 am,
Sat–Sun from 12 pm
Credit cards..Accepted
Type..Restaurant
Recommended for..Beer & food

"They have twenty-four rotating taps with over 500 new
beers. Talented fine-dining chefs highlight meats but also
have super-tasty vegetarian dishes. This is the place in
Helsinki where a beer geek would go for a gastronomic
experience with beer."—Pyry Hurula

VILLI WÄINÖ

Kalevankatu 4
Helsinki 00100, Finland
+358 503576704
www.villiwaino.fi

Recommended by
Juha-Pekka Jylhä

Opening hours.................................Sun–Fri from 2 pm,
Sat from 12 pm
Credit cards..Accepted
Type..Bar
Recommended for..Worth the travel

"I visit this place almost every time I'm in Helsinki. It's a
great place to sit down and grab a little Sahti and snacks
while planning your next step."—Juha-Pekka Jylhä

"THE BAR HAS A STAGGERING SELECTION OF VINTAGE LAMBICS, ABBEY ALES, RARE MIXED FERMENTATION BEERS, AND CHARM THAT CAN'T BE MATCHED." JONATHAN BOYCE P.127

"FEELS LIKE DRINKING IN A GYPSY BREWER'S UNDERGROUND BUNKER."

KEVIN RAUB P.127

COPENHAGEN

"ONE OF THE BEST SOUR-BEER LISTS IN THE UNIVERSE."

YUHANG LIN P.126

"THEY SERVE EXCELLENT OLD-SCHOOL NORDIC FOOD, AND THE ATMOSPHERE IS OUTSTANDING."

PATRICK EJLERSKOV P.127

"UNLIKE MOST OTHER BARS, THIS ONE IS A BRIGHT, SUNLIT, AIRY, LONG ROOM THAT TAKES AWAY THE INTIMIDATION FACTOR OF ENTERING A CRAFT-BEER BAR."

NATASHA HONG P.126

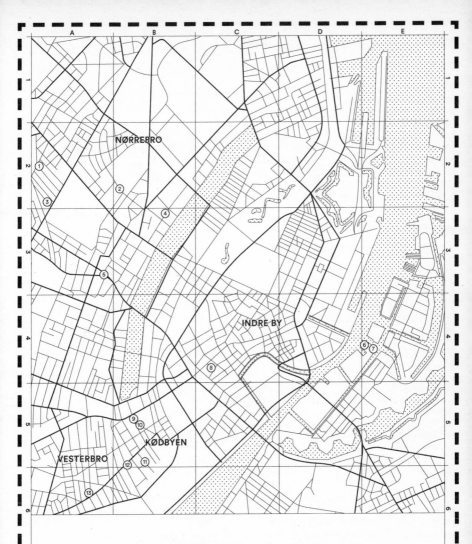

COPENHAGEN

N̂ SCALE

0   315   635   950
                        yd.

RESTAURANT BARR

Strandgade 93
Indre By
Copenhagen 1401, Denmark
+45 32963293
www.restaurantbarr.com

Recommended by
Linda Merete Skogholt

Opening hours	Mon–Thur from 5 pm, Fri–Sun from 12 pm
Credit cards	Accepted
Type	Bar and restaurant
Recommended for	Beer & food

RESTAURANT 108

Strandgade 108
Indre By
Copenhagen 1401, Denmark
+45 32963292
www.108.dk

Recommended by
Rasmus Seidler Krebs

Opening hours	Open 7 days from 5 pm
Credit cards	Accepted
Type	Restaurant
Recommended for	Unexpected

TAPHOUSE

Lavendelstræde 15
Indre By
Copenhagen 1462, Denmark
+45 88876543
www.taphouse.dk

Recommended by
Karol Sadłowski,
Leo E. Vasileiou,
Ladislav Vrtiš

Opening hours	Mon–Thur from 3 pm, Fri–Sun from 12 pm
Credit cards	Accepted
Type	Bar
Recommended for	Worth the travel

WARPIGS BREWPUB

Flæsketorvet 25
Kødbyen
Copenhagen 1711, Denmark
+45 43484848
www.warpigs.dk

Recommended by
Jonathan Boyce, Mike Goguen,
Roland Graber, Danny Hamilton,
Natasha Hong, Kris Li,
Maxim Polivanov,
Höskuldur Sæmundsson,
Chris Treanor

Opening hours	Mon–Wed from 11:30 am, Thur–Sun from 11 am
Credit cards	Accepted
Type	Brewpub
Recommended for	Wish I'd opened

"Unlike most other bars, this one is a bright, sunlit, airy, long room that takes away the intimidation factor of entering a craft-beer bar."—Natasha Hong

BRUS

Guldbergsgade 29
Nørrebro
Copenhagen 2200, Denmark
+45 75222200
www.tapperietbrus.dk

Recommended by
Jonathan Boyce,
Paraskevas Giagmouroglou,
Shannon McFarlane,
Thomas Palmer,
Christopher Pilkington

Opening hours	Mon–Thur from 3 pm, Fri–Sun from 12 pm
Credit cards	Accepted
Type	Bar and restaurant
Recommended for	Wish I'd opened

"A mix of bar, brewery, and restaurant all executed beautifully. Stylish interiors, fresh beers brewed on-site, and painstakingly crafted dishes. It challenges the idea of what a craft-beer bar and restaurant can be and never compromises on quality or atmosphere."—Jonathan Boyce

HIMMERIGET

Åboulevard 27
Nørrebro
Copenhagen 1960, Denmark
+45 35355100
www.himmeriget.dk

Recommended by
Yuhang Lin

Opening hours	Sun–Thur from 3 pm, Fri–Sat from 2 pm
Credit cards	Accepted
Type	Bar
Recommended for	Wish I'd opened

"One of the best sour-beer lists in the universe."
—Yuhang Lin

KOELSCHIP

Stefansgade 35
Nørrebro
Copenhagen 2200, Denmark
+45 35831020
www.mikkeller.dk/location/koelschip

Recommended by
Jonathan Boyce

Opening hours	Sun–Thur from 5 pm, Fri from 2 pm, Sat from 12 pm
Credit cards	Accepted
Type	Bar
Recommended for	Worth the travel

"All lit by candlelight. The bar has a staggering selection of vintage lambics, abbey ales, rare mixed fermentation beers, and charm that can't be matched."—Jonathan Boyce

KRONBORGGADE 3
Kronborggade 3
Nørrebro
Copenhagen 2200, Denmark

Recommended by
Rasmus Seidler Krebs

Opening hours	Mon–Sat from 2 pm
Credit cards	Accepted
Type	Bar
Recommended for	Local favorite

"When I go out, I often go for life, people, and atmosphere rather than the best selection of beer."
—Rasmus Seidler Krebs

NØRREBRO BRYGHUS
Ryesgade 3
Nørrebro
Copenhagen 2200, Denmark
+45 35300530
www.noerrebrobryghus.dk

Recommended by
Olli Majanen,
Höskuldur Sæmundsson

Opening hours	Open 7 days from 12 pm
Credit cards	Accepted
Type	Restaurant and brewery
Recommended for	Beer & food

"A busy brewery and restaurant with a relaxed feeling—well worth the visit. They have a creative and playful way of combining beer and food."—Olli Majanen

CAFÉ DYREHAVEN
Sønder Boulevard 72
Vesterbro
Copenhagen 1720, Denmark
www.dyrehavenkbh.dk

Recommended by
Patrick Ejlerskov

Opening hours	Open 7 days from 9 am
Credit cards	Accepted
Type	Restaurant
Recommended for	Wish I'd opened

"The bar is in the heart of Vesterbro. They serve excellent old-school Nordic food, and the atmosphere is outstanding."
—Patrick Ejlerskov

FERMENTOREN
Halmtorvet 29C
Vesterbro
Copenhagen 1700, Denmark
+45 23908677
www.fermentoren.com

Recommended by
Magnus Svensson

Opening hours	Mon–Wed from 3 pm, Thur–Sun from 2 pm
Credit cards	Accepted
Type	Beer garden and bar
Recommended for	Local favorite

"This is my watering hole when visiting Copenhagen. It's between a dive bar and craft-beer bar, with an amazing tap selection and Big Lebowski-themed bathrooms. They have a whole-roasted pig barbecue on Sundays!"
—Magnus Svensson

MIKKELLER BAR COPENHAGEN
Viktoriagade 8BC
Vesterbro
Copenhagen 1655, Denmark
+45 33310415
www.mikkeller.dk

Recommended by
Jack Cregan,
Øystein Krogtoft,
Aniko Lehtinen,
Kevin Raub,
Leo E. Vasileiou

Opening hours	Sun–Fri from 1 pm, Sat from 12 pm
Credit cards	Accepted
Type	Bar
Recommended for	Worth the travel

"They have so many beer taps."—Jack Cregan

"Mikkeller is almost mythical in status in the craft-beer world and their Copenhagen bar—candlelit, stylish, pure Danish aesthetic—feels like drinking in a gypsy brewer's underground bunker."—Kevin Raub

ØL & BRØD
Viktoriagade 6
Vesterbro
Copenhagen 1655, Denmark
+45 33314422
www.ologbrod.com

Recommended by
Patrick Ejlerskov

Opening hours	Tue–Sun from 12 pm
Credit cards	Accepted
Type	Restaurant
Recommended for	Beer & food

"The restaurant combines excellent Nordic-style food with amazing beers. They experiment in both food and beer, which is fantastic."—Patrick Ejlerskov

"THIS MIGHT SEEM LIKE YOUR ORDINARY PETROL STATION FROM THE OUTSIDE, BUT WALK IN AND YOU WILL BE GREETED WITH AN ABSOLUTELY AMAZING CRAFT-BEER SELECTION."

GEOFFREY JANSEN VAN VUUREN P.139

"I THINK THEY'RE MAKING SOME OF THE BEST BEERS IN THE UK AND ARE CRIMINALLY UNDERRATED. YOU WON'T FIND BETTER KEPT CASK BEER IN THE COUNTRY."

JEN FERGUSON P.133

UNITED KINGDOM & REPUBLIC OF IRELAND

"**ONE OF THE UK'S BEST-KEPT SECRETS.**"

KELLY RYAN P.132

"THE MOST BEAUTIFUL VEGETARIAN INDIAN STREET FOOD WITH THE BEST BEERS FROM BRITAIN AND AROUND THE WORLD."

STU MCKINLAY P.133

"THIS PUB IS THE JEWEL IN THE CROWN OF THE GALWAY BAY BREWERY BARS. IT'S COZY AND HAS A GREAT SELECTION OF BEERS AND A KNOWLEDGEABLE STAFF."

SIMON BRODERICK P.143

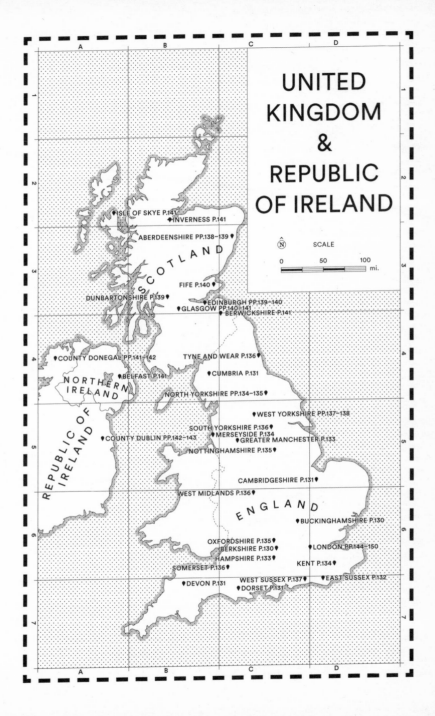

UNITED KINGDOM & REPUBLIC OF IRELAND

N̂   SCALE

0   50   100 mi.

ISLE OF SKYE P.141
INVERNESS P.141
ABERDEENSHIRE PP.138–139
SCOTLAND
FIFE P.140
DUNBARTONSHIRE P.139
EDINBURGH PP.139–140
GLASGOW PP.140–141
BERWICKSHIRE P.141
COUNTY DONEGAL PP.141–142
TYNE AND WEAR P.136
BELFAST P.141
CUMBRIA P.131
NORTHERN IRELAND
NORTH YORKSHIRE PP.134–135
WEST YORKSHIRE PP.137–138
SOUTH YORKSHIRE P.136
MERSEYSIDE P.134
GREATER MANCHESTER P.133
COUNTY DUBLIN PP.142–143
NOTTINGHAMSHIRE P.135
REPUBLIC OF IRELAND
CAMBRIDGESHIRE P.131
WEST MIDLANDS P.136
ENGLAND
BUCKINGHAMSHIRE P.130
OXFORDSHIRE P.135
BERKSHIRE P.130
LONDON PP.144–150
HAMPSHIRE P.133
KENT P.134
SOMERSET P.136
DEVON P.131
WEST SUSSEX P.137
EAST SUSSEX P.132
DORSET P.131

THE CROWN AT BRAY

High Street
Bray
Berkshire SL6 2AH, England
+44 1628621936
www.thecrownatbray.com

Recommended by
Jeppe Jarnit-Bjergsø

Opening hours	Open 7 days from 11:30 am
Credit cards	Accepted but not Amex
Type	Pub and beer garden
Recommended for	Beer & food

It's exactly as you would imagine a classic English pub owned by chef Heston Blumenthal. The food is obviously amazing, but it also has some great beers and a fantastic garden. You can even stay at the inn if you've had a few too many.

COBBS FARM SHOP & KITCHEN

Bath Road
Hungerford
Berkshire RG17 0SP, England
+44 1488686770
www.cobbsfarmshop.co.uk

Recommended by
Alexis Alexiou

Opening hours	Mon–Sat from 9 am, Sun from 10 am
Credit cards	Accepted
Type	Retail
Recommended for	Unexpected

THE BELL INN

Ambury Road
Reading
Berkshire RG8 9SE, England
+44 1635578272

Recommended by
Geoff Griggs

Opening hours	Tue–Sat from 11 am, Sun from 12 pm
Credit cards	Not accepted
Type	Beer garden and pub
Recommended for	Beer garden

BAG OF NAILS

141 Saint Georges Road
Bristol BS1 5UW, England
+44 7941521777

Recommended by
Simon Broderick

Opening hours	Open 7 days from 12 pm
Credit cards	Not accepted
Type	Pub
Recommended for	Worth the travel

BREWDOG BRISTOL

58 Baldwin Street
Bristol BS1 1QW, England
+44 1179279258
www.brewdog.com

Recommended by
Katy DeWinter

Opening hours	Open 7 days from 12 pm
Credit cards	Accepted
Type	Bar and restaurant
Recommended for	Worth the travel

WILD BEER AT WAPPING WHARF

6–8 Gaol Ferry Steps
Bristol BS1 6WE, England
+44 1173294997
www.wbwappingwharf.com

Recommended by
Andrew Cooper

Opening hours	Mon–Fri from 12 pm, Sat–Sun from 11 am
Credit cards	Accepted
Type	Brewery and restaurant
Recommended for	Local favorite

BEER BEAR

86 High Street
Milton Keynes
Buckinghamshire MK11 1AH, England
www.stonybeerbear.co.uk

Recommended by
Jack Cregan

Opening hours	Tue–Sat from 12 pm
Credit cards	Accepted but not Amex
Type	Retail
Recommended for	Unexpected

MOOGBREW

1 Copeland Cottages, Marsh Lane
Taplow
Buckinghamshire SL6 0DF, England
+44 7941241954
www.moogbrew.co.uk

Recommended by
David Williams

Opening hours	Alternate Saturdays from 12 pm
Credit cards	Accepted
Type	Beer garden and microbrewery
Recommended for	Beer garden

"A community-focused nanobrewery taproom in a tiny cottage garden."—David Williams

CALVERLEY'S BREWERY

23A Hooper Street
Cambridge
Cambridgeshire CB1 2NZ, England
+44 1223312370
www.calverleys.com

Recommended by
Patrick Ejlerskov

Opening hours............Thur–Fri from 6 pm, Sat from 11 am
Credit cards...Accepted
Type..Brewery and beer garden
Recommended for..Beer garden

BEER AMBLESIDE

8 Kelsick Road
Ambleside
Cumbria LA22 0BZ, England
+44 1539422290
www.beergb.com

Recommended by
Alastair Kirk

Opening hours.........Mon–Sat from 11 am, Sun from 10 am
Credit cards...Accepted
Type...Retail
Recommended for......................................Local favorite

"Friendly, small place, mainly a bottle shop with 300 plus beers and growler fills."—Alastair Kirk

THE DRUNKEN DUCK INN AND RESTAURANT

Barngates
Ambleside
Cumbria LA22 0NG, England
+44 1539436347
www.drunkenduckinn.co.uk/bar

Recommended by
Alastair Kirk

Opening hours.......................................By reservation
Credit cards...Accepted
Type..Bar and restaurant
Recommended for......................................Beer & food

THE FACTORY TAP

5 Aynam Road
Kendal
Cumbria LA9 7DE, England
+44 1539482541
www.thefactorytap.co.uk

Recommended by
Alastair Kirk

Opening hours....................................Wed–Thur from 4 pm,
Fri–Sun from 3 pm
Credit cards...Not accepted
Type..Pub
Recommended for...Wish I'd opened

"A large selection of the best local Cumbrian beers."
—Alastair Kirk

HAWKSHEAD BREWERY & BEER HALL

Staveley Mill Yard
Staveley
Cumbria LA8 9LR, England
+44 1539822644
www.hawksheadbrewery.co.uk

Recommended by
Tim Blades

Opening hours...Mon–Fri from 9 am,
Sat–Sun from 12 pm
Credit cards...Accepted
Type..Brewpub
Recommended for......................................Beer & food

THE SHIP INN DEVON

Passage Road
Noss Mayo
Devon PL8 1EW, England
+44 1752872387
www.nossmayo.com

Recommended by
Charles Guerrier

Opening hours.............................Open 7 days from 9:30 am
Credit cards...Accepted
Type..Pub
Recommended for..Beer garden

HIVE BEACH CAFÉ

Beach Road
Burton Bradstock
Dorset DT6 4RF, England
+44 1308897070
www.hivebeachcafe.co.uk

Recommended by
Andrew Cooper

Opening hours................................Open 7 days from 10 am
Credit cards...Accepted
Type...................................Bar, beer garden, and restaurant
Recommended for..Beer garden

"An amazing location on the beach, tucked away. An incredible place to spend the day."—Andrew Cooper

BRIGHTON BIERHAUS
161 Edward Street
Brighton
East Sussex BN2 0JB, England
+44 1273686386
www.brightonbierhaus.com

Recommended by
Stephen Whitehurst

Opening hours...................................Open 7 days from 12 pm
Credit cards...Accepted
Type...Brewpub
Recommended for...................................Local favorite

"The biggest and freshest range of Brighton Beer is at this brewery taproom, alongside imported German lagers and wheat beers, guest ales, and ciders. Make sure you pop by on a Wednesday for Kindred Spirits, the beer cocktail night."—Stephen Whitehurst

CURRY LEAF CAFE
60 Ship Street
Brighton
East Sussex BN1 1AE, England
+44 1273207070
www.curryleafcafe.com

Recommended by
David Williams

Opening hours...........Mon–Sat from 12 pm, Sun from 1 pm
Credit cards...Accepted
Type...Restaurant
Recommended for...................................Beer & food

"Great Indian street food with good beers."
—David Williams

THE EVENING STAR
55–56 Surrey Street
Brighton
East Sussex BN1 3PB, England
+44 1273328931
www.eveningstarbrighton.co.uk

Recommended by
Matteo Bonfanti

Opening hours..Sun–Fri from 12 pm,
Sat from 11 am
Credit cards..............................Accepted but not Amex
Type...Pub
Recommended for..........................Worth the travel

LUCKY BEACH
183 Kings Road Arches
Brighton
East Sussex BN1 1NB, England
+44 1273728280
www.luckybeach.co.uk

Recommended by
James Cuthbertson

Opening hours..Mon–Fri from 9 am,
Sat–Sun from 8:30 am
Credit cards...Accepted
Type...Restaurant
Recommended for...................................Unexpected

THE POND
49 Gloucester Road
Brighton
East Sussex BN1 4AQ, England
+44 1273660277
www.thepondbrighton.com

Recommended by
Jack Cregan

Opening hours...................................Open 7 days from 12 pm
Credit cards...Accepted
Type...Pub
Recommended for...................................Local favorite

THE BRUNSWICK
1–3 Holland Road
Hove
East Sussex BN3 1JF, England
+44 1273733984
www.thebrunswick.net

Recommended by
Jack Cregan

Opening hours...................................Open 7 days from 12 pm
Credit cards...Accepted
Type.......................................Beer garden and pub
Recommended for...................................Beer garden

THE SNOWDROP INN
119 South Street
Lewes
East Sussex BN7 2BU, England
+44 1273471018
www.thesnowdropinn.pub

Recommended by
Kelly Ryan

Opening hours...................................Open 7 days from 12 pm
Credit cards...Accepted
Type...Pub
Recommended for...................................Beer & food

"One of the UK's best-kept secrets. They serve some of the finest Scotch eggs you'll ever try. It showcases a lot of local beers, including Burning Sky, one of my favorites."
—Kelly Ryan

BUNDOBUST MANCHESTER

61 Piccadilly
Manchester
Greater Manchester M1 2AG, England
+44 1613596757
www.bundobust.com/manchester

Recommended by
Neil Bontoft,
Stu McKinlay

Opening hours	Open 7 days from 12 pm
Credit cards	Accepted
Type	Restaurant and bar
Recommended for	Beer & food

"The most beautiful vegetarian Indian street food with the best beers from Britain and around the world. What more do you want? Bundobust offers a refreshing difference."
—Stu McKinlay

CAFÉ BEERMOTH

Brown Street
Manchester
Greater Manchester M2 1DA, England
+44 1618352049
www.beermoth.co.uk/cafe

Recommended by
James Goulding

Opening hours	Open 7 days from 12 pm
Credit cards	Accepted
Type	Bar
Recommended for	Wish I'd opened

"They curate the best tap list in the UK."—James Goulding

THE MARBLE ARCH INN

73 Rochdale Road
Manchester
Greater Manchester M4 4HY, England
+44 1618325914
www.marblebeers.com

Recommended by
Jen Ferguson

Opening hours	Open 7 days from 12 pm
Credit cards	Accepted
Type	Pub
Recommended for	Local favorite

"I think they're making some of the best beers in the UK and are criminally underrated. You won't find better kept cask beer in the country."—Jen Ferguson

THE PILCROW PUB

Hanover Street
Manchester
Greater Manchester M60 0AB, England
United Kingdom
+44 1618344989
www.thepilcrowpub.com

Recommended by
Neil Bontoft

Opening hours	Open 7 days from 12 pm
Credit cards	Accepted
Type	Beer garden, pub, and restaurant
Recommended for	Beer garden

PORT STREET BEER HOUSE

39–41 Port Street
Manchester
Greater Manchester M1 2EQ, England
+44 1612379949
www.portstreetbeerhouse.co.uk

Recommended by
Jeppe Jarnit-Bjergsø

Opening hours	Open 7 days from 12 pm
Credit cards	Accepted
Type	Pub
Recommended for	Local favorite

Port Street is a very modern British beer bar. They highlight what's hot with current craft-beer trends and carry some really great cask beer. There is always a stellar selection to be found, and the owners are very friendly and welcoming.

MID HANTS RAILWAY WATERCRESS LINE

The Railway Station, Station Road
New Alresford
Hampshire SO24 9JG, England
United Kingdom
+44 1962733810
www.watercressline.co.uk

Recommended by
Bruno Aquino

Opening hours	Variable
Credit cards	Not accepted
Type	Bar
Recommended for	Unexpected

BOTTLE SHOP: CANTERBURY

Station Road West
Canterbury
Kent CT2 8AN, England
+44 2035832065
www.bottle-shop.co.uk

Recommended by
Antonis Moustakas

Opening hours	Tue–Sun from 9 am
Credit cards	Accepted
Type	Retail and bar
Recommended for	Unexpected

THE FOUNDRY BREW PUB

White Horse Lane
Canterbury
Kent CT1 2RU, England
+44 1227455899
www.thefoundrycanterbury.co.uk

Recommended by
Antonis Moustakas

Opening hours	Open 7 days from 12 pm
Credit cards	Accepted
Type	Brewpub and restaurant
Recommended for	Beer & food

THE SMUGGLERS ALE HOUSE

10 High Street
New Romney
Kent TN28 8BU, England
+44 7581230397
www.smugglersalehouse.co.uk

Recommended by
Rob Bright

Opening hours	Open 7 days from 12 pm
Credit cards	Not accepted
Type	Pub
Recommended for	Worth the travel

London, see pages 144–150

TAP & BOTTLES

19 Cambridge Walks
Chapel Street
Southport
Merseyside PR8 1EN, England
+44 1704544322

Recommended by
Neil Bontoft

Opening hours	Open 7 days from 12 pm
Credit cards	Not accepted
Type	Pub
Recommended for	Wish I'd opened

"A little gem."—Neil Bontoft

CRAVEN ARMS PUB & CRUCK BARN

Appletreewick
Yorkshire Dales National Park
Skipton
North Yorkshire BD23 6DA, England
+44 1756720270
www.craven-cruckbarn.co.uk

Recommended by
Richard Burhouse

Opening hours	Open 7 days from 11:30 am
Credit cards	Accepted
Type	Beer garden and pub
Recommended for	Beer garden

"A historic Yorkshire pub, with traditional features in a quiet Yorkshire village. They serve traditional cask beers, including some from wooden barrels. The setting is the key though, surrounded by the beautiful countryside."
—Richard Burhouse

THE BLACK SWAN AT OLDSTEAD

Oldstead
York
North Yorkshire YO61 4BL, England
+44 1347868387
www.blackswanoldstead.co.uk

Recommended by
Richard Burhouse

Opening hours	Mon–Fri from 6 pm, Sat from 12 pm, Sun from 6 pm
Credit cards	Accepted
Type	Restaurant
Recommended for	Unexpected

"Amazing food and fantastic service."—Richard Burhouse

HOUSE OF THE TREMBLING MADNESS

48 Stonegate
York
North Yorkshire YO1 8AS, England
+44 1904640009
www.tremblingmadness.co.uk

Recommended by
Tim Blades

Opening hours	Mon–Sat from 10 am, Sun from 11 am
Credit cards	Accepted
Type	Pub
Recommended for	Wish I'd opened

"A ramshackle medieval building, and everything about it is fun."—Tim Blades

THE SLIP INN

Recommended by
Venkatesh Iyer

20 Clementhorpe
York
North Yorkshire YO23 1AN, England
+44 1904621793
www.theslipinnyork.co.uk

Opening hours	Mon–Thur from 4 pm, Fri from 1 pm, Sat–Sun from 12 pm
Credit cards	Accepted
Type	Pub
Recommended for	Local favorite

ROCK CITY

Recommended by
Jaega Wise

8 Talbot Street
Nottingham
Nottinghamshire NG1 5GG, England
+44 1159506547
www.rock-city.co.uk

Opening hours	Wed–Sat from 10 pm, Sun from 7 pm
Credit cards	Accepted
Type	Bar
Recommended for	Unexpected

STRATFORD HAVEN

Recommended by
Jaega Wise

2 Stratford Road
Nottingham
Nottinghamshire NG2 6BA, England
+44 1159825981
www.castlerockbrewery.co.uk

Opening hours	Mon–Fri from 11 am, Sat–Sun from 10 am
Credit cards	Accepted
Type	Pub
Recommended for	Worth the travel

"The beer is always excellent here. Some of the best cask beer you will drink in the UK."—Jaega Wise

THE ARGYLL

Recommended by
Mark Hatherly

15 Market Place
Henley-on-Thames
Oxfordshire RG9 2AA, England
+44 1491573400
www.theargyllhenley.co.uk

Opening hours	Open 7 days from 11 am
Credit cards	Accepted
Type	Pub
Recommended for	Beer & food

THE BIRD IN HAND

Recommended by
Mark Hatherly

61 Greys Road
Henley-on-Thames
Oxfordshire RG9 1SB, England
+44 1491575775
www.henleybirdinhand.co.uk

Opening hours	Open 7 days from 12 pm
Credit cards	Accepted but not Amex
Type	Pub
Recommended for	Worth the travel

THE FALKLAND ARMS

Recommended by
Geoff Griggs

19–21 The Green
Oxford
Oxfordshire OX7 4DB, England
+44 1608683653
www.falklandarms.co.uk

Opening hours	Mon–Sat from 8 am, Sun from 9 am
Credit cards	Accepted
Type	Pub
Recommended for	Worth the travel

"A beautiful sixteenth-century pub with great beer in a Cotswolds village, complete with flagstone floors, oak beams, and an inglenook fireplace."—Geoff Griggs

TURF TAVERN

Recommended by
Amy Newell-Large

4–5 Bath Place
Oxford
Oxfordshire OX1 3SU, England
United Kingdom
+44 1865243235
www.turftavern-oxford.co.uk

Opening hours	Open 7 days from 11 am
Credit cards	Accepted
Type	Pub
Recommended for	Wish I'd opened

"A drinking establishment since 1381!" —Amy Newell-Large

HAUSER & WIRTH SOMERSET

Dropping Lane
Bruton
Somerset BA10 0NL, England
+44 1749814060
www.hauserwirthsomerset.com

Recommended by
Andrew Cooper

Opening hours	Tue–Sun from 11 am
Credit cards	Accepted
Type	Restaurant
Recommended for	Unexpected

"An art gallery in rural Somerset with an amazing restaurant and bar."—Andrew Cooper

AVALON INN AT GLASTONBURY FESTIVAL

Worthy Farm
Pilton
Somerset BA4 4BY, England

Recommended by
Jen Ferguson

Opening hours	Last weekend of June
Type	Pub
Recommended for	Unexpected

THE FAT CAT

23 Alma Street
Sheffield
South Yorkshire S3 8SA, England
+ 44 1142494801
www.thefatcat.co.uk

Recommended by
Tom Hanson

Opening hours	Open 7 days from 12 pm
Credit cards	Accepted
Type	Pub
Recommended for	Worth the travel

THE SHEFFIELD TAP

1B Sheffield Station
Sheaf Street
Sheffield
South Yorkshire S1 2BP, England
+44 1142737558
www.sheffieldtap.com

Recommended by
Kelly Ryan

Opening hours	Sun–Thur from 11 am, Sat–Sun from 10 am
Credit cards	Accepted
Type	Pub
Recommended for	Wish I'd opened

"This pub sits right on the platform of a busy train station. They always have great dark and unfiltered lagers on tap and have a brewery in the adjoining building."—Kelly Ryan

THE ANCHOR

Main Street
Walberswick
Suffolk IP18 6UA, England
+44 1502722112
www.anchoratwalberswick.com

Recommended by
Geoff Griggs

Opening hours	Open 7 days from 8:30 am
Credit cards	Accepted
Type	Pub
Recommended for	Beer & food

PITCHER & PIANO NEWCASTLE

108 Quayside
Newcastle Upon Tyne
Tyne and Wear NE1 3DX, England
+44 1912324110
www.pitcherandpiano.com/newcastle

Recommended by
Luis Arce

Opening hours	Open 7 days from 9 am
Credit cards	Accepted
Type	Bar and restaurant
Recommended for	Beer garden

"The view of Quayside and the Millennium Bridge and the atmosphere are amazing."—Luis Arce

THE BARTON ARMS

144 High Street
Birmingham
West Midlands B6 4UP, England
+44 1213335988
www.thebartonsarms.com

Recommended by
Paul Fallen

Opening hours	Open 7 days from 12 pm
Credit cards	Accepted
Type	Beer garden, pub, and restaurant
Recommended for	Unexpected

"A Thai restaurant serving perfectly conditioned Oakham cask beers."—Paul Fallen

THE UNICORN

145 Bridgnorth Road
Stourbridge
West Midlands DY8 3NX, England
+44 1384394823
www.bathams.co.uk/the-unicorn

Recommended by
Logan Plant

Opening hours	Mon–Sat from 12 pm
Credit cards	Not accepted
Type	Pub
Recommended for	Worth the travel

"It's where I first dreamed of starting a brewery."
—Logan Plant

THE LOCKHART TAVERN
Recommended by
James Cuthbertson

41 The Broadway
Haywards Heath
West Sussex LA22 0BZ, England
+44 1444440696
www.darkstarbrewing.co.uk

Opening hours............Sun–Fri from 12 pm, Sat from 9 am
Credit cards...................................Accepted but not Amex
Type..Pub and restaurant
Recommended for.................................Local favorite

"A great selection of beers, both cask and keg, alongside
fresh food."—James Cuthbertson

THE GROVE
Recommended by
Natasha Hong

2 Spring Grove Street
Huddersfield
West Yorkshire HD1 4BP, England
+44 1484430113
www.thegrove.pub

Opening hours.......................Mon–Thur from 2pm,
Fri–Sun from 12 pm
Credit cards..Accepted
Type..Pub
Recommended for.............................Worth the travel

"I love their wide range of craft beers on cask. It's not
something I've seen in a lot of the modern craft-beer bars in
the UK, much less in the rest of the world, and The Grove is
happy to march to their own beat in that way."
—Natasha Hong

MAGIC ROCK TAP
Recommended by
Richard Burhouse

Willow Park Business Centre
Willow Lane
Huddersfield
West Yorkshire HD1 5EB, England
+44 1484649823
www.magicrockbrewing.com/tap-room

Opening hours.......................Tue–Thur from 2 pm,
Fri from 1 pm, Sat–Sun from 12 pm
Credit cards..Accepted
Type..Brewery and bar
Recommended for.................................Local favorite

BUNDOBUST LEEDS
Recommended by
Aidy Fenwick,
Venkatesh Iyer,
Vasilia Venizelacou

6 Mill Hill
Leeds
West Yorkshire LS1 5DQ, England
+44 1132431248
www.bundobust.com

Opening hours.................Open 7 days from 12 pm
Credit cards..Accepted
Type..Restaurant and bar
Recommended for.................................Beer & food

"Bundobust does Indian street food that is vegetarian and
vegan-friendly, showcasing the vast spectrum of Indian
cooking past meat-inspired dishes. The beer selection is
always fantastic and pairs well with the food"
—Vasilia Venizelacou

FRIENDS OF HAM
Recommended by
Natasha Hong

4–8 New Station Street
Leeds
West Yorkshire LS1 5DL, England
+44 1132420275
www.friendsofham.co.uk

Opening hours..........Mon–Sat from 12 pm, Sun from 1 pm
Credit cards..Accepted
Type..Bar and restaurant
Recommended for.................................Beer & food

"Their love for craft beer and ham is infectious."
—Natasha Hong

HEADROW HOUSE
Recommended by
James Goulding

Bramleys Yard
19 The Headrow
Leeds
West Yorkshire LS1 6PU, England
+44 1132459370
www.headrowhouse.com

Opening hours.......................Mon–Fri from 12 pm,
Sat–Sun from 11 am
Credit cards...................................Accepted but not Amex
Type..................................Bar, beer garden, and restaurant
Recommended for.................................Beer garden

LAMB AND FLAG
1 Church Row
Leeds
West Yorkshire LS2 7HD, England
+44 1132431255
www.lambandflagleeds.co.uk

Recommended by
Venkatesh Iyer

Opening hours....................................Open 7 days from 11 am
Credit cards..Accepted
Type..Beer garden and pub
Recommended for..Beer garden

LITTLE LEEDS BEERHOUSE
Unit B3B, Leeds Corn Exchange
Leeds
West Yorkshire LS1 7BR, England
+44 1132456602
www.littleleedsbeerhouse.com

Recommended by
Aidy Fenwick

Opening hours....................................Mon–Sat from 10 am,
Sun from 11 am
Credit cards..Accepted
Type...Bar and retail
Recommended for..Wish I'd opened

NORTHERN MONK BREW COMPANY
The Old Flax Store
Marshall Mills, Marshall Street
Leeds
West Yorkshire LS11 9YJ, England
+44 1132430003
www.northernmonkbrewco.com

Recommended by
Vasilia Venizelacou

Opening hours....................................Tue–Sun from 11 am
Credit cards..Accepted
Type...Brewery and bar
Recommended for..Local favorite

PREMIER STORE FARSLEY
Water Lane
Leeds
West Yorkshire LS28 5LD, England
+44 1132553277
www.premier-stores.co.uk

Recommended by
Vasilia Venizelacou

Opening hours....................................Mon–Sat from 10 am,
Sun from 11 am
Credit cards..Accepted
Type..Retail
Recommended for..Unexpected

"From the outside it's under the Premier Store brand, a chain of convenience stores, but this one is a fantastic little craft beer bottle shop."—Vasilia Venizelacou

BREWDOG CASTLEGATE
5–9 Union Street
Aberdeen
Aberdeenshire AB11 5BU, Scotland
+44 1224586650
www.brewdog.com

Recommended by
Dave Grant

Opening hours....................................Mon–Fri from 11 am,
Sat–Sun from 10 am
Credit cards..Accepted
Type..Bar
Recommended for..Local favorite

"Great range of draft and international bottles. Always getting the best new bottles from around the world."
—Dave Grant

MUSA
33 Exchange Street
Aberdeen
Aberdeenshire AB11 6PH, Scotland
+44 1224571771
www.musaaberdeen.com

Recommended by
Dave Grant

Opening hours....................................Mon–Sat from 11 am
Credit cards..Accepted
Type..Restaurant
Recommended for..Local favorite

"Great traditional but edgy Scottish cuisine. They have fierce beer on tap and an awesome whisky selection."
—Dave Grant

SIX DEGREES NORTH
6 Littlejohn Street
Aberdeen
Aberdeenshire AB10 1FF, Scotland
+44 1224379192
www.sixdnorth.co.uk

Recommended by
Chris Mair

Opening hours...........Mon–Thur from 12 pm, Fri–Sat from
11 am, Sun from 12:30 pm
Credit cards....................................Accepted but not Amex
Type...Brewery and bar
Recommended for..Wish I'd opened

WESTHILL SERVICE STATION

Straik Road
Aberdeen
Aberdeenshire AB32 6TJ, Scotland
+44 1224742336
www.hopshopaberdeen.com

Recommended by
Tim Blades,
Geoffrey Jansen
van Vuuren

Opening hours.................................Mon–Sat from 7 am
Credit cards...Accepted
Type..Retail
Recommended for.....................................Unexpected

"The beers are nearly all cold-stored. Their passion and commitment is incredible."—Tim Blades

"This might seem like your ordinary petrol station from the outside, but walk in and you will be greeted with an absolutely amazing craft-beer selection, as well as a growler fill station."—Geoffrey Jansen van Vuuren

SUGAR BOAT

30 Colquhoun Square
Helensburgh
Dunbartonshire G84 8AQ, Scotland
+44 1436647522
www.sugarboat.co.uk

Recommended by
Paul Fallen

Opening hours.............Sun–Fri from 10 am, Sat from 11 am
Credit cards...Accepted
Type..Restaurant
Recommended for....................................Beer & food

"A restaurant with a beer selection and phenomenal food."
—Paul Fallen

THE BOW BAR

80 West Bow
Edinburgh EH1 2HH, Scotland
+44 1312267667
www.thebowbar.co.uk

Recommended by
Paul Fallen

Opening hours.................................Open 7 days from 12 pm
Credit cards...Accepted
Type...Bar
Recommended for................................Wish I'd opened

"It's an institution."—Paul Fallen

THE BRAUHAUS

105–107 Lauriston Place
Edinburgh EH3 9JG, Scotland
+44 1316295434

Recommended by
Joe Dick

Opening hours.......................................Sun–Thur from 3 pm,
Fri–Sat from 5 pm
Credit cards...Accepted
Type...Bar
Recommended for...............................Local favorite

"The passion and respect for every single drink in the bar is incredible."—Joe Dick

THE HOLYROOD 9A

9A Holyrood Road
Edinburgh EH8 8AE, Scotland
+44 1315565044
www.theholyrood.co.uk

Recommended by
Paul Fallen

Opening hours.................................Open 7 days from 9 am
Credit cards...Accepted
Type...Bar and restaurant
Recommended for...............................Local favorite

"They have a great selection of beers and some of the best burgers in Scotland."—Paul Fallen

THE LAST WORD SALOON

44 Saint Stephen Street
Edinburgh EH3 5AL, Scotland
+44 1312259009
www.lastwordsaloon.com

Recommended by
Ron Hoglund

Opening hours.................................Open 7 days from 4 pm
Credit cards...Accepted
Type...Bar
Recommended for...............................Worth the travel

THE ROYAL OAK

1 Infirmary Street
Edinburgh EH1 1LT, Scotland
+44 1315572976
www.royal-oak-folk.com

Recommended by
Stefán Pálsson

Opening hours.......................................Mon–Sat from 11:30 am,
Sun from 12:30 pm
Credit cards..Not accepted
Type...Pub
Recommended for...............................Worth the travel

SALT HORSE BEER SHOP & BAR

57–61 Blackfriars Street
Edinburgh EH1 1NB, Scotland
+44 1315588304
www.salthorse.beer

Recommended by
Tim Blades,
Chris Mair,
Shannon McFarlane

Opening hours	Mon–Thur from 4 pm, Fri–Sat from 12 pm, Sun from 12:30 pm
Credit cards	Accepted
Type	Bar and retail
Recommended for	Local favorite

"Some of the best beer available gets poured here, even beers that aren't normally on tap in Scotland. All the staff are super knowledgeable and the taps rotate."
—Shannon McFarlane

TEUCHTERS LANDING

1c Dock Place
Edinburgh EH6 6LU, Scotland
+44 1315547427
www.teuchtersbar.co.uk

Recommended by
Joe Dick

Opening hours	Open 7 days from 10:30 am
Credit cards	Accepted
Type	Beer garden and pub
Recommended for	Beer garden

THE SHIP INN FIFE

The Toft
Elie
Fife KY9 1DT, Scotland
+44 1333330246
www.shipinn.scot

Recommended by
Paul Fallen

Opening hours	Open 7 days from 10:30 am
Credit cards	Not accepted
Type	Beer garden and pub
Recommended for	Beer garden

BREWDOG GLASGOW

1397 Argyle Street
Glasgow G3 8AN, Scotland
+44 1413347175
www.brewdog.com

Recommended by
Nikki Ohanlon

Opening hours	Open 7 days from 12 pm
Credit cards	Accepted
Type	Bar
Recommended for	Local favorite

GRUNTING GROWLER

51 Old Dumbarton Road
Glasgow G3 8RF, Scotland
+44 1412584551
www.gruntinggrowler.com

Recommended by
Aidy Fenwick,
Jehad Hatu,
Steve Hindy

Opening hours	Tue–Thur from 12 pm, Fri–Sat from 10 am, Sun from 12 pm
Credit cards	Accepted
Type	Retail and pub
Recommended for	Local favorite

INN DEEP

445 Great Western Road
Glasgow G12 8HH, Scotland
+44 1413571075
www.inndeep.com

Recommended by
Nikki Ohanlon,
Christopher Williams

Opening hours	Mon–Sat from 12 pm, Sun from 12:30 pm
Credit cards	Accepted
Type	Bar and beer garden
Recommended for	Beer garden

KOELSCHIP YARD

686–688 Pollokshaws Road
Glasgow G41 2QB, Scotland
+44 1414232945
www.koelschipyard.beer

Recommended by
Nikki Ohanlon

Opening hours	Mon–Sat from 12 pm, Sun from 12:30 pm
Credit cards	Accepted
Type	Bar
Recommended for	Wish I'd opened

"A friendly bar that stocks great hard-to-find beer."
—Nikki Ohanlon

SHILLING BREWING COMPANY

92 West George Street
Glasgow G2 1PJ, Scotland
+44 1413531654
www.shillingbrewingcompany.co.uk

Recommended by
Shannon McFarlane

Opening hours	Open 7 days from 12 pm
Credit cards	Accepted
Type	Brewery and restaurant
Recommended for	Wish I'd opened

SIX°NORTH GLASGOW

566 Dumbarton Road
Glasgow G11 6RH, Scotland
+44 1413346677
www.sixdnorth.co.uk

Recommended by
Jehad Hatu

Opening hours.....................Mon–Sat from 12 pm,
Sun from 12:30 pm
Credit cards..Accepted
Type..Brewery and bar
Recommended for................................Beer & food

BLACK ISLE BAR AND ROOMS

68 Church Street
Inverness IV1 1EN, Scotland
+44 1463229920
www.blackislebar.com

Recommended by
Shaheen Budhrani

Opening hours.....................Open 7 days from 11 am
Credit cards..Accepted
Type...Pub
Recommended for................................Beer & food

"A great mix of hard-to-find beers both on tap and in bottles, paired with pizzas topped with ingredients grown eight miles away."—Shaheen Budhrani

SEUMAS' BAR

Sligachan Hotel
Sligachan
Isle of Skye IV47 8SW, Scotland
+44 1478650204
www.sligachan.co.uk/seumas-bar

Recommended by
Adam Watson

Opening hours.....................Open 7 days from 12 pm
Credit cards..Accepted
Type...Bar
Recommended for.........................Worth the travel

THE ANDERSON

Union Street
Fortrose
Ross and Cromarty IV10 8TD, Scotland
+44 1381620236
www.theanderson.co.uk

Recommended by
Chris Mair

Opening hours.....................Open 7 days from 4 pm
Credit cards...........................Accepted but not Amex
Type...Bar and restaurant
Recommended for...............................Unexpected

"Fortrose is a tiny place on the Black Isle and a good few miles from anywhere. The Anderson is a beer mecca. It's brilliant."—Chris Mair

HEMELVAART BIER CAFE

High Street
Ayton
Berwickshire
Roxburgh, Ettrick, and
Lauderdale TD14 5QL, Scotland
+44 7377364266
www.hemelvaart.co.uk

Recommended by
Aidy Fenwick

Opening hours.....................Mon from 5 pm, Thur–Fri from
1 pm, Sat–Sun from 12 pm
Credit cards..Accepted
Type...Pub
Recommended for...............................Unexpected

"A tiny town bar with an awesome Belgian selection, tasty food, and lovely staff."—Aidy Fenwick

SUNFLOWER PUBLIC HOUSE

65 Union Street
Belfast
County Antrim & County Down BT1 2JG
Northern Ireland
+44 2890232474
www.sunflowerbelfast.com

Recommended by
Rick LeVert

Opening hours..........Mon–Sat from 12 pm, Sun from 5 pm
Credit cards..Accepted
Type...Pub
Recommended for.........................Worth the travel

DONEGAL AIRPORT

Carrickfinn
Kincasslagh
County Donegal F94 X2RH, Republic of Ireland
+353 749548284
www.donegalairport.ie

Recommended by
Rick LeVert

Opening hours...Variable
Credit cards...........................Accepted but not Amex
Type...Bar and retail
Recommended for...............................Unexpected

"A stunningly beautiful location and nice to be able to drink a good beer in the middle of nowhere."—Rick LeVert

THE TAP ROOM AT RATHMULLAN HOUSE

Recommended by
Rick LeVert

Rathmullan Terrace, Kinnegar
Rathmullan
County Donegal F92 YA0F, Republic of Ireland
+353 749158188
www.rathmullanhouse.com/the-tap-room

Opening hours..Variable
Credit cards...Accepted
Type...Bar and restaurant
Recommended for..............................Beer & food

"Superb wood-fired pizzas and good beer with a very pleasant atmosphere."—Rick LeVert

THE BREW DOCK

Recommended by
Jonathan Boyce

1 Amiens Street
Dublin 1
County Dublin, Republic of Ireland
+353 18881842
www.galwaybaybrewery.com/brewdock

Opening hours....................Open 7 days from 12 pm
Credit cards.........................Accepted but not Amex
Type..Pub
Recommended for...........................Local favorite

URBAN BREWING

Recommended by
Leo E. Vasileiou

Vault C, CHQ Building
Custom House Quay
Dublin 1
County Dublin, Republic of Ireland
+353 15685989
www.urbanbrewing.ie

Opening hours....................Open 7 days from 12 pm
Credit cards...Accepted
Type........................Microbrewery and beer garden
Recommended for.............................Beer garden

ALFIE BYRNE'S BY GALWAY BAY BREWERY

Recommended by
Jehad Hatu

Earlsfort Terrace
Dublin 2
County Dublin, Republic of Ireland
+353 16028976
www.galwaybaybrewery.com/alfiebyrnes

Opening hours....................Open 7 days from 12 pm
Credit cards...Accepted
Type..Bar
Recommended for...............................Unexpected

"We stayed in the Conrad Hotel, and my mother-in-law said she saw a beer bar downstairs. It turned out to be a Galway Bay Brewery bar with some amazing beers on tap."
—Jehad Hatu

THE BERNARD SHAW

Recommended by
Rick LeVert

11–12 South Richmond Street
Dublin 2
County Dublin, Republic of Ireland
+353 19060218
www.thebernardshaw.com

Opening hours...................Open 7 days from 12 pm
Credit cards...Accepted
Type...Beer garden
Recommended for...........................Wish I'd opened

THE BULL AND CASTLE

Recommended by
Leo E. Vasileiou

5–7 Lord Edward Street
Dublin 2
County Dublin, Republic of Ireland
+353 14751122
www.fxbuckley.ie/bull-castle-bar

Opening hours.......Mon–Sat from 12:30 pm, Sun from 12 pm
Credit cards.........................Accepted but not Amex
Type...Restaurant
Recommended for...............................Unexpected

PORTERHOUSE CENTRAL

Recommended by
Francisco Oyarce

45 Nassau Street
Dublin 2
County Dublin, Republic of Ireland
+353 16797539
www.theporterhouse.ie

Opening hours....................Open 7 days from 11 am
Credit cards...Accepted
Type...Brewery and bar
Recommended for...........................Worth the travel

L. MULLIGAN GROCER

Recommended by
Simon Broderick,
John Duffy

18 Stoneybatter
Dublin 7
County Dublin, Republic of Ireland
+353 016709889
www.lmulligangrocer1.weebly.com

Opening hours.............................Mon–Fri from 4 pm,
Sat–Sun from 12:30 pm
Credit cards.........................Accepted but not Amex
Type..Pub
Recommended for..............................Beer & food

57 THE HEADLINE

Recommended by
John Duffy

56–57 Clanbrassil Street Lower
Dublin 8
County Dublin, Republic of Ireland
+353 015320279
www.57theheadline.com

Opening hours...Mon from 4 pm,
Tue–Sat from 3 pm, Sun from 1 pm
Credit cards...Accepted
Type...Restaurant
Recommended for...Local favorite

"Consistently an excellent range of beers, specializing in
new Irish releases."—John Duffy

THE SALT HOUSE

Recommended by
Simon Broderick,
Danny Hamilton

Raven Terrace
Galway
County Galway H91 D9Y2, Republic of Ireland
+353 091441550
www.galwaybaybrewery.com/salthouse

Opening hours...................................Mon–Thur from 3 pm,
Fri–Sun from 1 pm
Credit cards...Accepted
Type...Pub
Recommended for...Wish I'd opened

"This pub is the jewel in the crown of the Galway Bay
Brewery bars. It's cozy and has a great selection of beers
and a knowledgeable staff."—Simon Broderick

THE ROOST

Recommended by
Trevor Wirtanen

Main Street
Maynooth
County Kildare W23 E7T3, Republic of Ireland
+353 16289843

Opening hours.........Mon–Sat from 11 am, Sun from 12 pm
Credit cards...Accepted
Type...Pub and restaurant
Recommended for...Wish I'd opened

"Stay up front: a dimly-lit pub where you can go
through pints of Guinness while sitting by a fireplace or
watching football. The back is more modern and
restaurary."—Trevor Wirtanen

BREWERY CORNER

Recommended by
Leo E. Vasileiou

29 Parliament Street
Kilkenny
County Kilkenny R95 PV44, Republic of Ireland
+353 567805081
www.carlowbrewing.com

Opening hours...................................Open 7 days from 1 pm
Credit cards...Accepted but not Amex
Type...Pub
Recommended for...Local favorite

"A fantastic beer selection, an intimate setting, and live local
bands."—Leo E. Vasileiou

SEAN'S BAR

Recommended by
Simon Broderick

13 Main Street
Athlone
County Westmeath N37 V2C4, Republic of Ireland
+353 906492358
www.seansbar.ie

Opening hours...................................Mon–Sat from 10:30 am,
Sun from 12:30 pm
Credit cards...Accepted
Type...Beer garden and pub
Recommended for...Beer garden

"The beer garden is a lovely place to have a drink on a sunny
afternoon, and you can look out at the River Shannon. The
place is steeped in history, and it's in the 2004 *Guinness World
Records* as the oldest pub in Ireland."—Simon Broderick

SIMON LAMBERT & SONS

Recommended by
Simon Broderick

37 South Main Street
Wexford
County Wexford Y35 P772, Republic of Ireland
+353 539180041
www.simonlambertandsons.ie

Opening hours.........Mon–Sat from 9:30 am, Sun from 6 pm
Credit cards...Accepted but not Amex
Type...Pub
Recommended for...Local favorite

"This place serves their own amazing beer and a selection
of the best Irish craft beers. The bar has no frills, but the
atmosphere is great, thanks to the warm and welcoming
team who work there."—Simon Broderick

"THE BAR'S TAP LIST IS VARIED AND CONSTANTLY CHANGING. THE LINEUP IS ALWAYS ONE OF THE BEST IN LONDON."

JONATHAN BOYCE P.146

"A GREAT COMMUNITY PUB WITH A FANTASTIC RANGE OF BEERS."

JAMES CUTHBERTSON P.148

LONDON

"A CHAMPION OF GREAT BEER."

TOBY COOPER P.147

"A LITTLE HIDDEN GEM OVERLOOKING THE THAMES."

BRUNO AQUINO P.146

"A FANTASTIC SELECTION."

ZACH MACK P.149

LONDON

SCALE

0   465   930   1405
yd.

1. BEAVERTOWN BREWERY TAP ROOM (P.150)
2. WILD CARD BREWERY (P.150)
3. THE CHEQUERS (P.150)
4. RED LION & SUN (P.148)
5. THE DUKE'S HEAD (P.148)
6. THE FALTERING FULLBACK (P.147)
7. SOUTHAMPTON ARMS (P.148)
8. THE MERMAID CLAPTON (P.149)
9. HOWLING HOPS BREWERY AND TANK BAR (P.147)
10. CRATE BREWERY & PIZZERIA (P.147)
11. THE CRAFT BEER CO. ISLINGTON (P.148)
12. THE WENLOCK ARMS (P.148)
13. MOTHER KELLY'S (P.146)
14. EUSTON TAP (P.148)
15. BLOOMSBURY LANES (P.146)
16. CRAFT BEER CO (P.147)
17. ST. JOHN BAR AND RESTAURANT (P.147)
18. THE WATER POET (P.150)
19. THE ELGIN (P.149)
20. MEATLIQUOR (P.149)
21. PITT CUE (P.146)
22. YE OLDE CHESHIRE CHEESE (P.146)
23. THE HARP (P.147)
24. THE HOP LOCKER (P.149)
25. THE RAKE (P.149)
26. BOROUGH MARKET (P.150)
27. THE MAYFLOWER PUB (P.150)
28. CASK PUB & KITCHEN (P.150)
29. THE CITY BARGE (P.146)
30. BRITISH AIRWAYS (P.148)
31. THE WHITE HORSE (P.147)
32. STORMBIRD (P.146)
33. CROWN AND ANCHOR (P.146)
34. BUSSEY BEER GARDEN (P.150)
35. THE BEER SHOP LONDON (P.149)

MOTHER KELLY'S

251 Paradise Row
Bethnal Green
London E2 9LE, England
+44 2070121244
www.motherkellys.co.uk

Recommended by
Jonathan Boyce,
Jack Cregan,
Mikko Mäkelä,
Christopher Williams

Opening hours..........Mon from 4 pm, Tue–Sun from 12 pm
Credit cards..Accepted
Type..Bar and retail
Recommended for...Worth the travel

"It's in a great little spot in an old railway arch with outdoor seating and a fantastic atmosphere. It also has a street-food pop-up in the outdoor area on the weekends."
—Christopher Williams

"The bar's tap list is varied and constantly changing. The lineup is always one of the best in London."
—Jonathan Boyce

BLOOMSBURY LANES

Bedford Way
Basement of Tavistock Hotel
Bloomsbury
London WC1H 9EU, England
+44 2071831979
www.bloomsburybowling.com

Recommended by
Tony Barron

Opening hours....................................Open 7 days from 12 pm
Credit cards..Accepted
Type...Bar
Recommended for..Unexpected

CROWN AND ANCHOR

246 Brixton Road
Brixton
London SW9 6AQ, England
+44 2077370060
www.crownandanchorbrixton.co.uk

Recommended by
Thomas Palmer

Opening hours...Mon–Fri from 5 pm,
Sat–Sun from 12 pm
Credit cards............................Accepted but not Amex
Type...Pub
Recommended for..Local favorite

"A warm interior and large outdoor seating area that backs onto a park. They have a great staff and lots of local beer on tap."—Thomas Palmer

STORMBIRD

25 Camberwell Church Street
Camberwell
London SE5 8TR, England
+44 2077084460
www.thestormbirdpub.co.uk

Recommended by
Mario Canestrelli

Opening hours....................................Mon–Fri from 4 pm,
Sat–Sun from 12 pm
Credit cards..Accepted
Type...Pub
Recommended for..Local favorite

THE CITY BARGE

27 Strand-on-the-Green
Chiswick
London W4 3PH, England
+44 2089942148
www.citybargechiswick.com

Recommended by
Bruno Aquino

Opening hours....................................Mon–Fri from 12 pm,
Sat–Sun from 10 am
Credit cards..Accepted
Type....................Beer garden, pub, and restaurant
Recommended for.......................................Beer garden

"A little hidden gem overlooking the Thames."
—Bruno Aquino

PITT CUE

1 The Avenue
Devonshire Square
City of London
London EC2M 4YP, England
+44 2073247770
www.pittcue.co.uk

Recommended by
Jaega Wise

Opening hours...........Mon–Fri from 12 pm, Sat from 6 pm
Credit cards..Accepted
Type...Restaurant and bar
Recommended for....................................Beer & food

YE OLDE CHESHIRE CHEESE

145 Fleet Street
City of London
London EC4A 2BU, England
+44 2073536170

Recommended by
Charles Finkel

Opening hours...........Mon–Fri from 11 am, Sat from 12 pm
Credit cards..Accepted
Type...Pub
Recommended for..................................Wish I'd opened

CRAFT BEER CO.

82 Leather Lane
Clerkenwell
London EC1N 7TR, England
+44 2074077049
www.thecraftbeerco.com/clerkenwell

Recommended by
James Cuthbertson

Opening hours............................Mon–Sat from 12 pm
Credit cards...Accepted
Type..Pub
Recommended for.............................Wish I'd opened

"An amazing beer list and knowledgeable staff. They have a great cask-beer lineup."—James Cuthbertson

ST. JOHN BAR AND RESTAURANT

26 Saint John Street
Clerkenwell
London EC1M 4AY, England
+ 44 2072510848
www.stjohnrestaurant.com

Recommended by
Tom Hanson

Opening hours..........Mon–Sat from 9 am, Sun from 10 am
Credit cards...Accepted
Type..Bar and restaurant
Recommended for...................................Beer & food

THE HARP

47 Chandos Place
Covent Garden
London WC2N 4HS, England
+44 2078360291
www.harpcoventgarden.com

Recommended by
Toby Cooper

Opening hours............................Mon–Sat from 10:30 am,
Sun from 12 pm
Credit cards...Accepted
Type..Pub
Recommended for.............................Wish I'd opened

"A champion of great beer."—Toby Cooper

THE FALTERING FULLBACK

19 Perth Road
Finsbury Park
London N4 3HB, England
+44 2072725834
www.thefullback.co.uk

Recommended by
Rob Bright

Opening hours...........................Open 7 days from 12 pm
Credit cards...Accepted
Type..Pub and beer garden
Recommended for...................................Beer garden

"A huge, sprawling, multilevel beer garden with plenty of benches and greenery. A fantastic all-around experience." —Rob Bright

THE WHITE HORSE

1–3 Parsons Green
Fulham
London SW6 4UL, England
+44 2077362115
www.whitehorsesw6.com

Recommended by
Paul Anspach,
Olli Majanen

Opening hours.............................Open 7 days from 9:30 am
Credit cards...Accepted
Type...Pub and restaurant
Recommended for...................................Beer & food

"The pioneer of wide-range beer bars. Well-kept cask ales are also available. Their annual Old Ale Festival is exceptional."—Olli Majanen

CRATE BREWERY & PIZZERIA

Unit 7, Queen's Yard
The White Building
Hackney Wick
London E9 5EN, England
+44 2085333331
www.cratebrewery.com

Recommended by
Toby Cooper

Opening hours.............................Open 7 days from 12 pm
Credit cards..........................Accepted but not Amex
Type..........................Brewery and beer garden
Recommended for...................................Beer garden

HOWLING HOPS BREWERY AND TANK BAR

Unit 9A, Queen's Yard
White Post Lane
Hackney Wick
London E9 5EN, England
+44 2035838262
www.howlinghops.co.uk

Recommended by
Aitor Labrador

Opening hours.............................Open 7 days from 12 pm
Credit cards..........................Accepted but not Amex
Type..Beer garden
Recommended for.............................Wish I'd opened

"The UK's first dedicated tank bar and smokehouse, at Howling Hops brewery. The freshest beer you can get plus delicious food."—Aitor Labrador

THE DUKE'S HEAD

16 Highgate High Street
Highgate
London N6 5JG, England
+44 2083411310
www.thedukesheadhighgate.co.uk

Recommended by
Paul Anspach

Opening hours	Open 7 days from 12 pm
Credit cards	Accepted
Type	Pub
Recommended for	Wish I'd opened

"I haven't had a better cask beer than in the Duke's Head for a long time."—Paul Anspach

RED LION & SUN

25 North Road
Highgate
London N6 4BE, England
+44 2083401780
www.theredlionandsun.com

Recommended by
James Cuthbertson

Opening hours	Open 7 days from 12 pm
Credit cards	Accepted
Type	Beer garden, pub, and restaurant
Recommended for	Beer garden

"The best pub food in London and an amazing Sunday roast. They have a good selection of cans and bottles."
—James Cuthbertson

BRITISH AIRWAYS

Longford
Hillingdon
London TW6, England
+44 1914907901
www.britishairways.com

Recommended by
Arnau Rovira

Opening hours	Variable
Credit cards	Accepted
Type	Bar
Recommended for	Unexpected

"I was glad to find good beer during ten-hour flights from London to Singapore."—Arnau Rovira

THE CRAFT BEER CO. ISLINGTON

55 White Lion Street
Islington
London N1 9PP, England
+44 2078349988
www.thecraftbeerco.com

Recommended by
Antonis Moustakas

Opening hours	Mon–Thur from 4 pm, Fri–Sat from 12 pm, Sun from 2 pm
Credit cards	Accepted
Type	Pub
Recommended for	Wish I'd opened

THE WENLOCK ARMS

26 Wenlock Road
Islington
London N1 7TA, England
+44 2076083406
www.wenlockarms.com

Recommended by
James Cuthbertson,
Chuwy Phillips

Opening hours	Mon from 3 pm, Tue–Sun from 12 pm
Credit cards	Accepted
Type	Pub
Recommended for	Worth the travel

"A great community pub with a fantastic range of beers."
—James Cuthbertson

SOUTHAMPTON ARMS

139 Highgate Road
Kentish Town
London NW5 1LE, England
www.thesouthamptonarms.co.uk

Recommended by
Jen Ferguson

Opening hours	Open 7 days from 12 pm
Credit cards	Not accepted
Type	Beer garden and pub
Recommended for	Beer garden

EUSTON TAP

190 Euston Road
Kings Cross
London NW1 2EF, England
+44 2031378837
www.eustontap.com

Recommended by
Toby Cooper,
Paraskevas Giagmouroglou,
Zach Mack,
Thomas Palmer,
James Tai

Opening hours	Open 7 days from 12 pm
Credit cards	Accepted
Type	Bar
Recommended for	Wish I'd opened

"Housed in a tiny former station building, the Euston Tap probably has the highest beer selection per square meter of floor space in all the world. The building and size are unique, as is the physical setup of a copper-backed tap wall, flanked by single coolers of bottled and canned beer flanking the sides, effectively taking up the entire back wall of the space."—James Tai

"A fantastic selection in one of the most unique settings imaginable."—Zach Mack

---

THE HOP LOCKER

Southbank Centre Market
Belvedere Road
Lambeth
London SE1 8XX, England

Recommended by
Daniel Goh

Opening hours	Sun–Fri from 12 pm, Sat from 11 am
Credit cards	Accepted
Type	Bar
Recommended for	Unexpected

"A pop-up craft-beer bar in an outdoor food market."
—Daniel Goh

THE RAKE

14A Winchester Walk
London Bridge
London SE1 9AG, England
+44 2074070557
www.utobeer.co.uk

Recommended by
Dave Grant,
Stu McKinlay

Opening hours	Sun–Thur from 12 pm, Fri from 11 am, Sat from 10 am
Credit cards	Accepted
Type	Bar
Recommended for	Unexpected

THE MERMAID CLAPTON

181 Clarence Road
Lower Clapton
London E5 8EE, England
+44 2085339677
www.themermaidclapton.com

Recommended by
James Goulding

Opening hours	Open 7 days from 12 pm
Credit cards	Accepted
Type	Pub
Recommended for	Local favorite

MEATLIQUOR

74 Welbeck Street
Marylebone
London W1G 0BA, England
+44 2072244239
www.meatliquor.com

Recommended by
Erin Lowder

Opening hours	Sun–Thur from 12 pm, Fri–Sat from 11 am
Credit cards	Accepted
Type	Restaurant
Recommended for	Unexpected

"An insanely awesome atmosphere."—Erin Lowder

THE ELGIN

96 Ladbroke Grove
Notting Hill
London W11 1PY, England
+44 2072295663
www.theelginnottinghill.co.uk

Recommended by
James Goulding

Opening hours	Mon–Sat from 11 am, Sun from 12 pm
Credit cards	Accepted
Type	Pub
Recommended for	Beer & food

"I'm always blown away by the beer dinners here."
—James Goulding

THE BEER SHOP LONDON

40 Nunhead Green
Nunhead
London SE15 3QF, England
+44 2077325555
www.thebeershoplondon.co.uk

Recommended by
Paul Anspach

Opening hours	Tue–Fri from 4 pm, Sat–Sun from 12 pm
Credit cards	Accepted
Type	Bar and retail
Recommended for	Local favorite

"I love how honest this bar is. Set up by a local couple who created a space that's both a great neighborhood boozer and an up-to-date, relevant beer bar. A very comfortable place to sit and drink for hours in a quieter part of town."
—Paul Anspach

BUSSEY BEER GARDEN
Recommended by
Antonis Moustakas

133 Copeland Road
Peckham
London SE15 3SN, England
+44 2086707054
www.busseybeergarden.com

Opening hours................................Fri from 4 pm,
Sat–Sun from 12 pm (summer)
Credit cards..................................Accepted
Type...Beer garden
Recommended for.............................Beer garden

CASK PUB & KITCHEN
Recommended by
Bruno Aquino

6 Charlwood Street
Pimlico
London SW1V 2EE, England
+44 2076307225
www.caskpubandkitchen.com

Opening hours...................Open 7 days from 12 pm
Credit cards..................................Accepted
Type..Pub
Recommended for.......................Worth the travel

THE MAYFLOWER PUB
Recommended by
Paul Anspach,
Bruno Aquino

117 Rotherhithe Street
Rotherhithe
London SE16 4NF, England
+44 2072374088
www.mayflowerpub.co.uk

Opening hours.........Mon–Sat from 11 am, Sun from 12 pm
Credit cards..................................Accepted
Type.............................Beer garden and pub
Recommended for.............................Beer garden

BOROUGH MARKET
Recommended by
Flaviu Adrian Odorhean

8 Southwark Street
Southwark
London SE1 1TL, England
+44 2074071002
www.boroughmarket.org.uk

Opening hours............Mon–Fri from 10 am, Sat from 8 am
Credit cards..............................Not accepted
Type...Retail
Recommended for............................Unexpected

THE WATER POET
Recommended by
Shaheen Budhrani

9-11 Folgate Street
Spitalfields
London E1 6BX, England
+44 2074260495
www.waterpoet.co.uk

Opening hours...........................Mon–Fri from 11 am,
Sat–Sun from 12 pm
Credit cards..................................Accepted
Type.............................Beer garden and pub
Recommended for.............................Beer garden

BEAVERTOWN BREWERY TAP ROOM
Unit 17–18, Lockwood Industrial Park   Recommended by
Mill Mead Road
Logan Plant
Tottenham Hale
London N17 9QP, England
+44 2085259884
www.beavertownbrewery.co.uk

Opening hours.....................Open Sat from 2 pm
Credit cards..................................Accepted
Type...Brewery
Recommended for.........................Local favorite

THE CHEQUERS
Recommended by
Jaega Wise

145 High Street
Walthamstow
London E17 7BX, England
+44 2085036407
www.chequerse17.com

Opening hours...........................Mon–Fri from 5 pm,
Sat–Sun from 12 pm
Credit cards..................................Accepted
Type..Pub
Recommended for.........................Local favorite

WILD CARD BREWERY
Recommended by
Jaega Wise

Unit 7, Ravenswood Industrial Estate
Shernhall Street
Walthamstow
London E17 9HQ, England
+44 2089355560
www.wildcardbrewery.co.uk

Opening hours.............Fri from 5 pm, Sat–Sun from 12 pm
Credit cards..................................Accepted
Type.......................Beer garden, bar, and brewery
Recommended for.............................Beer garden

"IT'S ONE OF THE BEST CRAFT BEER BREWERIES IN THE NETHERLANDS."

NICK VAN BEUSEKOM P.155

"I LOVE THIS PLACE. IT'S A BREWPUB WITH THIRTY TAPS, INCLUDING GREAT DUTCH, EUROPEAN, AND INTERNATIONAL CRAFT BEERS."

JACOBO PÉREZ LLISO P.156

THE NETHERLANDS

"IT'S A BREWPUB IN A CHURCH IN THE CENTER OF THE CITY. A ONE-OF-A-KIND SETTING FOR CRAFT BEER AND A BEAUTIFUL VENUE."

PYRY HURULA P.155

"AN AMAZING SPOT: TREES, LONG TABLES, MUSIC, GREAT, BEER AND FOOD." DIEGO CASTRO P.154

THE NETHERLANDS

N

SCALE

0   25   50
mi.

♦NORTH HOLLAND P.155

♦AMSTERDAM PP.160−165

♦UTRECHT PP.157-158

♦GELDERLAND P.154

♦SOUTH HOLLAND PP.155−157

♦NORTH BRABANT PP.154−155

♦LIMBURG P.154

DE NIEUWE WINKEL

Hertogstraat 71
Nijmegen
Gelderland 6511 RW, The Netherlands
+31 243225093
www.denieuwewinkel.com

Recommended by
Kick van Hout

Opening hours................................Tue–Sat from 5:30 pm
Credit cards...Accepted
Type...Restaurant
Recommended for...Beer & food

STOOM BEER & FOOD

Waalbandijk 14D
Nijmegen
Gelderland 6541 AJ, The Netherlands
+31 242020010
www.stoomnijmegen.com

Recommended by
Kick van Hout

Opening hours...................................Tue–Thur from 4 pm,
Fri–Sun from 2 pm
Credit cards...Not accepted
Type..Restaurant and bar
Recommended for.......................................Local favorite

DE VLAAMSCHE REUS

Hoogstraat 21
Wageningen
Gelderland 6701 BL, The Netherlands
+31 317412834
www.vlaamschereus.nl

Recommended by
Antonis Moustakas

Opening hours....................................Tue–Fri from 3 pm,
Sat–Sun from 2pm
Credit cards...Accepted
Type..Bar
Recommended for..................................Worth the travel

CAFÉ FRAPE

Het Bat 7
Maastricht
Limburg 6211 EX, The Netherlands
+31 648658918

Recommended by
Mike Amidei

Opening hours...................Mon, Wed, Fri–Sat from 10 am,
Thur from 3 pm, Sun from 11 am
Type..Pub
Recommended for.......................................Local favorite

CAFÉ 'T POTHUISKE

Het Bat 1
Maastricht
Limburg 6211 EX, The Netherlands
+31 433216002
www.pothuiske.nl

Recommended by
Mike Amidei

Opening hours...................................Tue–Thur from 11 am,
Fri–Sun from 10 am
Type..Pub
Recommended for...Beer & food

PROEFLOKAAL GOESTING

Henseniusplein 13
Venray
Limburg 5801 BB, The Netherlands
+31 478855621
www.proeflokaalgoesting.nl

Recommended by
Kick van Hout

Opening hours...................................Mon–Thur from 4 pm,
Fri–Sun from 2 pm
Credit cards...Accepted
Type..Bar
Recommended for..................................Worth the travel

LA TRAPPE TRAPPIST

Eindhovenseweg 3
Berkel-Enschot
North Brabant 5056 RP, The Netherlands
+31 135358147
www.latrappetrappist.com

Recommended by
Diego Castro

Opening hours.........Mon–Sat from 11 am, Sun from 12 pm
Credit cards...Accepted
Type...Brewery and beer garden
Recommended for...Beer garden

"An amazing spot: trees, long tables, music, great beer, and food, all in front of one of the most important Abbeys in the world."—Diego Castro

BIERRECLAME MUSEUM

Haagweg 375
Breda
North Brabant 4813 XC, The Netherlands
+31 765220975
www.bierreclamemuseum.nl

Recommended by
Linda van Loon

Opening hours...Sun from 11 am
Credit cards...Not accepted
Type..Beer garden
Recommended for...Beer garden

"It's a very small and packed museum with a pub and a beer garden. The menu is very traditional but very good. But it's the setting that makes it an awesome place. It's a combination of an American barn with beer memorabilia. It's dark and cozy, and there is country music."
—Linda van Loon

CAFÉ RESTAURANT BROUWERIJ DE BEYERD

Boschstraat 26   Recommended by
Breda   Bruno Aquino
North Brabant 4811 GH, The Netherlands
+31 765214265
www.beyerd.nl

Opening hours	Sun–Tue from 10 am, Thur-Fri from 10 am, Sat from 12 pm
Credit cards	Accepted
Type	Bar and restaurant
Recommended for	Wish I'd opened

"A classic pub where everybody knows your name. A good range of styles to taste and fantastic food. They make you feel at home."—Bruno Aquino

JOPENKERK HAARLEM

Gedempte Voldersgracht 2   Recommended by
Haarlem   Pyry Hurula
North Holland 2011 WD, The Netherlands
+31 235334114
www.jopenkerk.nl

Opening hours	Open 7 days from 10 am
Credit cards	Accepted
Type	Brewpub
Recommended for	Wish I'd opened

"It's a brewpub in a church in the center of the city. A one-of-a-kind setting for craft beer and a beautiful venue."
—Pyry Hurula

UILTJE BAR

Zijlstraat 18   Recommended by
Haarlem   Nick van Beusekom
North Holland 2011 TN, The Netherlands
+31 238446227
www.uiltjecraftbeer.com

Opening hours	Mon–Fri from 4 pm, Sat–Sun from 2 pm
Credit cards	Accepted
Type	Pub
Recommended for	Worth the travel

"They have thirty taps, good service, great food, and a wide beer selection from all over the world. They love creations from microbreweries. The love for beer is all over this place."—Nick van Beusekom

UILTJE BREWERY & TAPROOM

Bingerweg 25   Recommended by
Haarlem   Nick van Beusekom
North Holland 2031 AZ, The Netherlands
+31 238446395
www.uiltjecraftbeer.com

Opening hours	Thur–Sun from 12 pm
Credit cards	Accepted
Type	Brewery and pub
Recommended for	Beer garden

"They have lots of events and a great food selection. It's one of the best craft-beer breweries in The Netherlands."
—Nick van Beusekom

BROUWCAFÉ DE MOLEN

Overtocht 43   Recommended by
Bodegraven   Anton Pligin
South Holland 2411 BT, The Netherlands
+31 172610848
www.brouwerijdemolen.nl

Opening hours	Wed–Sun from 12 pm
Credit cards	Accepted
Type	Brewery
Recommended for	Beer garden

"A great selection of local beer, wonderful views, and a relaxing location near the mill. The beer is really great. It's a must for beer lovers."—Anton Pligin

CAFÉ HET KLOOSTER

Vlamingstraat 2   Recommended by
Delft   Jeppe Jarnit-Bjergsø
South Holland 2611 KW, The Netherlands
+31 645694928

Opening hours	Mon–Fri from 4 pm, Sat–Sun from 2 pm
Credit cards	Not accepted
Type	Bar
Recommended for	Local favorite

BELGISCH BIERCAFÉ BOUDEWIJN

Nieuwe Binnenweg 53 A–B
Rotterdam
South Holland 3014 GD, The Netherlands
+31 104363562
www.bbcboudewijn.nl

Recommended by
Jeppe Jarnit-Bjergsø

Opening hours	Open 7 days from 12 pm
Credit cards	Accepted but not Amex
Type	Beer garden and restaurant
Recommended for	Local favorite

CIDERCIDER

Veerlaan 19D
Rotterdam
South Holland 3072 AN, The Netherlands
+31 618054512
www.cidercider.nl

Recommended by
Mike Amidei

Opening hours	Wed–Fri, Sun from 12 pm, Sat from 10 am
Type	Bar and retail
Recommended for	Wish I'd opened

FENIX FOOD FACTORY

Veerlaan 19D
Rotterdam
South Holland 3072 AB, The Netherlands
+31 646136799
www.fenixfoodfactory.nl

Recommended by
Edgars Melnis

Opening hours	Tue–Sat from 10 am, Sun from 12 pm
Credit cards	Accepted
Type	Pub
Recommended for	Beer & food

KAAPSE BROUWERS

Veerlaan 19-D
Rotterdam
South Holland 3072 AN, The Netherlands
+31 102180853
www.kaapsebrouwers.nl

Recommended by
Jacobo Pérez Lliso

Opening hours	Tue–Sun from 12 pm
Credit cards	Not accepted
Type	Brewpub
Recommended for	Worth the travel

"I love this place. It's a brewpub with thirty taps, including great Dutch, European, and international craft beers."
—Jacobo Pérez Lliso

KAAPSE MARIA

Mauritsweg 52
Rotterdam
South Holland 3012 JW
The Netherlands
+31 108423978
www.kaapsemaria.nl

Recommended by
Stephen Andrews,
Liubomir Chonos,
Razvan Costache

Opening hours	Wed–Fri from 3 pm, Sat–Sun from 12 pm
Credit cards	Accepted
Type	Bar and restaurant
Recommended for	Beer & food

"Maria is a special place, in the most incredible historic building. They have a well-curated list that always includes sparkling water, sake, and world-class beers from all over the world. The place is full of handmade wooden accents done by a local woodworker."—Stephen Andrews

SIJF

Oude Binnenweg 115
Rotterdam
South Holland 3012 JB, The Netherlands
+31 104332610
www.sijf.nl

Recommended by
Jeppe Jarnit-Bjergsø

Opening hours	Open 7 days from 10 am
Credit cards	Accepted
Type	Restaurant and bar
Recommended for	Local favorite

BIERSPECIAAL CAFÉ "DE PAAS"

Dunne Bierkade 16A
The Hague
South Holland 2512 BC, The Netherlands
+31 703600019
www.depaas.nl

Recommended by
Mike Amidei

Opening hours	Mon–Fri from 4 pm, Sat–Sun from 3 pm
Credit cards	Accepted
Type	Beer garden and pub
Recommended for	Beer garden

BRODY'S AMERICAN TAPHOUSE

Korte Molenstraat 2
The Hague
South Holland 2513 BM, The Netherlands
+31 702155827
www.brodys.nl

Recommended by
Mike Amidei

Opening hours	Tue–Thur from 4 pm, Sat–Sun from 2 pm
Credit cards	Accepted
Type	Pub
Recommended for	Local favorite

CAFÉ DE LA GARE

Nieuwe Schoolstraat 13A
The Hague
South Holland 2514 HT, The Netherlands
+31 707446255
www.delagare.nl

Recommended by
Mike Amidei

Opening hours	Tue–Thur from 4:30 pm, Fri–Sun from 4 pm
Credit cards	Not accepted
Type	Beer garden and pub
Recommended for	Beer garden

THE FIDDLER

Riviervismarkt 1
The Hague
South Holland 2513AM, The Netherlands
+31 703651955
www.fiddler.nl

Recommended by
Jeppe Jarnit-Bjergsø

Opening hours	Mon from 5 pm, Tue–Sun from 12 pm
Credit cards	Accepted
Type	Brewpub
Recommended for	Beer & food

KOMPAAN BEER BAR

Saturnusstraat 55
The Hague
South Holland 2516 AE, The Netherlands
+31 707622494
www.kompaanbier.nl/beer-bar

Recommended by
Jeppe Jarnit-Bjergsø

Opening hours	Thur–Fri from 4 pm, Sat–Sun from 2 pm
Credit cards	Accepted
Type	Brewery and bar
Recommended for	Local favorite

MURPHY'S LAW

Doctor Kuyperstraat 7
The Hague
South Holland 2514 BA, The Netherlands
+31 704272507
www.murphysjazz.nl

Recommended by
Jeppe Jarnit-Bjergsø

Opening hours	Mon–Sat from 4 pm
Credit cards	Accepted
Type	Pub
Recommended for	Local favorite

BREWPUB DE KROMME HARING

Europalaan 2C
Utrecht 3526 KS, The Netherlands
+31 616970399
www.dekrommeharing.nl

Recommended by
Mike Amidei

Opening hours	Wed–Fri from 4 pm, Sat–Sun from 2 pm
Credit cards	Accepted
Type	Brewpub
Recommended for	Local favorite

BROUWERIJ MAXIMUS

Pratumplaats 2A
Utrecht 3454 NA, The Netherlands
+31 307370800
www.brouwerijmaximus.nl

Recommended by
Jeppe Jarnit-Bjergsø

Opening hours	Tue–Thur from 4 pm, Fri–Sat from 2 pm, Sun from 1 pm
Credit cards	Not accepted
Type	Brewery and beer garden
Recommended for	Beer & food

CAFÉ DERAT

Lange Smeestraat 37
Utrecht 3511 PT, The Netherlands
+31 302319513
www.cafederat.nl

Recommended by
Linda van Loon

Opening hours.....................................Open 7 days from 2 pm
Credit cards..Not accepted
Type...Bar
Recommended for....................................Local favorite

"A cozy, traditional bar with a great, quiet atmosphere and two cats who love attention. The beer prices and the selection are very good. The bartenders are very friendly and know when to start a conversation and when to hold back. Not a modern hipster-style bar but a nice 70s-era atmosphere with a lot of wood."—Linda van Loon

CAFÉ JAN PRIMUS

Jan van Scorelstraat 27–31
Utrecht 3583 CJ, The Netherlands
+31 302514572

Recommended by
Mike Amidei

Opening hours.................................Open 7 days from 3 pm
Credit cards...Accepted
Type...Pub
Recommended for....................................Local favorite

DE DRIE DORSTIGE HERTEN

Lange Nieuwstraat 47
Utrecht 3512 PC, The Netherlands
+31 308884430
www.dedriedorstigeherten.nl

Recommended by
Mike Amidei

Opening hours.................................Wed–Sun from 3 pm
Type...Bar
Recommended for.................................Wish I'd opened

KAFÉ BELGIË

Oudegracht 196
Utrecht 3511 NR, The Netherlands
+31 302312666
www.kafebelgie.nl

Recommended by
Tom Hanson

Opening hours.....................................Sun–Mon from 1 pm,
Tue–Sat from 11 am
Credit cards...Accepted
Type...Beer garden and bar
Recommended for....................................Beer garden

"Not so much a beer garden as just outdoor seating, but I have really great memories of sitting with my girlfriend next to the canals in Utrecht (my grandparents live there, so we usually visit once a year) and trying to figure out what I should order from their huge beer selection. Loads of great beer and a great setting."—Tom Hanson

> "THE ONLY BAR IN THE NETHERLANDS WITH TRUE CRAFT BEER."
>
> PETER VAN DER AREND P.162

> "FORMER BATHHOUSE TURNED BREWERY UNDER THE NOSE OF A WINDMILL SANDWICHED BETWEEN TWO CANALS."
>
> KEVIN RAUB P.162

AMSTERDAM

> "IN DE WILDEMAN ARE TRULY AMBASSADORS OF GOOD BEER."
>
> AART VAN BERGEN P.163

> "THE PLACE IS BRILLIANT. IT'S AN OLD BUTCHER SHOP WITH A GREAT ATMOSPHERE AND AN UNDERGROUND, HIDDEN LOCATION. PLUS THE BEER IS VERY TASTY!"
>
> RORY MILLER P.165

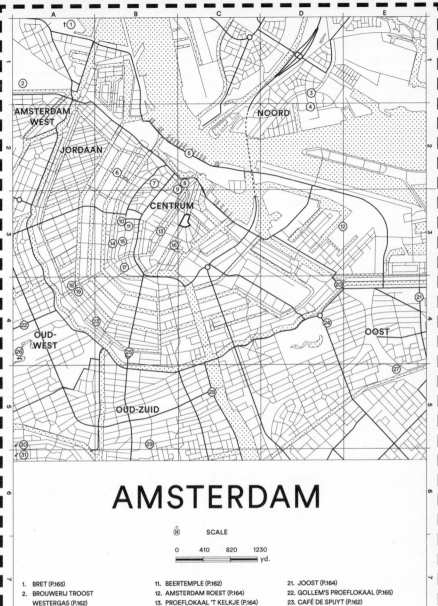

AMSTERDAM

N   SCALE

0   410   820   1230
                        yd.

BROUWERIJ TROOST WESTERGAS

Pazzanistraat 27
Amsterdam-West
Amsterdam 1014 DB, The Netherlands
+31 207371028
www.brouwerijtroost.nl/westergas-amsterdam

Recommended by
Mike Amidei, Peter
van der Arend,
Roberto Orano

Opening hours	Mon–Thur from 4pm, Sat–Sun from 12 pm
Type	Beer garden and brewpub
Recommended for	Beer garden

BEERTEMPLE

Nieuwezijds Voorburgwal 250
Centrum
Amsterdam 1012 RR, The Netherlands
+31 206271427
www.beertemple.nl

Recommended by
Peter van der Arend

Opening hours	Open 7 days from 12 pm
Credit cards	Accepted
Type	Bar and restaurant
Recommended for	Local favorite

"The only bar in The Netherlands with true craft beer."
—Peter van der Arend

BROUWERIJ DE PRAEL

Oudezijds Armsteeg 26
Centrum
Amsterdam 1012 GP, The Netherlands
+31 204084469
www.deprael.nl

Recommended by
Mike Amidei

Opening hours	Open 7 days from 12 pm
Type	Brewery and pub
Recommended for	Local favorite

BROUWERIJ 'T IJ

Funenkade 7
Centrum
Amsterdam 1018 AL, The Netherlands
+31 202619801
www.brouwerijhetij.nl

Recommended by
Ben Love,
Flaviu Adrian
Odorhean,
Kevin Raub

Opening hours	Open 7 days from 2 pm
Credit cards	Accepted
Type	Beer garden and brewery
Recommended for	Beer garden

"Former bathhouse turned brewery under the nose of a
windmill sandwiched between two canals."—Kevin Raub

CAFÉ DE ENGELBEWAARDER

Kloveniersburgwal 59HS
Centrum
Amsterdam 1011 JZ, The Netherlands
+31 206253772
www.cafe-de-engelbewaarder.nl

Recommended by
Mike Amidei

Opening hours	Open 7 days from 10 am
Credit cards	Accepted
Type	Pub and restaurant
Recommended for	Local favorite

CAFÉ DE SPUYT

Korte Leidsedwarsstraat 86
Centrum
Amsterdam 1017 RD, The Netherlands
+31 206248901
www.despuyt.nl

Recommended by
Mike Amidei

Opening hours	Mon–Thur from 4 pm, Fri–Sun from 3 pm
Type	Bar
Recommended for	Local favorite

CAFE GOLLEM RAAMSTEEG

Raamsteeg 4
Centrum
Amsterdam 1012 VZ, The Netherlands
+31 206129444
www.cafegollem.nl

Recommended by
Mike Amidei

Opening hours	Mon–Thur from 4 pm, Fri–Sun from 12 pm
Credit cards	Not accepted
Type	Pub
Recommended for	Wish I'd opened

CANNIBALE ROYALE HANDBOOGSTEEG

Handboogstraat 17a
Centrum
Amsterdam 1012 XM, The Netherlands
+31 202337160
www.cannibaleroyale.nl

Recommended by
Mike Amidei

Opening hours	Open 7 days from 12 pm
Credit cards	Accepted but not Amex
Type	Bar and restaurant
Recommended for	Beer & food

'CAUSE BEER LOVES FOOD

Lange Leidsedwarsstraat 4
Centrum
Amsterdam 1017 NL, The Netherlands
+31 202237562
www.causebeerlovesfood.nl

Recommended by
Aart van Bergen

Opening hours.....................................Open 7 days from 4 pm
Credit cards...Accepted
Type...Pub
Recommended for...Beer & food

DE BIERKONING

Paleisstraat 125
Centrum
Amsterdam 1012 ZL, The Netherlands
+31 206252336
www.bierkoning.nl

Recommended by
Mike Amidei

Opening hours.........Mon–Sat from 11 am, Sun from 12 pm
Type...Retail
Recommended for...Local favorite

DE ZOTTE

Raamstraat 29
Centrum
Amsterdam 1016 XL, The Netherlands
+31 206268694

Recommended by
Jeppe Jarnit-Bjergsø

Opening hours.....................................Open 7 days from 4 pm
Credit cards...Accepted
Type...Pub
Recommended for...Beer & food

HAARBARBAAR

Rosmarijnsteeg 4
Centrum
Amsterdam 1012 RP, The Netherlands
+31 204317683
www.haarbarbaar.nl

Recommended by
Aart van Bergen

Opening hours...Tue–Sat from 11 am
Credit cards...Accepted
Type...Retail
Recommended for...Unexpected

"This barbershop gives you a complimentary bottle of
Loki Golden IPA to accompany your fresh fade."
—Aart van Bergen

HET ELFDE GEBOD

Zeedijk 5
Centrum
Amsterdam 1012 AN, The Netherlands
+31 614630469

Recommended by
Jeppe Jarnit-Bjergsø

Opening hours.................................Mon–Thur from 4 pm,
                                                            Fri–Sun from 2 pm
Type...Bar
Recommended for...................................Worth the travel

IN DE WILDEMAN

Kolksteeg 3
Centrum
Amsterdam 1012 PT
The Netherlands
+31 206382348
www.indewildeman.nl

Recommended by
Aart van Bergen,
Christopher DeWolf,
Lasse Ericsson,
Kick van Hout,
Rick Nelson,
Raphael Rodrigues

Opening hours.......................................Mon–Sat from 12 pm
Credit cards...Accepted
Type...Pub
Recommended for...................................Worth the travel

"An institution in the Amsterdam beer scene. In de
Wildeman are truly ambassadors of good beer."
—Aart van Bergen

LITTLE DÉLIRIUM AMSTERDAM

De Ruyterkade 42A
Centrum
Amsterdam 1012 AA, The Netherlands
+31 203377971
www.littledelirium.nl

Recommended by
Jeppe Jarnit-Bjergsø

Opening hours.....................................Open 7 days from 11 am
Type...Bar
Recommended for...Local favorite

PROEFLOKAAL ARENDSNEST

Herengracht 90
Centrum
Amsterdam 1015 BS, The Netherlands
+31 204212057
www.arendsnest.nl

Recommended by
Flaviu Adrian Odorhean

Opening hours..................................Open 7 days from 12 pm
Credit cards..Accepted but not Amex
Type...Pub
Recommended for...Worth the travel

This place is the best of both worlds. It has that classic pub feeling, but instead of standard pub beer options, they provide a list of the best that Dutch craft beer has to offer. Highly recommended.

PROEFLOKAAL 'T KELKJE

Oudezijds Achterburgwal 164
Centrum
Amsterdam 1012 DW, The Netherlands
+31 625378104
www.kelkje.nl

Recommended by
Jeppe Jarnit-Bjergsø

Opening hours.......................................Tue–Thur from 4 pm,
                                                         Fri–Sun from 3 pm
Type...Pub
Recommended for...Local favorite

TAPROOM

Nieuwe Vijzelstraat 1
Centrum
Amsterdam 1017 HT, The Netherlands
+31 202212343
www.taproom.nl

Recommended by
Mike Amidei

Opening hours.....................................Mon–Thur from 3 pm,
                                                       Fri–Sun from 11:30 am
Type..Restaurant and bar
Recommended for...Local favorite

OEDIPUS BREWING

Gedempt Hamerkanaal 85
Noord
Amsterdam 1021KP, The Netherlands
www.oedipus.com

Recommended by
Rick Nelson

Opening hours.............Thur from 5 pm, Fri–Sun from 2 pm
Credit cards..Accepted but not Amex
Type..Beer garden and brewery
Recommended for...Beer garden

WALHALLA CRAFT BEER

Spijkerkade 10
Noord
Amsterdam 1021 JS, The Netherlands
+31 611391675
www.walhallacraftbeer.nl

Recommended by
Aart van Bergen

Opening hours...............Fri from 4pm, Sat–Sun from 2 pm
Type..Microbrewery
Recommended for...Local favorite

AMSTERDAM ROEST

Jacob Bontiusplaats 1
Oost
Amsterdam 1018 LL, The Netherlands
+31 203080283
www.amsterdamroest.nl

Recommended by
Liubomir Chonos

Opening hours..................................Fri–Sun from 12 pm
Credit cards..Accepted
Type..Bar and beer garden
Recommended for...Beer garden

"Great design, music, atmosphere, and location."
—Liubomir Chonos

DE BIERTUIN

Linnaeusstraat 29
Oost
Amsterdam 1093 EE, The Netherlands
+31 206650956
www.debiertuin.nl

Recommended by
Kick van Hout

Opening hours..................................Open 7 days from 11 am
Credit cards..Accepted
Type..Beer garden
Recommended for...Beer garden

"They have robust food like big chicken from the spit. They have a great selection of beers."—Kick van Hout

JOOST

Molukkenstraat 33
Oost
Amsterdam 1095 AT, The Netherlands
+31 643748787
www.joost-amsterdam.nl

Recommended by
Jeppe Jarnit-Bjergsø

Opening hours...Mon–Fri from 3 pm,
                                                             Sat–Sun from 1 pm
Type...Pub
Recommended for...Local favorite

POESIAT & KATER

Recommended by
Aart van Bergen

Polderweg 648
Oost
Amsterdam 1093 KP, The Netherlands
+31 203331050
www.poesiatenkater.nl

Opening hours..Tue–Fri from 11 am,
Sat–Sun from 10 am
Credit cards..Not accepted
Type...Beer garden and brewpub
Recommended for...Beer garden

CRAFT & DRAFT

Recommended by
Roberto Orano

Overtoom 147
Oud-West
Amsterdam 1054 JR, The Netherlands
+31 202230725
www.craftanddraft.nl

Opening hours..Mon–Fri from 4 pm,
Sat–Sun from 2 pm
Credit cards..Accepted
Type...Bar
Recommended for...........................Wish I'd opened

GOLLEM'S PROEFLOKAAL

Overtoom 160–162
Oud-West

Recommended by
Jeppe Jarnit-Bjergsø

Amsterdam 1054 HP, The Netherlands
+31 206129444
www.cafegollem.nl

Opening hours..Mon–Thur from 1 pm,
Fri–Sun from 12 pm
Credit cards.............................Accepted but not Amex
Type...Beer garden
Recommended for...........................Local favorite

BUTCHER'S TEARS

Recommended by
Rory Miller

Karperweg 45
Oud-Zuid
Amsterdam 1075 LB, The Netherlands
+31 653909777
www.butchers-tears.com

Opening hours.............................Wed–Sun from 4 pm
Credit cards..Not accepted
Type..Bar and brewery
Recommended for.............................Worth the travel

"The place is brilliant. It's an old butcher shop with a great atmosphere and an underground, hidden location. Plus the beer is very tasty!"—Rory Miller

DOPEY'S ELIXER

Recommended by
Mike Amidei

Lutmastraat 49
Oud-Zuid
Amsterdam 1072 JP, The Netherlands
+31 206716946
www.dopeyselixer.nl

Opening hours..Mon–Fri from 1 pm,
Sat–Sun from 4 pm
Type...Pub
Recommended for...............................Local favorite

FOEDERS

Recommended by
Jeppe Jarnit-Bjergsø

Ceintuurbaan 257
Oud-Zuid
Amsterdam 1074 CZ, The Netherlands
+31 636593100
www.foeders.amsterdam

Opening hours..Mon–Fri from 2 pm,
Sat–Sun from 12 pm
Type...Bar
Recommended for...........................Wish I'd opened

AMSTERDAM AIRPORT SCHIPHOL

Evert van de Beekstraat 202
Schipol

Recommended by
Nemanja Stefanovic

Amsterdam 1118, The Netherlands
www.schiphol.nl

Opening hours..Variable
Credit cards..Variable
Type...Bar
Recommended for.............................Unexpected

BRET

Recommended by
Alberto Gómez

Orlyplein 76
Westpoort
Amsterdam 1043 DP, The Netherlands
+31 850600060
www.bret.bar

Opening hours..Mon–Fri from 11 am,
Sat–Sun from 12 pm
Credit cards..Accepted
Type.............................Bar, beer garden, and restaurant
Recommended for.............................Beer garden

"THE BEST BEER MENU I'VE EVER SEEN. PERIOD."

JULIE RHODES P.169

"THEY HAVE A PHENOMENAL COLLECTION OF VINTAGE BELGIAN BEERS."

KRIS HERTELEER P.168

BELGIUM

"LAMBIC! GUEUZE! AND ALL OTHER FRUITED VARIANTS OF SPONTANEOUSLY FERMENTED BEER."

TIM ADAMS P.169

"A LEGENDARY PLACE WHERE YOU CAN FIND OLD TREASURES."

GABRIEL BOCANEGRA P.168

"BEING AT KULMINATOR IS LIKE BEING AT YOUR GRANDPARENTS' HOUSE — IN A GOOD WAY. IMAGINE A BAR WITH WOODEN FURNITURE, DRIED HOP PLANTS EVERYWHERE, AND EIGHT CATS. PLUS, THERE ARE OLD BEER BOTTLES AND ADVERTISEMENTS."

LINDA VAN LOON P.168

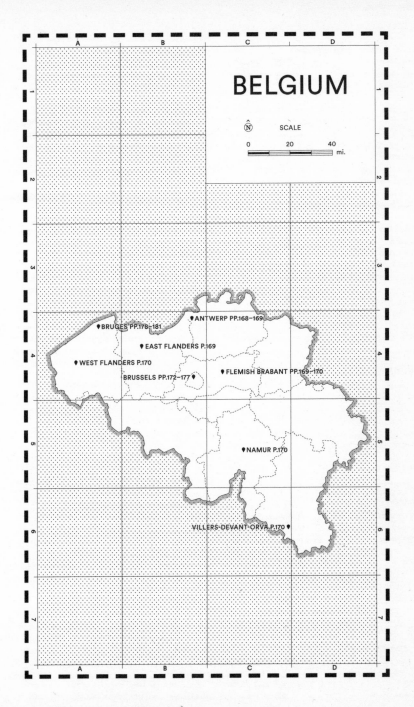

BELGIUM

N

SCALE

0   20   40
mi.

BRUGES PP.178-181

ANTWERP PP.168-169

EAST FLANDERS P.169

WEST FLANDERS P.170

BRUSSELS PP.172-177

FLEMISH BRABANT PP.169-170

NAMUR P.170

VILLERS-DEVANT-ORVA P.170

BILLIE'S BIER KAFÉTARIA

Kammenstraat 12

Antwerp 2000, Belgium
+32 32263183

Recommended by
Benny van Aerschot

Opening hours	Mon from 6 pm, Wed–Fri from 4 pm, Sat–Sun from 3 pm
Credit cards	Accepted
Type	Bar
Recommended for	Local favorite

"Billie's has a large beer collection and multiple rotating taps."—Benny van Aerschot

COHIBA ATMOSPHERE ANTWERP

Suikerrui 5

Antwerp 2000, Belgium
+32 470539846
www.cohibaatmosphere-antwerp.com

Recommended by
Yves Panneels

Opening hours	Mon–Fri from 9 am
Credit cards	Accepted
Type	Bar
Recommended for	Unexpected

GOLLEM

Suikerrui 28

Antwerp 2000, Belgium
+32 36894989

Recommended by
Benny van Aerschot

Opening hours	Open 7 days from 11 am
Credit cards	Accepted
Type	Bar and restaurant
Recommended for	Beer & food

KULMINATOR

32 Vleminckveld

Antwerp 2000, Belgium
+32 32324538

Recommended by
Benny van Aerschot,
Mike Amidei, Gabriel
Bocanegra, Diego Castro,
Andres Erazo, Molly Gunn,
Kris Herteleer, Linda van Loon
Shannon McFarlane, Brian Oakley,
Oliver San Antonio,
Linda Merete Skogholt,
Jens Skrubbe, Alan Sprints,
Eugene Tolstov

Opening hours	Mon from 8 pm, Tue–Sat from 4 pm
Credit cards	Not accepted
Type	Bar and beer garden
Recommended for	Worth the travel

"A legendary place where you can find old treasures."
—Gabriel Bocanegra

"They have a phenomenal collection of vintage Belgian beers."—Kris Herteleer

"Being at Kulminator is like being at your grandparents' house—in a good way. Imagine a bar with wooden furniture, dried hop plants everywhere, and eight cats. Plus, there are old beer bottles and advertisements."—Linda van Loon

"An amazing selection of the best beers from Belgium, many rare vintages, and special blends. A cozy and quiet atmosphere with friendly owners."—Linda Merete Skogholt

"It's a bit out of the way, but their bottle list is worth the travel from any distance."—Mike Amidei

"The best vintage list ever."—Molly Gunn

"The sheer number of aged bottles of Belgian beers makes this place unique. The beer list is encyclopedic."
—Oliver San Antonio

This bar feels as if you are hanging out in your living room (assuming you own cats). The difference of being in this living room is that you have access to an absolutely legendary cellar.

UNIVERSITY OF ANTWERP

Prinsstraat 13

Antwerp 2000, Belgium
+32 32654111
www.uantwerpen.be

Recommended by
Benny van Aerschot

Opening hours	Variable
Type	Bar
Recommended for	Unexpected

"The University of Antwerp has its own beer."
—Benny van Aerschot

IN DEN SPYTIGHEN DUVEL

Otterstraat 99

Turnhout
Antwerp 2300, Belgium
+32 14423500

Recommended by
Bart Cuypers

Opening hours	Tue–Fri, Sun from 2 pm, Sat from 3 pm
Credit cards	Not accepted
Type	Bar
Recommended for	Local favorite

"This is one of the oldest Belgian craft-beer bars. With a selection of over 400 beers, it has one of the largest collections. When visiting this bar you definitely need to try the beers of the local brewery Het Nest."—Bart Cuypers

Brussels, see pages 172–177

"A small bar that's also a bicycle museum, although finding the bikes can be tricky since it's very dark inside. The owner is fantastic and usually doesn't give a choice for what beer to buy. He charges a random amount for it. I love this place. The atmosphere is totally unique."—Valgeir Valgeirsson

DE HEEREN VAN LIEDEKERCKE

Kasteelstraat 33
Denderleeuw
East Flanders 9470, Belgium
+32 53680888
www.heerenvanliedekercke.be

Recommended by
Julie Rhodes,
Jens Skrubbe

Opening hours	Mon, Thur–Sat from 11:45 am, Sun from 12:30 pm
Credit cards	Accepted
Type	Pub
Recommended for	Worth the travel

"The best beer menu I've ever seen. Period. The staff knowledge level is off the charts, the food is to die for, the ambiance lasts for days—an elegant, historically epic beer experience."—Julie Rhodes

This is a world-class, very traditional lambic bar that completely lives up to its rightfully legendary status.

SINT-JORISHOF

Botermarkt 2
Ghent
East Flanders 9000, Belgium
+32 491378725
www.sint-jorishof.com

Recommended by
Julie Rhodes

Opening hours	Mon–Thur from 5 pm, Fri–Sun from 12 pm
Credit cards	Accepted
Type	Restaurant
Recommended for	Beer & food

"A wacky place, with the best steak in Belgium, an elegant beer menu, table-side butchery, and the best béarnaise sauce in the world."—Julie Rhodes

'T VELOOTJE BAR PECULIAR

Kalversteeg 2
Ghent
East Flanders 9000, Belgium
+32 486838648

Recommended by
Jens Skrubbe,
Valgeir Valgeirsson

Opening hours	Open 7 days from 6 pm
Credit cards	Not accepted
Type	Bar
Recommended for	Worth the travel

3 FONTEINEN

Herman Teirlinckplein 3
Beersel
Flemish Brabant 1650, Belgium
+32 23310652
www.3fonteinenrestaurant.com

Recommended by
Jeff Halvorson,
Josh Pfriem,
Alex Wallash

Opening hours	Thur–Mon from 12 pm
Credit cards	Accepted
Type	Restaurant
Recommended for	Beer & food

"A beautiful setting on a hill in the Brussels countryside. Amazing traditional Belgian cuisine with a great selection of wine, lambic, and beer."—Jeff Halvorson

Armand Debelder is an absolute legend. Even if you are nowhere near Beersel, Belgium, you should drop what you are doing and go. Drinking 3F beers at the 3 Fonteinen restaurant is the height of beer geekdom.

IN DE VERZEKERING TEGEN DE GROTE DORST

Frans Baetensstraat 45
Eizeringen
Flemish Brabant 1750, Belgium
+32 25325858
www.dorst.be

Recommended by
Tim Adams,
Yves Panneels,
Maxim Polivanov,
Eugene Tolstov

Opening hours	Sun from 10 am
Credit cards	Not accepted
Type	Bar
Recommended for	Worth the travel

"Lambic! Gueuze! And all other fruited variants of spontaneously fermented beer."—Tim Adams

"The best lambic bar in the world."—Yves Panneels

A fantastic family-run, very traditional Belgian bar. Make sure you have the hours right, since they are open only one day a week. The lambics available on their list will make it worth your effort.

BRUSSELS AIRPORT

Leopoldlaan
Zaventem
Flemish Brabant 1930, Belgium
+32 27532788
www.brusselsairport.be

Opening hours................................Open 7 days from 4 am
Credit cards..Accepted
Type..Retail
Recommended for......................................Unexpected

BARNABEER

Rue de Bruxelles 39
Namur 5000, Belgium
+32 475594384

Opening hours..........................Mon–Fri from 11 am,
Sat from 2 pm, Sun from 1 pm
Credit cards..Not accepted
Type...Bar
Recommended for......................................Unexpected

"Has the best selection of beer in a city where there aren't
many craft-beer bars."—Jaime Ojeda

ABBAYE D'ORVAL

Orval 1
Florenville
Villers-devant-Orval 6823, Belgium
+32 61311261
www.orval.be

Opening hours...Variable
Credit cards............................Accepted but not Amex
Type...Brewery
Recommended for......................................Unexpected

Bruges, see pages 178–181

OERBIER DE DOLLE BROUWERS
Roeselarestraat 12B

Esen
West Flanders 8600, Belgium
+32 51502781
www.dedollebrouwers.be

Opening hours................................Sat–Sun from 2 pm
Credit cards..Not accepted
Type...Brewery
Recommended for....................................Local favorite

EDISON

Koninklijke Baan 152
Koksijde
West Flanders 8670, Belgium
+32 478380799
www.brasserie-edison.be

Opening hours..........................Fri–Tue from 12 pm
Type..Restaurant
Recommended for....................................Beer & food

"Vincent Florizoone is Belgium's greatest beer chef."
—Yves Panneels

LOKAALMARKT ROESELARE
Sint-Amandskerk

De Coninckplein 3
Roeselare
West Flanders 8800, Belgium
+30 470609256
www.lokaalmarkt.be

Opening hours....................................Fri from 12 pm
Credit cards..Accepted
Type...Bar
Recommended for......................................Unexpected

"This is a farmers market in a former church. You would not
expect a bar in there!"—Kris Herteleer

IN DE VREDE

Donkerstraat 13
Vleteren
West Flanders 8640, Belgium
+32 57400377
www.indevrede.be

Opening hours............................Sat–Wed from 9:45 am
Credit cards..Accepted
Type...Bar
Recommended for....................................Beer & food

"A beautiful café near Westvleteren Abbey, a beautiful
setting, and three types of beer. It is a simple monk's cuisine
of bread, cheese, and pickles."—Maxim Polivanov

"BEAUTIFULLY PREPARED TRADITIONAL BELGIAN FARE WITH OUTSTANDING BEER-PAIRING SUGGESTIONS."

CHARLES GUERRIER P.177

"THEY SERVE THE FRESHEST ZINNEBIR IN TOWN."

YVAN DE BAETS P.175

BRUSSELS

"AROUND 150 OF BELGIUM'S GREATEST BEERS IN A DELIGHTFULLY CLUTTERED WARM ATMOSPHERE. IT ENTERTAINS THE EYE AND THE PALATE." ALASTAIR KIRK P.176

"CANTILLON STANDS OUT BECAUSE OF THE BALANCE BETWEEN TRADITION AND CRAZINESS."

PABLO SANTOS P.174

"I DON'T KNOW OF ANY BAR THAT HAS A MORE EXTENSIVE LIST OF RARE, AGED BEER IN THE WORLD."

ANGELO ORONA P.174

BRUSSELS

N

SCALE

0   330   660   985
yd.

JOSAPHAT

ILOT SACRÉ

ANNEESSENS

STALINGRAD

SABLON

CUREGHEM

BARRIÈRE DE SAINT GILLES

À LA MORT SUBITE

Rue Montagne aux
Herbes Potagères 7
Brussels 1000, Belgium
+32 25131318
www.alamortsubite.com

Recommended by
Barry Elwonger,
Em Sauter

Opening hours.........Mon–Sat from 11 am, Sun from 12 pm
Credit cards................................Accepted but not Amex
Type..Bar and restaurant
Recommended for..Worth the travel

"A well-known and historic beer bar that should be on every beer traveler's bucket list. It is very close to the renowned Cantillon Brewery. Great service with an intimate setting."
—Barry Elwonger

BISTROT BRUSSELS AIRPORT

Pier B, Brussels Airport
Brussels 1930, Belgium
+32 27197707
www.bistrot.com

Recommended by
Bart Cuypers

Opening hours.................................Open 7 days from 4 am
Credit cards...Accepted
Type...Restaurant
Recommended for...Unexpected

"They have a nice selection of lambics, oude gueuzes, and oude krieks."—Bart Cuypers

BOOZE 'N BLUES

Rue des Riches Claires 20
Brussels 1000, Belgium
+32 25139333

Recommended by
Lauren Grimm

Opening hours................................Mon–Fri from 11 am,
Sat–Sun from 5 pm
Type...Bar
Recommended for...Worth the travel

"Booze 'n Blues has a dive-bar aesthetic. Everything about it is pared down and spot on. They have fresh beer from Brasserie de la Senne on draft and a small selection of charcuterie. For music, there's a coin-operated classic rock jukebox that blares distorted 45s. There's also outdoor seating when the weather is nice. It doesn't get any better."
—Lauren Grimm

BREWDOG BRUSSELS

Putterie 20
Brussels 1000, Belgium
+32 25136355
www.brewdog.com

Recommended by
Razvan Costache

Opening hours...........Mon–Fri from 11 am, Sat from 12 pm
Credit cards..Accepted
Type...Bar
Recommended for...Wish I'd opened

CANTILLON BREWERY

Rue Gheude 56
Brussels 1070, Belgium
+32 25214928
www.cantillon.be

Recommended by
Alex Acker,
Paul Anspach,
Marie-Josée Lefebvre,
Pablo Santos

Opening hours.................................Mon–Tue from 10 am,
Thur–Sat from 10 am
Credit cards..Accepted
Type...Brewery
Recommended for...Worth the travel

"The bar is located inside the brewery, an old house modified to fit the whole brewery and lab. Belgium is a dreamland for any brewer—a lot of variety and beer diversity. Cantillon stands out because of the balance between tradition and craziness."—Pablo Santos

This is the holy grail of lambic. If you love lambic, this is where you need to be, with rare bottles on offer in a cozy and welcoming environment. It doesn't get any better.

DELIRIUM CAFÉ

Impasse de la Fidélité 4
Brussels 1000, Belgium
+32 25144434
www.deliriumcafe.be

Recommended by
Tim Besecker,
Matthew Buttigieg,
Stefano Di Gioacchino,
Ryan Evans, Amelia Franklin,
Danny Hamilton, Svilen Kirilovski,
Edgars Melnis, Angelo Orona, Josh Patton,
Sergio Ribenboim, Kelsey Roth,
Oliver San Antonio, Zac Triemert

Opening hours.................................Open 7 days from 10 am
Credit cards................................Accepted but not Amex
Type...Bar
Recommended for...Worth the travel

"The cellar list will make your head spin with its variety and quality. Delirium is a must-see for any serious beer traveler! I don't know of any bar that has a more extensive list of rare, aged beer in the world."—Angelo Orona

"Over 2,000 beers, three floors with different moods and beers, proper glassware, a comfortable basement area that is warm and exploding with personality, super fun and knowledgeable people serving in one of the most beautiful and underestimated cities in the world and a jaw-dropping cold room downstairs."—Stefano Di Gioacchino

DYNAMO - BAR DE SOIF

130 Chaussée d'Alsemberg
Brussels 1060, Belgium
+32 25391567
www.dynamobar.be

Recommended by
Sam Sarmad

Opening hours...........Wed–Sat from 5 pm, Sun from 4 pm
Credit cards...Accepted
Type..Bar
Recommended for...Local favorite

"Eighteen beers on tap, with Belgian and international craft beers."—Sam Sarmad

IN 'T SPINNEKOPKE

Place du Jardin aux Fleurs 1
Brussels 1000, Belgium
+32 25118695
www.spinnekopke.be

Recommended by
Flaviu Adrian Odorhean

Opening hours........Mon from 6:30 pm, Tue–Fri from 12pm,
Sat from 6:30 pm
Credit cards...Accepted
Type..Restaurant
Recommended for..Beer & food

"A cozy, old-school, and good-quality traditional restaurant with older waiters who are very attentive. It's in an old house, and the owner sells his own beers as well as others, they cook with beer, specifically with their traditional lambics."—Flaviu Adrian Odorhean

LA BUVETTE SAINT-SÉBASTIEN

Parc Josaphat 1030
Brussels 1030, Belgium
www.buvettesintsebastiaan.com

Recommended by
Yvan De Baets

Opening hours...Mon–Fri from 3 pm,
Sat–Sun from 2 pm
Credit cards...Not accepted
Type...Beer garden
Recommended for..Beer garden

"A perfect old-fashioned yet trendy family beer garden in the middle of a bucolic city park. They serve the freshest Zinnebir in town."—Yvan De Baets

LA FLEUR EN PAPIER DORÉ

55 Rue des Alexiens
Brussels 1000, Belgium
+32 25111659
www.lafleurenpapierdore.be

Recommended by
Yvan De Baets

Opening hours..Tue–Sun from 11 am
Credit cards...Accepted
Type..Restaurant
Recommended for..Wish I'd opened

LA TANA

Rue de l'Enseignement 10
Brussels 1000, Belgium
+32 489731916

Recommended by
Roberto Orano

Opening hours..Mon–Fri from 12 pm
Credit cards...Accepted
Type..Restaurant
Recommended for..Beer & food

"An Italian restaurant with craft beers from Italy and Belgium."—Roberto Orano

LE BAR DU MATIN

Chaussée d'Alsemberg 172
Brussels 1190, Belgium
+32 25377159
www.bardumatin.blogspot.com

Recommended by
Liubomir Chonos

Opening hours.....................................Open 7 days from 8 am
Credit cards...Accepted
Type..Bar
Recommended for..Wish I'd opened

"They have the capability to attract people who are sensitive about quality music and design. They know how to run a successful business."—Liubomir Chonos

LE COQ

Rue Auguste Orts 14
Brussels 1000, Belgium
+32 25142414
www.stoemplive.be

Recommended by
Yvan De Baets

Opening hours...........Mon–Sat from 12 pm, Sun from 4 pm
Credit cards..Not accepted
Type..Restaurant
Recommended for..................................Local favorite

LE POECHENELLEKELDER

5 Rue du Chêne
Brussels 1000, Belgium
+32 25119262
www.poechenellekelder.be

Recommended by
Alastair Kirk

Opening hours..........................Tue–Sun from 11 am
Credit cards..Accepted
Type..Bar
Recommended for............................Worth the travel

"Around 150 of Belgium's greatest beers in a delightfully cluttered warm atmosphere. It entertains the eye and the palate."—Alastair Kirk

LES BRIGITTINES

Place de la Chapelle 5
Brussels 1000, Belgium
+32 25126891
www.lesbrigittines.com

Recommended by
Yvan De Baets,
Jens Skrubbe

Opening hours...........Mon–Fri from 12 pm, Sat from 7 pm
Credit cards..Accepted
Type...Restaurant
Recommended for....................................Beer & food

"Dirk Miny, the chef and owner, is passionate about high-quality raw materials, and he cooks with a lot of love and finesse. He is equally passionate about craft beers and natural wines. They treat beer and wine equally, which is surprisingly rare in Belgium."—Yvan De Baets

MOEDER LAMBIC FONTAINAS

Place Fontainas 8
Brussels 1000, Belgium
+32 25036068
www.moederlambic.com

Recommended by
Ben Maeso, Bob Olson,
Francisco Pereira,
Josh Pfriem, John Rowley,
Linda Merete Skogholt, Jens
Skrubbe, Zaq Suarez, Polly
Watts, Christian Weber

Opening hours...................................Open 7 days from 11 am
Credit cards..Accepted
Type..Bar
Recommended for............................Worth the travel

"An incredible Belgian beer selection from classics to new-school breweries. It's a super cool spot in the heart of Brussels with a knowledgeable and friendly staff. They have a very well-catered list of beers, including special blends for them by Cantillon. This—combined with a really cool spot, rad folks, and food—accentuates the experience."
—Josh Pfriem

"An amazing selection of beers, both classic and modern. They have a knowledgeable and friendly staff, serving some of the best beers in the world when it comes to sours and wild ales."—Linda Merete Skogholt

"A great selection."—Polly Watts

"If you have a layover in Brussels and don't have time to get to all the legendary breweries in town, Moeder Lambic will have beer just as fresh in one central location. Their selection is just about unbeatable."—Zaq Suarez

MOEDER LAMBIC ORIGINAL

68 Rue de Savoie
Brussels 1060, Belgium
+32 25441699
www.moederlambic.com

Recommended by
Liubomir Chonos,
Laurent Cicurel, Joe Dick,
Kris Li, Lynn McIlwee,
Angelo Orona, Luke Pestl,
Valgeir Valgeirsson

Opening hours...................................Open 7 days from 4 pm
Credit cards..Accepted
Type..Bar
Recommended for............................Worth the travel

"This is the benchmark for any craft-beer bar in Europe: one of the first, high selections of craft beer. The service is an example of how beer should be served—the Belgian way."—Laurent Cicurel

"Basically a neighborhood café on a quiet street with the best lambic beer on tap and in bottle. They have other amazing beers from Belgium and beyond as well."
—Luke Pestl

This is truly lambic heaven. Rarities abound in their voluminous bottle list, with both hard-to-find beers and vintage classics.

NÜETNIGENOUGH

Rue du Lombard 25
Brussels 1000, Belgium
+32 25137884
www.nuetnigenough.be

Recommended by
Dorothée van Agt,
Bruno Aquino,
Matteo Bonfanti,
Mario Canestrelli,
Lynn McIlwee,
Sam Sarmad

Opening hours	Mon–Fri from 5 pm, Sat–Sun from 12 pm
Credit cards	Accepted
Type	Bar and restaurant
Recommended for	Beer & food

"Nüetnigenough is a small meat-centric restaurant that's worth lining up for. Whether you're looking for authentic Flemish stew or beef tongue, the flavors and textures are perfect. The servers are well versed in their beer list and readily offer an opinion on what would pair well with your meal."—Lynn McIlwee

"A really cozy place with beautiful decor and a small but great beer selection with classic Belgian food. I try to go every time I'm in Brussels."—Mario Canestrelli

---

'T KELDERKE

Grand Place 15
Brussels 1000
Belgium
+32 25137344
www.restaurant-het-kelderke.be

Recommended by
Charles Guerrier

Opening hours	Open 7 days from 12 pm
Credit cards	Accepted
Type	Restaurant
Recommended for	Beer & food

"Beautifully prepared traditional Belgian fare with outstanding beer-pairing suggestions."—Charles Guerrier

"THE FRIENDLY AND KNOWLEDGEABLE STAFF WELCOME YOU INTO THEIR CAFÉ, WHERE YOU COULD EASILY SPEND THE AFTERNOON SIPPING BEER AND EATING CHEESE."

LYNN MCILWEE P.180

"CRAZY-GOOD BEERS AND A TERRACE WHERE YOU CAN PLAY PÉTANQUE (BOULES OR BOCCE)."

LINDA MERETE SKOGHOLT P.180

BRUGES

"THIS IS ONE OF THE COOLEST BEER DESTINATIONS IN ALL OF EUROPE. THE LOCATION IS GORGEOUS AND FEELS HIDDEN."

RICHARD HINKLE P.180

"A DIMLY LIT STONE CELLAR WITH AN AMAZING TAP LIST OF BELGIAN CRAFT BEER, CHARCUTERIE PLATES, AND BOARD GAMES."

COLBY COX P.181

"YOU COULD SPEND DAYS HERE."

JEFF HALVORSON P.181

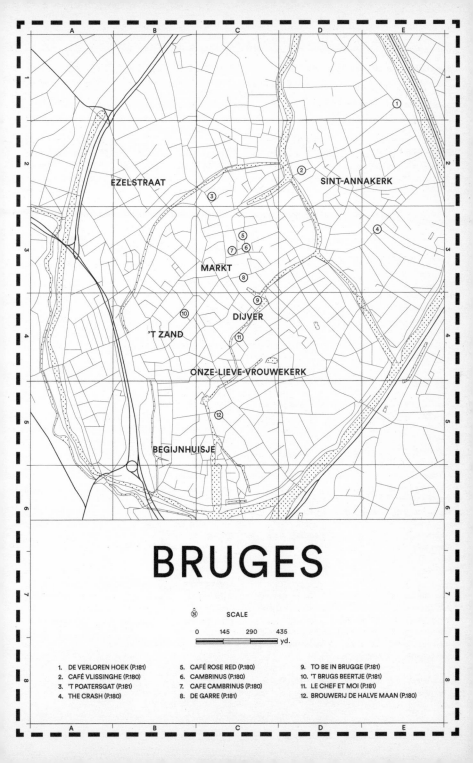

BRUGES

1. DE VERLOREN HOEK (P.181)
2. CAFÉ VLISSINGHE (P.180)
3. 'T POATERSGAT (P.181)
4. THE CRASH (P.180)
5. CAFÉ ROSE RED (P.180)
6. CAMBRINUS (P.180)
7. CAFE CAMBRINUS (P.180)
8. DE GARRE (P.181)
9. TO BE IN BRUGGE (P.181)
10. 'T BRUGS BEERTJE (P.181)
11. LE CHEF ET MOI (P.181)
12. BROUWERIJ DE HALVE MAAN (P.180)

BROUWERIJ DE HALVE MAANS

Walplein 26
Bruges
West Flanders 8000, Belgium
+32 50444222
www.halvemaan.be

Recomended by
Diego Castro

Opening hours	Open 7 days from 11 am
Credit cards	Accepted
Type	Brewery and restaurant
Recommended for	Beer & food

"Great beer and food pairing. They have an interesting guided tour to the brewery."—Diego Castro

CAFÉ CAMBRINUS

Philipstockstraat 7
Bruges
West Flanders 8000, Belgium
+32 50332328
www.cambrinus.eu

Recommended by
Mark Sigman

Opening hours	Open 7 days from 11 am
Credit cards	Accepted
Type	Restaurant and bar
Recommended for	Beer & food

"A complete integration of food and beer classics from the region."—Mark Sigman

CAFÉ ROSE RED

Cordoeaniersstraat 16
Bruges
West Flanders 8000, Belgium
+32 50339051
www.cordoeanier.be/rosered

Recommended by
Patrick Ejlerskov,
Lynn McIlwee

Opening hours	Wed–Mon from 11 am
Credit cards	Accepted
Type	Pub
Recommended for	Local favorite

"This café is in the heart of beautiful Bruges yet not in the busy tourist area. It has an extensive cellar, an adjoining quaint hotel, and a small tapas menu. The friendly and knowledgeable staff welcome you into their café, where you could easily spend the afternoon sipping beer and eating cheese."—Lynn McIlwee

"They had an amazing beer menu and very friendly and skilled bar staff."—Patrick Ejlerskov

CAFÉ VLISSINGHE

Blekersstraat 2
Bruges
West Flanders 8000, Belgium
+32 50343737
www.cafevlissinghe.be

Recommended by
Linda Merete Skogholt

Opening hours	Wed–Sun from 11 am
Credit cards	Not accepted
Type	Beer garden and pub
Recommended for	Beer garden

"Crazy-good beers and a terrace where you can play Pétanque (boules or bocce). A good variety of cheeses and meats if you need a snack. They serve all the classic Belgian beers on draft and bottle."—Linda Merete Skogholt

CAMBRINUS

Philipstockstraat 19
Bruges
West Flanders 8000, Belgium
+32 50332328
www.cambrinus.eu

Recommended by
Richard Hinkle

Opening hours	Open 7 days from 11 am
Credit cards	Accepted
Type	Bar
Recommended for	Worth the travel

"This is one of the coolest beer destinations in all of Europe. The location is gorgeous and feels hidden. The menu boasts several hundred beers, each served in its own special glass. They have the most diverse beer menu and delicious food."
—Richard Hinkle

THE CRASH

Langestraat 78
Bruges
West Flanders 8000, Belgium
+32 50347081

Recommended by
Trevor Wirtanen

Opening hours	Sat–Thur from 8 pm, Fri from 4 pm
Credit cards	Not accepted
Type	Bar
Recommended for	Worth the travel

"A tiny punk bar."—Trevor Wirtanen

DE GARRE

Recommended by
Luis Arce,
Bill Howell,
Matt Van Wyk

De Garre 1
Bruges
West Flanders 8000, Belgium
+32 50341029
www.degarre.be

Opening hours............Sun–Fri from 12 pm, Sat from 11 am
Credit cards..Accepted
Type...Bar
Recommended for..Worth the travel

"Simply being hard to find yet well sought after makes De Garre attractive. The coziness of this old building welcomes you, and the knowledgeable and friendly staff keeps you there."—Matt Van Wyk

DE VERLOREN HOEK

Recommended by
Alex Acker

Carmersstraat 178
Bruges
West Flanders 8000, Belgium
+32 50698019
www.deverlorenhoek.be

Opening hours.......................................Wed–Sun from 11 am
Credit cards..Accepted
Type..Restaurant
Recommended for...Beer & food

"Great Belgian home-style food with a small but excellent selection of draft and bottled Belgian beers. Great food, good beer selection, nice setting, nice owners."
—Alex Acker

LE CHEF ET MOI

Recommended by
Kris Herteleer

Dijver 13
Bruges
West Flanders 8000, Belgium
+32 50396011
www.lechefetmoi.be

Opening hours.......................................Tue–Sat from 12 pm
Credit cards..Accepted
Type..Restaurant
Recommended for...Beer & food

"Very nice classic French food with different beers in wineglasses. A great interior as well."—Kris Herteleer

'T BRUGS BEERTJE

Recommended by
Jeff Halvorson,
Jonathan Moxey

Kemelstraat 5
Bruges
West Flanders 8000, Belgium
+32 50339616
www.brugsbeertje.be

Opening hours..Thur–Tue from 4 pm
Credit cards..Not accepted
Type...Pub
Recommended for..Worth the travel

"Small and friendly, with an amazing assortment of world-class beer, right in the middle of one of the most picturesque cities of Europe. You could spend days here."
—Jeff Halvorson

It's one of my favorite places to drink beer anywhere."
—Jonathan Moxey

TO BE IN BRUGGE

Recommended by
Cindy DeRama

Wollestraat 53
Bruges
West Flanders 8000, Belgium
+32 050611222
www.2-be.biz

Opening hours...............................Open 7 days from 10 am
Credit cards..................................Accepted but not Amex
Type...Bar
Recommended for..Worth the travel

"The selection and scenery is amazing: on the canal in a beautiful historic city."—Cindy DeRama

'T POATERSGAT

Recommended by
Colby Cox

Vlamingstraat 82
Bruges
West Flanders 8000, Belgium
+32 495228650

Opening hours.......................................Tue–Wed from 5 pm,
Sun from 5 pm
Type...Bar
Recommended for..Worth the travel

"It's a little hard to find but worth the journey. A dimly-lit stone cellar with an amazing tap list of Belgian craft beer, charcuterie plates, and board games."—Colby Cox

"THIS WAS THE FIRST CRAFT-BEER BAR TO OPEN IN FRANCE. THEY HAVE A REALLY GOOD SELECTION."

LAURENT CICUREL P.185

"THE FRESHEST BEER IN THE COUNTRY."

ROLAND GRABER P.188

FRANCE, LUXEMBOURG & SWITZERLAND

"THE BAR IS LIKE THE EXTENSION OF YOUR LIVING ROOM IF YOU LIVE IN A MEDIEVAL CASTLE. IT'S SMALL AND RUN WITH LOVE BY A COUPLE WHO ARE TRUE BEER LOVERS."

CHRISTIAN JAUSLIN P.186

"THE OWNER IS SUCH A RAD DUDE. HE HAS A KILLER SELECTION OF BELGIAN BEERS, WITH A SECRET STASH OF HARD-TO-GET AMERICAN BEERS."

BRIAN OAKLEY P.185

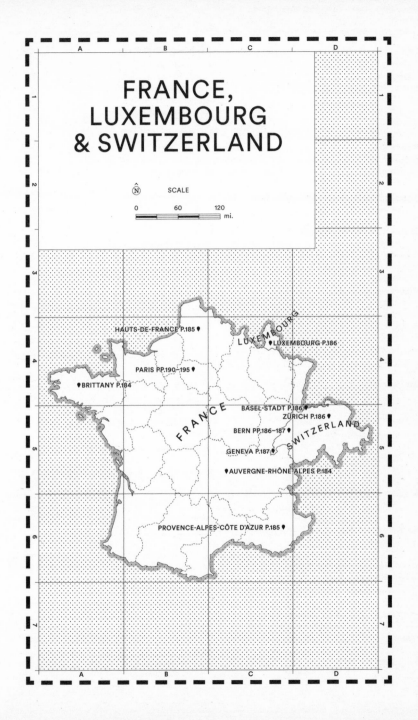

FRANCE, LUXEMBOURG & SWITZERLAND

SCALE

0   60   120 mi.

LUXEMBOURG

HAUTS-DE-FRANCE P.185 ♥

♥ LUXEMBOURG P.186

PARIS PP.190–195 ♥

♥ BRITTANY P.184

FRANCE

BASEL-STADT P.186 ♥

♥ ZÜRICH P.186

BERN PP.186–187 ♥

SWITZERLAND

GENEVA P.187 ♥

♥ AUVERGNE-RHÔNE-ALPES P.184

PROVENCE-ALPES-CÔTE D'AZUR P.185 ♥

LE K7

3 Route de la Peysse
Chambéry
Auvergne-Rhône-Alpes 73000, France
+33 479335168
www.lek7.fr

Recommended by
Rémi Brusa

Opening hours............Mon–Fri from 10 am, Sat from 2 pm
Credit cards..Accepted
Type..Restaurant
Recommended for...Unexpected

"This is a music studio and restaurant."—Rémi Brusa

LES BIÈRES DE MIDGARD

118 Rue Juiverie
Chambéry
Auvergne-Rhône-Alpes 73000, France
+33 967138365
www.bieres-midgard.com

Recommended by
Rémi Brusa

Opening hours............Mon–Fri from 3 pm, Sat from 12 pm
Credit cards..Accepted
Type..Bar and retail
Recommended for..Local favorite

BERLUCOQUET

98 Avenue de l'Aiguille du Midi
Chamonix-Mont-Blanc
Auvergne-Rhône-Alpes 74400, France
www.berlucoquet.unblog.fr

Recommended by
Mike Amidei

Opening hours..Tue–Sun from 5 pm
Credit cards...Not accepted
Type...Bar
Recommended for..Beer & food

DIKKENEK CAFÉ

3 Rue d'Austerlitz
Lyon
Auvergne-Rhône-Alpes 69004, France
+33 469679765
www.dikkenek-cafe.fr

Recommended by
Jeppe Jarnit-Bjergsø

Opening hours..................Tue–Fri from 8:30 am, Sat from
9 am, Sun from 4 pm, Mon from 5 pm
Credit cards............................Accepted but not Amex
Type..Pub
Recommended for..Local favorite

LA CHOPE DE LUG

9 Rue du Boeuf
Lyon
Auvergne-Rhône-Alpes 69005, France
+33 967105988
www.lachopedelug.fr

Recommended by
Mike Amidei

Opening hours....................................Tue–Fri from 2:30 pm,
Sat–Sun from 10:30 am
Type..Retail
Recommended for..Local favorite

LES BERTHOM

2 Place Ennemond Fousseret
Lyon
Auvergne-Rhône-Alpes 69005, France
+33 478284410
www.lesberthom.com

Recommended by
Mike Amidei

Opening hours..Mon–Fri from 5 pm,
Sat–Sun from 4 pm
Credit cards..Accepted
Type...Bar
Recommended for..Worth the travel

LES FLEURS DU MALT — LA MISE EN BIÈRE

15 Quai Romain Rolland
Lyon
Auvergne-Rhône-Alpes 69005, France
+33 472656416
www.lyon.lesfleursdumaltlebar.fr

Recommended by
Jeppe Jarnit-Bjergsø

Opening hours..Mon–Fri from 5 pm,
Sat–Sun from 2 pm
Credit cards..Accepted
Type...Bar
Recommended for..Beer & food

CHEZ ALAIN

18 Rue Poullain Duparc
Rennes
Brittany 35000, France
+33 299502830

Recommended by
Jeppe Jarnit-Bjergsø

Opening hours..Mon from 4 pm,
Tue from 3 pm, Wed–Sat from 11 am
Type..Retail
Recommended for..Local favorite

L'ABBAYE DES SAVEURS

13 Rue des Vieux Murs
Lille
Hauts-de-France 59800, France
+33 328077006

Recommended by
Mike Amidei

Opening hours................................Mon–Tue from 2 pm,
Wed–Sun from 11 am
Credit cards..Accepted
Type..Retail
Recommended for.............................Local favorite

LA CAPSULE

25 Rue des Trois Mollettes
Lille
Hauts-de-France 59800, France
+33 320421475
www.bar-la-capsule.fr

Recommended by
Stephane Bogaert,
Laurent Cicurel,
Brian Oakley

Opening hours...........................Mon–Fri from 5:30 pm,
Sat from 4 pm, Sun from 5:30 pm
Credit cards..Accepted
Type..Bar
Recommended for.............................Worth the travel

"The owner is such a rad dude. He has a killer selection of Belgian beers, with a secret stash of hard-to-get American beers."—Brian Oakley

"This was the first craft-beer bar to open in France. They have a really good selection. They promote the local beers from northern France."—Laurent Cicurel

LE BLOEMPOT

22 Rue des Bouchers
Lille
Hauts-de-France 59000, France
www.bloempot.fr

Recommended by
Stephane Bogaert

Opening hours..............................Tue–Sat from 12 pm
Credit cards..Accepted
Type...Restaurant
Recommended for..................................Beer & food

"A restaurant with a great chef who loves beers and is doing many great events around beer. They use local ingredients."
—Stephane Bogaert

Paris, see pages 190–195

FIETJE

143 Rue Sainte
Marseille
Provence-Alpes-Côte d'Azur 13007, France
+33 491588162
www.fietje.fr

Recommended by
Guillaume David

Opening hours................................Tue–Wed from 5 pm,
Thur–Sat from 6 pm
Credit cards..Accepted
Type..Bar
Recommended for.............................Worth the travel

LA CUISINE DE ZEBULINE ET ZIGOTO

1–5 Rue du Colonel Fabien
Martigues
Provence-Alpes-Côte d'Azur 13500, France
+33 695092093

Recommended by
Guillaume David

Opening hours..........................Open 7 days from 9 am
(May 1 to Oct 1)
Credit cards..Accepted
Type..Bar and restaurant
Recommended for..................................Beer & food

BRASSERIE DE SULAUZE

Chemin du Vieux Sulauze
Miramas
Provence-Alpes-Côte-d'Azur 13140, France
+33 490453948
www.brasseriedesulauze.com

Recommended by
Guillaume David

Opening hours...................................Mon from 3 pm,
Wed from 3 pm, Fri from 3 pm
Credit cards..Accepted
Type..............................Beer garden and brewery
Recommended for................................Beer garden

"In the middle of 600 hectares of nature, this brewery is like a farmer's beer garden."—Guillaume David

BOUNEWEGER STUFF

1 Rue du Cimetière
Luxembourg 1338, Luxembourg
+352 26190550
www.bounewegerstuff.lu

Recommended by
Mike Amidei

Opening hours................................Sun–Fri from 11 am,
Sat from 10 am
Credit cards..Accepted
Type..Bar
Recommended for..................................Beer & food

BRASSERIE LA CATHÉDRALE

9 Rue Beck
Luxembourg 1222, Luxembourg
+352 223784
www.restaurant-cathedrale.com

Recommended by
Mike Amidei

Opening hours	Mon–Sat from 6 am
Credit cards	Accepted
Type	Restaurant
Recommended for	Beer & food

CAFÉ ROCAS

33 Rue des Capucins
Luxembourg 1313, Luxembourg
+352 27478620
www.rocas.lu

Recommended by
Jeppe Jarnit-Bjergsø

Opening hours	Mon–Sat from 4:30 pm
Type	Bar
Recommended for	Local favorite

CENTS CAFÉ BEIM ZEUTZIUS

71 Rue de Treves
Luxembourg 2630, Luxembourg
+352 26430031

Recommended by
Jeppe Jarnit-Bjergsø

Opening hours	Mon–Sat from 11 am
Credit cards	Accepted but not Amex
Type	Pub
Recommended for	Local favorite

LIQUID BAR

15 Rue Münster
Luxembourg 2160, Luxembourg
+352 25884747
www.liquid.lu

Recommended by
Mark Hatherly

Opening hours	Mon–Fri from 5 pm,
	Sat–Sun from 1 pm
Credit cards	Accepted
Type	Pub
Recommended for	Local favorite

"A great beer selection—especially Belgian—plus great live music and a cool interior."—Mark Hatherly

PINGUIN ZEM BIER-HUUS

Schüetzenmattstrasse 21
Basel
Basel-Stadt 4051, Switzerland
+41 612613513

Recommended by
Jeppe Jarnit-Bjergsø

Opening hours	Mon–Fri from 7 am
Type	Pub
Recommended for	Local favorite

BARBIÈRE

Breitenrainplatz 40
Bern 3014, Switzerland
+41 315367077
www.barbiere-bern.ch

Recommended by
Roland Graber

Opening hours	Mon–Fri from 7 am,
	Sat from 9 am
Credit cards	Accepted
Type	Beer garden and brewpub
Recommended for	Beer garden

BIERCAFÉ AU TRAPPISTE

Rathausgasse 68
Bern 3011, Switzerland
+41 313110789
www.autrappiste.ch

Recommended by
Mike Amidei

Opening hours	Mon–Sat from 4 pm
Credit cards	Not accepted
Type	Bar and restaurant
Recommended for	Local favorite

BIERKELLER AU TRAPPISTE

Rathausgasse 53
Bern 3011, Switzerland
+41 315350874

Recommended by
Richard Burhouse,
Roland Graber, Christian
Jauslin, Chris Treanor,
Grant Waner

Opening hours	Tue–Fri from 5 pm,
	Sat from 3 pm, Sun from 4 pm
Credit cards	Not accepted
Type	Pub
Recommended for	Local favorite

"The bar is like the extension of your living room if you live in a medieval castle. It's small and run with love by a couple who are true beer lovers."—Christian Jauslin

"A historic building, great owners, friendly locals, and great food."—Richard Burhouse

"The best international beer in town, with six to twelve on tap and great food."—Roland Graber

CRAFTGALLERY
Marktgasse 38
Bern 3011, Switzerland
+41 313115494
www.craftgallery.ch

Recommended by
Roland Graber

Opening hours..Tue–Fri from 11 am,
Sat from 10 am
Credit cards...Accepted
Type...Retail
Recommended for...Beer & food

"The beer and food pairing events are one of a kind."
—Roland Graber

LITTLE THAI
Hauptstrasse 19
Matten bei Interlaken
Bern 3800, Switzerland
+41 338211017
www.mylittlethai.ch

Recommended by
Grant Waner

Opening hours.............................Wed–Sun from 11 am
Credit cards...Accepted
Type...Restaurant
Recommended for...Unexpected

"Excellent Thai food and beer menu."—Grant Waner

MOMENT
Postgasse 49
Bern 3011, Switzerland
+41 313321020
www.moment-bern.ch

Recommended by
Roland Graber

Opening hours..........................Tue–Fri from 11:30 am,
Sat from 5:30 pm
Credit cards...Accepted
Type...Restaurant
Recommended for...Unexpected

"Fresh food and fresh local beer."—Roland Graber

AU COIN MOUSSE
Rue Du Fort-Barreau 21
Geneva 1201, Switzerland
+41 227405750
www.aucoinmousse.ch

Recommended by
Mike Amidei

Opening hours...Tue–Sat from 5 pm,
Sun from 4 pm
Credit cards...Accepted
Type..Bar
Recommended for...Worth the travel

LA CITADELLE
Rue des Sources 20
Geneva 1205, Switzerland
+41 223215800
www.lacitadelle.ch

Recommended by
Mike Amidei

Opening hours..........Sun–Mon from 5 pm, Tue from 3 pm,
Wed–Fri from 5 pm, Sat from 3 pm
Credit cards..Not accepted
Type..Bar
Recommended for..Local favorite

BRASSERIE DES FRANCHES-MONTAGNES
Chemin des Buissons 8
Saignelégier
Jura 2350, Switzerland
+41 329512626
www.brasseriebfm.ch

Recommended by
Mike Amidei

Opening hours............Mon–Sat from 9:30 am (restaurant)
Wed, Fri–Sat from 4 pm (bar)
Credit cards...Accepted
Type..Restaurant and brewery
Recommended for...Worth the travel

WHITEFRONTIER TAPROOM
Rue du Levant 99
Martigny
Valais 1920, Switzerland
+41 277756918
www.whitefrontier.ch

Recommended by
Caterina Lodo,
Chris Treanor

Opening hours...Tue–Sat from 11 am
Credit cards...Accepted
Type...Brewery
Recommended for..Local favorite

PIBAR

Rue du Valentin 62
Lausanne
Vaud 1004, Switzerland
+41 216460228
www.pibar.ch

Recommended by
Mike Amidei

Opening hours...........................Tue–Fri from 5 pm,
Sat from 6 pm
Credit cards..Accepted
Type...Bar
Recommended for..............................Local favorite

THE ALEHOUSE – PALMHOF

Universitätstrasse 23
Zürich 8006, Switzerland
+41 445428745
www.alehouse.ch

Recommended by
Jeppe Jarnit-Bjergsø

Opening hours.........................Mon–Fri from 8:30 am,
Sat–Sun from 11:30 am
Credit cards..Accepted
Type...Pub
Recommended for..............................Local favorite

ANDORRA

Münstergasse 20
Zürich 8001, Switzerland
+41 442526570
www.andorra.ch

Recommended by
Mike Amidei

Opening hours..............................Sun–Thur from 5 pm,
Fri–Sat from 2 pm
Credit cards..Accepted
Type...Bar
Recommended for..............................Local favorite

BEERS'N'MORE

Universitätstrasse 25
Zürich 8006, Switzerland
+41 445428746
www.beersnmore.com

Recommended by
Jeppe Jarnit-Bjergsø

Opening hours...........................Tue–Thur from 4 pm,
Fri–Sat from 2 pm
Credit cards..Accepted
Type..Retail
Recommended for............................Worth the travel

DRINKS OF THE WORLD

Zurich Railway Station
Halle Landesmuseum
Zürich 8001, Switzerland
+41 442111051
www.beerworld.ch

Recommended by
Mike Amidei

Opening hours.......................Open 7 days from 9 am
Credit cards..Accepted
Type..Retail
Recommended for...........................Wish I'd opened

THE INTERNATIONAL BEER BAR

Luisenstrasse 7
Zürich 8005, Switzerland
www.theinternational.ch

Recommended by
Mike Goguen,
Roland Graber

Opening hours.......................Open 7 days from 5 pm
Credit cards..Accepted
Type...Bar
Recommended for...........................Wish I'd opened

"The freshest beer in the country. Servers are very
knowledgeable."—Roland Graber

RESTAURANT BAUSCHÄNZLI

Stadthausquai 2
Zürich 8001, Switzerland
+41 442124919
www.bauschaenzli.ch

Recommended by
Christian Jauslin

Opening hours.......................Open 7 days from 11 am
Credit cards..Accepted
Type...Beer garden
Recommended for.......................................Beer garden

"A great location in the middle of Zurich."—Christian Jauslin

ZEUGHAUSKELLER

Bahnhofstrasse 28A
Zürich 8001, Switzerland
+41 442201515
www.zeughauskeller.ch

Recommended by
Jeppe Jarnit-Bjergsø

Opening hours....................Open 7 days from 11:30 am
Credit cards..Accepted
Type...Restaurant
Recommended for............................Worth the travel

"A FRIENDLY PLACE."

EDWARD JALAT-DEHEN P.194

"THE BARMEN ARE VERY FUNNY."

DOROTHÉE VAN AGT P.195

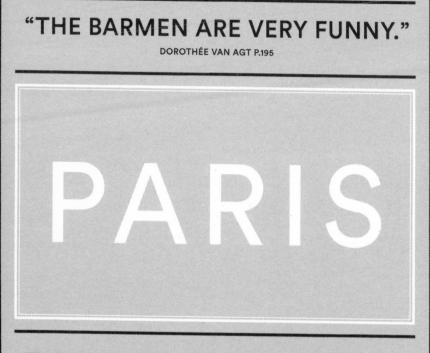

PARIS

"THEY HAVE TEN TAPS IN THE RESTAURANT AND A GREAT BOTTLE MENU. THEIR DELICIOUS CUISINE IS A FUSION OF INNOVATION AND TRADITION. THEY CREATE DISHES FOR PAIRING BEERS."

VALTER LOVERIER P.193

"IT'S A VERY SMALL BAR WITH ONLY CRAFT BEER AT A GOOD PRICE ON TAP."

DOROTHÉE VAN AGT P.195

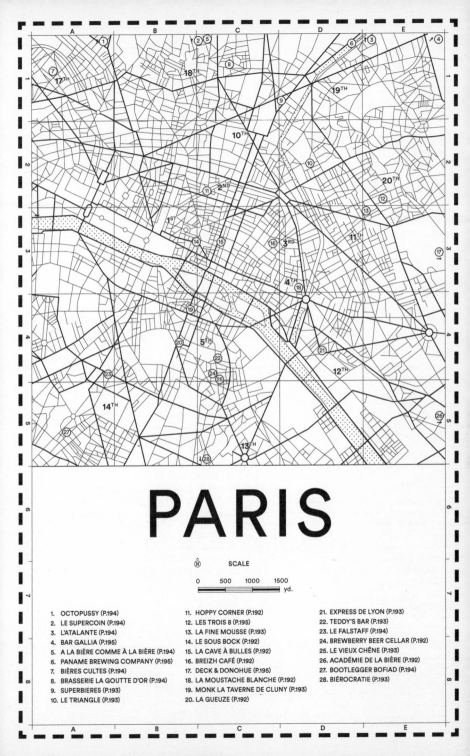

PARIS

$\hat{N}$ SCALE

0   500   1000   1500
|___|___|___|___|
                    yd.

LE SOUS BOCK

49 Rue Saint Honoré
1st Arrondissement
Paris 75001, France
+33 140264661

Recommended by
Mike Amidei

Opening hours	Open 7 days from 9 am
Credit cards	Accepted
Type	Bar
Recommended for	Local favorite

HOPPY CORNER

34 Rue des Petits Carreaux
2nd Arrondissement
Paris 75002, France
+33 983069039

Recommended by
Jeppe Jarnit-Bjergsø

Opening hours	Mon–Sat from 5 pm
Credit cards	Accepted
Type	Pub
Recommended for	Beer & food

BREIZH CAFÉ

109 Rue Vieille du Temple
3rd Arrondissement
Paris 75003, France
+33 142721377
www.breizhcafe.com

Recommended by
Jeppe Jarnit-Bjergsø

Opening hours	Mon–Fri from 11:30 am, Sat–Sun from 10 am
Credit cards	Accepted
Type	Restaurant
Recommended for	Beer & food

LA CAVE À BULLES

45 Rue Quincampoix
4th Arrondissement
Paris 75004, France
+33 140290369
www.caveabulles-paris.fr

Recommended by
Jeppe Jarnit-Bjergsø

Opening hours	Tue–Sat from 10 am
Credit cards	Accepted
Type	Retail
Recommended for	Worth the travel

LA MOUSTACHE BLANCHE

16 Rue des Tournelles
4th Arrondissement
Paris 75004, France
+33 175571506
www.lamoustacheblanche.fr

Recommended by
Mike Amidei

Opening hours	Tue–Sat from 1 pm, Sun from 2 pm
Credit cards	Accepted
Type	Retail
Recommended for	Worth the travel

ACADÉMIE DE LA BIÈRE

88B Boulevard de Port-Royal
5th Arrondissement
Paris 75005, France
+33 143546665
www.academie-biere.com

Recommended by
Jeppe Jarnit-Bjergsø

Opening hours	Open 7 days from 10 am
Credit cards	Accepted but not Amex
Type	Restaurant and pub
Recommended for	Worth the travel

BREWBERRY BEER CELLAR

18 Rue du Pot de Fer
5th Arrondissement
Paris 75005, France
+33 145311228
www.brewberry.fr

Recommended by
Mike Amidei

Opening hours	Tue–Sun from 5 pm
Credit cards	Accepted
Type	Bar
Recommended for	Worth the travel

LA GUEUZE

19 Rue Soufflot
5th Arrondissement
Paris 75005, France
+33 143546300

Recommended by
Jeppe Jarnit-Bjergsø

Opening hours	Open 7 days from 9 am
Credit cards	Accepted
Type	Bar
Recommended for	Wish I'd opened

LE VIEUX CHÊNE

69 Rue Mouffetard
5th Arrondissement
Paris 75005, France
+33 172607981

Recommended by
Jeppe Jarnit-Bjergsø

Opening hours....................................Open 7 days from 4 pm
Credit cards...Accepted
Type...Bar
Recommended for...Local favorite

MONK LA TAVERNE DE CLUNY

51 Rue de la Harpe
5th Arrondissement
Paris 75005, France
+33 143542888
www.latavernedecluny.com

Recommended by
Mike Amidei

Opening hours....................................Open 7 days from 9 am
Type...Bar
Recommended for...Wish I'd opened

TEDDY'S BAR

3 Rue Thouin
5th Arrondissement
Paris 75005, France
+33 950032222

Recommended by
Edward Jalat-Dehen

Opening hours.......Mon–Sat from 4:30 pm, Sun from 4 pm
Credit cards...Accepted
Type...Bar
Recommended for...Local favorite

LE TRIANGLE

13 Rue Jacques Louvel Tessier
10th Arrondissement
Paris 75010, France
+33 171395802
www.triangleparis.com

Recommended by
Mike Amidei

Opening hours...Tue–Sat from 6 pm
Credit cards...Accepted
Type...Restaurant and microbrewery
Recommended for...Local favorite

SUPERBIERES

203 Rue du Faubourg Saint-Martin
10th Arrondissement
Paris 75010, France
+33 982529888
www.superbieres.com

Recommended by
Jeppe
Jarnit-Bjergsø

Opening hours...............................Tue–Sat from 11 am
Credit cards...Accepted
Type..Retail
Recommended for....................................Worth the travel

LA FINE MOUSSE

6 Avenue Jean Aicard
11th Arrondissement
Paris 75011, France
+33 148064094
www.lafinemousse.fr

Recommended by
Laurent Cicurel,
Roberto Alves da Fonseca,
Valter Loverier,
Shiro Yamada,
Jason Zeeff

Opening hours....................................Open 7 days from 4 pm
Credit cards...Accepted
Type...Bar
Recommended for..Beer & food

"They have ten taps in the restaurant and a great bottle menu.
Their delicious cuisine is a fusion of innovation and tradition.
They create dishes for pairing beers."—Valter Loverier

EXPRESS DE LYON

1 Rue de Lyon
12th Arrondissement
Paris 75012, France
+33 143432132

Recommended by
Mike Amidei

Opening hours....................................Mon–Fri from 8:30 am,
Sat–Sun from 9:30 am
Credit cards.............................Accepted but not Amex
Type...Bar
Recommended for..Beer & food

BIÉROCRATIE

32 Rue de l'Espérance
13th Arrondissement
Paris 75013, France
+33 153801610
www.bierocratie.com

Recommended by
Mike Amidei

Opening hours...Tue from 11 am,
Wed from 4 pm, Thur–Sat from 11 am
Credit cards...Accepted
Type..Retail
Recommended for...Local favorite

BOOTLEGGER BOFIAD

82 Rue de l'Ouest
14th Arrondissement
Paris 75014, France
+33 143279402
www.bieres-bootlegger.fr

Recommended by
Jeppe Jarnit-Bjergsø

Opening hours.................................Tue–Sat from 10:30 am
Credit cards..Accepted
Type......................................Restaurant and retail
Recommended for.............................Local favorite

LE FALSTAFF

42 Rue du Montparnasse
14th Arrondissement
Paris 75014, France
+33 143353829

Recommended by
Jeppe Jarnit-Bjergsø

Opening hours.......................Open 7 days from 8:30 am
Credit cards..Accepted
Type...Pub
Recommended for...........................Worth the travel

BIÈRES CULTES

25 Rue Legendre
17th Arrondissement
Paris 75017, France
+33 142270319
www.bierescultes.fr

Recommended by
Jeppe Jarnit-Bjergsø

Opening hours...Mon from 3 pm,
Tue–Sat from 11 am
Credit cards..Accepted
Type..Retail
Recommended for............................Wish I'd opened

OCTOPUSSY

22 Rue de la Jonquière
17th Arrondissement
Paris 75017, France
+33 973668965
www.octopussyparis.com

Recommended by
Jeppe Jarnit-Bjergsø

Opening hours...........................Mon–Sat from 6 pm,
Sun from 5 pm
Credit cards..Accepted
Type..Bar
Recommended for............................Wish I'd opened

A LA BIÈRE COMME À LA BIÈRE

20 Rue Custine
18th Arrondissement
Paris 75018, France
+33 952805914
www.alabierecommealabiere.com/cave-paris-custine

Recommended by
Mike Amidei

Opening hours...........................Tue–Fri from 3 pm,
Sat from 12 pm, Sun from 3 pm
Credit cards..Accepted
Type..Bar and retail
Recommended for...........................Worth the travel

BRASSERIE LA GOUTTE D'OR

28 Rue de la Goutte d'Or
18th Arrondissement
Paris 75018, France
+33 980642351
www.brasserielagouttedor.com

Recommended by
Mike Amidei

Opening hours..............Thur–Fri from 6 pm, Sat from 2 pm
Credit cards..Accepted
Type..Restaurant
Recommended for.............................Local favorite

LE SUPERCOIN

3 Rue Baudelique
18th Arrondissement
Paris 75018, France
+33 950070490
www.supercoin.net

Recommended by
Jeppe Jarnit-Bjergsø

Opening hours...............................Tue–Sun from 5 pm
Credit cards..Accepted
Type..Bar
Recommended for...........................Worth the travel

L'ATALANTE

26 Quai de la Marne
19th Arrondissement
Paris 75019, France
+33 145261382
www.atalanteourcq.fr

Recommended by
Edward Jalat-Dehen

Opening hours...............................Open 7 days from 10 am
Credit cards..Accepted
Type..Beer garden
Recommended for.............................Beer garden

"A friendly place."—Edward Jalat-Dehen

PANAME BREWING COMPANY

41 bis Quai de la Loire
19th Arrondissement
Paris 75019, France
+33 140364355
www.panamebrewingcompany.com

Recommended by
Mike Amidei

Opening hours......................................Open 7 days from 11 am
Credit cards...Accepted
Type..Brewery
Recommended for...Local favorite

LES TROIS 8

11 Rue Victor Letalle
20th Arrondissement
Paris 75020, France
+33 140334770
www.lestrois8.fr

Recommended by
Dorothée van Agt,
Edward Jalat-Dehen

Opening hours......................................Open 7 days from 5 pm
Credit cards...Accepted
Type...Bar
Recommended for...Local favorite

"It's a very small bar with only craft beer at a good price on tap and natural wine. The barmen are very friendly and funny."—Dorothée van Agt

DECK & DONOHUE

71 Rue de la Fraternité
Montreuil
Île-de-France 93100, France
+33 967311596
www.deck-donohue.com

Recommended by
Mike Amidei

Opening hours..Sat from 11 am
Credit cards......................................Accepted but not Amex
Type..Brewery
Recommended for...Local favorite

BAR GALLIA

35 Rue Méhul
Pantin
Île-de-France 93500, France
+33 157145672
www.galliaparis.com/le-bar-gallia

Recommended by
Laurent Cicurel

Opening hours...............................Wed–Fri from 5:30 pm,
Sat–Sun from 3 pm
Credit cards...Accepted
Type..Beer garden
Recommended for...Beer garden

"A really nice and chilled place, always with a lot going on: concerts, DJs, workshops. They also brew their own beer. They began as gypsy brewers. Now that they have their own brewery, the quality improves each time I go. They have a really good Berliner Weisse and hoppy beers."
—Laurent Cicurel

"AN OLD BREWERY AT A MONASTERY FROM 1455! THE BEER IS DELICIOUS, THE FOOD IS WONDERFUL, BUT THE SETTING IS WHAT REALLY DOES IT."

TIM ADAMS P.198

"WORLD-CHAMPION BREWMASTER AND BEER PLUS GREAT FOOD—A TRUE BAVARIAN JEWEL."

JORG FINKELDEY P.201

GERMANY

"A QUINTESSENTIAL GERMAN BIERGARTEN."

JULIE RHODES P.198

"THEY DON'T CARE ABOUT TRENDS. THEY DO WHAT THEY'VE DONE SINCE 1699 (BEER) AND 1872 (FOOD). GET THE FRESH TROUT AND KARP; IF IT'S NOT FISH SEASON TRY THE SCHNITZEL."

ULRIKE GENZ P.201

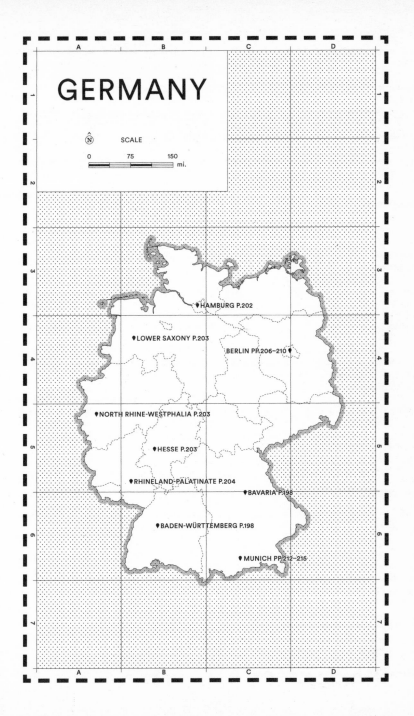

GERMANY

N SCALE

0   75   150
                    mi.

♦ HAMBURG P.202

♦ LOWER SAXONY P.203

BERLIN PP.206–210 ♦

♦ NORTH RHINE-WESTPHALIA P.203

♦ HESSE P.203

♦ RHINELAND-PALATINATE P.204

♦ BAVARIA P.198

♦ BADEN-WÜRTTEMBERG P.198

♦ MUNICH PP.212–215

TAPROOM JUNGBUSCH
Recommended by
Felix Schuessler
Beilstrasse 4
Mannheim
Baden-Württemberg 68159, Germany
+49 62131958881
www.taproomjungbusch.de

Opening hours	Tue–Sat from 6 pm
Credit cards	Accepted but not Amex
Type	Pub and brewery
Recommended for	Wish I'd opened

ANDECHS MONASTERY
Recommended by
Tim Adams
Bergstrasse 2
Andechs
Bavaria 82346, Germany
+49 8152376259
www.andechs.de

Opening hours	Open 7 days from 10 am
Credit cards	Not accepted
Type	Beer garden and brewery
Recommended for	Beer garden

"An old brewery at a monastery from 1455! The beer is delicious, the food (get the Schweinshaxe!) is wonderful, but the setting is what really does it."—Tim Adams

AYINGER BRÄUSTÜBERL
Recommended by
George Alexakis,
Charles Finkel,
Julie Rhodes
Münchener Strasse 2
Aying
Bavaria 85653, Germany
+49 80951345
www.ayinger-braeustueberl.de

Opening hours	Open 7 days from 10 am
Credit cards	Accepted
Type	Beer garden
Recommended for	Beer garden

"One of the world's classic beer gardens in the Bavarian tradition. They have extraordinary beer, in a garden with a giant chestnut tree and views of Brauereigasthof Aying, a hotel since 1385 with the largest maypole in Bavaria."
—Charles Finkel

"An amazing place under big trees. Great food and so traditional. You get the feeling of Bavaria."
—George Alexakis

"A quintessential German biergarten."—Julie Rhodes

BOOTSHAUS RESTAURANT IM HAIN
Recommended by
Fal Allen
Mühlwörth 18A
Bamberg
Bavaria 96047, Germany
+49 95124485
www.bootshaus-restaurant.de

Opening hours	Open 7 days from 11 am
Credit cards	Accepted
Type	Beer garden and restaurant
Recommended for	Beer garden

BRAUEREI GREIFENKLAU
Recommended by
Fal Allen,
Peter Eichhorn
Laurenziplatz 20
Bamberg
Bavaria 96049, Germany
+49 95153219
www.greifenklau.de

Opening hours	Tue–Sat from 10:30 am
Credit cards	Not accepted
Type	Beer garden
Recommended for	Worth the travel

"Delicious beer and food with a great beer garden that sits atop a hill, overlooking a picturesque valley with a castle on the opposite ridge."—Fal Allen

"Traditional and cozy with a great view over the landscape of the historic city of Bamberg and its green surroundings. It's one of the lesser-known breweries in Bamberg, but their beer is great and it's well worth the hike uphill."
—Peter Eichhorn

CAFÉ ABSEITS

Pödeldorfer Strasse 39
Bamberg
Bavaria 96052, Germany
+49 951303422
www.abseits-bamberg.de

Recommended by
Jussi Rokka

Opening hours..................................Open 7 days from 9 am
Credit cards...Not accepted
Type...Bar
Recommended for................................Wish I'd opened

MAHR'S BRÄU

Wunderburg 10
Bamberg
Bavaria 96050, Germany
+49 951915170
www.mahrs.de

Recommended by
Mario Canestrelli,
André Ek,
Dimitrij Jurisic,
Mike Murphy,
Rick Nelson

Opening hours.........Tue–Sun from 10 am, Mon from 4 pm
Credit cards...Not accepted
Type.................................Beer garden, brewery, and Pub
Recommended for.................................Beer garden

SCHLENKERLA

Dominikanerstrasse 6
Bamberg
Bavaria 96049, Germany
+49 95156060
www.schlenkerla.de

Recommended by
Danny Hamilton,
Jussi Rokka,
Sebastian Sauer

Opening hours...............................Open 7 days from 9:30 am
Credit cards...Not accepted
Type...Brewery and pub
Recommended for................................Worth the travel

"It's one of the most traditional pubs in the area of Franconia
and a world classic. The interior of the bar is old-fashioned,
rustic, and absolutely cozy. The selection of a gravity-
kegged smoked beer and some rustic German food can
never be wrong. A great experience and a unique place."
—Sebastian Sauer

Schlenkerla has been making beers the old-fashioned way for
a long, long time (since 1405!). To visit their brewery is to take
a step back in time. Their smoked beers are fantastic, and their
helles is one of the best pilsners in Germany. It tastes even
better when sitting at the brewery.

SPEZIAL-KELLER

Sternwartsrasse 8
Bamberg
Bavaria 96049, Germany
+49 95154887
www.spezial-keller.de

Recommended by
Lasse Ericsson,
Tomas Halberstad,
Olli Majanen,
Jussi Rokka

Opening hours..Tue–Sat from 3 pm,
Sun from 10:30 am
Credit cards..Accepted
Type...Beer garden
Recommended for...Beer garden

"On a hill overlooking the city, serving a great Bamberg
Rauchbier. It's always worth the hike up the hill."
—Jussi Rokka

"It's traditional Bamberg beer. If you enjoy that, then you're
in for a double treat because the setting is awesome."
—Tomas Halberstad

BRAUEREI-GASTHAUS ZUM MAX

Ampferbach 25
Burgebrach-Ampferbach
Bavaria 96138, Germany
+49 95461725
www.max-bier.de

Recommended by
Ulrike Genz

Opening hours..Tue from 5 pm,
Fri–Sun from 5 pm
Credit cards...Not accepted
Type...Pub and restaurant
Recommended for................................Worth the travel

ST. GEORGEN BRÄU KELLER

Marktstrasse 12
Buttenheim
Bavaria 96155, Germany
+49 95454460
www.georgenbraeu.de

Recommended by
Ulrike Genz

Opening hours.....................................Mon–Wed from 11 am,
Fri–Sun from 11 am
Credit cards..Accepted
Type.........................Beer garden, brewery, and restaurant
Recommended for...Beer garden

SCHMAUSENKELLER

Am Bahnhof 13
Frensdorf
Bavaria 96158, Germany
+49 9502608
www.schmausenkeller.de

Recommended by
Evan Doan

Opening hours	Mon, Fri–Sat from 4 pm, Sun from 11 am
Type	Brewery and beer garden
Recommended for	Beer garden

"A true example of a fantastic German beer garden. Fantastic ambiance and beer."—Evan Doan

KÖNIG LUDWIG SCHLOSSBRAUEREI

Augsburger Strasse 41
Fürstenfeldbruck
Bavaria 82256, Germany
+49 81412430
www.koenig-ludwig-brauerei.com

Recommended by
Marie-Josée Lefebvre

Opening hours	Mon–Fri from 8 am
Type	Beer garden and brewery
Recommended for	Beer garden

"I attended a horse show there and had a beer in the beautiful garden. They do have good beers, but the setup is magic."—Marie-Josée Lefebvre

CAMBA OLD FACTORY

An der Weberei 1
Gundelfingen an der Donau
Bavaria 89423, Germany
+49 90739971942
www.camba-bavaria.de

Recommended by
Georgi Hristov

Opening hours	Variable
Credit cards	Not accepted
Type	Beer garden and brewery
Recommended for	Beer garden

"I like this place because I was able to taste a lot of the beers from the brewery and also order pizza. The setting is really nice—a brewery hidden in the forest. Also, the beer from their brewer, Frau Gruber, exceeds all standards."
—Georgi Hristov

BIERKELLER ROPPELT

Stiebarlimbach 9
Hallerndorf
Bavaria 91352, Germany
+49 91957263
www.brauerei-roppelt.de/bierkeller

Recommended by
Sebastian Sauer

Opening hours	May–October Fri–Tue from 11 am, Wed–Thur from 3:30 pm
Credit cards	Not accepted
Type	Beer garden and restaurant
Recommended for	Beer garden

FRANZIS LIEBERTH'S KELLER

Kreuzberg
Hallerndorf
Bavaria 91352, Germany
+49 954570746
www.franzis-keller.de

Recommended by
Olivier Dupras

Opening hours	Mon–Fri from 4 pm, Sat–Sun from 11:30 am
Type	Beer garden
Recommended for	Beer garden

"Kreuzberg is a place near Bamberg located on top of a small hill, near a very old church. A couple of breweries of Hallerndorf have a beer garden there surrounded by forest. From Kreuzberg, you can take a short walk in the forest to Roppelt beer garden. I just love the Franconian way of doing things. Beer is life, and they create beautiful spots like this one to drink beer."—Olivier Dupras

WEISSES BRÄUHAUS KELHEIM

Emil-Ott-Strasse 3
Kehlheim
Bavaria 93309, Germany
+49 94413480
www.weisses-brauhaus-kelheim.de

Recommended by
Ronald Siemsgluess

Opening hours	Wed–Sun from 10 am
Credit cards	Accepted
Type	Beer garden
Recommended for	Beer garden

BRAUEREI-GASTHOF PLANK

Marktplatz 1
Laaber
Bavaria 93164, Germany
+49 943160889
www.brauerei-plank.de

Recommended by
Jorg Finkeldey

Opening hours................Thur–Mon from 8 am
Credit cards.................................Not accepted
Type...Restaurant
Recommended for...................Worth the travel

"World-champion brewmaster and beer plus great food—a true Bavarian jewel."—Jorg Finkeldey

Munich, see pages 212–215

SCHLÖSSLE BRAUEREI

Schlössleweg 3
Neu-Ulm
Bavaria 89231, Germany
+49 73177390
www.schloessle.com

Recommended by
Thomas Wagner

Opening hours.....................Mon–Wed from 5 pm,
Thur–Sun from 11 am
Credit cards.................................Not accepted
Type.............................Beer garden and brewery
Recommended for...........................Beer garden

"The best beer garden ever."—Thomas Wagner

SCHOENRAMER BREWERY

Salzberger Strasse 17
Petting
Bavaria 83367, Germany
+49 86869880
www.brauerei-schoenram.de

Recommended by
Ashleigh Carter

Opening hours....................Mon–Fri from 7 am
Credit cards....................................Accepted
Type...........................Brewery and restaurant
Recommended for...................Worth the travel

"A beautifully designed brewery and restaurant with perfect German lagers."—Ashleigh Carter

BRAUEREI-GASTHOF MÜLLER

Würzburger Strasse 1
Stegaurach
Bavaria 96135, Germany
+49 95129191
www.debringer-bier.de

Recommended by
Ulrike Genz

Opening hours...................Tue–Wed from 11 am, Thur from
4:30 pm, Fri–Sat from 11 am, Sun from 10 am
Credit cards.................................Not accepted
Type..........................Brewery and restaurant
Recommended for............................Beer & food

"They don't care about trends. They do what they've done since 1699 (beer) and 1872 (food). Get the fresh trout and karp; if it's not fish season try the schnitzel."—Ulrike Genz

CAMBA BIERERLEBNISWELT IN TRUCHTLACHING

Mühlweg 2
Truchtlaching
Bavaria 83376, Germany
+49 8667876800
www.camba-bavaria.de

Recommended by
Peter Krammer

Opening hours.........................Tue–Thur from 3 pm,
Fri–Sat from 10 am
Credit cards....................................Accepted
Type.............................Beer garden and brewery
Recommended for...........................Beer garden

"Great international beer styles brewed in their own brewery. A wonderful garden at the Alz river."
—Peter Krammer

CREW REPUBLIC

Andreas-Danzer-Weg 30
Unterschleißheim
Bavaria 85716, Germany
+49 89411471290
www.crewrepublic.de

Recommended by
Amy Newell-Large

Opening hours..............................Friday from 4 pm
Credit cards....................Accepted but not Amex
Type..Brewery
Recommended for...................Worth the travel

BRAUEREI HECKEL

Vorstadt 3
Waischenfeld
Bavaria 91344, Germany
+49 9202493
www.bierland-oberfranken.de

Recommended by
Olivier Dupras

Opening hours.................................Tue–Wed from 4:30 pm,
 Fri from 4:30 pm, Sat from 9:30 am, Sun from 10 am
Type...Brewery
Recommended for...Worth the travel

"This place is the guesthouse for the Heckel Brauerei, a
Franconian brewery that was family-run when I was there.
It's in a small village forty minutes from Bamberg. It's tiny
and kind of dark, with wooden walls. There is no music.
The five patrons quietly sip their beer. My friend and I order
the only beer brewed by the brewery, a golden Vollbier at
5.8% ABV from a classic Franconian cask. The beer is
perfect, their vollbier is the best I've ever drunk."
—Olivier Dupras

CAMPINGPLATZ WALLBERG

Rainerweg 10
Weißach am Tegernsee
Bavaria 83700, Germany
+49 80225371
www.campingplatz-wallberg.de

Recommended by
Rick Nelson

Opening hours...Always open
Credit cards...Not accepted
Type..Restaurant
Recommended for...Unexpected

"It has beer from Brauerei Tegernsee, known for one of the
best pilsners and helles in Germany. Next to that is a
campground with the best kitchen ever. It's a really good
Bayerisch kitchen. Go for the maultasche or kalb sauer
lunge, with a liter mug of helles."—Rick Nelson

Berlin, see pages 206–210

BEYOND BEER

Weidenallee 55
Hamburg 20357, Germany
+49 4044465424
www.beyondbeer.de

Recommended by
Ronald Siemsgluess

Opening hours..Tue–Fri from 1 pm,
 Sat from 10 am
Credit cards...Accepted
Type...Retail
Recommended for....................................Wish I'd opened

"The best beer selection in Germany, with great beer,
great service, and an outstanding atmosphere."
—Ronald Siemsgluess

BRAUGASTHAUS ALTES MÄDCHEN

Lagerstrasse 28B
Hamburg 20357, Germany
+49 40800077750
www.altes-maedchen.de

Recommended by
Birgit Rieber,
Daniel Thombansen

Opening hours.......................................Mon–Sat from 12 pm,
 Sun from 10 am
Credit cards...Accepted
Type...Brewery and restaurant
Recommended for..Local favorite

"Altes Mädchen is a taproom, a beer bar, and a restaurant of
Ratsherrn Brauerei. It was the first place in Germany with
such a great range of beers, not only Ratsherrn beers
but also others from all over the world. There's even a
bakery, which shows the historical relationship between
brewing and baking."—Birgit Rieber

GALOPPER DES JAHRES

Schulterblatt 73
Hamburg 20357, Germany
+49 4043093975
www.dreiundsiebzig.de

Recommended by
Gerrit Lerch

Opening hours.......................................Mon–Sat from 5 pm,
 Sun from 12 pm
Credit cards...Not accepted
Type..Bar
Recommended for..Local favorite

"A wide selection of draft beers and bottles, plus good
ambiance in a cool part of town."—Gerrit Lerch

ÜBERQUELL BRAUWERKSTÄTTEN

Saint Pauli Fischmarkt 28–32
Hamburg 20359, Germany
+49 40334421260
www.ueberquell.com

Recommended by
Michele Hengst,
Gerrit Lerch,
Ronald Siemsgluess

Opening hours......................................Mon–Thur from 5 pm,
Fri–Sun from 12 pm
Credit cards..Accepted
Type..Brewery and Pub
Recommended for..Beer & food

NAÏV

Fahrgasse 4
Frankfurt am Main
Hesse 60311, Germany
+49 6921006230
www.naiv-frankfurt.de

Recommended by
Felix Schuessler

Opening hours..Mon–Fri from 5 pm,
Sat–Sun from 12 pm
Credit cards..Accepted
Type..Bar and restaurant
Recommended for..Local favorite

HEINRICH - DAS WIRTSHAUS

Jasperallee 42
Braunschweig
Lower Saxony 38102, Germany
+49 53160946710
www.heinrich-braunschweig.de

Recommended by
Odin Paul

Opening hours..Mon–Sat from 3 pm,
Sun from 11 am
Credit cards..Accepted
Type..............................Beer garden and restaurant
Recommended for..Beer garden

SCHADT'S BRAUEREI GASTHAUS

Höhe 28
Braunschweig
Lower Saxony 38100, Germany
+49 531400349
www.schadts-brauerei-gasthaus.de

Recommended by
Odin Paul

Opening hours..Tue–Sat from 12 pm,
Sun–Mon from 5 pm
Credit cards..Accepted
Type..Brewery
Recommended for...Wish I'd opened

BRAUHAUS GOSLAR

Marktkirchhof 2
Goslar
Lower Saxony 38640, Germany
+49 5321685804
www.brauhaus-goslar.de

Recommended by
Odin Paul

Opening hours..................................Open 7 days from 11 am
Credit cards.............................Accepted but not Amex
Type..Brewery
Recommended for...Local favorite

SÜDSEE-BADEPARADIES KONTIKI-BAR

Südsee Camp 1
Wietzendorf
Lower Saxony 29649, Germany
+49 5196250351
www.suedsee-camp.de

Recommended by
Odin Paul

Opening hours......................................Mon–Fri from 12 pm,
Sat–Sun from 10 am
Credit cards...Not accepted
Type...Bar
Recommended for...Unexpected

"It's a campground, and they offer three special beers."
—Odin Paul

CRAFTBEER CORNER COELN

Martinstrasse 32
Cologne
North Rhine-Westphalia 50667, Germany
www.craftbeercorner.de

Recommended by
Sebastian Sauer

Opening hours......................................Mon–Thur from 6 pm,
Fri–Sat from 5 pm
Credit cards..Accepted
Type...Pub
Recommended for...Local favorite

"It's the first craft-beer-focused beer bar in the most populous German state. This bar gets the attention of anyone searching craft-beer destinations, with a dedicated beer list and a great atmosphere."—Sebastian Sauer

LOMMERZHEIM

Siegesstrasse 18
Cologne
North Rhine-Westphalia 50679, Germany
+49 221814392
www.lommerzheim.juisyfood.com

Recommended by
Lori Beck

Opening hours	Mon from 11 am, Wed–Sat from 11 am, Sun from 10:30 am
Credit cards	Not accepted
Type	Pub
Recommended for	Beer & food

"This is my favorite place to drink Kölsch and eat. They have a very small menu of traditional German foods, but it's all about the pork chop. The staff will make sure you have a great time. It doesn't get more authentic then this. No thinking necessary, and you'll end up with an epic, unforgettable pairing."—Lori Beck

BRAUHAUS THOMBANSEN

Lange Strasse 3
Lippstadt
North Rhine-Westphalia 59555, Germany
+49 2941800815
www.lippstaedter-brauerei.de

Recommended by
Daniel Thombansen

Opening hours	Tue–Sat from 5 pm
Credit cards	Accepted
Type	Brewery
Recommended for	Local favorite

"Nice food, like burger and schnitzel, and different home-brewed beers, from classic to craft beers." —Daniel Thombansen

GRIESS KELLER

Kellerweg 9
Strullendorf
Rhineland-Palatinate 96129, Germany
+49 1607865972
www.braueri-gress.de

Recommended by
Mario Canestrelli

Opening hours	Mon–Fri from 3 pm, Sat–Sun from 12 pm
Credit cards	Not accepted
Type	Beer garden
Recommended for	Beer garden

"Simply the most beautiful place to drink a beer anywhere. The Griess Kellerbier—a Franconian gem—an unfiltered lager brewed 150 meters down the road, served in stoneware mugs is absolute bliss."—Mario Canestrelli

KRAFT BRÄU

Hotel Blesius Garten
Olewiger Strasse 135
Trier
Rhineland-Palatinate 54295, Germany
+49 65136060
www.kraftbraeu.de

Recommended by
Felix Schuessler

Opening hours	Open 7 days from 11 am to 12 am
Credit cards	Accepted
Type	Brewery and restaurant
Recommended for	Beer & food

"A hotel, restaurant, and brewery in an old wine village outside of Trier. They have more than ten house-brewed beers on tap. Their annual house-run beer festival has twenty craft breweries from all over Germany. They also do tastings with their in-house beer sommelier in five-course-menus."—Felix Schuessler

ZAPOTEX

Am Pferdemarkt 1A
Trier
Rhineland-Palatinate 54290, Germany
+49 65175822
www.zapotex.de

Recommended by
Felix Schuessler

Opening hours	Mon–Sat from 7 pm, Sun from 8 pm
Credit cards	Not accepted
Type	Bar
Recommended for	Worth the travel

"A fantastic collection of craft beers, whiskeys, gins, and other fine spirits. They have regional and seasonal beers on tap all year, traditional lager beers, and imported and limited craft beers. It looks inconspicuous from the outside, but there's a lot of know-how on the inside. They have a great staff, and it's a meeting point for the local brewers scene." —Felix Schuessler

BERLIN

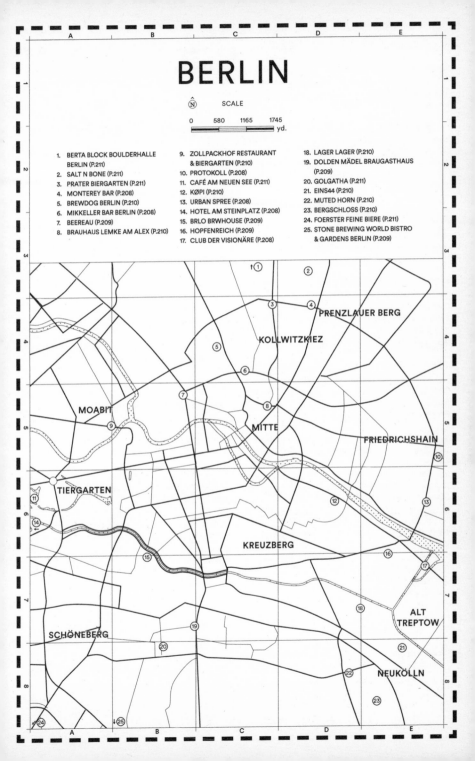

CLUB DER VISIONÄRE
Recommended by
Gabriela Velasco

Am Flutgraben 1
Schlesische Strasse
Alt-Treptow
Berlin 12435, Germany
+49 3069518942
www.clubdervisionaere.com

Opening hours..............................Mon–Thur from 2 pm,
Fri–Sun from 12 pm
Credit cards...Not accepted
Type...................................Beer garden and bar
Recommended for...................................Beer garden

"It's casual and relaxed—you can drink beer just sitting on the floor. It's next to the water."—Gabriela Velasco

HOTEL AM STEINPLATZ
Recommended by
Peter Eichhorn

Steinplatz 4
Charlottenburg
Berlin 10623, Germany
+49 305544447053
www.hotelsteinplatz.com

Opening hours..............................Mon–Fri from 12 pm,
Sat–Sun from 6 pm
Credit cards...Accepted
Type...Restaurant
Recommended for...................................Beer & food

"A great chef, Nicholas Hahn, prepares amazing food and creative dishes. The servers suggest beer pairings from the wonderful selection of international beers. One of the first high-class restaurants in Germany to offer outstanding beer pairings. This place has been the first in the country to put beer on the same level as wine."—Peter Eichhorn

PROTOKOLL
Recommended by
Vadim Gurov

Boxhagener Strasse 110
Friedrichshain
Berlin 10245, Germany
+49 17660886670
www.protokollberlin.de

Opening hours...................Open 7 days from 4 pm
Credit cards...Accepted
Type...Bar
Recommended for...................................Worth the travel

URBAN SPREE
Recommended by
Michele Hengst

Revaler Strasse 99
Friedrichshain
Berlin 10245, Germany
+49 3074078597
www.urbanspree.com

Opening hours.........................Tue–Sun from 12 pm
Credit cards...Not accepted
....Beer garden and bar
Recommended for...................................Beer garden

"It's in this supercool industrial area, a little arty—mostly street and graffiti art—good atmosphere."—Michele Hengst

MONTEREY BAR
Recommended by
Lea Lima

Danziger Strasse 61
Helmholtzkiez
Berlin 10435, Germany
+49 1753670536
www.montereybar.com

Opening hours.....................Open 7 days from 5 pm
Credit cards...Accepted
Type...Bar
Recommended for...................................Worth the travel

"I loved the beer selection and rock music."—Lea Lima

MIKKELLER BAR BERLIN
Recommended by
Milos Vuksic

Torstrasse 102
Kollwitzkiez
Berlin 10119, Germany
+49 17683141103
www.mikkeller.dk

Opening hours.....................Open 7 days from 3 pm
Credit cards...Accepted
Type...Bar
Recommended for...................................Wish I'd opened

BRLO BRWHOUSE

Schöneberger Strasse 16
Kreuzberg
Berlin 10963, Germany
+49 15174374235
www.brlo-brwhouse.de

Recommended by
Peter Eichhorn,
Svitlana Filatova,
Marisa Jackson,
Cristina Saez,
Martin Voigt

Opening hours............................Tue–Fri from 5 pm,
Sat–Sun from 12 pm
Credit cards...Accepted
Type...Beer garden, restaurant,
and brewery
Recommended for.................................Beer garden

"The main building is made from shipping containers where the brewery, taproom, and restaurant are located. The beer garden is outside in a recreational area close to the Berlin city center. It's a very unconventional place to meet and bring the kids and dogs. Have a decent dinner or just grab a beer. Anything goes, and it's very welcoming. Plus, they make their own ice cream in the summer—very yummy! They have some of the best beers in town. It's also worth it to come in winter for the indoor taproom."—Martin Voigt

"The place is a perfect embodiment of modern Berlin: trendy, youthful, and sleekly designed. It's both green and calm—drinking beer under real hop vines is an amazing experience. The food is amazing, and the chef is innovative and adventurous. Twenty taps represent the house beer, collaborations between BRLO and other breweries, and the finest examples of international craft beer. They do educational and fun events. Brewery tours are available."
—Svitlana Filatova

DOLDEN MÄDEL BRAUGASTHAUS

Mehringdamm 80
Kreuzberg
Berlin 10965, Germany
+49 3077326213
www.doldenmaedel.de

Recommended by
Birgit Rieber

Opening hours............................Open 7 days from 11:30 am
Credit cards...Accepted
Type...Pub
Recommended for.................................Worth the travel

"Great beers, atmosphere, and service with many beerkeepers. Many lines with local Berlin beer, often special versions not found elsewhere."—Birgit Rieber

HOPFENREICH

Sorauer Strasse 31
Kreuzberg
Berlin 10997, Germany
+49 3088061080
www.hopfenreich.de

Recommended by
Cristina Saez

Opening hours............................Open 7 days from 4 pm
Credit cards...Accepted
Type...Bar
Recommended for.................................Local favorite

"A nice atmosphere, with local breweries on tap."
—Cristina Saez

STONE BREWING WORLD BISTRO & GARDENS BERLIN

Im Marienpark 23
Mariendorf
Berlin 12107, Germany
+49 30212343100
www.stonebrewing.eu

Recommended by
Dorothée van Agt, Matthew
Buttigieg, Diego Castro,
Daniel Goh, Jamil Haddad,
Stefan Krueger, John Latta,
Gerrit Lerch, Odin Paul,
Andris Rasiņš, Estacio
Rodrigues, Cristina Saez

Opening hours........Mon–Sat from 12 pm, Sun from 10 am
Credit cards...Accepted
Type...Beer garden and brewery
Recommended for.................................Worth the travel

"What Stone has done in Berlin is amazing. It has converted a beautiful old gasworks into one of the most impressive beer gardens and breweries on the planet. The trip is well worth it. You'll find it hard to leave once you settle in, so plan to stay a while."—John Latta

"It has 100 taps with the freshest beer from all over the world. The very large space has great ambience, including gardens for outdoor dining and really nice food paired with beer."—Matthew Buttigieg

BEEREAU

Claire-Waldoff-Strasse 2–4
Mitte
Berlin 10117, Germany
+49 3031176081

Recommended by
Ulrike Genz

Opening hours............................Mon–Sat from 2 pm
Credit cards...Accepted
Type...Bar
Recommended for.................................Local favorite

BRAUHAUS LEMKE AM ALEX

Karl-Liebknecht-Strasse 13
Mitte
Berlin 10178, Germany
+49 3030878989
www.lemke.berlin

Recommended by
Odin Paul

Opening hours..................................Open 7 days from 12 pm
Credit cards...Accepted
Type..Pub
Recommended for......................................Beer & food

---

BREWDOG BERLIN

Ackerstrasse 29
Mitte
Berlin 10115, Germany
+49 3048477770
www.brewdog.com

Recommended by
Peter Eichhorn,
Stefan Krueger

Opening hours..................................Open 7 days from 12 pm
Credit cards...................................Accepted but not Amex
Type..Pub
Recommended for.................................Wish I'd opened

"A great mixture of people and amazing pizza."
—Peter Eichhorn

"Good beer selection. Open space. Good people."
—Stefan Krueger

KØPI

Köpenicker Strasse 137
Mitte
Berlin 10179, Germany
www.koepi137.net

Recommended by
Ulrike Genz

Opening hours.......................................Thur–Sat from 8 pm
Credit cards...Not accepted
Type..Bar
Recommended for.......................................Unexpected

---

ZOLLPACKHOF RESTAURANT & BIERGARTEN

Elisabeth-Abegg-Strasse 1
Moabit
Berlin 10557, Germany
+49 3033099720
www.zollpackhof.de

Recommended by
Øystein Krogtoft

Opening hours..................................Open 7 days from 10 am
Credit cards...Accepted
Type...Beer garden
Recommended for.....................................Beer garden

---

BERGSCHLOSS

Kopfstrasse 59
Neukölln
Berlin 12053, Germany
+49 3064435906

Recommended by
Michele Hengst

Opening hours.................................Thur–Sat from 7 pm
Credit cards...Not accepted
Type..Bar and brewery
Recommended for......................................Local favorite

"The cozy taproom of the Berliner Berg brewery. A relaxed atmosphere with candles and chilled music and great draft beers from nine taps."—Michele Hengst

---

EINS44

Elbestrasse 28/29
Neukölln
Berlin 12045, Germany
+49 3062981212
www.eins44.com

Recommended by
Michele Hengst

Opening hours........Tue–Fri from 12:30 pm, Sat from 7 pm
Credit cards...Accepted
Type...Restaurant
Recommended for......................................Beer & food

---

LAGER LAGER

Pflügerstrasse 68
Neukölln
Berlin 12047, Germany
+49 3023903919
www.lagerlagerberlin.de

Recommended by
Michele Hengst

Opening hours............Mon–Fri from 2 pm, Sat from 12 pm
Credit cards...Accepted
Type..Bar and retail
Recommended for.......................................Unexpected

---

MUTED HORN

Flughafenstrasse 49
Neukölln
Berlin 12053, Germany
+49 3091569256
www.themutedhorn.com

Recommended by
Tomas Halberstad,
Andris Rasiņš,
Ronald Siemsgluess,
Ben Whitney

Opening hours.......................................Mon–Fri from 5 pm,
Sat–Sun from 3 pm
Credit cards...Accepted
Type..Bar
Recommended for...................................Worth the travel

"Muted Horn consistently has one of the best tap and bottle lists in the city."—Ben Whitney

BERTA BLOCK BOULDERHALLE BERLIN

Mühlenstrasse 62
Pankow
Berlin 13187, Germany
+49 3091424730
www.bertablock.de

Recommended by
Ben Whitney

Opening hours................................Mon–Fri from 9 am
Sat–Sun from 10 am
Type...Bar
Recommended for....................................Unexpected

"A rock-climbing gym with craft beer on draft. You have to carb up after a nice climb."—Ben Whitney

PRATER BIERGARTEN

Kastanienallee 7–9
Prenzlauer Berg
Berlin 10435, Germany
+49 304485688
www.pratergarten.de

Recommended by
Lori Beck,
Gerrit Lerch,
Pablo Santos

Opening hours..........Mon–Sat from 6 pm, Sun from 12 pm
Credit cards.......................................Not accepted
Type.............................Beer garden and restaurant
Recommended for.................................Beer garden

"Great atmosphere and beautiful outdoor space. The setting is amazing."—Lori Beck

SALT N BONE

Schliemannstrasse 31
Prenzlauer Berg
Berlin 10437, Germany
+49 3091448885
www.saltnbone.de

Recommended by
Joe Dick

Opening hours..............Tue–Fri from 6 pm, Sat from 5 pm,
Sun from 2 pm
Credit cards.......................................Not accepted
Type...Pub
Recommended for.................................Beer & food

"An excellent local and imported range, and the menu and atmosphere are perfect. They have a tight menu of five rotating keg beers that turn over nicely."—Joe Dick

GOLGATHA

Dudenstrasse 40–64
Schöneberg
Berlin 10965, Germany
+49 307852453
www.golgatha-berlin.de

Recommended by
Rick LeVert

Opening hours.................................Open 7 days from 9 am
Credit cards.......................................Not accepted
Type...Beer garden
Recommended for.................................Beer garden

FOERSTERS FEINE BIERE

Bornstrasse 20
Steglitz
Berlin 12163, Germany
www.foerstersfeinebiere.de

Recommended by
Peter Eichhorn

Opening hours.................................Mon–Sat from 4 pm
Credit cards.......................................Not accepted
Type...Bar
Recommended for.................................Local favorite

"The owner takes his beer seriously. Great selection and wonderful recommendations and balance between classic and craft. They have a nice yard in the summertime."
—Peter Eichhorn

CAFÉ AM NEUEN SEE

Lichtensteinallee 2
Tiergarten
Berlin 10787, Germany
+49 302544930
www.cafeamneuensee.de

Recommended by
Vasilia Venizelacou

Opening hours.................................Open 7 days from 9 am
Credit cards.......................................Not accepted
Type...Beer garden
Recommended for.................................Beer garden

"The beer garden is lit with festoon lighting, next to a beautiful lake surrounded by trees. It has little paddle boats that are free to use, and it's so calming to sit there. The atmosphere is buzzing too. The venue has traditional German beer, but it's the setting that takes your breath away."—Vasilia Venizelacou

"WELCOMING AND JOLLY, WITH EXCELLENT BEER AND FOOD."
JOHN DUFFY P.215

"A CRAZY, NOISY ATMOSPHERE WHERE YOU CAN BEFRIEND LOCALS AND TOURISTS."
OLIVER SAN ANTONIO P.214

MUNICH

"A BEAUTIFUL BEER GARDEN WITH AMAZING GERMAN FOOD."
ASHLEIGH CARTER P.214

"MAGICAL BEER."
JORG FINKELDEY P.215

"A MUST-NOT-MISS IN MUNICH. GREAT BEER AND SETTING, GOOD SERVICE, PLUS SWING SETS FOR THE KIDS. BIERGARTEN PERFECTION."
STEPHEN ROGINSON P.214

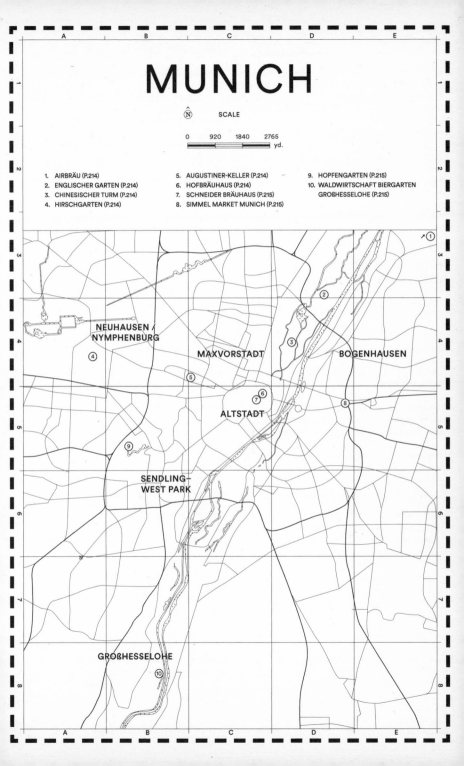

AIRBRÄU

Terminalstrasse Mitte 18
Munich International Airport
Munich 85356, Germany
+49 8997593111
www.munich-airport.de

Recommended by
Simon Broderick,
Olivier Dupras,
Jaanis Tammela

Opening hours......................................Open 7 days from 8 am
Credit cards...Accepted
Type..Bar
Recommended for...Unexpected

"I didn't expect to find a brewery in the airport. They do
some very good seasonal specials."—Simon Broderick

AUGUSTINER-KELLER

Arnulfstrasse 52
Munich 80335, Germany
+49 89594393
www.augustinerkeller.de

Recommended by
John Duffy,
Josh Pfriem,
Stephen Roginson,
Höskuldur Sæmundsson,
Leo Sewald

Opening hours..................................Open 7 days from 10 am
Credit cards...Accepted
Type...Restaurant and beer garden
Recommended for...Beer garden

"A huge beer garden, with easy access to liters of
world-class helles lager and food to go with it. It's a place to
gather with friends and have a blast."—Josh Pfriem

"A must-not-miss in Munich. Great beer and setting, good
service, plus swing sets for the kids. Biergarten perfection."
—Stephen Roginson

CHINESISCHER TURM

Englischer Garten 3
Munich 80538, Germany
+49 89383820
www.chinaturm.de

Recommended by
Adam Bruckman Watson

Opening hours..................................Open 7 days from 10 am
Credit cards...Accepted
Type..Beer garden
Recommended for...Beer garden

"I was lucky enough to have a few liters of dunkle and a
bratwurst here."—Adam Bruckman Watson

ENGLISCHER GARTEN

Englischer Garten 2
Munich 80538, Germany
+49 8938666390
www.muenchen.de

Recommended by
Estacio Rodrigues,
Ben Self

Opening hours...............................Wed–Sun from 10:30 am
Credit cards...Accepted
Type..Beer garden
Recommended for...Beer garden

"It's hard to find a better atmosphere than sitting in a public
park with dozens of other people, casually enjoying a
traditional helles, pretzels, and spiral-cut radishes. Sure,
there are plenty of places with a more diverse selection or
craftier beers, but I'll take that atmosphere before anyplace
else in the world."—Ben Self

HIRSCHGARTEN

Hirschgarten 1
Munich 80639, Germany
+49 89179119
www.hirschgarten.de

Recommended by
Ashleigh Carter

Opening hours...............................Open 7 days from 11:30 am
Credit cards...Accepted
Type...Beer garden and restaurant
Recommended for...Beer garden

"A beautiful beer garden with amazing German food. Big
trees and deer to watch!"—Ashleigh Carter

HOFBRÄUHAUS

Platzl 9
Munich 80331, Germany
+49 89290136100
www.hofbraeuhaus.de

Recommended by
Brian Boyer, Kevin Drake,
Rick Green, Nathan Hoeft,
Ron Hoglund, Oliver San
Antonio, Felipe Valenciano,
Jaega Wise

Opening hours......................................Open 7 days from 9 am
Credit cards...Accepted
Type..Beer garden
Recommended for...Beer garden

"A crazy, noisy atmosphere where you can befriend locals
and tourists. It's the best beer experience in Munich, outside
Oktoberfest. Both the setting and the beer are great. The
food is wonderful as well, especially the German
sausages."—Oliver San Antonio

HOPFENGARTEN

Siegenburger Strasse 43
Munich 81373, Germany
+49 897608846
www.hopfen-garten.de

Recommended by
Kris Li

Opening hours	Open 7 days from 11 am (summer)
Type	Beer garden
Recommended for	Beer garden

"A true German beer garden experience. Not touristy, lots of great local food options, and excellent pilsner."—Kris Li

SCHNEIDER BRÄUHAUS

Tal 7
Munich 80331, Germany
+49 892901380
www.schneider-brauhaus.de

Recommended by
John Duffy,
Camilo Rojas Sanchez

Opening hours	Open 7 days from 8 am
Credit cards	Accepted
Type	Beer garden and restaurant
Recommended for	Worth the travel

"Welcoming and jolly, with excellent beer and food."
—John Duffy

SIMMEL MARKET MUNICH

Einsteinstrasse 130
Munich 81675, Germany
+49 8941188862
www.simmel.de

Recommended by
Will Fisher

Opening hours	Open 7 days from 7 am
Credit cards	Accepted
Type	Retail
Recommended for	Unexpected

"A neighborhood market. I flew into Munich for work and was staying in Ingolstadt. I went to this store to pick up some beer and found bottles of Ayinger and Schneider and thought I'd died and gone to heaven."—Will Fisher

WALDWIRTSCHAFT BIERGARTEN GROßHESSELOHE

Georg-Kalb-Strasse 3
Munich 82049, Germany
+49 8974994030
www.waldwirtschaft.de

Recommended by
Jorg Finkeldey

Opening hours	Open 7 days from 10 am
Credit cards	Accepted
Type	Beer garden
Recommended for	Beer garden

"A great beer garden where you can bring your own food. They have awesome live music and magical beer."
—Jorg Finkeldey

"UTOPIA!"

TOD MOTT P.222

"FIFTEEN TAPS, MORE THAN 700 BOTTLE AND CAN BEERS, ROCK MUSIC, AND THE BEST PEOPLE."

JUAN FERNÁNDEZ P.218

SPAIN, PORTUGAL & MALTA

"YOU CAN EAT AMAZING LOCAL DISHES LIKE TXULETON BEEF IN THE MIDDLE OF THE MOUNTAINS AND DRINK GOOD CRAFT BEER."

JACOBO PÉREZ LLISO P.218

"REALLY GREAT BURGERS—PROBABLY THE BEST IN TOWN—WITH A GREAT CURATED AND ALWAYS UP-TO-DATE BEER MENU."

BRUNO CARRILHO P.221

SPAIN, PORTUGAL & MALTA

N SCALE

0   75   150
mi.

A B C D

1

2

3

♦ ASTURIAS P.218   ♦ BASQUE COUNTRY P.218

♦ GALICIA P.219   S P A I N

CATALONIA P.218 ♦

♦ PORTO P.221   BARCELONA PP.224–227 ♦

P O R T U G A L   ♦ MADRID P.219

VALENCIAN COMMUNITY P.219 ♦

♦ LISBON P.220

4

5

6

M A L T A

S Ã O   M I G U E L   NORTHERN REGION P.222 ♦
CENTRAL REGION P.222 ♦
SOUTH EASTERN REGION P.222 ♦

♦ RIBEIRA GRANDE P.222

7

A B C D

EL LÚPULO FEROZ
Recommended by
Juan Fernández

Calle Ildefonso Sánchez del Río 8
Oviedo
Asturias 33001, Spain
+34 667675857

Opening hours.....................................Open 7 days from 6 pm
Credit cards...Accepted but not Amex
Type..Bar
Recommended for..Local favorite

"Fifteen taps, more than 700 bottle and can beers, rock music, and the best people."—Juan Fernández

ESTEBENEA
Recommended by
Jacobo Pérez Lliso

Barrio Olaberria 51
Irun
Basque Country 20303, Spain
+34 943621962

Opening hours.....................................Open 7 days from 12 pm
Credit cards...Accepted but not Amex
Type..Restaurant
Recommended for...Unexpected

"You can eat amazing local dishes like Txuleton beef in the middle of the mountains and drink good craft beer."
—Jacobo Pérez Lliso

BAR DESY
Recommended by
Richard Burhouse

Ronda Kalea 4
San Sebastian
Basque Country 20001, Spain
+34 943293763

Opening hours.......................................Mon–Sat from 6 am
Credit cards...Accepted
Type..Bar
Recommended for..Beer & food

Barcelona, see pages 224–227

LA LLÚDRIGA
Recommended by
Aitor Labrador

Parque del Ter
Carretera Costa Brava, s/n
Colomers
Catalonia 17144, Spain
+34 629756246

Opening hours....................................Thur–Tue from 9 am
Credit cards...Accepted but not Amex
Type..Bar and restaurant
Recommended for...Unexpected

"A beach bar–restaurant next to a river with eighty craft-beer lines? Yes, at La Llúdriga. Incredible beer."
—Aitor Labrador

EL BIRROT
Recommended by
Aitor Labrador

Carrer la Creu 5
Jafre
Catalonia 17143, Spain
+34 635624726

Opening hours.......................................Thur–Mon from 6 pm
Credit cards...Accepted
Type...Beer garden
Recommended for..Beer garden

"A hidden gem. A real beer garden in a small town next to Costa Brava. Enjoy one of the best local and international beer menus in Catalonia, under the shadow of hundred-year-old trees and paired with the best rustic food."
—Aitor Labrador

LA BARRICONA
Recommended by
Aitor Labrador

Carretera de Sant Joan
de les Abadesses, km 3'6
Ripoll
Catalonia 17500, Spain
+34 972702352
www.labarricona.cat

Opening hours.....................................Open 7 days from 1 pm
Credit cards...Accepted but not Amex
Type..Restaurant
Recommended for..Beer & food

"Located in a Catalan Masia (country house), La Barricona-Traficant de Menjars is a cooperative featuring local farmers, ranchers, and producers like Catalan brewers La Calavera."—Aitor Labrador

CERVEZOTECA MALTE

Rúa Galera 47
A Coruña
Galicia 15003, Spain
+34 981205751
www.cervezotecamalte.com

Recommended by
Alberto Gómez

Opening hours	Tue–Sun from 1 pm, Mon from 6 pm
Credit cards	Accepted
Type	Bar and restaurant
Recommended for	Beer & food

BEE BEER

Calle de Augusto Figueroa 30
Centro
Madrid 28004, Spain
+34 911296955

Recommended by
Lana Svitankova

Opening hours	Tue–Sat from 12 pm, Sun from 5 pm
Credit cards	Accepted
Type	Bar
Recommended for	Beer & food

BREW WILD PIZZA BAR

Calle Echegaray 23
Centro
Madrid 28014, Spain
+34 913483586
www.brewwildpizzabar.com

Recommended by
Alberto Gómez,
Jacobo Pérez Lliso

Opening hours	Tue–Fri from 6 pm, Sat–Sun from 1 pm
Credit cards	Accepted
Type	Bar and restaurant
Recommended for	Wish I'd opened

"A great atmosphere and a good combination of amazing craft beer and great pizza. They also have a cave inside the bar."—Alberto Gómez

"An awesome bar with fifteen taps (four from La Quince Brewery) and eleven guest taps with the best craft-beer selection from Spain, Europe, and the United States. They also have a nice selection of bottles, including many lambic beers—and amazing Sicilian pizzas, which is my favorite beer pairing. There's punk rock music and a nice ambience across two floors. Upstairs is an American-style taproom, and downstairs is a cave. Perfect location if you want to visit Madrid (close to Plaza Santa Ana and Puerta del Sol)."
—Jacobo Pérez Lliso

MAD GRILL

Calle de Campoamor 13
Centro
Madrid 28004, Spain
+34 910126430
www.madrestaurants.com

Recommended by
Aniko Lehtinen

Opening hours	Open 7 days from 1:30 pm
Credit cards	Accepted
Type	Restaurant
Recommended for	Beer & food

"The restaurant serves nice American-style food with good-quality Spanish craft beer, and the beers go really well with the food."—Aniko Lehtinen

CERVEZAS LA VIRGEN

P.I. Európolis
Calle Turín 13
Las Rozas
Madrid 28232, Spain
+34 910804742
www.cervezaslavirgen.com

Recommended by
Ruben Martinez

Opening hours	Tue–Sun from 12:30 pm
Credit cards	Accepted
Type	Bar and brewery
Recommended for	Beer & food

"An amazing location inside the brewery, with incredible food from a food truck."—Ruben Martinez

CERVEZAS ALTHAIA ARTESANA

Plaça dels Furs 1
Altea
Valencian Community 03590, Spain
+34 965840605
www.althaiaartesana.com

Recommended by
Mayte Pardo

Opening hours	Mon–Sat from 9:30 am
Credit cards	Accepted
Type	Bar and microbrewery
Recommended for	Unexpected

"The taproom of the microbrewery in the pretty village of Altea. Fresh, high-quality beer in a cozy atmosphere. It was unexpected to find a microbrewery of this quality in such a small tourist village in the Costa Blanca."—Mayte Pardo

LA BOUTIQUE DE LA CERVEZA

Carrer de Lluís de Santàngel 19
Valencia
Valencian Community 46005, Spain
+34 963810807
www.estucerveza.com

Recommended by
Mayte Pardo

Opening hours............................Mon–Fri from 10:30 am
Credit cards..Accepted
Type...Bar
Recommended for...........................Worth the travel

LLÚPOL CELLER DE CERVESES

Carrer del Moro Zeid 2
Valencia
Valencian Community 46001, Spain
+34 639036006

Recommended by
Mayte Pardo

Opening hours..............................Tue–Sat from 11 am
Credit cards...Not accepted
Type...Bar and retail
Recommended for..............................Wish I'd opened

MARKET CRAFT BEER

Carrer de les Danses 5
Valencia
Valencian Community 46001, Spain
+34 644333127

Recommended by
Paul Anspach

Opening hours...............................Tue–Sun from 6 pm
Credit cards............................Accepted but not Amex
Type...Pub
Recommended for.................................Unexpected

RUZANUVOL CERVECERIA
ARTESANAL RUZAFA

Carrer de Lluís de Santàngel 3
Valencia
Valencian Community 46005, Spain
+34 680993892
www.ruzanuvol.com

Recommended by
Mayte Pardo

Opening hours.............................Open 7 days from 7 pm
Credit cards..Accepted
Type..Restaurant
Recommended for................................Beer & food

"Italian home cooking of the highest quality and craft beer
on tap."—Mayte Pardo

CRUZES CREDO

Rua Cruzes da Sé 29
Alfama
Lisbon 1100-192, Portugal
+351 218822296

Recommended by
Francisco Pereira

Opening hours................................Open 7 days from 12 pm
Credit cards............................Accepted but not Amex
Type...Pub
Recommended for.................................Unexpected

"Great food and a good selection of Portuguese craft
bottles."—Francisco Pereira

28 CAFÉ

Rua de Santa Cruz do Castelo 45
Alfama
Lisbon 1100-129, Portugal

Recommended by
Olli Majanen

Type...Bar and restaurant
Recommended for.................................Unexpected

"When walking up and down in Bairro Alto in Lisbon and just
wanting to have a refreshment in a random café, I was glad
to find local craft beer here."—Olli Majanen

CERVETECA LISBOA

Praça das Flores 62
Bairro Alto
Lisbon 1200-192, Portugal
www.cervetecalisboa.com

Recommended by
Bruno Aquino,
Ana Dias,
Hugo Gonçalves,
Lea Lima

Opening hours..............................Open 7 days from 3:30 pm
Credit cards..Accepted
Type...Bar
Recommended for.............................Local favorite

"A small spot but with the best beer selection in Lisbon.
The staff are friendly and passionate about beer."
—Hugo Gonçalves

CERVEJA MUSA

Rua do Açucar 83
Beato
Lisbon 1950-006, Portugal
+351 213877777
www.cervejamusa.com

Recommended by
Bruno Carrilho

Opening hours...........................Tue–Sun from 4 pm
Credit cards..Accepted
Type...Brewery
Recommended for.............................Local favorite

"A great atmosphere with a view over the production facilities, plus twelve beers on tap (all produced there). There is also musical programming, including live gigs with some of the hottest new Portuguese musicians."
—Bruno Carrilho

DOIS CORVOS CERVEJEIRA

Rua Capitão Leitão 94
Beato
Lisbon 1950-052, Portugal
+351 211284366
www.doiscorvos.pt

Recommended by
Hugo Gonçalves

Opening hours	Open 7 days from 2 pm
Credit cards	Accepted
Type	Bar
Recommended for	Wish I'd opened

"They were the first taproom in Lisbon and started the Lisbon Beer District in the Marvila neighborhood."
—Hugo Gonçalves

GROUND BURGER

Avenida António
Augusto de Aguiar 148
Praça de Espanha
Lisbon 1050-021, Portugal
+351 213717171
www.groundburger.com

Recommended by
Bruno Carrilho

Opening hours	Tue–Sat from 12 pm
Credit cards	Accepted
Type	Restaurant
Recommended for	Beer & food

"Really great burgers—probably the best in town—with a great curated and always up-to-date beer menu. Plus, very good advice on how to best combine specific burgers and beers, both domestic and international."—Bruno Carrilho

ADUELA

Rua das Oliveiras 36
Porto 4050-157, Portugal
+351 222084398

Recommended by
Ricardo Santos

Opening hours	Sun–Mon from 3 pm, Tue–Sat from 12 pm
Credit cards	Accepted
Type	Beer garden
Recommended for	Beer garden

CATRAIO

Rua de Cedofeita 256
Porto 4050-174, Portugal
+351 222010320

Recommended by
Ricardo Santos

Opening hours	Tue–Sat from 4 pm
Credit cards	Accepted
Type	Bar and retail
Recommended for	Worth the travel

"This was the first craft-beer bar and shop to open in Porto. They have a huge range of national and international craft beers on tap and in bottle. They are very selective, so whatever the beer style, quality is guaranteed. The owners and staff are great and friendly. It is a meeting point for beer lovers, and it's common to see brewers gather there, talking about beer among themselves or with the public."
—Ricardo Santos

EMBAIXADA DO PORTO

Praça de Carlos Alberto 121
Porto 4050-158, Portugal
+351 912133034
www.embaixadaporto.com

Recommended by
Bruno Carrilho

Opening hours	Mon–Sat from 12 pm, Sun from 9 pm
Credit cards	Not accepted
Type	Bar
Recommended for	Unexpected

"It caters mostly to the artist and international students, who typically want to drink as cheaply as possible. Yet it has a decent craft-beer selection."—Bruno Carrilho

LETRARIA CRAFT BEER GARDEN PORTO

Rua da Alegria 101
Porto 4000-033, Portugal
+351 939348069
www.cervejaletra.pt

Recommended by
Ana Dias,
Juan Fernández,
Francisco Pereira,
André Pintado,
Ricardo Santos,
Jaanis Tammela

Opening hours	Mon, Wed–Sat from 5 pm, Sun from 4 pm
Credit cards	Not accepted
Type	Beer garden
Recommended for	Beer garden

"Forty taps of Portuguese craft beers, with a lot of food-pairing options. It's an outstanding beer garden with 300 square meters in the center of Porto."—Francisco Pereira

SANTA BARBARA ECO-BEACH RESORT

Estrada Regional 1 — Recommended by
1 Morro de Baixo — Tod Mott
Ribeira Grande Azores 9600-219, Portugal
+351 296470360
www.santabarbaraazores.com

Opening hours	Always open
Credit cards	Accepted
Type	Restaurant
Recommended for	Unexpected

"Utopia! The best food and views on the island."—Tod Mott

RYAN'S PUB

3 Triq Wied Ghomor — Recommended by
Saint Julian's — Matthew Buttigieg
Central Region STJ 2041, Malta
+356 27139173
www.ryanspub.com

Opening hours	Tue–Fri from 7 pm, Sat–Sun from 12 pm
Credit cards	Accepted
Type	Pub
Recommended for	Local favorite

"This bar installed its own tap system, one of the first in Malta that's independently owned and, more important, one of the only bars with cold storage for its kegs. It's definitely poised to revolutionize the craft-beer bar scene in Malta. It has a nice rotation of beers on its eight taps and offers beer flights. The pub grub is delicious, with amazing burgers, ribs, and grilled meats."—Matthew Buttigieg

BADASS BURGERS – RAZZETT L-AHMAR

Durumblat Street — Recommended by
Mosta — Matthew Buttigieg
Northern Region MST 4812, Malta
+356 21416460
www.badassburgers.eu

Opening hours	Wed–Thur from 6 pm, Sat–Sun from 12 pm
Credit cards	Accepted
Type	Beer garden
Recommended for	Beer garden

"A versatile place—unusual for Malta—with a large outdoor space, which is excellent for chilling. There's an extensive menu which appeals to both young people and families (pizza, burgers, vegetarian-friendly). It also includes a cool game room and a space for live music events. They have great beer—Evil Twin, Stone, De La Senne, To Ol, Birra del Borgo—though only industrial beers on tap now"
—Matthew Buttigieg

67 KAPITALI

67 Old Bakery Street — Recommended by
Valletta — Matthew Buttigieg
South Eastern Region VLT 1427, Malta
+356 27380010
www.67kapitali.com

Opening hours	Mon–Fri from 12 pm, Sat–Sun from 9:30 am
Credit cards	Accepted
Type	Bar
Recommended for	Unexpected

"It's a very small, cozy place that feels more like a café, but it has slowly evolved to stock a wide range of craft beers. The owners are nice and knowledgeable in beer. It's in a corner in the bustling old city, where people-watching is easy and very relaxing."—Matthew Buttigieg

"THEY HAVE INCREDIBLY FRIENDLY AND KNOWLEDGEABLE BARTENDERS, WHO ARE ALWAYS EXCITED TO DISCUSS ALL THINGS BEER. PLUS THERE ARE FIFTEEN TAPS OF BEER FROM AROUND THE WORLD."

SARA SARTANG P.226

BARCELONA

"AN INSANE BEER SELECTION."

LAURI ELANGO P.226

"NAPARBCN ELEVATES THE ART OF PAIRING BEER AND FOOD. THE OWNERS AND CHEFS UNDERSTAND THAT BEER IS AN EVEN BETTER BEVERAGE TO PAIR WITH FINE CUISINE THAN WINE."

CHRIS MAESTRO P.227

"AT BIERCAB, YOU FEEL AT HOME."

GABRIEL BOCANEGRA P.226

BARCELONA

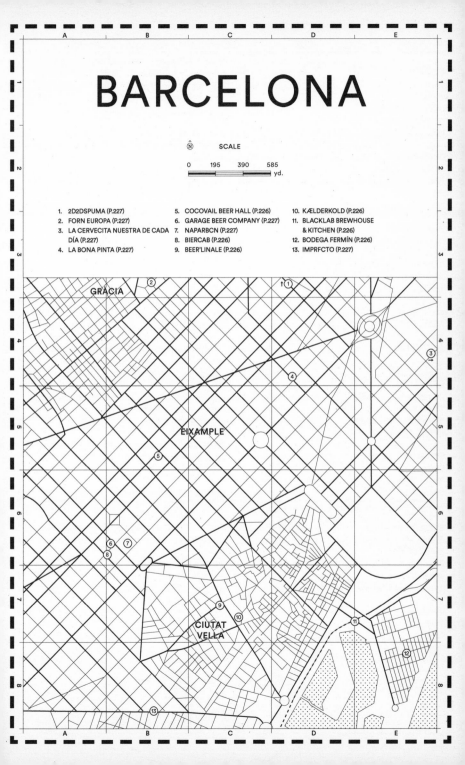

N   SCALE

0   195   390   585
yd.

GRÀCIA

EIXAMPLE

CIUTAT VELLA

BEER'LINALE

Carrer del Carme 7
Ciutat Vella
Barcelona 08001, Spain
+34 936393479
www.beerlinale.com

Recommended by
Arnau Rovira

Opening hours	Open 7 days from 11 am
Credit cards	Accepted
Type	Restaurant and brewery
Opening hours	Beer & food

BLACKLAB BREWHOUSE & KITCHEN

Palau de Mar, Plaça Pau Vila 1
Ciutat Vella
Barcelona 08039, Spain
+34 932218360
www.blacklab.es

Recommended by
Jing Chen,
Jaanis Tammela

Opening hours	Open 7 days from 12 pm
Credit cards	Accepted but not Amex
Type	Bar
Opening hours	Beer & food

BODEGA FERMÍN

Carrer de Sant Carles 18
Ciutat Vella
Barcelona 08003, Spain
+34 931124303

Recommended by
David Pié Aliana

Opening hours	Wed–Mon from 10 am
Credit cards	Accepted
Type	Bar
Opening hours	Worth the travel

KÆLDERKOLD

Carrer del Cardenal Casañas 7
Ciutat Vella
Barcelona 08002, Spain
+34 932779671
www.kaelderkold.com

Recommended by
Sara Sartang

Opening hours	Open 7 days from 12:30 pm
Credit cards	Accepted
Type	Bar
Opening hours	Worth the travel

"They have incredibly friendly and knowledgeable bartenders, who are always excited to discuss all things beer. Plus there are fifteen taps of beer from around the world."—Sara Sartang

BIERCAB

Carrer de Muntaner 55
Eixample
Barcelona 08011, Spain
+34 644689045
www.biercab.com

Recommended by
Benny van Aerschot,
George Alexakis,
Olof Andersson, Gabriel
Bocanegra, André Ek,
Lauri Elango, Juan Fernández,
Mike Goguen, Alberto Gómez,
Aitor Labrador, Valter Loverier,
Olli Majanen, David Pié Aliana,
Anton Pligin, Arnau Rovira,
Chris Treanor, Felipe Valenciano

Opening hours	Mon–Sat from 12 pm, Sun from 5 pm
Credit cards	Accepted
Type	Brewery and Pub
Opening hours	Worth the travel

"The interior is amazing and the choice of beers is excellent, with a lot of beers on draft."—Benny van Aerschot

"Manuel Baltasar, one of the owners, has a lot of knowledge. He offers the best beers in the world, including specific and peculiar beers that are very difficult to get."
—Felipo Valenciano

"At BierCaB, you feel at home. This is a world-class beer bar, with thirty taps of amazing rotating beers and perfect food to pair your beer."—Gabriel Bocanegra

"An insane beer selection."—Lauri Elango

COCOVAIL BEER HALL

Carrer d'Aragó 284
Eixample
Barcelona 08009, Spain
+34 937822479
www.cocovailbeerhall.com

Recommended by
Arnau Rovira

Opening hours	Mon–Thur from 11:30 am, Sat–Sun from 1 pm
Credit cards	Accepted
Type	Bar
Credit cards	Local favorite

GARAGE BEER COMPANY

Carrer del Consell de Cent 261
Eixample
Barcelona 08011, Spain
+34 935285989
www.garagebeer.co

Recommended by
Bruno Carrilho,
Juan Fernández

Opening hours	Open 7 days from 12 pm
Credit cards	Accepted
Type	Microbrewery
Credit cards	Wish I'd opened

"A great concept that truly lives up to the beer it produces and the personality of the owners. The food, beer, and service are way above average."—Bruno Carrilho

IMPRFCTO

Avenue del Parallel 104
Eixample
Barcelona 08015, Spain
+34 932229801
www.imprfcto.com

Recommended by
Jonathan Boyce

Opening hours	Open 7 days from 5 pm
Credit cards	Accepted
Type	Bar
Credit cards	Unexpected

LA BONA PINTA

Carrer de la Diputació 433
Eixample
Barcelona 08013, Spain
+34 932316703
www.labonapinta.com

Recommended by
David Pié Aliana

Opening hours	Tue–Sat from 11:30 am, Sun from 5:30 pm
Credit cards	Accepted but not Amex
Type	Bar
Credit cards	Local favorite

NAPARBCN

Carrer de la Diputació 223
Eixample
Barcelona 08011, Spain
+34 934089162
www.naparbcn.com

Recommended by
Chris Maestro,
Francisco Pereira,
Felipe Valenciano

Opening hours	Tue–Sun from 12 pm
Credit cards	Accepted
Type	Pub
Credit cards	Worth the travel

"NaparBCN elevates the art of pairing beer and food. The owners and chefs understand that beer is an even better beverage to pair with fine cuisine than wine. The Naparbier options and the other beers on tap were excellent. Their beer cellar, which customers can view, contains Trappist bottles from over thirty years ago. The various small plates we enjoyed were impressive."—Chris Maestro

FORN EUROPA

Carrer del Pare Làinez 13
Gràcia
Barcelona 08003, Spain
+34 932840136
www.forneuropa.es

Recommended by
David Pié Aliana

Opening hours	Mon–Sat from 7 am
Credit cards	Accepted
Type	Bar and restaurant
Recommended for	Unexpected

2D2DSPUMA

Carrer de la Manigua 8
Sant Andreu
Barcelona 08027, Spain
+34 654241581
www.2d2dspuma.com

Recommended by
Mayte Pardo

Opening hours	Mon–Sat from 6 pm
Credit cards	Not accepted
Type	Beer garden, brewery, and retail
Recommended for	Beer garden

"Great professionals, personalized attention, and beers of great quality."—Mayte Pardo

LA CERVECITA NUESTRA DE CADA DÍA

Carrer de Llull 184
Sant Martí
Barcelona 08005, Spain
+34 934869271

Recommended by
David Pié Aliana

Opening hours	Tue–Sat from 11:30 am, Sun–Mon from 5:30 pm
Credit cards	Accepted
Type	Beer garden, bar, and retail
Recommended for	Beer garden

> "THE ATMOSPHERE IS INCREDIBLE BECAUSE IT IS SMALL AND SHABBY BUT HAS A GREAT SOUL. IT'S PERFECT FOR THE BEER GEEK BUT EQUALLY SUITED TO THE TRADITIONAL DRINKER."

VALTER LOVERIER P.234

> "THEY PRODUCE SOME OF THE MOST PROGRESSIVE AND THOUGHTFUL BEERS IN ITALY, ALL BREWED AND BOTTLED IN THE BUILDING NEXT DOOR."

STEPHEN ANDREWS P.235

ITALY & SAN MARINO

> "A SUPER-RELAXING PUB IN THE MONFERRAT HILLS WITH GOOD BEER, GOOD MUSIC, AND AN AMAZING VIEW."

ALESSIO GATTI P.232

> "IT'S THE CRADLE OF THE ROME CRAFT-BEER SCENE."

PIETRO DI PILATO P.234

ITALY
& SAN
MARINO

N

SCALE

0   80   160
mi.

LA FONTELINA RESTAURANT

Via Faraglioni 2 | Recommended by
Capri | Isaac Showaki
Campania 80073, Italy
+39 0818370845
www.fontelina-capri.com/restaurant

Opening hours...................Open 7 days from 12:30 pm
Credit cards..Accepted
Type..Restaurant
Recommended for............................Worth the travel

"You are in this magical place in a tiny island. You cannot beat being in Capri sorrounded by the Mediterranean." —Isaac Showaki

HOPPY ENDING

| | Recommended by
Via Santa Maria della Libera 30 | Neil Bontoft
Naples
Campania 80127, Italy
+39 08118779206
www.hoppyending.it

Opening hours.......................Open 7 days from 5 pm
Credit cards..Accepted
Type...Bar
Recommended for......................................Unexpected

BALADIN BOLOGNA

| | Recommended by
Via Clavature 12 | Lea Lima
Bologna
Emilia-Romagna 40124, Italy
+39 051232919
www.baladin.it

Opening hours....................Open 7 days from 11:30 am
Credit cards..Accepted
Type..Pub
Recommended for..................................Beer & food

BIRRA CERQUA

| | Recommended by
Via Broccaindosso 5/C | Eleonora Rigato
Bologna
Emilia-Romagna 40125, Italy
+39 0510286107
www.birracerqua.com

Opening hours.......................Mon–Sat from 6:30 pm
Credit cards..Accepted
Type..Brewpub
Recommended for..............................Local favorite

"It's the only brewpub in the center of Bologna. They produce and sell great craft beer with passion. A special tiny place with great music."—Eleonora Rigato

RANZANI13

| | Recommended by
Via Camillo Ranzani 5/12H | Alessio Gatti,
Bologna | Dimitrij Jurisic,
Emilia-Romagna 40127, Italy | Eleonora Rigato
+39 0518493743
www.ranzani13.it

Opening hours..............................Mon–Fri from 11 am,
Sat–Sun from 7 pm
Credit cards..Accepted
Type..Restaurant
Recommended for....................................Beer & food

"Some of the best pizzas in Italy, with great craft beers on tap."—Dimitrij Jurisic

"They make very good pizza and sell very good craft beer."—Eleonora Rigato

AGRITURISMO I MURETTI

Via Sarciano 5 | Recommended by
Montecolombo | Andrea Mina
Emilia-Romagna 47854, Italy
+39 0541985146
www.imuretti.it

Opening hours.....................Mon, Wed–Sat from 10 am,
Tue from 5 pm, Sun from 12 pm
Credit cards..Accepted
Type..Restaurant
Recommended for......................................Unexpected

FOB

| | Recommended by
Via Castracane 17 | Georgi Hristov
Rimini
Emilia-Romagna 47921, Italy
+39 0541784933

Opening hours.......................Open 7 days from 12 pm
Credit cards..Accepted
Type..Restaurant
Recommended for............................Worth the travel

"It has an extensive selection of craft beer on tap and in bottle. The last time I was there, it was full of brewers from around the continent, and you could speak with them and share ideas. It was awesome. They have around forty craft beers on tap."—Georgi Hristov

O'OSCIAD PUB

Via San Francesco 1
Verucchio
Emilia-Romagna 47826, Italy
+39 05411492906

Recommended by
Andrea Mina

Opening hours.....................Mon–Fri from 7:30 pm,
Sat–Sun from 6 pm
Credit cards..Accepted
Type...Pub
Recommended for.........................Wish I'd opened

MASTRO BIRRAIO

Via Venezian Felice 24
Trieste
Friuli-Venezia Giulia 34121, Italy
+39 3498356201

Recommended by
Olof Andersson,
Marco Vidmar,
Alessandro
Zecchinati

Opening hours..........Tue from 12 pm, Wed–Sat from 6 pm
Credit cards..Accepted
Type...Bar
Recommended for...............................Beer & food

"A hidden craft-beer spot in Trieste. The beers are great:
diverse, fascinating, and interesting. The food is also great:
fresh, tasty, and plentiful."—Marco Vidmar

TAVERNA AI MASTRI D'ARME

Via di Tor Bandena 3/a
Trieste
Friuli-Venezia Giulia 34121, Italy
+39 0403478112

Recommended by
Dimitrij Jurisic

Opening hours........Mon from 6 pm, Wed–Sun from 6 pm
Credit cards..Accepted
Type...Bar
Recommended for..............................Local favorite

BEERSHOP MADDALENA

Via della Maddalena 50R C
Genoa
Liguria 16124, Italy
+39 0107980430
www.beershopmaddalena.it

Recommended by
Alessio Gatti

Opening hours....................................Mon–Sat from 8 am
Type..Retail
Recommended for................................Unexpected

"A vegetable shop in the tiny old-town streets of Genoa.
Ten years ago they started to sell craft beer in bottles,
and they now have more than 250 selected craft beers."
—Alessio Gatti

SCURRERIA BEER & BAGEL

Via Scurreria 22R
Genoa
Liguria 16123, Italy
+39 3296903690
www.scurreria.com

Recommended by
Alessio Gatti

Opening hours..........................Mon–Fri from 6 pm,
Sat–Sun from 12 pm
Type...Bar
Recommended for..............................Local favorite

"A good rotating beer selection, both tap and bottle."
—Alessio Gatti

BALADIN CASELLE AEROPORTO

Torino Airport, Strada Aeroporto 12
Caselle Torinese
Lombardy 10072, Italy
www.baladin.it

Recommended by
Teo Musso

Opening hours....................Open 7 days from 10 am
Credit cards..Accepted
Type...Pub
Recommended for................................Unexpected

THE WELLINGTON PUB

Via Felice Cavallotti 17
Lodi
Lombardy 26900, Italy
+39 3479422767

Recommended by
Pietro Di Pilato

Opening hours.....................................Mon–Sat from 8 pm,
Sun from 5 pm
Credit cards..Accepted
Type...Pub
Recommended for..............................Local favorite

BIRRERIA CASSINA

Piazza Silvio Pellico 1
Merate
Lombardy 23807, Italy
+39 3335242113

Recommended by
Matteo Bonfanti

Opening hours...................................Mon–Sat from 5:30 pm
Credit cards..............................Accepted but not Amex
Type...................................Beer garden and bar
Recommended for.............................Beer garden

BIRRA DEL CARROBIOLO
Piazza Indipendenza 1
Monza
Lombardy 20900, Italy
+39 039325100
www.birradelcarrobiolo.it

Recommended by
Matteo Bonfanti

Opening hours	Mon–Fri from 12 pm, Sat–Sun from 6:30 pm
Credit cards	Accepted
Type	Pub
Recommended for	Local favorite

BERE BUONA BIRRA
Via Adige 13
Milan 20135, Italy
+39 3926206679
www.berebuonabirra.com

Recommended by
Alessio Gatti

Opening hours	Mon–Fri from 12 pm, Sat–Sun from 10 am
Credit cards	Accepted
Type	Pub
Recommended for	Wish I'd opened

BIRRIFICIO LAMBRATE ADELCHI
Via Adelchi 5
Milan 20131, Italy
+39 0270638678
www.birrificiolambrate.com

Recommended by
Pietro Di Pilato, Alessio
Gatti, Itay Marom,
Christopher Pilkington,
Eleonora Rigato

Opening hours	Tue–Sun from 6 pm
Credit cards	Not accepted
Type	Brewery and pub
Recommended for	Worth the travel

"Birrificio Lambrate is one of the Italian craft-beer pioneers. They've been an inspiration for many years."
—Pietro Di Pilato

LAMBICZOON
Via Friuli 46
Milan 20135, Italy
+39 0236534840
www.lambiczoon.com

Recommended by
Nicolò Musso

Opening hours	Sun–Fri from 6:30 pm, Sat from 12:30 pm
Credit cards	Accepted but not Amex
Type	Pub
Recommended for	Worth the travel

"A unique place in Italy. They have a huge selection of spontaneous fermentation and sour beer from all over the world."—Nicolò Musso

BIRRERIA LUNA TURCA
Strada Comunale della Collina 43
Masio
Piedmont 15024, Italy
+39 3332870242

Recommended by
Alessio Gatti

Opening hours	Tue–Sat from 8 pm
Credit cards	Not accepted
Type	Beer garden and pub
Recommended for	Beer garden

"A super-relaxing pub in the Monferrat hills with good beer, good music, and an amazing view."—Alessio Gatti

BIRRERIA LE BALADIN
Piazza V Luglio 1944 15
Piozzo
Piedmont 12060, Italy
+39 0173795431
www.baladin.it

Recommended by
Tony Forder,
Marie-Josée Lefebvre,
Nicolò Musso,
Teo Musso

Opening hours	Tue–Sat from 6 pm, Sun from 11 am
Credit cards	Accepted
Type	Beer garden and brewery
Recommended for	Beer & food

"It's the only beer garden in Italy."—Nicolò Musso

"This is where you can join the Baladin World. Visit the brewery every Sunday and during the summer. It's a great space to spend time with friends and family. The choice of summer food and beers are a milestone in the Italian craft-beer scene."—Teo Musso

BICI & BIRRA
Corso Regina Margherita 108
Turin
Piedmont 10152, Italy
+39 115799709
www.biciebirra.com

Recommended by
Valter Loverier

Opening hours...............Tue–Fri from 4 pm, Sat from 11 am
Credit cards..Accepted
Type..Bar
Recommended for..Unexpected

"It's a bike repair shop, you can taste some of the best Italian beers while they fix your bike."—Valter Loverier

DOGANA TORINO
Via Rocciamelone 12/a
Turin
Piedmont 10143, Italy
+39 1119580798

Recommended by
Valter Loverier

Opening hours...Mon–Sat from 4 pm
Credit cards..............................Accepted but not Amex
Type..Pub
Recommended for..Local favorite

"They are passionate and skilled enough to propose which beer you'd like best. Diego and Fulvio are veterans of the craft-beer market."—Valter Loverier

OPEN BALADIN TORINO
Piazzale Valdo Fusi
Turin
Piedmont 10123, Italy
+39 011835863
www.baladin.it

Recommended by
Nicolò Musso,
Teo Musso

Opening hours.............................Sun–Fri from 12:15 pm,
Sat from 6:30 pm
Credit cards..Accepted
Type..Pub
Recommended for...Beer & food

"It's the best spot in town and the only one that offers a great selection of craft beer from Italy and all over the world with thirty-eight taps."—Nicolò Musso

TRIPEL B
Via Valprato 68
Turin
Piedmont 10155, Italy
+39 3738891831
www.tripelb.com

Recommended by
Lana Svitankova

Opening hours.......................................Tue–Thur from 4 pm,
Fri from 12 pm, Sat from 3 pm
Credit cards..Accepted
Type...Retail
Recommended for..Unexpected

"A huge selection of specialties, classics, and new-wave brews. They have rare gems you can't even find in Belgium."
—Lana Svitankova

BEERCODE KITCHEN & BAR
Leonardo da Vinci–Fiumicino Airport
Via Leonardo da Vinci 320
Rome 00054, Italy
+39 800606666

Recommended by
Felix Schuessler

Opening hours...............................Open 7 days from 8 am
Credit cards..Accepted
Type..Bar and restaurant
Recommended for..Unexpected

BIR & FUD
Via Benedetta 23
Rome 00153, Italy
+39 065894016
www.birdandfud.it

Recommended by
Rafi Chaudry,
Jaroslaw Guzda

Opening hours...................................Mon–Thur from 6 pm,
Fri–Sun from 12 pm
Credit cards..Accepted
Type......................................Beer garden and restaurant
Recommended for...Beer & food

IL SERPENTE
Via dei Marsi 21
Rome 00185, Italy
+39 064909463

Recommended by
Jaroslaw Guzda

Opening hours...............................Open 7 days from 6 pm
Credit cards..Accepted
Type..Pub
Recommended for..Unexpected

"A small pub in the student area. A great owner."
—Jaroslaw Guzda

LA BIRRERIA AT EATALY

Piazzale XII Ottobre 1492
Rome 00154, Italy
+39 0690279201
www.eataly.net

Opening hours.....................................Open 7 days from 9 am
Credit cards...Accepted
Type...Bar
Recommended for...Wish I'd opened

"A huge place near an abandoned metro station in Rome.
Great food and craft-beer selection. Strongly
recommend."—Pablo Santos

MA CHE SIETE VENUTI A FÀ

Via Benedetta 25
Rome 00153, Italy
+39 0664562046
www.football-pub.com

Recommended by
Alex Acker, George Alexakis,
Olof Andersson, Gabriel
Bocanegra, Mario Canestrelli,
Pietro Di Pilato, Dimitrij Jurisic,
Caterina Lodo, Valter Loverier,
Kim Mercado, Mike Murphy

Opening hours...................................Open 7 days from 11 am
Credit cards..Not accepted
Type...Pub
Recommended for...Worth the travel

"One of the smallest places I've ever been. They always have
a great selection, and the beers are so amazingly well
conditioned. People from all over the planet are enjoying
beers here."—George Alexakis

"They have the perfect balance between the beer selection
and atmosphere. They play good jams, throw good events,
and have super friendly, attentive, and knowledgeable
staff."—Kim Mercado

"The best spot for getting the best beers in the world."
—Mike Murphy

"It's the cradle of the Rome craft-beer scene."
—Pietro Di Pilato

"When I started, everything I knew was thanks to these
guys. The atmosphere is incredible because it is small and
shabby but has a great soul. It's perfect for the beer geek
but equally suited to the traditional drinker."
—Valter Loverier

This place looks like a hole-in-the-wall, but they serve the
best beers available. It's a superhip place to spend time
in Rome.

NEL BUCO DEL MULO

Via della Scala 33
Rome 00153, Italy
+39 3386631251

Opening hours.............................Open 7 days from 11:30 am
Credit cards...Accepted
Type...Restaurant
Recommended for...Unexpected

OPEN BALADIN ROMA

Via degli Specchi 6
Rome 00186, Italy
+39 066838989
www.openbaladinroma.it

Opening hours...................................Open 7 days from 12 pm
Credit cards...Accepted
Type...Pub
Recommended for...Beer & food

"The best burgers in Italy."—Nicolò Musso

PIZZARIUM

Via della Meloria 43
Rome 00136, Italy
+39 0639745426
www.bonci.it

Opening hours......................................Mon–Sat from 11 am,
Sun from 12 pm
Credit cards...Accepted
Type...Restaurant
Recommended for...Unexpected

"This is a place where you get a quick bite of pizza taglio,
where they cut up a square pizza, weigh it, and charge
per 100 grams. I met the owner, and he told me he loves
fermentation. He had a pretty decent beer selection as well.
I highly recommend it if you go to Rome."
—Mike Murphy

FORSTERBRÄU MERAN

Recommended by
Daniel Thombansen

Corso Libertà 90
Meran
Trentino-South Tyrol 39012, Italy
+39 473236535
www.forsterbrau.it

Opening hours.....................................Open 7 days from 10 am
Credit cards...Accepted
Type..Beer garden and restaurant
Recommended for...Beer garden

"A fantastic view of the Alps. Beers are made in-house."
—Daniel Thombansen

MOSTODULCE

Recommended by
Joe Ploof

Via Nazionale 114/R
Florence
Tuscany 50123, Italy
+39 0552302928

Opening hours...Mon–Sun from 11 am
Credit cards...Accepted
Type...Bar and brewery
Recommended for...Unexpected

"This punk brewery in Florence serves Italian takes on
American, German, and English styles."—Joe Ploof

ELFO'S PUB

Recommended by
Sam Sarmad

Via Sant'Agata 20
Perugia
Umbria 06123, Italy
+39 3470785981

Opening hours.................................Open 7 days from 6 pm
Credit cards...Accepted
Type...Pub
Recommended for...Worth the travel

PROSCIUTTERIA DEL CORSO

Recommended by
Sam Sarmad

Corso G. Mazzini 73
Spoleto
Umbria 06049
Italy
+39 0743224014

Opening hours.................................Open 7 days from 12 pm
Credit cards...Not accepted
Type...Restaurant
Recommended for...Unexpected

"Small with a great choice of both bottle and tap beers.
Great antipasti!"—Sam Sarmad

CRAK TAPROOM

Recommended by
Stephen Andrews,
Caterina Lodo,
Chris Treanor

Via Pontarola 9
Campodarsego
Veneto 35011, Italy
+39 3661134713
www.crakbrewery.com/tap-room

Opening hours.................................Wed–Sun from 5:30 pm
Credit cards...Accepted
Type...Brewery
Recommended for...Wish I'd opened

"This place is a hidden gem. The taproom is a massive space
filled with vintage furniture and lighting. The back garden is
the real stunner. It's the best place to grab some of the most
mind-blowing homemade pizza you've ever had. And there's
great beer. They produce some of the most progressive and
thoughtful beers in Italy, all brewed and bottled in the
building next door."—Stephen Andrews

NIDABA

Recommended by
Pietro Di Pilato

Via Argine 15
Montebelluna
Veneto 31044, Italy
+39 0423609937
www.nidabaspirit.it

Opening hours...Mon–Sat from 6 pm
Credit cards...Accepted
Type...Restaurant and pub
Recommended for..Beer & food

"Everything they do is just perfect. It's hard to say if it is
a pub, a restaurant, or a club. They have amazing food with
a great beer selection in a very cool location. It's hard
to find another place offering such a complete experience.
The food is contemporary with great local ingredients."
—Pietro Di Pilato

WHITE PONY PUB

Recommended by
Roberto Orano

Corso Vittorio Emanuele II 185
Padua
Veneto 35123, Italy
+39 3472492689
www.whiteponymicrobrewery.com

Opening hours	Tue–Sat from 5 pm, Sun from 6 pm
Credit cards	Accepted
Type	Pub
Recommended for	Local favorite

"The best beer choice in town with eight to twelve taps and about 250 bottles. Half the taps are from White Pony, and the rest are guest beers. A friendly atmosphere and staff."—Roberto Orano

ORMESINI DA ALDO

Recommended by
Richard Ammerman

Fondamenta dei Ormesini 2710
Venice
Veneto 30121, Italy
+39 041715834

Opening hours	Mon–Sat from 11 am
Credit cards	Not accepted
Type	Bar and retail
Recommended for	Unexpected

"A hidden gem that took me many years to recognize. I used to walk by this place daily when I was in grade school. For a city full of tourist trap bars, Ormesini da Aldo is an unpretentious one-man shop with four self-serve bottle fridges, a couple of taps, and some simple cicchetti-style beer snacks. Grab one of the many interesting Italian craft beers, and enjoy it alongside the canal."
—Richard Ammerman

BIRRIFICIO ABUSIVO

Recommended by
Andrea Mina

Via Venticinque Marzo 29/A
Domagnano
Castello di Domagnano 47895, San Marino
+39 3662014538
www.birrificioabusivo.com

Opening hours	By appointment
Credit cards	Not accepted
Type	Brewery
Recommended for	Local favorite

ROXY BAR

Recommended by
Andrea Mina

Via Consiglio Dei Sessanta 115
Dogana
Castello di Serravalle 47899, San Marino
+39 0549908711
www.roxybar.sm

Opening hours	Mon–Sat from 6 am, Sun from 7 am
Credit cards	Not accepted
Type	Beer garden, bar, and restaurant
Recommended for	Beer garden

"This bar and pizzeria is frequented by local workers and citizens. It's near a park and a soccer field."—Andrea Mina

L'INSOLITO POSTO

Recommended by
Andrea Mina

Piazza Giovanni Bertoldi 1–5
Serravalle
Castello di Serravalle 47899, San Marino
+39 3391978255

Opening hours	Open 7 days from 6 am
Credit cards	Not accepted
Type	Bar and restaurant
Recommended for	Worth the travel

"This is a local bar with a wood-burning oven for pizza. Beers are available in bottles and on draft."—Andrea Mina

CAFFÈ DIVINO

Recommended by
Andrea Mina

Via Salita alla Cesta 7
San Marino 47890, San Marino
+378 0549992714

Type	Bar
Recommended for	Beer & food

"Caffè Divino is a bar in the historical center of San Marino, almost on the top of Titano mountain. You can find a fresh meal with our typical bread, piadina romagnola, with local ham and cheese. Hot and fresh dishes."—Andrea Mina

"THIS BREWERY IS A REAL OLD-WORLD EXPERIENCE. THEY USE OLD-SCHOOL LAGER FERMENTATION AND PROCESSING TECHNIQUES, INCLUDING OPEN FERMENTATION, HORIZONTAL LAGERING, AND STORING BEER IN WOODEN BARRELS. THEY SERVE THE BEER STRAIGHT FROM THESE BARRELS INTO YOUR STONE PIT."

DJ MCCREADY P.242

POLAND, CZECH REPUBLIC, AUSTRIA & HUNGARY

"A BEAUTIFUL 300-YEAR-OLD BREWERY THAT HAS BEEN RENOVATED AND IS BREWING GREAT BEER AGAIN."

ALEXIS ALEXIOU P.241

"THE BEST SELECTION OF CRAFT BEER IN THE COUNTRY."

LADISLAV VRTIŠ P.241

"THE ENERGETIC AND KNOWLEDGEABLE STAFF MADE THIS PLACE A FANTASTIC EXPERIENCE."

HÖSKULDUR SÆMUNDSSON P.243

POLAND,
CZECH
REPUBLIC,
AUSTRIA &
HUNGARY

N SCALE

0   75   150
mi.

A   B   C   D

1

2

MASOVIA P.240

3   P O L A N D

LESSER POLAND P.240

LOWER SILESIA P.240

4

OLOMOUC P.240

C Z E C H   R E P U B L I C

PRAGUE P.241

SOUTH MORAVIAN REGION P.242

PILSEN P.241   BUDAPEST P.243

VIENNA P.243

UPPER AUSTRIA P.242

H U N G A R Y

SALZBURG P.242

A U S T R I A

TYROL P.242

OMERTA PUB

Kupa 3
Kraków
Lesser Poland 31-057, Poland
+48 501508227
www.omerta.com.pl

Recommended by
Jaroslaw Guzda

Opening hours	Open 7 days from 4 pm
Credit cards	Not accepted
Type	Pub
Recommended for	Local favorite

"It has twenty-eight taps, featuring beers from all over the world. It's the oldest craft-beer pub in Kraków and possibly in Poland."—Jaroslaw Guzda

VIVA LA PINTA

Floriańska 13
Kraków
Lesser Poland 31-019, Poland
+48 123789722
www.browarpinta.pl

Recommended by
Jaroslaw Guzda

Opening hours	Mon–Fri from 4 pm, Sat–Sun from 2 pm
Credit cards	Accepted
Type	Beer garden and brewery
Recommended for	Beer garden

BISTRO NAROŻNIK

Ludwika Rydygiera 30
Wroclaw
Lower Silesia 50-001, Poland
+48 575885050

Recommended by
Karol Sadłowski

Opening hours	Open 7 days from 10 am
Credit cards	Accepted but not Amex
Type	Bar
Recommended for	Local favorite

KURNA CHATA

Odrzańska 17
Wroclaw
Lower Silesia 50-113, Poland
+48 713410668
www.kurnachata.pl

Recommended by
Karol Sadłowski

Opening hours	Open 7 days from 7 am
Credit cards	Not accepted
Type	Beer garden and restaurant
Recommended for	Beer garden

PROFESJA BAR

Kwidzyńska 6
Wroclaw
Lower Silesia 51-416, Poland
+48 883167341
www.browarprofesja.pl

Recommended by
Karol Sadłowski

Type	Bar
Recommended for	Wish I'd opened

TARGOWA – CRAFT BEER AND FOOD

Piaskowa 17
Wroclaw
Lower Silesia 50-158, Poland
+48 533330551
www.targowa.eu

Recommended by
Karol Sadłowski

Opening hours	Mon–Fri from 12 pm, Sat–Sun from 10 am
Credit cards	Accepted
Type	Pub
Recommended for	Beer & food

"In the basement of an ancient building with a modern interior."—Karol Sadłowski

JABEERWOCKY CRAFT BEER PUB

Nowogrodzka 12
Warsaw
Masovia 00-511, Poland
+48 222543107
www.taproom.pl

Recommended by
Jehad Hatu

Opening hours	Mon–Sat from 2 pm, Sun from 3 pm
Credit cards	Accepted
Type	Pub
Recommended for	Worth the travel

PIVOVAR CHOMOUT

Dalimilova 18/92
Olomouc 783 35, Czech Republic
+420 608778348
www.pivochomout.cz

Recommended by
Jura Omelka

Opening hours	Open 7 days from 11 am (summer)
Credit cards	Not accepted
Type	Restaurant
Recommended for	Local favorite

BEER FACTORY

Dominikánská 8
Pilsen 301 00, Czech Republic
+420 379422526
www.beerfactoryplzen.cz

Recommended by
Alexis Alexiou

Opening hours	Open 7 days from 11 am
Type	Brewery
Recommended for	Beer & food

"This is a great brewhouse in the middle of the historic beer city of Pilsen. They serve traditional beer, cheeses, sausages, and pâté made with quality ingredients."
—Alexis Alexiou

BEERGEEK BAR

Vinohradská 62
Prague 130 00, Czech Republic
+420 776827068
www.beergeek.cz

Recommended by
Ondrej Pernica,
Ladislav Vrtiš

Opening hours	Open 7 days from 3 pm
Credit cards	Accepted
Type	Bar
Recommended for	Local favorite

"The best selection of craft beer in the country."
—Ladislav Vrtiš

KINO SVĚTOZOR

Vodičkova 791/41
Prague 110 00, Czech Republic
+420 224946824
www.kinosvetozor.cz

Recommended by
Ondrej Pernica

Opening hours	Mon–Fri from 12:30 pm, Sat–Sun from 10:30 am
Credit cards	Accepted
Type	Bar
Recommended for	Unexpected

"An independent cinema in the center of Prague has a small, cozy bar with a movie-theme setting—for example, red curtains suggesting David Lynch. They have rotating taps with a fair selection of beers, always serving at least one craft brew."—Ondrej Pernica

LETNÁ BEER GARDEN

Letenské Sady
Prague 170 00, Czech Republic
+420 233378200
www.letenskyzamecek.cz/restaurants/letna-garden

Recommended by
Shawn Decker,
Ondrej Pernica

Opening hours	Open 7 days from 11 am
Credit cards	Not accepted
Type	Beer garden
Recommended for	Beer garden

T-ANKER SUNNY TERRACE

Náměstí Republiky 656/8
Prague 110 00, Czech Republic
+420 722445474
www.t-anker.cz

Recommended by
Ladislav Vrtiš

Opening hours	Open 7 days from 11 am
Credit cards	Accepted
Type	Beer garden and restaurant
Recommended for	Beer garden

"Located in downtown Prague on the rooftop of a department store. The view from this place is just phenomenal."—Ladislav Vrtiš

ÚNĚTICE BREWERY

Rýznerova 19/5
Prague 252 62, Czech Republic
+420 220515687
www.unetickypivovar.cz

Recommended by
Alexis Alexiou

Opening hours	Open 7 days from 11 am
Credit cards	Accepted
Type	Brewery
Recommended for	Worth the travel

"It's a beautiful 300-year-old brewery that has been renovated and is brewing great beer again."—Alexis Alexiou

ZLÝ ČASY

Cestmirova 390/5
Prague 140 00, Czech Republic
+420 723339995
www.zlycasy.eu

Recommended by
Jura Omelka

Opening hours	Mon–Fri from 2 pm, Sat–Sun from 5 pm
Credit cards	Not accepted
Type	Bar
Recommended for	Beer & food

GREEN CAT PIVÁRIUM

Recommended by
Alexis Alexiou

Dvořákova 3
Brno
South Moravian Region 602 00, Czech Republic
+420 775566602
www.zelenakocka.cz

Opening hours	Mon–Sat from 4 pm, Sun from 5 pm
Credit cards	Not accepted
Type	Restaurant
Recommended for	Wish I'd opened

"They have a great selection of craft beers every day and nice food that complements the beer."—Alexis Alexiou

AUGUSTINER BRÄU

Recommended by
DJ McCready,
Birgit Rieber,
Lana Svitankova,
Marco Vidmar

7 Lindhofstrasse
Salzburg
Salzburg 5020, Austria
+43 662431246
www.augustinerbier.at

Opening hours	Mon–Fri from 3 pm, Sat–Sun from 2:30 pm
Credit cards	Not accepted
Type	Beer garden and brewery
Recommended for	Beer garden

"This brewery is a real old-world experience. People have been drinking here since 1621. They use old-school lager fermentation and processing techniques, including open fermentation, horizontal lagering, and storing beer in wooden barrels. They serve the beer straight from these barrels into your stone pit. Sitting at long wooden tables with hundreds of locals in a massive beer hall decorated with deer heads, you feel the community spirit of the place, even on a weeknight."—DJ McCready

TRIBAUN

Recommended by
Martin Voigt

Museumstrasse 5
Innsbruck
Tyrol 6020, Austria
+43 512238559
www.tribaun.com

Opening hours	Mon–Sat from 5 pm
Credit cards	Not accepted
Type	Bar
Recommended for	Wish I'd opened

"This underground bar is in the heart of the city and brings together all generations in the name of beer. There's regular live music by local bands, great small snacks, and an awesome selection of drafts that you can't get anywhere else in the country."—Martin Voigt

KÖGLERHOF

Recommended by
Peter Krammer

Am Grossamberg 7
Grossamberg
Upper Austria 4040, Austria
+43 72395256
www.koeglerhof.at

Opening hours	Thur–Fri from 5 pm, Sat from 2 pm
Credit cards	Accepted
Type	Restaurant
Recommended for	Beer & food

"The owner produces cider himself and has the great gift for perfectly combining food with beer—including sour beers—and drinks. They also run a farm and cook with regional and organic ingredients."—Peter Krammer

CHELSEA PUB

Recommended by
Peter Krammer

Domgasse 5
Linz
Upper Austria 4020, Austria
+43 732779409

Opening hours	Open 7 days from 6 pm
Credit cards	Not accepted
Type	Pub
Recommended for	Local favorite

THE BRICKMAKERS PUB & KITCHEN

Zieglergasse 42
Vienna 1070, Austria
+43 19974414
www.brickmakers.at

Recommended by
Peter Krammer,
Birgit Rieber,
Martin Voigt

Opening hours..Mon–Fri from 4 pm,
Sat–Sun from 10 am
Credit cards..Accepted
Type..Restaurant and pub
Recommended for...Worth the travel

"A wide variety of craft beer on tap, an international community of guests, and excellent food paired with beer. They serve their own beer and rotate taps, selecting the most interesting Portuguese craft beers. The well-trained staff are awesome and speak English. They support the local beer community with events and tastings."—Martin Voigt

"Great food and gypsy brewing from Me and Uwe by Brian Patton. They have a chef who combines beers with food. A great range of local and international beers."
—Peter Krammer

7STERN BRÄU

Siebensterngasse 19
Vienna 1070, Austria
+43 15238697
www.7stern.at

Recommended by
Aniko Lehtinen,
Felix Schuessler

Opening hours.............................Open 7 days from 11 am
Credit cards..Accepted
Type..Beer garden
Recommended for...Beer garden

"It has a superb terrace, where you can enjoy your beer. They brew their own beer."—Aniko Lehtinen

ÉLESZTŐ

Tuzolto utca 22
Budapest 1094, Hungary
+36 703361279
www.elesztohaz.hu

Recommended by
Höskuldur Sæmundsson,
Marco Vidmar

Opening hours.............................Open 7 days from 3 pm
Credit cards..Not accepted
Type..Bar
Recommended for...Worth the travel

"The energetic and knowledgeable staff made this place a fantastic experience. I went there every night of my Budapest stay. Fantastic rotating selection of beers, good food, and a great atmosphere, not unlike Warpigs in Copenhagen."—Höskuldur Sæmundsson

"A great craft-beer selection in a fantastic environment with good service."—Marco Vidmar

SZIMPLA KERT

Kazinczy utca 14
Budapest 1075, Hungary
+36 202618669
www.szimpla.hu

Recommended by
Fal Allen

Opening hours...................Mon–Thur and Sat from 12 pm,
Fri from 10 am, Sun from 9 am
Credit cards..Not accepted
Type..Bar
Recommended for...Wish I'd opened

"This bar is eclectic—a strange yet awesome collection of stuff hidden away on a side street."—Fal Allen

FELSŐ KOCSMA

Dobogókői út
Pilisszentkereszt
Pest 2098, Hungary

Recommended by
Aniko Lehtinen

Opening hours...Mon–Fri from 7 am
Type..Bar
Recommended for...Unexpected

"A bar for village locals, with local craft IPA."
—Aniko Lehtinen

> "PROBABLY THE BEST AND THE WIDEST SELECTION OF TOP-NOTCH BEERS IN MOSCOW."
> EUGENE TOLSTOV P.246

> "A MINUSCULE BAR IN A MEDIEVAL BUILDING IN THE HISTORIC OLD TOWN OF TALLINN, IT'S ONE OF THE LAST NON-TOURIST PLACES LEFT IN THE NEIGHBORHOOD."
> LAURI ELANGO P.246

RUSSIA, ESTONIA, LATVIA, LITHUANIA, UKRAINE & ROMANIA

> "A LUXURIOUS EUROPEAN INTERIOR, TRADITIONAL BAVARIAN AND UKRAINIAN CUISINE, AND LIVE MUSIC SOME EVENINGS." VLADIMIR KUSHNIREV P.249

> "A ROMANIAN CRAFT-BEER BAR FROM ZAGANU, THE PIONEERS OF CRAFT BREWING IN ROMANIA."
> LAURENTIU BANESC P.249

> "IT IS REALLY A BEER LIBRARY, STYLED LIKE A LIBRARY WITH SHELVES OF BOOKS AND BEER, LIBRARY LAMPS, AND BEER MAGAZINES."
> LANA SVITANKOVA P.248

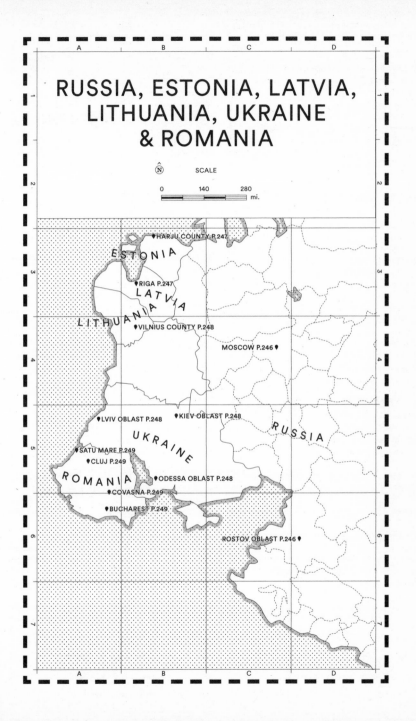

RUSSIA, ESTONIA, LATVIA, LITHUANIA, UKRAINE & ROMANIA

N

SCALE

0   140   280 mi.

ESTONIA

♥HARJU COUNTY P.247

LATVIA

♥RIGA P.247

LITHUANIA

♥VILNIUS COUNTY P.248

MOSCOW P.246 ♥

♥LVIV OBLAST P.248   ♥KIEV OBLAST P.248

RUSSIA

UKRAINE

♥SATU MARE P.249

♥CLUJ P.249

♥ODESSA OBLAST P.248

ROMANIA

♥COVASNA P.249

♥BUCHAREST P.249

ROSTOV OBLAST P.246 ♥

CRAFT REPUBLIC

Malyy Gnezdnikovskiy Pereulok 9/7
Moscow 125009, Russia
+7 9651126671
www.craftrepublic.ru

Recommended by
Anton Pligin,
Eugene Tolstov

Opening hours................................Open 7 days from 2 pm
Credit cards...Accepted
Type..Pub
Recommended for..Local favorite

"Probably the best and the widest selection of top-notch beers in Moscow and most likely in Russia."
—Eugene Tolstov

LOS BANDIDOS

Ulitsa Maroseyka 2/15
Moscow 101000, Russia
+7 9032854004

Recommended by
Alberto Gómez

Opening hours................................Open 7 days from 1 pm
Credit cards...Accepted
Type...Restaurant
Recommended for..Unexpected

"Sixty taps inside an underground cave."—Alberto Gómez

RULE TAPROOM

Starovagankovskiy Lane 19
Moscow 119019, Russia
+7 9851680819
www.ruletaproom.ru

Recommended by
Vadim Gurov

Opening hours................................Open 7 days from 4 pm
Credit cards...Accepted
Type..Bar
Recommended for..Local favorite

"RULE Taproom is the Zagovor Brewery headquarters with twenty-seven carefully selected beers and more than 500 rare bottles. It has the vibe of an underground music scene community. It's a few minutes from the Kremlin."
—Vadim Gurov

GOLODRANETS

Ulitsa Shaumyana 67
Rostov-on-Don
Rostov Oblast 344002, Russia
+7 9895386633
www.vk.com/golodranetsbarvk

Recommended by
Maxim Polivanov

Opening hours................................Open 7 days from 3 pm
Credit cards...Accepted
Type..Bar
Recommended for..Local favorite

"One of the first craft-beer bars in Russia, with lots of lambics and imperial stouts in a small place."
—Maxim Polivanov

BREWDOG TALLINN

Rotermanni 2
Tallinn
Harju County 10111, Estonia
+372 5579787
www.brewdog.com

Recommended by
Jaanis Tammela

Opening hours................................Mon–Wed from 5 pm,
Thur–Sat from 2 pm
Credit cards...Accepted
Type..Bar
Recommended for..Wish I'd opened

"A small bar in a historic building, presenting the old architecture combined with a modern bar."
—Jaanis Tammela

KOHT

Lai 8
Tallinn
Harju County 10133, Estonia
+372 6443302

Recommended by
Lauri Elango,
Christopher Pilkington,
Jaanis Tammela

Opening hours................................Open 7 days from 5 pm
Credit cards...Accepted
Type..Bar
Recommended for..Local favorite

"A minuscule bar in a medieval building in the historic Old Town of Tallinn, it's one of the last non-tourist places left in the neighborhood. The bar and the even smaller shop attached to it boast a bottle selection of more than 650 beers and twelve rotating taps, boasting the best of Estonian and international beers."—Lauri Elango

LEIB RESTO JA AED
Uus 31
Tallinn
Harju County 10111, Estonia
+372 6119026
www.leibresto.ee

Recommended by
Lauri Elango

Opening hours	Tue–Fri from 6 pm, Sat from 12 pm
Credit cards	Accepted
Type	Restaurant
Recommended for	Beer & food

PUDEL BAAR
Telliskivi 60a
Tallinn
Harju County 10412, Estonia
+372 58664496
www.pudel.ee

Recommended by
Lauri Elango

Opening hours	Sun–Fri from 4 pm, Sat from 12 pm
Credit cards	Accepted
Type	Beer garden and bar
Recommended for	Beer garden

"The first proper craft-beer bar in town. Not really a beer garden per se, but when the weather is nice there's a ton of seating outside. Fourteen taps and multiple fridges of international goodies in the coolest, hippest, most quickly gentrifying area of town."—Lauri Elango

TALLINN AIRPORT
Tartu maantee 101
Tallinn
Harju County 10112, Estonia
+372 6058888
www.tallinn-airport.ee

Recommended by
Lauri Elango

Opening hours	Open 7 days from 40 minutes before the first departure
Credit cards	Accepted
Type	Bar
Recommended for	Unexpected

"There are ample options to drink great local beers at the tiny, cozy Tallinn Airport. It has become a preflight and postflight tradition to sit in one of the cafés and have a fresh local IPA or gose."—Lauri Elango

TALLINN FERRY
Tallinn D-Terminal, Lootsi 13
Tallinn
Harju County 10151, Estonia
+358 6318320
www.tallinksilja.fi

Recommended by
Pyry Hurula

Opening hours	Open 7 days from 6 am
Credit cards	Accepted
Type	Bar
Recommended for	Unexpected

"This is an unusual place for craft beer. These ferries have around two dozen craft beers and it's getting better and better."—Pyry Hurula

ALUS CELLE
Baznīcas iela 35
Riga LV-1010, Latvia
+371 24118556

Recommended by
Andris Rasiņš

Opening hours	Open 7 days from 12 pm
Credit cards	Accepted
Type	Bar
Recommended for	Local favorite

"In my opinion, this is one of the best craft-beer bars in the Baltics, perhaps in all of eastern Europe."—Andris Rasiņš

FOLKKLUBS ALA PAGRABS
Peldu iela 19
Riga LV-1050, Latvia
+371 27796914
www.folkklubs.lv

Recommended by
Krisjanis Zelgis

Opening hours	Mon–Fri from 12 pm, Sat–Sun from 2 pm
Credit cards	Accepted
Type	Bar
Recommended for	Beer & food

"They have a huge local beer selection, and the food pairs well. A must-have is the Murbudu cider, made by the bar's owner."—Krisjanis Zelgis

LABIETIS

Aristida Briana 9A-2
Riga LV-1001, Latvia
+371 25655958
www.labietis.lv

Recommended by
Edgars Melnis

Opening hours	Mon from 4 pm, Tue–Fri from 3 pm, Sat–Sun from 1 pm
Credit cards	Accepted
Type	Brewery
Recommended for	Local favorite

TAKA

Miera iela 10
Riga LV-1001, Latvia
+371 29230508

Recommended by
Krisjanis Zelgis

Opening hours	Tue–Fri from 3 pm, Sat from 2 pm, Sun from 6 pm, Mon from 2 pm
Credit cards	Accepted
Type	Bar
Recommended for	Local favorite

"A place for local Latvian craft beer and craft beer from nearby Estonia, Russia, Lithuania, and Nordic countries."
—Krisjanis Zelgis

TRIS VIRI LAIVA

Avotu iela 35
Riga LV-1009, Latvia
+371 29671741

Recommended by
Krisjanis Zelgis

Opening hours	Mon–Fri from 11 am, Sat–Sun from 2 pm
Credit cards	Accepted
Type	Beer garden and restaurant
Recommended for	Beer garden

ALAUS BIBLIOTEKA

Traku 4
Vilnius
Vilnius County 01132, Lithuania
+370 52126874

Recommended by
Lana Svitankova

Opening hours	Tue–Fri from 5 pm, Sat from 3 pm
Credit cards	Accepted
Type	Bar
Recommended for	Wish I'd opened

"It is really a beer library, styled like a library with shelves of books and beer, library lamps, and beer magazines. You can get your own library card to check out different styles of beer you've tried."—Lana Svitankova

ŠPUNKA

Užupio gatve 9
Vilnius
Vilnius County 01202, Lithuania
+370 65232361
www.spunka.lt

Recommended by
Krisjanis Zelgis

Opening hours	Mon from 5 pm, Tue–Sun from 3 pm
Credit cards	Accepted
Type	Pub
Recommended for	Unexpected

"A small room with some five taps and a good selection of local Dundulis brewery beers."—Krisjanis Zelgis

VARVAR BAR

108/16 Saksaganskogo Street
Kiev
Kiev Oblast 02000, Ukraine
+380 676215511

Recommended by
Lana Svitankova

Opening hours	Open 7 days from 2 pm
Credit cards	Accepted
Type	Bar
Recommended for	Local favorite

ARSENAL RIBS

5 Pidvalna Street
Lviv
Lviv Oblast 79000, Ukraine
+380 673734151

Recommended by
Vladimir Kushnirev

Opening hours	Open 7 days from 12 pm
Credit cards	Accepted but not Amex
Type	Restaurant
Recommended for	Unexpected

"Inexpressible atmosphere combined with delicious ribs and fresh beer. You cannot come in a tie."—Vladimir Kushnirev

FRIENDS AND BEER

9 Deribasovskaya Street
Odessa
Odessa Oblast 65000, Ukraine
+380 487601998
www.friendsandbeer.com.ua

Recommended by
Vladimir Kushnirev

Opening hours	Open 7 days from 12 pm
Credit cards	Accepted but not Amex
Type	Pub
Recommended for	Worth the travel

PYVNOY SAD

Recommended by
Vladimir Kushnirev

6 Havanna Street
Odessa
Odessa Oblast 65000, Ukraine
+380 48777888

Opening hours	Open 7 days from 10 am
Credit cards	Not accepted
Type	Beer garden
Recommended for	Beer garden

"A luxurious European interior, traditional Bavarian and Ukrainian cuisine, and live music some evenings. Also four kinds of craft beer."—Vladimir Kushnirev

TROUBADUR

Recommended by
Vladimir Kushnirev

Zhukovsky 13
Odessa
Odessa Oblast 65000, Ukraine
+380 487855863
www.troubadur.com.ua

Opening hours	Open 7 days from 9 am
Credit cards	Accepted
Type	Bar
Recommended for	Local favorite

MIKKELLER BAR BUCHAREST

Piața Charles de Gaulle 3
Bucharest 011857, Romania
+40 757574977
www.mikkeller.ro

Recommended by
Razvan Costache,
Flaviu Adrian Odorhean

Opening hours	Mon–Fri from 5 pm, Sat–Sun from 1 pm
Credit cards	Accepted
Type	Bar
Recommended for	Local favorite

ROMANIAN CRAFT BEER BAR

Calea Victoriei 91–93
Bucharest 010091, Romania
+40 770550234
www.bere-zaganu.ro

Recommended by
Laurentiu Banescu

Opening hours	Open 7 days from 12 pm
Credit cards	Accepted but not Amex
Type	Brewery
Recommended for	Local favorite

"A Romanian craft-beer bar from Zaganu, the pioneers of craft brewing in Romania. They serve all the best Romanian craft beers on ten taps and in bottles as well."
—Laurentiu Banescu

BLEND. BREWS & BITES

Recommended by
Flaviu Adrian Odorhean

Strada Piezişă 8
Cluj Napoca
Cluj 400000, Romania
+40 770552957

Opening hours	Mon–Fri from 10 am, Sat–Sun from 11 am
Credit cards	Accepted but not Amex
Type	Restaurant
Recommended for	Local favorite

"The widest beer variety in town, with a nice big terrace, a central location, good finger food, and a nice design."
—Flaviu Adrian Odorhean

SZIMPLA

Recommended by
Ionut Ciobota

Strada 1 Decembrie 1918, Number 37
Sfântu Gheorghe
Covasna 520023, Romania
+40 745901671
www.szimpla.ro

Opening hours	7 days from 8 am
Credit cards	Accepted
Type	Bar
Recommended for	Local favorite

LE PETIT NAPLES

Recommended by
Ionut Ciobota

Strada Horea 4
Satu Mare 440004, Romania
+40 261713579

Opening hours	Mon from 6 pm, Tue–Sat from 8 am
Credit cards	Accepted
Type	Restaurant
Recommended for	Beer & food

"Real artisanal cuisine—the owner personally prepares all the seasonal food."—Ionut Ciobota

"BEER IS SERVED DIRECTLY FROM THE MATURATION TANKS WITH NO FILTRATION OR PASTEURIZATION."
ALEXIS ALEXIOU P.256

SLOVENIA, CROATIA, SERBIA, KOSOVO, BULGARIA, GREECE & CYPRUS

"THE BEST TRUE CRAFT-BEER PUB IN GREECE."
NIKOS KOCHYLIS P.254

"OUTSTANDING FOOD PAIRED WITH BEERS."
DIMITRIJ JURISIC P.252

"THIS SPOT IS COMPLETELY SECLUDED, WITH A SPECTACULAR VIEW OF THE ŠUMADIJA HILLS, SOME FORTY MINUTES FROM THE CAPITAL. IT IS A NEVER-ENDING SOURCE OF INSPIRATION."
KOSARA DANGIĆ MELENTIJEVIĆ P.253

SLOVENIA, CROATIA, SERBIA, KOSOVO, BULGARIA, GREECE & CYPRUS

N

SCALE

0   30   60
mi.

SLOVENIA

LJUBLJANA P.252
ZAGREB P.252
KOPER P.252
ISTRIA P.252

CROATIA

BELGRADE P.253

SERBIA

DUBROVNIK-NERETVA P.252

BURGAS P.253
SOFIA P.254
BULGARIA
PAZARDZHIK P.253
PRISTINA P.253
KOSOVO
CENTRAL MACEDONIA P.255

GREECE

ATHENS P.254
ATTICA P.255
SOUTH AEGEAN P.256

CYPRUS
NICOSIA P.256

RESTAURANT NORO

Kolaričeva ulica 1
Koper 6000, Slovenia
+386 40869696

Recommended by
Dimitrij Jurisic

Opening hours................................Tue–Sat from 12 pm
Credit cards...Accepted
Type..Restaurant
Recommended for...................................Unexpected

"Outstanding food paired with beers."—Dimitrij Jurisic

SIR WILLIAM'S PUB

Tavčarjeva ulica 8a
Ljubljana 1101, Slovenia
+386 59944825
www.sirwilliamspub.webs.com

Recommended by
Marco Vidmar

Opening hours.................................Mon–Fri from 8 am,
Sat from 10 am, Sun from 5 pm
Credit cards...Accepted
Type...Pub
Recommended for..............................Local favorite

"Sir William's Pub was one of the first craft-beer bars in
Slovenia in 1998."—Marco Vidmar

GLAM CAFÉ

Palmotićeva ulica 5
Dubrovnik
Dubrovnik-Neretva 20000, Croatia
+385 911518257

Recommended by
André Ek,
Tomas Halberstad,
Nicole Pearce

Opening hours.............................Open 7 days from 9 am
Credit cards..Not accepted
Type...Pub
Recommended for...................................Unexpected

"This little place in Dubrovnik has all the best Croatian beers
in one spot."—Nicole Pearce

BEER GARDEN PUB

Brenobića 2
Poreč
Istria 52440, Croatia
+385 996784242

Recommended by
Alessandro Zecchinati

Opening hours.............................Open 7 days from 5 pm
Credit cards..Not accepted
Type...Beer garden
Recommended for..................................Beer garden

BURA BREW

Ulica Mate Vlašića 26/19
Poreč
Istria 52440, Croatia
+385 916014006
www.burabrew.hr

Recommended by
Alessandro Zecchinati

Opening hours.............................Mon–Fri from 9:30 am
Credit cards..Not accepted
Type...Brewery
Recommended for.............................Wish I'd opened

CRAFT ROOM

Ulica Opatovina 35
Zagreb 10000, Croatia
+385 14845390

Recommended by
Alessandro Zecchinati

Opening hours............................Open 7 days from 10 am
Credit cards...Accepted
Type...Pub
Recommended for..............................Local favorite

"A good selection of Croatian craft beer."
—Alessandro Zecchinati

BAR SAŠA

Gospodar Jevremova 40
Belgrade 11000, Serbia
+381 112637103

Recommended by
Nemanja Stefanovic

Opening hours.............................Tue–Sun from 10 am
Credit cards...Accepted
Type..Bar and restaurant
Recommended for.................................Beer & food

ENDORFIN BAR & RESTAURANT

Braće Jugovića 3
Belgrade 11000, Serbia
+381 63220611
www.endorfingastropub.com

Recommended by
Kosara Dangić Melentijević,
Milos Vuksic

Opening hours............................Open 7 days from 10 am
Credit cards...Accepted
Type..Restaurant
Recommended for.................................Beer & food

"Chef Vanja Puškar is eager to play with local, long-
forgotten flavors and to refresh them with new techniques.
He also uses spent grains bread and beer-based sauces.
Beer is king here. They are cooking with it and using the
aromas as an inspiration for the food choices."
—Kosara Dangić Melentijević

MAJSTOR ZA PIVO
Recommended by
Kosara Dangić Melentijević,
Milos Vuksic

Žorža Klemansoa 18
Belgrade 11000, Serbia
+381 112419161
www.majstorzapivo.com

Opening hours................................Mon–Sat from 12 pm
Credit cards...Accepted
Type..Bar and retail
Recommended for..................................Local favorite

PIVO I KOBAJA
Recommended by
Nemanja Stefanovic

Ruzveltova 36
Belgrade 11000, Serbia
+381 62404885
www.pivoikobaja.rs

Opening hours..................................Open 7 days from 8 am
Credit cards...Accepted
Type......................................Beer garden and restaurant
Recommended for..Beer garden

SAMO PIVO
Recommended by
Kosara Dangić Melentijević,
Nemanja Stefanovic

Balkanska 13
Belgrade 11000, Serbia
www.samopivo.rs

Opening hours.....................................Open 7 days from 12 pm
Credit cards...Not accepted
Type..Bar
Recommended for...................................Local favorite

"They serve only beer. They have twenty-three taps and always serve new beers from all over the world."
—Nemanja Stefanovic

KABINET BREWERY
Recommended by
Kosara Dangić
Melentijević

Despota Stevana Lazarevića 11
Nemenikuće
Belgrade 11450, Serbia
+381 112424478
www.kabinet.rs

Type..Brewery
Recommended for...................................Worth the travel

"This spot is completely secluded, with a spectacular view of the Šumadija hills, some forty minutes from the capital. It is a never-ending source of inspiration."
—Kosara Dangić Melentijević

KOD TOME I NADE
Recommended by
Kosara Dangić Melentijević

Kosmajski Put
Nemenikuće
Belgrade 11450, Serbia
+381 118255155

Opening hours................................Open 7 days from 8 am
Credit cards...Not accepted
Type...Restaurant
Recommended for..................................Unexpected

"This very traditional family restaurant, in a village near the Kosmaj mountain. It has craft beer on tap and serves only split-roasted lamb and suckling pig."
—Kosara Dangić Melentijević

SOMA BOOK STATION
Recommended by
Alex Butler

4/A Fazli Grajqevci
Pristina 10000, Kosovo
+381 38748818
www.somabookstation.com

Opening hours................................Mon–Sat from 8 am
Credit cards.........................Accepted but not Amex
Type..Bar and retail
Recommended for..................................Local favorite

TAVERN RUBIN
Recommended by
Rory Miller

Ulitsa Perla 2008
Primorsko
Burgas 8180, Bulgaria

Type...Restaurant
Recommended for..................................Unexpected

RHOMBUS BREWERY
Recommended by
Svilen Kirilovski

Ivaylovsko shose 4
Pazardzhik 4400, Bulgaria
+359 899189638
www.rhombusbrewery.com

Opening hours................................Open 7 days from 3 pm
Credit cards...Accepted
Type..Brewery
Recommended for...Beer & food

N'DEY BARA TANGRA
Bulevard Tsar Simeon 37
Sliven 8801, Bulgaria
+359 885443595

Recommended by
Svilen Kirilovski

Opening hours.................................Tue–Sat from 8 pm
Credit cards.......................................Not accepted
Type...Bar
Recommended for.................................Unexpected

BAGRI RESTAURANT
Ulitsa Dobrudzja 10
Sofia 1000, Bulgaria
+359 885077927
www.bagri-restaurant.bg

Recommended by
Georgi Hristov

Opening hours...........................Open 7 days from 11 am
Credit cards...Accepted
Type...Restaurant
Recommended for.............................Beer & food

HALBITE
Ulitsa Neofit Rilski 72
Sofia 1000, Bulgaria
+359 29804147
www.halbite.com

Recommended by
Svilen Kirilovski

Opening hours...........................Open 7 days from 11 am
Credit cards.......................................Not accepted
Type.................................Beer garden and bar
Recommended for.............................Beer garden

KANAAL
Bulevard Madrid 2
Sofia 1505, Bulgaria
+359 882856346
www.kanaal.bg

Recommended by
George Alexakis,
Liubomir Chonos,
Georgi Hristov,
Svilen Kirilovski,
Ofer Ronen

Opening hours.......................Mon–Sat from 5:30 pm,
Sun from 3 pm
Credit cards.......................................Not accepted
Type...Bar
Recommended for.............................Local favorite

"Bar KANAAL is the first real craft-beer bar in Sofia and
Bulgaria, contributing greatly to the development
of the beer culture in the city. You can always find at least
150 beers, and there are thirteen taps for draft beer."
—Svilen Kirilovski

100 BEERS
Ulitsa Yuri Venelin 1
Sofia 1000, Bulgaria
+359 879864667
www.100beers.bg

Recommended by
Rory Miller

Opening hours..........................Open 7 days from 10 am
Credit cards...Accepted
Type..Retail
Recommended for.............................Local favorite

"This is the closest place to my apartment with craft beer.
I can always rely on a great up-to-date selection of tasty
beers from all over. It's technically a shop, but they often
have great options on draft."—Rory Miller

BEERTIME
1 Plateia Iroon
Athens 105 54, Greece
+30 2103228443
www.beertime.gr

Recommended by
Todd Beal,
Jussi Rokka

Opening hours...........................Open 7 days from 4 pm
Credit cards...Accepted
Type...Bar
Recommended for.................................Unexpected

THE LAZY BULLDOG PUB
Orfeos 2 ke Persefonis 13
Athens 118 54, Greece
+30 6975026836

Recommended by
Paraskevas Giagmouroglou,
Nikos Kochylis,
Vassilis Segos

Opening hours.............................Open 7 days from 1 pm
Credit cards...Accepted
Type.................................Restaurant and pub
Recommended for.............................Beer & food

THE LOCAL PUB
Chaimanta 25
Athens 152 34, Greece
+30 6940864443

Recommended by
Paraskevas Giagmouroglou,
Nikos Kochylis,
Vassilis Segos

Opening hours.............................Tue–Sun from 6 pm
Credit cards.......................................Not accepted
Type..Pub
Recommended for.............................Local favorite

"The best true craft-beer pub in Greece."—Nikos Kochylis

ARCH BEER HOUSE

Recommended by
Nikos Kochylis

Ethnikis Antistaseos 91
Peristeri
Attica 121 34, Greece
+30 2105752992
www.archbeerhouse.gr

Opening hours....................................Open 7 days from 7 pm
Credit cards..Not accepted
Type...Beer garden and bar
Recommended for...Beer garden

BIBERE

Recommended by
Vassilis Segos

5 Aggelou Metaxa Street
Piraeus
Attica 185 34, Greece
+30 2104110004

Opening hours....................................Open 7 days from 9 am
Credit cards...Accepted
Type...Beer garden and restaurant
Recommended for...Unexpected

THE BAR L.A.B.

Recommended by
Aggelos Kaniatsakis

Nik. Plastira ke Mistakidou 2
Kalamaria
Central Macedonia 551 32, Greece
+30 2310443595

Opening hours....................................Open 7 days from 9 am
Credit cards...Accepted
Type...Restaurant
Recommended for...Wish I'd opened

AUGUST BAR

Recommended by
Aggelos Kaniatsakis

Mavrokordatou 2
Thessaloniki
Central Macedonia 546 43, Greece
+30 2310850750
www.avgoustos.gr

Opening hours....................................Open 7 days from 9 pm
Credit cards..Not accepted
Type..Bar
Recommended for...Worth the travel

BEER FABRICA

Recommended by
Aggelos Kaniatsakis

Eptapirgiou 69
Thessaloniki
Central Macedonia 566 26, Greece
+30 2310209943
www.beerfabrica.gr

Opening hours....................................Open 7 days from 5 pm
Credit cards...Accepted
Type..Bar and retail
Recommended for...Local favorite

"Thessaloniki's original beer and food store."
—Aggelos Kaniatsakis

EXTRAVAGANZA

Recommended by
Aggelos Kaniatsakis

Episkopou Amvrosiou 8
Thessaloniki
Central Macedonia 546 30, Greece
+30 2310529791

Opening hours...Wed–Mon from 1 pm
Credit cards..Not accepted
Type....................................Beer garden, bar, and restaurant
Recommended for...Beer garden

THE HOPPY PUB

Recommended by
George Alexakis,
Aggelos Kaniatsakis,
Antonis Moustakas

Nikiforou Foka 6
Thessaloniki
Central Macedonia 546 21, Greece
+30 2310269203

Opening hours....................................Tue–Sun from 5:30 pm
Credit cards...Accepted
Type..Pub
Recommended for...Local favorite

PRIMATE DRAFT

Recommended by
Aggelos Kaniatsakis

25 Martiou 12
Thessaloniki
Central Macedonia 546 46, Greece
+30 2310413038

Opening hours....................................Open 7 days from 9 am
Credit cards..Not accepted
Type..Bar and restaurant
Recommended for...Beer & food

SANTORINI BREWING COMPANY

Mesa Gonia
Santorini
South Aegean 847 00, Greece
+30 2268030268
www.santorinibrewingcompany.gr

Recommended by
Itay Marom

Opening hours	Mon–Sat from 12 pm
Credit cards	Not accepted
Type	Brewery
Recommended for	Unexpected

"It was surprising to find good craft beer on such a small
island. You can find their beer all over Santorini."
—Itay Marom

PIVO MICROBREWERY

Asklipiou 36
Nicosia
Nicosia 1011, Cyprus
+357 22377088
www.pivomicrobrewery.com.cy

Recommended by
Alexis Alexiou

Opening hours	Wed–Sun from 7 pm
Credit cards	Accepted
Type	Microbrewery
Recommended for	Local favorite

"A nice old house with brewing technology visible to
everyone. Beer is served directly from the maturation
tanks with no filtration or pasteurization. There are four
year-round signature beers and two seasonal beers on tap."
—Alexis Alexiou

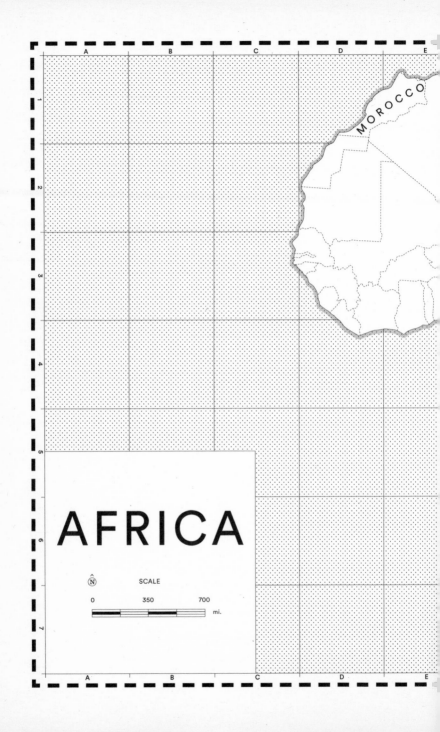

MOROCCO

AFRICA

N

SCALE

0   350   700
mi.

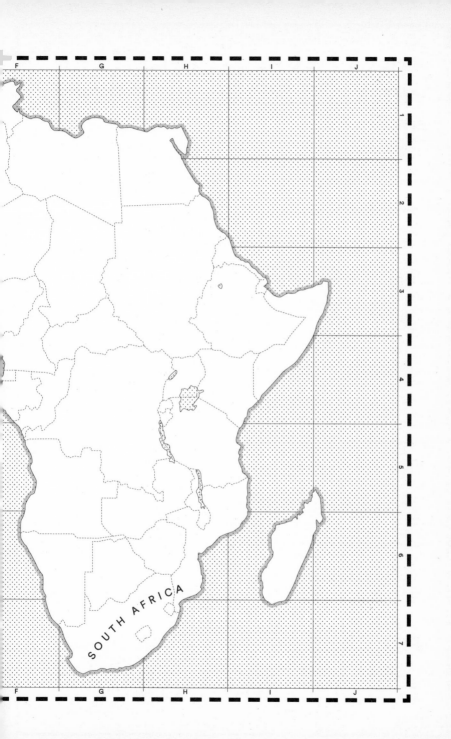

SOUTH AFRICA

"THEY SERVE MULTI-AWARD-WINNING BEERS WITH GOOD AND UNPRETENTIOUS FOOD."

THEO DE BEER P.262

MOROCCO & SOUTH AFRICA

"A GREAT ATMOSPHERE WHERE IT'S EASY TO STAY AND RELAX."

MARCI MULLEN P.262

"GREAT VIBE, AWESOME MUSIC, HOMEY FEEL, AND GREAT BEERS WITH A FRIENDLY STAFF."

JORG FINKELDEY P.263

"THEIR SELECTION IS BETTER THAN ANY OTHER BAR ON THE CONTINENT."

FRANS VAN STADEN P.262

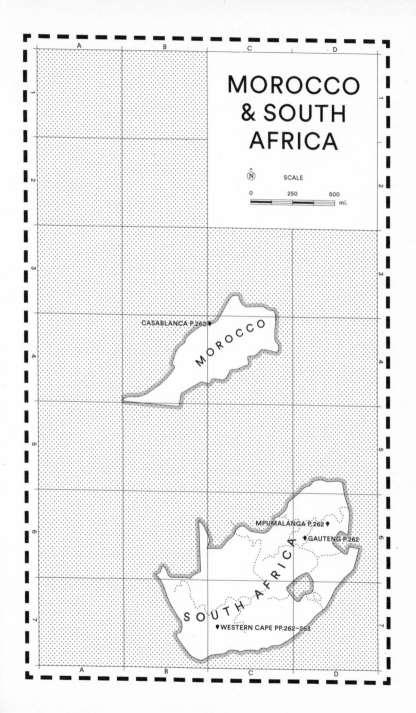

MOROCCO
& SOUTH
AFRICA

N   SCALE

0   250   500 mi.

CASABLANCA P.262

MOROCCO

MPUMALANGA P.262
GAUTENG P.262

SOUTH AFRICA

WESTERN CAPE PP.262–263

LA BODEGA

Recommended by
Marci Mullen

129 Rue Allal Ben Abdallah
Casablanca 20250, Morocco
+212 522541842
www.bodega.ma

Opening hours........Mon–Sat from 12 pm, Sun from 7 pm
Credit cards..Accepted
Type..Bar
Recommended for..Worth the travel

"A great atmosphere where it's easy to stay and relax."
—Marci Mullen

MAD GIANT

Recommended by
Jorg Finkeldey

1 Fox Street
Johannesburg
Gauteng 2048, South Africa
+27 114920901
www.madgiant.co.za

Opening hours................................Open 7 days from 12 pm
Credit cards..Accepted
Type..Brewery
Recommended for...Unexpected

ANVIL ALE HOUSE & BREWERY

Naledi Drive
Dullstroom
Mpumalanga 1110, South Africa
+27 132540197
www.anvilbrewery.com

Recommended by
Theo de Beer

Opening hours....................................Wed–Mon from 8 am
Credit cards......................................Accepted but not Amex
Type.....................................Beer garden and brewery
Recommended for...Beer garden

"They serve multi-award-winning beers in a child-
and pet-friendly garden setting, with good and
unpretentious food."—Theo de Beer

AFRO CARIBBEAN BREWERY

Recommended by
Theo de Beer

157 2nd Avenue
Cape Town
Western Cape 7708, South Africa
+27 216740186
www.acbc.co.za

Opening hours..................................Open 7 days from 5 pm
Credit cards......................................Accepted but not Amex
Type..Microbrewery
Recommended for..Worth the travel

BANANA JAM CAFE

Recommended by
Theo de Beer,
Mike Goguen,
Frans van Staden

157 2nd Avenue
Cape Town
Western Cape 7708, South Africa
+27 216740186
www.bananajamcafe.co.za

Opening hours..Tue–Sun from 11 am
Credit cards..Accepted
Type..Restaurant
Recommended for..Worth the travel

"Their selection is better than any other bar on the
continent."—Frans van Staden

"New brews are always on tap with an Afro-Caribbean
brewery on-site. A great beer selection."—Theo de Beer

BEERHOUSE

Recommended by
Nicholas Bush

223 Long Street
Cape Town
Western Cape 8000, South Africa
+27 874700593
www.beerhouse.co.za

Opening hours..................................Open 7 days from 11 am
Credit cards......................................Accepted but not Amex
Type..Bar
Recommended for..Worth the travel

DRIFTER BREWING COMPANY

Recommended by
Nicholas Bush

156 Victoria Road
Cape Town
Western Cape 7806, South Africa
+27 614217340
www.drifterbrewing.co.za

Opening hours..Friday from 5 pm
Credit cards......................................Accepted but not Amex
Type..Brewery
Recommended for..Local favorite

JACK BLACK'S TAPROOM

10 Brigid Road
Cape Town
Western Cape 7945, South Africa
+27 214474151
www.jackblackbeer.com/taproom

Recommended by
Frans van Staden

Opening hours	Wed–Sat from 10 am
Credit cards	Accepted
Type	Bar and brewery
Recommended for	Beer & food

"Every month they host food pairing events, burger nights, and food truck Fridays. They always have something new and exciting to try."—Frans van Staden

MOTHERLAND BREWERS

Mandela Rhodes Building
Corner of Wale and
St George's Mall Street
Cape Town
Western Cape 8001, South Africa
+27 214220960

Recommended by
Frans van Staden

Opening hours	Mon–Fri from 12 pm
Credit cards	Accepted but not Amex
Type	Brewery
Recommended for	Unexpected

"It's small, quirky, and in such an unexpected location."
—Frans van Staden

URBAN BREWING COMPANY

31 Harbour Road
Cape Town
Western Cape 7872, South Africa
+27 217911130
www.urbanbrewery.co.za

Recommended by
Jorg Finkeldey

Opening hours	Mon from 5 pm, Tue–Sun from 11 am
Credit cards	Accepted but not Amex
Type	Brewery
Recommended for	Wish I'd opened

"They have an award-winning German-inspired beer portfolio."—Jorg Finkeldey

BERG RIVER BREWERY

1, 36 Westhoven
Paarl
Western Cape 7646, South Africa
+27 218711390
www.bergriverbrewery.co.za

Recommended by
Jorg Finkeldey

Opening hours	Mon–Sat from 9 am
Credit cards	Accepted
Type	Brewery
Recommended for	Local favorite

"Great vibe, awesome music, homey feel, and great beers with a friendly staff."—Jorg Finkeldey

SEDGEFIELD CRAFT BREWERY

Scarab Village
N2 Highway
Sedgefield
Western Cape 6573, South Africa
+27 829014268
www.sedgefieldbrewery.co.za

Recommended by
Theo de Beer

Opening hours	Mon–Sat from 8 am
Credit cards	Accepted but not Amex
Type	Brewery
Recommended for	Unexpected

"A tiny (nano) brewery with the owner/brewer in attendance."—Theo de Beer

CRAFT WHEAT & HOPS

16 Andringa Street
Stellenbosch
Western Cape 7600, South Africa
+27 218828069
www.craftstellenbosch.co.za

Recommended by
Toby Cooper

Opening hours	Open 7 days from 10 am
Credit cards	Accepted
Type	Microbrewery
Recommended for	Unexpected

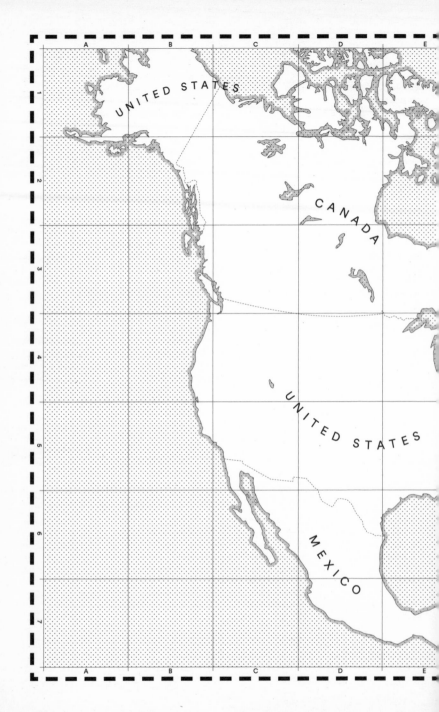

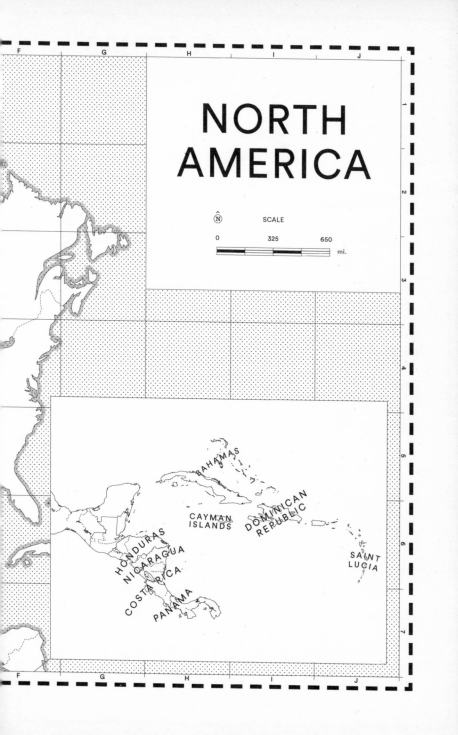

NORTH AMERICA

N

SCALE

0   325   650
mi.

BAHAMAS

CAYMAN ISLANDS

DOMINICAN REPUBLIC

SAINT LUCIA

HONDURAS

NICARAGUA

COSTA RICA

PANAMA

“THIS LITTLE SPOT HAS EVERYTHING A BEER LOVER COULD ASK FOR.” JEFF ORR P.269

“A KILLER BEER MENU, ALWAYS ROTATING WITH NEW WORLD-CLASS PRODUCTS. THEY ALSO HAVE A SMALL, ARTISANAL, AND AMAZINGLY TASTY FOOD MENU.” DAN MASON P.270

CANADA

“SOME OF THE FINEST BEER ON THE CONTINENT.” ZACH MACK P.271

“THE BEST BREWPUB IN THE WORLD.” DOROTHÉE VAN AGT P.271

“THE QUALITY IS JUST OUTSTANDING.” MARTIN VOIGT P.269

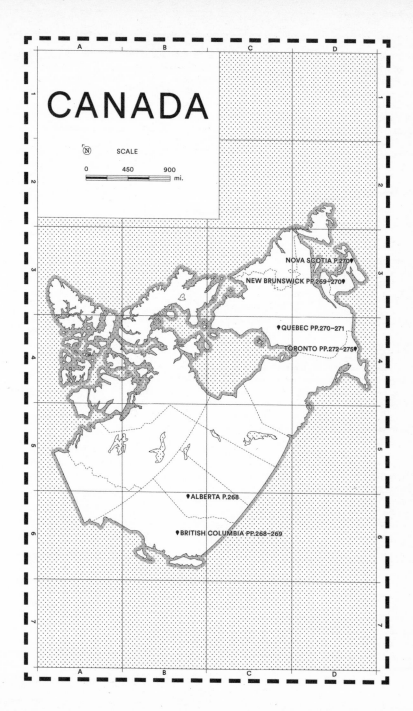

CANADA

N SCALE

0   450   900
mi.

CHILI'S GRILL & BAR CALGARY AIRPORT

2000 Airport Road Northeast
Calgary
Alberta T2E 6Z8, Canada
+1 4032502072
www.chilis.com

Recommended by
Jeff Orr

Opening hours	Open 7 days from 4:30 am
Credit cards	Accepted
Type	Restaurant
Recommended for	Unexpected

CRAFT BEER MARKET

345 10th Avenue Southwest
Calgary
Alberta T2R 0A5, Canada
+1 4035142337
www.craftbeermarket.ca

Recommended by
Craig Cooper,
Jeff Orr

Opening hours	Mon–Fri from 11 am, Sat–Sun from 10 am
Credit cards	Accepted
Type	Restaurant
Recommended for	Beer & food

"They have over 100 beers on tap, and the pipework from the glass-front keg room into a central bar is amazing theater. They also have great pub food."
—Craig Cooper

"Craft holds regular brewmaster dinners, which have absolutely fantastic pairings."—Jeff Orr

NATIONAL ON 17TH

550 17th Avenue Southwest
Calgary
Alberta T2S 0B1, Canada
+1 4032290226
www.ntnl.ca/national-17th

Recommended by
Jeff Orr

Opening hours	Mon–Sat from 11 am, Sun from 10 am
Credit cards	Accepted
Type	Bar
Recommended for	Local favorite

"When National on 17th opened it was a beacon of great beer, focused on independently owned breweries. Even with an emerging craft-beer scene, it stands apart with a diverse beer list, delicious beer, and a casual and comfortable atmosphere."—Jeff Orr

THE SUGAR BOWL CAFE

10922 88 Avenue Northwest
Edmonton
Alberta T6G 0Z1, Canada
+1 7804338369
www.thesugarbowl.org

Recommended by
Kirk Zembal

Opening hours	Open 7 days from 8 am
Credit cards	Accepted
Type	Restaurant
Recommended for	Local favorite

DAGERAAD BREWING

3191 Thunderbird Crescent #114
Burnaby
British Columbia V5A 3G1, Canada
+1 6044202050
www.dageraadbrewing.com

Recommended by
Aaron Johnson

Opening hours	Open 7 days from 12 pm
Credit cards	Accepted
Type	Brewery
Recommended for	Unexpected

VANCOUVER ISLAND LIQUOR NANAIMO

2875 Departure Bay Road
Nanaimo
British Columbia V9S 3X1, Canada
+1 2507568817

Recommended by
Christian Jauslin

Opening hours	Open 7 days from 9 am
Credit cards	Accepted
Type	Retail
Recommended for	Unexpected

"This is a liquor store next to a gas station that has a good selection of local beers."—Christian Jauslin

ALIBI ROOM

157 Alexander Street
Gastown
Vancouver
British Columbia V6A 1B8, Canada
+1 6046233383
www.alibi.ca

Recommended by
Evan Doan,
Aaron Johnson,
Ben Love,
Lynn McIlwee,
Jeff Orr,
Martin Voigt

Opening hours	Mon–Fri from 5 pm, Sat–Sun from 10 am
Credit cards	Accepted
Type	Pub
Recommended for	Beer & food

"One of the original craft-beer bars in Vancouver, it is always guaranteed to have countless amazing beers on tap, with great people and fantastic food."—Evan Doan

"This little spot has everything a beer lover could ask for." —Jeff Orr

"A great variety of beers: 99.9% Canadian. The quality is just outstanding."—Martin Voigt

CRAFT BEER MARKET VANCOUVER

85 West 1st Avenue
Mount Pleasant
Vancouver
British Columbia V5Y 3K8, Canada
+1 6047092337
www.craftbeermarket.ca/vancouver

Recommended by
Thomas Lau

Opening hours	Mon–Fri from 11 am, Sat–Sun from 10 am
Credit cards	Accepted
Type	Bar and restaurant
Recommended for	Wish I'd opened

PARALLEL 49 BREWING COMPANY

1950 Triumph Street
Hastings-Sunrise
Vancouver
British Columbia V5L 1K5, Canada
+1 6045582739
www.parallel49brewing.com

Recommended by
Marissa Mills

Opening hours	Open 7 days from 11 am
Credit cards	Accepted
Type	Brewery
Recommended for	Beer & food

"Forty beers on tap and a food truck menu." —Marissa Mills

33 ACRES BREWING COMPANY

15 West 8th Avenue
Mount Pleasant
Vancouver
British Columbia V5Y 1M8, Canada
+1 6046204589
www.33acresbrewing.com

Recommended by
Travis Richards

Opening hours	Mon–Fri from 9 am, Sat–Sun from 10 am
Credit cards	Accepted
Type	Brewery
Recommended for	Unexpected

"Great beer tucked into a tiny storefront. Unpretentious, and their house-made coffee is great as well." —Travis Richards

THE DRAKE EATERY

517 Pandora Avenue
Victoria
British Columbia V8W 1N6, Canada
+1 2505909075
www.drakeeatery.com

Recommended by
Evan Doan,
Danny Hamilton

Opening hours	Open 7 days from 11:30 am
Credit cards	Accepted
Type	Pub
Recommended for	Beer & food

SPINNAKERS GASTRO BREWPUB & GUESTHOUSES

308 Catherine Street
Victoria
British Columbia V9A 3S8, Canada
+1 2503862739
www.spinnakers.com

Recommended by
Rick Green,
Aaron Johnson

Opening hours	Open 7 days from 11 am
Credit cards	Accepted
Type	Brewpub
Recommended for	Beer & food

"Located in British Columbia's capital, Spinnakers is Canada's first brewpub. They brew a range of styles, from classic real ales to barrel-aged sours and ciders. Their food is excellent, with a focus on local, seasonal, and sustainable. They even have an in-house chocolatier. You could easily spend an entire weekend there."—Rick Green

540 KITCHEN AND BAR

540 Queen Street
Fredericton
New Brunswick E3B 1B9, Canada
+1 5064495400
www.540kitchenandbar.com

Recommended by
Dan Mason

Opening hours	Mon–Fri from 11:30 am, Sat from 5 pm
Credit cards	Accepted
Type	Bar and restaurant
Recommended for	Beer & food

"An absolute killer small-food menu that constantly rotates, incorporating local fresh quality products everywhere. The food competes with any place I've been. What makes it special is a 100% local craft-beer menu serving only the finest brews."—Dan Mason

JAMES JOYCE PUB

659 Queen Street
Fredericton
New Brunswick E3B 586, Canada
+1 5064509820
www.jamesjoycepub.com

Recommended by
Paul Maybee

Opening hours...................................Mon–Fri from 11:30 am,
Sat–Sun from 3 pm
Credit cards...Accepted
Type...Pub
Recommended for...................................Local favorite

"Over thirty New Brunswick beers."—Paul Maybee

BISHOP'S CELLAR

1477 Lower Water Street
Bishop's Landing
Halifax
Nova Scotia B3J 3Z4, Canada
+1 9024902675
www.bishopscellar.com

Recommended by
Dan Mason

Opening hours...................................Mon–Fri from 10 am,
Sat from 8 am, Sun from 12 pm
Credit cards...Accepted
Type...Retail
Recommended for...................................Unexpected

"The best selection of rare and local brews in Atlantic Canada."—Dan Mason

STILLWELL

1672 Barrington Street
Halifax
Nova Scotia B3J 2A2, Canada
+1 9024211672
www.barstillwell.com

Recommended by
Todd Beal,
Dan Mason,
Paul Maybee

Opening hours...................................Sun–Thur from 4 pm,
Fri–Sat from 12 pm
Credit cards...Accepted
Type...Bar
Recommended for...................................Wish I'd opened

"A killer beer menu, always rotating with new world-class products. They also have a small, artisanal, and amazingly tasty food menu."—Dan Mason

STILLWELL BEERGARDEN

5688 Spring Garden Road
Halifax
Nova Scotia B3H 1H5, Canada
+1 9024784211
www.barstillwell.com/beergarden

Recommended by
Dan Mason,
Paul Maybee

Opening hours...................................Open 7 days from 12 pm
Credit cards...Accepted
Type...Beer garden
Recommended for...................................Beer garden

Toronto, see pages 272–275

BRASSERIE DUNHAM

3809 Rue Principale
Dunham
Quebec J0E 1M0, Canada
+1 4502840516
www.brasseriedunham.com

Recommended by
Eloi Deit

Opening hours...................................Thur–Sun from 12 pm
Credit cards...Accepted
Type...Restaurant and pub
Recommended for...................................Local favorite

BRASSERIE HARRICANA

95 Rue Jean-Talon Ouest
La Petite-Patrie
Montreal
Quebec H2R 2W8, Canada
+1 5143033039
www.brasserieharricana.com

Recommended by
Marie-Pier Veilleux

Opening hours...................................Open 7 days from 12 pm
Credit cards.................................Accepted but not Amex
Type...............................Restaurant and microbrewery
Recommended for...................................Beer & food

ISLE DE GARDE BRASSERIE

1039 Rue Beaubien Est
La Petite-Patrie
Montreal
Quebec H2S 1T3, Canada
+1 5143031661
www.isledegarde.com

Recommended by
Marie-Pier Veilleux

Opening hours...................................Sat–Wed from 1 pm,
Thur–Fri from 11:30 am
Credit cards...Accepted
Type...Restaurant
Recommended for...................................Local favorite

L'AMÈRE À BOIRE

2049 Rue Saint-Denis
La Petite-Patrie
Montreal
Quebec H2X 3K8, Canada
+1 5142827448
www.amereaboire.com

Recommended by
Olivier Dupras

Opening hours.....................................Open 7 days from 1 pm
Credit cards...Accepted
Type...Brewpub
Recommended for......................................Local favorite

"One of the oldest brewpubs in the city. You go there to drink the Cerna Hora—a classic Czech pils—or to have a pint of their English pale ale served in a hand pump."—Olivier Dupras

VICES & VERSA

6631 Saint Laurent Boulevard
Little Italy
Montreal
Quebec H2S 3C5, Canada
+1 5142722498
www.vicesetversa.com

Recommended by
Neil Callaghan,
Christopher DeWolf,
Stefano Di Gioacchino,
Shawna O'Flaherty

Opening hours.......................................Mon–Tue from 3 pm,
Wed–Sun from 11:30 am
Credit cards...Accepted
Type..Pub
Recommended for...............................Worth the travel

"A beautiful garden next to a park. The best beer selection in Montreal."—Stefano Di Gioacchino

"This little pub is far from Montreal's downtown neighborhoods, far enough off the beaten track that it's primarily locals. They feature an extremely well-curated tap list of Quebecois beers, and live music that includes French Canadian fiddle nights. They also have lively food pairings. They do cask ales year-round."—Shawna O'Flaherty

DIEU DU CIEL

29 Avenue Laurier Ouest
Mile End
Montreal
Quebec H2T 2N2, Canada
+1 5144909555
www.dieuduciel.com

Recommended by
Dorothée van Agt,
Hugo Gonçalves,
Zach Mack,
Ofer Ronen

Opening hours.........Mon–Thur from 3 pm, Fri–Sun from 1 pm
Credit cards...Accepted
Type...Brewpub
Recommended for...............................Worth the travel

"The best brewpub in the world."—Dorothée van Agt

"Some of the finest beer on the continent —across the entire spectrum of styles—plus a great ambiance."
—Zach Mack

LE BATEAU DE NUIT

275 Rue Saint-Jean
Quebec City
Quebec G1R 1N8, Canada
+1 4189772626
www.bateaudenuit.com

Recommended by
Eloi Deit

Opening hours......................Mon–Tue from 7 pm, Wed–Fri
from 5 pm, Sat–Sun from 8 pm
Credit cards...Not accepted
Type..Pub
Recommended for...Unexpected

"A hidden gem with great owners."—Eloi Deit

AUBERGE FESTIVE SEA SHACK

292 Boulevard Perron Est
Sainte-Anne-des-Monts
Quebec G4V 3A7, Canada
+1 8669632999
www.aubergefestive.com

Recommended by
Marie-Pier Veilleux

Opening hours..Always open
Credit cards...Accepted
Type..Bar
Recommended for...Unexpected

"A hostel with a camping site and a tiki bar outside by the water. They have a great selection of beer."
—Marie-Pier Veilleux

TÊTE D'ALLUMETTE MICROBRASSERIE

265 Route 132 Ouest
St-André de Kamouraska
Quebec G0L 2H0, Canada
+1 4184932222
www.tetedallumette.com

Recommended by
Olivier Dupras

Opening hours...Thur–Fri from 2 pm,
Sat–Sun from 12 pm
Credit cards...Accepted
Type...Microbrewery and pub
Recommended for......................................Wish I'd opened

"EVERYTHING IS JUST PERFECT."

MARIE-PIER VEILLEUX P.275

TORONTO

"AN AMAZING DRAFT AND BOTTLE SELECTION FROM ALL OVER THE WORLD."

ELOI DEIT P.274

"THIS PLACE BLEW ME AWAY."

ERIK MOYNIHAN P.275

"THEIR LIST IS FANTASTICALLY CURATED, WITH MOSTLY LOCAL BEER AND A NICE BOTTLE PROGRAM. THE FOOD IS DELICIOUS AS WELL."

SHAWNA O'FLAHERTY P.275

TORONTO

1. MILL STREET BREW PUB (P.275)
2. THE JERSEY GIANT
   PUB & RESTAURANT (P.275)
3. BEERBISTRO (P.275)

4. BAR HOP BREWCO (P.275)
5. MADAME BOEUF AND FLEA (P.274)
6. BIRRERIA VOLO (P.274)
7. BELLWOODS BREWERY (P.275)

8. DANDYLION (P.274)
9. BURDOCK BREWERY (P.274)
10. RAINHARD BREWING
    COMPANY (P.274)

BURDOCK BREWERY

1184 Bloor Street West
Bloordale Village
Toronto
Ontario M6H 1N2, Canada
+1 4165464033
www.burdockto.com

Recommended by
Shawna O'Flaherty

Opening hours......................................Mon–Thur from 5 pm,
Fri–Sun from 2 pm
Credit cards..Accepted
Type..Microbrewery and
entertainment venue
Recommended for...Wish I'd opened

"Half the venue is a concert hall and event space that
supports local artists and musicians, and they offer fantastic
beer made on-site. It's soundproofed, so you can enjoy food
in the restaurant half without being disturbed. The menu
changes constantly, based on what's in season. Beers rotate
constantly, too, and are always seasonal and creative. It's a
nice place to have a more upscale craft-beer experience."
—Shawna O'Flaherty

MADAME BOEUF AND FLEA

252 Dupont Street
Christie Pits
Toronto
Ontario M5R 1V7, Canada
+1 6473523337
www.madameboeuf.com

Recommended by
Marie-Pier Veilleux

Opening hours..Mon–Fri from 4 pm,
Sat–Sun from 11 am
Credit cards..Accepted
Type..Bar and beer garden
Recommended for..Beer garden

RAINHARD BREWING COMPANY

100 Symes Road
Harwood
Toronto
Ontario M6N 3T1, Canada
+1 4167632337
www.rainhardbrewing.com

Recommended by
Shawna O'Flaherty

Opening hours....................................Wed–Sun from 12 pm
Credit cards..Accepted
Type..Brewery
Recommended for.......................................Local favorite

"Rainhard is a taproom for the Rainhard brewery. The owner
and brewmaster, Jordan, is often on-site pouring beers and
chatting with his guests. He always has something new,
seasonal, and fun on tap. Weekends involve a lot of pop-up
parties featuring bluegrass bands, vinyl launch parties,
movie nights, food trucks, and communal barbecues in the
parking lot with his two brewery neighbors (Shacklands
Brewing and Junction Craft Brewing). You'll be glad to have
made the journey through a postindustrial wasteland to get
here."—Shawna O'Flaherty

BIRRERIA VOLO

612 College Street
Little Italy
Toronto
Ontario M6G 1B4, Canada
+1 4164985786
www.birreriavolo.com

Recommended by
Eloi Deit,
Kris Li,
Paul Maybee,
Malia Paasch,
Luke Pestl

Opening hours..Tue–Fri from 4 pm,
Sat–Sun from 2 pm
Credit cards..Accepted
Type..Bar
Recommended for...Wish I'd opened

"An amazing draft and bottle selection from all over the
world."—Eloi Deit

"It's a very intimate setting in the best way possible. It
almost forces you to converse with the people around you.
It's also walking distance to dozens of other great venues."
—Luke Pestl

"They put on cask days and an amazing cask-beer festival
held every year in Toronto."—Malia Paasch

"Speciality beers on tap and an amazing bottle list, plus
sours on draft."—Paul Maybee

DANDYLION

1198 Queen Street West
Little Portugal
Toronto
Ontario M6J 1J6, Canada
+1 6474649100
www.restaurantdandylion.com

Recommended by
Luke Pestl

Opening hours....................................Tue–Sat from 5:30 pm
Credit cards..Accepted
Type...Restaurant
Recommended for....................................Beer & food

"Small menu and small beer list in a small neighborhood restaurant. Everything is absolutely world class—food, beer, service, space, wine, and neighborhood."—Luke Pestl

BAR HOP BREWCO

Recommended by
Shawna O'Flaherty

137 Peter Street
Old Toronto
Toronto
Ontario M5V 2H3, Canada
+1 6473527476
www.barhopbar.com

Opening hours	Open 7 days from 12 pm
Credit cards	Accepted
Type	Beer garden and pub
Recommended for	Beer garden

"A large and comfortable rooftop patio with an extremely knowledgeable staff. Their list is fantastically curated, with mostly local beer and a nice bottle program. The food is delicious as well."—Shawna O'Flaherty

BEERBISTRO

Recommended by
Ethan Cox

18 King Street East
Old Toronto
Toronto
Ontario M5C 1C4, Canada
+1 4168619872
www.beerbistro.com

Opening hours	Mon–Fri from 11:30 am, Sat–Sun from 11 am
Credit cards	Accepted
Type	Restaurant
Recommended for	Beer & food

THE JERSEY GIANT PUB & RESTAURANT

Recommended by
Mischa Smith

71 Front Street East
Old Toronto
Toronto
Ontario M5E 1T9, Canada
+1 4163684095
www.jerseygiant.ca

Opening hours	Mon–Fri from 11 am, Sat–Sun from 10 am
Credit cards	Accepted
Type	Restaurant and pub
Recommended for	Worth the travel

"The epitome of a local pub—great barkeep, fresh Guinness, and pub food fit for a king."—Mischa Smith

MILL STREET BREW PUB

Recommended by
Mischa Smith

21 Tank House Lane
Old Toronto
Toronto
Ontario M5A 3C4, Canada
+1 4166810338
www.millstreetbrewery.com/toronto-brew-pub

Opening hours	Mon–Fri from 11 am, Sat–Sun from 10 am
Credit cards	Accepted
Type	Beer garden and pub
Recommended for	Beer garden

"Sitting in the Victorian-era distillery is my favorite outdoor place to have good craft beers straight from the source. The setting makes it a winner, as do a couple of my favorite Canadian craft brews—try the Stock Ale, Stock Alestick, and Helles Bock."—Mischa Smith

BELLWOODS BREWERY

Recommended by
Erin Lowder,
Erik Moynihan,
Marie-Pier Veilleux

124 Ossington Avenue
Trinity-Bellwoods
Toronto
Ontario M6J 2Z5, Canada
+1 4165354586
www.bellwoodsbrewery.com

Opening hours	Mon–Thur from 5 pm, Fri–Sun from 2 pm
Credit cards	Accepted
Type	Brewery
Recommended for	Worth the travel

"This place blew me away—great beers, great food, awesome staff, and a cool vintage bottle selection."
—Erik Moynihan

"Everything is just perfect. Accessible to everyone and high-quality beers."—Marie-Pier Veilleux

USA WEST

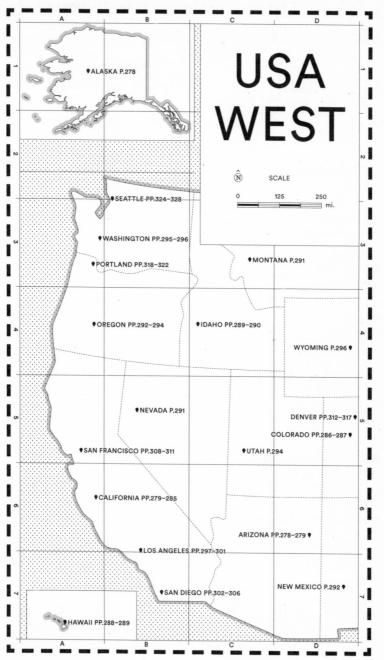

USA
WEST

Ⓝ   SCALE

0   125   250
mi.

ALASKA P.278

SEATTLE PP.324–328

WASHINGTON PP.295–296

PORTLAND PP.318–322

MONTANA P.291

OREGON PP.292–294

IDAHO PP.289–290

WYOMING P.296

NEVADA P.291

DENVER PP.312–317

COLORADO PP.286–287

SAN FRANCISCO PP.308–311

UTAH P.294

CALIFORNIA PP.279–285

ARIZONA PP.278–279

LOS ANGELES PP.297–301

SAN DIEGO PP.302–306

NEW MEXICO P.292

HAWAII PP.288–289

ANCHORAGE BREWING COMPANY

148 West 91st Street
Anchorage
Alaska 99515, United States
+1 9076772739
www.anchoragebrewing.company

Recommended by
Dave Grant

Opening hours	Wed–Sun from 2 pm
Credit cards	Accepted
Type	Beer garden and brewery
Recommended for	Beer garden

"They serve all Anchorage Brewing beers, which are my favorite."—Dave Grant

CAFÉ AMSTERDAM

530 East Benson Boulevard #3
Anchorage
Alaska 99508, United States
+1 9072740074
www.cafe-amsterdam.com

Recommended by
Bill Howell

Opening hours	Tue–Sun from 7 am
Credit cards	Accepted
Type	Restaurant
Recommended for	Local favorite

HUMPY'S GREAT ALASKAN ALEHOUSE

610 West 6th Avenue
Anchorage
Alaska 99517, United States
+1 9072762337
www.humpysalaska.com

Recommended by
Nicole Pearce

Opening hours	Mon–Fri from 11 am, Sat–Sun from 9 am
Credit cards	Accepted
Type	Restaurant
Recommended for	Local favorite

"You'll find things here that no one else in Alaska has on tap."
—Nicole Pearce

GOLDEN EAGLE SALOON

3630 Main Street
Ester
Alaska 99725, United States
+1 9074790809

Recommended by
Bill Howell

Opening hours	Mon–Fri from 5:30 pm, Sat–Sun from 12 pm
Credit cards	Not accepted
Type	Pub
Recommended for	Unexpected

MAJESTIC MARKETPLACE

601 East Piccadilly Drive #95
Flagstaff
Arizona 86001, United States
+1 9287730313
www.majesticmarketplaceaz.com

Recommended by
John Rowley

Opening hours	Open 7 days from 9 am
Credit cards	Accepted
Type	Retail
Recommended for	Unexpected

KINGS BEER AND WINE

2811 North Central Avenue
Phoenix
Arizona 85004, United States
+1 6022651777

Recommended by
Cody Wilson

Opening hours	Mon–Fri from 10 am, Sat–Sun from 11 am
Credit cards	Accepted
Type	Retail
Recommended for	Unexpected

"It's a corner store with the best selection in Arizona and growler fills."—Cody Wilson

SCOTTSDALE BEER COMPANY

8608 East Shea Boulevard
Scottsdale
Arizona 85260, United States
+1 4802191844
www.scottsdalebeercompany.com

Recommended by
Brian Boyer

Opening hours	Sun from 10 am, Mon–Thur from 3 pm, Fri–Sat from 11 am
Credit cards	Accepted
Type	Bar and brewery
Recommended for	Beer & food

ERMANOS CRAFT BEER & WINE BAR

220 North 4th Avenue
Tucson
Arizona 85705, United States
+1 5204456625
www.ermanosbrew.com

Recommended by
Kyle Jefferson

Opening hours	Open 7 days from 11 am
Credit cards	Accepted
Type	Bar and restaurant
Recommended for	Local favorite

"Ermanos consistently curates one of the best draft selections in Tucson. Eric's persistence and eye for quality, both locally and regionally, always keep us coming back." —Kyle Jefferson

LOEWS VENTANA CANYON RESORT

7000 North Resort Drive
Tucson
Arizona 85750, United States
+1 5202992020
www.loewshotels.com/ventana-canyon

Recommended by
Tristan White

Opening hours	Always open
Credit cards	Accepted
Type	Restaurant
Recommended for	Beer & food

REILLY CRAFT PIZZA & DRINK

101 East Pennington Street
Tucson
Arizona 85701, United States
+1 5208825550
www.reillypizza.com

Recommended by
Tristan White

Opening hours	Mon–Fri from 11 am, Sat–Sun from 12 pm
Credit cards	Accepted
Type	Beer garden and restaurant
Recommended for	Beer garden

"Absolutely amazing food and a great beer garden, all tucked into a recently renovated historic building in downtown Tucson."—Tristan White

SAINT CHARLES TAVERN

1632 South 4th Avenue
Tucson
Arizona 85713, United States
+1 5208885925

Recommended by
Tristan White

Opening hours	Open 7 days from 10 am
Credit cards	Accepted
Type	Pub
Recommended for	Unexpected

"It's a neighborhood bar with a great drink program. There's an outdoor beer garden with a stage that features live music a handful times a week, and the selection of beer is surprisingly well thought out. It's also one of the few places to get Underberg."—Tristan White

TAP & BOTTLE DOWNTOWN

403 North 6th Avenue #135
Tucson
Arizona 85705, United States
+1 5203448999
www.thetapandbottle.com

Recommended by
Tristan White

Opening hours	Mon–Thur from 2 pm, Fri–Sun from 12 pm
Credit cards	Accepted
Type	Pub
Recommended for	Local favorite

LADYFACE ALE COMPANIE ALEHOUSE & BRASSERIE

29281 Agoura Road
Agoura Hills
California 91301, United States
+1 8184774566
www.ladyfaceale.com

Recommended by
Devon Randall

Opening hours	Open 7 days from 11:30 am
Credit cards	Accepted
Type	Pub
Recommended for	Beer & food

HOPSY

1137 Solano Avenue
Albany
California 94706, United States
+1 5109220353
www.hopsy.beer

Recommended by
Josemari Cuervo

Opening hours	Open 7 days from 11 am
Credit cards	Accepted
Type	Retail
Recommended for	Unexpected

THE BEAR'S LAIR

2495 Bancroft Way
Berkeley
California 94720, United States
+1 5106653968
www.bearslairberkeley.com

Recommended by
Bruno Carrilho

Opening hours	Mon–Sat from 11 am, Sun from 12 pm
Credit cards	Accepted
Type	Beer garden and restaurant
Recommended for	Beer garden

"Sun, friends, atmosphere, great beer. I almost weep just to remember it."—Bruno Carrilho

JUPITER TAPROOM

Recommended by
James Tai

2181 Shattuck Avenue
Berkeley
California 94704, United States
+1 5108438277
www.jupiterbeer.com

Opening hours	Mon–Fri from 11:30 am, Sat–Sun from 12 pm
Credit cards	Accepted
Type	Beer garden and bar
Recommended for	Beer garden

NEPENTHE

Recommended by
Mark Hodges

48510 State Highway 1
Big Sur
California 93920, United States
+1 8316672345
www.nepenthe.com

Opening hours	Open 7 days from 11:30 am
Credit cards	Accepted
Type	Restaurant
Recommended for	Unexpected

"Having a pint here while looking down the coast of Big Sur is truly majestic."—Mark Hodges

THE BREWING LAIR

Recommended by
Justin Walsh

67007 State Highway 70
Blairsden
California 96103, United States
+1 5303940940
www.thebrewinglair.com

Opening hours	Open 7 days from 12 pm
Credit cards	Accepted
Type	Beer garden and brewery
Recommended for	Beer garden

"Rad beer is made on-site and, there's an amazing open facility with disk golf, cornhole, and a picnic area."
—Justin Walsh

FIRESTONE WALKER BREWING COMPANY

Recommended by
Chris Mair,
Reid Ramsay

620 McMurray Road
Buellton
California 93427, United States
+1 8056974777
www.firestonebeer.com

Opening hours	Mon–Sun from 11 am
Credit cards	Accepted
Type	Brewery
Recommended for	Beer & food

"The best burger I've ever had. Everything about my visit was great. Superb staff, tasty beer, and a burger that still stands out as being incredible, years later."—Chris Mair

"Firestone Walker has an incredible wild and sour program. They have an amazing tap lineup that speaks for itself. The brewery really took its time crafting an incredible restaurant with some of the best food I've had in 800 breweries visited. Many of the dishes are designed to pair with the wild ales on tap. Quality food and chef-driven inspired dishes."—Reid Ramsay

PIZZA PORT CARLSBAD

Recommended by
Rafi Chaudry,
Sebastian Sauer,
Justin Walsh

571 Carlsbad Village Drive
Carlsbad
California 92008, United States
+1 7607207007
www.pizzaport.com

Opening hours	Open 7 days from 11 am
Credit cards	Accepted
Type	Brewery
Recommended for	Worth the travel

"You can sit here in paradise and drink probably the best IPAs in the whole area."—Sebastian Sauer

PHANTOM CARRIAGE BREWERY

18525 South Main Street
Carson
California 90248, United States
+1 3105385834
www.phantomcarriage.com

Recommended by
Pyry Hurula

Opening hours	Mon from 3 pm, Tue–Fri from 11:30 am, Sat from 12 pm, Sun from 11 am
Credit cards	Accepted
Type	Brewery
Recommended for	Worth the travel

"This is one of the places you want to recommend to everyone—it's part horror movie, part sour brewery, part restaurant. It's like stepping into a year-round Halloween party."—Pyry Hurula

SIERRA NEVADA TAPROOM AND RESTAURANT

1075 East 20th Street
Chico
California 95928, United States
+1 5303452739
www.sierranevada.com

Recommended by
Camilo Rojas Sanchez

Opening hours	Open 7 days from 11 am
Credit cards	Accepted
Type	Restaurant and brewery
Recommended for	Beer & food

CORONADO BREW PUB

170 Orange Avenue
Coronado
California 92118, United States
+1 6194374452
www.coronadobrewing.com

Recommended by
Nathaniel Schmidt

Opening hours	Open 7 days from 10:30 am
Credit cards	Accepted
Type	Brewpub
Recommended for	Worth the travel

DAVIS BEER SHOPPE

211 G Street
Davis
California 95616, United States
+1 5307565212

Recommended by
Canaan Khoury

Opening hours	Open 7 days from 11 am
Credit cards	Accepted
Type	Pub
Recommended for	Worth the travel

UNCLE HENRY'S DELI

7400 Florence Avenue
Downey
California 90240, United States
+1 5629270114
www.unclehenrysdeli.com

Recommended by
Sarah Bennett

Opening hours	Mon–Sat from 11 am, Sun from 12 pm
Credit cards	Accepted
Type	Restaurant
Recommended for	Unexpected

"An old-school Polish deli, with 250 taps of local, regional, and national rarities crammed on the wall, and fridges and shelves filled with special-release and hard-to-find bottles."—Sarah Bennett

STONE BREWING WORLD BISTRO & GARDENS ESCONDIDO

1999 Citracado Parkway
Escondido
California 92029
United States
+1 7602947866
www.stonebrewing.com

Recommended by
Paul Fallen, Dave Grant,
Mark Hodges, Bill Howell,
Pyry Hurula, Toshi Ishii,
Marisa Jackson,
Qi Jiang, John Latta,
Ben Maeso, Chris Mair,
Amy Newell-Large,
Nicole Pearce, Jacobo Pérez Lliso,
Devon Randall, Darren (Doc)
Robinson, Nathaniel Schmidt,
Brett Tate, Del Vance,
Chris Vandergrift, Scott Wood

Opening hours	Open 7 days from 11 am
Credit cards	Accepted
Type	Beer garden and brewery
Recommended for	Beer garden

"There is nothing like this in the world of craft beer. A stunning place made with no expenses spared." —Pyry Hurula

HUMBOLDT CIDER COMPANY TAP ROOM

517 F Street
Eureka
California 95501, United States
+1 7074976320
www.humboldtcidercompany.com

Recommended by
Tracy Teach

Opening hours	Open 7 days from 2 pm
Credit cards	Accepted
Type	Brewery
Recommended for	Wish I'd opened

"They have award-winning local ciders on tap." —Tracy Teach

GOLDEN WEST SALOON

Recommended by
Fal Allen

128 East Redwood Avenue
Fort Bragg
California 95437, United States
+ 1 7079645914

Opening hours..................................Open 7 days from 12 pm
Credit cards...Accepted
Type...Bar
Recommended for...Local favorite

LITTLE RIVER INN

Recommended by
Fal Allen

7901 State North Highway 1
Little River
California 95456, United States
+1 7079375942
www.littleriverinn.com

Opening hours...Always open
Credit cards...Accepted
Type...Restaurant
Recommended for...Unexpected

BEACHWOOD BBQ AND BREWING
LONG BEACH

Recommended by
Yuhang Lin

210 East 3rd Street
Long Beach
California 90802, United States
+1 5624364020
www.beachwoodbbq.com

Opening hours....................................Tue–Sun from 11:30 am
Credit cards...Accepted
Type...Beer garden and restaurant
Recommended for.......................................Beer garden

"A world-class craft-beer selection. I have been there many
times and have never been disappointed with the quality."
—Yuhang Lin

Los Angeles, see pages 298–301

CLOCKTOWER CELLAR

Recommended by
Justin Walsh

6080 Minaret Road
Mammoth Lakes
California 93546, United States
+1 7609342725
www.clocktowercellar.com

Opening hours....................................Open 7 days from 4 pm
Credit cards...Accepted
Type...Bar
Recommended for...Local favorite

ALVARADO STREET BREWERY
& GRILL

Recommended by
Brett Tate

426 Alvarado Street
Monterey
California 93940, United States
+1 8316552337
www.alvaradostreetbrewery.com

Opening hours...........................Open 7 days from 11:30 am
Credit cards...Accepted
Type...Brewery
Recommended for..................................Wish I'd opened

"It stands out because of its location, nestled near the
famous landmarks of Cannery Row and Fisherman's Wharf
in Monterey, California. A creative and high-quality beer
menu."—Brett Tate

TIED HOUSE

Recommended by
Ofer Ronen

954 Villa Street
Mountain View
California 94041, United States
+1 6509652739
www.tiedhouse.com

Opening hours...........................Open 7 days from 11:30 am
Credit cards...Accepted
Type...Brewpub
Recommended for..................................Wish I'd opened

"One of the earliest brewpubs. Great beer and food."
—Ofer Ronen

BEER REVOLUTION

464 3rd Street
Oakland
California 94607, United States
+1 5104522337
www.beer-revolution.com

Recommended by
Em Sauter

Opening hours.................................Open 7 days from 12 pm
Credit cards..Accepted
Type..Bar
Recommended for..Wish I'd opened

THE TRAPPIST

460 8th Street
Oakland
California 94607, United States
+1 5102388900
www.thetrappist.com

Recommended by
Jeppe Jarnit-Bjergsø

Opening hours.................................Open 7 days from 12 pm
Credit cards..Accepted
Type..Pub
Recommended for..Local favorite

If you're in Oakland looking for a crazy-good tap list and friendly service, The Trappist is what you're looking for. It has a decidedly Belgian vibe and amazing beers.

ACE HOTEL & SWIM CLUB

701 East Palm Canyon Drive
Palm Springs
California 92264, United States
+1 7603259900
www.acehotel.com/palmsprings

Recommended by
Luke Pestl

Opening hours..Always open
Credit cards..Accepted
Type..Bar
Recommended for..Unexpected

"I was expecting decent beer, but they had a tremendous selection."—Luke Pestl

LAGUNITAS BREWING COMPANY

1280 North McDowell Boulevard
Petaluma
California 94954, United States
+1 7077694495
www.lagunitas.com

Recommended by
Todd Beal,
Matthew Kelly,
Jeff Orr

Opening hours.................................Wed–Fri from 2 pm,
Sat–Sun from 11:30 am
Credit cards..Accepted
Type........................Beer garden, bar, and brewery
Recommended for...Beer garden

"Amazing beer and a beer garden that puts the rest to shame."—Jeff Orr

San Diego, see pages 302–306

San Francisco, see pages 308–311

SAN JOSE ORIGINAL JOE'S

301 South 1st Street
San Jose
California 95113, United States
+1 4082927030
www.sanjoseoriginaljoes.com

Recommended by
Mark Hatherly

Opening hours.................................Open 7 days from 11 am
Credit cards..Accepted
Type...Restaurant
Recommended for..Wish I'd opened

DOCENT BREWING

33049 Calle Aviador #C
San Juan Capistrano
California 92675, United States
+1 9492188488
www.docentbrewing.com

Recommended by
Patrick Rue

Opening hours.................................Mon–Thur from 3 pm,
Fri–Sun from 12 pm
Credit cards..Accepted
Type...Brewery
Recommended for..Local favorite

CHURCHILL'S PUB & GRILLE

887 West San Marcos Boulevard
San Marcos
California 92069, United States
+1 7604718773
www.churchillspub.us

Recommended by
Mark Hodges

Opening hours	Open 7 days from 11 am
Credit cards	Accepted
Type	Pub
Recommended for	Beer & food

SANTA BARBARA BOWL

1122 North Milpas Street
Santa Barbara
California 93103, United States
+1 8059627411
www.sbbowl.com

Recommended by
Logan Plant

Opening hours	Variable
Credit cards	Not accepted
Type	Bar
Recommended for	Unexpected

THE OASIS TASTING ROOM & KITCHEN

415A River Street
Santa Cruz
California 95060, United States
+1 8316218040
www.oasissantacruz.com

Recommended by
Alec Stefansky

Opening hours	Wed–Sun from 11 am
Credit cards	Accepted
Type	Restaurant and brewery
Recommended for	Local favorite

FATHER'S OFFICE

1018 Montana Avenue
Santa Monica
California 90403, United States
+1 3107362224
www.fathersoffice.com

Recommended by
Devin Kimble,
David Newman,
Kevin Raub

Opening hours	Mon–Thur from 5 pm, Frid from 4 pm, Sat–Sun from 12 pm
Credit cards	Accepted
Type	Restaurant and pub
Recommended for	Wish I'd opened

"Oh my God, that burger! Belgian beers! So good!
A neighborhood bar that has awesome food and was
so far ahead of its time."—David Newman

"It's worth the wait."—Kevin Raub

COOPERAGE BREWING COMPANY

981 Airway Court #G
Santa Rosa
California 95403, United States
+1 7072939787
www.cooperagebrewing.com

Recommended by
James Larson

Opening hours	Mon–Fri from 2 pm, Sat–Sun from 12 pm
Credit cards	Accepted
Type	Brewery
Recommended for	Worth the travel

"We went to Russian River, and it was packed, so I snuck in
the back door and asked where the employees go to drink.
They pointed me to Cooperage."—James Larson

RUSSIAN RIVER BREWERY

725 4th Street
Santa Rosa
California 95404, United States
+1 7075452337
www.russianriverbrewing.com

Recommended by
Josemari Cuervo,
Mike Goguen,
Canaan Khoury,
Logan Plant,
Oliver San Antonio,
Geoffrey Seideman,
Ling Wan Chang

Opening hours	Open 7 days from 11 am
Credit cards	Accepted
Type	Brewery and pub
Recommended for	Beer & food

"They brew the best IPAs in the world."—Ling Wan Chang

"A beer mecca for me, so to drink Pliny from the source was
a truly magnificent moment. The array and quality of beers
Vinnie and the team brew is outstanding."—Logan Plant

BEACHWOOD BBQ

Recommended by
Sarah Bennett

131 Main Street
Seal Beach
California 90740, United States
+1 5624934500
www.beachwoodbbq.com

Opening hours.....................................Tue–Sun from 11:30 am
Credit cards...Accepted
Type...Restaurant
Recommended for...Local favorite

"Beachwood has always been on the forefront of good craft
beer, since it opened as a barbecue restaurant with a tiny
attached bar in Seal Beach. Now it has a brewpub and an
experimental barrel room to call its own in Long Beach.
Combined, the three provide the ultimate craft-beer
drinking experience. They invented the flux capacitor, a gas
and pressure control panel that is licensed and used in some
of the top beer bars all over the country."—Sarah Bennett

PIZZA PORT SOLANA BEACH

Recommended by
Jacobo Pérez Lliso

135 State Highway North 101
Solana Beach
California 90725, United States
+1 8584817332
www.pizzaport.com

Opening hours.....................................Open 7 days from 11 am
Credit cards...Accepted
Type...Restaurant
Recommended for...Beer & food

MONKISH BREWING CO.

Recommended by
Jeppe Jarnit-Bjergsø

20311 South Western Avenue
Torrance
California 90501, United States
+1 3102952157
www.monkishbrewing.com

Opening hours............Mon–Thur from 4 pm, Fri from 1 pm,
Sat from 12 pm, Sun from 1 pm
Credit cards...Accepted
Type...Brewery
Recommended for...Local favorite

Monkish is famous in beer-nerd circles for good reason. Their
beers are fantastic. They are rightly famous for their IPAs, but
their Belgian beers are not to be missed. Their tasting room is
a lot of fun to hang out in. Great staff.

ALIBI ALE WORKS – TRUCKEE PUBLIC HOUSE

Recommended by
Kevin Drake

10069 Bridge Street
Truckee
California 96161, United States
+1 5305365029
www.alibialeworks.com

Opening hours.....................................Open 7 days from 12 pm
Credit cards...Accepted
Type...Brewery
Recommended for...Local favorite

DUST BOWL BREWERY TAPROOM

Recommended by
Brett Tate

3000 Fulkerth Road
Turlock
California 95380, United States
+1 2092502043
www.dustbowlbrewing.com

Opening hours.....................................Open 7 days from 11 am
Credit cards...Accepted
Type...Brewery
Recommended for...Local favorite

MENDOCINO BREWING COMPANY ALE HOUSE

Recommended by
Nathaniel Schmidt

1252 Airport Road
Ukiah
California 95482, United States
+1 7074672337
www.mendobrew.com

Opening hours............Thur from 1 pm, Fri–Sat from 12 pm,
Sun from 1 pm
Credit cards...Accepted
Type...Beer garden and bar
Recommended for...Beer garden

"Great location and good beers."—Nathaniel Schmidt

FLUID STATE BEER GARDEN

Recommended by
Katherine Kyle

692 East Main Street
Ventura
California 93001, United States
+1 8056283107
www.fluidstatebeer.com

Opening hours...Tue–Thur from 3 pm,
Fri–Sun from 11:30 am
Credit cards...Accepted
Type...Beer garden
Recommended for...Worth the travel

DRY DOCK BREWING CO.
– NORTH DOCK
2801 Tower Road
Aurora
Colorado 80011, United States
+1 3034005606
www.drydockbrewing.com

Recommended by
Richard Hinkle

Opening hours.....................................Wed–Thur from 2 pm,
Fri–Sat from 12 pm
Credit cards....................................Accepted but not Amex
Type..Bar and brewery
Recommended for...Local favorite

"This taproom is great because they always have a large variety of award-winning beers on tap and the friendliest staff in town. They have a Frisbee golf course and an indoor patio looking directly at the production brewery."
—Richard Hinkle

AVERY BREWING COMPANY
4910 Nautilus Court
Boulder
Colorado 80301, United States
+1 7207739817
www.averybrewing.com

Recommended by
Larry Cook,
Amy Newell-Large,
Zac Triemert

Opening hours..........Tue–Sun from 11 am, Mon from 3 pm
Credit cards...Accepted
Type..Brewery
Recommended for.......................................Beer & food

BACKCOUNTRY PIZZA & TAPHOUSE
2319 Arapahoe Avenue
Boulder
Colorado 80302, United States
+1 3034494285
www.backcountrypizzaandtaphouse.com

Recommended by
Jeffrey Stuffings

Opening hours..........Mon–Sat from 11 am, Sun from 10 am
Credit cards...Accepted
Type...Bar and restaurant
Recommended for...Worth the travel

"Backcountry has one of the best beer lists in the world, in about the most unpretentious environment you could create. Where else can you drink Fantôme Saison and play Golden Tee?"—Jeffrey Stuffings

Denver, see pages 312–317

JOYRIDE BREWING COMPANY
2501 Sheridan Boulevard
Edgewater
Colorado 80214, United States
+1 7204327560
www.joyridebrewing.com

Recommended by
Richard Hinkle

Opening hours....................................Mon–Thur from 12 pm,
Fri–Sun from 11 am
Credit cards...Accepted
Type...Brewery and Bar
Recommended for...Wish I'd opened

CHOICE CITY BUTCHER & DELI
104 West Olive Street
Fort Collins
Colorado 80524, United States
+1 9704902489
www.choicecitybutcher.com

Recommended by
John Stewart

Opening hours..................................Open 7 days from 7 am
Credit cards...Accepted
Type...Restaurant and retail
Recommended for...Worth the travel

NEW BELGIUM BREWING COMPANY
500 Linden Street
Fort Collins
Colorado 80524, United States
+1 9702210524
www.newbelgium.com

Recommended by
James Renwick,
Rob Zellermayer

Opening hours..................................Open 7 days from 11 am
Credit cards...Accepted
Type...Beer garden and brewery
Recommended for...Beer garden

"Brilliant beers and venue and a sustainability minded ethos."—James Renwick

ODELL
800 East Lincoln Avenue
Fort Collins
Colorado 80524, United States
+1 9704989070
www.odellbrewing.com

Recommended by
Nathan Keffer

Opening hours..................................Open 7 days from 11 am
Credit cards...Accepted
Type.................................Beer garden, bar, and brewery
Recommended for...Beer garden

"The beer garden located just outside the taproom is a great place to relax on a Colorado summer day. The mountains are all around and the brewing facility spreads across the background."—Nathan Keffer

BARRELS & BOTTLES BREWERY

600 12th Street #160 Recommended by
Golden Ashleigh Carter
Colorado 80401, United States
+1 7203283643
www.barrelsbottles.com

Opening hours.....................................Open 7 days from 11 am
Credit cards..Accepted but not Amex
Type..Brewery and pub
Recommended for..Local favorite

"One of the most well-thought-out tap lists."
—Ashleigh Carter

WELDWERKS BREWING COMPANY

508 8th Avenue Recommended by
Greeley Neil Fisher
Colorado 80631, United States
+1 9704606345
www.weldwerksbrewing.com

Opening hours...Mon–Tue from 2 pm,
Wed–Sun from 12 pm
Credit cards...Accepted
Type..Beer garden and brewery
Recommended for..Worth the travel

FRONT RANGE BREWING COMPANY

400 West South Boulder Road Recommended by
Suite 1650 Ron Hoglund
Lafayette
Colorado 80026, United States
+1 3033390767
www.frontrangebrewingcompany.com

Opening hours...Mon–Fri from 3 pm,
Sat from 12 pm, Sun from 2 pm
Credit cards...Accepted
Type...Brewery
Recommended for..Beer & food

PARRY'S PIZZERIA & BAR LONGMONT

1232 South Hover Road Recommended by
Longmont Joe Dick
Colorado 80501, United States
+1 3036511010
www.parryspizza.com

Opening hours.........Mon–Sat from 11 am, Sun from 12 pm
Credit cards...Accepted
Type...Restaurant
Recommended for..Unexpected

"A pizza place in a parking lot with 100 amazing taps."
—Joe Dick

WIBBY BREWING

209 Emery Street Recommended by
Longmont Amy Newell-Large
Colorado 80501, United States
+1 3037764594
www.wibbybrewing.com

Opening hours.................................Mon–Thur from 11:30 am,
Fri–Sun from 11 am
Credit cards...Accepted
Type...Brewery
Recommended for..Local favorite

PAGOSA BREWING COMPANY & GRILL

118 North Pagosa Boulevard Recommended by
Pagosa Springs Leif Rotsaert
Colorado 81147, United States
+1 9707312739
www.pagosabrewing.com

Opening hours.....................................Open 7 days from 11 am
Credit cards..Accepted but not Amex
Type..Beer garden and brewery
Recommended for..Beer garden

"Consider a beer garden in a small mountain town in late fall, surrounded by fresh hops, and you get the feeling of total isolation from the busy world."—Leif Rotsaert

HONOLULU BEERWORKS

328 Cooke Street
Honolulu
Hawaii 96813, United States
+1 8085892337
www.honolulubeerworks.com

Recommended by
Rob Bright,
Nate Ilaoa,
Geoffrey Seideman

Opening hours.............................Mon–Sat from 11 am
Credit cards..Accepted
Type...Brewery
Recommended for.................................Beer & food

MURPHY'S BAR & GRILL

Recommended by
David Newman

2 Merchant Street
Honolulu
Hawaii 96813, United States
+1 8085310422
www.murphyshawaii.com

Opening hours...........................Mon–Fri from 11 am,
Sat from 5:30 pm, Sun from 5 pm
Credit cards..Accepted
Type..Pub
Recommended for.................................Unexpected

"The best hospitality in the business. They've been serving craft beer way before it was the hip thing to do."
—David Newman

PINT AND JIGGER

Recommended by
David Newman

1936 South King Street
Honolulu
Hawaii 96826, United States
+1 8087449593
www.pintandjigger.com

Opening hours....................................Mon–Fri from 4:30 pm,
Sat–Sun from 8 am
Credit cards..Accepted
Type..Pub
Recommended for.................................Beer & food

SHIROKIYA JAPAN VILLAGE WALK

1450 Ala Moana Boulevard #1360
Honolulu
Hawaii 96814, United States
+1 8089739111
www.shirokiya.com

Recommended by
Nate Ilaoa

Opening hours.............................Open 7 days from 10 am
Credit cards..Accepted
Type...Beer garden
Recommended for.................................Beer garden

"Great Japanese food and very cheap beer."—Nate Ilaoa

SIDE STREET INN

614 Kapahulu Avenue #100
Honolulu
Hawaii 96815, United States
+1 8087393939
www.sidestreetinn.com

Recommended by
Nate Ilaoa

Opening hours.............................Mon–Fri from 4 pm,
Sat–Sun from 1 pm
Credit cards..Accepted
Type...Bar
Recommended for.................................Unexpected

"A good beer selection on tap and the best fried pork chops in the state."—Nate Ilaoa

VILLAGE BOTTLE SHOP & TASTING ROOM

675 Auahi Street #121
Honolulu
Hawaii 96813, United States
+1 8083690688
www.villagebeerhawaii.com

Recommended by
David Newman

Opening hours.............................Open 7 days from 11 am
Credit cards..Accepted
Type...Bar and retail
Recommended for.................................Local favorite

YARD HOUSE HONOLULU

226 Lewers Street
Honolulu
Hawaii 96815, United States
+1 8089239273

Recommended by
Brett Tieman

Opening hours.........Mon–Sat from 11 am, Sun from 10 am
Credit cards..Accepted
Type...........................Beer garden and restaurant
Recommended for.................................Beer garden

MAUI BREWING COMPANY

605 Lipoa Parkway
Kihei
Hawaii 96753, United States
+1 8082133002
www.mauibrewingco.com

Recommended by
Nate Ilaoa,
Erick Ramirez

Opening hours................................Open 7 days from 11 am
Credit cards..Accepted
Type...Brewery
Recommended for..............................Worth the travel

KOHOLA BREWERY

910 Honoapiilani Highway #55
Lahaina
Hawaii 96761, United States
+1 8088683198
www.koholabrewery.com

Recommended by
Nate Ilaoa

Opening hours................................Open 7 days from 12 pm
Credit cards..Accepted
Type...Brewery
Recommended for..............................Worth the travel

"My favorite craft-beer spot."—Nate Ilaoa

ROCK & BREWS PAIA

120 Hana Highway
Maui
Hawaii 96779, United States
+1 8085799011
www.rockandbrews.com/paia

Recommended by
David Stein

Opening hours................................Open 7 days from 11 am
Credit cards..Accepted
Type..Bar and restaurant
Recommended for..............................Wish I'd opened

BIG ISLAND BREWHAUS

64-1066 Mamalahoa Highway
Waimea
Hawaii 96743, United States
+1 8088871717
www.bigislandbrewhaus.com

Recommended by
Fal Allen

Opening hours.........Mon–Sat from 11 am, Sun from 12 pm
Credit cards..Accepted
Type...Restaurant
Recommended for..................................Beer & food

BARBARIAN BREWING DOWNTOWN TAP ROOM

1022 West Main Street
Boise
Idaho 83702, United States
+1 2083872739
www.barbarianbrewing.com

Recommended by
Hannah Barnett

Opening hours................................Mon–Thur from 2 pm,
Fri–Sun from 12 pm
Credit cards..Accepted
Type...Brewery
Recommended for..............................Local favorite

"Barbarian is one of the up-and-coming breweries in Boise. They're one of the only breweries in Idaho that I know of focusing on sour and barrel-aged beers. Their downtown taproom always has over twenty delicious beers on tap. Bre and James, the founders, are two of the most hard-working people I know. This is the bar where I take my beer industry friends when they come to town."
—Hannah Barnett

BAR GERNIKA

202 South Capitol Boulevard
Boise
Idaho 83702, United States
+1 2083442175
www.bargernika.com

Recommended by
Hannah Barnett,
David Roberts

Opening hours................................Mon–Fri from 11 am,
Sat from 11:30 am
Credit cards..Accepted
Type..Bar
Recommended for..............................Unexpected

"Bar Gernika is a unique Boise experience, and they have been doing traditional Basque bar food for more than twenty-five years. A beer and food experience that can't be had anywhere else. Make sure to try the croquettes."
—David Roberts

BITTERCREEK ALEHOUSE

246 North 8th Street
Boise
Idaho 83702, United States
+1 2084296340
www.bcrfl.com/bittercreek

Recommended by
Hannah Barnett,
Matt Gelsthorpe,
David Roberts

Opening hours................................Open 7 days from 11 am
Credit cards..Accepted
Type...Restaurant
Recommended for..............................Local favorite

"Bittercreek is the hot spot for Boise locals. Their happy hour is next level."—Hannah Barnett

THE HANDLEBAR BOISE

Recommended by
James Long

1519 West Main Street
Boise
Idaho 83702, United States
+1 2083440068

Opening hours	Mon–Fri from 2 pm, Sat–Sun from 12 pm
Credit cards	Accepted
Type	Bar
Recommended for	Local favorite

STATE & LEMP

Recommended by
James Long

2870 West State Street
Boise
Idaho 83702, United States
+1 2084296735
www.stateandlemp.com

Opening hours	Wed–Sat from 6 pm
Credit cards	Accepted
Type	Restaurant
Recommended for	Beer & food

"Amazing beer and wine pairings."—James Long

IDAHO CITY GROCERY

Recommended by
James Long

3868 Idaho Highway 21
Idaho City
Idaho 83631, United States
+1 2083924426
www.idahocitygrocery.com

Opening hours	Open 7 days from 8 am
Credit cards	Accepted but not Amex
Type	Retail
Recommended for	Unexpected

WARFIELD DISTILLERY & BREWERY

Recommended by
Ben Bradley

280 North Main Street
Ketchum
Idaho 83340, United States
+1 2087262739
www.warfielddistillery.com

Opening hours	Open 7 days from 4 pm
Credit cards	Accepted
Type	Brewery
Recommended for	Local favorite

"Great beer made with organic malt and whole-leaf hops. The rooftop bar has the best view in town."—Ben Bradley

RANTS AND RAVES BREWERY

Recommended by
Neil Marzolf

308 North Jackson Street
Moscow
Idaho 83843, United States
+1 2085964061
www.rrbrew.pub

Opening hours	Open 7 days from 11 am
Credit cards	Accepted but not Amex
Type	Brewery
Recommended for	Local favorite

"Great setting in the middle of town. The best beer ever!"
—Neil Marzolf

PREFUNK BEER BAR NAMPA

Recommended by
Matt Gelsthorpe,
James Long

1214 1st Street South
Nampa
Idaho 83651, United States
+1 2084660981

Opening hours	Mon–Sat from 11 am, Sun from 12 pm
Credit cards	Accepted
Type	Bar
Recommended for	Wish I'd opened

WILDLIFE BREWING

Recommended by
Leif Rotsaert

145 South Main Street
Victor
Idaho 83455, United States
+1 2087872623
www.wildlifebrewing.com

Opening hours	Wed–Sun from 4 pm
Credit cards	Accepted
Type	Microbrewery
Recommended for	Local favorite

BACKSLOPE BREWING
Recommended by
Carla Fisher
1107 9th Street West
Columbia Falls
Montana 59912, United States
+1 4068972850
www.backslopebrewing.com

Opening hours............................Mon–Sat from 11 am
Credit cards...Accepted
Type...Brewery
Recommended for.................................Local favorite

HA BREWING CO.
Recommended by
Carla Fisher
2525 Grave Creek Road
Eureka
Montana 59917, United States
+1 4068893950
www.habrewing.com

Opening hours.........................Wed–Sun from 3 pm
Credit cards...Accepted
Type...Brewery
Recommended for..............................Worth the travel

BONSAI BREWING PROJECT
549 Wisconsin Avenue
Recommended by
Carla Fisher
Whitefish
Montana 59937, United States
+1 4067301717

Opening hours............................Tue–Sun from 12 pm
Credit cards...Accepted
Type..............................Beer garden and brewery
Recommended for.................................Local favorite

INCLINE SPIRITS & CIGARS
120 Country Club Drive #25
Recommended by
Brett Tate
Incline Village
Nevada 89451, United States
+1 7758319292
www.inclinespirits.com

Opening hours.........................Open 7 days from 10 am
Credit cards...Accepted
Type...Retail
Recommended for.................................Local favorite

"It's small and tucked away in a strip mall. I stumbled on it and was pleasantly surprised at their dedication to craft beer and whiskey."—Brett Tate

ATOMIC LIQUORS
Recommended by
Bryan Brushmiller
917 Fremont Street
Las Vegas
Nevada 89101, United States
+1 7029823000
www.atomic.vegas

Opening hours............................Mon–Wed from 4 pm,
Thur–Fri from 2 pm, Sat–Sun from 12 pm
Credit cards...Accepted
Type..Bar and retail
Recommended for...................................Unexpected

"Great history and an even better selection of beer from breweries around the world."—Bryan Brushmiller

KHOURY'S FINE WINE & SPIRITS
9915 South Eastern Avenue #110
Recommended by
Mark Drutman
Las Vegas
Nevada 89183, United States
+1 7024359463
www.khourysfinewine.com

Opening hours.........Mon–Sat from 10 am, Sun from 12 pm
Credit cards...Accepted
Type..Bar
Recommended for...................................Unexpected

SAGE
Recommended by
Kellan Bartosch
3730 South Las Vegas Boulevard
Las Vegas
Nevada 89109, United States
+1 7025908690
www.aria.com/en/restaurants/sage

Opening hours..............................Mon–Sat from 6 pm
Credit cards...Accepted
Type...Restaurant
Recommended for................................Beer & food

"Incredible food, beverages, and service."—Kellan Bartosch

MINDEN MEAT AND DELI
1595 U.S. Highway 395 North
Recommended by
Justin Walsh
Minden
Nevada 89423, United States
+1 7757839999
www.mindenmeat.com

Opening hours.........................Open 7 days from 9 am
Credit cards...Accepted
Type...Retail
Recommended for...................................Unexpected

BOSQUE BREWING COMPANY

8900 San Mateo Boulevard Northeast
Albuquerque
New Mexico 87113, United States
+1 5054333889
www.bosquebrewing.com

Recommended by
Chris Jackson

Opening hours.........Mon–Sat from 11 am, Sun from 12 pm
Credit cards...Accepted
Type..Brewery
Recommended for......................................Local favorite

"A variety of creative and innovative beer styles."
—Chris Jackson

NEXUS RESTAURANT AND BREWERY

4730 Pan American Freeway
Northeast #D
Albuquerque
New Mexico 87109, United States
+1 5052424100
www.nexusbrewery.com

Recommended by
Chris Jackson

Opening hours....................................Open 7 days from 11 am
Credit cards...Accepted
Type..Brewery
Recommended for......................................Beer & food

"Amazing food, a mix of Southern and New Mexico styles,
combined with award-winning beers made on-site."
—Chris Jackson

SISTER BAR

407 Central Avenue Northwest
Albuquerque
New Mexico 87102, United States
+1 5052424900
www.sisterthebar.com

Recommended by
Angelo Orona

Opening hours....................................Open 7 days from 11 am
Credit cards...Accepted
Type...Bar
Recommended for......................................Local favorite

"Sister is a huge supporter of the local craft-beer scene. The
variety of beers they offer is thoughtful and ever changing."
—Angelo Orona

COMANCHE CREEK BREWERY

225 Comanche Creek Road
Eagle Nest
New Mexico 87718, United States
+1 5753772337
www.comanchecreekbrewingco.com

Recommended by
Chris Jackson

Opening hours.......................................Wed–Sat from 12 pm
Credit cards...Accepted
Type..Brewery
Recommended for......................................Unexpected

"A tiny brewery in a log cabin at the end of a dirt road, in an
alpine meadow at the foot of the Sangre de Cristo
mountains."—Chris Jackson

ROWLEY FARMHOUSE ALES

1405 Maclovia Street
Santa Fe
New Mexico 87505, United States
+1 5054280719
www.rowleyfarmhouse.com

Recommended by
John Rowley

Opening hours............................Open 7 days from 11:30 am
Credit cards...Accepted
Type...Pub
Recommended for......................................Wish I'd opened

SECOND STREET BREWERY

1814 2nd Street
Santa Fe
New Mexico 87505, United States
+1 5059823030
www.secondstreetbrewery.com

Recommended by
Chris Jackson,
Leif Rotsaert

Opening hours.........Mon–Sat from 11 am, Sun from 12 pm
Credit cards...Accepted
Type.................................Beer garden and brewery
Recommended for......................................Beer garden

BUOY BEER COMPANY

18th Street
Astoria
Oregon 97103, United States
+1 5033254540
www.buoybeer.com

Recommended by
Stuart Keating

Opening hours....................................Open 7 days from 11 am
Credit cards...Accepted
Type..Brewery
Recommended for......................................Wish I'd opened

"Perhaps the best Czech-style pilsner I've had in the U.S., in a beautiful building that overlooks the Columbia River and the Pacific Ocean."—Stuart Keating

CROW'S FEET COMMONS

875 Northwest Brooks Street
Bend
Oregon 97701, United States
+1 5417280066
www.crowsfeetcommons.com

Recommended by
Josh Ruffin

Opening hours	Open 7 days from 8 am
Credit cards	Accepted
Type	Beer garden and bar
Recommended for	Beer garden

CRUX FERMENTATION PROJECT

50 Southwest Division Street
Bend
Oregon 97702, United States
+1 5413853333
www.cruxfermentation.com

Recommended by
Alex Acker,
Cameron Johnson

Opening hours	Tue–Sun from 11:30 am, Mon from 4 pm
Credit cards	Accepted
Type	Brewery
Recommended for	Worth the travel

GOODLIFE BREWING COMPANY

70 Southwest Century Drive
Bend
Oregon 97702, United States
+1 5417280749
www.goodlifebrewing.com

Recommended by
Hannah Barnett

Opening hours	Open 7 days from 12 pm
Credit cards	Accepted
Type	Beer garden, bar, and brewery
Recommended for	Beer garden

"GoodLife Brewing has an awesome lawn behind their brewery with cornhole, horseshoes, and plenty of great beer."—Hannah Barnett

SPOKEN MOTO

310 Southwest Industrial Way
Bend
Oregon 97702, United States
+1 5423066689
www.spokenmoto.com

Recommended by
Hannah Barnett

Opening hours	Open 7 days from 8 am
Credit cards	Accepted
Type	Bar and restaurant
Recommended for	Wish I'd opened

"Spoken Moto is way more than a craft-beer bar. It's also a coffee shop, a motorcycle shop, and a food truck lot." —Hannah Barnett

GREENBERRY STORE & TAVERN

29974 Oregon State Highway 99 West
Corvallis
Oregon 97333, United States
+1 5417523796

Recommended by
Matt Van Wyk

Opening hours	Tue–Thur from 2 pm, Fri from 3 pm, Sat from 8 am
Credit cards	Accepted
Type	Retail and bar
Recommended for	Unexpected

"In the middle of rural Oregon fields, Greenberry Tavern is a meeting place for locals, with a great list of Northwest American craft beers. Pair any of them with Viv's daily food specials, and you can't go wrong."—Matt Van Wyk

BEERGARDEN

777 West 6th Avenue
Eugene
Oregon 97402, United States
+1 5415059432
www.beergardenme.com

Recommended by
Matt Van Wyk

Opening hours	Open 7 days from 11 am
Credit cards	Accepted
Type	Beer garden
Recommended for	Beer garden

"Beergarden is simple. Great beer is served in a welcoming bar with a massive beer garden surrounded by six to seven food carts of different cuisines. The seating includes communal tables and smaller private ones. The beer is always great, and there's a huge variety, but the setting with food carts makes it a must."—Matt Van Wyk

Portland, see pages 318–322

THE BIER STEIN
Recommended by
Matt Van Wyk

1591 Willamette Street
Eugene
Oregon 97401, United States
+1 5414852437
www.thebierstein.com

Opening hours..........Mon–Sat from 11 am, Sun from 12 pm
Credit cards...Accepted
Type...Pub
Recommended for.....................................Local favorite

"Loaded with hundreds of the best bottles from around the
Northwest and the world and a carefully selected thirty-tap
draft list. Second to none."—Matt Van Wyk

HIGH STREET BREWERY
Recommended by
Zach Warren

1243 High Street
Eugene
Oregon 97401, United States
+1 5413454905
www.mcmenamins.com

Opening hours..........Mon–Sat from 11 am, Sun from 12 pm
Credit cards...Accepted
Type.........................Beer garden, microbrewery, and pub
Recommended for................................Beer garden

SOLERA BREWERY
Recommended by
Patrick Lively

4945 Baseline Road
Mount Hood
Oregon 97041, United States
+1 5413525500
www.solerabrewery.com

Opening hours............................Mon–Tue, Thur from 4 pm,
Fri–Sun from 12 pm
Credit cards...Accepted
Type.............................Beer garden and brewery
Recommended for................................Beer garden

PELICAN BREWING
Recommended by
Dimitrij Jurisic

33180 Cape Kiwanda Drive
Pacific City
Oregon 97135, United States
+1 5039657007
www.pelicanbrewing.com

Opening hours....................................Open 7 days from 8 am
Credit cards...Accepted
Type...Brewery
Recommended for.............................Wish I'd opened

VENTI'S CAFE & BASEMENT BAR
Recommended by
Nathan Keffer

325 Court Street Northeast
Salem
Oregon 97301, United States
+1 5033998733
www.ventiscafe.com

Opening hours....................................Open 7 days from 11 am
Credit cards...Accepted
Type..Restaurant
Recommended for.....................................Unexpected

"A true find."—Nathan Keffer

MCMENAMINS EDGEFIELD
Recommended by
Brett Tate,
Casey Workman,
Del Vance

2126 Southwest Halsey Street
Troutdale
Oregon 97060, United States
+1 5036698610
www.mcmenamins.com/edgefield

Opening hours....................................Open 7 days from 7 am
Credit cards...Accepted
Type...Brewery
Recommended for.....................................Beer & food

"A historic hotel with several pubs, fine-dining restaurants,
and a brewery, a winery, and a distillery. There are hidden
little beer bars all over."—Del Vance

BEERHIVE PUB
Recommended by
Del Vance

128 Main Street
Salt Lake City
Utah 84101, United States
+1 8013644268

Opening hours....................................Open 7 days from 12 pm
Credit cards...Accepted
Type...Pub
Recommended for.....................................Local favorite

"Over 250 beers to choose from, and 95 percent of them are
U.S. craft brands. A strip of ice along the entire bar keeps
the beer cold till the last sip."—Del Vance

BOUNDARY BAY BREWERY & BISTRO

1107 Railroad Avenue
Bellingham
Washington 98225, United States
+1 3606475593
www.bbaybrewery.com

Recommended by
Aaron Johnson,
Cameron Johnson

Opening hours...................................Open 7 days from 11 am
Credit cards...Accepted but not Amex
Type..........................Beer garden, restaurant, and brewery
Recommended for...Beer garden

"Great beer and food and the greatest view of the Puget
Sound. Their nationally award-winning beer is brewed
on-site."—Cameron Johnson

ELIZABETH STATION

1400 West Holly Street
Bellingham
Washington 98225, United States
+1 3607338982
www.elizabethstation.es

Recommended by
Aaron Johnson,
Amy Newell-Large

Opening hours...................................Open 7 days from 10 am
Credit cards...Accepted
Type...Bar and retail
Recommended for...Worth the travel

"A fantastic beer store, beer bar, and convenience store.
They offer one of the widest varieties of bottled beer I've
ever seen! Enjoy the sunshine along Washington's beautiful
coast."—Amy Newell-Large

STONES THROW BREWERY

1009 Larrabee Avenue
Bellingham
Washington 98225, United States
+1 3603625058
www.stonesthrowbrewco.com

Recommended by
Aaron Johnson

Opening hours...................................Mon–Fri from 12 pm,
Sat–Sun from 11 am
Credit cards...Accepted
Type...Brewery
Recommended for...Local favorite

NORTH FORK BREWERY

6186 Mount Baker Highway
Deming
Washington 98244, United States
+1 3605992337
www.northforkbrewery.com

Recommended by
Cameron Johnson

Opening hours...................................Open 7 days from 12 pm
Credit cards...Accepted
Type...Brewery and pub
Recommended for...Unexpected

"Fantastic beer and giant housemade pizzas."
—Cameron Johnson

HAMA HAMA OYSTER SALOON

35846 U.S. Highway 101
Lilliwaup
Washington 98555, United States
+1 3608775811
www.hamahamaoysters.com

Recommended by
Kyle Jefferson

Opening hours...Fri–Sun from 12 pm
Credit cards...Accepted
Type..Bar and restaurant
Recommended for...Beer & food

TIPSY COW

16345 Cleveland Street
Redmond
Washington 98052, United States
+1 4258968716
www.tipsycowburgerbar.com

Recommended by
Leo Sewald

Opening hours...................................Open 7 days from 11 am
Credit cards...Accepted
Type...Restaurant
Recommended for...Beer & food

"The best burgers I've ever had. Period. They offer beer,
cider, and wine pairings for all their hamburgers."
—Leo Sewald

Seattle, see pages 324–328

PERRY STREET BREWING

1025 South Perry Street #2   Recommended by
Spokane   Cameron Johnson
Washington 99202, United States
+1 5092792820
www.perrystreetbrewing.com

Opening hours...............................Tue–Thur from 2 pm,
    Fri–Sun from 11:30 am
Credit cards..Accepted but not Amex
Type..Brewery and pub
Recommended for.......................................Beer & food

STEEL BARREL TAPROOM

154 South Madison Street #100   Recommended by
Spokane   Cameron Johnson
Washington 99201, United States
+1 5093159879
www.thesteelbarrel.com

Opening hours..........Tue–Sun from 11 am, Mon from 4 pm
Credit cards..Accepted
Type..Brewery and pub
Recommended for.......................................Local favorite

"There is ceviche from chef Chad White with thirty taps, craft cocktails, multiple in-house breweries, and shuffleboard."—Cameron Johnson

ENGINE HOUSE NO. 9

Recommended by
Rory Miller

611 North Pine Street
Tacoma
Washington 98406, United States
+1 2532723435
www.ehouse9.com

Opening hours........Mon–Fri from 11 am, Sat–Sun from 8 am
Credit cards..Accepted
Type..Beer garden and pub
Recommended for.......................................Beer garden

ROADHOUSE BREWING COMPANY PUB & EATERY

Recommended by
Colby Cox

20 East Broadway
Jackson Hole
Wyoming 83001, United States
+1 3077390700
www.roadhousebrewery.com

Opening hours....................................Open 7 days from 4 pm
Credit cards..Accepted
Type..Brewery and pub
Recommended for.......................................Local favorite

"Small-batch beers, locally sourced eats, and improvisational jam bands. What else needs to be said?"—Colby Cox

SNOWY MOUNTAIN BREWERY & PUB

601 Pic Pike Road   Recommended by
Saratoga   Richard Hinkle
Wyoming 82331, United States
+1 8005940178
www.snowymountainbrewery.com

Opening hours....................................Open 7 days from 11 am
Credit cards..Accepted
Type..Beer garden and brewery
Recommended for.......................................Beer garden

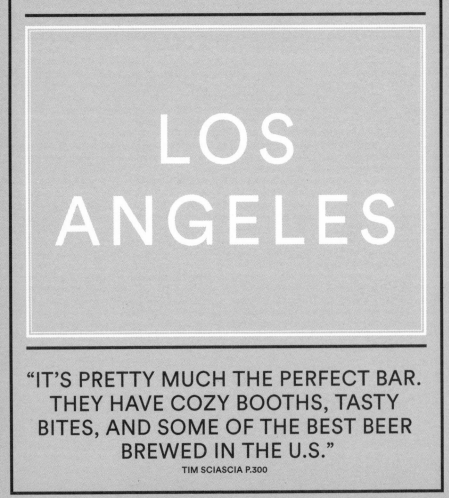

"A HAVEN FOR LOW-KEY COOL. THEY MAKE WORLD-CLASS BEER IN THE BACK OF A REVAMPED LOCAL DIVE."
SARAH BENNETT P.300

"UNBELIEVABLY GREAT BEER."
PATRICK MORSE P.300

"I DIDN'T EXPECT TO LOVE THE TASTING-ROOM VIBE AS MUCH AS I DO." DEVON RANDALL P.300

LOS ANGELES

"IT'S PRETTY MUCH THE PERFECT BAR. THEY HAVE COZY BOOTHS, TASTY BITES, AND SOME OF THE BEST BEER BREWED IN THE U.S."
TIM SCIASCIA P.300

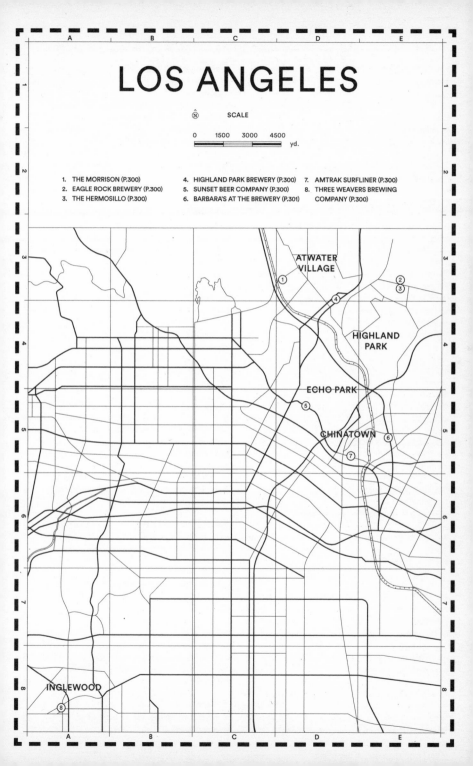

LOS ANGELES

N

SCALE

0   1500   3000   4500   yd.

1. THE MORRISON (P.300)
2. EAGLE ROCK BREWERY (P.300)
3. THE HERMOSILLO (P.300)
4. HIGHLAND PARK BREWERY (P.300)
5. SUNSET BEER COMPANY (P.300)
6. BARBARA'S AT THE BREWERY (P.301)
7. AMTRAK SURFLINER (P.300)
8. THREE WEAVERS BREWING COMPANY (P.300)

ATWATER VILLAGE

HIGHLAND PARK

ECHO PARK

CHINATOWN

INGLEWOOD

EAGLE ROCK BREWERY

Recommended by
Patrick Morse

3056 Roswell Street
Atwater Village
Los Angeles
California 90065, United States
+1 3232577866
www.eaglerockbrewery.com

Opening hours	Tue–Fri from 4 pm, Sat–Sun from 12 pm
Credit cards	Accepted
Type	Brewery
Recommended for	Unexpected

"Unbelievably great beer."—Patrick Morse

THE MORRISON

Recommended by
Stefan Krueger

3179 Los Feliz Boulevard
Atwater Village
Los Angeles
California 90039, United States
+1 3236671839
www.themorrisonla.com

Opening hours	Mon–Thur from 3 pm, Fri–Sat from 12 pm, Sun from 10 am
Credit cards	Accepted
Type	Pub
Recommended for	Unexpected

AMTRAK SURFLINER

Recommended by
Thomas Palmer

800 North Alameda Street
Chinatown
Los Angeles
California 90012, United States
+1 8008727245
www.amtrak.com/pacific-surfliner-train

Opening hours	Variable
Type	Bar
Recommended for	Unexpected

SUNSET BEER COMPANY

Recommended by
Katie Andrews,
Rob Zellermayer

1498 West Sunset Boulevard
Echo Park
Los Angeles
California 90026, United States
+1 2134812337
www.sunsetbeerco.com

Opening hours	Open 7 days from 12 pm
Credit cards	Accepted
Type	Bar and retail
Recommended for	Wish I'd opened

THE HERMOSILLO

Recommended by
Tim Sciascia

5125 York Boulevard
Highland Park
Los Angeles
California 90042, United States
+1 3237396459
www.thehermosillo.com

Opening hours	Mon–Thur from 5 pm, Fri–Sun from 12 pm
Credit cards	Accepted
Type	Bar and brewery
Recommended for	Worth the travel

"It's pretty much the perfect bar. They have cozy booths, tasty bites, and some of the best beer brewed in the U.S."
—Tim Sciascia

HIGHLAND PARK BREWERY

The Hermosillo

Recommended by
Sarah Bennett

5127 York Boulevard
Highland Park
Los Angeles
California 90042, United States
+1 3237396459
www.hpb.la

Opening hours	Mon–Thur from 5 pm, Fri–Sun from 12 pm
Credit cards	Accepted
Type	Brewery
Recommended for	Wish I'd opened

"A haven for low-key cool. They make world-class beer in the back of a revamped local dive."—Sarah Bennett

THREE WEAVERS BREWING COMPANY

Recommended by
Devon Randall

1031 West Manchester Boulevard A–B
Inglewood
Los Angeles
California 90301, United States
+1 3104005830
www.threeweavers.la

Opening hours	Mon–Thur from 3 pm, Fri–Sun from 12 pm
Credit cards	Accepted
Type	Brewery and bar
Recommended for	Unexpected

"I knew Alex's beers would be great, though I didn't expect to love the tasting-room vibe as much as I do."
—Devon Randall

BARBARA'S AT THE BREWERY

620 Moulton Avenue #110
Lincoln Heights
Los Angeles
California 90031, United States
+1 3232219204
www.barbarasatthebrewery.com

Recommended by
Devon Randall

Opening hours...................................Mon–Fri from 11:30 am,
                                                     Sat–Sun from 11 am
Credit cards..Accepted
Type...Pub
Recommended for..Local favorite

"A BEER GARDEN WITH AMAZING FOOD, NESTLED IN A BACKYARD THAT LOOKS LIKE A NATIONAL PARK OR LIKE MR. MIYAGI'S BACKYARD IN *THE KARATE KID*."

REID RAMSAY P.305

SAN DIEGO

"YOU FEEL AS IF YOU'RE SITTING IN A BEER GARDEN IN THE CENTER OF HAVANA."

TIM SCIASCIA P.305

"IF YOU WANT SOME HOPPY GOODNESS, THIS IS THE SPOT TO CHECK OUT. THEIR IPA ROTATION IS AMAZING."

MARK HODGES P.304

"THIS PLACE IS SO LAID-BACK AND UNASSUMING— I JUST LOVE IT."

SCOTT WOOD P.304

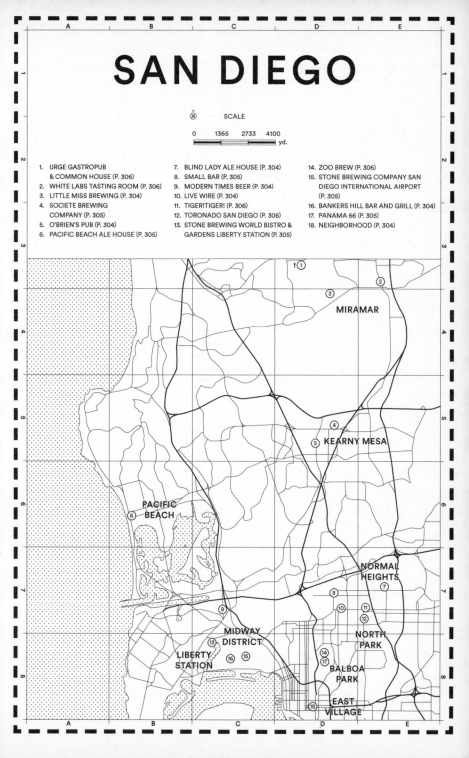

SAN DIEGO

N   SCALE

0   1365   2733   4100
yd.

1. URGE GASTROPUB
   & COMMON HOUSE (P. 306)
2. WHITE LABS TASTING ROOM (P. 306)
3. LITTLE MISS BREWING (P. 304)
4. SOCIETE BREWING
   COMPANY (P. 305)
5. O'BRIEN'S PUB (P. 304)
6. PACIFIC BEACH ALE HOUSE (P. 305)
7. BLIND LADY ALE HOUSE (P. 304)
8. SMALL BAR (P. 305)
9. MODERN TIMES BEER (P. 304)
10. LIVE WIRE (P. 304)
11. TIGER!TIGER! (P. 306)
12. TORONADO SAN DIEGO (P. 306)
13. STONE BREWING WORLD BISTRO &
    GARDENS LIBERTY STATION (P. 305)
14. ZOO BREW (P. 306)
15. STONE BREWING COMPANY SAN
    DIEGO INTERNATIONAL AIRPORT
    (P. 305)
16. BANKERS HILL BAR AND GRILL (P. 304)
17. PANAMA 66 (P. 305)
18. NEIGHBORHOOD (P. 304)

MIRAMAR

KEARNY MESA

PACIFIC
BEACH

NORMAL
HEIGHTS

MIDWAY
DISTRICT

LIBERTY
STATION

NORTH
PARK

BALBOA
PARK

EAST
VILLAGE

BANKERS HILL BAR AND GRILL

San Diego International Airport
3225 North Harbor Drive
Terminal 1 East, Floor 2, Gate 7
San Diego
California 92101, United States
+1 6194002404
www.san.org

Recommended by
Phillip MacNitt

Opening hours..................................Open 7 days from 6 am
Credit cards...Accepted
Type..Bar and restaurant
Recommended for...Unexpected

BLIND LADY ALE HOUSE

3416 Adams Avenue
San Diego
California 92116, United States
+1 6192552491
www.blindladyalehouse.com

Recommended by
Toshi Ishii,
Gabriela Velasco,
Justin Walsh

Opening hours.....................................Mon–Thur from 5 pm,
Fri–Sun from 11:30 am
Credit cards...Accepted
Type...Pub
Recommended for...Beer & food

LITTLE MISS BREWING

7949 Stromesa Court #Y
San Diego
California 92126, United States
+1 6198802752
www.littlemissbrewing.com

Recommended by
Isaac Aroche

Opening hours................................Mon–Wed from 4:30 pm,
Thur–Fri from 4 pm, Sat from 12 pm
Credit cards...Accepted
Type...Brewery
Recommended for...Unexpected

LIVE WIRE

2103 El Cajon Boulevard
San Diego
California 92104, United States
+1 6192917450
www.livewirebar.com

Recommended by
Phillip MacNitt

Opening hours..................................Open 7 days from 5 pm
Credit cards...Accepted
Type...Bar
Recommended for...Local favorite

MODERN TIMES BEER

3725 Greenwood Street
San Diego
California 92110, United States
+1 6195469694
www.moderntimesbeer.com

Recommended by
Tony Barron

Opening hours..................................Open 7 days from 12 pm
Credit cards...Accepted
Type...Brewery
Recommended for...Local favorite

"The beer is brewed and the coffee is brewed and roasted
on-site. They have a huge variety of beer styles, all canned
fresh on the premises. There's amazing artwork on the walls
made of Post-its and comic book pages."—Tony Barron

NEIGHBORHOOD

777 G Street
San Diego
California 92101, United States
+1 6194460002
www.neighborhoodsd.com

Recommended by
Christian Jauslin,
Scott Wood

Opening hours............................Open 7 days from 11:30 am
Credit cards...Accepted
Type...Bar
Recommended for...Beer & food

"This place is so laid-back and unassuming—I just love it.
The beer list is stellar. And there's a speakeasy in the back
that's utterly fantastic."—Scott Wood

O'BRIEN'S PUB

4646 Convoy Street
San Diego
California 92111, United States
+1 8587151745
www.obrienspub.net

Recommended by
Mark Hodges

Opening hours..................................Mon–Fri from 10:30 am,
Sat–Sun from 11 am
Credit cards...Accepted
Type...Pub
Recommended for...Worth the travel

"If you want some hoppy goodness, this is the spot to check
out. Their IPA rotation is amazing."—Mark Hodges

PACIFIC BEACH ALE HOUSE

721 Grand Avenue
San Diego
California 92109, United States
+1 8585812337
www.pbalehouse.com

Recommended by
Leo Sewald

Opening hours.................................Mon–Fri from 11 am,
Sat–Sun from 9 am
Credit cards..Accepted
Type...Restaurant
Recommended for.............................Wish I'd opened

PANAMA 66

1450 El Prado
San Diego
California 92101, United States
+1 6196961966
www.panama66.blogspot.com

Recommended by
Tim Sciascia

Opening hours.................................Mon–Fri from 11 am,
Sat–Sun from 10 am
Credit cards..Accepted
Type.............................Beer garden and restaurant
Recommended for.....................................Beer garden

"It's in the middle of the Plaza de Panama in Balboa Park.
When you're there, you feel as if you're sitting in a beer
garden in the center of Havana. The beer is good, but it's
more about sitting in this beautiful location with great
weather and live nightly music."—Tim Sciascia

SMALL BAR

4628 Park Boulevard
San Diego
California 92116, United States
+1 6197957998
www.smallbarsd.com

Recommended by
Katy DeWinter

Opening hours...................Open 7 days from 10 am
Credit cards..Accepted
Type..Bar
Recommended for.............................Wish I'd opened

SOCIETE BREWING COMPANY

8262 Clairemont Mesa Boulevard
San Diego
California 92111, United States
+1 8585985409
www.societebrewing.com

Recommended by
Alex Wallash

Opening hours.....................Open 7 days from 12 pm
Credit cards..Accepted
Type...Brewery
Recommended for...............................Local favorite

"There is a short list of places you can go where every beer
is perfectly made, and Societe is definitely on that list."
—Alex Wallash

STONE BREWING COMPANY SAN DIEGO INTERNATIONAL AIRPORT

3225 North Harbor Drive
San Diego
California 92101, United States
+1 6196868533
www.stonebrewing.com

Recommended by
Pietro Di Pilato

Opening hours.....................Open 7 days from 6 am
Credit cards..Accepted
Type...Bar and restaurant
Recommended for..................................Unexpected

STONE BREWING WORLD BISTRO & GARDENS LIBERTY STATION

2816 Historic Decatur Road
San Diego
California 92106
United States
+1 6192692100
www.stonebrewing.com

Recommended by
Tony Barron, Evan Doan,
Andres Erazo, Dustin Jeffers,
Valter Loverier, Pablo Mejia,
Thomas Palmer, Reid Ramsay,
Eugenio Romero,
Zac Triemert

Opening hours..................Open 7 days from 11:30 am
Credit cards..Accepted
Type...............................Beer garden and brewery
Recommended for.....................................Beer garden

"It's Stone, so you know everything is going to be
immaculate. The attention to detail at Liberty Station is
amazing. They have a giant beer garden surrounded
by flowing water, big stones, and hanging lights. Plus, it's
San Diego, so the whether is beautiful 99 percent of the
time."—Dustin Jeffers

"A beer garden with amazing food, nestled in a backyard
that looks like a national park or like Mr. Miyagi's backyard
in The Karate Kid."—Reid Ramsay

TIGER!TIGER!

3025 El Cajon Boulevard
San Diego
California 92104, United States
+1 6194870401
www.tigertigertavern.com

Recommended by
Katy DeWinter,
Gabriela Velasco

Opening hours	Tue–Thur from 5 pm, Fri from 3 pm, Sat from 11:30 am, Sun from 10:30 am
Credit cards	Accepted
Type	Bar
Recommended for	Beer & food

TORONADO SAN DIEGO

4026 30th Street
San Diego
California 92104, United States
+1 6192820456
www.toronadosd.com

Recommended by
Phillip MacNitt,
Devon Randall,
Tim Sciascia,
Scott Wood

Opening hours	Open 7 days from 11:30 am
Credit cards	Accepted
Type	Bar
Recommended for	Wish I'd opened

URGE GASTROPUB & COMMON HOUSE

255 Redel Road
San Diego
California 92078, United States
+1 7607988822
www.sm.urgegastropub.com

Recommended by
Mark Hodges

Opening hours	Open 7 days from 11:30 am
Credit cards	Accepted
Type	Beer garden and brewery
Recommended for	Wish I'd opened

"This has everything I love in one spot—it's a brewery, a restaurant, and a whiskey bar with bowling."—Mark Hodges

WHITE LABS TASTING ROOM

9495 Candida Street
San Diego
California 92126, United States
+1 8885932785
www.whitelabs.com

Recommended by
Hannah Barnett

Opening hours	Mon–Fri from 9 am
Credit cards	Accepted
Type	Brewery
Recommended for	Worth the travel

"White Labs is actually a yeast company with a tasting room. They have some of the coolest taster flights I've ever seen. This creates an experience unlike any other."
—Hannah Barnett

ZOO BREW

2920 Zoo Drive
San Diego Zoo
San Diego
California 92101, United States
+1 6192311515
www.zoo.sandiegozoo.org

Recommended by
Matthew Kelly

Opening hours	Open 7 days from 9 am
Credit cards	Accepted
Type	Bar
Recommended for	Unexpected

"I had a full range of stone beers in cans on a sunny day while looking at animals."—Matthew Kelly

"THE BEER IS GRISETTE-INSPIRED, WITH SPELT, WHEAT, AND LOCALLY FORAGED GRAPEFRUIT."
JAMES TAI P.310

"A PIONEER FOR AMERICAN CRAFT BEER." PATRICK RUE P.310

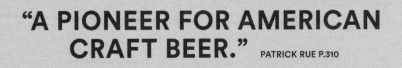

SAN FRANCISCO

"AN EXCEPTIONAL BEER LIST PAIRED WITH FANTASTIC BELGIAN-INSPIRED DISHES. A TRUE MARRIAGE OF BEER AND FOOD." BILL HOWELL P.310

"WITHOUT A DOUBT, THE BEST RANGE OF BOTTLED BEER ANYWHERE."
DAVE GRANT P.311

"IT MARRIES A DIVEY, PUNK-ROCK ATMOSPHERE WITH A WORLD-CLASS BEER LIST."
JOSHUA M. BERNSTEIN P.310

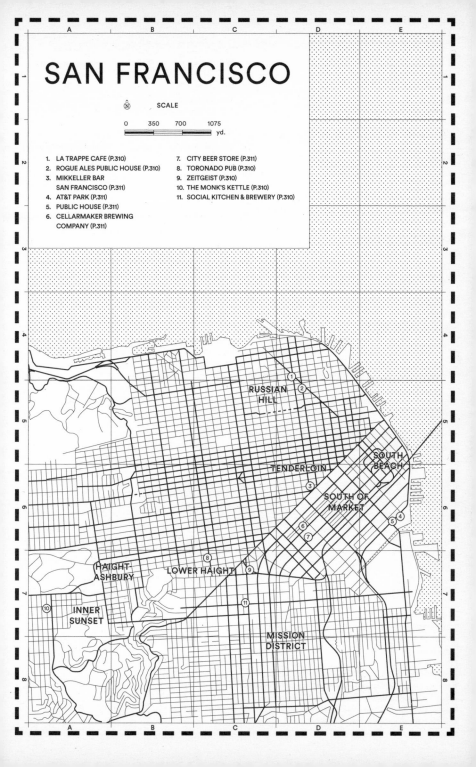

SAN FRANCISCO

N

SCALE

0   350   700   1075
yd.

1. LA TRAPPE CAFE (P.310)
2. ROGUE ALES PUBLIC HOUSE (P.310)
3. MIKKELLER BAR
   SAN FRANCISCO (P.311)
4. AT&T PARK (P.311)
5. PUBLIC HOUSE (P.311)
6. CELLARMAKER BREWING
   COMPANY (P.311)
7. CITY BEER STORE (P.311)
8. TORONADO PUB (P.310)
9. ZEITGEIST (P.310)
10. THE MONK'S KETTLE (P.310)
11. SOCIAL KITCHEN & BREWERY (P.310)

RUSSIAN
HILL

TENDERLOIN

SOUTH
BEACH

SOUTH OF
MARKET

HAIGHT-
ASHBURY

LOWER HAIGHT

INNER
SUNSET

MISSION
DISTRICT

SOCIAL KITCHEN & BREWERY

1326 9th Avenue
Inner Sunset
San Francisco
California 94122, United States
+1 4156810330
www.socialkitchenandbrewery.com

Recommended by
Todd Beal

Opening hours..........................Mon–Thur from 5 pm,
Fri from 4 pm, Sat–Sun from 11:30 am
Credit cards...Accepted
Type.......................................Restaurant and brewery
Recommended for.......................................Beer & food

TORONADO PUB

547 Haight Street
Lower Haight
San Francisco
California 94117
United States
+1 4158632276
www.toronado.com

Recommended by
Peter van der Arend,
Ryan Bedford, Joshua M.
Bernstein, Ethan Cox, Patrick
Ejlerskov, Chris Frosaker,
Lawrence George,
Matthew Kelly, Luke Nicholas,
Patrick Rue, James Tai,
Jared Welch, Tristan White,
Christopher Wong

Opening hours.............................Open 7 days from 11:30 am
Credit cards...Not accepted
Type...Pub
Recommended for.....................................Wish I'd opened

"Fresh pours of Russian River's Pliny the Elder for the eternal win. It marries a divey, punk-rock atmosphere with a world-class beer list."—Joshua M. Bernstein

"A pioneer for American craft beer."—Patrick Rue

THE MONK'S KETTLE

3141 16th Street
Mission District
San Francisco
California 94103, United States
+1 4158659523
www.monkskettle.com

Recommended by
Stefano Di Gioacchino,
Mike Goguen, Erin Lowder
Phillip MacNitt,
Luke Nicholas,
Vassilis Segos,
James Tai

Opening hours...................................Open 7 days from 12 pm
Credit cards...Accepted
Type...Pub
Recommended for.......................................Beer & food

"An incredibly well-curated beer program coupled with an equally well-executed, seasonally driven menu. A sandwich uses a sweet mild hake for its fish atop a pineapple tartar sauce, and the beer is grisette-inspired, with spelt, wheat, and locally foraged grapefruit."—James Tai

ZEITGEIST

199 Valencia Street
Mission District
San Francisco
California 94103, United States
+1 4152557505

Recommended by
Will Fisher,
Phillip MacNitt,
Ruben Martinez

Opening hours...................................Open 7 days from 9 am
Credit cards...Not accepted
Type...Beer garden and bar
Recommended for.......................................Beer garden

LA TRAPPE CAFÉ

800 Greenwich Street
Russian Hill
San Francisco
California 94133, United States
+1 4154408727
www.latrappecafe800.com

Recommended by
Bill Howell

Opening hours...................................Tue–Wed from 5 pm,
Thur–Sat from 6 pm
Credit cards...Accepted
Type..Restaurant
Recommended for.......................................Beer & food

"An exceptional beer list paired with fantastic Belgian-inspired dishes. A true marriage of beer and food."
—Bill Howell

ROGUE ALES PUBLIC HOUSE

673 Union Street
Russian Hill
San Francisco
California 94133, United States
+1 4153627880
www.rogue.com

Recommended by
Ruben Martinez,
David Williams

Opening hours...................................Open 7 days from 12 pm
Credit cards...Accepted
Type...Pub
Recommended for.......................................Beer garden

AT&T PARK

24 Willie Mays Plaza
South Beach
San Francisco
California 94107, United States
+1 4159722000
www.mlb.com/giants

Recommended by
Alex Acker

Opening hours..Variable
Credit cards..Accepted
Type..................................Entertainment venue
Recommended for....................................Unexpected

"A decent selection of local craft beer."—Alex Acker

PUBLIC HOUSE

24 Willie Mays Plaza
South Beach
San Francisco
California 94107, United States
+1 4156440240
www.publichousesf.com

Recommended by
Tim Sciascia

Opening hours...........Tue–Sat from 11 am, Sun from 10 am
Credit cards..Accepted
Type..Pub
Recommended for....................................Unexpected

"This is a great gastropub attached to AT&T Park, where the
San Francisco Giants play baseball. They have a great
selection of draft and bottles that you can purchase and
bring into the ballpark. Imagine drinking a Russian River
Blind Pig or a Rodenbach Grand Cru while enjoying the
national pastime."—Tim Sciascia

CELLARMAKER BREWING COMPANY

1150 Howard Street
South of Market
San Francisco
California 94103, United States
+1 4158633940
www.cellarmakerbrewing.com

Recommended by
Laurentiu Banescu

Opening hours..Tue–Thur from 3 pm,
Fri–Sat from 12 pm, Sun from 1 pm
Credit cards......................................Accepted but not Amex
Type..Brewery
Recommended for..Worth the travel

CITY BEER STORE

1168 Folsom Street #101
South of Market
San Francisco
California 94103, United States
+1 4155031033
www.citybeerstore.com

Recommended by
Dave Grant,
Tim Sciascia

Opening hours................................Open 7 days from 12 pm
Credit cards..Accepted
Type..Bar
Recommended for..Worth the travel

"Without a doubt, the best range of bottled beer anywhere."
—Dave Grant

"Their beer lineup is world-class."—Tim Sciascia

MIKKELLER BAR SAN FRANCISCO

34 Mason Street
Tenderloin
San Francisco
California 94102, United States
+1 4159840279
www.mikkellerbar.com/sf

Recommended by
Todd Beal,
Stefano Di Gioacchino,
Matthew Kelly,
Francisco Oyarce,
André Pintado

Opening hours..Mon–Fri from 12 pm,
Sat–Sun from 11 am
Credit cards..Accepted
Type..Bar and restaurant
Recommended for..Beer & food

"A lot of draft beer and a variety of food options, including
beer pairings."—Francisco Oyarce

"Great tap and bottle list with outstanding food. Plus, they
have sours in the basement."—Todd Beal

"PARADISE ON EARTH."

MARTIN VOIGT P.315

DENVER

"OVER 200 RETRO VIDEO GAMES AND PINBALL MACHINES AND A FULL BAR."

REID RAMSAY P.316

"'NO CRAP ON TAP' IS THEIR MOTTO, AND THEY LIVE BY IT."

TAYLOR REES P.315

"A TREMENDOUS SELECTION OF RARE AND EXCLUSIVE BEERS."

CHRIS JACKSON P.314

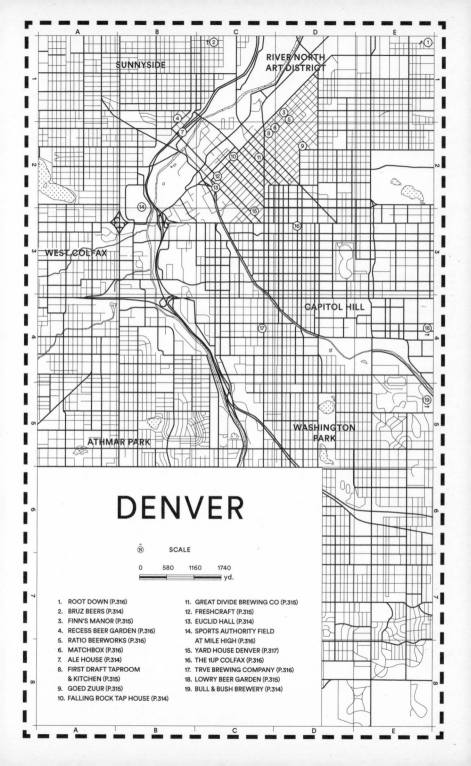

DENVER

N   SCALE

0   580   1160   1740
yd.

ALE HOUSE
Recommended by
Ryan Evans

2501 16th Street
Denver
Colorado 80211, United States
+1 3034339734
www.alehousedenver.com

Opening hours	Open 7 days from 11 am
Credit cards	Accepted
Type	Bar and restaurant
Recommended for	Beer & food

"Great food, view of the city, and beer selection."
—Ryan Evans

BRUZ BEERS
Recommended by
Ryan Evans

1675 West 67th Avenue #100
Denver
Colorado 80221, United States
+1 3036502337
www.bruzbeers.com

Opening hours	Mon–Fri from 3 pm, Sat–Sun from 12 pm
Credit cards	Accepted
Type	Brewery and pub
Recommended for	Local favorite

"High-quality Belgian-style beers in the middle of the United States—excellent."—Ryan Evans

BULL & BUSH BREWERY
Recommended by
David Lin,
Brian Sauer

4700 Cherry Creek Drive South
Denver
Colorado 80246, United States
+1 3037590333
www.bullandbush.com

Opening hours	Mon–Fri from 11 am, Sat–Sun from 10 am
Credit cards	Accepted
Type	Brewery and pub
Recommended for	Beer & food

"A great selection of beer and hundreds of whiskeys in a cozy British-style pub."—David Lin

EUCLID HALL
Recommended by
Chris Frosaker,
Patrick Lively,
Scott Shor,
Mark Sigman,
Brett Tate

1317 14th Street
Denver
Colorado 80202, United States
+1 3035954255
www.euclidhall.com

Opening hours	Open 7 days from 11:30 am
Credit cards	Accepted
Type	Restaurant
Recommended for	Beer & food

"Euclid Hall is in an 1883 building. It oozes of history along with dynamic and creative food, all intertwined with craft beer and whiskey pairings. As per their slogan 'Crafted, Not Cranked Out,' the food is unique, even for a hip city like Denver."—Brett Tate

"Euclid Hall utilizes a rotating menu on both the food and beer side, so every experience can be new and different. Quality is of the highest concern with both the food and beverage program."—Patrick Lively

"Dinosaur beef-marrow bones. A fantastic sour beer bottle list."—Scott Shor

FALLING ROCK TAP HOUSE
Recommended by
Bryan Brushmiller, Larry Cook,
Tony Forder, Ron Hoglund,
Bill Howell, Chris Jackson,
David Lin, David Newman,
Taylor Rees, Trip Ruvane,
Jesse Scheitler,
Michiko Tsutsui,
Martin Voigt

1919 Blake Street
Denver
Colorado 80202
United States
+1 3032938338
www.fallingrocktaphouse.com

Opening hours	Open 7 days from 11 am
Credit cards	Accepted
Type	Pub
Recommended for	Worth the travel

"It's a bloody legend with hard-to-find beers."—Bill Howell

"A great selection of beers and a nice open atmosphere."
—Bryan Brushmiller

"A tremendous selection of rare and exclusive beers."
—Chris Jackson

"Best selection of draft and bottles in the least pretentious atmosphere. This bar is amazing. They've been in the game so long that their relationships with all the craft brewers is like family. This is evident in the selection they have."—David Newman

"Paradise on earth."—Martin Voigt

"'No Crap on Tap' is their motto, and they live by it."
—Taylor Rees

FINN'S MANOR

	Recommended by
2927 Larimer Street	Collin Castore

Denver
Colorado 80205, United States
www.finnsmanor.net

Opening hours	Tue–Thur from 5 pm, Fri–Sun from 2 pm
Credit cards	Accepted
Type	Beer garden
Recommended for	Beer garden

FIRST DRAFT TAPROOM & KITCHEN

1309 26th Street	Recommended by
Denver	Kyle Hurst

Colorado 80205, United States
+1 3037368400
www.firstdraftdenver.com

Opening hours	Open 7 days from 11 am
Credit cards	Accepted
Type	Bar
Recommended for	Wish I'd opened

"Self-serve craft beer is an amazing concept. As little or as much as you'd like. It's up to you. Pay by the ounce."
—Kyle Hurst

FRESHCRAFT

	Recommended by
1530 Blake Street	Tony Barron

Denver
Colorado 80202, United States
+1 3037589608
www.freshcraft.com

Opening hours	Open 7 days from 11 am
Credit cards	Accepted
Type	Bar and restaurant
Recommended for	Worth the travel

"An incredible little venue in the Denver city center. They always give first-class service, and their knowledge is second to none."—Tony Barron

GOED ZUUR

	Recommended by
2801 Welton Street	Taylor Rees,
Denver	Julie Rhodes,
Colorado 80205, United States	Jesse Scheitler,
+1 7207492709	Jared Welch,
www.goedzuur.com	Matt Van Wyk

Opening hours	Mon–Fri from 3 pm, Sat–Sun from 1 pm
Credit cards	Accepted
Type	Pub
Recommended for	Beer & food

"A 100 percent sour and funky beer bar with a world-class selection of drafts and bottles; not to mention some of the special events they throw bring in the best beer in the world. The food, cheese, charcuterie, and butter—yes, they have a butter flight—is top notch."—Jared Welch

"The first sour-only beer bar in the United States."
—Taylor Rees

GREAT DIVIDE BREWING CO.

	Recommended by
2201 Arapahoe Street	Nathan Keffer

Denver
Colorado 80205, United States
+1 3032969460
www.greatdivide.com

Opening hours	Open 7 days from 12 pm
Credit cards	Accepted
Type	Bar and brewery
Recommended for	Worth the travel

LOWRY BEER GARDEN

	Recommended by
7577 East Academy Boulevard	Yazan M. Karadsheh

Denver
Colorado 80203, United States
+1 3033660114
www.lowrybeergarden.com

Opening hours	Open 7 days from 11 am
Credit cards	Accepted
Type	Beer garden and restaurant
Recommended for	Beer garden

MATCHBOX

Recommended by
Ashleigh Carter

2625 Larimer Street
Denver
Colorado 80205, United States
+1 7204379100
www.matchboxdenver.com

Opening hours.................................Mon–Fri from 12 pm,
Sat–Sun from 4 pm
Credit cards...Accepted
Type..Bar
Recommended for....................................Unexpected

THE 1UP COLFAX

Recommended by
Reid Ramsay

717 East Colfax Avenue
Denver
Colorado 80203, United States
+1 3037362230
www.the-1up.com

Opening hours.................................Mon–Fri from 3 pm,
Sat–Sun from 11 am
Credit cards...Accepted
Type..Bar
Recommended for................................Wish I'd opened

"Over 200 retro video games and pinball machines and a full
bar with craft beer on tap and cocktails."—Reid Ramsay

RATIO BEERWORKS

Recommended by
Vadim Gurov

2920 Larimer Street
Denver
Colorado 80205, United States
+1 3039978288
www.ratiobeerworks.com

Opening hours.................................Open 7 days from 12 pm
Credit cards...Accepted
Type.............................Beer garden and microbrewery
Recommended for....................................Beer garden

RECESS BEER GARDEN

Recommended by
Ryan Evans

2715 17th Street #103
Denver
Colorado 80211, United States
+1 7206380020
www.recessbeergarden.com

Opening hours.................................Mon–Fri from 11 am,
Sat–Sun from 10 am
Credit cards...Accepted
Type..Beer garden and restaurant
Recommended for....................................Beer garden

"An excellent outdoor beer garden. The food is great too."
—Ryan Evans

ROOT DOWN

Recommended by
Jacob Landry

Denver International Airport
Concourse C
Denver
Colorado 80249, United States
+1 3033426959
www.rootdowndia.com

Opening hours.................................Open 7 days from 7 am
Credit cards...Accepted
Type...Restaurant
Recommended for....................................Unexpected

"A gem—it's a restaurant with great food and a local beer
and cider selection unlike any other airport restaurant in the
country."—Jacob Landry

SPORTS AUTHORITY FIELD
AT MILE HIGH

Recommended by
Martin Voigt

1701 Bryant Street
Denver
Colorado 80204, United States
+1 3035344476
www.sportsauthorityfieldatmilehigh.com

Opening hours...Variable
Credit cards...Accepted
Type...Entertainment venue
Recommended for....................................Unexpected

TRVE BREWING COMPANY

227 Broadway #101
Denver
Colorado 80203, United States
+1 3033511021
www.trvebrewing.com

Recommended by
Chris Jackson

Opening hours..................................Mon–Wed from 3 pm,
Thur–Sun from 12 pm
Credit cards...Accepted
Type...Brewery
Recommended for...Wish I'd opened

"A heavy metal-themed brewery."—Chris Jackson

YARD HOUSE DENVER

1555 Court Place
Denver
Colorado 80202, United States
+1 3035729273
www.yardhouse.com

Recommended by
Ron Hoglund

Opening hours..................................Open 7 days from 11 am
Credit cards...Accepted
Type...Restaurant
Recommended for...Wish I'd opened

"A great location with wonderful international and local beer
options. The service and atmosphere are first-rate."
—Ron Hoglund

> "LEGENDARY BOTTLE SHARES AND EIGHT TAPS OF GREATNESS."
>
> KIRK ZEMBAL P.320

> "IT'S PURE HAPPINESS."
>
> EVAN DOAN P.320

PORTLAND

> "JUST AMAZING BEER."
>
> MOLLY GUNN P.320

> "ONE OF THE FIRST PLACES TO MERGE THE TAPROOM AND BOTTLE-SHOP CONCEPTS, AND IT'S STILL ONE OF THE BEST."
>
> JOSH RUFFIN P.320

> "AWESOME VIBE, AND THE BIKE THEME IS FULLY ENTRENCHED IN EVERYTHING THE BAR DOES."
>
> NATHAN KEFFER P.321

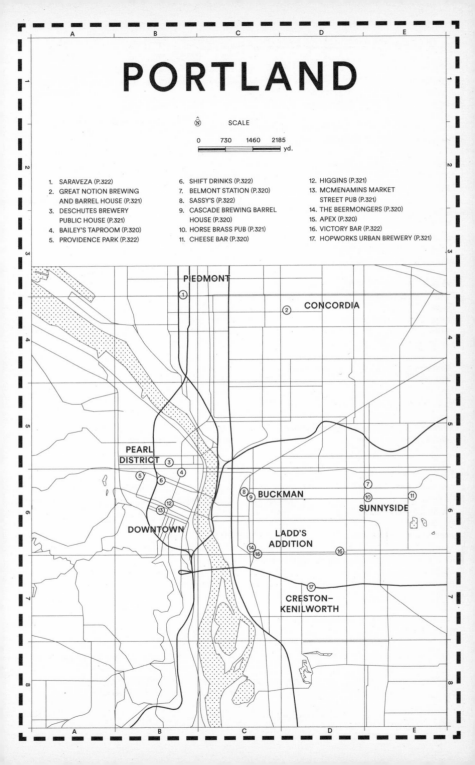

PORTLAND

N   SCALE

0   730   1460   2185
━━━━━━━━━━━━━━━━ yd.

1. SARAVEZA (P.322)
2. GREAT NOTION BREWING AND BARREL HOUSE (P.321)
3. DESCHUTES BREWERY PUBLIC HOUSE (P.321)
4. BAILEY'S TAPROOM (P.320)
5. PROVIDENCE PARK (P.322)
6. SHIFT DRINKS (P.322)
7. BELMONT STATION (P.320)
8. SASSY'S (P.322)
9. CASCADE BREWING BARREL HOUSE (P.320)
10. HORSE BRASS PUB (P.321)
11. CHEESE BAR (P.320)
12. HIGGINS (P.321)
13. MCMENAMINS MARKET STREET PUB (P.321)
14. THE BEERMONGERS (P.320)
15. APEX (P.320)
16. VICTORY BAR (P.322)
17. HOPWORKS URBAN BREWERY (P.321)

PIEDMONT

CONCORDIA

PEARL DISTRICT

BUCKMAN

SUNNYSIDE

DOWNTOWN

LADD'S ADDITION

CRESTON–KENILWORTH

APEX

1216 Southeast Division Street
Portland
Oregon 97202
United States
+1 5032739227
www.apexbar.com

Recommended by
Christopher DeWolf,
Evan Doan, Tim Gormley,
Molly Gunn, Sang Jun Lee,
Katherine Kyle,
Cody Morris, Alan Sprints,
Casey Workman, Kirk Zembal

Opening hours.............................Open 7 days from 11:30 am
Credit cards...Not accepted
Type...Beer garden
Recommended for...Beer garden

"It's pure happiness."—Evan Doan

"Just amazing beer."—Molly Gunn

BAILEY'S TAPROOM

213 Southwest Broadway
Portland
Oregon 97205, United States
+1 5032951004
www.baileystaproom.com

Recommended by
Kirk Zembal

Opening hours..................................Open 7 days from 12 pm
Credit cards..Accepted
Type...Bar
Recommended for...Beer & food

"A fantastic beer and bottle list, especially upstairs."
—Kirk Zembal

THE BEERMONGERS

1125 Southeast Division Street
Portland
Oregon 97202, United States
+1 5032346012
www.thebeermongers.com

Recommended by
Casey Workman,
Kirk Zembal

Opening hours...................................Open 7 days from 11 am
Credit cards..Accepted
Type...Bar
Recommended for...................................Worth the travel

"Legendary bottle shares and eight taps of greatness."
—Kirk Zembal

BELMONT STATION

4500 Southeast Stark Street
Portland
Oregon 97215, United States
+1 5032328538
www.belmont-station.com

Recommended by
Rick Nelson,
Josh Pfriem,
Josh Ruffin

Opening hours..Mon–Sat from 10 am,
Sun from 11 am
Credit cards..Accepted
Type..Bar and retail
Recommended for...................................Wish I'd opened

"An incredible selection of draft and bottled beers. They are
very in touch with the heartbeat of the Portland beer scene."
—Josh Pfriem

"One of the first places to merge the taproom and
bottle-shop concepts, and it's still one of the best."
—Josh Ruffin

Belmont Station is a Portland institution, and for good reason.
They have a huge, well-curated selection of beers and a very
friendly staff.

CASCADE BREWING BARREL HOUSE

939 Southeast Belmont Street
Portland
Oregon 97214, United States
+1 5032658603
www.cascadebrewingbarrelhouse.com

Recommended by
Danny Hamilton,
Cameron Johnson,
Sang Jun Lee

Opening hours...................................Open 7 days from 12 pm
Credit cards..Accepted
Type.................................Beer garden, brewery, and pub
Recommended for...Beer garden

CHEESE BAR

6031 Southeast Belmont Street
Portland
Oregon 97215, United States
+1 5032226014
www.cheese-bar.com

Recommended by
Kirk Zembal

Opening hours......................................Tue–Sun from 11 am
Credit cards..Accepted
Type...Bar
Recommended for...Unexpected

"A crazy good Belgian beer list. Grab some cheese and a
fantastic bottle, and go."—Kirk Zembal

DESCHUTES BREWERY PUBLIC HOUSE

Recommended by
Matt Gelsthorpe

210 Northwest 11th Avenue
Portland
Oregon 97209, United States
+1 5032964906
www.deschutesbrewery.com/portland

Opening hours......................................Open 7 days from 11 am
Credit cards..Accepted
Type...Pub
Recommended for...Beer & food

GREAT NOTION BREWING AND BARREL HOUSE

Recommended by
Collin Castore,
Casey Workman

2204 Northeast Alberta Street #101
Portland
Oregon 97211, United States
+1 5035484491
www.greatnotionpdx.com

Opening hours......................................Open 7 days from 12 pm
Credit cards..Accepted
Type..Bar and brewery
Recommended for...Beer & food

"I loved all their New England IPAs."—Casey Workman

HIGGINS

Recommended by
Kevin Drake

1239 Southwest Broadway
Portland
Oregon 97205, United States
+1 5032229070
www.higginsportland.com

Opening hours...............................Mon–Sat from 11:30 am,
Sun from 4 pm
Credit cards..Accepted
Type..Bar and restaurant
Recommended for...Beer & food

"Incredible seasonal farm-to-table food with one of the oldest craft-beer programs in Portland's fine-dining community."—Kevin Drake

HOPWORKS URBAN BREWERY

2944 Southeast Powell Boulevard
Portland

Recommended by
Nathan Keffer,
Nikki Ohanlon

Oregon 97202, United States
+1 5032324677
www.hopworksbeer.com

Opening hours......................................Open 7 days from 11 am
Credit cards..Accepted
Type...Microbrewery
Recommended for...Beer & food

"An awesome vibe, and the bike theme is fully entrenched in everything the bar does."—Nathan Keffer

HORSE BRASS PUB

4534 Southeast Belmont Street
Portland

Recommended by
Evan Doan,
Kevin Drake,
James Landers,
Alan Sprints

Oregon 97215, United States
+1 5032322202
www.horsebrass.com

Opening hours......................................Open 7 days from 11 am
Credit cards..Accepted
Type...Pub
Recommended for...Worth the travel

"It's an original pioneer of craft beer in the Northwest with a top-notch selection and food."—James Landers

MCMENAMINS MARKET STREET PUB

1526 Southwest 10th Avenue
Portland

Recommended by
Rory Miller

Oregon 97201, United States
+1 5034970160
www.mcmenamins.com/market-street-pub

Opening hours......................................Open 7 days from 11 am
Credit cards..Accepted
Type...Pub
Recommended for...Beer & food

PROVIDENCE PARK

1844 Southwest Morrison Street
Portland
Oregon 97205, United States
+1 5035535400
www.providenceparkpdx.com

Recommended by
Ben Love

Opening hours	Variable
Credit cards	Accepted
Type	Entertainment venue
Recommended for	Unexpected

"The only stadium in the U.S. where craft outsells domestic for any sport."—Ben Love

SARAVEZA

1004 North Killingsworth Street
Portland
Oregon 97217, United States
+1 5032064252
www.saraveza.com

Recommended by
Matt Van Wyk

Opening hours	Open 7 days from 11 am
Credit cards	Accepted
Type	Pub
Recommended for	Worth the travel

SASSY'S

927 Southeast Morrison Street
Portland
Oregon 97214, United States
+1 5032311606
www.sassysbar.com

Recommended by
Jerry Gnagy

Opening hours	Open 7 days from 10:30 am
Credit cards	Accepted
Type	Bar
Recommended for	Wish I'd opened

"Great beer selection and performance art."—Jerry Gnagy

SHIFT DRINKS

1200 Southwest Morrison Street
Portland
Oregon 97205, United States
+1 5039223933
www.shiftdrinkspdx.com

Recommended by
Zach Warren

Opening hours	Mon–Fri from 4 pm, Sat–Sun from 5 pm
Credit cards	Accepted
Type	Bar
Recommended for	Wish I'd opened

"Shift Drinks caters to those in the hospitality industry. They offer quality libations at reasonable prices."—Zach Warren

VICTORY BAR

3652 Southeast Division Street
Portland
Oregon 97202, United States
+1 5032868755
www.thevictorybar.com

Recommended by
Ben Love

Opening hours	Open 7 days from 5:30 pm
Credit cards	Accepted
Type	Bar
Recommended for	Local favorite

"Victory has an eclectic beer selection and intriguing art and decor."—Ben Love

"THE ULTIMATE GASTROPUB. THE BEER IS SERVED DIRECTLY FROM BREWERY TANKS."

CHARLES FINKEL P.328

"THE ATMOSPHERE IS UNMATCHED AND THE MURALS ARE STUNNING." ANNA ELLIS P.327

SEATTLE

"THIS PLACE CHECKS ALL THE BOXES FOR ME. QUIET AND AUSTERE, THIS BAR DELIVERS AN EXPERIENCE THAT IS FOCUSED 100 PERCENT ON THE BEER."

STEPHEN ANDREWS P.327

"SAFECO FIELD, THE HOME OF THE SEATTLE MARINERS BASEBALL TEAM, HAS AN UNBELIEVABLE LINEUP OF CRAFT BEER. A SURREAL EXPERIENCE"

KYLE JEFFERSON P.327

"ALWAYS ON THE CUTTING EDGE OF THE BEER REVOLUTION."

ALAN SPRINTS P.326

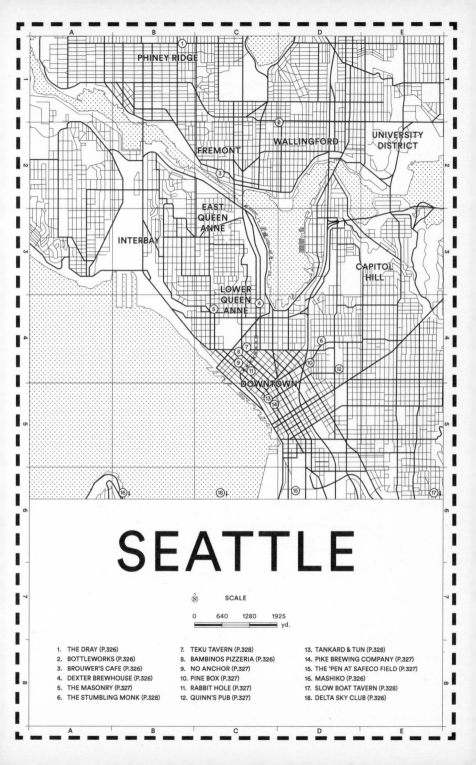

SEATTLE

PHINEY RIDGE

WALLINGFORD

UNIVERSITY DISTRICT

FREMONT

EAST QUEEN ANNE

INTERBAY

CAPITOL HILL

LOWER QUEEN ANNE

DOWNTOWN

$\hat{N}$ SCALE

0   640   1280   1925
yd.

BAMBINOS PIZZERIA
Recommended by
Tim Gormley

401 Cedar Street
Seattle
Washington 98121, United States
+1 2062692222
www.bambinosseattle.com

Opening hours.............................Open 7 days from 11:30 am
Credit cards...Accepted
Type...Restaurant
Recommended for..Unexpected

BOTTLEWORKS
Recommended by
Cody Morris

1710 North 45th Street #3
Seattle
Washington 98103, United States
+1 2066332437
www.bottleworks.com

Opening hours...................................Open 7 days from 11 am
Credit cards...Accepted
Type..Retail
Recommended for..Local favorite

BROUWER'S CAFE
Recommended by
James Landers,
Yuhang Lin,
Cody Morris

400 North 35th Street
Seattle
Washington 98103, United States
+1 2062672437
www.brouwerscafe.com

Opening hours...................................Open 7 days from 11 am
Credit cards...Accepted
Type...Pub
Recommended for..Worth the travel

"They have sixty-four craft beers on draft and a selection of
over 400 bottles from the U.S. and abroad. Craft-beer lovers
can easily find what they need."—Yuhang Lin

DELTA SKY CLUB
Recommended by
Charles Finkel

Seattle-Tacoma International Airport
17801 International Boulevard
Terminal A
Seattle
Washington 98158, United States
+1 8004962225

Opening hours.............................Open 7 days from 5:30 am
Credit cards...Accepted
Type...Bar
Recommended for..Unexpected

DEXTER BREWHOUSE
Recommended by
Alan Sprints

803 Dexter Avenue North
Seattle
Washington 98109, United States
+1 2064031228
www.dexterbrewhouse.com

Opening hours..Mon–Fri from 11 am,
Sat–Sun from 10 am
Credit cards...Accepted
Type...Brewpub
Recommended for..Beer & food

"Always on the cutting edge of the beer revolution."
—Alan Sprints

THE DRAY
Recommended by
Tim Gormley

708 Northwest 65th Street
Seattle
Washington 98107, United States
+1 2064534527
www.thedray.com

Opening hours...................................Open 7 days from 11 am
Credit cards..Accepted but not Amex
Type...Bar
Recommended for...Wish I'd opened

MASHIKO
Recommended by
Cody Morris

4725 California Avenue Southwest
Seattle
Washington 98116, United States
+1 2069354339
www.mashikorestaurant.com

Opening hours...................................Open 7 days from 5 pm
Credit cards...Accepted
Type...Restaurant
Recommended for..Beer & food

"A fantastic local sushi restaurant with a house shiso beer."
—Cody Morris

THE MASONRY

Recommended by
Tim Sciascia

20 Roy Street
Seattle
Washington 98109, United States
+1 2064534375
www.themasonryseattle.com

Opening hours	Open 7 days from 11:30 am
Credit cards	Accepted
Type	Bar and restaurant
Recommended for	Beer & food

NO ANCHOR

Recommended by
Stephen Andrews,
Mike Murphy

2505 2nd Avenue #105
Seattle
Washington 98121, United States
+1 2064482610
www.noanchorbar.com

Opening hours	Mon–Fri from 12 pm, Sat–Sun from 11 am
Credit cards	Accepted
Type	Bar
Recommended for	Beer & food

"Everything at No Anchor is meticulously curated—the beer, cocktails, the food menu, even the oddities lining the walls. The staff and owners are extremely knowledgeable and passionate about finding the perfect pairing that brings out the best in both the beer and the dish."—Mike Murphy

"This place checks all the boxes for me. Quiet and austere, this bar delivers an experience that is focused 100 percent on the beer."—Stephen Andrews

THE 'PEN AT SAFECO FIELD

Recommended by
Kyle Jefferson,
Lynn McIlwee,
Yuhang Lin

1250 1st Avenue South
Seattle
Washington 98134, United States
+1 2063464001
www.mlb.com/mariners

Opening hours	Variable
Credit cards	Accepted
Type	Entertainment venue
Recommended for	Unexpected

"Safeco Field, the home of the Seattle Mariners baseball team, has an unbelievable lineup of craft beer. A surreal experience."—Kyle Jefferson

PIKE BREWING COMPANY

1415 1st Avenue
Seattle Recommended by
Charles Finkel
Washington 98101, United States
+1 2066226044
www.pikebrewing.com

Opening hours	Open 7 days from 11 am
Credit cards	Accepted
Type	Brewery
Recommended for	Worth the travel

PINE BOX

Recommended by
John Stewart

1600 Melrose Avenue
Seattle
Washington 98122, United States
+1 2065880375
www.pineboxbar.com

Opening hours	Mon–Fri from 3 pm, Sat–Sun from 11 am
Credit cards	Accepted
Type	Restaurant and pub
Recommended for	Wish I'd opened

QUINN'S PUB

Recommended by
Tim Gormley

1001 East Pike Street
Seattle
Washington 98122, United States
+1 2063257711
www.quinnspubseattle.com

Opening hours	Open 7 days from 4 pm
Credit cards	Accepted
Type	Pub
Recommended for	Beer & food

RABBIT HOLE

Recommended by
Anna Ellis

2222 2nd Avenue
Seattle
Washington 98121, United States
+1 2069564653
www.rabbitholeseattle.com

Opening hours	Open 7 days from 4 pm
Credit cards	Accepted
Type	Bar
Recommended for	Wish I'd opened

"The atmosphere is unmatched and the murals are stunning. They have Skee-Ball for a quarter."—Anna Ellis

SLOW BOAT TAVERN

Recommended by
Mike Murphy

5701 Rainier Avenue South
Seattle
Washington 98118, United States
+1 2062356023
www.slowboattavern.com

Opening hours..Open 7 days from 2 pm
Credit cards...Accepted
Type...Bar
Recommended for...Local favorite

THE STUMBLING MONK

Recommended by
Matt Gelsthorpe

1635 East Olive Way
Seattle
Washington 98102, United States
+1 2068600916

Opening hours..Open 7 days from 6 pm
Credit cards...Accepted
Type...Pub
Recommended for...Worth the travel

TANKARD & TUN

Recommended by
Charles Finkel

1415 1st Avenue
Seattle
Washington 98101, United States
+1 2068126619
www.pikebrewing.com/tankard-tun

Opening hours..Open 7 days from 11 am
Credit cards...Accepted
Type...Restaurant
Recommended for...Beer & food

"The ultimate gastropub, a part of the Pike Brewing
Company. The beer is served directly from brewery
tanks."—Charles Finkel

TEKU TAVERN

Recommended by
Nicole Pearce

552 Denny Way
Seattle
Washington 98109, United States
+1 2064661764
www.tekutavern.beer

Opening hours................................Mon–Thur from 12 pm,
Fri–Sun from 11 am
Credit cards...Accepted
Type...Bar
Recommended for...Wish I'd opened

"The space and location are great. I love the coolers with all
the bottled beer. They have an extensive collection of draft
and bottles, takeout available too."—Nicole Pearce

"AS IF YOU'VE BEEN TRANSPORTED TO A SMALL CITY IN GERMANY."
SUZANNE HAYS P.333

"THE COOLEST TAPROOM EVER."
MATT WINJUM P.342

USA MIDWEST

"RIGHT ON THE RIVER, THIS BEER GARDEN IS A HIDDEN GEM."
JAMES LARSON P.345

"THE COUNTRY BAR TO TOP ALL COUNTRY BARS."
MARIKA JOSEPHSON P.332

"THIS BREWERY HAS ONE OF THE BEST PUBLIC TOURS IN THE INDUSTRY AND A VAST BEER HALL. PAIR IT WITH A LIVE POLKA BAND, PINTS OF THE BREWERY'S AMBER LAGER, AND THE GENERAL INFECTIOUS SPIRIT OF CAMARADERIE AND CELEBRATION, AND YOU'LL HAVE A NIGHT TO REMEMBER."
JOHN HOLL P.345

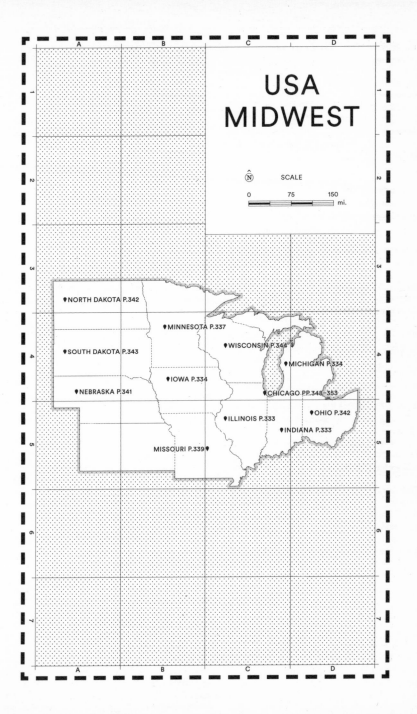

USA
MIDWEST

N   SCALE

0   75   150
                         mi.

NORTH DAKOTA P.342

MINNESOTA P.337

SOUTH DAKOTA P.343

WISCONSIN P.344

MICHIGAN P.334

IOWA P.334

NEBRASKA P.341

CHICAGO PP.348–353

OHIO P.342

ILLINOIS P.333

INDIANA P.333

MISSOURI P.339

SCRATCH BREWING COMPANY

264 Thompson Road
Ava
Illinois 62907, United States
+1 6184261415
www.scratchbeer.com

Recommended by
Stuart Keating

Opening hours..Thur from 5 pm,
Fri from 4 pm, Sat–Sun from 12 pm
Credit cards..Not accepted
Type...Microbrewery
Recommended for...............................Worth the travel

"Groundbreaking beer of phenomenal quality made by
wonderful people in an idyllic setting."—Stuart Keating

MAPLE TREE INN

13301 South Old Western Avenue
Blue Island
Illinois 60406, United States
+1 7083883461
www.mapletreeinnrestaurant.com

Recommended by
Steve Kamp

Opening hours................Tue–Fri from 5 pm, Sat from 3 pm
Credit cards...Accepted
Type..Restaurant
Recommended for.......................................Wish I'd opened

BRICK STONE BREWERY

557 William R Latham Senior Drive
Bourbonnais
Illinois 60914, United States
+1 8159369277
www.brickstonebrewery.com

Recommended by
Steve Kamp

Opening hours...........................Open 7 days from 10:30 am
Credit cards...Accepted
Type..Beer garden and brewery
Recommended for...Beer & food

Chicago, see pages 348–353

EVIL HORSE BREWING COMPANY

1338 Main Street
Crete
Illinois 60417, United States
+1 7083042907
www.evilhorsebrewing.com

Recommended by
Steve Kamp

Opening hours..Mon–Fri from 3 pm,
Sat–Sun from 12 pm
Credit cards...Accepted
Type..Brewery
Recommended for.......................................Local favorite

THE VETERAN'S INN

304 Union Avenue
Dowell
Illinois 62927, United States
+1 6185681251

Recommended by
Marika Josephson

Opening hours..........Mon–Sat from 7 am, Sun from 12 pm
Credit cards...Not accepted
Type...Bar
Recommended for.......................................Local favorite

"The country bar to top all country bars."
—Marika Josephson

ST. NICHOLAS BREWING COMPANY

12 South Oak Street
Du Quoin
Illinois 62832, United States
+1 6187909212
www.stnicholasbrewco.com

Recommended by
Paul Plett

Opening hours...Tue–Sun from 11 am
Credit cards...Accepted
Type..Brewery
Recommended for.......................................Local favorite

"I love their Wee Heavy. The setting is an old hotel and has
great character. Also, the beer is amazing!"—Paul Plett

ROPER'S REGAL BEAGLE

3043 Godfrey Road
Godfrey
Illinois 62035, United States
+1 6184662112
www.ropersregalbeagle.com

Recommended by
Matt Gelsthorpe

Opening hours....................................Open 7 days from 11 am
Credit cards...Accepted
Type...Bar
Recommended for.......................................Unexpected

EMMETT'S BREWING COMPANY
WEST DUNDEE

Recommended by
Jaime Ojeda

128 West Main Street
West Dundee
Illinois 60118, United States
+1 8474284500
www.emmettsbrewingco.com

Opening hours	Open 7 days from 11:30 am
Credit cards	Accepted
Type	Brewery and pub
Recommended for	Beer & food

THE PINT ROOM BAR

Recommended by
Kevin Smolar

110 West Main Street
Carmel
Indiana 46032, United States
+1 3175718400
www.pintroomcarmel.com

Opening hours	Open 7 days from 11 am
Credit cards	Accepted
Type	Restaurant
Recommended for	Local favorite

BEER GEEKS

Recommended by
Kevin Smolar

3030 45th Street
Highland
Indiana 46322, United States
+1 2195139795
www.beergeekspub.com

Opening hours	Open 7 days from 3 pm
Credit cards	Accepted but not Amex
Type	Pub
Recommended for	Worth the travel

BREWFEST

Recommended by
Kevin Smolar

8347 Kennedy Avenue
Highland
Indiana 46322, United States
+1 2192372682

Opening hours	Open 7 days from 3 pm
Credit cards	Accepted
Type	Pub
Recommended for	Wish I'd opened

"It's a serve yourself type of place. They have twenty taps.
You get a card preloaded with two pints' worth of beer, and
you pour however much you'd like."
—Kevin Smolar

KAHN'S FINE WINES AND SPIRITS

Recommended by
Suzanne Hays

5341 North Keystone Avenue
Indianapolis
Indiana 46220, United States
+1 3172519463
www.kahnsfinewines.com

Opening hours	Mon–Sat from 9 am
Credit cards	Accepted
Type	Retail
Recommended for	Unexpected

THE KOELSCHIP

Recommended by
Erin Thompson

2505 North Delaware Street
Indianapolis
Indiana 46205, United States
+1 3174149539
www.thekoelschip.com

Opening hours	Mon–Thur from 2 pm, Fri–Sun from 12 pm
Credit cards	Accepted
Type	Bar
Recommended for	Wish I'd opened

THE RATHSKELLER

Recommended by
Suzanne Hays,
Kevin Smolar,
Erin Thompson

401 East Michigan Street
Indianapolis
Indiana 46204, United States
+1 3176360396
www.rathskeller.com

Opening hours	Open 7 days from 11 am
Credit cards	Accepted
Type	Beer garden and restaurant
Recommended for	Beer garden

"A stellar list of German brews. In the summer you can enjoy
a Schlenkerla in the outdoor space while listening to live
music, as if you've been transported to a small city in
Germany."—Suzanne Hays

THE HEOROT

Recommended by
Maxon Cox

219 South Walnut Street
Muncie
Indiana 47305, United States
+1 7652870173

Opening hours.............Mon–Fri from 11 am, Sun from 12 pm
Credit cards..Accepted
Type...Pub
Recommended for................................Local favorite

3 FLOYDS BREWPUB

Recommended by
Kevin Smolar

9750 Indiana Parkway
Munster
Indiana 46321, United States
+1 2199224425
www.3floyds.com

Opening hours....................Open 7 days from 11 am
Credit cards..Accepted
Type..Brewpub
Recommended for...............................Beer & food

TGI FRIDAYS

Recommended by
Kevin Smolar

3401 South U.S. Highway 41
Terre Haute
Indiana 47802, United States
+1 8122328444
www.tgifridays.com

Opening hours....................Open 7 days from 11 am
Credit cards..Accepted
Type...Restaurant
Recommended for................................Unexpected

"For a chain restaurant, they have an amazing beer list. I was
blown away by the options and selection."—Kevin Smolar

SCHERA'S ALGERIAN-AMERICAN
RESTAURANT & BAR

Recommended by
Jeffrey Stuffings

107 South Main Street
Elkader
Iowa 52043, United States
+1 5632451992
www.scheras.com

Opening hours.........................Mon–Sat from 11 am,
Sun from 11:30 am
Credit cards..Accepted
Type...Restaurant
Recommended for................................Unexpected

"A really great selection of beers from the Shelton brothers
and 12 Percent Imports in a small town in rural Iowa. Chef
Brian Bruening and Frederique Boudouani of Abu Nawas
have created a wonderful place for food and drink right on
the beautiful Turkey River."—Jeffrey Stuffings

JOLLY PUMPKIN

Recommended by
Rob Zellermayer

311 South Main Street
Ann Arbor
Michigan 48104, United States
+1 7349132730
www.jollypumpkin.com

Opening hours.........................Mon–Fri from 11 am,
Sat–Sun from 10 am
Credit cards..Accepted
Type...Bar and brewery
Recommended for...............................Beer & food

"Unusual sandwiches complementing an eccentric tap
list."—Rob Zellermayer

GRIFFIN CLAW BREWING COMPANY

575 South Eton Street
Birmingham

Recommended by
Ben Whitney

Michigan 48009, United States
+1 2487124050
www.griffinclawbrewingcompany.com

Opening hours...........................Tue–Fri from 2 pm,
Sat–Sun from 12 pm
Credit cards..Accepted
Type...Brewery
Recommended for...............................Beer & food

TRANSIENT ARTISAN ALES

4229 Lake Street
Bridgman

Recommended by
Peter Crowley

Michigan 49106, United States
+1 8152364116
www.transientartisanales.com

Opening hours.........................Sat–Sun from 12 pm
Credit cards..Accepted
Type...Microbrewery
Recommended for................................Unexpected

"A tiny hole-in-the-wall with extremely solid beers and an
extensive wild barrel program. Chris is a totally chill and
unassuming dude. He should have a giant ego, but he just
lets his beers talk."—Peter Crowley

8 DEGREES PLATO

Recommended by
Stephen Roginson

3409 Cass Avenue
Detroit
Michigan 48201, United States
+1 3138889972
www.8degreesplato.com

Opening hours	Open 7 days from 11 am
Credit cards	Accepted
Type	Bar and retail
Recommended for	Local favorite

PLUM MARKET

Recommended by
Christopher Williams

Detroit Metro Airport
McNamara Terminal, Gate A36
Detroit
Michigan 48242, United States
+1 7349423126
www.plummarket.com

Opening hours	Open 7 days from 5 am
Credit cards	Accepted
Type	Restaurant and retail
Recommended for	Unexpected

FITZGERALD'S HOTEL AND RESTAURANT

Recommended by
Nicole Pearce

5033 Front Street
Eagle River
Michigan 49950, United States
+1 9063370666
www.fitzgeralds-mi.com

Opening hours	Mon–Thur from 3 pm, Fri–Sun from 12 pm
Credit cards	Accepted
Type	Restaurant
Recommended for	Unexpected

AXLE BREWING COMPANY LIVERNOIS TAP

Recommended by
Dominic Calzetta

567 Livernois Avenue
Ferndale
Michigan 48220, United States
+1 2482842422
www.axlebrewing.com

Opening hours	Tue–Fri from 4 pm, Sat from 12 pm, Sun from 10 am
Credit cards	Accepted
Type	Beer garden and brewery
Recommended for	Beer garden

"Well-made, approachable beer that keeps style in mind, paired with a well-rounded creative menu. The beer is top-notch classic beer, and the setting is very comfortable."
—Dominic Calzetta

FOUNDERS BREWING COMPANY GRAND RAPIDS

Recommended by
John Stewart,
Jason Zeeff

235 Grandville Avenue Southwest
Grand Rapids
Michigan 49503, United States
+1 6167761195
www.foundersbrewing.com

Opening hours	Mon–Sat from 11 am, Sun from 12 pm
Credit cards	Accepted
Type	Brewery
Recommended for	Local favorite

HOPCAT

Recommended by
Stephen Roginson

25 Ionia Avenue Southwest
Grand Rapids
Michigan 49503, United States
+1 6164514677
www.hopcat.com

Opening hours	Open 7 days from 11 am
Credit cards	Accepted
Type	Bar
Recommended for	Wish I'd opened

"The scale of choice is staggering. Recycling and compost divert over 90 percent of their waste."—Stephen Roginson

MARATHON GRAND RAPIDS

205 28th Street Southwest
Grand Rapids
Michigan 49548, United States
+1 6162411330
www.mymarathonstation.com

Recommended by
Dominic Calzetta

Opening hours	Mon–Fri from 6 am, Sat–Sun from 7 am
Credit cards	Accepted
Type	Retail
Recommended for	Unexpected

"Since this is in Beer City USA you half expect to find beer everywhere. Sure enough, even the gas stations have great craft selections."—Dominic Calzetta

REZERVOIR LOUNGE

Recommended by
John Stewart

1418 Plainfield Avenue Northeast
Grand Rapids
Michigan 49505, United States
+1 6164510010
www.rezlounge.com

Opening hours	Mon–Thur from 4 pm, Fri–Sun from 11 am
Credit cards	Accepted
Type	Bar and restaurant
Recommended for	Local favorite

"A good mix of local Michigan beers with special national offerings."—John Stewart

THE SØVENGÅRD

Recommended by
Stephen Roginson

443 Bridge Street Northwest #1
Grand Rapids
Michigan 49504, United States
+1 6162147207
www.sovengard.com

Opening hours	Tue–Fri from 4 pm, Sat from 12 pm, Sun from 10 am
Credit cards	Accepted
Type	Beer garden
Recommended for	Beer & food

CELLARMEN'S

Recommended by
Dominic Calzetta

24310 John R Road
Hazel Park
Michigan 48030, United States
+1 5864134206
www.cellarmens.com

Opening hours	Wed–Thur from 5 pm, Fri from 4 pm, Sat–Sun from 1 pm
Credit cards	Accepted
Type	Brewery
Recommended for	Local favorite

KOZY LOUNGE

Recommended by
Dominic Calzetta

150 East 10 Mile Road
Hazel Park
Michigan 48030, United States
+1 2485475017
www.kozylounge.com

Opening hours	Mon–Sat from 10 am, Sun from 12 pm
Credit cards	Accepted
Type	Bar
Recommended for	Worth the travel

"The world's greatest dive bar. They welcome everybody."
—Dominic Calzetta

MABEL GRAY

Recommended by
Dominic Calzetta

23825 John R Road
Hazel Park
Michigan 48030, United States
+1 2483984300
www.mabelgraykitchen.com

Opening hours	Tue–Fri from 5 pm, Sat from 4 pm
Credit cards	Accepted
Type	Restaurant
Recommended for	Beer & food

KALAMAZOO BEER EXCHANGE

Recommended by
Neil Callaghan

211 East Water Street
Kalamazoo
Michigan 49007, United States
+1 2695321188
www.kalamazoobeerexchange.com

Opening hours	Mon–Sat from 11 am
Credit cards	Accepted
Type	Pub
Recommended for	Wish I'd opened

"A great beer selection, but the stock market tie-in is really fun. The beers that move quickly go up in price; the ones that aren't selling go down in price."—Neil Callaghan

WATER TOWER SPORTS PUB

Recommended by
Del Vance

7245 Lakeshore Road
Lexington
Michigan 48450, United States
+1 8103593310
www.watertowersportspub.com

Opening hours	Wed–Thur from 4 pm, Fri–Sun from 12 pm
Credit cards	Accepted
Type	Beer garden and pub
Recommended for	Unexpected

"In eastern Michigan, you'll be psyched to find this place They have over 100 great craft beers and pizza."—Del Vance

JOLLY PUMPKIN RESTAURANT & BREWERY TRAVERSE CITY

13512 Peninsula Drive
Traverse City
Michigan 49686, United States
+1 2312234333
www.jollypumpkin.com

Recommended by
Jason Zeeff

Opening hours.................................Mon–Fri from 4 pm,
Sat from 11:30 am, Sun from 10 am
Credit cards...Accepted
Type... Restaurant and brewery
Recommended for...Beer & food

"Situated in one of the most beautiful parts of Michigan, across from the bay, the Jolly Pumpkin Traverse City location is a must-stop for anyone who loves sour beer and great food."—Jason Zeeff

LUPULIN BREWING

570 Humboldt Drive #107
Big Lake
Minnesota 55309, United States
+1 7632639549
www.lupulinbrewing.com

Recommended by
Eric Wentling

Opening hours.........Mon–Thur from 4 pm, Fri from 3 pm,
Sat from 12 pm, Sun from 11 am
Credit cards...Accepted
Type...Brewery
Recommended for...Unexpected

"This is a small local brewery in a distant suburb of the Twin Cities in a nondescript strip mall. I was blown away by the quality of the beers and the wonderful staff."—Eric Wentling

BURRITO UNION

1332 East 4th Street
Duluth
Minnesota 55805, United States
+1 2187284414
www.burritounion.com

Recommended by
Amelia Franklin

Opening hours...Mon–Fri from 11 am,
Sat–Sun from 10 am
Credit cards...Accepted
Type...Restaurant
Recommended for...Beer & food

FITGERS BREWHOUSE

600 East Superior Street
Duluth
Minnesota 55802, United States
+1 2182792739
www.fitgersbrewhouse.com

Recommended by
Jing Chen

Opening hours.................................Open 7 days from 11 am
Credit cards...Accepted
Type...Brewery
Recommended for...Local favorite

BLUE MOOSE BAR & GRILL

507 2nd Street Northwest
East Grand Forks
Minnesota 56721, United States
+1 2187736516
www.thebluemoose.net

Recommended by
Matt Winjum

Opening hours.................................Open 7 days from 11 am
Credit cards...Accepted
Type...Pub
Recommended for...Wish I'd opened

VOYAGEUR BREWING COMPANY

233 West Highway 61
Grand Marais
Minnesota 55604, United States
+1 2183873163
www.voyageurbrewing.com

Recommended by
Susan Prom

Opening hours...........Wed–Thur 3 pm, Fri–Sun from 11 am
Credit cards...Accepted
Type......................................Beer garden, brewery, and pub
Recommended for...Beer garden

INDEED BREWING COMPANY AND TAPROOM

711 Northeast 15th Avenue
Minneapolis
Minnesota 55413, United States
+1 6128435090
www.indeedbrewing.com

Recommended by
Eric Wentling

Opening hours....................................Wed–Thur from 3 pm,
Fri–Sun from 12 pm
Credit cards...Accepted
Type...Brewery
Recommended for...Local favorite

REPUBLIC

221 Cedar Avenue South
Minneapolis
Minnesota 55454, United States
+1 6123386146
www.republicmn.com

Recommended by
Jeff Halvorson

Opening hours................Mon–Fri from 11 am,
Sat–Sun from 10 am
Credit cards................................Accepted
Type..Bar
Recommended for................Local favorite

SURLY BREWING COMPANY

520 Malcom Avenue Southeast
Minneapolis
Minnesota 55414, United States
+1 7639994040
www.surlybrewing.com

Recommended by
Razvan Costache,
Jerry Hauck,
Nicole Pearce,
Eric Wentling

Opening hours................Open 7 days from 11 am
Credit cards................................Accepted
Type................Brewery and beer garden
Recommended for................Beer & food

TARGET FIELD

1 Twins Way
Minneapolis
Minnesota 55403, United States
+1 6126593400
www.mlb.com/twins/ballpark

Recommended by
Zac Triemert

Opening hours................................Variable
Credit cards................................Accepted
Type................Entertainment venue
Recommended for................Unexpected

MINNEAPOLIS–SAINT PAUL INTERNATIONAL AIRPORT

4300 Glumack Drive
Saint Paul
Minnesota 55111, United States
+1 6127265555
www.mspairport.com

Recommended by
Richard Hinkle,
Erin Thompson

Opening hours................................Always open
Credit cards................................Accepted
Type..Retail
Recommended for................Unexpected

THE HAPPY GNOME

498 Selby Avenue
Saint Paul
Minnesota 55102, United States
+1 6512872018
www.thehappygnome.com

Recommended by
Eric Wentling

Opening hours................Mon–Sat from 11 am,
Sun from 10 am
Credit cards................................Accepted
Type................Bar and restaurant
Recommended for................Worth the travel

"All eighty-nine taps are craft beer, and they have a very knowledgeable staff. The locally sourced seasonal cuisine has an emphasis on game meats."—Eric Wentling

STONE ARCH

4300 Glumack Drive
Minneapolis–Saint Paul Airport
Saint Paul
Minnesota 55111, United States
+1 6514609328
www.aeroservicegrp.com

Recommended by
Razvan Costache

Opening hours................Open 7 days from 4:30 am
Credit cards................................Accepted
Type................Bar and restaurant
Recommended for................Unexpected

GASTHAUS BAVARIAN HUNTER

8390 Lofton Avenue North
Stillwater
Minnesota 55082, United States
+1 6514397128
www.gasthausbavarianhunter.com

Recommended by
Trevor Wirtanen

Opening hours................Wed–Fri from 11 am,
Sat–Sun from 12 pm
Credit cards................................Accepted
Type................Beer garden and restaurant
Recommended for................Beer garden

LOLO AMERICAN KITCHEN AND CRAFT BAR STILLWATER

233 Main Street South
Stillwater
Minnesota 55082, United States
+1 6513422461
www.loloamericankitchen.com/stillwater

Recommended by
Trevor Wirtanen

Opening hours............................Open 7 days from 11:30 am
Credit cards...Accepted
Type..Restaurant
Recommended for...Beer & food

"They have phenomenal small plates, a great local beer selection, and amazing cocktails. But the food, man. It's always more fun to drink somewhere that has taste explosion."—Trevor Wirtanen

BIER STATION

120 East Gregory Boulevard
Kansas City
Missouri 64114, United States
+1 8165483870
www.bierstation.com

Recommended by
Chris Meyers

Opening hours.......................................Mon—Sat from 11 am,
Sun from 12 pm
Credit cards...Accepted
Type...Beer garden and bar
Recommended for...Beer garden

BOULEVARD BREWING COMPANY

2501 Southwest Boulevard
Kansas City
Missouri 64108, United States
+1 8164747095
www.boulevard.com

Recommended by
Jared Rudy

Opening hours............................Open 7 days from 8:30 am
Credit cards...Accepted
Type..Brewery
Recommended for...Wish I'd opened

BOULEVARD BREWING TOURS & RECREATION CENTER

2534 Madison Avenue
Kansas City
Missouri 64108, United States
+1 8167017247
www.boulevard.com

Recommended by
Jared Rudy

Opening hours............Sun—Fri from 11 am, Sat from 10 am
Credit cards...Accepted
Type..Pub
Recommended for...Worth the travel

BREWERY EMPERIAL

1829 Oak Street
Kansas City
Missouri 64108, United States
+1 8169459625
www.breweryemperial.com

Recommended by
Chris Meyers

Opening hours.........Mon—Sat from 11 am, Sun from 12 pm
Credit cards...Accepted
Type.................................Beer garden and restaurant
Recommended for...Beer & food

DOUBLE SHIFT BREWING COMPANY

412 East 18th Street
Kansas City
Missouri 64108, United States
+1 8163047028
www.doubleshiftbrewing.com

Recommended by
Rafi Chaudry

Opening hours...Tue—Fri from 4 pm,
Sat—Sun from 12 pm
Credit cards...Accepted
Type..Brewery
Recommended for...Local favorite

TAPCADE

1701 McGee Street #200
Kansas City
Missouri 64108, United States
+1 8164926577
www.tapcadekc.com

Recommended by
Chris Meyers

Opening hours......................................Mon—Thur from 4 pm,
Fri—Sun from 11 am
Credit cards...Accepted
Type..Bar
Recommended for...Wish I'd opened

CRANE BREWING

6515 Railroad Street
Raytown
Missouri 64133, United States
+1 8167434132
www.cranebrewing.com

Recommended by
Chris Meyers

Opening hours......................................Tue–Thur from 4 pm,
Fri from 2 pm, Sat from 12 pm
Credit cards..Accepted
Type...Brewery
Recommended for....................................Worth the travel

IRISH PUB HOUSE

6332 Raytown Road
Raytown
Missouri 64133, United States
+1 9135389080

Recommended by
Chris Meyers

Opening hours..........................Open 7 days from 10 am
Credit cards..Accepted
Type...Pub
Recommended for..Unexpected

BRIDGE TAP HOUSE AND WINE BAR

1004 Locust Street
St. Louis
Missouri 63101, United States
+1 3142418141
www.thebridgestl.com

Recommended by
Stuart Keating

Opening hours...........................Open 7 days from 11 am
Credit cards..Accepted
Type...Bar
Recommended for..Beer & food

BUSCH STADIUM

700 Clark Avenue
St. Louis
Missouri 63102, United States
+1 3143459600
www.mlb.com/cardinals

Recommended by
Marika Josephson

Opening hours...........................Open 7 days from 11 am
Credit cards..Accepted
Type..Entertainment venue
Recommended for..Unexpected

CIVIL LIFE BREWING COMPANY

3714 Holt Avenue
St. Louis
Missouri 63116, United States
www.thecivillife.com

Recommended by
Stuart Keating,
Jonathan Moxey

Opening hours...........................Tue–Thur from 4 pm,
Fri from 12 pm, Sat–Sun from 11 am
Credit cards...Not accepted
Type.................................Beer garden, brewery, and pub
Recommended for......................................Beer garden

"The best traditional malt-forward beer in St. Louis is on draft at this fine establishment."—Stuart Keating

SAINT LOUIS HOP SHOP

2606 Cherokee Street
St. Louis
Missouri 63118, United States
+1 3142614011
www.saintlouishopshop.com

Recommended by
Stuart Keating

Opening hours......................................Tue–Sun from 12 pm
Credit cards..Accepted
Type..Retail
Recommended for....................................Local favorite

THE SIDE PROJECT CELLAR

7373 Marietta Avenue
St. Louis
Missouri 63143, United States
+1 3142245211
www.thesideprojectcellar.com

Recommended by
Paul Kim

Opening hours......................................Tue–Thur from 3 pm,
Fri–Sat from 1 pm
Credit cards..Accepted
Type...Brewery
Recommended for....................................Worth the travel

"A beautiful bar that pours the best beers available. They feature drafts at different temperatures to make sure you're enjoying your beer in ideal conditions. The staff are incredibly knowledgeable and hospitable and are just great human beings. They have a world-class selection of beer, served perfectly and paired with the finest Midwestern hospitality. It feels as if you're at your best friend's house. That is, if your best friend is an amazing brewer named Cory King."—Paul Kim

This very friendly and welcoming bar just happens to pour the delicious and rare beers from Side Project Brewing. Truly one-of-a-kind!

URBAN CHESTNUT BREWING COMPANY

3229 Washington Avenue
St. Louis
Missouri 63103, United States
+1 3142220143
www.urbanchestnut.com

Recommended by
Matt Gelsthorpe

Opening hours	Open 7 days from 11 am
Credit cards	Accepted
Type	Beer garden
Recommended for	Beer garden

"Urban Chestnut takes an understated approach to the beer garden—lots of communal seating, good beer, and perfect beer snacks."—Matt Gelsthorpe

FAIRFIELD OPERA HOUSE BREWERY & GRILL

415 D Street
Fairfield
Nebraska 68938, United States
+1 4027262447
www.fairfieldoperahouse.com

Recommended by
Nathan Hoeft

Opening hours	Tue–Sat from 5 pm
Credit cards	Accepted
Type	Restaurant
Recommended for	Unexpected

"When we moved to Nebraska, we stayed in Glenville, and this place was close by. We stopped in for a meal and found they had local beer on tap. At the time, the beer they had was from Gottberg Brewpub, but now the owner has started brewing his own beer."—Nathan Hoeft

FIRST STREET BREWING COMPANY

119 North Saint Joseph Avenue
Hastings
Nebraska 68901, United States
+1 4028342400
www.firststreetbrewing.com

Recommended by
Nathan Hoeft

Opening hours	Thur–Fri from 4 pm, Sat from 12 pm, Sun from 2 pm
Credit cards	Accepted
Type	Brewery
Recommended for	Wish I'd opened

SOZO AMERICAN CUISINE

110 South 2nd Avenue
Kearney
Nebraska 68847, United States
+1 3084553444
www.sozokearney.com

Recommended by
Nathan Hoeft

Opening hours	Mon–Fri from 6:30 am, Sat–Sun from 7 am
Credit cards	Accepted
Type	Restaurant
Recommended for	Beer & food

BRICKWAY BREWERY & DISTILLERY

1116 Jackson Street
Omaha
Nebraska 68102, United States
+1 4029332613
www.drinkbrickway.com

Recommended by
Zac Triemert

Opening hours	Mon–Thur from 2 pm, Fri–Sun from 11 am
Credit cards	Accepted
Type	Brewery
Recommended for	Local favorite

LOCAL BEER, PATIO AND KITCHEN DOWNTOWN

902 Dodge Street
Omaha
Nebraska 68102, United States
+1 4023154301
www.localbeer.co

Recommended by
Zac Triemert

Opening hours	Open 7 days from 11 am
Credit cards	Accepted
Type	Bar and restaurant
Recommended for	Wish I'd opened

"The complete focus is on local Nebraska beer: Of the sixty-plus taps, over 90 percent are beers brewed in the state."—Zac Triemert

RHOMBUS GUYS

312 Kittson Avenue
Grand Forks
North Dakota 58201, United States
+1 7017877317
www.rhombuspizza.com

Opening hours.................................Open 7 days from 11 am
Credit cards...Accepted
Type...Pub
Recommended for..Local favorite

"Built in the late 1800s as the largest opera house from
Minneapolis to Seattle, Rhombus Guys is the coolest
taproom ever."—Matt Winjum

RHOMBUS GUYS BREWING COMPANY

116 South 3rd Street
Grand Forks
North Dakota 58201, United States
+1 7017570598
www.rhombusguysbrewing.com

Recommended by
Matt Winjum

Opening hours.................................Open 7 days from 11 am
Credit cards...Accepted
Type..Brewery
Recommended for..................................Worth the travel

JACKIE O'S

22–24 West Union Street
Athens
Ohio 45701, United States
+1 7405929686
www.jackieos.com

Recommended by
Brad Clark

Opening hours.................................Open 7 days from 11 am
Credit cards...Accepted
Type...Brewery and pub
Recommended for..Local favorite

GREAT AMERICAN BALL PARK

100 Joe Nuxhall Way
Cincinnati
Ohio 45202, United States
+1 5137657000
www.mlb.com/reds

Recommended by
Jesse Scheitler

Opening hours...Variable
Credit cards...Accepted
Type...Bar
Recommended for....................................Unexpected

RHINEGEIST BREWERY

1910 Elm Street
Cincinnati
Ohio 45202, United States
+1 5133811367
www.rhinegeist.com

Recommended by
Erich Phillips

Opening hours.................................Mon–Fri from 3 pm,
Sat–Sun from 12 pm
Credit cards...Accepted
Type..Brewery
Recommended for..................................Worth the travel

THE GREENHOUSE TAVERN

2038 East 4th Street
Cleveland
Ohio 44115, United States
+1 2164430511
www.thegreenhousetavern.com

Recommended by
Brad Clark

Opening hours.................................Open 7 days from 11 am
Credit cards...Accepted
Type...Restaurant
Recommended for..Beer & food

TREMONT TAPHOUSE

2572 Scranton Road
Cleveland
Ohio 44113, United States
+1 2162944451
www.tremonttaphouse.com

Recommended by
Daniel Kravitz

Opening hours.................................Mon–Fri from 4 pm,
Sat from 11 am, Sun from 10 am
Credit cards...Accepted
Type...Bar and restaurant
Recommended for..................................Worth the travel

SEVENTH SON BREWING COMPANY

1101 North 4th Street
Columbus
Ohio 43201, United States
+1 6144212337
www.seventhsonbrewing.com

Recommended by
Collin Castore

Opening hours.................................Tue–Thur from 3:30 pm,
Fri–Sun from 11 am
Credit cards...Accepted
Type..Brewery
Recommended for..Local favorite

HARMAR TAVERN
205 Maple Street
Marietta
Ohio 45750, United States
+1 7403738727

Recommended by
Brad Clark

Opening hours	Mon–Thur from 10 am,
	Fri–Sat from 7 am, Sun from 8 am
Credit cards	Accepted but not Amex
Type	Bar
Recommended for	Unexpected

"Operating since 1905!"—Brad Clark

AJ'S ORE CAR SALOON
537 Mount Rushmore Road
Custer
South Dakota 57730, United States
+1 6056733051

Recommended by
Brian Boyer

Opening hours	Wed–Sun from 3 pm
Credit cards	Not accepted
Type	Retail
Recommended for	Wish I'd opened

"This is the hangout to drink a cheap beer and catch a NASCAR race."—Brian Boyer

BUGLIN' BULL RESTAURANT AND SPORTS BAR
511 Mount Rushmore Road
Custer
South Dakota 57730, United States
+1 6056734477
www.buglinbull.com

Recommended by
Brian Boyer

Opening hours	Wed–Sun from 11 am
Credit cards	Accepted
Type	Bar and restaurant
Recommended for	Worth the travel

INDEPENDENT ALE HOUSE
625 Saint Joseph Street
Rapid City
South Dakota 57701, United States
+1 6057489492
www.independentalehouse.com

Recommended by
Jesse Scheitler

Opening hours	Sun–Thur from 3 pm,
	Fri–Sat from 11 am
Credit cards	Accepted
Type	Pub
Recommended for	Worth the travel

"There are forty craft beers, with constantly rotating taps. Killer pizza and awesome taps."—Jesse Scheitler

LOST CABIN BEER CO.
1401 West Omaha Street #3
Rapid City
South Dakota 57701, United States
+1 6051785678
www.lostcabin.beer

Recommended by
Jesse Scheitler

Opening hours	Tue–Thur from 3 pm,
	Fri–Sun from 12 pm
Credit cards	Accepted
Type	Brewery and pub
Recommended for	Local favorite

MOONSHINE GULCH SALOON
22635 North Rochford Road
Rochford
South Dakota 57745, United States
+1 6055842743

Recommended by
Brian Boyer

Opening hours	Variable
Credit cards	Not accepted
Type	Bar
Recommended for	Unexpected

"The place is wallpapered with thousands of business cards from visitors from all over the world. Betsy is the owner, operator, and bartender. When she's not cooking your burger, she's nursing an abandoned fawn back to health."—Brian Boyer

MONKS HOUSE OF ALE REPUTE AND GANDY DANCER BREW WORKS
420 East 8th Street
Sioux Falls
South Dakota 57103, United States
+1 6053382328
www.monkshouseofalerepute.com

Recommended by
Jerry Hauck

Opening hours	Sun–Thur from 3 pm,
	Fri–Sat from 1 pm
Credit cards	Accepted
Type	Bar and brewery
Recommended for	Worth the travel

"The first craft-beer bar in South Dakota. They have forty taps that change frequently, as well as 125 bottles, excellent pizza, and sandwiches."—Jerry Hauck

MILWAUKEE BURGER COMPANY

2620 East Clairemont Avenue
Eau Claire
Wisconsin 54701, United States
+1 7158346503
www.milwaukeeburgercompany.com

Recommended by
Kyle Hurst

Opening hours..................................Open 7 days from 11 am
Credit cards..Accepted
Type..Restaurant
Recommended for..Beer & food

"They have the best burgers anywhere—ever. They also have cheese curds and beer."—Kyle Hurst

THE EXPLORIUM BREWPUB

5300 South 76th Street #1450A
Greendale
Wisconsin 53129, United States
+1 4144231365
www.exploriumbrew.com

Recommended by
Barry Elwonger

Opening hours..................................Open 7 days from 11 am
Credit cards..Accepted
Type...Restaurant and brewery
Recommended for..Beer & food

"A great family-run business with a cool atmosphere and solid beer."—Barry Elwonger

FOX HOLLOW GOLF COURSE

North 3287 County Trunk OA
La Crosse
Wisconsin 54601, United States
+1 6087864635
www.foxhollowgolfandbanquets.com

Recommended by
Clay Keel

Opening hours....................................Open 7 days from 8 am
Credit cards..Accepted
Type..Bar
Recommended for..Unexpected

"They offer dozens of excellent beers on tap and dozens more bottled beers from the best craft and historical breweries around the world. Food offerings include some local dishes from Wisconsin, like fried pickles and fried Wisconsin cheese."—Clay Keel

TOM'S BURNED DOWN CAFE

234 Middle Road
La Pointe
Wisconsin 54850, United States
+1 7157476100

Recommended by
Trevor Wirtanen

Opening hours..................................Open 7 days from 11 am
Credit cards..Not accepted
Type..Bar
Recommended for..Unexpected

BRASSERIE V

1923 Monroe Street
Madison
Wisconsin 53711, United States
+1 6082558500
www.brasseriev.com

Recommended by
John Stewart

Opening hours.....................................Mon–Sat from 11 am
Credit cards..Accepted
Type..Bar and restaurant
Recommended for..Unexpected

CASK & ALE

212 State Street
Madison
Wisconsin 53703, United States
+1 6084679450
www.caskandalemadison.com

Recommended by
Josh Ruffin

Opening hours.......................................Mon–Fri from 4 pm,
Sat from 2 pm, Sun from 5 pm
Credit cards..Accepted
Type..Bar
Recommended for...Local favorite

MERCHANT MADISON

121 South Pinckney Street
Madison
Wisconsin 53703, United States
+1 6082599799
www.merchantmadison.com

Recommended by
Isaac Showaki

Opening hours..Mon–Fri from 3 pm,
Sat–Sun from 9 am
Credit cards..Accepted
Type...Restaurant and retail
Recommended for...Local favorite

BURNHEARTS

Recommended by
Brian Sauer

2599 South Logan Avenue
Milwaukee
Wisconsin 53207, United States
+1 4142940490
www.burnheartsbar.com

Opening hours	Mon–Fri from 3 pm, Sat–Sun from 12 pm
Credit cards	Accepted
Type	Bar
Recommended for	Worth the travel

DRAFT AND VESSEL

Recommended by
James Larson

4417 North Oakland Avenue
Milwaukee
Wisconsin 53211, United States
+1 4145335599
www.draftandvessel.com

Opening hours	Mon–Thur from 3 pm, Fri from 1 pm, Sat–Sun from 11 am
Credit cards	Accepted
Type	Bar
Recommended for	Wish I'd opened

GOODKIND

Recommended by
James Larson

2457 South Wentworth Avenue
Milwaukee
Wisconsin 53207, United States
+1 4147634706
www.goodkindbayview.com

Opening hours	Mon–Sat from 4 pm, Sun from 10 am
Credit cards	Accepted
Type	Restaurant
Recommended for	Beer & food

HUBBARD PARK LODGE

Recommended by
James Larson

3565 North Morris Boulevard
Milwaukee
Wisconsin 53211, United States
+1 4143324207
www.hubbardlodge.com

Opening hours	Mon–Fri from 3 pm, Sat–Sun from 12 pm
Credit cards	Accepted
Type	Beer garden
Recommended for	Beer garden

"Right on the river, this beer garden is a hidden gem."
—James Larson

LAKEFRONT BREWERY

Recommended by
John Holl

1872 North Commerce Street
Milwaukee
Wisconsin 53212, United States
+1 4143728800
www.lakefrontbrewery.com

Opening hours	Mon–Fri from 11 am, Sat from 9 am, Sun from 10 am
Credit cards	Accepted
Type	Beer garden and brewery
Recommended for	Beer garden

"This brewery has one of the best public tours in the industry and a vast beer hall that models the German tradition and embraces the charm and cuisine of the Midwest. On Friday it hosts the weekly fish fry (cod or perch) paired with a heaping pile of fresh-cut fries. Or opt for the cheese curds—the best in the city. Pair it with a live polka band, pints of the brewery's amber lager, and the general infectious spirit of camaraderie and celebration, and you'll have a night to remember."—John Holl

MILLER PARK

Recommended by
James Larson

1 Brewers Way
Milwaukee
Wisconsin 53214, United States
+1 4149024452
www.millerpark.com

Opening hours	Variable
Credit cards	Accepted
Type	Entertainment venue
Recommended for	Unexpected

PALM TAVERN

Recommended by
James Larson,
Rob Zellermayer

2989 South Kinnickinnic Avenue
Milwaukee
Wisconsin 53207, United States
+1 4147440393
www.palm-tavern.com

Opening hours	Mon–Sat from 5 pm, Sun from 7 pm
Credit cards	Accepted
Type	Beer garden and pub
Recommended for	Local favorite

"Some of the best draft beer on tap in the city. A very small bar with a dark and cozy atmosphere. It's a good place for brewers to hide out and drink awesome beer."
—James Larson

ÜBER TAP ROOM & CHEESE BAR

1048 North Old World Third Street
Milwaukee
Wisconsin 53203, United States
+1 4147552424
www.ubertaproom.com

Recommended by
Colby Cox

Opening hours..................................Open 7 days from 11 am
Credit cards..Accepted
Type...Bar
Recommended for...Beer & food

"They offer an amazing selection of craft beers and grilled cheese. They play with cheese as only Wisconsinites can. Try the five-cheese, sun-dried tomato, and garlic grilled cheese with one of more than forty local beers on tap."
—Colby Cox

NEW GLARUS BREWING COMPANY

2400 State Highway 69
New Glarus
Wisconsin 53574, United States
+1 6085275850
www.newglarusbrewing.com

Recommended by
Jeff Halvorson

Opening hours.......................................Mon–Sat from 10 am,
Sun from 12 pm
Credit cards..Accepted
Type...Beer garden and brewery
Recommended for...Beer garden

"This is a destination beer garden in the United States. What New Glarus Brewing has done is remarkable. It's classic, expansive, and inviting, and it's worth staying in town just to get the whole Swiss experience in Wisconsin."
—Jeff Halvorson

OLIPHANT BREWING

350 Main Street #2
Somerset
Wisconsin 54025, United States
+1 6517056070
www.oliphantbrewing.com

Recommended by
Trevor Wirtanen

Opening hours.......................................Wed–Thur from 4 pm,
Fri from 2 pm, Sat–Sun from 12 pm
Credit cards..Accepted
Type..Brewery and pub
Recommended for...Local favorite

"A small taproom with rad art and a massive VHS tape collection."—Trevor Wirtanen

OCTOPI BREWING

1131 Uniek Drive
Waunakee
Wisconsin 53597, United States
+1 6086204705
www.octopibrewing.com

Recommended by
Isaac Showaki

Opening hours...Tue–Fri from 4 pm,
Sat from 1 pm, Sun from 12 pm
Credit cards..Accepted
Type.....................................Beer garden, bar, and brewery
Recommended for...Beer garden

"Their chicken biscuit sandwich with maple reduction is outstanding. Rotating beers pair incredibly well with the food."—Isaac Showaki

"PROBABLY RESPONSIBLE FOR SINGLE-HANDEDLY CREATING THE CRAFT-BEER BAR SCENE IN CHICAGO."

KELSEY ROTH P.352

CHICAGO

"DEATH METAL, GOURMET BURGERS, AND A KILLER BEER SELECTION."

JULIE RHODES P.350

"GREAT FOOD AND BUILT-IN BEER PAIRINGS. EVERYTHING IS PERFECTION."

MOLLY GUNN P.353

"A MICHELIN-STARRED RESTAURANT WITH AN UNBELIEVABLE DRINK PROGRAM."

JARED WELCH P.351

"THE BEER IS IMPECCABLY CURATED."

PAUL KIM P.353

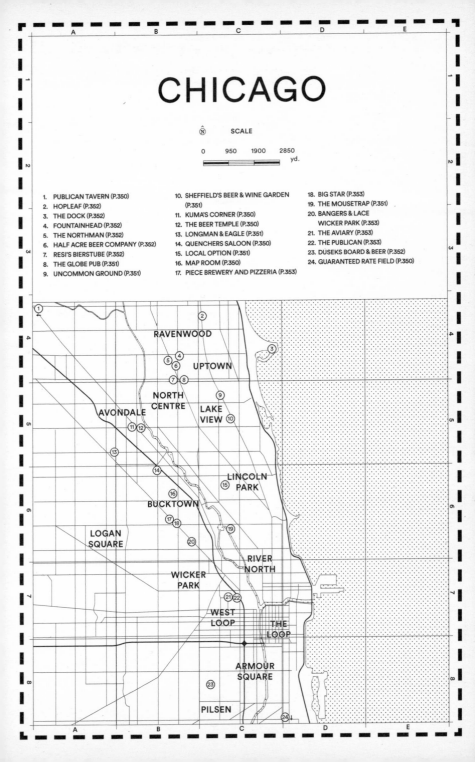

CHICAGO

$\hat{N}$ SCALE

0   950   1900   2850
                              yd.

1. PUBLICAN TAVERN (P.350)
2. HOPLEAF (P.352)
3. THE DOCK (P.352)
4. FOUNTAINHEAD (P.352)
5. THE NORTHMAN (P.352)
6. HALF ACRE BEER COMPANY (P.352)
7. RESI'S BIERSTUBE (P.352)
8. THE GLOBE PUB (P.351)
9. UNCOMMON GROUND (P.351)

10. SHEFFIELD'S BEER & WINE GARDEN (P.351)
11. KUMA'S CORNER (P.350)
12. THE BEER TEMPLE (P.350)
13. LONGMAN & EAGLE (P.351)
14. QUENCHERS SALOON (P.350)
15. LOCAL OPTION (P.351)
16. MAP ROOM (P.350)
17. PIECE BREWERY AND PIZZERIA (P.353)

18. BIG STAR (P.353)
19. THE MOUSETRAP (P.351)
20. BANGERS & LACE WICKER PARK (P.353)
21. THE AVIARY (P.353)
22. THE PUBLICAN (P.353)
23. DUSEKS BOARD & BEER (P.352)
24. GUARANTEED RATE FIELD (P.350)

RAVENWOOD

UPTOWN

NORTH CENTRE

AVONDALE

LAKE VIEW

LINCOLN PARK

BUCKTOWN

LOGAN SQUARE

WICKER PARK

RIVER NORTH

WEST LOOP

THE LOOP

ARMOUR SQUARE

PILSEN

PUBLICAN TAVERN
Recommended by
Tim Adams,
Patrick Rue

Chicago O'Hare International Airport
Terminal 3
Chicago
Illinois 60666, United States
+1 8776727467

Opening hours	Open 7 days from 5:30 am
Credit cards	Accepted
Type	Bar and restaurant
Recommended for	Unexpected

"Orval in the airport? Yes."—Tim Adams

GUARANTEED RATE FIELD
Recommended by
Steve Kamp,
Paul Kim

333 West 35th Street
Armour Square
Chicago
Illinois 60616, United States
+1 3126745875
www.theguaranteedratefield.com

Opening hours	Open 7 days from 5:30 pm
Credit cards	Accepted
Type	Entertainment venue
Recommended for	Unexpected

"You can enjoy seventy-five local craft beers while watching White Sox baseball."—Paul Kim

THE BEER TEMPLE
Recommended by
Marika Josephson

3173 North Elston Avenue
Avondale
Chicago
Illinois 60618, United States
+1 7737540907
www.craftbeertemple.com

Opening hours	Open 7 days from 11 am
Credit cards	Accepted
Type	Bar and retail
Recommended for	Wish I'd opened

KUMA'S CORNER
Recommended by
Julie Rhodes

2900 West Belmont Avenue
Avondale
Chicago
Illinois 60618, United States
+1 7736048769
www.kumascorner.com

Opening hours	Mon–Sat from 11:30 am, Sun from 12 pm
Credit cards	Accepted
Type	Pub
Recommended for	Wish I'd opened

"They have death metal, gourmet burgers, and a killer beer selection."—Julie Rhodes

MAP ROOM
Recommended by
Kevin Blodger,
Brad Clark,
Erin Lowder

1949 North Hoyne Avenue
Bucktown
Chicago
Illinois 60647, United States
+1 7732527636
www.maproom.com

Opening hours	Mon–Fri from 6:30 am, Sat from 7:30 am, Sun from 11 am
Credit cards	Accepted
Type	Bar
Recommended for	Worth the travel

QUENCHERS SALOON
Recommended by
Steve Kamp

2401 North Western Avenue
Bucktown
Chicago
Illinois 60647, United States
+1 7732769730
www.quenchers.com

Opening hours	Mon–Fri from 12 pm, Sat–Sun from 11 am
Credit cards	Not accepted
Type	Bar
Recommended for	Worth the travel

SHEFFIELD'S BEER & WINE GARDEN

3258 North Sheffield Avenue
Lake View
Chicago
Illinois 60657, United States
+1 7732814989
www.sheffieldschicago.com

Recommended by
Ben Bradley,
Steve Kamp

Opening hours	Mon–Fri from 11 am, Sat–Sun from 10 am
Credit cards	Accepted
Type	Beer garden
Recommended for	Beer garden

"An epic beer selection."—Ben Bradley

UNCOMMON GROUND

3800 North Clark Street
Lake View
Chicago
Illinois 60613, United States
+1 7739293680
www.uncommonground.com

Recommended by
Martin Coad

Opening hours	Mon–Fri from 11 am, Sat–Sun from 9 am
Credit cards	Accepted
Type	Restaurant
Recommended for	Local favorite

LOCAL OPTION

1102 West Webster Avenue
Lincoln Park
Chicago
Illinois 60614, United States
+1 7733482008
www.localoptionbier.com

Recommended by
Aidy Fenwick,
Jerry Gnagy,
Jason Zeeff

Opening hours	Open 7 days from 12 pm
Credit cards	Accepted
Type	Pub
Recommended for	Wish I'd opened

"An awesome beer selection in a unique space, with metal music playing and a rocking staff with great service."
—Aidy Fenwick

If you love heavy metal *and* craft beer, there are few better places to enjoy both passions. It feels like a dive bar, in the best way possible.

THE MOUSETRAP

1460 North Kingsbury Street
Lincoln Park
Chicago
Illinois 60642, United States
+1 3129292916
www.offcolorbrewing.com

Recommended by
Paul Kim

Opening hours	Open 7 days from 11 am
Credit cards	Accepted
Type	Brewery
Recommended for	Local favorite

"Home to Off Color's wild and funky fermentation brewery. They feature a vast variety of Off Color, though the taproom also pours guest drafts from brewery friends from across the country and the globe."—Paul Kim

LONGMAN & EAGLE

2657 North Kedzie Avenue
Logan Square
Chicago
Illinois 60647, United States
+1 7732767110
www.longmanandeagle.com

Recommended by
Jared Welch

Opening hours	Open 7 days from 9 am
Credit cards	Accepted
Type	Restaurant and pub
Recommended for	Beer & food

"A Michelin-starred restaurant with an unbelievable drink program. There is also a bar area hidden at the back available for anyone to walk in."—Jared Welch

THE GLOBE PUB

1934 West Irving Park Road
North Center
Chicago
Illinois 60613, United States
+1 7738713757
www.theglobepub.com

Recommended by
Rob Zellermayer

Opening hours	Mon–Fri from 11 am, Sat–Sun from 7 am
Credit cards	Accepted
Type	Pub
Recommended for	Unexpected

"I went to watch World Cup soccer. I ended up with pints of world-class beer."—Rob Zellermayer

HALF ACRE BEER COMPANY

4257 North Lincoln Avenue
North Center
Chicago
Illinois 60618, United States
+1 7737548488
www.halfacrebeer.com

Recommended by
Peter Crowley

Opening hours..Tue–Sun from 11 am
Credit cards...Accepted
Type...Bar and brewery
Recommended for..Local favorite

THE NORTHMAN

4337 North Lincoln Avenue
North Center
Chicago
Illinois 60618, United States
+1 7739352255
www.thenorthman.com

Recommended by
Dominic Calzetta

Opening hours..Mon–Fri from 4 pm,
                                                          Sat–Sun from 11:30 am
Credit cards...Accepted
Type...Pub
Recommended for..Wish I'd opened

"This is the first all-cider bar in Chicago. The selection
of cider is more diverse than anywhere else."
—Dominic Calzetta

RESI'S BIERSTUBE

2034 West Irving Park Road
North Center
Chicago
Illinois 60618, United States
+1 7734721749

Recommended by
Martin Coad,
Ethan Cox

Opening hours..Open 7 days from 2 pm
Credit cards...Accepted
Type...Beer garden
Recommended for..Beer garden

DUSEKS BOARD & BEER

1227 West 18th Street
Pilsen
Chicago
Illinois 60608, United States
+1 3125263851
www.dusekschicago.com

Recommended by
Martin Coad

Opening hours..Mon–Fri from 11 am,
                                                          Sat–Sun from 9 am
Credit cards...Accepted
Type...Restaurant
Recommended for..Beer & food

FOUNTAINHEAD

1970 West Montrose Avenue
Ravenswood
Chicago
Illinois 60613, United States
+1 7736978204
www.fountainheadchicago.com

Recommended by
Shawn Decker

Opening hours..Mon–Fri from 4 pm,
                                                          Sat–Sun from 11 am
Credit cards...Accepted
Type...Bar
Recommended for..Local favorite

HOPLEAF

5148 North Clark Street
Ravenswood
Chicago
Illinois 60640,
United States
+1 7733349851
www.hopleafbar.com

Recommended by
Collin Castore, Martin
Coad, Peter Crowley, Mark
Drutman, Clay Keel, Paul Kim,
Stephen Roginson, Kelsey
Roth, Kraig Torres, Jeremiah
Tracy, Chris Vandergrift,
Rob Zellermayer

Opening hours..Open 7 days from 12 pm
Credit cards...Accepted
Type...Bar
Recommended for..Wish I'd opened

"Probably responsible for single-handedly creating the
craft-beer bar scene in Chicago."—Kelsey Roth

"This bar led the way in Chicago for craft beer. Michael
Roper took a seedy dive bar and transformed it into a beer
and food mecca. Every brewery in Chicago wants to be
on their list—it means you've made it to the big leagues.
They have an expansive beer selection, a knowledgeable
staff, and a scratch kitchen that puts out phenomenal
food."—Paul Kim

THE DOCK
200 West Montrose Harbor Drive
Uptown
Chicago
Illinois 60640, United States
+1 7737048435
www.thedockatmontrosebeach.com

Recommended by
Martin Coad

Opening hours.................................Mon–Fri from 11 am,
Sat–Sun from 10 am (summer only)
Credit cards...Accepted
Type..Bar
Recommended for.................................Unexpected

"Seasonally on the lake, this bar transports you to the Caribbean, and they serve delicious local craft beer."
—Martin Coad

THE AVIARY
955 West Fulton Market
West Loop
Chicago
Illinois 60607, United States
+1 3122260868
www.theaviary.com

Recommended by
Jeppe Jarnit-Bjergsø

Opening hours.....................Open 7 days from 5 pm
Credit cards...Accepted
Type..Bar
Recommended for.........................Worth the travel

A world-renowned cocktail bar with an amazing beer list, with many specialty beers that you can get only at the Aviary.

THE PUBLICAN
837 West Fulton Market
West Loop
Chicago
Illinois 60607, United States
+1 3127339555
www.thepublicanrestaurant.com

Recommended by
Neil Callaghan,
Eloi Deit, Molly Gunn, Marika
Josephson, Paul Kim,
Ben Love, Jonathan
Moxey, Sebastian Sauer,
John Stewart

Opening hours.................................Mon–Fri from 3:30 pm,
Sat from 10 am, Sun from 9 am
Credit cards...Accepted
Type...Restaurant
Recommended for.........................Beer & food

"It's one of my favorite places to go when I'm feeling gluttonous—ham sampler, pork rinds, all sorts of cured pork, oysters, and plenty of great beer to wash it all down."—Jonathan Moxey

"Great food and built-in beer pairings. Everything is perfection."—Molly Gunn

"The beer is impeccably curated."—Paul Kim

BANGERS & LACE WICKER PARK
1670 West Division Street
Wicker Park
Chicago
Illinois 60622, United States
+1 7732526499
www.bangersandlacebar.com

Recommended by
Keegan Konkoski Kramer

Opening hours.................................Mon–Fri from 2 pm,
Sat–Sun from 11 am
Credit cards...Accepted
Type...Restaurant
Recommended for.........................Wish I'd opened

"Great look, feel, vibe, and food and drink selection."
—Keegan Konkoski Kramer

BIG STAR
1531 North Damen Avenue
Wicker Park
Chicago
Illinois 60622, United States
+1 7732354039
www.bigstarchicago.com

Recommended by
Kelsey Roth

Opening hours.....................Open 7 days from 11:30 am
Credit cards...Accepted
Type.......................................Beer garden and bar
Recommended for.........................Beer garden

"A cool vibe with a great outdoor patio. You can't beat their quality craft beer and delicious tacos. They have a good selection of Midwestern and national beers."
—Kelsey Roth

PIECE BREWERY AND PIZZERIA
1927 West North Avenue
Wicker Park
Chicago
Illinois 60622, United States
+1 7737724422
www.piecechicago.com

Recommended by
Kevin Blodger,
Martin Coad,
Isaac Showaki

Opening hours.....................Open 7 days from 11 am
Credit cards...Accepted
Type.......................................Restaurant and brewery
Recommended for.........................Wish I'd opened

"EXCEPTIONAL."

KIM MERCADO P.357

"UNBELIEVABLE FOOD AND WORLD-CLASS BEER TO MATCH. UNLIKE ANYTHING ELSE IN ITS CLASS."

LAWRENCE GEORGE P.361

USA NORTHEAST

"AN IMPECCABLE BEER PROGRAM. THE BOTTLE SHOP IS A WORLD-CLASS PROVISIONS STORE THAT BLOWS MY MIND."

WILL GROVES P.370

"ONE OF THE BEST BEER CELLARS IN THE COUNTRY, REALLY GOOD FOOD, A COMFORTABLE AND RELAXED ATMOSPHERE, AND A CHARASMATIC AND PASSIONATE FAMILY."

MIKE AMIDEI P.356

"IF I COULD, I WOULD GO OUT OF MY WAY EVERY DAY TO BE HERE. EVERYTHING FROM THE FOOD TO THE BEER TO THE PEOPLE IS EXCEPTIONAL."

SUZANNE HAYS P.361

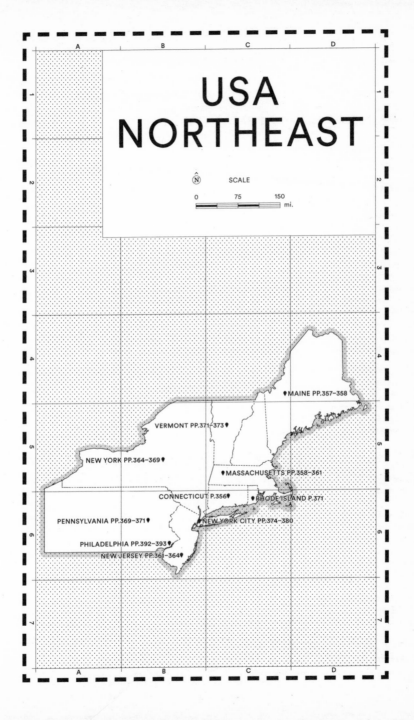

USA
NORTHEAST

(N) SCALE

0   75   150
mi.

MAINE PP.357–358

VERMONT PP.371–373

NEW YORK PP.364–369

MASSACHUSETTS PP.358–361

CONNECTICUT P.356

RHODE ISLAND P.371

PENNSYLVANIA PP.369–371

NEW YORK CITY PP.374–380

PHILADELPHIA PP.392–393

NEW JERSEY PP.361–364

THE SPIGOT

468 Prospect Avenue
Hartford
Connecticut 06105, United States
+1 8602367663

Recommended by
Joe Ploof

Opening hours................................Sun–Thur from 6 pm,
Fri–Sat from 4 pm
Credit cards...Not accepted
Type..Bar
Recommended for.................................Local favorite

EAST SIDE RESTAURANT

131 Dwight Street
New Britain
Connecticut 06051, United States
+1 8602231188
www.eastsiderestaurant.com

Recommended by
Em Sauter

Opening hours.........................Tue–Sat from 11:30 am,
Sun from 12 pm
Credit cards..Accepted
Type.......................................Beer garden and restaurant
Recommended for.................................Beer garden

CASK REPUBLIC

179 Crown Street
New Haven
Connecticut 06510, United States
+1 4752388335
www.caskrepublic.com

Recommended by
Anastasia Howell

Opening hours...........................Open 7 days from 11:30 am
Credit cards..Accepted
Type...Beer garden and pub
Recommended for.................................Beer garden

"The woodwork inside is breathtaking."
—Anastasia Howell

J TIMOTHY'S TAVERNE

143 New Britain Avenue
Plainville
Connecticut 06062, United States
+1 8607476813
www.jtimothys.com

Recommended by
Em Sauter,
Mark Sigman

Opening hours...........................Open 7 days from 11:30 am
Credit cards..Accepted
Type...Bar and restaurant
Recommended for.................................Local favorite

"An excellent selection of hard-to-get local beers and, their
beer manager, Nikki, is awesome. They also have the best
wings in America."—Em Sauter

MCKAYS PUBLIC HOUSE

231 Main Street
Bar Harbor
Maine 04609, United States
+1 2072882002
www.mckayspublichouse.com

Recommended by
Marci Mullen

Opening hours.............................Wed–Sat from 5 pm
Credit cards..Accepted
Type...Beer garden and pub
Recommended for.................................Beer garden

FRONT STREET PUB

37 Front Street
Belfast
Maine 04915, United States
+1 2073388900
www.frontstreetpub.com

Recommended by
Marci Mullen

Opening hours...........................Open 7 days from 11 am
Credit cards..Accepted
Type..Pub
Recommended for.................................Local favorite

EBENEZER'S PUB

44 Allen Road
Lovell
Maine 04051, United States
+1 2079253200
www.ebenezerspub.net

Recommended by
Mike Amidei,
Tod Mott,
Yves Panneels,
John Rowley

Opening hours.............................Fri–Sun from 11:30 am
Credit cards..Accepted
Type...Restaurant and pub
Recommended for.................................Worth the travel

"One of the best beer cellars in the country, really good
food, a comfortable and relaxed atmosphere, and a
charismatic and passionate family."—Mike Amidei

This legendary spot in the middle of rural Maine is one of a
kind. It definitely has one of the best bottle lists this side of the
Atlantic. It's a hike to get here, but it's worth the trip!

MONHEGAN BREWING COMPANY

1 Boody Lane
Monhegan
Maine 04852, United States
+1 2075960011
www.monheganbrewing.com

Recommended by
Shawn Decker

Opening hours...Variable
Credit cards..Accepted
Type...Brewery
Recommended for.....................................Unexpected

"A brewery on a tiny island ten miles off the coast of Maine. There is barely electricity out there, so it's pretty remarkable that someone put a brewery there. It's a very good place to hang after a day of hiking."—Shawn Decker

OXBOW BREWING COMPANY

274 Jones Woods Road
Newcastle
Maine 04553, United States
+1 2073155962
www.oxbowbeer.com

Recommended by
Brad Clark,
Shawn Decker,
Kim Mercado

Opening hours..........................Thur–Sun from 12 pm
Credit cards..Accepted
Type......................................Beer garden and brewery
Recommended for.............................Wish I'd opened

"Exceptional. It's deep in the woods away from anything, the air is fresh and crisp, and at night you can see the stars."—Kim Mercado

EVENTIDE OYSTER COMPANY

86 Middle Street
Portland
Maine 04101, United States
+1 2077748538
www.eventideoysterco.com

Recommended by
Tim Adams,
Phil Cassella

Opening hours..............................Open 7 days from 11 am
Credit cards..Accepted
Type...Bar and restaurant
Recommended for.......................................Beer & food

"Eventide is where I had my most memorable beer and food pairing. Their New England Clam Bake with lobster tails, potatoes, salt pork, mussels, and steamers on a frigid March day paired with Allagash Tripel is an experience I crave when the weather gets colder."—Phil Cassella

NOVARE RES BIER CAFÉ

4 Canal Plaza
Portland
Maine 04101, United States
+1 2077612437
www.novareresbiercafe.com

Recommended by
Tim Adams, Todd Beal,
Joshua M. Bernstein,
Phil Cassella, Will Fisher,
Patrick Lively, Tod Mott,
Mark Sigman, Jeffrey
Stuffings, Dave Witham

Opening hours.......................Mon–Thur from 4 pm,
Fri from 3 pm, Sat–Sun from 12 pm
Credit cards..Accepted
Type...Bar
Recommended for............................Wish I'd opened

"I wish I'd opened this bar, mainly so I could hang out with Shahin Khojastehzad all the time. Incredible, thoughtfully curated beer list in a cool, cavernous setting. Very knowledgeable staff and house-made fernet if you get tired of beer."—Jeffrey Stuffings

"Head down a nearly hidden side street in Portland's historic Old Port and you'll find Novare, where world-class Belgian beers are matched to the best of Maine beer."
—Joshua M. Bernstein

"They deserve considerable credit for the vibrant beer scene that Portland enjoys today."—Tim Adams

Novare Res simply does things right. They have a solid list of draft beers and an extensive bottle menu of hard-to-find beers. The staff are very knowledgeable, and they make finding the perfect beer easy. In a town of great beer destinations, this place stands out.

OXBOW BLENDING & BOTTLING

49 Washington Avenue
Portland
Maine 04101, United States
+1 2073500025
www.oxbowbeer.com

Recommended by
Will Fisher

Opening hours..............................Open 7 days from 12 pm
Credit cards..Accepted
Type...Brewery
Recommended for...................................Local favorite

PORTLAND LOBSTER COMPANY

180 Commercial Street
Portland
Maine 04101, United States
+1 2077752112
www.portlandlobstercompany.com

Recommended by
Josh Pfriem

Opening hours................................Open 7 days from 11 am
Credit cards...Accepted
Type...Restaurant
Recommended for..Unexpected

RAMEN SUZUKIYA

229 Congress Street
Portland
Maine 04101, United States
+1 2077610905
www.ramensuzukiya.com

Recommended by
Bryan Brushmiller

Opening hours................................Tue–Thur from 5 pm,
Fri–Sat from 12 pm
Credit cards...Accepted
Type...Restaurant
Recommended for..Beer & food

"Small and intimate. They have ramen!"—Bryan Brushmiller

SLAB

25 Preble Street Extension
Portland
Maine 04101, United States
+1 2072453088
www.slabportland.com

Recommended by
Matt DeLuca,
Will Fisher

Opening hours...........Mon–Sat from 11 am, Sun from 3 pm
Credit cards...Accepted
Type...Bar and restaurant
Recommended for.................................Wish I'd opened

DEEP ELLUM

477 Cambridge Street
Allston
Massachusetts 02134, United States
+1 6177872337
www.deepellum-boston.com

Recommended by
Scott Drake

Opening hours................................Mon–Fri from 11 am,
Sat–Sun from 10 am
Credit cards...Accepted
Type...Pub
Recommended for..............................Worth the travel

BREWER'S FORK

7 Moulton Street
Boston
Massachusetts 02129, United States
+1 6173375703
www.brewersfork.com

Recommended by
Suzanne Hays

Opening hours................................Mon–Fri from 2:30 pm,
Sat–Sun from 5 pm
Credit cards...Accepted
Type...............................Beer garden and restaurant
Recommended for.....................................Local favorite

"This place feels like home. The vibe is casual, unpretentious, and inviting. There's a diversity in the list that makes it appealing, and the wood-fired pizzas can't be beat."
—Suzanne Hays

THE LOWER DEPTHS

476 Commonwealth Avenue
Boston
Massachusetts 02215, United States
+1 6172666662
www.thelowerdepths.com

Recommended by
Scott Drake

Opening hours................................Open 7 days from 11:30 am
Credit cards...Not accepted
Type..Bar
Recommended for.................................Wish I'd opened

ROW 34

383 Congress Street
Boston
Massachusetts 02210
United States
+1 6175535900
www.row34.com

Recommended by
Ryan Bedford,
Andrew Cooper,
André Ek, Ben Maeso,
Kelsey Roth, Magnus
Svensson, Karl Volstad

Opening hours................................Mon–Sat from 11:30 am,
Sun from 10:30 am
Credit cards...Accepted
Type...Restaurant
Recommended for..Beer & food

"This astonishing seafood bar in Boston has it all: superfresh seafood and shellfish, and tremendous sliders and tacos. It's all paired beautifully with the best craft beer from the area and beyond."—Magnus Svensson

TRILLIUM BREWING COMPANY

369 Congress Street
Boston
Massachusetts 02110, United States
+1 6174538745
www.trilliumbrewing.com

Recommended by
Aidy Fenwick,
Matthew
Steinberg,
Jared Welch

Opening hours...Mon–Sat from 11 am,
Sun from 12 pm
Credit cards...Accepted
Type...Beer garden and brewery
Recommended for...Beer garden

A visit to Boston is not complete without a stop at Trillium.
Flawless beers, great people, and several very cool locations
to visit. If their Wild Ales are around when you visit, buy your
maximum allotment.

THE LOBSTER TRAP RESTAURANT

290 Shore Road
Bourne
Massachusetts 02532, United States
+1 5087597600
www.lobstertrap.net

Recommended by
Kraig Torres

Opening hours...................................Open 7 days from 11 am
Credit cards...Accepted
Type...Restaurant
Recommended for..Unexpected

"A touristy seafood place with great beer on tap, including
Lord Hobo and Trillium."—Kraig Torres

THE PUBLICK HOUSE

1648 Beacon Street
Brookline
Massachusetts 02445, United States
+1 6172772880
www.thepublickhousebeerbar.com

Recommended by
Suzanne Hays,
Matthew Steinberg

Opening hours...Mon–Fri from 5 pm,
Sat–Sun from 12 pm
Credit cards.............................Accepted but not Amex
Type...Pub
Recommended for...Worth the travel

"With nearly twenty years under their belt, the Publick
House has been a standout in the Boston beer scene from
day one. Proudly servicing an array of local and international
beers, they focus on hops and Belgians."
—Matthew Steinberg

"This bar is a dream come true for me. There's nothing I love
more than German and Belgian beer. The Publick House has
been a beer lover's staple for years. The selection of
European beers cannot be beat."—Suzanne Hays

CHARLIE'S KITCHEN

10 Eliot Street
Cambridge
Massachusetts 02138, United States
+1 6174929646
www.charlieskitchen.com

Recommended by
Scott Drake

Opening hours...................................Open 7 days from 11 am
Credit cards...Accepted
Type...Beer garden and pub
Recommended for...Beer garden

"A railcar-style interior and a beautiful sunken beer garden
in a back alley, all in the heart of Harvard Square. At night,
wooden trellises are lit with hanging lights."—Scott Drake

MAMALEH'S DELICATESSEN

1 Kendall Square
15 Hampshire Street
Cambridge
Massachusetts 02139, United States
+1 6179583354
www.mamalehs.com

Recommended by
Scott Drake

Opening hours.....................................Open 7 days from 8 am
Credit cards...Accepted
Type...Restaurant
Recommended for...Beer & food

THE MUDDY CHARLES PUB

Walker Memorial
142 Memorial Drive
Cambridge
Massachusetts 02139, United States
+1 6172532086
www.muddy.mit.edu

Recommended by
Roberto Alves da Fonseca

Opening hours........Mon–Thurs from 2 pm, Fri from 12 pm
Credit cards...Not accepted
Type...Pub
Recommended for..Unexpected

TREE HOUSE BREWING COMPANY

129 Sturbridge Road
Charlton
Massachusetts 01507, United States
+1 4135232367
www.treehousebrew.com

Opening hours	Wed from 12 pm, Thur–Fri from 2 pm, Sat from 11 am
Credit cards	Accepted
Type	Brewery
Recommended for	Wish I'd opened

JACK'S ABBY CRAFT LAGERS

100 Clinton Street
Framingham
Massachusetts 01702, United States
+1 5088720900
www.jacksabby.com

Recommended by
Andris Rasiņš

Opening hours	Tue–Sat from 11:30 am, Sun from 10 am
Credit cards	Accepted
Type	Restaurant and brewery
Recommended for	Beer & food

SEYMOUR THE PUB

5 Bank Row Street
Greenfield
Massachusetts 01301, United States
+1 4133258555

Recommended by
Matthew Steinberg

Opening hours	Mon–Sat from 5 pm, Sun from 1 pm
Credit cards	Accepted but not Amex
Type	Pub
Recommended for	Local favorite

"With light-colored wood and hand-built tables and chairs, a shelf of books, a handmade chess board, small jars of snacks, and a truly beer-passionate crew, this place is so special. Extras like choice lighting, music from actual records, and most importantly, an undeniable humility and humble feeling make this place a favorite of mine."
—Matthew Steinberg

THE QUARTERS

8 Railroad Street
Hadley
Massachusetts 01035, United States
+1 4134294263
www.hadleyquarters.com

Recommended by
Kelsey Roth

Opening hours	Mon from 5 pm, Tue–Fri from 12 pm, Sat from 10 am, Sun from 11 am
Credit cards	Accepted
Type	Bar
Recommended for	Unexpected

LUKE'S BEER AND WINE CONVENIENCE STORE

1478 North Main Street
Palmer
Massachusetts 01069, United States
+1 4132834765

Recommended by
Matthew Steinberg

Opening hours	Mon–Sat from 8:30 am, Sun from 10 am
Credit cards	Accepted
Type	Retail
Recommended for	Unexpected

"This is kind of a hole in the wall that's just a regular convenience store from the outside."—Matthew Steinberg

NOTCH BREWERY & TAP ROOM

283 Derby Street
Salem
Massachusetts 01970, United States
+1 9782389060
www.notchbrewing.com

Recommended by
Suzanne Hays

Opening hours	Wed–Thur from 4 pm, Fri–Sun from 12 pm
Credit cards	Accepted
Type	Beer garden and brewery
Recommended for	Beer garden

OLDE MAGOUN'S SALOON

518 Medford Street
Somerville
Massachusetts 02145, United States
+1 6177762600
www.magounssaloon.com

Recommended by
Kelsey Roth

Opening hours	Mon–Fri from 11:30 am, Sat–Sun from 10 am
Credit cards	Accepted
Type	Bar
Recommended for	Local favorite

"September and October are amazing, with ten authentic German Oktoberfest beers on draft."—Kelsey Roth

THIRSTY SCHOLAR PUB

Recommended by
Scott Drake

70 Beacon Street
Somerville
Massachusetts 02143, United States
+1 6174972294
www.thethirstyscholarpub.com

Opening hours......................................Mon–Thur from 5 pm,
Fri–Sun from 11 am
Credit cards...Accepted
Type..Pub
Recommended for...Unexpected

FIVE EYED FOX

Recommended by
Lawrence George

37 3rd Street
Turners Falls
Massachusetts 01376, United States
+1 4138635654
www.fiveeyedfox.com

Opening hours...............................Wed–Fri from 11:30 am,
Sat–Sun from 10 am
Credit cards...Accepted
Type..Bar
Recommended for.......................................Local favorite

"The perfect cozy room for dinner, brunch, or afternoon beers. Always welcoming, always comfortable, and free of pretense. The passion and personality of the owners are evident in the decor, food menu, and beer list. Every detail was meticulously planned."—Lawrence George

ARMSBY ABBEY

Recommended by
Lawrence George,
Suzanne Hays,
Brian Oakley,
Patrick Rue,
Matthew Steinberg,
Dave Witham

144 North Main Street
Worcester
Massachusetts 01608, United States
+1 5087951012
www.armsbyabbey.com

Opening hours...............................Mon–Fri from 11:30 am,
Sat–Sun from 10 am
Credit cards...Accepted
Type...Bar and restaurant
Recommended for.....................................Beer & food

"This place really showed me how a tomato is the perfect pairing with an IPA."—Brian Oakley

"Unbelievable food and world-class beer to match. Unlike anything else in its class."—Lawrence George

"They put as much attention into their beer selection as they do their food, and both are amazing."—Patrick Rue

"If I could, I would go out of my way every day to be here. Everything from the food to the beer to the people is exceptional."—Suzanne Hays

Armsby Abbey in Worcester is a great bar. They feature a very well-curated selection of drafts—typically including multiple Hill Farmstead offerings—and bottles, great food, great bread, and an unpretentious and very helpful staff.

THE DIVE BAR

Recommended by
Scott Drake,
Matthew Steinberg

34 Green Street
Worcester
Massachusetts 01604, United States
+1 5087525802
www.thedivebarworcester.com

Opening hours....................................Open 7 days from 6 pm
Credit cards...Not accepted
Type..Bar
Recommended for.......................................Local favorite

ASBURY FESTHALLE & BIERGARTEN

527 Lake Avenue
Asbury Park
New Jersey 7712, United States
+1 7329978767
www.asburybiergarten.com

Recommended by
Augie Carton,
Jason Carty

Opening hours....................................Mon–Thur from 4 pm,
Fri–Sun from 12 pm
Credit cards...Accepted
Type...Beer garden and restaurant
Recommended for.................................Beer garden

THE ASBURY HOTEL

Recommended by
John Merklin

210 5th Avenue
Asbury Park
New Jersey 07712, United States
+1 7327747100
www.theasburyhotel.com

Opening hours..May–October
Credit cards...Accepted
Type...Beer garden
Recommended for.................................Beer garden

BRICKWALL TAVERN & DINING ROOM

Recommended by
John Merklin

522 Cookman Avenue
Asbury Park
New Jersey 07712, United States
+1 7327741264
www.brickwalltavern.com

Opening hours	Open 7 days from 11 am
Credit cards	Accepted
Type	Pub
Recommended for	Local favorite

THE CLOVERLEAF TAVERN

395 Bloomfield Avenue
Caldwell

Recommended by
Blake Crawford

New Jersey 07006, United States
+1 9732269812
www.cloverleaftavern.com

Opening hours	Mon–Sat from 11 am, Sun from 10 am
Credit cards	Accepted
Type	Pub
Recommended for	Local favorite

"Cloverleaf focuses on New Jersey beers and consistently has the best beer in the state."—Blake Crawford

CAPITAL CRAFT

171 U.S. Highway 22
Green Brook

Recommended by
John Merklin,
Bob Olson

New Jersey 08812, United States
+1 7329685700
www.capitalcraftnj.com

Opening hours	Open 7 days from 11:30 am
Credit cards	Accepted
Type	Beer garden and restaurant
Recommended for	Beer & food

BLEND BAR & BISTRO

911 Highway 33
Hamilton

Recommended by
John Merklin

New Jersey 08690, United States
+1 6092458887
www.blendbar.com

Opening hours	Open 7 days from 12 pm
Credit cards	Accepted
Type	Bar
Recommended for	Worth the travel

PILSENER HAUS & BIERGARTEN

1422 Grand Street
Hoboken

Recommended by
Bob Olson

New Jersey 07030, United States
+1 2016835465
www.pilsenerhaus.com

Opening hours	Mon–Thur from 5 pm, Fri from 4 pm, Sat–Sun from 12 pm
Credit cards	Accepted
Type	Beer garden and restaurant
Recommended for	Beer garden

BARCADE JERSEY CITY

163 Newark Avenue
Jersey City

Recommended by
Tim Besecker,
Bob Olson

New Jersey 07302, United States
+1 2013324555
www.barcadejerseycity.com

Opening hours	Open 7 days from 12 pm
Credit cards	Accepted
Type	Bar
Recommended for	Wish I'd opened

"Awesome mix of local beers from the surrounding states with old-school video games. Good vibe, tasty bites to eat, and knowledgeable staff."—Bob Olson

"Video games, video games, video games. Drinking good beer and playing old-school video games is the perfect combo."—Tim Besecker

WÜRSTBAR

516 Jersey Avenue
Jersey City

Recommended by
John Holl

New Jersey 07302, United States
+1 2014798396
www.wurstbarjc.com

Opening hours	Open 7 days from 12 pm
Credit cards	Accepted
Type	Bar
Recommended for	Local favorite

"Housemade sausages with both traditional and inventive toppings fully complement the craft-beer selection that leans heavily on wild, sour, and cider."—John Holl

JAY'S ELBOW ROOM

2806 Route 73
Maple Shade
New Jersey 08052, United States
+1 8562353687
www.jayselbowroom.com

Recommended by
Jason Carty,
Dustin Jeffers

Opening hours	Mon–Sat from 10 am, Sun from 11 am
Credit cards	Accepted
Type	Bar and restaurant
Recommended for	Unexpected

"From 99-cent daily lunch specials to the closing time of 3 am, this place is a hole-in-the-wall paradise for craft-beer connoisseurs. This place is a gem. Fresh beer from New Jersey brewing staples like Kane, Carton, Cape May, and Tonewood are always available."—Jason Carty

BOYLE'S TAVERN

2 Willow Avenue
Monmouth Beach
New Jersey 07750, United States

Recommended by
Augie Carton

Opening hours	Open 7 days from 3 pm
Type	Bar
Recommended for	Local favorite

JOCKEY HOLLOW BAR & KITCHEN

110 South Street
Morristown
New Jersey 07960, United States
+1 9736443180
www.jockeyhollowbarandkitchen.com

Recommended by
Blake Crawford

Opening hours	Tue–Fri from 12 pm, Sat from 4 pm, Sun from 11 am
Credit cards	Accepted
Type	Restaurant
Recommended for	Beer & food

THE LOCAL EATERY AND PUB

64 High Street
Mount Holly
New Jersey 08060, United States
+1 6097848684
www.thelocal-nj.com

Recommended by
Jason Carty

Opening hours	Tue–Sat from 11:30 am, Sun from 12 pm
Credit cards	Accepted
Type	Pub
Recommended for	Wish I'd opened

"As the name states, everything is local—the beer, spirits, wine, and menu. The chalkboard highlights fourteen New Jersey beers."—Jason Carty

NEWARK LIBERTY INTERNATIONAL AIRPORT

Terminal C, 3 Brewster Road
Newark
New Jersey 07114, United States
+1 9739616000
www.panynj.gov/airports/newark-liberty

Recommended by
Augie Carton,
Katherine Kyle,
Kevin Raub

Opening hours	Always open
Credit cards	Accepted
Type	Retail
Recommended for	Unexpected

PRUDENTIAL CENTER

25 Lafayette Street
Newark
New Jersey 07102, United States
+1 9737576500
www.prucenter.com

Recommended by
Bob Olson

Opening hours	Variable
Credit cards	Accepted
Type	Entertainment venue
Recommended for	Unexpected

AMENDMENT 21

521 Arnold Avenue
Point Pleasant Beach
New Jersey 08742, United States
+1 7322959619
www.amendmenttwentyone.com

Recommended by
John Merklin,
Bob Olson

Opening hours	Mon–Sat from 11:30 am, Sun from 12 pm
Credit cards	Accepted
Type	Bar
Recommended for	Wish I'd opened

THE DOG & CASK

55 State Route 17 South
Rochelle Park
New Jersey 07662, United States
+1 2018455101
www.thedogandcask.com

Recommended by
Bob Olson

Opening hours	Mon–Sat from 11:30 am, Sun from 11 am
Credit cards	Accepted
Type	Restaurant and pub
Recommended for	Local favorite

THE STIRLING HOTEL

227 Main Avenue
Stirling
New Jersey 07980, United States
+1 9086476919
www.thestirlinghotel.com

Recommended by
Tim Besecker,
Cindy DeRama

Opening hours	Open 7 days from 11:30 am
Credit cards	Accepted
Type	Bar
Recommended for	Local favorite

DEBONAIR MUSIC HALL

1409 Queen Anne Road
Teaneck
New Jersey 07666, United States
+1 2018330011
www.debonairmusichall.showare.com

Recommended by
Blake Crawford

Opening hours	Variable
Credit cards	Accepted
Type	Bar and entertainment venue
Recommended for	Unexpected

"A live music venue with a focus on local beers. Good shows and great beer, so what's not to love about that?"
—Blake Crawford

New York City, see pages 374–389

THE CITY BEER HALL

42 Howard Street
Albany
New York 12207, United States
+1 5184492337
www.thecitybeerhall.com

Recommended by
Christian Weber

Opening hours	Open 7 days from 11 am
Credit cards	Accepted
Type	Beer garden and restaurant
Recommended for	Beer & food

"The chef and restaurant/bar manager are extremely beer and food savvy. The menu and beer list are always unique and changing."—Christian Weber

WOLFF'S BIERGARTEN ALBANY

895 Broadway
Albany
New York 12207, United States
+1 5184272461
www.wolffsbiergarten.com

Recommended by
Christian Weber

Opening hours	Mon–Fri from 11 am, Sat–Sun from 9 am
Credit cards	Not accepted
Type	Beer garden
Recommended for	Beer garden

BANK SQUARE COFFEEHOUSE

129 Main Street
Beacon
New York 12508, United States
+1 8454407165
www.banksquarecoffeehouse.com

Recommended by
Adam Watson

Opening hours	Mon–Fri from 6 am, Sat–Sun from 7 am
Credit cards	Accepted
Type	Bar
Recommended for	Unexpected

BRUSHLAND EATING HOUSE

1927 County Highway 6
Bovina Center
New York 13740, United States
+1 6078324861
www.brushlandeatinghouse.com

Recommended by
Kim Mercado

Opening hours	Wed–Fri from 5:30 pm, Sat–Sun from 5:30 pm
Credit cards	Accepted
Type	Restaurant
Recommended for	Unexpected

"In a town where the population is only 500, you walk into this dimly lit restaurant and find a list with Stillwater, Evil Twin, and other known craft beers. The food was amazing and the service even better. I try to make it out there every other month or so because it's that good."—Kim Mercado

KEYBANK CENTER

1 Seymour H. Knox III Plaza
Buffalo
New York 14203, United States
+1 7168554100
www.keybankcenter.com

Recommended by
Ethan Cox

Opening hours	Variable
Credit cards	Accepted
Type	Entertainment venue
Recommended for	Unexpected

MR. GOODBAR

1110 Elmwood Avenue
Buffalo
New York 14222, United States
+1 7168824000
www.mrgoodbarbuffalo.com

Recommended by
Ethan Cox,
Clay Keel

Opening hours	Open 7 days from 12 pm
Credit cards	Accepted
Type	Bar
Recommended for	Local favorite

RESURGENCE BREWING COMPANY

1250 Niagara Street
Buffalo
New York 14213, United States
+1 7163819868
www.resurgencebrewing.com

Recommended by
Anna Ellis

Opening hours	Tue–Fri from 4 pm, Sat–Sun from 12 pm
Credit cards	Accepted
Type	Brewery
Recommended for	Local favorite

CONSTELLATION BRANDS MARVIN SANDS PERFORMING ARTS CENTER

3355 Marvin Sands Drive
Canandaigua
New York 14424, United States
+1 5853944400
www.cmacevents.com

Recommended by
Alex Butler

Opening hours	Variable
Credit cards	Accepted
Type	Entertainment venue
Recommended for	Unexpected

YOUNG LION BREWING COMPANY TAPROOM

26 Lakeshore Drive
Canandaigua
New York 14424, United States
+1 5854126065
www.younglionbrewing.com

Recommended by
Alex Butler

Opening hours	Wed–Thur from 2 pm, Fri–Sun from 12 pm
Credit cards	Accepted
Type	Bar and brewery
Recommended for	Wish I'd opened

BREWERY OMMEGANG

656 County Highway 33
Cooperstown
New York 13326, United States
+1 6075441800
www.ommegang.com

Recommended by
Richard Ammerman

Opening hours	Open 7 days from 12 pm
Credit cards	Accepted
Type	Beer garden, brewery, and restaurant
Recommended for	Beer garden

GABLE INN

14 Port Watson Street
Cortland
New York 13045, United States
+1 6077565453

Recommended by
Mike Amidei

Opening hours	Mon–Sat from 6 pm
Credit cards	Not accepted
Type	Bar
Recommended for	Unexpected

"A great local drinking establishment. They have exactly the beer you want, served in a clean environment, by a bartender who understands service."—Mike Amidei

THE COUNTRY CORNER
Recommended by
Zoe Williams

270 Main Street
East Setauket
New York 11733, United States
+1 6317512800
www.countrycornerli.com

Opening hours...................................Open 7 days from 11 am
Credit cards...Accepted
Type..Bar and restaurant
Recommended for...Unexpected

"A little hole-in-the-wall spot with amazing beer and food."
—Zoe Williams

PORTS CAFE
Recommended by
Alex Butler

4432 West Lake Road
Geneva
New York 14456, United States
+1 3157892020
www.portscafe.com

Opening hours................................Tue–Sat from 5 pm
Credit cards...Accepted
Type..Restaurant
Recommended for...Beer & food

SUAREZ FAMILY BREWERY
Recommended by
Luke Pestl

2278 U.S. 9
Hudson
New York 12534, United States
+1 5185376464
www.suarezfamilybrewery.com

Opening hours............Wed from 3 pm, Fri–Sun from 1 pm
Credit cards...Accepted
Type..Brewery
Recommended for...Wish I'd opened

"It is perfect. A quiet area overlooking farm fields with
world-class beers."—Luke Pestl

ITHACA BEER COMPANY
Recommended by
Tony Forder

122 Ithaca Beer Drive
Ithaca
New York 14850, United States
+1 6072730766
www.ithacabeer.com

Opening hours..Wed–Sun from 12 pm
Credit cards...Accepted
Type...Beer garden
Recommended for...Beer garden

LIQUIDS AND SOLIDS AT THE HANDLEBAR
Recommended by
Dylan Badger

6115 Sentinel Road
Lake Placid
New York 12946, United States
+1 5188975012
www.liquidsandsolids.com

Opening hours...Tue–Sun from 4 pm
Credit cards...Accepted
Type..Restaurant
Recommended for.......................................Local favorite

DECICCO & SONS
Recommended by
James Tai

2141 Palmer Avenue
Larchmont
New York 10538, United States
+1 9148734447
www.deciccoandsons.com

Opening hours..............................Open 7 days from 7:30 am
Credit cards...Accepted
Type...Retail
Recommended for...Unexpected

AMBULANCE BREW HOUSE

202 Main Street
Nanuet
New York 10954, United States
+1 8455017100
www.ambulancebrewhouse.com

Recommended by
Blake Crawford

Opening hours..............................Open 7 days from 11:30 am
Credit cards...Accepted
Type...Beer garden
Recommended for...Beer garden

"Walk through the tasting room to the big secret—an
excellent outdoor beer garden tucked behind the main bar.
Such a great surprise and always filled with friendly people."
—Blake Crawford

DEFIANT BREWING COMPANY

6 East Dexter Plaza
Pearl River
New York 10965, United States
+1 8459208602
www.defiantbrewing.com

Recommended by
Tony Forder

Opening hours........Mon–Fri from 2 pm, Sat–Sun from 12 pm
Credit cards...Not accepted
Type..Brewery
Recommended for.......................................Local favorite

SHELL STATION

443 State Route 3
Plattsburgh
New York 12901, United States
+1 5185630043

Recommended by
Tony Forder

Opening hours..Always open
Credit cards..Accepted
Type..Retail
Recommended for.....................................Unexpected

C'EST CHEESE

216B Main Street
Port Jefferson
New York 11777, United States
+1 6314034944
www.cestcheesepj.com

Recommended by
Chris Maestro,
Zoe Williams

Opening hours.........Mon–Sat from 11 am, Sun from 12 pm
Credit cards..Accepted
Type..Restaurant
Recommended for.....................................Unexpected

TOMMY'S PLACE

109 Main Street
Port Jefferson
New York 11777, United States
+1 6314738778
www.tommysplace.com

Recommended by
Zoe Williams

Opening hours............................Open 7 days from 11:30 am
Credit cards..Accepted
Type..Beer garden and pub
Recommended for.................................Beer garden

PLAN BEE FARM BREWERY

115 Underhill Road
Poughkeepsie
New York 12603, United States
+1 8452429562
www.planbeefarmbrewery.com

Recommended by
Marika Josephson

Opening hours..........................Fri–Sun from 12 pm
Credit cards..Accepted
Type..Beer garden
Recommended for.................................Beer garden

SCHATZI'S PUB & BIER GARDEN

202 Main Street
Poughkeepsie
New York 12601, United States
+1 8454541179
www.iloveschatzis.com/schatzispk

Recommended by
Adam Watson

Opening hours...........................Mon–Fri from 3 pm,
Sat from 12 pm, Sun from 11 am
Credit cards..Accepted
Type..Beer garden and pub
Recommended for.................................Local favorite

GENESEE BREW HOUSE

25 Cataract Street
Rochester
New York 14605, United States
+1 5852639200
www.geneseebeer.com

Recommended by
Anna Ellis

Opening hours.......................Open 7 days from 11 am
Credit cards..Accepted
Type..Brewery
Recommended for.................................Beer & food

"Amazing burgers. The whole brewery is set up almost like
a museum."—Anna Ellis

LUX LOUNGE

666 South Avenue
Rochester
New York 14620, United States
+1 5852329030
www.lux666.com

Recommended by
Johnnie Compton

Opening hours.........................Mon–Thur from 5 pm,
Fri from 4:30 pm, Sat–Sun from 4 pm
Credit cards..Accepted
Type..Beer garden and bar
Recommended for.................................Beer & food

TAP & MALLET

381 Gregory Street
Rochester
New York 14620, United States
+1 5854730503
www.tapandmallet.com

Recommended by
Alex Butler,
Ben Maeso

Opening hours.........................Mon–Sat from 11:30 am,
Sun from 12 pm
Credit cards..Accepted
Type..Pub
Recommended for.................................Worth the travel

ARTISANAL BREW WORKS

41 Geyser Road
Saratoga Springs
New York 12866, United States
+1 5185942337
www.artisanalbrewworks.com

Recommended by
Daniel Kravitz

Opening hours.................................Tue–Thur from 3:30 pm,
Fri from 3 pm, Sat–Sun from 12 pm
Credit cards...Accepted
Type...............................Beer garden and brewery
Recommended for...Beer garden

HENRY STREET TAPROOM

86 Henry Street
Saratoga Springs
New York 12866, United States
+1 5188868938
www.henrystreettaproom.com

Recommended by
Christian Weber

Opening hours.................................Mon–Fri from 4 pm,
Sat from 12 pm, Sun from 10 am
Credit cards...Accepted
Type...Pub
Recommended for.......................................Local favorite

CANDLELIGHT INN

519 Central Park Avenue
Scarsdale
New York 10583, United States
+1 9144729706

Recommended by
Tracy Teach

Opening hours.........................Open 7 days from 11 am
Credit cards..Not accepted
Type..Restaurant
Recommended for..Beer & food

"The most amazing wings, fries, and bar menu. Ever."
—Tracy Teach

MOHAWK TAPROOM & GRILL

153 Mohawk Avenue
Scotia
New York 12302, United States
+1 5183578005
www.mohawktaproom.com

Recommended by
Phil Cassella

Opening hours.................................Tue–Sat from 11 am,
Sun from 12 pm
Credit cards...Accepted
Type..Restaurant
Recommended for.......................................Local favorite

"Owners Mike and Stephanie Martini wow you with what really matters: really good pub food and an incredibly curated draft list. Mike often goes out of his way to bring back kegs, bottles, and cans directly from breweries that we typically don't see in upstate New York. Mohawk has the best wings in the Capitol Region."—Phil Cassella

TAP & BARREL

558 Smithtown Bypass
Smithtown
New York 11787, United States
+1 6317805474
www.tapandbarrelny.com

Recommended by
Zoe Williams

Opening hours.................................Mon–Fri from 4 pm,
Sat–Sun from 1 pm
Credit cards...Accepted
Type...Pub
Recommended for......................................Worth the travel

NOW & LATER

620 Ulster Street
Syracuse
New York 13204, United States
+1 3154220606
www.nowandlaterbar.com

Recommended by
Ben Maeso

Opening hours...........................Open 7 days from 1 pm
Credit cards...Accepted
Type..Bar and retail
Recommended for.......................................Local favorite

WOLFF'S BIERGARTEN SYRACUSE

106 Montgomery Street
Syracuse
New York 13210, United States
+1 3152997789
www.wolffsbiergarten.com/syracuse-new-york

Recommended by
Anna Ellis

Opening hours.................................Mon–Fri from 11 am,
Sat–Sun from 9 am
Credit cards..Not accepted
Type..................................Beer garden and bar
Recommended for...Beer garden

THE RUCK

104 3rd Street
Troy
New York 12180, United States
+1 5182731872
www.getrucked.com

Recommended by
John Holl,
Daniel Kravitz

Opening hours.............................Mon–Tue from 4 pm,
Wed–Sun from 11 am
Credit cards...Accepted
Type...Bar
Recommended for................................Local favorite

FOREST AND MAIN BREWING CO.

61 North Main Street
Ambler
Pennsylvania 19002, United States
+1 2155421776
www.forestandmain.com

Recommended by
Mike Amidei

Opening hours..........................Tue–Fri from 4 pm,
Sat–Sun from 11:30 am
Credit cards...Accepted
Type..Beer garden and brewery
Recommended for.................................Beer garden

"On a late-summer trip to Tired Hands, we also stopped at
Forest and Main, and I was very impressed. I've always liked
their beers, and the brewery is very quaint and full of charm.
It's in a converted home, in the middle of a suburban
neighborhood. They have a fair amount of outdoor seating
on a porch and several picnic tables in the front yard. It's a
great place to while away the time on a late-summer day."
—Mike Amidei

TIRED HANDS BREW CAFÉ

16 Ardmore Avenue
Ardmore
Pennsylvania 19003, United States
+1 6108967621
www.tiredhands.com/cafe

Recommended by
Chelsie Markel

Opening hours............................Tue–Fri from 4 pm,
Sat–Sun from 12 pm
Credit cards...Accepted
Type...Brewery
Recommended for................................Local favorite

"It's art in a glass. The beer here never disappoints, and the
food is addictive."—Chelsie Markel

TIRED HANDS FERMENTARIA

35 Cricket Terrace
Ardmore
Pennsylvania 19003, United States
+1 4844132983
www.tiredhands.com/fermentaria

Recommended by
Jillian Antonelli,
Yuko Odashima,
Thomas Palmer,
PJ Sullivan

Opening hours...............................Open 7 days from 12 pm
Credit cards...Accepted
Type...Brewery
Recommended for............................Worth the travel

"Tired Hands Fermentaria has some of the best beers on the
East Coast. I like how they incorporate wild foraged
ingredients and go out on a limb with new ideas and
recipes."—Jillian Antonelli

BONN PLACE BREWING

310 Taylor Street
Bethlehem
Pennsylvania 18015, United States
+1 6104196660
www.bonnbrewing.com

Recommended by
Matty Eck

Opening hours..........Wed–Thur from 4 pm, Fri from 3 pm,
Sat–Sun from 12 pm
Credit cards...Accepted
Type..Brewery and pub
Recommended for................................Local favorite

HIDDEN RIVER BREWING COMPANY

1808 West Schuylkill Road
Douglassville
Pennsylvania 19518, United States
+1 4848801167
www.hiddenriverbrewing.com

Recommended by
Jillian Antonelli

Opening hours.........................Thur–Fri from 4 pm,
Sat–Sun from 2 pm
Credit cards...Accepted
Type...Brewery
Recommended for................................Local favorite

"Set in a 300-year-old historic lodge furnished with antiques
and creepy portraits, HRB's small-batch brewery tap list and
vibe are always eclectic. I had a smoked butternut squash
and habanero brown ale, a golden beet Saison, and a
blackberry raspberry dark Saison—all while enjoying live
music from a traditional South American folk music trio."
—Jillian Antonelli

POP'S KITCHEN AND TAPROOM

480 Industrial Drive
Easton
Pennsylvania 18042, United States
+1 6105591962
www.popskitchen.biz

Recommended by
John Holl

Opening hours	Mon–Fri from 5 am, Sat from 6 am, Sun from 7 am
Credit cards	Accepted
Type	Restaurant
Recommended for	Unexpected

SABATINI'S PIZZA

1925 Wyoming Avenue
Exeter
Pennsylvania 18643, United States
+1 5706932270
www.sabatinis.com

Recommended by
Chelsie Markel

Opening hours	Open 7 days from 10 am
Credit cards	Not accepted
Type	Bar
Recommended for	Wish I'd opened

PAXTANG GRILL

3323 Derry Street
Harrisburg
Pennsylvania 17111, United States
+1 7175642738
www.paxtanggrill.com

Recommended by
Jesse Prall

Opening hours	Mon–Sat from 11 am
Credit cards	Accepted
Type	Bar
Recommended for	Unexpected

TRÖEGS INDEPENDENT BREWING

200 East Hershey Park Drive
Hershey
Pennsylvania 17033, United States
+1 7175341297
www.troegs.com

Recommended by
Joseph Finkenbinder,
Chelsie Markel,
Jesse Prall

Opening hours	Open 7 days from 11 am
Credit cards	Accepted
Type	Beer garden and brewery
Recommended for	Beer garden

HUNGER-N-THIRST

920 Landis Avenue
Lancaster
Pennsylvania 17603, United States
+1 7172083808
www.hungernthirst.com

Recommended by
Johnnie Compton,
Chelsie Markel

Opening hours	Tue–Sun from 11 am
Credit cards	Accepted
Type	Retail and pub
Recommended for	Beer & food

"Andrew runs an impeccable beer program. The bottle shop is a world-class provisions store that blows my mind. The chef is on another level."—Johnnie Compton

MASTRACCHIO'S RESTAURANT & LOUNGE

344 Juniata Parkway East
Newport
Pennsylvania 17074, United States
+1 7175677511
www.mastracchiosrestaurantandlounge.com

Recommended by
Johnnie Compton

Opening hours	Mon–Sat from 10 am
Credit cards	Accepted but not Amex
Type	Bar
Recommended for	Unexpected

"It's a dive with a beer museum."—Johnnie Compton

Philadelphia, see pages 390–393

THE CHURCH BREW WORKS

3525 Liberty Avenue
Pittsburgh
Pennsylvania 15201, United States
+1 4126888200

Recommended by
Amelia Franklin

Opening hours	Open 7 days from 11:30 am
Credit cards	Accepted
Type	Pub
Recommended for	Wish I'd opened

"It's in an old church!"—Amelia Franklin

MARI'S 6 PAC N MORE

835 Hiesters Lane
Reading
Pennsylvania 19605, United States
+1 6107506430

Recommended by
Jillian Antonelli

Opening hours.................................Open 7 days from 11 am
Credit cards..Accepted
Type...Bar and retail
Recommended for...Unexpected

"In a strip mall, Mari's 6 Pac is primarily a bottle shop,
though it has a full liquor bar and about a dozen taps with a
tiny bar. They have rare beers, local beers, world-class
beers, and beers from different countries."—Jillian Antonelli

COOPER'S SEAFOOD HOUSE

701 North Washington Avenue
Scranton
Pennsylvania 18509, United States
+1 5703466883
www.coopers-seafood.com

Recommended by
Trip Ruvane

Opening hours.........Mon–Sat from 11 am, Sun from 12 pm
Credit cards..Accepted
Type...Restaurant
Recommended for...Unexpected

BARLEY CREEK BREWING COMPANY

1774 Sullivan Trail
Tannersville
Pennsylvania 18372, United States
+1 5706299399
www.barleycreek.com

Recommended by
Trip Ruvane

Opening hours.....................................Open 7 days from 8 am
Credit cards..Accepted
Type.....................................Beer garden and microbrewery
Recommended for...Beer garden

TERESA'S NEXT DOOR

124 North Wayne Avenue
Wayne
Pennsylvania 19087, United States
+1 6102939909
www.teresas-cafe.com

Recommended by
Jillian Antonelli,
Bart Cuypers

Opening hours....................................Mon–Sat from 11:30 am,
Sun from 4 pm
Credit cards..Accepted
Type...Bar and restaurant
Recommended for..Beer & food

NEWPORT STORM BREWERY

293 J.T. Connell Highway
Newport
Rhode Island 02840, United States
+1 4018495232
www.newportstorm.com

Recommended by
Theresa Malafronte

Opening hours..Wed–Mon 12 pm
Credit cards..Accepted
Type..Brewery
Recommended for...Local favorite

THE SCURVY DOG

1718 Westminster Street
Providence
Rhode Island 02909, United States
+41 4012707980
www.scurvydogbar.com

Recommended by
Brian Oakley

Opening hours.................................Open 7 days from 5 pm
Credit cards..Accepted
Type..Bar
Recommended for...Local favorite

"It is a rock-and-roll dive bar with a righteous patio and
always a good beer list. And there's free pool until 10 pm."
—Brian Oakley

PROCLAMATION ALE COMPANY

298 Kilvert Street
Warwick
Rhode Island 02886, United States
+1 4017876450
www.proclamationale.com

Recommended by
Dave Witham

Opening hours......................................Wed–Fri from 3 pm,
Sat–Sun from 12 pm
Credit cards..Accepted
Type...Bar and brewery
Recommended for...Local favorite

THE FARMHOUSE TAP & GRILL

160 Bank Street
Burlington
Vermont 05401, United States
+1 8028590888
www.farmhousetg.com

Recommended by
Dylan Badger,
Christian Weber

Opening hours......................................Mon–Fri from 11 am,
Sat–Sun from 10 am
Credit cards..Accepted
Type...Restaurant
Recommended for.......................................Wish I'd opened

FOAM BREWERS

112 Lake Street
Burlington
Vermont 05401, United States
+1 8023992511
www.foambrewers.com

Recommended by
Mark Drutman

Opening hours.........Mon–Sat from 12 pm, Sun from 11 am
Credit cards..Accepted
Type........................Beer garden and brewery
Recommended for....................................Beer garden

HEN OF THE WOOD

55 Cherry Street
Burlington
Vermont 05401, United States
+1 8025400534
www.henofthewood.com

Recommended by
Keegan Konkoski Kramer

Opening hours....................................Open 7 days from 5 pm
Credit cards..Accepted
Type...Bar and restaurant
Recommended for..................................Local favorite

MANHATTAN PIZZA & PUB

167 Main Street
Burlington
Vermont 05401, United States
+1 8026586776
www.manhattanpizzaandpubvt.com

Recommended by
Dylan Badger

Opening hours....................................Mon from 8 pm,
Tue–Thur from 4:30 pm,
Fri–Sat from 11:30 am, Sun from 12:30 pm
Credit cards..Accepted
Type...Restaurant
Recommended for..........................Wish I'd opened

THREE NEEDS BREWERY & TAPROOM

185 Pearl Street
Burlington
Vermont 05401, United States
+1 8024970119

Recommended by
Matt DeLuca

Opening hours....................................Open 7 days from 4 pm
Credit cards........................Accepted but not Amex
Type.....................................Microbrewery and pub
Recommended for..................................Local favorite

HILL FARMSTEAD BREWERY

403 Hill Road
Greensboro
Vermont 05842, United States
+1 8025337450
www.hillfarmstead.com

Recommended by
Doug Dozark

Opening hours..Wed–Sat from 12 pm
Credit cards..Accepted
Type......................................Brewery and retail
Recommended for..........................Worth the travel

What more is there to say about Hill Farmstead? It is such
a beautiful location in rural Vermont. That the beers are
incredible goes without saying. They simply don't make a bad
beer. Their tasting room also offers rare bottles from other
breweries, along with Hill Farmstead favorites, and the entire
team is extremly welcoming.

THREE PENNY TAPROOM

108 Main Street
Montpelier
Vermont 05602, United States
+1 8022238277
www.threepennytaproom.com

Recommended by
Brad Clark

Opening hours..Mon–Fri from 11 am
Sat–Sun from 12 pm
Credit cards........................Accepted but not Amex
Type..Pub
Recommended for..........................Wish I'd opened

LOST NATION BREWING

87 Creamery Road
Morrisville
Vermont 05661, United States
+1 8028518041
www.lostnationbrewing.com

Recommended by
Keegan Konkoski Kramer

Opening hours..................................Wed–Sun from 11:30 am
Credit cards..Accepted
Type........................Beer garden and brewery
Recommended for....................................Beer garden

THE SKINNY PANCAKE

Burlington International Airport
1200 Airport Drive
South Burlington
Vermont 05401, United States
+1 8027526761
www.skinnypancake.com

Recommended by
Dylan Badger,
Michiko Tsutsui

Opening hours..............................Open 7 days from 4:30am
Credit cards...Accepted
Type...Restaurant
Recommended for.....................................Unexpected

THE ALCHEMIST

100 Cottage Club Road
Stowe
Vermont 05672, United States
+1 8028828165
www.alchemistbeer.com

Recommended by
Anton Pligin

Opening hours..Tue–Sat from 11 am
Credit cards...Accepted
Type...Microbrewery
Recommended for............................Wish I'd opened

SUNSET GRILLE & TAP ROOM

140 Cottage Club Road
Stowe
Vermont 05672, United States
+1 8022539281
www.sunsetgrillevt.com

Recommended by
Vadim Gurov

Opening hours..........................Open 7 days from 11:30 am
Credit cards...Accepted
Type...Restaurant
Recommended for....................................Beer & food

SUGARBUSH RESORT

102 Forest Drive
Warren
Vermont 05674, United States
+1 8005378427
www.sugarbush.com

Recommended by
Christian Weber

Opening hours.................................Open 7 days from 8 am
Credit cards...Accepted
Type..Bar
Recommended for.....................................Unexpected

"Not my normal ski spot, but most of their lift lodges have
great Vermont sought-after cans on their menus."
—Christian Weber

THE BLACKBACK PUB

1 Stowe Street
Waterbury
Vermont 05676, United States
+1 8022440123
www.theblackbackpub.com

Recommended by
Mark Drutman

Opening hours...Tue–Sun from 12 pm
Credit cards...Accepted
Type..Pub
Recommended for................................Local favorite

PROHIBITION PIG

23 South Main Street
Waterbury
Vermont 05676, United States
+1 8022444120
www.prohibitionpig.com

Recommended by
Tim Besecker,
Matt DeLuca,
Cindy DeRama,
Chelsie Markel

Opening hours.....................................Mon–Thur from 4 pm,
Fri–Sun from 11:30 am
Credit cards...Accepted
Type...Bar and restaurant
Recommended for..............................Worth the travel

"Not only do they have their own brewery, but the
ever-changing beer list is well curated. It's a common
occurrence to see Hill Farmstead, Lawson's, Allagash, and
other heavy hitters in the beer lineup. Four words: fried
pimento cheese balls."—Chelsie Markel

In Waterbury, you go to where the old Alchemist brewpub
used to be, you'll find this awesome, bar and brewery with
great food, very friendly service, and many great local beers.
Their in-house beers are well worth trying.

PARKER PIE COMPANY

161 County Road
West Glover
Vermont 05875, United States
+1 8025253366
www.parkerpie.com

Recommended by
Daniel Kravitz,
Ben Maeso,
Kim Mercado

Opening hours...Tue–Sun from 11 am
Credit cards............................Accepted but not Amex
Type..Pub
Recommended for....................................Beer & food

"Hands down the best pizza in Vermont. The draft list always
has exceptional local offerings, including Hill Farmstead."
—Daniel Kravitz

"IF THERE IS A MORE AUTHENTIC BIERGARTEN EXPERIENCE OUTSIDE GERMANY, I'VE NEVER SEEN IT."

ZACH MACK P.376

"AN INCREDIBLE SUMMER BEER GARDEN IN THE MIDDLE OF THE CITY."

STEVE HINDY P.378

NEW YORK CITY

"A BOWLING ALLEY WITH A CRAFT-BEER SELECTION. WHAT ELSE DO YOU NEED?"

KYLE HURST P.379

"WHEN YOU STEP INTO THIS BEER GARDEN, YOU SUDDENLY FEEL TRANSPORTED OUT OF QUEENS."

RYAN BEDFORD P.379

"A BEER LIST TO DIE FOR."

JEN FERGUSON P.376

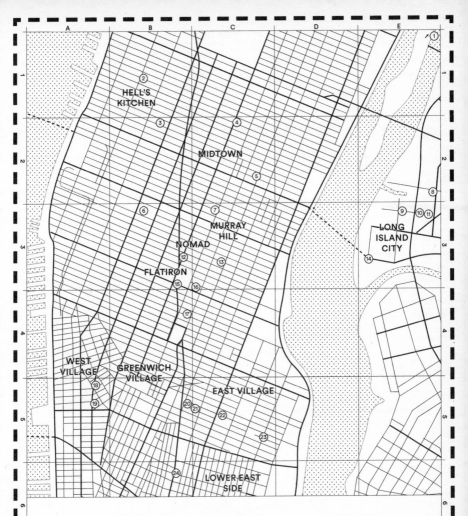

NEW YORK CITY

MANHATTAN & QUEENS

N̂   SCALE

0   290   580   870
yd.

1. BOHEMIAN HALL AND BEER GARDEN (P.379)
2. AS IS NYC (P.377)
3. BEER CULTURE (P.377)
4. ROCK CENTER CAFÉ (P.378)
5. BEER TABLE (P.377)
6. MADISON SQUARE GARDEN (P.378)
7. THE GINGER MAN NEW YORK (P.378)
8. JOHN BROWN SMOKEHOUSE (P.379)

9. ROCKAWAY BREWING COMPANY (P.380)
10. THE GUTTER BAR LIC (P.379)
11. FIFTH HAMMER BREWING COMPANY (P.379)
12. THE NOMAD BAR (P.378)
13. THE CANNIBAL BEER & BUTCHER (P.378)
14. LIC LANDING BY COFFEED (P.380)
15. EATALY NYC FLATIRON (P.376)

16. ELEVEN MADISON PARK (P.376)
17. GRAMERCY TAVERN (P.377)
18. BLIND TIGER ALE HOUSE (P.377)
19. CARMINE STREET BEERS (P.379)
20. MCSORLEY'S OLD ALE HOUSE (P.376)
21. JIMMY'S NO. 43 (P.376)
22. PROLETARIAT (P.376)
23. ZUM SCHNEIDER NYC (P.376)
24. LORELEY BEER GARDEN (P.377)

JIMMY'S NO. 43

43 East 7th Street
East Village
Manhattan
New York 10003, United States
+1 2129823006
www.jimmysno43.com

Recommended by
Katie Andrews

Opening hours.....................................Mon–Thur from 2 pm,
Fri–Sun from 1 pm
Credit cards...Accepted
Type...Pub
Recommended for...Worth the travel

MCSORLEY'S OLD ALE HOUSE

15 East 7th Street
East Village
Manhattan
New York 10003, United States
+1 2124739148
www.mcsorleysoldalehouse.nyc

Recommended by
Anna Ellis,
Phillip MacNitt,
Del Vance

Opening hours............Mon–Sat from 11 am, Sun from 1 pm
Credit cards...Not accepted
Type...Bar
Recommended for..Wish I'd opened

"This bar was opened in 1854 and pours only two types of
beer: light and dark. And they serve them two at a time.
They say Abraham Lincoln drank there, so if I'd opened it
maybe I would have met him."—Phillip MacNitt

PROLETARIAT

102 Saint Marks Place
East Village
Manhattan
New York 10009, United States
+1 2127776707
www.proletariatny.com

Recommended by
Ryan Bedford,
Jen Ferguson,
Zach Mack,
Chris Mair,
Josh Ruffin

Opening hours.....................................Mon–Thur from 5 pm,
Fri–Sun from 2 pm
Credit cards...Accepted
Type...Bar
Recommended for..Wish I'd opened

"The moment we walked into Proletariat it became the
benchmark—the bar we wished we owned. Deliciously
dark, cozy, a beer list to die for. It manages to effortlessly
tread the line between craft bar and dive bar."
—Jen Ferguson

ZUM SCHNEIDER NYC

107 Avenue C
East Village
Manhattan
New York 10009, United States
+1 2125981098
www.nyc.zumschneider.com

Recommended by
Zach Mack

Opening hours.....................................Mon–Thur from 5 pm,
Fri from 4 pm, Sat–Sun from 1 pm
Credit cards...Not accepted
Type..Beer garden
Recommended for...Beer garden

"If there is a more authentic biergarten experience outside
Germany, I've never seen it."—Zach Mack

EATALY NYC FLATIRON

200 5th Avenue
Flatiron
Manhattan
New York 10010, United States
+1 2122292560
www.eataly.com

Recommended by
Tod Mott

Opening hours.....................................Open 7 days from 9 am
Credit cards...Accepted
Type...Beer garden, retail, and restaurant
Recommended for...Beer garden

ELEVEN MADISON PARK

11 Madison Avenue
Flatiron
Manhattan
New York 10010, United States
+1 2128890905
www.elevenmadisonpark.com

Recommended by
Andrew Cooper

Opening hours............................Mon–Thur from 5:30 pm,
Fri–Sun from 12 pm
Credit cards...Accepted
Type..Restaurant
Recommended for...Beer & food

"The food is off the charts, and the beer list is amazing for
a quality restaurant. Crazy! The most amazing taste
experience of my life."—Andrew Cooper

GRAMERCY TAVERN

42 East 20th Street
Flatiron
Manhattan
New York 10003, United States
+1 2124770777
www.grammercytavern.com

Recommended by
Steve Hindy,
Katherine Kyle

Opening hours...................................Open 7 days from 11:30 am
Credit cards...Accepted
Type..Restaurant
Recommended for..Beer & food

"The highest-quality food with a beer list that pairs well with every course. The food is always inspired, and the beer can keep up."—Katherine Kyle

"Great food and great beer list, including vintage years of many strong beers."—Steve Hindy

BLIND TIGER ALE HOUSE

281 Bleecker Street
Greenwich Village
Manhattan
New York 10014, United States
+1 2124624682
www.blindtigeralehouse.com

Recommended by
Augie Carton, Razvan
Costache, Peter Eichhorn,
Molly Gunn, Yuya
Hayashi, Steve Hindy,
John Holl, Tod Mott,
James Tai, Michiko Tsutsui

Opening hours...................................Open 7 days from 11:30 am
Credit cards...Accepted
Type..Bar
Recommended for..Worth the travel

"If there ever was a neighborhood bar where everyone knows your name, it would certainly be Blind Tiger. An industry institution for two decades and very much a vanguard for the North American craft-beer scene, The Tiger offers a relaxed, unpretentious atmosphere that focuses on the people and beer."—James Tai

AS IS NYC

734 10th Avenue
Hell's Kitchen
Manhattan
New York 10019, United States
+1 6468581153
www.asisnyc.com

Recommended by
Matthew Pene

Opening hours...................................Open 7 days from 12 pm
Credit cards...Accepted
Type..Bar
Recommended for..Wish I'd opened

LORELEY BEER GARDEN

7 Rivington Street
Lower East Side
Manhattan
New York 10002, United States
+1 2122537077
www.loreleynyc.com

Recommended by
Jonathan Moxey

Opening hours...................................Open 7 days from 12 pm
Credit cards...Accepted
Type...Beer garden
Recommended for..Beer garden

BEER CULTURE

328 West 45th Street
Midtown
Manhattan
New York 10036, United States
+1 6465902139
www.beerculturenyc.com

Recommended by
Blake Crawford

Opening hours...................................Open 7 days from 11:30 am
Credit cards..Accepted but not Amex
Type..Restaurant and pub
Recommended for...Wish I'd opened

"Feels like a tucked-away little secret. Good beer in Times Square? Yeah."—Blake Crawford

BEER TABLE

Grand Central Terminal
Graybar Passage
Midtown
Manhattan
New York 10017, United States
+1 2129220008
www.beertable.com

Recommended by
Lauren Grimm

Opening hours...Mon–Fri from 8 am,
Sat from 10 am, Sun from 12 pm
Credit cards...Accepted
Type...Retail
Recommended for...Unexpected

"Beer Table is a bottle shop in Grand Central Terminal, the endpoint of the Metro-North railroad, which runs along the Hudson River—and you can drink beer on the train. The location and beer selection at Beer Table make it the perfect place to grab beer for the ride. They offer growlers of local draft beer, as well as bottles from around the world."
—Lauren Grimm

MADISON SQUARE GARDEN

4 Pennsylvania Plaza
Midtown
Manhattan
New York 10001, United States
+1 2124656225
www.msg.com/madison-square-garden

Recommended by
Ryan Bedford

Opening hours	Variable
Credit cards	Accepted
Type	Entertainment venue
Recommended for	Unexpected

"Madison Square Garden has embraced the local craft scene. They added a nice selection of beers, which are poured alongside the usual mass-produced products."
—Ryan Bedford

ROCK CENTER CAFÉ

Rockefeller Center
20 West 50th Street
Midtown
Manhattan
New York 10020, United States
+1 2123327620
www.rockcentercafe.com

Recommended by
Steve Hindy

Opening hours	Mon–Fri from 7:30 am, Sat–Sun from 9:30 am
Credit cards	Accepted
Type	Beer garden and restaurant
Recommended for	Beer garden

"An incredible summer beer garden in the middle of the city. Have a nice beer under the fountain of Prometheus."
—Steve Hindy

THE CANNIBAL BEER & BUTCHER

113 East 29th Street
Murray Hill
Manhattan
New York 10016, United States
+1 2126865480
www.thecannibalnyc.com

Recommended by
Matthew Pene

Opening hours	Open 7 days from 11 am
Credit cards	Accepted
Type	Restaurant
Recommended for	Beer & food

"I love that they have four reach-in coolers so you can browse the beer inventory. You can grab a beer and take it back to your table. Their intelligent staff won't lead you astray. They also have small snacks like beef jerky and chicharones to a half pig's head for two. Their more scientific approach to pairing food and beer down to a molecular level was a paradigm shift for me."
—Matthew Pene

THE GINGER MAN NEW YORK

11 East 36th Street
Murray Hill
Manhattan
New York 10016, United States
+1 2125323740
www.gingerman-ny.com

Recommended by
Yuya Hayashi,
Marie-Josée Lefebvre

Opening hours	Mon–Fri from 11:30 am, Sat–Sun from 12:30 pm
Credit cards	Accepted
Type	Bar
Recommended for	Local favorite

"A lot of Belgian beer and beer from breweries from around the world. The ambiance is awesome. The bartenders and waiters know about beer."—Marie-Josée Lefebvre

THE NOMAD BAR

10 West 28th Street
NoMad
Manhattan
New York 10001, United States
+1 2127961500
www.thenomadhotel.com

Recommended by
Dean Myers

Opening hours	Mon–Fri from 12 pm, Sat–Sun from 5 pm
Credit cards	Accepted
Type	Bar
Recommended for	Worth the travel

"This is a cocktail mecca. Does that take away from why I love it as a beer destination? Absolutely not. As a reformed sommelier, I'm always on the lookout for the next steps in beer's elevation to the pedestal wine culture occupies in America. Late at night, grab a table in the library if possible."—Dean Myers

The NoMad is one of my favorite places to hang out in New York City. They run a fantastic beverage program. They have a great selection of craft beer—including NoMader Weisse from Evil Twin made especially for the NoMad—creative cocktails, and very nice wines. All in a cozy atmosphere with that textbook NYC buzz. An amazingly hospitable staff also helps.

CARMINE STREET BEERS

52A Carmine Street
West Village
Manhattan
New York 10014, United States
+1 2126332337

Recommended by
Matthew Pene

Opening hours	Mon–Sat from 11:30 am, Sun from 12 pm
Credit cards	Accepted
Type	Bar
Recommended for	Local favorite

"A massive selection of current beers and rare allocations, with tons of hidden gems. They also have a great tasting room, with beers on tap and growler fills."—Matthew Pene

BOHEMIAN HALL AND BEER GARDEN

29–19 24th Avenue
Astoria
Queens
New York 11102, United States
+1 7182744925
www.bohemianhall.com

Recommended by
Ryan Bedford,
Joshua M. Bernstein,
Alex Butler, Kyle Hurst,
Patrick Morse,
Samuel Richardson

Opening hours	Mon–Fri from 5 pm, Sat–Sun from 12 pm
Credit cards	Accepted
Type	Beer garden
Recommended for	Beer garden

"One of the classic spots to hit in New York City—great beer, atmosphere, and sausage, with a focus on Czech heritage."—Alex Butler

"The leafy refuge is as close as you'll come to drinking in a classic German beer garden without booking a flight."
—Joshua M. Bernstein

"When you step into this beer garden, you suddenly feel transported out of Queens. It's a large space with plenty of shade and seating, along with authentic Czech beers."
—Ryan Bedford

FIFTH HAMMER BREWING COMPANY

10–28 46th Avenue
Long Island City
Queens
New York 11101, United States
+1 7186632084
www.fifthhammerbrewing.com

Recommended by
Katherine Kyle

Opening hours	Mon–Thur from 4 pm, Fri from 3 pm, Sat–Sun from 12 pm
Credit cards	Accepted
Type	Brewery
Recommended for	Local favorite

"Great beer, great people. The whole operation reminds me of great jazz. No coincidence that Chris Cuzme is an accomplished jazz musician. There's even a piano. Though it's the beer that drives people here."—Katherine Kyle

THE GUTTER BAR LIC

10–22 46th Avenue
Long Island City
Queens
New York 11101, United States
+1 9293280409
www.thegutterbrooklyn.com/lic

Recommended by
Kyle Hurst

Opening hours	Mon–Thur from 5 pm, Fri from 2 pm, Sat–Sun from 12 pm
Credit cards	Accepted
Type	Bar
Recommended for	Local favorite

"A bowling alley with a craft-beer selection. What else do you need?"—Kyle Hurst

JOHN BROWN SMOKEHOUSE

10–43 44th Drive
Long Island City
Queens
New York 11101, United States
+1 3476171120
www.johnbrownseriousbbq.com

Recommended by
Kyle Hurst

Opening hours	Mon–Fri from 11:30 am, Sat–Sun from 12 pm
Credit cards	Accepted
Type	Restaurant
Recommended for	Unexpected

"Amazing barbecue with a killer beer selection in the back."
—Kyle Hurst

LIC LANDING BY COFFEED

52–10 Center Boulevard
Long Island City
Queens
New York 11101, United States
+1 3477064696
www.coffeednyc.com/liclanding

Recommended by
Kyle Hurst

Opening hours......................................Open 7 days from 7 am
Credit cards..Accepted
Type...Beer garden
Recommended for..Worth the travel

"The view is amazing. This is my favorite place to have a
beer and watch the sunset."—Kyle Hurst

ROCKAWAY BREWING COMPANY

46-01 5th Street
Long Island City
Queens
New York 11101, United States
+1 7184826528
www.rockawaybrewco.com

Recommended by
Cristina Saez

Opening hours....................................Mon–Wed from 5 pm,
            Thur–Fri from 3 pm, Sat–Sun from 12 pm
Credit cards..Accepted
Type...Bar and brewery
Recommended for..Worth the travel

"A small, friendly taproom and brewery."—Cristina Saez

"MEKELBURG'S FEELS LIKE A SECRET. THE BAR IS IN THE BASEMENT OF A BUILDING BEHIND THEIR ARTISANAL GROCERY STORE."

LAUREN GRIMM P.384

"THE BEST NEIGHBORHOOD BAR IN NEW YORK CITY, PERIOD!"

MIKE AMIDEI P.385

NEW YORK CITY

"ANY BAR THAT DOESN'T HAVE MIKE IS CAPABLE OF BEING ONLY THE SECOND-BEST BAR IN THE WORLD."

ZAQ SUAREZ P.386

"TØRST HAS BEEN MY ABSOLUTE FAVORITE BAR IN NEW YORK CITY SINCE ITS INCEPTION. THE TAP LIST IS SUPERB AND UNLIKE ANY OTHER BAR IN NEW YORK."

CHRIS MAESTRO P.386

"WALK INTO THIS LAUNDROMAT AND WALK PAST THE WASHERS AND DRYERS AND THROUGH THE BACK DOOR WITH TWO WASHER WINDOWS. YOU'LL FIND A BAR SERVING GREAT PINTS AND CANS OF CRAFT BEERS, SURROUNDED BY THE HOLY GRAIL OF PINBALL MACHINES. BEER + PINBALL MACHINES = HEAVEN."

KIM MERCADO P.385

NEW YORK CITY

BROOKLYN & STATEN ISLAND

Ⓝ   SCALE

0   875   1750   2630
yd.

HANK'S SALOON

46 3rd Avenue
Boerum Hill
Brooklyn
New York 11217, United States
www.hankssaloon.com

Recommended by
Joe Ploof

Opening hours..........Mon–Sat from 11 am, Sun from 12 pm
Credit cards...Not accepted
Type...Bar
Recommended for...............................Worth the travel

BROOKLYN CIDER HOUSE

1100 Flushing Avenue
Bushwick
Brooklyn
New York 11237, United States
+1 3472950308
www.brooklynciderhouse.com

Recommended by
Joshua M. Bernstein

Opening hours.................................Tue–Sun from 5 pm
Credit cards..Accepted
Type......................................Bar and restaurant
Recommended for....................................Beer & food

BAR GREAT HARRY

280 Smith Street
Carroll Gardens
Brooklyn
New York 11231, United States
+1 3474575650
www.bargreatharry.com

Recommended by
Samuel Richardson

Opening hours................................Mon–Fri from 2 pm,
Sat–Sun from 12:30 pm
Credit cards..Accepted
Type...Bar
Recommended for...............................Local favorite

OTHER HALF BREWING

195 Centre Street
Carroll Gardens
Brooklyn
New York 11231, United States
+1 9177656107
www.otherhalfbrewing.com

Recommended by
Krisjanis Zelgis

Opening hours..........Mon–Wed from 3 pm, Thur–Fri from
12 pm, Sat from 10 am, Sun from 11 am
Credit cards..Accepted
Type..Brewery
Recommended for..............................Wish I'd opened

CARDIFF GIANT

415 Myrtle Avenue
Clinton Hill
Brooklyn
New York 11205, United States
+1 9293377873
www.cardiffgiantny.com

Recommended by
Yuko Odashima

Opening hours.................................Mon–Fri from 4pm,
Sat–Sun from 12 pm
Credit cards..Accepted
Type...Bar
Recommended for...............................Local favorite

MEKELBURG'S

293 Grand Avenue
Clinton Hill
Brooklyn
New York 11238, United States
+1 7183992337
www.mekelburgs.com

Recommended by
Lauren Grimm,
Patrick Morse,
Yuko Odashima,
Merlin Ward,
Adam Watson,
Cody Wilson

Opening hours.................................Mon–Fri from 8 am,
Sat–Sun from 10 am
Credit cards..Accepted
Type..Bar and retail
Recommended for....................................Beer & food

"Mekelburg's feels like a secret. The bar is in the basement
of a building behind their artisanal grocery store. Comfort
foods like banh mi and porchetta sandwiches fill the menu,
and their beer list is always well curated."—Lauren Grimm

COVENHOVEN

730 Classon Avenue
Crown Heights
Brooklyn
New York 11238, United States
+1 7184839950
www.covenhovennyc.com

Recommended by
Joshua M. Bernstein,
Shawn Decker,
Paul Kim

Opening hours................................Mon–Fri from 2 pm,
Sat–Sun from 12 pm
Credit cards..Accepted
Type...Bar
Recommended for...............................Local favorite

"Covenhoven is the quintessential mom-and-pop shop—the
owners live upstairs. The candlelit room is always filled with
regulars, happily sipping through the sixteen local-focused
drafts or plucking one of the couple of hundred cans or
bottles from the fridge. When the weather is nice, there's a
grassy backyard."—Joshua M. Bernstein

NAHSHEL GROCERY

539 Park Place
Crown Heights
Brooklyn
New York 11238, United States

Recommended by
Joshua M. Bernstein

Opening hours..Variable
Type..Retail
Recommended for...Unexpected

"Years ago, my corner bodega was the place to go for tall
boys of Coors and turkey sandwiches, served through a
bulletproof window at all hours of the night. Then, slowly
and steadily, the bodega started stocking beers from Ballast
Point, Cigar City, Stone, and others. It's still a disconnect to
visit the bodega that got me drunk on cheap domestic lagers
and walk out with a sixer of Jai Alai IPA."
—Joshua M. Bernstein

THREES BREWING

333 Douglass Street
Gowanus
Brooklyn
New York 11217, United States
+17185222110
www.threesbrewing.com

Recommended by
Katie Andrews,
Phil Cassella,
Rasmus Seidler Krebs

Opening hours.....................................Mon–Thur from 5 pm,
Fri from 3 pm, Sat–Sun from 12 pm
Credit cards..Accepted
Type......................................Beer garden, bar, and brewery
Recommended for...Beer garden

"It's huge and awesome, with a great atmosphere and local
brews on tap. Plus they serve drinks, which gives it a
broader and more mixed crowd, which I love. I also love the
Budweiser thing they have going on. The opposite of a
pretentious and snobby beer bar. It's the perfect mix of
geeks, regulars, walk-ins, and party people, combined with
basic and shitty beer, world-class beer, booze, and drinks."
—Rasmus Seidler Krebs

BROUWERIJ LANE

78 Greenpoint Avenue
Greenpoint
Brooklyn
New York 11222, United States
+1 3475296133
www.brouwerijlane.com

Recommended by
Mike Amidei,
Cindy DeRama,
Yazan M. Karadsheh

Opening hours.....................................Mon–Thur from 2 pm,
Fri–Sun from 12 pm
Credit cards..Accepted
Type...Bar and retail
Recommended for...Wish I'd opened

"The best neighborhood bar in New York City, period!
In the summer they have a small outdoor courtyard, and in
the winter it's supercozy with the wood stove cranking
away."—Mike Amidei

SUNSHINE LAUNDRY & PINBALL EMPORIUM

860 Manhattan Avenue
Greenpoint
Brooklyn
New York 11222, United States
+1 7184752055
www.sunshinelaundromat.com

Recommended by
Kim Mercado

Opening hours............Mon–Sat from 7 am, Sun from 8 am
Credit cards..Accepted
Type..Pub
Recommended for...Local favorite

"Walk into this Laundromat and walk past the washers and
dryers and through the back door with two washer
windows. You'll find a bar serving great pints and cans of
craft beers, surrounded by the holy grail of pinball
machines. Beer + pinball machines = heaven."
—Kim Mercado

TØRST

615 Manhattan Avenue
Greenpoint
Brooklyn
New York 11222
United States
+1 7183896034
www.torstnyc.com

Recommended by
Katie Andrews,
Sarah Bennett,
Neil Bontoft, Chris Frosaker,
Hugo Gonçalves, Rick Green,
Tomas Halberstad, Christian Jauslin,
Yazan M. Karadsheh, Clay Keel,
Nathan Keffer, Aniko Lehtinen,
Yuhang Lin, Chris Maestro,
DJ McCready, Pablo Mejia,
Shawna O'Flaherty, Nikki Ohanlon,
Josh Pfriem, Rasmus Seidler Krebs,
Scott Shor, Zaq Suarez, Michiko Tsutsui,
Valgeir Valgeirsson, Marie-Pier Veilleux,
Grant Waner, Kirk Zembal

Opening hours..................................Open 7 days from 12 pm
Credit cards...Accepted
Type...Bar and restaurant
Recommended for......................................Worth the travel

"Tørst has been my absolute favorite bar in New York City since its inception. Even though I consider myself a beer geek, I always leave Tørst learning something new about beer. The tap list is superb and unlike any other bar in New York. The decor and Tørst aesthetic are gorgeous."
—Chris Maestro

"I've never seen a more professionally run operation. Every detail has been thought through, from the bar design to the tap handles to the storage and the serving of the beer. This combo means you're likely to go for one but stay for many. They have one of the best selections of beer in the world, and it's made approachable for even the craft-beer novice by a helpful and insightful staff."—DJ McCready

"A super-rad spot in Brooklyn with a high-level focus on food and an incredible beer selection."—Josh Pfriem

"An insane bottle list. Great atmosphere and a cutting-edge selection."—Scott Shor

"Any bar that doesn't have Mike is capable of being only the second-best bar in the world. I heard Mike never gets too cold or too hot. I heard that sweaters were invented by a guy who met Mike and wanted to make some kind of clothes that made people feel as comfortable and supported as Mike makes you feel. I heard that the Writers Guild went on strike in 2007–8 because Mike didn't like what was on TV. Mike is a pair of shoes that are on sale, fit perfectly, and look really good. This bar does Mike Amidei better than anyone else. Does Mike work at other bars? No."—Zaq Suarez

Mike Amidei's curation of the draft and bottle list at Tørst make it one of the top beer destinations in the world. The service also makes it special. There's an amazing rotating draft and bottle list and unpretentious service. If you are in New York City, pay them a visit.

GREENWOOD PARK

555 7th Avenue
Greenwood
Brooklyn
New York 11215, United States
+1 7184997999
www.greenwoodparkbk.com

Recommended by
Merlin Ward

Opening hours.....................................Mon–Wed from 4 pm,
Thur–Sun from 12 pm
Credit cards...Not accepted
Type..Beer garden and bar
Recommended for.......................................Beer garden

BAR TOTO

411 11th Street
Park Slope
Brooklyn
New York 11215, United States
+1 7187684698
www.bartoto.com

Recommended by
Milos Vuksic

Opening hours.......................................Mon–Fri from 12 pm,
Sat–Sun from 11 am
Credit cards...Accepted
Type..Restaurant
Recommended for......................................Worth the travel

THE GATE

321 5th Aveue
Park Slope
Brooklyn
New York 11215, United States
+1 7187684329
www.thegatebrooklyn.com

Recommended by
Joe Ploof

Opening hours.......................................Mon–Fri from 3 pm,
Sat–Sun from 1 pm
Credit cards...Accepted
Type..Pub
Recommended for...................................Wish I'd opened

"An unpretentious yet knowledgeable bar staff and a great and well-curated beer list. It has a patio and is dog friendly. They were well ahead of the game in Brooklyn as far as craft goes. There's a reason Bell's and Ninkasi did New York City release parties there. It's perfect."—Joe Ploof

MISSION DOLORES

Recommended by
Yuko Odashima

249 4th Avenue
Park Slope
Brooklyn
New York 11215, United States
+1 3474575606
www.missiondolores.com

Opening hours	Mon–Tue from 4 pm, Wed–Fri from 2 pm, Sat–Sun from 12:30 pm
Credit cards	Accepted
Type	Bar and beer garden
Recommended for	Beer garden

"Beer and pinball."—Yuko Odashima

THE OWL FARM

Recommended by
Jonathan Moxey

297 9th Street
Park Slope
Brooklyn
New York 11215, United States
+1 7184994988
www.theowlfarm.com

Opening hours	Mon–Fri from 2 pm, Sat–Sun from 12:30 pm
Credit cards	Accepted
Type	Bar
Recommended for	Wish I'd opened

GOLD STAR BEER COUNTER

Recommended by
Lauren Grimm

176 Underhill Avenue
Prospect Heights
Brooklyn
New York 11238, United States
www.goldstarbeercounter.com

Opening hours	Mon–Fri from 4 pm, Sat–Sun from 2 pm
Credit cards	Accepted
Type	Bar
Recommended for	Local favorite

"Gold Star has amazing beer. Bartenders DJ from a
well-curated selection of classic records, and potted plants
line the walls. They also have a to-go window, where
passersby can order growlers and bottles."—Lauren Grimm

WARTEGA BREWING

Recommended by
Merlin Ward

33 35th Street #6A
Sunset Park
Brooklyn
New York 11232, United States
+1 9173971171
www.wartega.com

Opening hours	Fri–Sat from 4 pm
Credit cards	Accepted
Type	Brewery
Recommended for	Local favorite

BARCADE WILLIAMSBURG

Recommended by
Daniel Kravitz,
Erik Moynihan

388 Union Avenue
Williamsburg
Brooklyn
New York 11211, United States
+1 7183026464
www.barcadebrooklyn.com

Opening hours	Mon–Thur from 4 pm, Fri from 2 pm, Sat–Sun from 12 pm
Credit cards	Accepted
Type	Bar
Recommended for	Wish I'd opened

BROOKLYN BREWERY

Recommended by
Eleonora Rigato

79 North 11th Street
Williamsburg
Brooklyn
New York 11249, United States
+1 7184867422
www.brooklynbrewery.com

Opening hours	Fri from 6 pm, Sat–Sun from 12 pm
Credit cards	Accepted
Type	Brewery
Recommended for	Worth the travel

"It's a brewery, but you can visit and taste their great beers.
I loved that place."—Eleonora Rigato

BROOKLYN HARVEST MARKET
UNION AVENUE

204 Union Avenue
Williamsburg
Brooklyn
New York 11249, United States
+1 7184863300
www.brooklynharvestmarkets.com

Recommended by
Matthew Pene

Opening hours	Open 7 days from 7 am
Credit cards	Accepted
Type	Retail
Recommended for	Unexpected

"They gave a young man named Rico free rein to put together an insanely large beer section, and he crushes it on what he brings in."—Matthew Pene

FETTE SAU

354 Metropolitan Avenue
Williamsburg
Brooklyn
New York 11211, United States
+1 7189633404
www.fettesaubbq.com

Recommended by
John Latta,
Brett Tieman,
Christopher Williams

Opening hours	Mon from 5 pm, Tue–Sun from 12 pm
Credit cards	Accepted
Type	Restaurant
Recommended for	Beer & food

"If you love slow-cooked meat and love beer, then this is heaven. With its iconic bar layout and tap handles using old butcher knives, you'll be salivating as soon as you step through the door. It's an immersive meat experience in a relaxed and casual environment."—John Latta

RADEGAST HALL & BIERGARTEN

113 North 3rd Street
Williamsburg
Brooklyn
New York 11249, United States
+1 7189633973
www.radegasthall.com

Recommended by
Tim Besecker,
Matt DeLuca,
Cindy DeRama,
Matthew Pene

Opening hours	Mon–Fri from 12 pm, Sat–Sun from 11 am
Credit cards	Accepted
Type	Beer garden
Recommended for	Beer garden

"There is no better array of rooms and spaces to drink fine beer. There's an open-air roof, delicious food, liter steins, giant tables, and live music."—Matthew Pene

SPUYTEN DUYVIL

359 Metropolitan Avenue
Williamsburg
Brooklyn
New York 11211, United States
+1 7189634140
www.spuytenduyvilnyc.com

Recommended by
Stephen Andrews,
Stephane Bogaert,
Malia Paasch,
Rasmus Seidler Krebs,
Cody Wilson

Opening hours	Mon–Fri from 5 pm, Sat–Sun from 12 pm
Credit cards	Accepted
Type	Beer garden and bar
Recommended for	Beer garden

"It feels as if you're walking into a house. They have a limited draft selection but nothing shy of a perfect bottle list. It's immediately relaxing with a backyard feel."—Cody Wilson

"This place is an institution in New York City. No other bar falls into this category for me. It's a simple no-nonsense bar with a small tap list that's always different and never predictable. An amazing staff and the best back garden in Brooklyn hands down."—Stephen Andrews

Spuyten always has an amazing bottle list. Drinking rare bottles in a hip Brooklyn bar is always fun. They also have one of the best back patios of any bar in New York City.

THE WELL
272 Meserole Street
Williamsburg
Brooklyn
New York 11206, United States
+1 3473383612
www.thewellbrooklyn.com

Recommended by
Ethan Cox,
Lauren Grimm

Opening hours...Mon–Fri from 4 pm,
Sat–Sun from 12 pm
Credit cards..Accepted
Type...Beer garden and pub
Recommended for..Worth the travel

"The Well is in a historic brewery (Hittleman). It has a
large, light-filled backyard, where they host events and
performances. There are often food trucks parked in the
back."—Lauren Grimm

DOUBLE WINDSOR
210 Prospect Park West
Windsor Terrace
Brooklyn
New York 11215, United States
+1 3477253479
www.doublewindsorbklyn.com

Recommended by
Brett Tieman

Opening hours...Mon–Fri from 3 pm,
Sat–Sun from 12 pm
Credit cards...Not accepted
Type...Bar
Recommended for..Worth the travel

ADOBE BLUES
63 Lafayette Avenue
New Brighton
Staten Island
New York 10301, United States
+1 7187202583
www.adobeblues.com

Recommended by
Patrick Morse

Opening hours..............................Mon–Sat from 11:30 am,
Sun from 12 pm
Credit cards..Accepted
Type..Restaurant
Recommended for...Local favorite

"Tex-Mex atmosphere and menu. A small draft system but
always with great choices, including rare bottles and cans."
—Patrick Morse

"BREWERS DISTRIBUTE TO PENNSYLVANIA JUST TO BE REPRESENTED AT MONK'S. IT HAS THE BEST BOTTLE LIST I'VE EVER SEEN."

KYLE JEFFERSON P.392

"I LIKE THEIR ATTENTION TO DETAIL AND THE FEEL OF THIS PLACE."

MATTY ECK P.392

PHILADELPHIA

"IT'S WHERE I WANT TO EAT ALWAYS. TIM IS KNOWN IN THE WINE WORLD, BUT IT ALWAYS HAS A SMALL AMAZING HYPER-LOCAL BEER LIST, WITH BALANCED AND WELL-CURATED FLAVORED BEERS THAT ALWAYS INSPIRE. IT ALSO HAS AN IN-HOUSE BUTCHER SHOP."

JOHNNIE COMPTON P.392

"AN OLD-SCHOOL JAZZ BAR AT THE OLD ORTLIEB'S BREWERY."

GEOFFREY SEIDEMAN P.393

"MY GO-TO LOCAL PLACE FOR GOOD GERMAN FOOD AND BEER."

MATTY ECK P.392

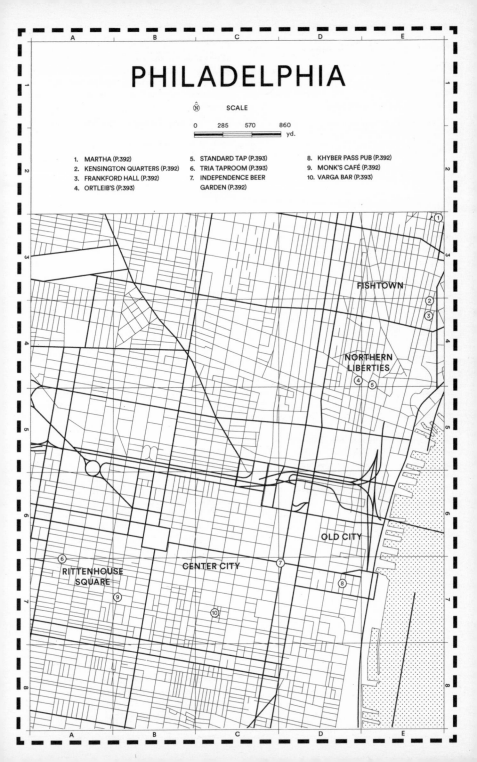

FRANKFORD HALL

1210 Frankford Avenue
Philadelphia
Pennsylvania 19125, United States
+1 2156343338
www.frankfordhall.com

Recommended by
Matty Eck,
Jesse Prall

Opening hours	Mon–Fri from 4 pm,
	Sat–Sun from 12 pm
Credit cards	Accepted
Type	Beer garden
Recommended for	Beer garden

"A big, open, beer garden that is great for hanging out during the nice times of year. It's my go-to local place for good German food and beer."—Matty Eck

INDEPENDENCE BEER GARDEN

100 South Independence
Mall West
Philadelphia
Pennsylvania 19106, United States
+1 2159227100
www.phlbeergarden.com

Recommended by
Geoffrey Seideman,
Mark Sigman,
Jason Zeeff

Opening hours	Variable
Credit cards	Accepted
Type	Beer garden
Recommended for	Beer garden

"Tucked around the base of an office building, this beer garden feels like an impromptu party, with ping-pong tables, yard games, and plenty of seating. They have a good selection of craft beers, some of which are in shipping containers. One corner of the space has a great view of Independence Hall."—Jason Zeeff

KENSINGTON QUARTERS

1310 Frankfort Avenue
Philadelphia
Pennsylvania 19125, United States
+1 2673145086
www.kensingtonquarters.com

Recommended by
Johnnie Compton

Opening hours	Mon–Thur from 5 pm,
	Fri from 12 pm, Sat–Sun from 11 am
Credit cards	Accepted
Type	Bar and restaurant
Recommended for	Beer & food

"It's where I want to eat always. Tim is known in the wine world, but it always has a small amazing hyper-local beer list, with balanced and well-curated flavored beers that always inspire. It also has an in-house butcher shop."
—Johnnie Compton

KHYBER PASS PUB

56 South 2nd Street
Philadelphia
Pennsylvania 19106, United States
+1 2152385888
www.khyberpasspub.com

Recommended by
Kellan Bartosch,
Mark Sigman

Opening hours	Open 7 days from 10 am
Credit cards	Accepted
Type	Pub
Recommended for	Unexpected

MARTHA

2113 East York Street
Philadelphia
Pennsylvania 19125, United States
+1 2158678881
www.marthakensington.com

Recommended by
Matty Eck

Opening hours	Mon, Wed–Sat from 4:30 pm,
	Sun from 12 pm
Credit cards	Accepted
Type	Bar
Recommended for	Wish I'd opened

"I like their attention to detail and the feel of this place. They have the extraordinary beer that I love to drink."—Matty Eck

MONK'S CAFÉ

264 South 16th Street
Philadelphia
Pennsylvania 19102, United States
+1 2155457005
www.monkscafe.com

Recommended by
Johnnie Compton,
Peter Crowley,
Bart Cuypers,
Neil Fisher,
Jeff Halvorson,
Dustin Jeffers,
Kyle Jefferson,
Mike Murphy

Opening hours	Open 7 days from 11:30 am
Credit cards	Accepted
Type	Pub
Recommended for	Worth the travel

"Brewers distribute to Pennsylvania just to be represented at Monk's. It has the best bottle list I've ever seen."
—Kyle Jefferson

ORTLEIB'S

847 North 3rd Street
Philadelphia
Pennsylvania 19123, United States
+1 2673243348
www.ortliebsphilly.com

Recommended by
Geoffrey Seideman

Opening hours.............................Tue–Sat from 5 pm,
Sun from 8 pm
Credit cards...Accepted
Type...Bar
Recommended for.........................Worth the travel

"An old-school jazz bar at the old Ortlieb's Brewery."
—Geoffrey Seideman

STANDARD TAP

901 North 2nd Street
Philadelphia
Pennsylvania 19123, United States
+1 2152380630
www.standardtap.com

Recommended by
Matty Eck,
Mike Murphy

Opening hours.........................Mon–Fri from 4 pm,
Sat–Sun from 11 am
Credit cards...Accepted
Type...Pub
Recommended for.........................Wish I'd opened

"I haven't been in years. But I have fond memories of great
beer and food, and there's something about it I can't put my
finger on. I just wished it was mine."—Mike Murphy

TRIA TAPROOM

2005 Walnut Street
Philadelphia
Pennsylvania 19103, United States
+1 2155578277
www.triaphilly.com

Recommended by
Kyle Jefferson

Opening hours.........................Mon–Fri from 12 pm,
Sat–Sun from 11 am
Credit cards...Accepted
Type...Bar and restaurant
Recommended for.........................Worth the travel

"As a brewer and a brewery owner, I find it refreshing to see
Tria take such care and attention to their service, beer
selection, beer serving, atmosphere, and food creates an
absolute beer drinking experience."—Kyle Jefferson

VARGA BAR

941 Spruce Street
Philadelphia
Pennsylvania 19107, United States
+1 2156275200
www.vargabar.com

Recommended by
Jason Carty

Opening hours.........................Mon–Thur from 4 pm,
Fri–Sun from 11 am
Credit cards...Accepted
Type...Pub
Recommended for.............................Beer & food

USA SOUTH

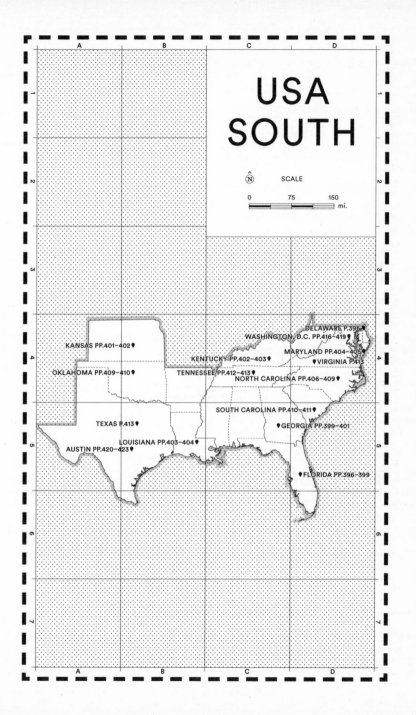

USA
SOUTH

N

SCALE

0   75   150
mi.

KANSAS PP.401–402 ♥

DELAWARE P.396 ♥
WASHINGTON, D.C. PP.416–419 ♥
MARYLAND PP.404–405 ♥
KENTUCKY PP.402–403 ♥
♥ VIRGINIA P.413
OKLAHOMA PP.409–410 ♥
TENNESSEE PP.412–413 ♥
NORTH CAROLINA PP.406–409 ♥

SOUTH CAROLINA PP.410–411 ♥

TEXAS P.413 ♥
♥ GEORGIA PP.399–401

LOUISIANA PP.403–404 ♥
AUSTIN PP.420–423 ♥

♥ FLORIDA PP.396–399

BOTTLE & CORK

1807 State Highway 1
Dewey Beach
Delaware 19971, United States
+1 3022277272
www.bottleandcorkdewey.com

Recommended by
Colby Cox

Opening hours................................Open 7 days from 2 pm
Credit cards..Not accepted
Type................................Bar and entertainment venue
Recommended for................................Wish I'd opened

"An indoor-outdoor medium-size music venue with four
bars, sand for a floor, a pretty good craft selection, and
some amazing live acts. It's also half a block from the ocean
and from the bay."—Colby Cox

JESSOP'S TAVERN

114 Delaware Street
New Castle
Delaware 19720, United States
+1 3023226111
www.jessops-tavern.com

Recommended by
Jason Carty

Opening hours..............................Open 7 days from 11:30 am
Credit cards..Accepted
Type..Restaurant and pub
Recommended for..............................Worth the travel

"A colonial-themed establishment with no TVs and the staff
dressed in traditional colonial attire. They have one of the
best beer lists on the East Coast, including a great selection
of Belgian beers you can't find easily in the U.S."
—Jason Carty

HENLOPEN CITY OYSTER HOUSE

50 Wilmington Avenue
Rehoboth Beach
Delaware 19971, United States
+1 3022609193
www.hcoysterhouse.com

Recommended by
Chelsie Markel

Opening hours................................Open 7 days from 12 pm
Credit cards..Accepted
Type..Restaurant
Recommended for................................Unexpected

"Fresh seafood, amazing food, a short walk to the beach,
a fantastic happy hour that folks line up to get into, and local
beer, plus some harder-to-find beers from all over the
globe."—Chelsie Markel

THE PICKLED PIG PUB

18756 Coastal Highway #3
Rehoboth Beach
Delaware 19971, United States
+1 3026455444
www.pickledpigpub.com

Recommended by
Jesse Prall

Opening hours................................Open 7 days from 11 am
Credit cards..Accepted
Type..Pub
Recommended for................................Local favorite

Washington, D.C., see pages 416–419

TWO GEORGES WATERFRONT GRILLE

728 Casa Loma Boulevard
Boynton Beach
Florida 33435, United States
+1 5617362717
www.twogeorgesrestaurant.com/boynton

Recommended by
Matt DeLuca

Opening hours................................Open 7 days from 11 am
Credit cards..Accepted
Type..Bar and restaurant
Recommended for................................Unexpected

THE STEIN & VINE

827 West Bloomingdale Avenue
Brandon
Florida 33511, United States
+1 8136554786
www.thesteinandvine.com

Recommended by
Clay Keel

Opening hours................................Open 7 days from 12 pm
Credit cards..Accepted
Type..Pub
Recommended for..............................Worth the travel

RC OTTER'S EATS

11506 Andy Rosse Lane
Captiva
Florida 33924, United States
+1 2393951142
www.captivaislandinn.com

Recommended by
Zach Mack

Opening hours................................Open 7 days from 8 am
Credit cards..Accepted
Type..Bar and restaurant
Recommended for................................Unexpected

7VENTH SUN BREWING COMPANY

1012 Broadway
Dunedin
Florida 34698, United States
+1 7277333013
www.7venthsun.com

Recommended by
Jared Welch

Opening hours	Open 7 days from 12 pm
Credit cards	Accepted
Type	Bar and brewery
Recommended for	Unexpected

"I have yet to find a brewery less than a year old that impressed me as much as 7venth Sun. That experience was so memorable that I used many of the features to shape my own taproom and drinking environment when I opened Southern Grist Brewing (in Nashville)."—Jared Welch

THE RIVERSIDE MARKET CAFÉ

608 Southwest 12th Avenue
Fort Lauderdale
Florida 33312, United States
+1 9543588333
www.theriversidemarket.com

Recommended by
Dustin Jeffers

Opening hours	Open 7 days from 8 am
Credit cards	Accepted
Type	Bar and retail
Recommended for	Local favorite

"Riverside Market is a great place to go when you want to have a good beer, pizza, and conversation without distractions. There are no TVs, so you actually have to talk to people. The walls are lined with coolers so you can pick out your beers (you bring up all your empties at the end and pay). They also have a good-size rotating tap list."
—Dustin Jeffers

JETBLUE PARK

11500 Fenway South Drive
Fort Myers
Florida 33913, United States
+1 2393344700
www.mlb.com/redsox

Recommended by
Marci Mullen

Opening hours	Variable
Credit cards	Accepted
Type	Entertainment venue
Recommended for	Unexpected

"This is the spring home of the Red Sox. They serve our Lobster Ale!"—Marci Mullen

KICKBACKS GASTROPUB

910 King Street
Jacksonville
Florida 32204, United States
+1 9043889551
www.kickbacksgastropub.com

Recommended by
Barry Elwonger,
Dustin Jeffers

Opening hours	Open 7 days from 7 am
Credit cards	Accepted
Type	Restaurant
Recommended for	Wish I'd opened

THE PORCH

429 Caroline Street
Key West
Florida 33040, United States
+1 3055176358
www.theporchkw.com

Recommended by
Collin Castore

Opening hours	Open 7 days from 11 am
Credit cards	Accepted
Type	Bar
Recommended for	Unexpected

BOXELDER CRAFT BEER MARKET

2817 North West 2nd Avenue
Miami
Florida 33127, United States
+1 3059427769
www.bxldr.com

Recommended by
Karl Volstad

Opening hours	Mon from 4 pm, Tue–Sun from 1 pm
Credit cards	Accepted
Type	Retail
Recommended for	Local favorite

J. WAKEFIELD BREWING

120 Northwest 24th Street
Miami
Florida 33127, United States
+1 7862544779
www.jwakefieldbrewing.com

Recommended by
Jeppe Jarnit-Bjergsø

Opening hours	Mon–Thur from 2 pm, Fri–Sun from 12 pm
Credit cards	Accepted
Type	Brewery
Recommended for	Local favorite

If you find yourself in beautiful South Florida, a visit to Wakefield is an absolute must. Great people and delicious beers tailor-made for the weather.

AMWAY CENTER
400 West Church Street #200
Orlando
Florida 32801, United States
+1 4074407000
www.amwaycenter.com

Recommended by
Valgeir Valgeirsson

Opening hours..Variable
Credit cards..Accepted
Type..Bar
Recommended for..Unexpected

GB'S BOTTLE SHOP AND TASTING BAR
531 Virginia Drive
Orlando
Florida 32803, United States
+1 4076340110
www.gbbottleshop.com

Recommended by
Josh Ruffin

Opening hours..Mon–Fri from 3 pm,
Sat–Sun from 12 pm
Credit cards..Accepted
Type..Bar and retail
Recommended for..Unexpected

"The draft and bottle selection is outstanding. On my visit,
I sampled Crooked Stave Colorado Wild Sage, Prairie Bomb,
and Mikkeller San Diego Raspberry Blush."—Josh Ruffin

THE GNARLY BARLEY
7431 South Orange Avenue
Orlando
Florida 32809, United States
+1 4078544999
www.thegnarlybarley.com

Recommended by
Christian Jauslin

Opening hours..Tue–Fri from 11 am,
Sat–Sun from 12 pm
Credit cards..Accepted
Type..Bar
Recommended for..Worth the travel

"It's tiny and off the beaten track, and it was hard for me to
leave. There is inside and outside seating and a good
selection of food and beers (from local craft beers to beer
from other places in the United States and Europe)."
—Christian Jauslin

RED LIGHT RED LIGHT
2810 Corrine Drive
Orlando
Florida 32803, United States
+1 4078939832
www.redlightredlightbeerparlour.com

Recommended by
Ron Raike

Opening hours..Open 7 days from 5 pm
Credit cards..Accepted
Type..Beer garden
Recommended for..Worth the travel

CYCLE BREWING
534 Central Avenue
St. Petersburg
Florida 33701, United States
www.cyclebrewing.com

Recommended by
Doug Dozark,
Magnus Svensson

Opening hours........Mon–Thur from 3 pm, Fri–Sun from 12 pm
Credit cards..Accepted
Type..Brewery
Recommended for..Worth the travel

"The guys at Cycle Brewing are probably the nicest dudes in
all the land—Eric Trinosky and the infamous Charlie Meers
are amazing. Sitting with those two in the Florida sunshine
with one of their amazingly crushable beers in the very
relaxed and unpretentious downtown Saint Petersburg is my
favorite thing to do."—Magnus Svensson

GREEN BENCH BREWING COMPANY
1133 Baum Avenue North
St. Petersburg
Florida 33705, United States
+1 7278009836
www.greenbenchbrewing.com

Recommended by
Jillian Antonelli

Opening hours..Tue–Sun from 12 pm
Credit cards..Accepted
Type..Beer garden and brewery
Recommended for..Beer garden

TROPICANA FIELD
1 Tropicana Drive
St. Petersburg
Florida 33705, United States
+1 7278253137
www.mlb.com/rays/ballpark

Recommended by
Barry Elwonger

Opening hours..Variable
Credit cards..Accepted
Type..Entertainment venue
Recommended for..Unexpected

COCK & BULL FARMHOUSE

975 Cattlemen Road
Sarasota
Florida 34232, United States
+1 9413631262
www.cnbpub.com

Recommended by
Jeff Halvorson

Opening hours........................Open 7 days from 5 pm
Credit cards...Accepted
Type...Pub
Recommended for.....................................Unexpected

AMALIE ARENA

401 Channelside Drive
Tampa
Florida 33602, United States
+1 8133016500
www.amaliearena.com

Recommended by
Doug Dozark

Opening hours..Variable
Credit cards...Accepted
Type....................................Entertainment venue
Recommended for.....................................Unexpected

CIGAR CITY BREWING

Tampa International Airport
Airside C
Tampa
Florida 33607, United States
+1 8138708700
www.cigarcitybrewing.com

Recommended by
Cindy DeRama

Opening hours........................Open 7 days from 10 am
Credit cards...Accepted
Type...Brewery
Recommended for.....................................Unexpected

"It was great to see a craft-beer space inside the airport."
—Cindy DeRama

CIGAR CITY BREWING COMPANY

3924 West Spruce Street
Tampa
Florida 33607, United States
+1 8133486363
www.cigarcitybrewing.com

Recommended by
Neil Callaghan

Opening hours........................Open 7 days from 11 am
Credit cards...Accepted
Type..Bar and brewery
Recommended for...................................Local favorite

THE INDEPENDENT BAR AND CAFÉ

5016 North Florida Avenue
Tampa
Florida 33603, United States
+1 8133414883
www.independentbartampa.com

Recommended by
Barry Elwonger

Opening hours.........................Open 7 days from 9 am
Credit cards...Accepted
Type...Bar
Recommended for...................................Local favorite

TAMPA BAY BREWING COMPANY

1600 East 8th Avenue
Tampa -
Florida 33605, United States
+1 8132471422
www.tbbc.beer

Recommended by
Jaanis Tammela

Opening hours........................Open 7 days from 11 am
Credit cards...Accepted
Type...Brewery
Recommended for..............................Worth the travel

PLAYALINDA BREWING COMPANY BRIX PROJECT

5220 South Washington Avenue
Titusville
Florida 32780, United States
+1 3215675974
www.playalindabrewingcompany.com

Recommended by
Ron Raike

Opening hours.................................Mon–Thur from 4 pm,
Fri from 3 pm, Sat–Sun from 12 pm
Credit cards...Accepted
Type.....................................Microbrewery and pub
Recommended for.............................Beer & food

BARLEYGARDEN KITCHEN & CRAFT BAR

900 Avalon Boulevard
Alpharetta
Georgia 30009, United States
+1 6782666218
www.barleygardenkitchen.com

Recommended by
Kraig Torres

Opening hours.................................Mon–Sat from 11 am,
Sun from 12:30 pm
Credit cards...Accepted
Type....................................Beer garden and bar
Recommended for.............................Beer garden

ONE FLEW SOUTH

Hartsfield-Jackson Airport
Terminal E
Atlanta
Georgia 30320, United States
+1 4042098209
www.oneflewsouthatl.com

Recommended by
Molly Gunn

Opening hours.................................Open 7 days from 11 am
Credit cards..Accepted
Type...Restaurant
Recommended for..Unexpected

THE PORTER BEER BAR

1156 Euclid Avenue Northeast
Atlanta
Georgia 30307, United States
+1 4042230393
www.theporterbeerbar.com

Recommended by
Adam Bruckman,
André Ek, Molly Gunn,
Marisa Jackson, Aaron
McClain, Shannon
McFarlane, Josh Ruffin,
Kraig Torres

Opening hours...............................Mon–Fri from 11:30 am,
Sat–Sun from 11 am
Credit cards..Accepted
Type..Bar
Recommended for...............................Worth the travel

"Their selection is almost beyond comparison in the
Southeast, with regional standouts like Creature Comforts
routinely sharing tap space alongside De Molen and
Cloudwater. They have some of the best shrimp and grits
I've ever had."—Josh Ruffin

"The best selection of fresh, vintage, and draft beers
anywhere in the world, with a commitment to glassware and
amazing creative food."—Molly Gunn

"Nothing compares with the Porter. It looks like this
hole-in-the-wall bar has nothing special about it, but then
you go in."—Shannon McFarlane

The Porter is one of the best beer bars in America. A world-
class cellar and vintage bottle selection, an extensive draft list,
and a thoroughly engaged and knowledgeable staff. Beer bars
don't get much better than this. The fact that Nick and Molly
are two fantastic people makes it even better to love.

TACO MAC

573 Main Street Northeast
Atlanta
Georgia 30324, United States
+1 4045745813
www.tacomac.com

Recommended by
Tim Scott

Opening hours.................................Open 7 days from 11 am
Credit cards..Accepted
Type...Bar and restaurant
Recommended for...................................Wish I'd opened

"A hundred craft beers on tap."—Tim Scott

WRECKING BAR BREWPUB

292 Moreland Avenue Northeast
Atlanta
Georgia 30307, United States
+1 4042212600
www.wreckingbarbrewpub.com

Recommended by
Adam Bruckman

Opening hours.................................Mon–Thur from 4 pm,
Fri–Sun from 12 pm
Credit cards..Accepted
Type...Brewpub
Recommended for...................................Beer & food

"The best brewpub I've been to. The food is top notch as
well."—Adam Bruckman

BRICK STORE PUB

125 East Court Square
Decatur
Georgia 30030, United States
+1 4046870990
www.brickstorepub.com

Recommended by
Chris Brown,
Adam Bruckman,
Neil Callaghan, Reid
Ramsay, Kevin Ryan,
David Stein, Kraig Torres

Opening hours.................................Mon–Sat from 11 am,
Sun from 12 pm
Credit cards..Accepted
Type..Pub
Recommended for...............................Worth the travel

"This was one of the first real beer bars in Atlanta. They have
a world-class Belgian beer bar upstairs."—Adam Bruckman

THE COMET PUB & LANES

2619 North Decatur Road
Decatur
Georgia 30033, United States
+1 4702251931
www.cometpubandlanes.com

Recommended by
Reid Ramsay

Opening hours	Mon from 5 pm, Tue–Sat from 10 am, Sun from 11 am
Credit cards	Accepted
Type	Pub
Recommended for	Unexpected

"Bowling lanes with local craft and Evil Twin."
—Reid Ramsay

BEN'S NEIGHBORHOOD GRILL & TAP

7080 Hodgson Memorial Drive
Savannah
Georgia 31406, United States
+1 9123519008
www.bensgrill.com

Recommended by
Kevin Ryan

Opening hours	Mon from 9 am, Tue–Sat from 11 am
Credit cards	Accepted but not Amex
Type	Pub
Recommended for	Unexpected

"In the middle of a strip mall, Ben's has an amazing craft selection that constantly changes. It's a hidden gem in midtown Savannah that will surprise you with the craft-beer selection and the Greek burger. Definitely get the sweet potato waffle fries."—Kevin Ryan

CRYSTAL BEER PARLOR

301 West Jones Street
Savannah
Georgia 31401, United States
+1 9123491000
www.crystalbeerparlor.com

Recommended by
Kevin Ryan

Opening hours	Open 7 days from 11 am
Credit cards	Accepted
Type	Bar and restaurant
Recommended for	Beer & food

THE WAREHOUSE BAR & GRILLE

18 East River Street
Savannah
Georgia 31401, United States
+1 9122346003
www.thewarehousebarandgrille.com

Recommended by
Kevin Ryan

Opening hours	Mon–Sat from 11 am, Sun from 12:30 pm
Credit cards	Accepted
Type	Bar and restaurant
Recommended for	Local favorite

KANSAS CITY RENAISSANCE FESTIVAL

633 North 130th Street
Bonner Springs
Kansas 66012, United States
+1 9137212110
www.kcrenfest.com

Recommended by
Jared Rudy

Opening hours	Variable
Credit cards	Accepted
Type	Beer garden
Recommended for	Unexpected

DODGE CITY BREWING

701 3rd Avenue
Dodge City
Kansas 67801, United States
+1 6203713999
www.dodgecitybrewing.com

Recommended by
Larry Cook

Opening hours	Wed–Thur from 4 pm, Fri–Sun from 11 am
Credit cards	Accepted
Type	Brewery
Recommended for	Local favorite

GELLA'S DINER & LB BREWING COMPANY

117 East 11th Street
Hays
Kansas 67601, United States
+1 7856212739
www.lbbrewing.com

Recommended by
Larry Cook,
Jared Rudy

Opening hours	Open 7 days from 11 am
Credit cards	Accepted
Type	Restaurant
Recommended for	Beer & food

"The food is insanely good, and the beer is too. It's the best brewpub I've ever been too. The quality of food and beer is A+."—Jared Rudy

NORSEMEN BREWING COMPANY

830 North Kansas Avenue
Topeka
Kansas 66608, United States
+1 7857833999
www.norsemenbrewingco.com

Recommended by
Jared Rudy

Opening hours................Tue–Fri from 4 pm, Sat from 11 am
Credit cards...Accepted
Type..Brewery
Recommended for..Local favorite

CENTRAL STANDARD BREWING

156 South Greenwood Street
Wichita
Kansas 67211, United States
+1 3162608515
www.centralstandardbrewing.com

Recommended by
Larry Cook

Opening hours.......................................Tue–Fri from 3 pm,
Sat–Sun from 12 pm
Credit cards...Accepted
Type..Beer garden and brewery
Recommended for...Beer garden

3RD TURN OLDHAM GARDENS

6300 Old Lagrange Road
Crestwood
Kentucky 40014, United States
+1 5024823373
www.3rdturnbrewing.com

Recommended by
Ben Shinkle

Opening hours....................................Thur–Sat from 3 pm
Credit cards...Accepted
Type..Beer garden and brewery
Recommended for...Beer garden

KENTUCKY NATIVE CAFÉ

417 East Maxwell Street
Lexington
Kentucky 40508, United States
+1 8592811718
www.michlers.com

Recommended by
Ben Self

Opening hours.......................................Mon–Fri from 4 pm,
Sat–Sun from 11am (spring–summer)
Credit cards...Accepted
Type...Beer garden
Recommended for...Beer garden

WEST SIXTH BREWING

501 West 6th Street
Lexington
Kentucky 40508, United States
+1 8597050915
www.westsixth.com

Recommended by
Ben Self,
Chris Vandergrift

Opening hours.................................Open 7 days from 11 am
Credit cards...Accepted
Type..Brewery
Recommended for..Local favorite

"The beer is incredible and the staff are the friendliest and
most informative in the city."—Chris Vandergrift

AGAINST THE GRAIN

401 East Main Street
Louisville Slugger Field
Louisville
Kentucky 40202, United States
+1 5025150174
www.atgbrewery.com

Recommended by
Jeppe Jarnit-Bjergsø

Opening hours.................................Open 7 days from 11 am
Credit cards...Accepted
Type..Restaurant and brewpub
Recommended for..Local favorite

The owners of this brewpub in a baseball stadium are the
coolest. I am a big fan, plus they have some of the best beer
names in the business.

HOLY GRALE

1034 Bardstown Road
Louisville
Kentucky 40204
United States
+1 5024599939
www.holygralelouisville.com

Recommended by
Pietro Di Pilato,
Jerry Gnagy, Marika
Josephson, Rick Nelson,
Jeffrey Stuffings, Erin
Thompson, Cody Wilson

Opening hours.......................................Mon–Fri from 4 pm,
Sat–Sun from 12 pm
Credit cards...Accepted
Type..Bar and restaurant
Recommended for..Beer & food

"The beer list is simply incredible, and the food and setting
are very special. I could live here."—Jeffrey Stuffings

A great selection of draft beer in a cool setting. Who hasn't
dreamed of drinking in church?

MONNIK BEER COMPANY

1036 East Burnett Avenue
Louisville
Kentucky 40217, United States
+1 5027426564
www.monnikbeer.com

Recommended by
Ben Shinkle

Opening hours................................Tue–Sun from 11 am
Credit cards...Accepted
Type...............................Restaurant and brewpub
Recommended for.............................Beer & food

"An outstanding combination of beers and local cuisine."
—Ben Shinkle

PROOF ON MAIN

21c Museum Hotel
702 West Main Street
Louisville
Kentucky 40202, United States
+1 5022176360
www.proofonmain.com

Recommended by
Ben Self

Opening hours.......................Open 7 days from 7 am
Credit cards..Accepted
Type...Bar and restaurant
Recommended for...............................Beer & food

SERGIO'S WORLD BEERS

1605 Story Avenue
Louisville
Kentucky 40206, United States
+1 5026182337
www.sergiosworldbeers.com

Recommended by
Sergio Ribenboim

Opening hours.......................Open 7 days from 2 pm
Credit cards...Not accepted
Type..Restaurant and pub
Recommended for............................Local favorite

THIRD STREET DIVE

442 South 3rd Street
Louisville
Kentucky 40202, United States
+1 5027493483

Recommended by
Zach Warren

Opening hours...................................Mon–Fri from 4 pm,
Sat–Sun from 6 pm
Credit cards....................Accepted but not Amex
Type...Bar
Recommended for................................Unexpected

THE AVENUE PUB

1732 Saint Charles Avenue
New Orleans
Louisiana 70130, United States
+1 5045869243
www.theavenuepub.com

Recommended by
Yvan De Baets,
Devin Kimble,
Jacob Landry,
David Stein,
Polly Watts

Opening hours...Always open
Credit cards..Accepted
Type...Pub
Recommended for............................Local favorite

Until the Avenue Pub opened, craft beer was a bit difficult to find in New Orleans. They're open 24-7, which gives you plenty of opportunity to visit. They have over forty drafts, many of them constantly rotating, and a stellar bottle list of interesting and hard-to-find beers. Polly has created a real gem that should not be missed.

COCHON BUTCHER

930 Tchoupitoulas Street
New Orleans
Louisiana 70130, United States
+1 5045887675
www.cochonbutcher.com

Recommended by
Angelo Orona

Opening hours.......................Open 7 days from 10 am
Credit cards..Accepted
Type...Retail
Recommended for...............................Beer & food

THE COURTYARD BREWERY

1020 Erato Street
New Orleans
Louisiana 70130, United States
www.courtyardbrewing.com

Recommended by
Joe Ploof

Opening hours.......................Mon–Wed from 4 pm,
Thur–Sun from 11 am
Credit cards..Accepted
Type.....................Beer garden and microbrewery
Recommended for......................................Beer garden

PARLEAUX BEER LAB

634 Lesseps Street
New Orleans
Louisiana 70117, United States
+1 5047028433
www.parleauxbeerlab.com

Recommended by
Scott Wood

Opening hours..........Mon from 3 pm, Thur–Fri from 3 pm,
Sat from 11 am, Sun from 12 pm
Credit cards..Accepted
Type..Brewery
Recommended for.................................Local favorite

STEIN'S MARKET AND DELI

2207 Magazine Street
New Orleans
Louisiana 70130, United States
+1 5045270771
www.steinsdeli.com

Recommended by
David Stein,
Scott Wood

Opening hours.......................................Tue–Fri from 7 am,
Sat–Sun from 9 am
Credit cards..Accepted
Type..Retail
Recommended for...............................Unexpected

"It's a Jewish deli that happens to have one of the best beer
selections I've ever seen."—David Stein

URBAN SOUTH BREWERY

1645 Tchoupitoulas Street
New Orleans
Louisiana 70130, United States
+1 5042674852
www.urbansouthbrewery.com

Recommended by
Jacob Landry

Opening hours....................................Mon–Wed from 4 pm,
Thur–Fri from 12 pm, Sat–Sun from 11 am
Credit cards..Accepted
Type..Brewery
Recommended for.................................Local favorite

"Urban South is making the highest-quality beer in New
Orleans."—Jacob Landry

BLUE PIT BBQ & WHISKEY BAR

1601 Union Avenue
Baltimore
Maryland 21211, United States
+1 4439485590
www.bluepitbbq.com

Recommended by
Kevin Blodger

Opening hours...................................Mon–Fri from 11:30 am,
Sat–Sun from 4 pm
Credit cards..Accepted
Type.........................Beer garden and restaurant
Recommended for.................................Beer garden

"This restaurant is about a block from my brewery, and
every time I step into their beer garden, I forget I'm still in
the neighborhood. I love sitting out on hot summer nights
drinking a bunch of beers among the trees and lush setting
back there and forgetting I'm in Baltimore."—Kevin Blodger

THE BREWER'S ART

1106 North Charles Street
Baltimore
Maryland 21201, United States
+1 4105476925
www.thebrewersart.com

Recommended by
Kevin Blodger

Opening hours..Mon–Fri from 4 pm,
Sat–Sun from 12 pm
Credit cards..Accepted
Type..Brewpub
Recommended for.................................Beer & food

MAX'S TAPHOUSE

737 South Broadway
Baltimore
Maryland 21231, United States
+1 4106756297
www.maxs.com

Recommended by
Kevin Blodger,
Malia Paasch

Opening hours.................................Open 7 days from 11 am
Credit cards..Accepted
Type..Pub
Recommended for...Worth the travel

"Max's always offers a great draft selection filled with great
beers you don't see at other places, and they really care for
the beer. They throw great events, like German Beer Fest,
Belgian Beer Fest, Wild and Sour Day, and even Italian Fest.
The staff have been there for years, and they're all great
people and so knowledgeable about beer."—Kevin Blodger

OF LOVE & REGRET

1028 South Conkling Street
Baltimore
Maryland 21224
United States
+1 4103270760
www.ofloveandregret.com

Recommended by
Christopher Williams

Opening hours........Mon–Fri from 4 pm, Sat–Sun from 11 am
Credit cards..Accepted
Type...Pub
Recommended for......................................Beer & food

"Brian Strumke's love and understanding of beer, food, art,
and music all sing in perfect harmony here."
—Christopher Williams

ORIOLE PARK AT CAMDEN YARDS

333 West Camden Street
Baltimore
Maryland 21201, United States
+1 4106859800
www.mlb.com/orioles

Recommended by
Amelia Franklin

Opening hours..Variable
Credit cards..Accepted
Type...Entertainment venue
Recommended for....................................Unexpected

VENICE TAVERN

339 South Conkling Street
Baltimore
Maryland 21224, United States
+1 4107323045

Recommended by
PJ Sullivan

Opening hours.........................Open 7 days from 8 am
Credit cards...Not accepted
Type..Bar
Recommended for....................................Unexpected

WET CITY

223 West Chase Street
Baltimore
Maryland 21201, United States
+1 4438736699
www.wetcitybrewing.com

Recommended by
PJ Sullivan

Opening hours.............................Mon–Thur from 5 pm,
Fri from 4 pm, Sat from 5 pm
Credit cards..Accepted
Type..Bar
Recommended for..............................Local favorite

BURLEY OAK BREWING COMPANY

10016 Old Ocean City Boulevard
Berlin
Maryland 21811, United States
+1 4435134647
www.burleyoak.com

Recommended by
Bryan Brushmiller

Opening hours....................................Open 7 days from 11 am
Credit cards.............................Accepted but not Amex
Type..Bar
Recommended for..............................Local favorite

ROCK BOTTOM RESTAURANT & BREWERY

7900 Norfolk Avenue
Bethesda
Maryland 20814, United States
+1 3016521311
www.rockbottom.com

Recommended by
Mark Hatherly

Opening hours....................................Open 7 days from 11 am
Credit cards..Accepted
Type...Restaurant
Recommended for....................................Unexpected

FRANKLINS RESTAURANT, BREWERY, AND GENERAL STORE

5123 Baltimore Avenue
Hyattsville
Maryland 20781, United States
+1 3019272740
www.franklinsbrewery.com

Recommended by
Amelia Franklin

Opening hours....................................Open 7 days from 11 am
Credit cards..Accepted
Type...Restaurant
Recommended for..............................Local favorite

"Twenty beers in a local business that's been around for
twenty-five years. Attached is a crazy toy store. What's not
to like?"—Amelia Franklin

APPALACHIAN VINTNER
745 Biltmore Avenue #121
Asheville
North Carolina 28803, United States
+1 8285057500
www.appalachianvintner.com

Recommended by
Chris Frosaker

Opening hours................................Mon–Sun from 10:15 am,
Sun from 12 pm
Credit cards...Accepted
Type...Retail
Recommended for.................................Local favorite

"They consistently have the best beer list in town and
rare beers on tap you can't get anywhere else."
—Chris Frosaker

THE BREW PUMP
760 Haywood Road
Asheville
North Carolina 28806, United States
+1 8287745550
www.thebrewpump.com

Recommended by
Jeremiah Tracy

Opening hours...................................Mon–Thur from 4 pm,
Fri–Sun from 2 pm
Credit cards...Accepted
Type...Bar
Recommended for.................................Local favorite

BURIAL BEER COMPANY
40 Collier Avenue
Asheville
North Carolina 28801, United States
+1 8284752739
www.burialbeer.com

Recommended by
Mike Murphy,
Kevin Raub

Opening hours...................................Mon–Thur from 2 pm,
Fri–Sun from 12 pm
Credit cards...Accepted
Type..Brewery
Recommended for.................................Local favorite

"The culmination of Asheville's exploding craft-beer scene.
It nails the combination of edgy and daring brews with
convivial atmosphere."—Kevin Raub

FUNKATORIUM
147 Coxe Avenue
Asheville
North Carolina 28801, United States
+1 8285523203
www.wickedweedbrewing.com

Recommended by
Kevin Raub

Opening hours.......................................Mon–Thur from 2 pm,
Fri–Sat from 12 pm, Sun from 11 am
Credit cards...Accepted
Type...Pub
Recommended for...............................Wish I'd opened

"A pilgrimage-worthy rustic pub dedicated to funky, sour,
and brett beers (twenty taps), backed by 600 plus aging
barrels. For fans of funk, it's North America's most important
beer destination. It's astonishing."—Kevin Raub

THIRSTY MONK
92 Patton Avenue
Asheville
North Carolina 28801, United States
+1 8282545470
www.monkpub.com

Recommended by
Aaron McClain,
Jaime Perez,
Kevin Ryan,
Ben Shinkle

Opening hours...................................Mon–Thur from 4 pm,
Fri–Sun from 12 pm
Credit cards...Accepted
Type...Brewery and pub
Recommended for...............................Wish I'd opened

"An awesome selection of beers and a wonderful selection
of Belgian beers in the cellar."—Ben Shinkle

WEDGE BREWING COMPANY
37 Paynes Way #001
Asheville
North Carolina 28801, United States
+1 8285052792
www.wedgebrewing.com

Recommended by
Rafi Chaudry,
Tim Gormley,
Aaron McClain

Opening hours.......................................Open 7 days from 12 pm
Credit cards...Accepted
Type...Beer garden and brewery
Recommended for.................................Local favorite

"They have great beer and a really cool industrial vibe, with
rustic materials and world-class street art."—Tim Gormley

THE WHALE

Recommended by
Zaq Suarez

507 Haywood Road
Asheville
North Carolina 28806, United States
+1 8285759888
www.thewhaleavl.com

Opening hours.................................Mon–Thur from 2 pm,
Fri–Sun from 12 pm
Credit cards...Accepted
Type...Bar
Recommended for...............................Local favorite

"Everyone has already deemed it the only place in town we
want to drink cool beers."—Zaq Suarez

WICKED WEED BREWING PUB

91 Biltmore Avenue
Asheville
North Carolina 28801, United States
+1 8285759599
www.wickedweedbrewing.com

Recommended by
Jaime Perez

Opening hours.................................Mon–Sat from 11:30 am,
Sun from 12 pm
Credit cards...Accepted
Type...Pub
Recommended for................................Beer & food

MILLTOWN

307 East Main Street
Carrboro
North Carolina 27510, United States
+1 9199682460
www.dininganddrinking.com

Recommended by
Jaime Perez

Opening hours...........Mon from 5 pm, Tue–Fri from 11 am,
Sat–Sun from 10:30 am
Credit cards...Accepted
Type.................................Beer garden, bar, and restaurant
Recommended for................................Beer garden

BEER STUDY

106 North Graham Street
Chapel Hill
North Carolina 27516, United States
+1 9192405423
www.beerstudy.com

Recommended by
Jaime Perez

Opening hours.........Mon–Sat from 11 am, Sun from 12 pm
Credit cards...Accepted
Type...Bar
Recommended for..............................Worth the travel

BRAWLEY'S BEVERAGE

4620 Park Road
Charlotte
North Carolina 28209, United States
+1 7045211300

Recommended by
Josh Patton

Opening hours.............Sun–Fri from 12 pm, Sat from 11 am
Credit cards...Accepted
Type..Bar and retail
Recommended for...............................Local favorite

THE OLDE MECKLENBURG BREWERY

4150 Yancey Road
Charlotte
North Carolina 28217, United States
+1 7045255644
www.oldebeckbrew.com

Recommended by
Dylan Badger

Opening hours...................................Open 7 days from 11 am
Credit cards...Accepted
Type...................................Beer garden and pub
Recommended for................................Beer garden

WHOLE FOODS MARKET CHARLOTTE

6610 Fairview Road
Charlotte
North Carolina 28210, United States
+1 9802132400
www.wholefoodsmarket.com/charlotte

Recommended by
Taylor Rees

Opening hours...................................Open 7 days from 7 am
Credit cards...Accepted
Type...Retail
Recommended for................................Unexpected

WOODEN ROBOT BREWERY

1440 South Tryon Street #110
Charlotte
North Carolina 28203, United States
+1 9808197875
www.woodenrobotbrewery.com

Recommended by
Josh Patton

Opening hours.............Tue–Thur from 4 pm, Fri from 3 pm,
Sat–Sun from 12 pm
Credit cards...Accepted
Type...Brewery
Recommended for................................Beer & food

JAKE'S BILLIARDS

1712 Spring Garden Street
Greensboro
North Carolina 27403, United States
+1 3363731303

Recommended by
Jeremiah Tracy

Opening hours..................................Open 7 days from 11 am
Credit cards...Accepted
Type..Bar
Recommended for...Wish I'd opened

THE PIPE AND PINT

3716 Spring Garden Street
Greensboro
North Carolina 27407, United States
+1 3362188610
www.thepipeandpint.com

Recommended by
Jaime Perez

Opening hours...................................Mon–Sat from 10 am
Credit cards...Accepted
Type..Retail
Recommended for...Unexpected

THE BREWER'S KETTLE

308 East Mountain Street
Kernersville
North Carolina 27284, United States
+1 3369923333
www.thebrewerskettle.com/kernersville

Recommended by
Jeremiah Tracy

Opening hours..........Mon–Sat from 12 pm, Sun from 2 pm
Credit cards...Accepted
Type..Beer garden and retail
Recommended for.....................................Beer garden

"Kernersville is (conveniently located) just minutes from two
of North Carolina's largest cities yet retains its quaint charm.
Behind this bottle shop and tasting room is a huge shaded
beer garden complete with a music stage, hammocks, and
fire pits. Nightly food trucks and a down-home vibe make
this my favorite place to drink outside. The beer selection is
second to none, with classic imports and the best of
American craft beer."—Jeremiah Tracy

SIERRA NEVADA TAPROOM

100 Sierra Nevada Way
Mills River
North Carolina 28732, United States
+1 8287086242
www.sierranevada.com

Recommended by
Julio Subero

Opening hours..................................Open 7 days from 11 am
Credit cards...Accepted
Type..Brewery
Recommended for..Beer & food

FISH HEADS BAR AND GRILL

8901 South Old Oregon Inlet Road
Nags Head
North Carolina 27959, United States
+1 2524415740
www.fishheadsobx.com

Recommended by
Chris Frosaker

Opening hours............................Open 7 days from 11:30 am
Credit cards...Accepted
Type..Pub
Recommended for...Unexpected

"It's located on a pier over the ocean."—Chris Frosaker

ZILLIE'S ISLAND PANTRY

538 Back Road
Ocracoke
North Carolina 27960, United States
+1 2529289036
www.zillies.com

Recommended by
Jeremiah Tracy

Opening hours..................................Open 7 days from 4 pm
Credit cards...Accepted
Type..Retail
Recommended for...Unexpected

"Set on a remote thirteen-mile-long barrier island in North
Carolina's Outer Banks. Zillie's has an awesome selection of
bottles, as well as a few great beers on tap, to enjoy on the
porch or while you shop."—Jeremiah Tracy

BREWERY BHAVANA

218 South Blount Street
Raleigh
North Carolina 27601, United States
+1 9198299998
www.brewerybhavana.com

Recommended by
Olivier Dupras

Opening hours	Tue from 5 pm, Wed–Sun from 11:30 am
Credit cards	Accepted
Type	Restaurant and brewery
Recommended for	Beer & food

"This is a restaurant, a beer bar, a bookshop, a library, and a flower shop. It's just beautiful, with natural light coming into the center of the place. I was impressed by the quality and the balance of the beers, and they pair very well with the Asian food served."—Olivier Dupras

STATE OF BEER

401A Hillsborough Street
Raleigh
North Carolina 27603, United States
+1 9195469116
www.stateof.beer

Recommended by
Jerry Gnagy

Opening hours	Mon–Sat from 11 am, Sun from 12 pm
Credit cards	Accepted
Type	Restaurant and retail
Recommended for	Unexpected

PJ'S FAST FOOD MART

237 Asheville Highway
Sylva
North Carolina 28779, United States
+1 8285869645

Recommended by
Zaq Suarez

Opening hours	Always open
Credit cards	Accepted
Type	Retail
Recommended for	Unexpected

"It's just a gas station forty-five minutes from anything but nature, but they have so much craft beer."—Zaq Suarez

THE PATRIARCH CRAFT BEER HOUSE & LAWN

9 East Edwards Street
Edmond
Oklahoma 73034, United States
+1 4052856670
www.thepatriarchedmond.com

Recommended by
Patrick Lively

Opening hours	Mon–Fri from 3 pm
Credit cards	Accepted
Type	Bar
Recommended for	Wish I'd opened

"Incredible all-Oklahoma craft inside an old house. Their cultivation of a great local tap selection makes it a premier location."—Patrick Lively

THE BUNKER CLUB

433 Northwest 23rd Street
Oklahoma City
Oklahoma 73103, United States
+1 4057028898
www.bunkerclubokc.com

Recommended by
Cody Wilson

Opening hours	Mon–Fri from 4 pm, Sat–Sun from 12 pm
Credit cards	Accepted
Type	Bar
Recommended for	Local favorite

"It's a cold war–themed dive bar with craft beer and free arcade games."—Cody Wilson

OAK & ORE

1732 Northwest 16th Street
Oklahoma City
Oklahoma 73106, United States
+1 4056062030
www.oakandore.com

Recommended by
Travis Richards

Opening hours	Mon from 4 pm, Tue–Sun from 11 am
Credit cards	Accepted
Type	Pub
Recommended for	Beer & food

"The upscale pub food combined with an amazing wall of rotating taps make this a new experience every time you visit."—Travis Richards

TAPWERKS ALE HOUSE & CAFE

121 East Sheridan Avenue
Oklahoma City
Oklahoma 73104, United States
+1 4053199599
www.tapwerks.com

Recommended by
Patrick Lively

Opening hours................................Open 7 days from 11 am
Credit cards..Accepted
Type..Bar and restaurant
Recommended for................................Local favorite

WILL ROGERS WORLD AIRPORT

7100 Terminal Drive
Oklahoma City
Oklahoma 73159, United States
+1 4053163271
www.flyokc.com

Recommended by
Stuart Keating

Opening hours..Always open
Credit cards..Accepted
Type..Retail
Recommended for................................Unexpected

FASSLER HALL

304 South Elgin Avenue
Tulsa
Oklahoma 74120, United States
+1 9185767898
www.fasslerhall.com/tulsa

Recommended by
Travis Richards

Opening hours................................Open 7 days from 11 am
Credit cards..Accepted
Type................................Beer garden and restaurant
Recommended for................................Beer garden

MCNELLIE'S SOUTH CITY

7031 South Zurich Avenue
Tulsa
Oklahoma 74136, United States
+1 9189335250
www.mcnelliessouthcity.com

Recommended by
Travis Richards

Opening hours................................Open 7 days from 11 am
Credit cards..Accepted
Type..Pub
Recommended for................................Local favorite

"The pub atmosphere and extensive beer list really give this bar a relaxing atmosphere, where you can sit back with a few friends and enjoy yourself."—Travis Richards

NOTHING'S LEFT BREWING CO.

1502 East 6th Street
Tulsa
Oklahoma 74120, United States
+1 9186456171
www.nothingsleftbrew.co

Recommended by
Travis Richards

Credit cards..Accepted
Type..Brewery
Recommended for................................Worth the travel

PRAIRIE BREWPUB

223 North Main Street
Tulsa
Oklahoma 74103, United States
+1 9189364395
www.prairiepub.com

Recommended by
Travis Richards

Opening hours.........Mon–Sat from 11 am, Sun from 10 am
Credit cards..Accepted
Type..Brewpub
Recommended for................................Wish I'd opened

THE BARREL

1859 Folly Road
Charleston
South Carolina 29412, United States
+1 8437322337
www.thebarrelcharleston.com

Recommended by
Malia Paasch

Opening hours................................Mon–Fri from 3 pm,
Sat–Sun from 12 pm
Credit cards..Accepted
Type..Beer garden
Recommended for................................Unexpected

"A dog park! It has a wonderful selection of craft beer, including a few I'd never had before."—Malia Paasch

CRAFTSMEN KITCHEN & TAP HOUSE

12 Cumberland Street
Charleston
South Carolina 29401, United States
+1 8435779699
www.craftsmentaphouse.com

Recommended by
Chris Brown

Opening hours................................Open 7 days from 11:30 am
Credit cards..Accepted
Type................................Beer garden, bar, and restaurant
Recommended for................................Beer garden

EDMUND'S OAST RESTAURANT

1081 Morrison Drive
Charleston
South Carolina 29403
United States
+1 8437271145
www.edmundsoast.com/restaurant

Recommended by
Mike Amidei, Jerry Gnagy,
Tim Gormley, Jacob Landry,
Malia Paasch, Scott Shor,
David Stein, Zaq Suarez,
Chris Vandergrift

Opening hours........Mon–Sat from 4:30 pm, Sun from 10 am
Credit cards...Accepted
Type...Restaurant
Recommended for..Beer & food

"Impeccable food, beer, and people. I am constantly amazed by Edmund's Oast. The attention to detail and hospitality is second to none."—Jerry Gnagy

"Their in-house beers are excellent, and they always have a great selection of guest taps, not to mention one of the best cocktail programs of any restaurant anywhere. The food at Edmund's Oast is amazing, and the staff are well versed in pairings. The house-made charcuterie is not to be missed. You are made to feel at home the moment you walk in. One of my favorite restaurants in the country."—Mike Amidei

Everything they do at Edmund's Oast is world-class. A huge list of draft beers (both guest beers and in-house), hard-to-find bottles, memorable cocktails, and an amazing staff all make it an experience to remember. It also has some of the best food in Charleston.

KUDU COFFEE AND CRAFT BEER

4 Vanderhorst Sreet
Charleston
South Carolina 29403, United States
+1 8438537186
www.kuducoffeeandcraftbeer.com

Recommended by
Chris Brown,
Scott Shor

Opening hours....................................Mon–Fri from 6:45 am,
Sat from 7 am, Sun from 8 am
Credit cards...Accepted
Type...Bar
Recommended for..Local favorite

ROYAL AMERICAN

970 Morrison Drive
Charleston
South Carolina 29403, United States
+1 8438176925
www.theroyalamerican.com

Recommended by
Zaq Suarez

Opening hours..Mon–Fri from 4 pm,
Sat–Sun from 12 pm
Credit cards...Accepted
Type..............................Beer garden, bar, and restaurant
Recommended for...Beer garden

"This place is a dive bar. They have music when they feel like it. I've lost many hours at the Royal American. There are definitely some good options to drink."—Zaq Suarez

THE DINGHY

8 J.C. Long Boulevard
Isle of Palms
South Carolina 29451, United States
+1 8432428310
www.dinghyiop.com

Recommended by
Brian Oakley

Opening hours....................................Mon–Thur from 11 am,
Fri–Sat from 11:30 am
Credit cards...Accepted
Type...Bar
Recommended for..Unexpected

EVO PIZZERIA

1075 East Montague Avenue
North Charleston
South Carolina 29405, United States
+1 8432251796
www.evopizza.com

Recommended by
Chris Brown

Opening hours.........Mon–Sat from 11 am, Sun from 12 pm
Credit cards...Accepted
Type...Restaurant
Recommended for..Beer & food

"Only craft beer—a good local selection—and the best pizza in South Carolina."—Chris Brown

CRAFTY BASTARD BREWERY

6 Emory Place
Knoxville
Tennessee 37917, United States
+1 8657552358
www.craftybastardbrewery.com

Recommended by
Aaron McClain

Opening hours	Tue–Fri from 4 pm, Sat–Sun from 2 pm
Credit cards	Accepted
Type	Brewery
Recommended for	Local favorite

ECHELON BICYCLES

138 West End Avenue
Knoxville
Tennessee 37934, United States
+1 8653921392
www.echelonbicycles.com

Recommended by
Aaron McClain

Opening hours	Mon–Sat from 11 am
Credit cards	Accepted
Type	Bar
Recommended for	Unexpected

SUTTREE'S HIGH GRAVITY TAVERN

409 South Gay Street
Knoxville
Tennessee 37902, United States
+1 8659343814
www.suttreeshighgravitytavern.com

Recommended by
Aaron McClain

Opening hours	Mon–Sat from 3 pm, Sun from 5 pm
Credit cards	Accepted
Type	Bar
Recommended for	Beer & food

"Constantly rotating taps and killer ramen."
—Aaron McClain

WISEACRE BREWING COMPANY

2783 Broad Avenue
Memphis
Tennessee 38112, United States
+1 9018887000
www.wiseacrebrew.com

Recommended by
Kellan Bartosch

Opening hours	Mon–Thur from 4 pm, Fri–Sat from 1 pm
Credit cards	Accepted
Type	Brewery
Recommended for	Local favorite

YOUNG AVENUE DELI

2119 Young Avenue
Memphis
Tennessee 38104, United States
+1 9012780034
www.youngavenuedeli.com

Recommended by
Kellan Bartosch

Opening hours	Open 7 days from 11 am
Credit cards	Accepted
Type	Bar
Recommended for	Worth the travel

12 SOUTH TAPROOM & GRILL

2318 12th Avenue South
Nashville
Tennessee 37204, United States
+1 6154637552
www.12southtaproom.com

Recommended by
Kellan Bartosch

Opening hours	Open 7 days from 11 am
Credit cards	Accepted
Type	Pub
Recommended for	Wish I'd opened

"A laid-back place to get beer and good food."
—Kellan Bartosch

CRAFT BREWED

2502 8th Avenue South
Nashville
Tennessee 37204, United States
+1 6158731992
www.craftbrewednashville.com

Recommended by
Jared Welch

Opening hours	Mon–Sat from 11 am, Sun from 12 pm
Credit cards	Accepted
Type	Bar and retail
Recommended for	Local favorite

THE FILLING STATION

1118 Halcyon Avenue
Nashville
Tennessee 37206, United States
+1 6154573535
www.brewstogo.com

Recommended by
Katy DeWinter

Opening hours	Mon–Sat from 11 am, Sun from 12 pm
Credit cards	Accepted
Type	Retail
Recommended for	Local favorite

THE PHARMACY BURGER PARLOR & BEER GARDEN

Recommended by
Katy DeWinter

731 McFerrin Avenue
Nashville
Tennessee 37206, United States
+1 6157129517
www.thepharmacynashville.com

Opening hours................................Open 7 days from 11 am
Credit cards..Accepted
Type...Beer garden and restaurant
Recommended for..Beer garden

"They have awesome burgers and a large selection of local beer. The beer garden area feels like you're in Europe."
—Katy DeWinter

Austin, see pages 420–423

HALLS WINE & SPIRITS

Recommended by
David Lin,
Patrick Lively

4200 West Glade Road
Colleyville
Texas 76034, United States
+1 8172676803
www.garrisonbros.com/halls-wine-spirits

Opening hours.................................Mon–Sat from 8 am
Credit cards..Accepted
Type...Retail
Recommended for...Unexpected

"This place boasts one of the best selections of craft beer, and it's tucked away in a Valero gas station."—Patrick Lively

MEDDLESOME MOTH

Recommended by
Tony Barron

1621 Oak Lawn Avenue
Dallas
Texas 75207, United States
+1 2146287900
www.mothinthe.net

Opening hours.........Mon–Sat from 11 am, Sun from 10 am
Credit cards..Accepted
Type..Bar and restaurant
Recommended for......................................Wish I'd opened

"Amazing decor with an extensive food and beer menu in the awesome design district of the city. The staff are incredibly helpful and service is top-class."—Tony Barron

PECAN LODGE

Recommended by
Erick Ramirez

2702 Main Sreet
Dallas
Texas 75226, United States
+1 2147488900
www.pecanlodge.com

Opening hours.......................................Tue–Sun from 11 am
Credit cards..Accepted
Type...Restaurant
Recommended for.......................................Beer & food

TROPHY RANCH

Recommended by
Eugene Tolstov

2800 Bledsoe Street #100
Fort Worth
Texas 76107, United States
+1 8178826966
www.thetrophyranch.com

Opening hours......Mon–Fri from 5 pm, Sat–Sun from 2 pm
Credit cards..Accepted
Type..............................Beer garden, bar, and restaurant
Recommended for..Beer garden

EVENING STAR CAFE

Recommended by
Dean Myers

2000 Mount Vernon Avenue
Alexandria
Virginia 22301, United States
+1 7035495051
www.eveningstarcafe.net

Opening hours...................................Mon–Fri from 5:30 pm,
Sat–Sun from 10 am
Credit cards..Accepted
Type...Restaurant
Recommended for...Unexpected

AW SHUCKS COUNTRY STORE

6100 Pouncey Tract Road
Glen Allen
Virginia 23059, United States
+1 8043640977
www.awshuckscountrystores.com

Recommended by
Grayson Shepard

Opening hours...................................Open 7 days from 6 am
Credit cards..Accepted
Type...Retail
Recommended for...Unexpected

"It's essentially a country gas station and convenience store with barbecue smoked on-site, sixteen taps of craft beer, and dozens of bottles and cans. The selection is quite good, with a Virginia focus."—Grayson Shepard

COELACANTH BREWING COMPANY

760 A West 22nd Street
Norfolk
Virginia 23517, United States
+1 7573836438
www.coelacanth.com

Recommended by
Kevin Erskine

Opening hours..................................Wed–Fri from 4:30 pm,
Sat from 12 pm, Sun from 1 pm
Credit cards...Accepted
Type...Brewery
Recommended for.....................................Local favorite

THE BIER GARDEN

438 High Street
Portsmouth
Virginia 23704, United States
+1 7573936022
www.biergarden.com

Recommended by
Dean Myers

Opening hours..........Mon–Sat from 11 am, Sun from 12 pm
Credit cards...Accepted
Type...Beer garden
Recommended for...Beer garden

THE ANSWER BREWPUB

6008 West Broad Street
Richmond
Virginia 23230, United States
+1 8042821248
www.theanswerbrewpub.com

Recommended by
Grayson Shepard,
Zach Warren

Opening hours....................................Mon–Wed from 4 pm,
Thur–Sun from 12 pm
Credit cards...Accepted
Type..................................Restaurant and brewpub
Recommended for...............................Worth the travel

"Not just a bar but also a brewpub, with fifty-six taps split
and a great selection from around the U.S. and Europe,
especially Belgium. They produce some of the best IPAs,
goses, and stouts in the U.S. The Vietnamese-influenced
bar food pairs well with the beer. The family owns Mekong
Restaurant in the same building."—Grayson Shepard

MEKONG RESTAURANT

6004 West Broad Street
Richmond
Virginia 23230, United States
+1 8042888929
www.mekongisforbeerlovers.com

Recommended by
Neil Callaghan,
Matty Eck,
Kevin Erskine,
Daniel Goh,
Zach Warren

Opening hours...............................Open 7 days from 11 am
Credit cards...Accepted
Type..Bar and restaurant
Recommended for...................................Unexpected

"A very unassuming Vietnamese restaurant in a strip mall,
with one of the best beer selections on the East Coast."
—Neil Callaghan

Mekong is a tasty Vietnamese restaurant in a strip mall in the
suburbs of Richmond, Virginia, that has over fifty beers on tap.
It doesn't make sense on paper, but when you show up it all
becomes crystal clear. An is a very gracious host, and he hires
very knowledgeable bartenders. There is a lot to like here, the
food is good, his draft list is impressive, and they brew their
own beers at the Answer, which is next door.

THE VEIL BREWING COMPANY

1301 Roseneath Road
Richmond
Virginia 23230, United States
www.theveilbrewing.com

Recommended by
Jeppe Jarnit-Bjergsø

Opening hours...Tue–Fri from 4 pm,
Sat–Sun from 12 pm
Credit cards...Accepted
Type...Brewery
Recommended for.....................................Local favorite

What more could you want? There is a great selection of
outstanding IPAs and sour beers and a cool place to drink
outside. Perfect.

COMMONWEALTH BREWING COMPANY

2444 Pleasure House Road
Virginia Beach
Virginia 23455, United States
+1 7573059652
www.commonwealthbrewingcompany.com

Recommended by
Malia Paasch

Opening hours..Mon–Fri from 3 pm,
Sat–Sun from 11 am
Credit cards...Accepted
Type...............................Beer garden and brewery
Recommended for.....................................Local favorite

"ONE OF THE MOST STUNNING PLACES I HAVE EVER SEEN. IT TRULY IS BEAUTIFUL. THE BEER IS DELICIOUS, AND THE FOOD MENU IS WELL THOUGHT OUT AND PERFECTLY EXECUTED."

JEFF ORR P.418

WASHINGTON, D.C.

ONE OF THE BEST BEVERAGE PROGRAMS IN THE COUNTRY, TRULY IMPRESSIVE."

MARK DRUTMAN P.418

"IT'S SO COOL TO TRAVEL WITHIN THE U.S. IN THOSE BIG TRAINS WHILE SIPPING A 60 MINUTES IPA!"

YVAN DE BAETS P.418

"AN INCREDIBLE, UNEXPECTED BEER LIST. THE BEST BREWERIES SEND SPECIAL KEGS TO THIS PLACE, WHERE YOU WILL FIND THE BEST CURATED LIST OF THE BEST CRAFT BEER IN THE U.S."

ISAAC SHOWAKI P.419

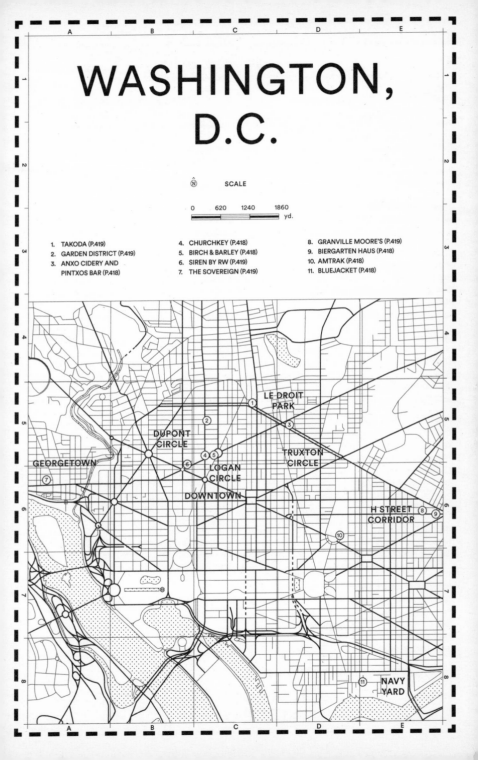

WASHINGTON, D.C.

N̂   SCALE

0   620   1240   1860
yd.

LE DROIT PARK

DUPONT CIRCLE

TRUXTON CIRCLE

GEORGETOWN

LOGAN CIRCLE

DOWNTOWN

H STREET CORRIDOR

NAVY YARD

AMTRAK
Recommended by
Yvan De Baets

60 Massachusetts Avenue Northeast
Washington
District of Columbia 20002, United States
+1 2029063000
www.amtrak.com

Opening hours...Variable
Credit cards...Accepted
Type...Bar
Recommended for...................................Unexpected

"It's so cool to travel within the U.S. in those big trains while
sipping a 60 Minutes IPA!"—Yvan De Baets

ANXO CIDERY AND PINTXOS BAR
Recommended by
Joe Ploof

300 Florida Avenue Northwest
Washington
District of Columbia 20001, United States
+1 2029863795
www.anxodc.com

Opening hours...................................Mon–Fri from 5 pm,
Sat–Sun from 10 am
Credit cards...Accepted
Type...Restaurant and pub
Recommended for.....................................Beer & food

BIERGARTEN HAUS
Recommended by
Jesse Scheitler

1355 H Street Northeast
Washington
District of Columbia 20002, United States
+1 2023884053
www.biergartenhaus.com

Opening hours...................................Mon–Fri from 4 pm,
Sat–Sun from 11 am
Credit cards...Accepted
Type...Beer garden
Recommended for.................................Beer garden

BIRCH & BARLEY
Recommended by
Anton Pligin

1337 14th Street Northwest
Washington
District of Columbia 20005, United States
+1 2025672576
www.birchandbarley.com

Opening hours...................................Tue–Fri from 5:30 pm,
Sat–Sun from 11 am
Credit cards...Accepted
Type..Restaurant
Recommended for..............................Local favorite

BLUEJACKET
Recommended by
Jeff Orr

300 Tingey Street Southeast
Washington
District of Columbia 20003, United States
+1 2025244862
www.bluejacketdc.com

Opening hours....................Open 7 days from 11 am
Credit cards...Accepted
Type...Restaurant and brewery
Recommended for...............................Wish I'd opened

"One of the most stunning places I have ever seen. It truly is
beautiful. The beer is delicious, and the food menu is well
thought out and perfectly executed."—Jeff Orr

CHURCHKEY
Recommended by
Bryan Brushmiller,
Mark Drutman,
Matty Eck, Alexa Penton,
Camilo Rojas Sanchez,
Patrick Rue, Brian Sauer,
Kraig Torres, Zach Warren,
Polly Watts, Cody Wilson

1337 14th Street Northwest
Washington
District of Columbia 20005
United States
+1 2025672576
www.churchkeydc.com

Opening hours...................................Mon–Fri from 4 pm,
Sat–Sun from 11:30 am
Credit cards...Accepted
Type...Bar
Recommended for...............................Worth the travel

"An amazing beer list with very rare beers on tap."
—Camilo Rojas Sanchez

"My one experience here was truly outstanding. The tap list
was one of the most amazing I've ever seen. One of the best
beverage programs in the country, truly impressive."
—Mark Drutman

A well-executed range of beers can always be found at
Churchkey. There is a long list of local and also international
beers, plus beers that don't see much distribution in the U.S.

GARDEN DISTRICT

Recommended by
Bryan Brushmiller,
Dean Myers,
Angelo Orona

1801 14th Street Northwest
Washington
District of Columbia 20009
United States
www.gardendistrictdc.com

Opening hours..Mon–Fri from 5 pm,
Sat–Sun from 12 pm
Credit cards...Accepted
Type...Beer garden
Recommended for...Beer garden

GRANVILLE MOORE'S

Recommended by
Bryan Brushmiller,
Dean Myers

1238 H Street Northeast
Washington
District of Columbia 20002, United States
+1 2023992546
www.granvillemoores.com

Opening hours........Mon–Fri from 5 pm, Sat–Sun from 11 am
Credit cards...Accepted
Type..Pub
Recommended for..Wish I'd opened

SIREN BY RW

Recommended by
Dean Myers

1515 Rhode Island Avenue Northwest
Washington
District of Columbia 20005, United States
+1 2025217171
www.sirenbyrw.com

Opening hours.......................................Mon–Fri from 4 pm,
Sat from 11:30 am, Sun from 11 am
Credit cards...Accepted
Type...Restaurant
Recommended for..Beer & food

THE SOVEREIGN

Recommended by
Em Sauter,
Isaac Showaki,
Chris Treanor

1206 Wisconsin Avenue Northwest
Washington
District of Columbia 20007
United States
+1 2027745875
www.thesovereigndc.com

Opening hours......................................Mon–Thur from 5 pm,
Fri from 11:30 am, Sat–Sun from 11 am
Credit cards...Accepted
Type...Bar and restaurant
Recommended for..Beer & food

"An incredible, unexpected beer list. The best breweries
send special kegs to this place, where you will find the best
curated list of the best craft beer in the U.S."
—Isaac Showaki

TAKODA

Recommended by
Amelia Franklin

715 Florida Avenue Northwest
Washington
District of Columbia 20001, United States
+1 2025251252
www.takodadc.com

Opening hours..Mon–Fri from 5 pm,
Sat–Sun from 11 am
Credit cards...Accepted
Type...Beer garden
Recommended for...Beer garden

"THEY NAILED THE CHILL OUTDOORS AND DRINK-BEER-ALL-DAY SCENE." KEEGAN KONKOSKI KRAMER P.423

AUSTIN

"CRAFT PRIDE HAS A SPECIAL PLACE IN MY HEART, WITH FIFTY-FOUR DRAFTS, ALL TEXAS-CRAFTED BEER."

BEN WHITNEY P.422

"THIS PLACE IS SO RAD."

SCOTT WOOD P.423

"A GREAT SETTING UNDER OAK TREES NEAR THE MISSOURI PACIFIC RAILROAD. SOME OF THE BEST PILSNER AND HELLES YOU'LL FIND ANYWHERE."

JEFFREY STUFFINGS P.422

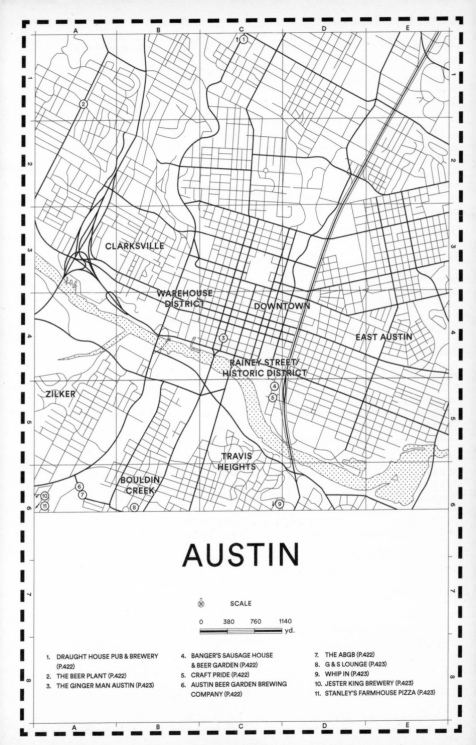

AUSTIN

SCALE

N̂

0   380   760   1140
yd.

1. DRAUGHT HOUSE PUB & BREWERY
    (P.422)
2. THE BEER PLANT (P.422)
3. THE GINGER MAN AUSTIN (P.423)

4. BANGER'S SAUSAGE HOUSE
    & BEER GARDEN (P.422)
5. CRAFT PRIDE (P.422)
6. AUSTIN BEER GARDEN BREWING
    COMPANY (P.422)

7. THE ABGB (P.422)
8. G & S LOUNGE (P.423)
9. WHIP IN (P.423)
10. JESTER KING BREWERY (P.423)
11. STANLEY'S FARMHOUSE PIZZA (P.423)

THE ABGB

1305 West Oltorf Street
Austin
Texas 78704, United States
+1 5122982242
www.theabgb.com

Recommended by
Michiko Tsutsui

Opening hours............................Tue–Fri from 11:30 am,
Sat–Sun from 12 pm
Credit cards...Accepted
Type.............................Beer garden and brewery
Recommended for.............................Beer garden

AUSTIN BEER GARDEN BREWING COMPANY

1305 West Oltorf Street
Austin
Texas 78704, United States
+1 5122982242
www.theabgb.com

Recommended by
Eloi Deit,
Jeffrey Stuffings

Opening hours............................Tue–Fri from 11:30 am,
Sat–Sun from 12 pm
Credit cards...Accepted
Type.............................Beer garden and brewery
Recommended for.............................Beer garden

"A great setting under oak trees near the Missouri Pacific Railroad. Some of the best pilsner and helles you'll find anywhere."—Jeffrey Stuffings

BANGER'S SAUSAGE HOUSE & BEER GARDEN

79 & 81 Rainey Street
Austin
Texas 78701, United States
+1 5123861656
www.bangersaustin.com

Recommended by
Chris Frosaker, David
Newman, John Rowley,
Kevin Ryan, David Stein,
PJ Sullivan, Ben Whitney

Opening hours.........Mon–Sat from 11 am, Sun from 10 am
Credit cards...Accepted
Type.............................Beer garden and pub
Recommended for.............................Beer garden

"Over 100 taps of beer from all over the world, house-made sausage, and a huge outdoor beer garden with an awesome atmosphere."—Chris Frosaker

THE BEER PLANT

3110 Windsor Road
Austin
Texas 78703, United States
+1 5125241800
www.thebeerplant.com

Recommended by
Eugene Tolstov

Opening hours....................Open 7 days from 11 am
Credit cards...Accepted
Type..Bar and restaurant
Recommended for.............................Beer & food

"This was my first vegan beer restaurant, and I was quite impressed."—Eugene Tolstov

CRAFT PRIDE

61 Rainey Street
Austin
Texas 78701, United States
+1 5124285571
www.craftprideaustin.com

Recommended by
Ben Whitney

Opening hours..............................Mon–Fri from 4 pm,
Sat from 1 pm, Sun from 12 pm
Credit cards...Accepted
Type..Bar
Recommended for...........................Worth the travel

"Craft Pride has a special place in my heart, with fifty-four drafts, all Texas-crafted beer. The bottle shop has over three hundred bottles from around the world."—Ben Whitney

DRAUGHT HOUSE PUB & BREWERY

4112 Medical Parkway
Austin
Texas 78756, United States
+1 5124526258
www.draughthouse.com

Recommended by
Jeffrey Stuffings,
Ben Whitney

Opening hours.................................Mon–Thur from 3 pm,
Fri–Sun from 1 pm
Credit cards...Accepted
Type..Brewery and pub
Recommended for.............................Local favorite

"The Draught House brings the Austin beer community together in a cool old-English setting. Great house beers too!"—Jeffrey Stuffings

G & S LOUNGE

Recommended by
James Landers

2420 South 1st Street
Austin
Texas 78704, United States
+1 5127078702
www.gandslounge.com

Opening hours...................................Mon–Sat from 3:30 pm,
Sun from 6 pm
Credit cards...Accepted
Type..Bar
Recommended for...Unexpected

"A gratifying yet surreal experience."—James Landers

THE GINGER MAN AUSTIN

301 Lavaca Street
Austin
Texas 78701, United States
+1 5124738801
www.thegingerman.com/austin

Recommended by
Dylan Badger

Opening hours.......................................Mon–Thur from 2 pm,
Fri–Sun from 1 pm
Credit cards...Accepted
Type..Pub
Recommended for.....................................Worth the travel

JESTER KING BREWERY

Recommended by
Barry Elwonger,
Richard Hinkle,
Clay Keel, Keegan
Konkoski Kramer,
Patrick Rue

13187 Fitzhugh Road
Austin
Texas 78736, United States
+1 5128297766
www.jesterkingbrewery.com

Opening hours.............Fri from 4 pm, Sat–Sun from 12 pm
Credit cards...Accepted
Type...Beer garden and brewery
Recommended for.......................................Beer garden

"Amazing beer from the on-site brewery, plus so many other
bottles. They nailed the chill outdoors and drink-beer-all-
day scene."—Keegan Konkoski Kramer

"Beautiful in a rustic, rural setting and world-class beer."
—Patrick Rue

Jester King has it all—beautiful scenery, an amazing place to
hang outdoors, very friendly service, and great food from
Stanley's Farmhouse Pizza, which is adjacent to the brewery.

STANLEY'S FARMHOUSE PIZZA

13187 Fitzhugh Road
Austin
Texas 78736, United States
+1 5129009079
www.stanleysfarmhousepizza.com

Recommended by
Kellan Bartosch

Opening hours..Fri from 5 pm,
Sat–Sun from 11:30 am
Credit cards...Accepted
Type...Beer garden and restaurant
Recommended for...Beer garden

WHIP IN

1950 South IH 35
Austin
Texas 78704, United States
+1 5124425337
www.whipin.com

Recommended by
Julie Rhodes,
Scott Wood

Opening hours.................................Open 7 days from 11 am
Credit cards...Accepted
Type..Pub
Recommended for...Unexpected

"This place is so rad. It's a bar, a bottle shop, a wine store, a
restaurant, and a live music venue."—Scott Wood

"IT'S SO RELAXING THAT YOU CAN EVEN NAP THERE."

JACOBO IGUÍNIZ MINUTTI P.432

"LOOKING OUT ON A VOLCANIC CRATER WHILE SOMEONE BROUGHT ME FRESHLY MADE MYTOS KELLERBIER WHILE ON A LOUNGE CHAIR. AMAZING."

EM SAUTER P.432

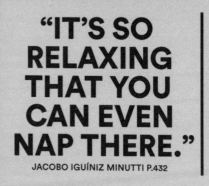

CENTRAL AMERICA & CARIBBEAN

"THE PERFECT SPACE AND SETTING TO DISCOVER NEW BEERS FROM AROUND THE WORLD."

JULIO SUBERO P.426

"AN IRISH PUB IN COSTA RICA WITH OVER FIFTY LOCAL CRAFT BEERS ON TAP AND OVER 100 BOTTLES."

STEFANO DI GIOACCHINO P.433

"WHEN I RETIRE, I WOULD LIKE TO OWN A PLACE LIKE THIS."

LUIS ARCE P.434

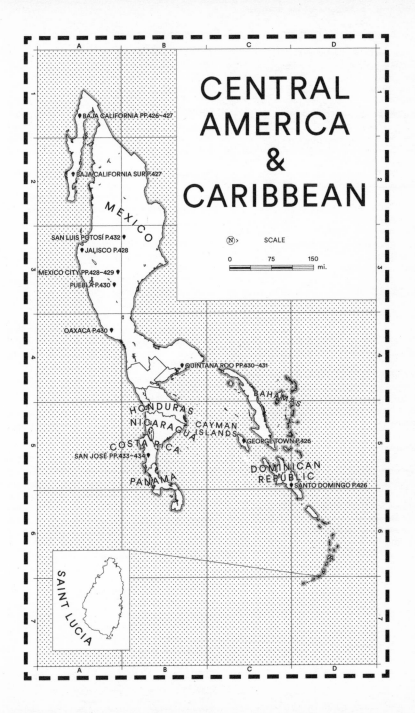

CENTRAL AMERICA & CARIBBEAN

SCALE

0   75   150
mi.

SAINT LUCIA

PIRATE REPUBLIC BREWING

Woodes Rogers Walk
Nassau
New Providence, Bahamas
+1 2423280612
www.piraterepublicbahamas.com

Recommended by
Brian Sauer

Opening hours.................................Open 7 days from 10 am
Credit cards...Accepted
Type...Brewery
Recommended for...Local favorite

CRAFT FOOD & BEVERAGE CO.

489 West Bay Road
George Town
Grand Cayman 33166, Cayman Islands
+1 3456400004
www.craftcayman.com

Recommended by
Jason Zeeff

Opening hours.................................Mon–Fri from 11:30 am,
Sat–Sun from 10:30 am
Credit cards...Accepted
Type..Pub
Recommended for...Unexpected

CULTURA CERVECERA

Calle Rafael Augusto Sánchez #96B
Santo Domingo
Distrito Nacional 10210, Dominican Republic
+1 8095339436

Recommended by
Julio Subero

Opening hours...................................Open 7 days from 4 pm
Credit cards...Accepted
Type...Bar
Recommended for...Worth the travel

"It has the widest variety of beer in the Dominican
Republic and offers the perfect space and setting to
discover new beers from around the world."
—Julio Subero

COASTLINE BEACH BAR

Micoud Highway
Vieux Fort LC12 201, Saint Lucia
+1 7584545300

Recommended by
Daniel Kravitz

Opening hours.................................Open 7 days from 9 am
Credit cards...Accepted
Type...Bar
Recommended for...Unexpected

"An absolutely pristine beachfront bar on the Atlantic
Ocean side of Saint Lucia. They serve Heineken that's
brewed and canned on the island—the freshest Heineken
I've had outside of the Netherlands."—Daniel Kravitz

MICROBREWERY AGUAMALA

Carretera Tijuana – Ensenada Km 104
El Sauzal
Baja California 22760, Mexico
+52 6461746068
www.aguamala.com.mx

Recommended by
Nathaniel Schmidt

Opening hours.............Tue–Sat from 2 pm, Sun from 1 pm
Credit cards...Accepted
Type..Microbrewery
Recommended for...Wish I'd opened

WENDLANDT EL SAUZAL

Calle 10 385
El Sauzal
Baja California 22760, Mexico
+52 6461747660
www.wendlandt.com.mx

Recommended by
Eugenio Romero

Opening hours.....................Wed from 7 am, Fri from 4 pm,
Sat from 10 am, Sun from 12 pm
Credit cards...Accepted
Type..Pub
Recommended for...Worth the travel

"Great beers and an ocean view."—Eugenio Romero

WENDLANDT ENSENADA

Boulevard Costero 248
Ensenada
Baja California 22870, Mexico
+52 6461782938
www.wendlandt.com.mx

Recommended by
Eugenio Romero

Opening hours.................................Tue–Sat from 6 pm
Credit cards...Accepted
Type..Pub
Recommended for...Local favorite

DECKMAN'S

Ensenada – Tecate Highway
Km 85.5
San Antonio de Las Minas
Baja California 22766, Mexico
+52 16461883960
www.deckmans.com

Recommended by
Nathaniel Schmidt

Opening hours........................Wed–Mon from 1 pm
Credit cards...Accepted
Type...Restaurant
Recommended for..................................Unexpected

BAJA CRAFT BEERS

Avenida Orizaba 10335
Tijuana
Baja California 22020, Mexico
+52 6646569405
www.bajacraftbeers.com

Recommended by
Jeppe Jarnit-Bjergsø

Opening hours........................Open 7 days from 1 pm
Credit cards...Accepted
Type..Pub
Recommended for............................Local favorite

BORDER PSYCHO TAPROOM

Erasmo Castellanos 9440
Tijuana
Baja California 22010, Mexico
+52 6643791235
www.borderpsychobrewery.com

Recommended by
Mike Amidei

Opening hours..........................Mon–Fri from 9 am
Credit cards...Accepted
Type...Brewery and pub
Recommended for............................Local favorite

CERVECERÍA INSURGENTE

Juan Cordero 10021
Tijuana
Baja California 22010, Mexico
+52 6646341242
www.cervezainsurgente.com

Recommended by
Jeppe Jarnit-Bjergsø

Opening hours..........................Mon–Fri from 9 am
Credit cards......................Accepted but not Amex
Type..Bar and brewery
Recommended for............................Local favorite

CERVECERÍA MAMUT

Calle Tercera #8161
Tijuana
Baja California 22000, Mexico
+52 6646850137

Recommended by
Mike Amidei

Opening hours........................Mon–Sat from 4 pm
Credit cards......................Accepted but not Amex
Type...Brewery and pub
Recommended for............................Beer & food

CERVECERÍA TIJUANA LA TABERNA

Boulevard Fundadores 2951
Tijuana
Baja California 22040, Mexico
+52 6646341111
www.cerveza-tijuana.com.mx

Recommended by
Mike Amidei

Opening hours..........Mon from 3 pm, Tue–Sun from 1 pm
Type..Bar and brewery
Recommended for............................Beer & food

CERVECERÍA RÁMURI

Boulevard Lázaro Cárdenas s/n
Cabo San Lucas
Baja California Sur 23479, Mexico
+52 6646268809
www.cervezaramuri.com

Recommended by
Mike Amidei

Opening hours............................Tue–Sun from 1 pm
Credit cards......................Accepted but not Amex
Type..Bar and brewery
Recommended for............................Beer & food

THE BEERBOX LA PAZ

Calle Independencia 201
La Paz
Baja California Sur 23000, Mexico
+52 6121297299

Recommended by
Jeppe Jarnit-Bjergsø

Opening hours..........................Mon–Sat from 5 pm
Credit cards......................Accepted but not Amex
Type...Restaurant and pub
Recommended for............................Local favorite

CASA MUSA

Calle Lapizlázuli 2581
Guadalajara
Jalisco 44580, Mexico
+52 3319837399

Recommended by
Jeppe Jarnit-Bjergsø

Opening hours	Tue–Sun from 6:30 pm
Credit cards	Accepted but not Amex
Type	Bar and restaurant
Recommended for	Beer & food

EL GRILLO

Av Chapultepec Sur 215
Guadalajara
Jalisco 44160, Mexico
+52 3338273090

Recommended by
Gabriela Velasco

Opening hours	Open 7 days from 12 pm
Credit cards	Accepted
Type	Pub
Recommended for	Worth the travel

"This local bar was the first to focus on Mexican craft beer and has supported the local and national beer movement."—Gabriela Velasco

PATAN ALE HOUSE

Calle Morelos 1281
Guadalajara
Jalisco 44160, Mexico
+52 3338266613

Recommended by
Gabriela Velasco

Opening hours	Tue–Sat from 2 pm, Sun from 3 pm
Credit cards	Accepted
Type	Beer garden and pub
Recommended for	Local favorite

PIGS PEARLS

Calle General Coronado 79
Guadalajara
Jalisco 44160, Mexico
+52 3338255933
www.pigspearls.com

Recommended by
Gabriela Velasco

Opening hours	Open 7 days from 1 pm
Credit cards	Accepted but not Amex
Type	Bar
Recommended for	Unexpected

THE BEER FACTORY CUICUILCO

Plaza Cuicuilco
Insurgentes Sur 3500
Peña Pobre
Mexico City 14060, Mexico
+52 5556060612
www.beerfactory.com

Recommended by
Jeppe Jarnit-Bjergsø

Opening hours	Open 7 days from 12 pm
Credit cards	Accepted
Type	Bar
Recommended for	Beer & food

BIERGARTEN

Calle Querétaro 225
Mexico City 06700, Mexico
+52 15552643478
www.biergartenroma.com

Recommended by
Isaac Aroche

Opening hours	Mon–Wed from 1 pm, Thur–Sun from 11 am
Credit cards	Accepted
Type	Beer garden
Recommended for	Beer garden

"Bar with an open view and a great food selection from the local market."—Isaac Aroche

BIZARRO CAFÉ COYOACAN

Cuauhtémoc 170
Mexico City 04100, Mexico
+52 5552643411

Recommended by
Mike Amidei

Opening hours	Mon–Sat from 9 am, Sun from 4 pm
Credit cards	Accepted
Type	Pub
Recommended for	Local favorite

CERVECERÍA CRISANTA

Plaza de la República 51
Mexico City 06030, Mexico
+52 5555356372
www.crisantamx.com

Recommended by
Jeppe Jarnit-Bjergsø

Opening hours	Mon–Fri from 1 pm, Sat from 10 am, Sun from 11 am
Credit cards	Accepted
Type	Bar and restaurant
Recommended for	Beer & food

EL DEPOSITO

Avenida Baja California 375
Mexico City 06170, Mexico
+52 5552710716
www.eldeposito.com.mx

Recommended by
Isaac Aroche

Opening hours	Open 7 days from 12 pm
Credit cards	Accepted
Type	Bar and retail
Recommended for	Wish I'd opened

EL TRAPPIST

Avenida Álvaro Obregón 298
Mexico City 06100, Mexico
+52 5559164260

Recommended by
Mike Amidei

Opening hours	Mon from 3:30 pm, Tue–Sat from 4:30 pm
Credit cards	Accepted but not Amex
Type	Bar and brewery
Recommended for	Local favorite

HOP THE BEER EXPERIENCE 2

Avenida Cuauhtémoc 870
Mexico City 03020, Mexico
+52 5540483408

Recommended by
Isaac Aroche,
Jacobo Iguíniz Minutti

Opening hours	Open 7 days from 2 pm
Credit cards	Accepted
Type	Bar
Recommended for	Worth the travel

"The greatest number of faucets in a bar in Mexico City
and probably Latin America."—Isaac Aroche

LA BELGA

95 Calle Querétaro
Mexico City 06700, Mexico
+52 5535479558
www.labelga.com.mx

Recommended by
Mike Amidei

Opening hours	Mon–Sat from 12 pm
Credit cards	Accepted but not Amex
Type	Retail
Recommended for	Worth the travel

LA GRACIELA TALLER DE CERVEZA

Orizaba 163
Mexico City 06700, Mexico
+52 5555842728
www.graciela.mx

Recommended by
Jeppe Jarnit-Bjergsø

Opening hours	Mon–Sat from 12 pm, Sun from 2 pm
Credit cards	Accepted
Type	Pub
Recommended for	Local favorite

PUJOL

Tennyson 133
Mexico City 11550, Mexico
+52 5555454111
www.pujol.com.mx

Recommended by
Jeppe Jarnit-Bjergsø

Opening hours	Mon–Sat from 1:30 pm
Credit cards	Accepted
Type	Restaurant
Recommended for	Beer & food

TASTING ROOM

Calle de Chiapas 173
Mexico City 06700, Mexico
+52 5571598388

Recommended by
Isaac Aroche

Opening hours	Mon–Sat from 3 pm
Credit cards	Accepted
Type	Bar
Recommended for	Local favorite

TERRAZA CRU CRU

Calle Milán P-4 44
Mexico City 06600, Mexico
+52 5550878782
www.casacerveceracrucru.com

Recommended by
Isaac Aroche

Opening hours	Open 7 days from 11 am
Credit cards	Accepted
Type	Bar and restaurant
Recommended for	Beer & food

"A great spot with a nice view of the city."—Isaac Aroche

CASA CERVECERA TIERRA BLANCA

Mártires de Tacubaya 517
Oaxaca 68000, Mexico
+52 9511328345
www.cervezatierrablanca.com

Recommended by
Mike Amidei

Opening hours............................Wed–Sun from 4 pm
Credit cards...Not accepted
Type...............................Restaurant and brewery
Recommended for........................Wish I'd opened

LA MEZCALERITA

Calle Macedonio Alcalá 706
Oaxaca 68000, Mexico
+52 9513997301

Recommended by
Jeppe Jarnit-Bjergsø

Opening hours.........................Open 7 days from 2 pm
Credit cards..Not accepted
Type...Bar and retail
Recommended for........................Wish I'd opened

SANTÍSIMA FLOR DE LÚPULO

Calle Ignacio Allende 215
Oaxaca 68000, Mexico
+52 9515164435

Recommended by
Jeppe Jarnit-Bjergsø

Opening hours..........................Mon–Sat from 4 pm
Credit cards...........................Accepted but not Amex
Type...Bar and restaurant
Recommended for.................................Beer & food

CERVECERÍA BRIGAL

Camino Nacional 220
Puebla 72120, Mexico
+52 8005522673

Recommended by
Jeppe Jarnit-Bjergsø

Opening hours..........................Mon–Fri from 10 am,
Sat–Sun from 6 pm
Credit cards..Not accepted
Type...Retail
Recommended for............................Local Favorite

DRAFT GASTROPUB

Avenida Rosendo Márquez 19
Puebla 72160, Mexico
+52 2222304450

Recommended by
Mike Amidei

Opening hours.........................Open 7 days from 12 pm
Credit cards...........................Accepted but not Amex
Type.........................Brewery, pub, and restaurant
Recommended for.................................Beer & food

UTOPÍA: BELGIAN BEER AND BISTRO

Avenida 9 Oriente #1
Puebla 72000, Mexico
+52 2222461147

Recommended by
Jeppe Jarnit-Bjergsø

Opening hours...........................Mon–Sat from 7 pm
Credit cards..Not accepted
Type...Bar
Recommended for...........................Worth the travel

CIERVA DORADA

Calle 6 Ote 2
Centro San Andrés Cholula
Puebla 72810, Mexico

Recommended by
Jacobo Iguíniz Minutti

Opening hours..........................Tue–Sun from 2 pm
Credit cards...Accepted
Type..Restaurant
Recommended for.............................Local favorite

EL DIABLITO CHOLULA

Calle 6 Norte 408
San Pedro Cholula
Puebla 72760, Mexico
+52 2221252795

Recommended by
Jacobo Iguíniz Minutti

Opening hours..........................Tue–Sat from 8 pm
Credit cards...Accepted
Type..Pub
Recommended for.................................Unexpected

EL ESTADIO CERVECERIA & RESTAURANT

Avenida Kabah
Manzana 3 Lote 12
Cancún
Quintana Roo 67500, Mexico
+52 9982722603
www.elestadio.restaurantwebexperts.com

Recommended by
Mike Amidei

Opening hours............................Tue–Sat from 1 pm,
Sun–Mon from 6 pm
Credit cards...Accepted
Type...Bar
Recommended for.............................Local favorite

EL SOCIO NAIZ TAQUERÍA

Avenida Nader #74
Manzana 3 Lote 4
Cancún
Quintana Roo 77500, Mexico
+52 9982556814

Recommended by
Mike Amidei

Opening hours...................................Open 7 days from 5 pm
Credit cards.......................................Accepted but not Amex
Type...Restaurant
Recommended for......................................Beer & food

THEBEERBOX CANCÚN

Avenida Nichupté
Super Manzana 19 Manzana 4 Lote 119
Cancún
Quintana Roo 77505, Mexico
+52 9982727782
www.thebeerbox.com

Recommended by
Jeppe
Jarnit-Bjergsø

Opening hours...Mon–Sat from 5 pm
Credit cards..Accepted
Type...Restaurant and pub
Recommended for......................................Local favorite

LA INTERNACIONAL CERVECERÍA

Avenida General Rafael E. Melgar 602
Cozumel
Quintana Roo 77600, Mexico
+52 9878691289

Recommended by
Jeppe Jarnit-Bjergsø

Opening hours..........Mon–Sat from 10 am, Sun from 5 pm
Credit cards..Accepted
Type...Bar
Recommended for......................................Local favorite

CERVEZA AKUMAL

E Norte 17, Mundo Hábitat
Playa del Carmen
Quintana Roo 77710, Mexico
+52 9841094108
www.cervezaakumal.mx

Recommended by
Pablo Santos

Opening hours...Mon–Fri from 8 am
Credit cards..Not accepted
Type...Bar
Recommended for...Unexpected

CLUB DE LA CERVEZA – WORLD BEER CLUB

5ta Avenida
Between Calles 34 and 38 Norte
Playa del Carmen
Quintana Roo 77710, Mexico
+52 9841470635
www.clubdelacerveza.mx

Recommended by
Mike Amidei

Opening hours...................................Open 7 days from 4 pm
Credit cards.......................................Accepted but not Amex
Type...Bar and brewery
Recommended for......................................Local favorite

PUERTO COCINA URBANA

5ta Avenida
Between Calle 34 and 38
Plaza San Pedro
Playa del Carmen
Quintana Roo 77710, Mexico
+52 9841473073

Recommended by
Jeppe Jarnit-Bjergsø

Opening hours...................................Open 7 days from 12 pm
Credit cards..Accepted
Type...Bar and restaurant
Recommended for......................................Beer & food

LA LEGENDARIA

Libramiento Sur Anillo
Periférico 720
San Luis Potosí 78294, Mexico
+52 4448335374
www.lalegendaria.com

Recommended by
Jacobo Iguíniz Minutti

Opening hours................Mon from 4 pm,
Tue–Sun from 2 pm
Credit cards................Accepted
Type................Beer garden
Recommended for................Beer garden

"A true beer garden. It's so relaxing that you can even nap there."—Jacobo Iguíniz Minutti

SOL DE COPÁN

Avenida El Mirador
Copán Ruinas
Copán 41120, Honduras
+504 26514758

Recommended by
Thomas Wagner

Opening hours................Tue–Sat from 4 pm
Credit cards................Not accepted
Type................Beer garden, restaurant, and
microbrewery
Recommended for................Local favorite

BOTANICOS BEER GARDEN

Plaza Eclipse
Contiguo al Hotel Holiday Inn
Managua 13002, Nicaragua
+505 22556010

Recommended by
Martin Serra

Opening hours................Mon–Fri from 4 pm,
Sat from 12 pm, Sun from 3 pm
Credit cards................Accepted
Type................Beer garden
Recommended for................Beer garden

"This is the first beer garden created for local beer in Nicaragua."—Martin Serra

LA ESTACIÓN CENTRAL

Recommended by
Martin Serra

Avenida Gabriel Cardenal
Managua 14038, Nicaragua
+505 22253274

Opening hours................Open 7 days from 4 pm
Credit cards................Accepted
Type................Restaurant
Recommended for................Beer & food

HOTEL POSADA ECOLÓGICA LA ABUELA

Laguna de Apoyo
Masaya 14241, Nicaragua
+505 88800368
www.posadaecologicalaabuela.com.ni

Recommended by
Em Sauter

Opening hours................Open 7 days from 8 am
Credit cards................Accepted
Type................Beer garden and restaurant
Recommended for................Unexpected

"Looking out on a volcanic crater when someone brought me freshly made Mytos Kellerbier while I was on a lounge chair. Amazing."—Em Sauter

SAN JUAN DEL SUR CERVECERÍA

Avenida Mercado
San Juan del Sur
Rivas 48600, Nicaragua
+505 25682683
www.sjdsbrewers.com

Recommended by
Martin Serra

Opening hours................Mon–Fri from 11 am,
Sat–Sun from 10 am
Credit cards................Accepted
Type................Brewpub
Recommended for................Local favorite

TOTOCO ECO-LODGE

Volcán Maderas, Balgüe
Isla de Ometepe
Rivas 48800, Nicaragua
+505 83587718
www.totoco.com.ni

Recommended by
Ben Bradley

Opening hours................Always open
Credit cards................Accepted
Type................Restaurant
Recommended for................Unexpected

PIZZERIA A LA LEÑA IL GIARDINO

Paraiso de Cartago 3
Orosi
Cartago, Costa Rica
+506 25332022

Recommended by
Luis Arce

Opening hours................Thur–Tue from 2 pm
Type................Restaurant
Recommended for................Unexpected

"Costa Rica has a very vibrant craft-beer scene. The day I came to Il Giardino, in my hometown of Orosi (a very small rural town) and found out they had craft beer, it was a great surprise but also a nice reminder of the hard work of many brewers to make this movement grow in the country."—Luis Arce

COCONUTZ SPORTS BAR

Main Street 2670–1982
Playas del Coco
Guanacaste 5019, Costa Rica
+506 26701982
www.coconutzbar.com

Recommended by
Ben Shinkle

Opening hours...................................Open 7 days from 9 am
Credit cards..Accepted
Type...Bar and microbrewery
Recommended for...Unexpected

"A treehouse-like setting with a small brewery on-site that brings craft beer to Costa Rica."—Ben Shinkle

EL VAQUERO BREWPUB

Playa Tamarindo 152
Tamarindo
Guanacaste 50309, Costa Rica
+506 26531238
www.witchsrocksurfcamp.com/el-vaquero-brewpub

Recommended by
Luis Arce

Opening hours.................................Open 7 days from 11 am
Credit cards..Accepted
Type..Brewpub
Recommended for..Local favorite

APOTECARIO

Calle 31 Avenido 9
San José 10101, Costa Rica
+506 40346485

Recommended by
Luis Arce

Opening hours.................................Tue–Sat from 11:30 am
Type..Beer garden
Recommended for..Beer & food

"The food is delicious, and they do very interesting combinations of ingredients. They experiment with fermentation and curing techniques. This place is home to Calle Cimarrona brewery, the guys love to experiment with sour beers and use local ingredients."—Luis Arce

CASA BREW GARDEN

Avenida Central Paseo Ruben Dario
San José, Costa Rica

Recommended by
Erick Ramirez

Opening hours..................................Mon–Sat from 6 pm
Credit cards..Accepted
Type...Beer garden and pub
Recommended for...Beer garden

"Their tap beers are the best in the country."
—Erick Ramirez

CASA FÉLIX

Calle 21
San José 10104, Costa Rica

Recommended by
Felipe Valenciano

Opening hours......................................Fri–Sat from 9 am
Type..Bar
Recommended for..Local favorite

CRAIC IRISH PUB

Calle 25 83
San José 10104, Costa Rica
+506 22219320
www.craicirishpub.com

Recommended by
Stefano Di Gioacchino

Opening hours..................................Mon–Sat from 6 pm
Credit cards..Accepted
Type...Pub
Recommended for...Unexpected

"An Irish pub in Costa Rica with over fifty local craft beers on tap and over 100 bottles."—Stefano Di Gioacchino

LUPULUS BEER SHOP

Calle 35, Avenida 9
San José 10101, Costa Rica
+506 22346392
www.lupuluscr.com

Recommended by
Daniel Moraga Leon

Opening hours....................................Tue–Thur from 6 pm,
Fri from 5 pm, Sat from 1 pm
Credit cards..Accepted
Type...Bar and restaurant
Recommended for..Beer & food

MERCADO LA CALIFORNIA

Calle 21
San José 10104, Costa Rica

<u>Recommended by</u>
Felipe Valenciano

Opening hours............Thur–Sat from 6 pm, Sun from 4 pm
Type..Bar
Recommended for...Unexpected

STIEFEL PUB

Avenida 7, 50 Este de la Casa Amarilla
San José, Costa Rica

<u>Recommended by</u>
Erick Ramirez

Opening hours....................................Mon–Fri from 11:30 am
Credit cards...Accepted
Type..Pub
Recommended for...Local favorite

"This is where the craft-beer culture began in Costa Rica."
—Erick Ramirez

WILK CRAFT BEER

Avenida 9, Calle 33
San José 10101, Costa Rica
+506 25243155

<u>Recommended by</u>
Stefano Di Gioacchino,
Daniel Moraga Leon,
Jaime Perez

Opening hours..Tue–Sat from 4 pm
Credit cards...Accepted
Type...Restaurant and brewpub
Recommended for...Local favorite

"Wilk is a brewpub dedicated exclusively to the
production and sale of artisanal beer, both national and
foreign."—Daniel Moraga Leon

HOPPY'S PLACE

Plaza Koros, Calle 5 200–298
Santa Ana
San José 10906, Costa Rica
+506 21008960
www.hoppysplace.com

<u>Recommended by</u>
Daniel Moraga Leon

Opening hours..............Tue–Sat from 5 pm, Sun from 2 pm
Credit cards...Accepted
Type........................Beer garden, brewpub, and restaurant
Recommended for...Beer garden

LB BIEREN

Calle 67 Este
Panama City, Panama
+507 3909259
www.lbbieren.com

<u>Recommended by</u>
Luis Arce,
Daniel Moraga Leon

Opening hours....................................Tue–Sat from 11:30 am
Credit cards...Accepted
Type...Bar and retail
Recommended for...Unexpected

"A wide selection of Belgian beers in Panama City. When
I retire, I would like to own a place like this."—Luis Arce

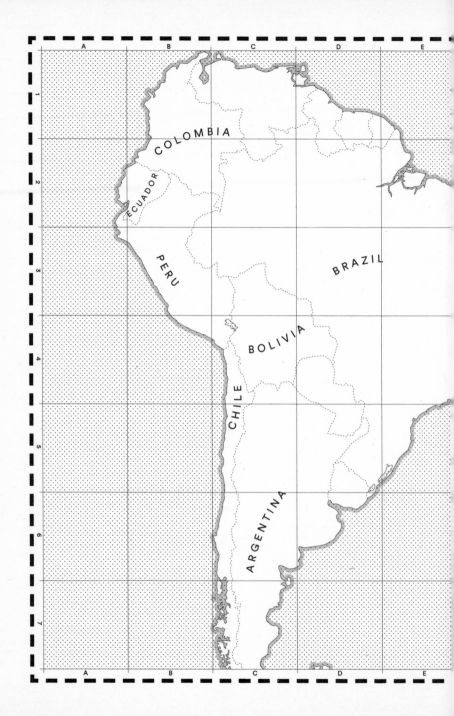

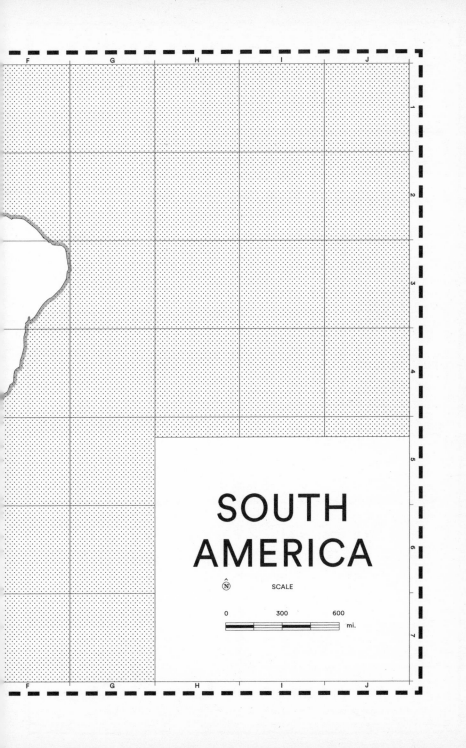

SOUTH
AMERICA

N

SCALE

0   300   600
                        mi.

"THE NITRO STOUT ON TAP IS ABSOLUTELY AMAZING!"
TRACY TEACH P.442

"IT'S AT THE ENTRANCE TO HUASCARÁN NATIONAL PARK IN THE CORDILLERA BLANCA. AN AMAZING ANDEAN SETTING TO DRINK CRAFT BEER."
CASEY WORKMAN P.441

SOUTH AMERICA NORTH

"AN AUTHENTIC BAR WITHOUT ANY BEER-SNOBBISM OR PRETENTION."
PABLO SANTOS P.440

"I HAD A VERY NICE QUINOA BEER AND WAS BLOWN AWAY BY THE FRUITY ESTERS."
CAMILO ROJAS SANCHEZ P.442

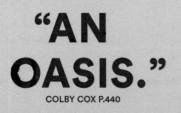

"AN OASIS."
COLBY COX P.440

A · B · C · D

BOGOTÁ P.440

VALLE DEL CAUCA P.440

COLOMBIA

QUITO PP.440–441

ECUADOR

ANCASH P.441

PERU

LIMA PP.441–442

AREQUIPA P.441 · LA PAZ P.442

COCHABAMBA P.442

BOLIVIA

SOUTH
AMERICA
NORTH

N

SCALE

0 · 225 · 450
mi.

CEVICHERÍA CENTRAL 118

Carrera 19 #118–92
Bogotá
Capital District 110221, Colombia
+57 16447766
www.centralcevicheria.com

Recommended by
Pablo Santos

Opening hours	Open 7 days from 12 pm
Credit cards	Accepted
Type	Restaurant
Recommended for	Beer & food

"Amazing seafood and an interesting food supplier program that focuses on sustainability and support of local fisherman (the MarViva certification). On the beer side, they make an outstanding local beer cocktail called Refajo with fresh grapefruit, syrup, soda and Zipa IPA (a local IPA by Moonshine)."—Pablo Santos

CHELARTE

Carrera 14 93B–45
Bogotá
Capital District 101, Colombia
+57 6160174
www.chelarte.com

Recommended by
Camilo Rojas Sanchez

Opening hours	Mon–Sat from 12 pm
Credit cards	Accepted
Type	Pub
Recommended for	Local favorite

EL MONO BANDIDO

Carrera 10 A #69–38
Bogotá
Capital District 110231, Colombia
+57 3105801751
www.elmonobandido.com

Recommended by
Pablo Santos

Opening hours	Mon–Sat from 4 pm
Credit cards	Accepted
Type	Bar
Recommended for	Local favorite

"El Mono Bandido is one of our favorite bars for craft beer. It is family hosted and owned, with a very friendly atmosphere and an excellent selection of local craft beer on tap from Bogotá and sometimes other cities, like Medellín. An authentic bar without any beer-snobbism or pretention."—Pablo Santos

HOTEL CLOUDBASE

Carrera 9 #8–65
Roldanillo
Valle del Cauca 761550, Colombia
+57 3188768999
www.cloudbasecolombia.com

Recommended by
Colby Cox

Opening hours	Open 7 days from 12 pm
Credit cards	Not accepted
Type	Brewpub
Recommended for	Unexpected

"Hotel Cloudbase is in a really cool mountain town in Colombia, in the Valle de Cauca. It's one of the best places to paraglide in the world, and it also produces some of the best coffee, bananas, and mangoes in the world. In the heart of this small town is a little hotel owned by a Swiss expat who loves beer. He sources quality craft beer from a friend with a brewpub. You won't find this beer outside Colombia. It's pretty good, and this is probably the only place between Cali and Medellín that has craft beer. An oasis."—Colby Cox

ALTAR CERVECERÍA

Olmedo y Vincente León
Centro Histórico
Quito
Pichincha 170136, Ecuador
+593 997721197
www.altarcerveceria.com

Recommended by
James Renwick

Opening hours	Tue–Sat from 5 pm
Credit cards	Accepted
Type	Brewery
Recommended for	Unexpected

"While backpacking in South America, I discovered this unexpected craft brewery. There were fantastic beers and atmosphere. Their porter hit the spot."—James Renwick

CERVEZA ARTESANAL SANTA ROSA

N23-y, Luis Cordero & Andalucía
Quito
Pichincha 170525, Ecuador
+593 998526112

Recommended by
Nathan Keffer

Opening hours	Tue–Sat from 4 pm
Credit cards	Not accepted
Type	Brewery and pub
Recommended for	Local favorite

"The bar is located in an old traditional neighborhood of Quito called La Floresta, which has recently seen the emergence of a strong gastronomy focus as well as an influx of youth. The second-story bar is a blend of modern and traditional colonial decor and architecture. The interior is beautifully designed with dark woods, metal, and a plaster wall chiseled by hand to reveal the brick beneath it. Santa Rosa usually sells only their own beer but occasionally has a guest tap, and everything they serve is worth trying."—Nathan Keffer

LA CANDELARIA

Recommended by
Stefan Nieto

Avenue República del Salvador N34–421
Quito
Pichincha 170505, Ecuador
+593 992785717

Opening hours	Mon–Sat from 12:30 pm
Credit cards	Accepted
Type	Pub
Recommended for	Beer & food

"The best craft-beer selection (taps and bottles), in a good neighborhood in Quito, with great food and good prices. They have friendly and fast service, good music, free Wi-Fi, art exhibitions, and great daily specials on the menu (including vegetarian ones). They speak Spanish and English, and the owners work there. They also have outdoor and indoor tables and are pet-friendly."
—Stefan Nieto

QUITEÑA CRAFT BEER COMPANY

Recommended by
Andres Erazo

Valladolid E13–142 y Guipúzcoa
Quito
Pichincha 170143, Ecuador
+593 995528651

Opening hours	Tue–Sat from 4 pm
Credit cards	Not accepted
Type	Bar and brewery
Recommended for	Local favorite

"A small cozy place where you can find samples of the freshly produced beers from the Quiteña brewery and some small batches of sours, IPAs, and brett beers. You can pair the beers with homemade sausages."
—Andres Erazo

SIERRA ANDINA BREWING COMPANY

Recommended by
Casey Workman

Avenida Centenario 1690 Cascapampa
Huaraz
Ancash 02250, Peru
+51 043221419
www.sierraandina.com

Opening hours	Mon–Fri from 9 am
Credit cards	Not accepted
Type	Microbrewery
Recommended for	Unexpected

"It's at the entrance to Huascarán National Park in the Cordillera Blanca. An amazing Andean setting to drink craft beer."—Casey Workman

CHELAWASI PUBLIC HOUSE

104 Campo Redondow
Arequipa 04001, Peru
+51 51232778

Opening hours	Tue–Fri from 4 pm, Sat–Sun from 12 pm
Credit cards	Accepted
Type	Pub
Recommended for	Local favorite

"Chelawasi is an Oregon-inspired craft-beer pub with an Oregonian owner. They sell mostly Andean beers (rather than Lima or jungle beers). They have twelve taps and more than thirty-five beers in bottle, all only Peruvian craft beers, no macros or imports."—Casey Workman

CERVECERÍA BARBARIAN

Recommended by
Jeppe Jarnit-Bjergsø

Andrés Cáceres K-7
Lima 15468, Peru
+51 013710643
www.barbarian.pe

Opening hours	Open 7 days from 12 pm
Credit cards	Accepted
Type	Microbrewery
Recommended for	Local favorite

Barbarian is a lot of fun and has a very Bohemian feel to it. There is a great selection of regional beers, and their in-house beers are really good.

EL RINCÓN DE BIGOTE

José Gálvez 529
Lima 18, Peru
+51 12412484
www.elrincondebigote.com

Recommended by
Tracy Teach

Opening hours..................................Tue–Sun from 11 am
Credit cards.............................Accepted but not Amex
Type...Restaurant
Recommended for...Unexpected

MOLLY'S IRISH BAR & RESTAURANT

Calle Berlín 172
Lima 15074, Peru
+51 945321332

Recommended by
Tracy Teach

Opening hours....................................Mon–Fri from 12 pm,
Sat–Sun from 9 am
Credit cards..Accepted
Type...Restaurant and pub
Recommended for..................................Local favorite

"The nitro stout on tap is absolutely amazing!"
—Tracy Teach

CLEMENTINA

Calle Juan Capriles
Cochabamba, Bolivia
+591 4252152
www.clementina.com.bo

Recommended by
Liam Lowdon

Opening hours..................................Tue–Sat from 7 pm
Credit cards...Not accepted
Type...Restaurant
Recommended for.........................Wish I'd opened

F HOUSE

Avenida América 652
Cochabamba, Bolivia
+591 44485776

Recommended by
Liam Lowdon

Opening hours..........................Open 7 days from 11 am
Type...Bar
Recommended for..............................Local favorite

"Great variety of craft beers and good food."
—Liam Lowdon

LA CAMPANA

Avenida América
Cochabamba, Bolivia
+591 44508910

Recommended by
Liam Lowdon

Opening hours............Tue–Sat from 5 pm, Sun from 12 pm
Credit cards..Not accepted
Type..Beer garden and bar
Recommended for................................Beer garden

"A great variety of craft beers and cocktails."
—Liam Lowdon

RUNNING CHASKI HOSTEL

Calle España 449
Cochabamba, Bolivia
+591 44250559
www.runningchaski.com.bo

Recommended by
Liam Lowdon

Opening hours.....................................Wed–Thur from 3 pm,
Fri–Sat from 4 pm, Sun–Mon from 3 pm
Credit cards...Accepted
Type..Bar
Recommended for.................................Worth the travel

"A great variety of Bolivian craft beers and good pizza."
—Liam Lowdon

THE SPITTING LLAMA BOOKSTORE AND OUTFITTER COCHABAMBA

Calle España 301
Cochabamba, Bolivia
+591 44522147

Recommended by
Liam Lowdon

Opening hours....................................Mon–Sat from 9 am
Type..Retail
Recommended for..Unexpected

GUSTU

Calle 10 300
La Paz, Bolivia
+591 22117491
www.restaurantgustu.com

Recommended by
Liam Lowdon,
Camilo Rojas Sanchez

Opening hours....................................Mon–Sat from 12 pm
Credit cards..Accepted
Type...Restaurant
Recommended for...................................Beer & food

"The food was amazing. I had a very nice quinoa beer
and was blown away by the fruity esters."
—Camilo Rojas Sanchez

"FANTASTIC BURGERS AND LOCAL BEERS."
ESTACIO RODRIGUES P.447

"THIS IS AN UNDERGROUND PLACE. THE PEOPLE THEN DRINK A PINT OF FRESH IPA ON THE STREET AND DANCE SAMBA ON FRIDAY NIGHTS."
VANESSA SOBRAL P.448

SOUTH AMERICA SOUTH

"IT HAS SOUL."
ROBERTO ALVES DA FONSECA P.446

"ELBOWING YOUR WAY THROUGH THE BUSTLING MASS OF THIRSTY PEOPLE TO MAKE IT TO CERVEJARIA SANTA THEREZINHA IS HALF THE FUN."
ANGELO ORONA P.446

"THIS BAR IS VERY WELCOMING AND A GOOD PLACE TO MAKE NEW FRIENDS."
STEFAN NIETO P.448

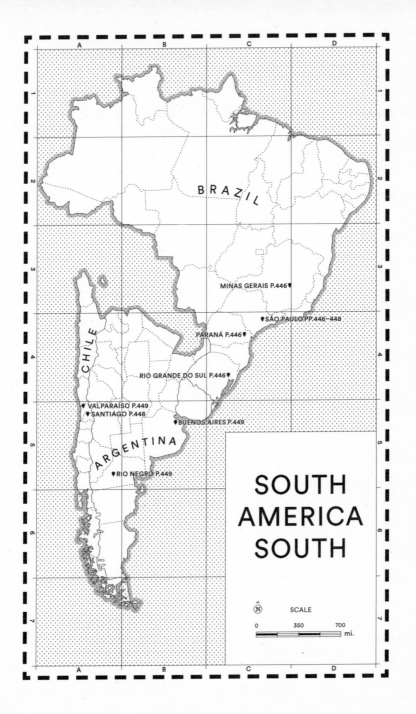

A | B | C | D

1

2

BRAZIL

3

MINAS GERAIS P.446 ♥

♥ SÃO PAULO PP.446–448

PARANÁ P.446 ♥

CHILE

RIO GRANDE DO SUL P.446 ♥

♥ VALPARAÍSO P.449
♥ SANTIAGO P.448

♥ BUENOS AIRES P.449

ARGENTINA

♥ RIO NEGRO P.449

SOUTH
AMERICA
SOUTH

N̂

SCALE

0   350   700
                              mi.

ATELIÊ WÄLS

Rua Gabriela de Melo 566
Belo Horizonte
Minas Gerais 30390-080, Brazil
+55 3131972450
www.wals.com.br/atelie

Recommended by
Jaime Ojeda

Opening hours	Tue–Thur from 5 pm, Fri–Sun from 11 am
Type	Restaurant and brewery
Recommended for	Wish I'd opened

"A great idea and place with a good selection of barrels."
—Jaime Ojeda

MERCADO MUNICIPAL DE CURITIBA

Avenida Sete de Setembro 1865
Curitiba
Paraná 80050-315, Brazil
+55 4133633764
www.mercadomunicipaldecuritiba.com.br

Recommended by
Vanessa Sobral

Opening hours	Open 7 days from 7 am
Credit cards	Accepted
Type	Restaurant
Recommended for	Unexpected

"This is a typical food market of Curitiba. There is a lot of good food, fruits, and meat. They have Way beer."
—Vanessa Sobral

BIER KELLER

Rua João Abott 596
Porto Alegre
Rio Grande do Sul 94150-610, Brazil
+55 5130842360

Recommended by
Roberto Alves da Fonseca,
Leo Sewald

Opening hours	Mon–Sat from 5:30 pm
Credit cards	Not accepted
Type	Pub
Recommended for	Worth the travel

"First of all, it's not a bar in the sense that you cannot walk in if the owner, Vittorio Lewandowski, doesn't know you and if you know nothing about beer. The idea is to keep the place familiar among the people who know it or, as he describes it, "a place just for friends." It is in an old house from the 1920s that used to be a shop—the tile floor and wooden counter are original. Vittorio carefully collected old beer memorabilia over the years and has spread it around Bier Keller, along with old records and wooden box coolers. There are some appetizers, but Vittorio lets people use the kitchen to cook if they feel like it. The little

world he has created is the highlight of the place, something hard to find in other beer bars. It has soul."
—Roberto Alves da Fonseca

"You enter only if you either know the owners or get an invitation. There are no waiters—you do your own stuff. Get your beer from the fridges and get, order, or sometimes even cook your own food. Kind of feels like home."
—Leo Sewald

BIER MARKT VOM FASS

Rua Barão de Santo Angelo 497
Porto Alegre
Rio Grande do Sul 90570-090, Brazil
+55 35740927
www.biermarkt.com.br

Recommended by
Leo Sewald

Opening hours	Mon–Sat from 6 pm
Credit cards	Accepted
Type	Bar
Recommended for	Local favorite

"The owner, Pedro, is a very approachable guy. This was one of the first craft-beer bars in my hometown. A good beer selection, nice food, and a cozy place."—Leo Sewald

CERVEJARIA SANTA THEREZINHA

Rua da Cantareira 306
Centro
São Paulo 01024-000, Brazil
+55 1132285501
www.statherezinha.com.br

Recommended by
Angelo Orona

Opening hours	Tue–Sun from 10 am
Credit cards	Accepted
Type	Brewery, retail, and pub
Recommended for	Unexpected

"Elbowing your way through the bustling mass of thirsty people to make it to Cervejaria Santa Therezinha is half the fun. Located in São Paulo's famed Mercadão, Cervejaria Santa Therezinha is a showcase of local and regional Brazilian brewing talent. Both draught and bottle offerings are well curated but offer enough variety to appeal to the masses. I paired a local witbier with Pastel de Bacalhau, a delightful cod-stuffed pastry common in Brazil. Hanging around Cervejaria Santa Therezinha is a great opportunity to take in the beautiful stained glass that throws soft light on the market floor, while enjoying the endless variety of Brazilian characters, beer in hand." —Angelo Orona

ICB FACTORY BREWERY
Rua Topazio 60
Indaiatuba
São Paulo 13346-620, Brazil
+55 1150979497
www.institutodacerveja.com.br

Recommended by
Estacio Rodrigues

Opening hours...................................Mon–Sat from 9 am
Credit cards...Accepted
Type...Beer garden
Recommended for.....................................Wish I'd opened

"A biergarten within a gypsy brewery."
—Estacio Rodrigues

AMBAR CRAFT BEERS
Rua Cunha Gago 129
Pinheiros
São Paulo 03178-200, Brazil
+55 1130311274
www.barambar.com.br

Recommended by
Estacio Rodrigues,
Vanessa Sobral

Opening hours.............................Open 7 days from 12 pm
Credit cards...Accepted
Type...Bar
Recommended for.................................Local favorite

"A nice local bar serving beers from local breweries."
—Estacio Rodrigues

CATETO PINHEIROS
Rua Francisco Leitão 272
Pinheiros
São Paulo 05414-020, Brazil
+55 1130635220

Recommended by
Roberto Alves da
Fonseca

Opening hours.............................Tue–Fri from 6 pm,
Sat–Sun from 1 pm
Credit cards...Accepted
Type...Bar
Recommended for.....................................Wish I'd opened

"They are a bar with four taps and a focus on cured meats, barbecue, and cheese, which they get from craft producers. Unlike other beer bars, they have a very interesting cocktail space on the first floor where they experiment with beer and spirits."—Roberto Alves da Fonseca

EMPÓRIO ALTO DOS PINHEIROS
Rua Vupabuçu 305
Pinheiros
São Paulo 05429-040, Brazil
+55 1130314328
www.eapsp.com.br

Recommended by
Roberto Alves da Fonseca,
Edward Jalat-Dehen,
Estacio Rodrigues, Raphael
Rodrigues, Vanessa Sobral

Opening hours...................................Mon–Fri from 12 pm,
Sat–Sun from 11 am
Credit cards...Accepted
Type...Bar
Recommended for.................................Local favorite

"Empório (EAP) started as a delicatessen. It attracted homebrewers and expanded its beer selection. Today it has around forty taps and a big bottle selection (local and imported, about half refrigerated). They gather beer geeks, people working nearby, and beginners too. I go there because there's always something new to sample and they have 5 oz (150 ml) pours. Unlike other beer places in Brazil, they also have a big food selection."—Roberto Alves da Fonseca

CERVEJARIA WALFÄNGER
Rua Carlos Ribeiro de Souza 115
Ribeirão Preto
São Paulo 14110-000, Brazil
+55 1633253660
www.walfanger.com.br

Recommended by
Roberto Alves da Fonseca

Opening hours...................................Wed–Fri from 6 pm,
Sat–Sun from 12 pm
Credit cards...Accepted
Type...Beer garden and brewery
Recommended for.....................................Beer garden

"This is a small brewery in Northwest São Paulo (state), and it has a small but cozy and typical German biergarten across the street, where you can see the brewery through large glass windows."—Roberto Alves da Fonseca

THE BURGER MAP
Rua das Aroeiras 442
Santo André
São Paulo 09090-000, Brazil
+55 1125340747
www.theburgermap.com.br

Recommended by
Estacio Rodrigues

Opening hours...................................Mon–Tue from 7 pm,
Wed–Sun from 12 pm
Credit cards...Accepted
Type...Restaurant
Recommended for.................................Beer & food

"Fantastic burgers and local beers."—Estacio Rodrigues

TITO BIERGARTEN

Recommended by
Vanessa Sobral

Rua Cuxiponés 210
Vila Anglo Brasileira
São Paulo 05030-020, Brazil
+55 11984460624
www.titobier.com

Opening hours..Variable
Credit cards.............................Accepted but not Amex
Type...Beer garden
Recommended for.....................................Beer garden

"Tito is the best biergarten in São Paulo. They have Marx
IPA and Goethe Kolsch, among other great beers."
—Vanessa Sobral

CERVEJARIA DOGMA

Recommended by
Vanessa Sobral

Rua Fortunato 236
Vila Buarque
São Paulo 01224-030, Brazil
www.loja.cervejariadogma.com.br

Opening hours.............................Wed–Fri from 5 pm,
Sat from 12 pm, Sun from 2 pm
Credit cards...Accepted
Type..Brewery
Recommended for.................................Local favorite

"The best tasting room in São Paulo."—Vanessa Sobral

CALDERETA CERVEJAS ARTESANAIS

Recommended by
Vanessa Sobral

Rua Wisard 397
Vila Madalena
São Paulo 05434-080, Brazil
+55 11954971110
www.caldereta.com.br

Opening hours.............................Tue–Sat from 3 pm
Type..Bar and retail
Recommended for.................................Wish I'd opened

"This is an underground place. The people then drink
a pint of fresh IPA on the street and dance samba on Friday
nights."—Vanessa Sobral

BARBUDO BEER GARDEN

Recommended by
Stefan Nieto

Jorge Washington 176, Plaza Ñuñoa
Santiago 7790827, Chile
+56 229060179
www.barbudo.cl

Opening hours.........................Mon–Fri from 5:30 pm,
Sat from 6:30 pm, Sun from 3 pm
Credit cards...Not accepted
Type...Beer garden
Recommended for.....................................Beer garden

"Great craft beer, great food, and close to residential
neighborhoods. This bar is very welcoming and a good
place to make new friends."—Stefan Nieto

FUENTE ITALIA

Recommended by
Stefan Nieto

Condell 1694
Santiago 7770209, Chile
+56 978883518

Opening hours.............................Tue–Sun from 1 pm
Credit cards...Accepted
Type..Restaurant
Recommended for.....................................Unexpected

LOOM

Recommended by
Jaime Ojeda

Bellavista 0360
Santiago, Chile
+56 232033123
www.loom.cl

Opening hours.........................Mon–Sat from 12:30 pm
Credit cards...Accepted
Type..Brewpub
Recommended for.................................Local favorite

"The first brewpub in Santiago."—Jaime Ojeda

PEPPERLAND BAR

Recommended by
Pablo Mejia

261 Santa Isabel
Santiago 8320000, Chile
+56 28134608

Opening hours.............................Mon–Sat from 1 pm
Credit cards...Accepted
Type...Bar
Recommended for.................................Local favorite

"A large selection of Chilean craft beers with a vegan-
friendly menu."—Pablo Mejia

BAR EL IRLANDÉS

Blanco 1279
Valparaíso 2362657, Chile
+56 323469757

Recommended by
Francisco Oyarce

Opening hours.........................Tue–Wed from 5 pm,
Thur from 6:30 pm, Fri–Sat from 4 pm
Credit cards...Accepted
Type...Pub
Recommended for...........................Local favorite

"This is the only real Irish-porteño (*porteño* is a person born in Valparaíso) bar in Valparaiso. They have local beers, Chilean award-winning beers, and a lot of international beers. They import Mikkeller, Amager, and To Øl. They also sell Evil Twin. The last few years, a new Peruvian chef has changed the food menu. She makes the best *lomo saltado*, among other things, in town. This is a very multicultural bar."—Francisco Oyarce

BARDENOR

Agua Santa
Viña del Mar
Valparaíso 2362657, Chile

Recommended by
Francisco Oyarce

Opening hours............Mon–Fri from 5 pm, Sat from 6 pm
Credit cards...Accepted
Type...Bar
Recommended for...........................Unexpected

"It's a bar for metal heads. It's dark. You don't expect a lot from it, but they have a really good selection of tap and bottled beers. My friends didn't believe me about this place, until they tried it."—Francisco Oyarce

BRUDER BEER GARDEN

Bartolomé Mitre 3188
Mar del Plata
Buenos Aires B7602BWH, Argentina
+54 2234955274
www.bruderbeergarden.com

Recommended by
Nicolas Rodriguez Etchelet

Opening hours.................................Open 7 days from 7 pm
Credit cards...Accepted
Type...Beer garden
Recommended for.............................Beer garden

"It's the first multibrand bar in Argentina, with more than twenty taps. It's always crowded."
—Nicolas Rodriguez Etchelet

BREOGHAN BREW BAR

Bolívar 860
San Telmo
Buenos Aires C1066AAR, Argentina
+54 1143009439

Recommended by
Diego Castro,
Nicolas Rodriguez Etchelet

Opening hours.................................Open 7 days from 6 pm
Credit cards...Not accepted
Type...Bar
Recommended for...........................Local favorite

"They carry the best international beers, plus the best beers from Argentina."—Nicolas Rodriguez Etchelet

THE GIBRALTAR

Perú 895
San Telmo
Buenos Aires C1068AAG, Argentina
+54 1143625310

Recommended by
Nicolas Rodriguez Etchelet

Opening hours.................................Open 7 days from 12 pm
Credit cards...Accepted
Type...Bar
Recommended for...........................Unexpected

"It's the only English pub in Buenos Aires."
—Nicolas Rodriguez Etchelet

CERVECERÍA LA CRUZ

Calle Nilpi 789
San Carlos de Bariloche
Río Negro 8400, Argentina
+54 294444634
www.cervecerialacruz.com.ar

Recommended by
Martin Serra

Opening hours.................................Tue–Sun from 6 pm
Credit cards...Accepted
Type...Bar
Recommended for...........................Worth the travel

"It's located a few blocks from the Nahuel Huapi Lake, a warm place with tasty food. I feel at home here."
—Martin Serra

INDEX BY VENUE

INDEX BY RECOMMENDATION CATEGORY

INDEX BY TYPE

INDEX BY COUNTRY